The Process of Economic Development

The Process of Economic Development is a textbook with a story to tell. It examines development obstacles from the colonial era to the present in Latin America, Asia, and Africa. Utilizing a fluid blend of classical development ideas and current theory, the book enables students to gain the type of balanced picture unavailable to them in other textbooks.

A close examination of recent events is integral to the book, with discussions ranging from the environment to the debt crisis, and from export-led industrialization to import substitution, endogenous growth theory, and technological capability. With a readable style and format, the authors focus on institutional transformation, income distribution, poverty, peasant agriculture and numerous current socio-economic issues.

Plentiful diagrams, boxes and user-friendly summaries and end of chapter questions help the reader to grasp many-faceted topics. Building upon the impressive and popular first edition, Cypher and Dietz have accomplished that rarity in textbook publishing: a book which will leave students with a framework of understanding empowering them to go on to interpret a broad range of "North–South" issues and controversies.

James M. Cypher is Professor of Economics at California State University in Fresno, USA. **James L. Dietz** is Professor of Economics at California State University in Fullerton, USA.

The Process of Economic Development
2nd Edition

James M. Cypher and James L. Dietz

Routledge
Taylor & Francis Group

LONDON AND NEW YORK

First published 1997
by Routledge
2 Park Square, Milton Park, Abingdon, Oxon OX14 4RN

Simultaneously published in the USA and Canada
by Routledge
270 Madison Ave, New York, NY 10016

Second edition first published 2004

Reprinted 2005 (three times), 2006 (twice)

Routledge is an imprint of the Taylor & Francis Group, an informa business

Typeset in Times by Wearset Ltd, Boldon, Tyne and Wear
Printed and bound in Great Britain by T.J. International Ltd, Padstow, Cornwall

British Library Cataloguing in Publication Data
A catalogue record for this book is available from the British Library

Library of Congress Cataloging in Publication Data
A catalog record for this book has been requested

ISBN10: 0-415-25415-9 (hbk)
ISBN10: 0-415-25416-7 (pbk)

ISBN13: 978-0-415-25415-1 (hbk)
ISBN13: 978-0-415-25416-8 (pbk)

Contents

Figures

Tables

Boxes

Focuses

Preface to the second edition

In writing the second edition of *Process of Economic Development* we have deliberated over every page of the first edition. We have found that the basic organization and sequencing of the book has been well received. We have not sought to alter the major themes examined in the first edition. Nonetheless, extensive changes too numerous to summarize have been introduced in virtually every chapter. We have attempted to include new research in every area. Yet, we are aware of the vastness of the field of economic development and the likelihood that we may have overlooked more than one important new research finding. Wherever possible data and tables have been brought up to date, or new tables have been created.

We were both pleased and surprised to find that the field of economic development seems, in some respects, to be moving closer to many of the core ideas highlighted in the first edition of the book. Specifically, it is currently stylish to acknowledge that any analysis of developing nations should include a serious examination of "institutions." (What exactly is meant by institutions is often not clearly defined or expressed.) Our thinking and research on issues of economic development has been profoundly influenced by institutionalist analysis. We thus welcome this "new" focus, which has long been a crucial component of our frame of reference when dealing with development issues.

A second change that we also welcome has been the revival of interest in the early "developmentalist" ideas of the core thinkers in the still-young field of development: Paul Rosenstein-Rodan, Albert Hirschman, Ragnar Nurkse, Arthur Lewis, and, more rarely, Gunnar Myrdal.

We are also encouraged by some of the broader indicators of development that suggest forward movement in developing nations, such as the 45 percent decline in infant mortality between 1970 and 1999. The World Bank notes that life expectancy in poor nations has improved by 20 years over the past four decades and illiteracy has been cut in half. These are changes of a magnitude that is hard to imagine. Other encouraging signs are to be found – the percent of the world's population below an inflation-adjusted income of one dollar a day dropped by 4 points between 1987 and 1998 – suggesting that some 240 million people were lifted out of the most extreme poverty. The two most populous nations in the world, India and China, have experienced rapid change. The World Bank registers China's economic growth at 10 percent a year, 1990–2001. (There is a debate over the accuracy of these numbers, but none over the fact that China has experienced explosive growth for a respectable period.) In the same period India had extremely strong economic growth of 5.9 percent per year. With these two nations accounting for an astonishing

45 percent of the 5.177 *billion* human beings with incomes below $2,975 (US) per year, it is easy to understand that the strong performance of these two giants has shaped the aggregate statistics reflecting the course of economic development.

Unfortunately broad data can often convey an impression that is not entirely accurate: Africa has suffered tremendously – even by historical standards that have registered brutal circumstances – and signs of hope in this vast area are few and far between. The Asian crisis of 1997 upset the forward movement of several nations in South East Asia bringing devastating consequences to the large nation of Indonesia (population 214 million). The Middle East, too, has experienced, at best, very modest gains after adjusting for relatively high population rates of growth in the region.

Latin America went through the "lost decade" of the 1980s only to experience the "lost half-decade" of the 1990s. The two giants of the region, Brazil and Mexico, had struggled to overcome serious setbacks in the 1980s and 1990s with a very modest degree of success. In the past five years (1998–2002) Latin America's average per capita income has declined, while in 2002 open unemployment reached the highest level ever registered in Latin America. At the same time, for non-oil exporters, in the new era of "export at all cost," Latin America has experienced declining terms of trade. Twenty million more Latin Americans fell below the poverty line in the past five years. And, in spite of the rhetoric lauding "emerging nations" that suggested a new era of "globalization" would lift many poor nations through financial flows that would facilitate a boost in investment and growth, Latin America has since 1999 sent more money *to* wealthy nations than it has received. That is, "net transfers" of funds – taking into account all inflows and outflows (such as payment of interest and repatriation of profits by transnational corporations) – have left Latin America in a net losing position in the new era of "globalization."

When the first edition of this book was published it was thought that "capital flows" to "emerging markets" would be so strong that "globalization" would (through some yet to be defined alchemy) "develop" much of the low income regions of the world. Such views have failed to coincide with the facts as we know them. For this, and other reasons, it appears that the field of development economics is opening up to new ideas once again – after a dark age wherein neoliberal dogma was often allowed to pass as a form of newfound wisdom that would sweep away underdevelopment through the "magic of the market." A new era of open debate and rethinking of development economics seems to beckon – a possibility that, if realized, could initiate a renewed focus on overcoming some of the most critical needs in developing nations.

A final change to be noted is the new, critical, focus on development institutions such as the IMF and the World Bank. Once obscure to most, these multilaterals have now come to the foreground due to the heated and sometimes violent discussion that has occurred since the interrupted meeting of the World Trade Organization in Seattle, Washington in 1999. When the first edition of this book was published in 1997 one often, unfortunately, encountered otherwise well-educated individuals with only the most shaky grasp of the function of the IMF and World Bank. We welcome the fact that these powerful institutions are now being held accountable by numerous concerned individuals (including Joseph Stiglitz the 2001 Nobel Award recipient in economics) throughout the world.

Preface to the first edition

The newspapers in the advanced nations regularly recount frightful events somewhere in Africa, Asia, or Latin America – famine in Africa, cholera in Latin America, or child labor in Asia – tragic stories that seem to have no beginning, no context, no history, and no end. This portrayal of events is not false, per se, but it is a distorted perception of life in the less-developed poor nations where the bulk of the world's population lives. Most of the daily life of the masses of people – their routines, hopes, struggles, accommodations, and work – fails to be reported. It is well to remember, however, that the people of these regions struggle to maintain their dignity, their humanity, and their grace.

This is a book about much that is important in determining the material well-being of vast numbers of individuals who live in the less-developed nations. Economic development demands enormous changes in the ways in which people organize their lives, and it requires transformations in the distribution of income, the sources of wealth, and in political, social, and economic power. In every poor country, there are people who benefit from economic underdevelopment, and they may be relative or even absolute losers if their society and economy are transformed. These elites have a compelling interest in preserving the status quo. But change in the less-developed world, however halting and however misguided at times, is occurring.

Economic development is concerned with both learning and doing. It is necessary to learn to master the relevant ideas which have been offered to interpret and analyze issues of development. It is also necessary to critically examine and contest inappropriate and erroneous ideas that have too often been presented as incontrovertible truths regarding development. But that is not enough. Economic development does not happen on its own, and never has. Good public policy is at the core of the process of economic development. Such policy, however, operates along a "knife edge," working within the limits and constraints of the conditions of the present, ever mindful of the mistakes of the past which have shaped the economy and society and its initial endowments. Even having put good policies into place is not enough; it is also important for policy-makers to know when and how to leave them behind for even better strategies.

This is a book about a vast and complex subject which involves investigating issues and problems from the perspective of economics, with insights from political science, history, sociology, environmental studies, and geography. We have concentrated primarily, on matters which have as their primary focus economic phenomena. Our approach to this area is much broader than examining prices, quantities, and markets. We are concerned with the forces *behind* these elements of economic behavior. This book weighs the institutional structure of the developing nations, as well as their history, in order to apply economic analysis to particular issues and problems. It is intended as a text for undergraduate courses in economic development. However, we have sought to make it accessible for use in courses taught in a range of fields, including the sociology of development, international relations and international political economy.

We have struggled to understand the fundamental issues of development economics for decades. This work has been done while we were students, while we were living and working in poor nations, conducting field research in several developing nations, studying decades of research conducted by scholars, examining case studies and country-specific accounts of development policies and strategies in many nations, and while teaching students over two decades. We have been in factories and artisan workshops, on small farms and in agribusiness facilities, in schools, hospitals, and health clinics, in government ministries and in universities in many different countries. We have exchanged ideas with and listened to people of every type, class, and background, including top political leaders and their policy advisers, corporate owners and their managers, union leaders, and members of the rank and file, small farmers and landless peasants, human rights leaders and victims of human rights abuse, bankers and stockbrokers and environmental activists. These experiences frame our thinking and guide our analysis every step of the way through this book.

An overview

This book begins with a basic introduction to the development problem and to the methods conventionally employed to measure economic development and human development. After completing this overview in Chapters 1 and 2, we depart from traditional treatment by analyzing the historical context of economic backwardness. We believe that the legacy of colonialism must be understood in order to have a proper context for interpreting and understanding the barriers facing poor nations today.

After positioning our analysis of the process of economic development within a historical context organized around the concept of path dependence, we next explore the body of economic thought devoted to the question of growth and development. In that section of the book, we first introduce the classical economists and their very sweeping ideas regarding growth, distribution, and equity. This is followed by two chapters which cover the full range of ideas presented by development economists from the end of the Second World War through to the early 1970s. The following chapter takes up the debate over the role of the state in the development process, a topic of some centrality in the 1980s. This book is concerned with much more than a careful recounting of the past. The remainder of the text thus is devoted to the present and to how successful development policies can be achieved.

Chapter 8 offers some of the latest theoretical thinking on development: the endogenous growth models. We have utilized the fertile possibilities of the endogenous growth approach to show how our treatment of history and institutions can actually strengthen and deepen the insights presented in the endogenous approach. We also show how many of the ideas of the early development economists can be constructively utilized to broaden the applicability of the endogenous growth analysis. We then use this material as a basic component in our presentation of the structural transformation toward industrialization in Chapters 9 and 10. These are core chapters which show how the experiences of the East Asian economies can be understood within a given institutional and historical context. As we shall see, they are far from "miracle economies," as some have called them. Rather, the East Asian economies are successful stories of good policy, which teach important lessons regarding the process of development.

We cover much of the vast terrain of agricultural development in Chapter 11. Here the discussion ranges over a number of matters, including land reform, the particular problems of the peasantry, the Green Revolution, land degradation and environmental destruction, and the role of transnational agribusiness.

The development of human skills and human potential is the focus of Chapters 12 and 13. Chapter 13 is unusual in that it is devoted to a range of problems which less developed nations must confront regarding their mastery of technology. Chapter 14 covers the full range of issues pertaining to transnational corporations operating in the less developed nations, including a discussion of export processing zones (EPZs), the rise of subcontracting arrangements, and a comparison of transnational activities in Asia and Latin America.

Chapter 15 is concerned with domestic and international macroeconomic policy. Such policies must be concerned with the ability to stabilize the economy and to stimulate growth via fiscal and monetary policy. Good policy-making demands close attention to the balance of payments and to the proper exchange rate. These macroeconomic policy variables receive a full treatment in this chapter. Finally, we go deeper into the foreign sector and macroeconomic management by way of an analysis of the debt crisis in Chapter 16 and a thorough treatment of the goals, objectives and strategies of the International Monetary Fund and the World Bank in Chapter 17.

We have made every effort to write a coherent book, rather than a series of non-integrated topics. We believe that the "process of development" cannot be understood as other than a set of interrelated and interacting phenomena. That is, the needs of agriculture cannot be understood without considering the requirements for industrialization, and industrialization cannot be understood without considering the necessity for independent technological development, and these three cannot be understood without knowledge of best practice, policies regarding the foreign sector, exchange rates, fiscal and monetary management, and so on.

We have not treated the issues of women in development and the environment as separable from the topics mentioned above. Instead, we have sought to weave these themes into our presentation of the topics and issues outlined above. Nor have we treated equity and social justice as separate issues, but rather as bound up with the totality of the development process.

There are many issues that we have not covered. To do so would be impossible. Each issue we take up could easily be expanded into a book of several volumes. Colonial history could easily involve a lifetime of study. The particular case studies of successful and failed industrialization are nearly endless. We have treated the issues we believe are most important and most pressing if one is to understand the complexity of the process of economic development, but not everything that might be covered, or covered in the detail that we, or others, might wish.

Above all, we hope that students will find this book useful and insightful. And we hope that some will become the policy-makers of tomorrow who are engaged in the ongoing struggle to bring human development to the many millions of the world who need, and deserve, a better life.

Using the book

One can read the book straight through, but we also have taught from it by covering Chapters 1–5 first; proceeding to read Chapters 9–11 in conjunction with Chapters 6 and 7; then reading Chapters 8, 12, 13 and 14 and on through the remainder of the text in sequence. We have included questions at the end of each chapter, many of which ask the reader to further analyze material covered, often including collecting additional data and interpreting it. We have found that as students work through the questions, their understanding of the complexity of the issues is greatly enhanced. It involves a major effort to answer each and every question, but the reward is large.

Acknowledgments

As is always the case, this book could not have been written without the help of many individuals. As is also the case, none should be held responsible in any way for the existing book.

To begin, we sincerely thank the five anonymous reviewers who labored over the needed revisions for the second edition offering detailed and well-thought-out comments. Their guidance, prompting and misgivings, as well as their praise, helped greatly in establishing the broad parameters for this edition.

Next, we thank our students. Nothing, in the academic world, could be more immediate than the give-and-take of the classroom along with the painful self-knowledge that arises from the act of reading exams. On the whole we have been pleased with the results of the first edition after many years of "testing" it with numerous students. We have trimmed, adjusted and amplified (and in some cases jettisoned) chapters on the basis of our students needs and wants. To our surprise, the new world of the internet has created the possibility for students around the globe to comment on the book. These serendipitous virtual encounters have also commonly resulted in new insights – some of which found their way into the second edition.

Many colleagues played a role in the years of research that have gone into the preparation and writing of the second edition – far more than we can formally recognize here. Nonetheless, for assistance (which came in various forms) we wish to thank – in no particular order – the following individuals: M. Shahid Alam, Paul Dale Bush, Al Campbell, Juan Castaings Teillery, Eugenia Correa, Willy Cortez, Enrique Dussel Peters, David Fairris, Sasan Fayazmanesh, Raul Fernandez, Ross Gandy, Rodolfo Garcia Zamora, Alicia Gíron, Arturo Guillén, Martin Hart-Landsberg, Peter Ho, Barney Hope, Marc Humbert, Kathy Kopinak, Fred Lee, Oscar Muñoz, Robert Pollin, Skye Stephenson, Carolina Stefoni, Miguel Angel Rivera, Cesar Ross, Howard Stein, Linda Shaffer, Janet Tanski, Marc Tool, Mayo Toruño, Gregorio Vidal, and Eduardo Zepeda.

At Routledge we have experienced the best of all possible worlds – excellent editors, ever forgiving of the interminable delays in meeting deadlines. Editors Terry Clague and Robert Langham have facilitated the second edition with aplomb and dispatch. Alan Jarvis, who first accepted our outline for the original manuscript, along with Alison Kirk and Kate Smith, who edited the first edition, are not to be forgotten. Unlike so many in the corporatized world of publishing, Routledge has given us wide latitude in every aspect of this book, sensible editing and clear, crisp communication. What else could we ask?

For institutional support we thank the Departments of Economics at California State University, Fresno and Fullerton. At both Universities we have availed ourselves of the excellent and untiring services provided by the ever-efficient library staff. At California State University, Fresno Administrative Assistant Sherry McCulloch has unstintingly found a way and time to take care of numerous matters. We also thank the Office of the Provost at this University for two University Research Grants. In addition the Dean of the College of Social Sciences facilitated travel to both Brazil and Chile to participate in Faculty Development Seminars in 1999 and 2001. FLACSO (Chile) deserves special thanks for support in the penultimate stages of this project.

Finally, our families should receive the greatest thanks for their assistance of every type, above and beyond anything we might have hoped for, or deserved.

JMC
JLD

Part 1

An overview of economic development

1 The development imperative

No society can surely be flourishing and happy, of which the far greater part of the members are poor and miserable.

Adam Smith, *The Wealth of Nations*

Our Dream is a World Free of Poverty
Aphorism heading the World Bank's Mission Statement

After studying this chapter, you should understand:
- the relative magnitude of poverty in the less-developed nations and some of its human and social costs;
- differences in relative incomes and development levels between regions of the less-developed world and compared to more-developed regions;
- trends in economic growth in different regions of the world;
- the extent of inequality in the distribution of income, in wealth and in participation in economic and social life of the world's poor in different regions of the world;
- the range of barriers to development, both internal and external, that tend to thwart economic, social, and human development;
- the importance of structural change, of technology and of institutional innovation to more rapid progress in the future in the less-developed world.

Why study economic development?

Throughout the 1990s, some eleven million children under the age of five were dying every year in the less-developed nations from preventable illnesses (UNDP 2001: 9; WHO 1994; World Bank 1993a: 1). These are sobering numbers and are difficult to grasp as aggregate abstractions. They translate to more than 35,000 deaths daily, more than 1,400 children dying every hour of every day of every week and of every month of the year, children whose lives ended before they really had an opportunity to begin. More than half of these deaths were due to respiratory illnesses and to diarrhoea and the severe dehydration that can ensue, exacerbated by malnutrition in a vicious circle of hunger and disease (see Focus 1.1 Saving Lives: ORT).[1] Roughly, in the ten seconds it has taken you to read this paragraph, five

---

FOCUS 1.1   SAVING LIVES: ORT

Imagine yourself for a moment as a poor rural villager in a less-developed nation with a young child in your care who develops diarrhoea. What would you do to prevent the illness from becoming life threatening?

Diarrhoea causes the body to throw off more water than can be reabsorbed. Death can result if more than 15 percent of the body's fluid is lost. What does this child need? What can you do to prevent dehydration and death? Clinics, phone calls, medicine, and a visit to a pharmacy are not options! You must come up with a home remedy. And fast! Think carefully about what you would do before reading on.

Along with the loss of water, sodium (salt) is also lost with diarrhoea. There is a fairly precise concentration of sodium in the human blood supply required for the body to function properly. With diarrhoea, this balance is upset as the kidneys, which normally regulate the salt level in the blood supply, are unable to maintain the proper balance. What the sick body needs is both sodium *and* more liquid, but the illness disturbs this delicate equilibrium and threatens survival.

The remedy is "oral rehydration therapy" or ORT. Simply providing the sick child with water to drink – which may have been the immediate cause of the diarrhoea in the first instance – is not enough. Nor, interestingly, is water mixed with salt. Because of the diarrhoea, the body cannot absorb the salt properly with the result that excess salt gets stored in the intestinal track and causes more water to pass into the intestine, actually worsening the diarrhoea. However, a mixture of water, salt, and sugar (glucose) *will* work, allowing the salt to be properly processed by the body and for water retention to be increased and the dehydration process halted.

A mixture of glucose (20 grams), sodium chloride (salt, 3.5 grams), sodium citrate (2.5 grams), and potassium chloride (1.5 grams) in one litre of clean water provides the ideal mixture for ORT. ORT must be initiated quickly before the dehydration becomes too severe. If it is not, intravenous rehydration may be the only alternative.

Source: Foster 1992: 197–198

---

more children in the less-developed world will have perished, and they too will have perished unnecessarily.[2]

Adults also die in pointless numbers in the less-developed world: more than seven million each year from illnesses such as tuberculosis and other contagious diseases that could be prevented or cured at a relatively small cost to society. Most of these deaths are rooted in extreme poverty and deprivation, including famine and sometimes civil war. They are human losses that, in our modern and affluent times, are not the result of any lack of human knowledge about how to prevent them.[3] The means to prevent this waste of human life is at hand; what is lacking seems to be the will.

If all this were not bad enough, since the 1980s an HIV/AIDS epidemic in many African countries has decimated what limited progress there had been on the health and poverty fronts with some countries, such as Botswana and Zimbabwe, especially hard hit. In confronting these and other problems, many of the barriers to progress in the less-developed countries seem to continue to be found in obstinate economic, political and social structures that remain resistant to the changes that could make extreme poverty and privation – and millions of deaths from poverty-related illnesses each year – the relics of history they deserve to be (World Bank 1993a: 116; 2000: 4–5).

Poverty in the less-developed world

Table 1.1 provides an overview of the extent of poverty facing the less-developed nations. In 1985, one out of every three persons, some 1,116 million men, women, and children, were "poor" by the World Bank's classification of having less than the equivalent of $370 per year available to meet their needs. By 1993, this number had risen to more than 1,300 million persons in poverty, and by 1998, preliminary statistics by the World Bank using the same roughly $1/day standard, found 1,198.9 million living in poverty, more than had been so living in 1985. If the cut-off line for poverty is extended to $2 a day, some 2.8 billion individuals fell below that standard in 1998, nearly half the world's 6 billion population (World Bank 2000: 3, 13).

Part I of Table 1.1 provides even more detail. Among those counted as poor in 1985, nearly one in five (633 million) were classified as "extremely poor" with an annual average per person income of less than $275. Former World Bank President, Robert McNamara, called these people the "absolute poor," human beings who suffer "a condition of life so degraded by disease, illiteracy, malnutrition, and squalor as to deny its victims basic human necessities." ... (It) "is life at the very

Table 1.1 Extent of world poverty and the poverty gap

Part I. 1985 Region	Extremely poor[a] (%)	Poor[b] (%)	Millions of poor	Poverty gap[c]
Sub-Saharan Africa	30	47	180	11
Eastern Asia	9	20	280	1
China	8	20	210	3
Southern Asia	29	51	520	10
India	33	55	420	12
Middle East and North Africa	21	31	60	2
Latin America and the Caribbean	12	19	70	1
All less-developed countries	*18*	*33*	*1,116*	*3*

Part II. 1990–1998 Percent of Population living on less than $1/day	1987	1990	1993	1998	Millions of poor, 1998
Sub-Saharan Africa	46.6	47.7	49.7	46.3	290.9
Eastern Asia	26.6	27.6	25.2	15.3	278.3
excluding China	23.9	18.5	15.9	11.3	65.1
Southern Asia	44.4	44.0	42.4	40.0	522.0
Middle East and North Africa	4.3	2.4	1.9	1.9	5.5
Latin America and the Caribbean	15.3	16.8	15.3	15.6	46.3
All less-developed countries	*28.3*	*29.0*	*28.1*	*24.0*	*1,198.9*

Sources: World Bank 1990: 29, Table 2.1; 2000: 13, Table A.1. Europe and Central Asia are excluded from table values. The roughly $1 a day (actually $1.08 in 1998) standard is based on a fixed, real base, that is, it is adjusted for inflation.

Notes
a Annual average income <$275 in 1985.
b Annual average income <$370 in 1985. The "Poor" category includes the "Extremely poor" as a sub-category.
c The "poverty gap" is the percentage by which the aggregate income of the poor falls short of the poverty line as a percentage of a region's (or country's) total consumption. It is the amount, in percentage terms, of additional income that would be needed to raise all the poor above the poverty line.

margin of physical existence." As McNamara suggested, the wretched condition of life of the absolute poor is almost beyond the power of understanding of those who live in developed countries (McNamara 1976: 5).

Almost one-half of the less-developed world's poor lived in southern Asia in 1985, with the greatest number in India. Part II of Table 1.1 shows that southern Asia's share of the less-developed world's total number of poor had not fallen in the 1990s (522 million out of a total 1,198.9 million poor). Sub-Saharan Africa, on the other hand, accounted for almost one-fourth of all the poor in the less-developed world by 1998, compared to 16 percent in 1985, as the incidence of poverty there worsened compared to trends in the rest of the world.

What is disheartening is the relatively small decrease in poverty in most of the regions shown in Part II of Table 1.1, not to mention the rise in poverty in Africa in the early 1990s. The decline in the incidence of poverty in East Asia from 20 percent of the region's population in 1985 (Part I of Table 1.1) to 15.3 percent in 1998 (and even lower when China is excluded; Part II) is one of the success stories of the past two decades, one that will be highlighted throughout this text. Still, poverty levels remain agonizingly high, reducing opportunities for the poor and their children over the future in a vicious circle. Quoting the World Bank from more than a decade past: "more than 1 billion people, one-fifth of the world's population, live on less than one dollar a day – a standard that Western Europe and the United States attained two hundred years ago" (World Bank 1991: 1). This is still true today. It is also important to recognize that the incidence of poverty is not gender-neutral, something the aggregate figures in the table obscure. "Poverty has a woman's face – of 1.3 billion people in poverty 70% are women [female]" (UNDP 1995: 4).

With the exception of the last column of Part I, the numbers in Table 1.1 provide what is called a "headcount" of the numbers of poor falling below the poverty line. Such a measure does not distinguish between those persons whose incomes are far below the poverty line and who hence need more assistance to reach the poverty threshold from those whose incomes already have brought them closer to the income level needed to escape official poverty. The headcount measure of poverty simply counts all persons below some income level as poor. The headcount measure is thus not at all sensitive to the *severity* of the poverty situation of those counted as poor; it treats all poor as if they were somehow the same.

The condition of being poor, however, is not similar for all those who are so classified. Imagine, for example, one country with half its population below the poverty line, but each is only $5 per year away from the poverty level of income. That is poverty of quite a different magnitude than another country which also has half its population below the poverty line, but each is $100 per year away from escaping poverty. The headcount measure of poverty, by simply adding up how many people fall below the poverty line, fails to capture this distinction and both countries will be counted as having 50 percent of their citizens in poverty by the headcount measure. Obviously, however, the severity of poverty in the first country is substantially less than in the second. There is another way to measure poverty that considers this issue.

The last column of Table 1.1 Part II, provides this alternative perspective on measuring poverty. The concept of the "poverty gap" captures the severity of the poor's plight. It is the additional amount of consumption (or income) that must be generated by a country to bring all the poor above the poverty line. The poverty gap is measured as a percent of a region's (or a country's) total current consumption (or it could be measured as a percent of income) that must be created and received by the poor in the right amounts to bring each family's income above the poverty line. For some regions of the world and for some countries the poverty gap was as low as 1–2 percent of current consumption; in other regions, the poverty gap was as high as 10–12 percent of total consumption. Data that is more recent is available on the poverty gap for individual economies, as the note to this paragraph notes, but it is not uniform by years and thus is not so easily displayed for comparison.[4]

For all the less-developed nations, an increase in income equivalent to about 3–4 percent of current consumption received in the right amounts by each family or individual in poverty would have been sufficient to shift all the poor above the World Bank's $2 per day poverty line in 1985. It is not unreasonable to assume that this amount is not substantially different now. Obviously, to accomplish the long-term goal of a world without poverty, a simple transfer of income from better-off citizens to the poor is not the ultimate means or goal. Reducing poverty is not about transfers of income, except in the short-run to alleviate the worst kinds of suffering. Rather, a *permanent reduction* in poverty requires a sufficient increase in production, jobs and incomes for the now poor such that they are no longer poverty-stricken and remain non-poor through their own efforts, not handouts.

This objective of a permanent increase in income and output that reaches the poor in the magnitudes shown in the table would not seem to be an overwhelmingly large technical barrier. For example, India could resolve to generate sufficient extra income and output in the economy over a generation to contribute to an increase in the income of the poor in the amount equal to 12 percent of total consumption. Over 25 years, this does not seem to be a technically unattainable goal, amounting to an increase in total consumption on the order of well less than 1 percent per year.

The possibility of fully eradicating poverty would seem to be within reach. It is not an impossible aspiration requiring super-human efforts beyond current resource capabilities. Greater productivity of labor and a better distribution of the world's productive resources, both human and physical, are what are needed to effect a long-term decrease in the poverty profile. It is a reasonable and humane objective for all the less-developed nations to target the elimination of absolute poverty from within their borders. It is a goal that the World Bank has embraced, with the target of cutting poverty in half by 2015 (World Bank 2001: 5–6; also see UNDP 2001: 22–25). Even for the poorest nations, the magnitude of the increase in output and income required to reduce poverty is within their grasp over a medium-range period of time with the right policies, the right decisions and the requisite political will.

The relatively modest size of the poverty gap compared to current incomes in the less-developed world strongly suggests that poverty is a problem of distribution, and not only of income, but especially of access to society's productive resources, particularly human capital-enhancing assets like education and other training. The existence of world poverty does not appear to be the consequence of a fundamental shortfall in aggregate productive capacity given the fairly small size of the poverty gap in most regions. Eradication of absolute poverty is a political economic problem, not a technical matter. Ending absolute poverty is a challenge of political will and to existing political and economic power structures.

Poverty is not just measured by a shortfall in income, of course. Low incomes have real consequences. For example, of the approximately 4.6 billion people in the less-developed countries, 968 million persons lacked access "to improved water sources"; 2.4 million were without proper sanitation; 854 million adults were illiterate (64 percent of these were women); 34 million were infected with HIV/AIDS, the great majority of these in Africa; and 2.2 million persons were dying annually from indoor air pollution, particularly, from exposure to toxic fumes from wood-burning cooking (the data is for the late 1990s and 2000; UNDP 2001: 9, 13).

The good news, despite these sobering statistics, is that there have been undeniable improvements in living standards in the less-developed world since 1970. Life expectancy at birth rose absolutely and relatively compared to the developed world, from 46 years in 1960 when it was equal to 67 percent of life expectancy in the developed nations to 64 years in 2000, which is equal to 82 percent of the level achieved in the developed countries. Infant mortality between birth and age one fell from 149 per 1,000 live births in 1960 to 59 in 1998, though, unfortunately, this number was higher at the end of the 1990s than at the beginning, showing that progress is not always a linear process. Adult literacy rose from 46 percent to about 75 percent over the same period to 2000, though in the least-developed nations 70 percent of all adults and only half of adult females could be classified as literate (see Focus 1.2 Progress and Regress, Winners and Losers).

Except for the last figures, all of the above are average values. In general, women do not fare as well as men on these social indicators. Rural areas suffer relative to urban areas, and ethnic groups and different social classes often have widely diverging outcomes as well. One can find nations that have made, at best, only modest

---

FOCUS 1.2   PROGRESS AND REGRESS, WINNERS AND LOSERS

We have relied above on some statistical data to get a "snap-shot" of the situation of poverty in the less-developed world. It is important and instructive to collect and try to understand some of this data yourself.

To get you started in that direction, and if you have access to the Internet, go to http://www.worldbank.org, the website of the World Bank (alternatively, look for a recent issue of the World Bank's *World Development Report*, which will have similar data, though what is now available is substantially less in the print edition than was available in the past). Click on "Data and Statistics" and then "Data by Country." Then go to "Country at a Glance tables."

Find data for Brazil, China, Costa Rica, Kenya, Korea (Rep.), Mexico, Pakistan, Sri Lanka, and Zimbabwe for the following social and economic variables: infant mortality rate; child malnutrition; life expectancy at birth; access to an improved water source; gross primary enrollment ratio; and the population growth rate.

What "picture" does this data give you about each of these countries? What general conclusions can you make about these countries just using this data as your source of information? Which country do you think is "best off"? Which is "worst off"? Rank these countries from best to worst using these indicators alone as your guide. You will have to decide which indicators are more important to your ranking and which are less important.

Which of these countries do you suspect has a greater incidence of poverty? Which has the least poverty? Now, find the poverty level for each of these countries as well as their income (GNI) per capita from the same tables. Rank the countries again from best to worst using the GNI per capita data. Is this ranking of countries substantially different from the first ranking you did using the social and economic variables? Explain why that might be the case if there is any difference.

progress on the path toward fuller economic and social development (examine, for example, the data on Niger, Pakistan or Yemen at the World Bank site noted at the end of this chapter). But there are reasons to be hopeful in many nations.

There remains much to be done to bring as many persons as possible out of poverty and the deprivation it produces and that is one reason why understanding how economic development takes place is so important.

The development enigma

It was the disturbing reality of world poverty, of a sharp division between rich nations and poor nations and within nations, and of so much human suffering in far too many countries that first brought us, in the late 1960s and early 1970s, to be keenly interested in development economics and the problems of what was then called the "Third World."[5] Why, we asked ourselves, when crossing the international border between the United States and Mexico from San Diego to Tijuana, did we witness such a dramatic and obvious change in incomes, living standards, and levels of human development? After all, the boundary between these two nations is an artificial political division. The geography on one side of the frontier is much like that on the other; in fact, in the mid-1800s, these lands were all part of one nation, Mexico. Why, then, does one enter after only a few steps or a short drive across the boundary into Mexico, not only a different world culturally and linguistically, but also one so unquestionably poorer and with fewer possibilities for individuals to realize their full potential when compared to the United States?

Other similar enigmas come easily to mind. Why is so much of Africa substantially less developed and poorer than Latin America (see Table 1.2 below), though both regions are considered part of the less-developed world? What accounts for the recent economic success of some East Asian countries, like South Korea and Taiwan, or taking a slightly longer time frame, of Japan, such that they seem to have passed over the threshold from underdevelopment to development? Why does India, which has such a promising human resource base with its large number of highly educated citizens and its immense potential market, remain one of the most

Table 1.2 Average income per capita and growth rates of per capita income

	Income per capita,[a]	Annual % change[b]	
	2001	1980–1990	1990–2001
Less-developed world	1,160	1.5	1.9
Sub-Saharan Africa	470	−1.2	0.0
East Asia and Pacific	900	6.4	6.3
South Asia	450	3.5	3.6
Middle East and North Africa	2,000	−1.1	0.9
Latin America and the Caribbean	3,560	−0.3	1.7
Developed world	26,710	2.5	1.8

Source: World Bank 2000: 275, Table 1, 279, Table 3, 295, Table 11; 2003: 235, Table 1, 239, Table 3.

Notes
a As measured by Gross National Product (GNP) per capita, in US dollars.
b Of per capita Gross Domestic Product (GDP).

impoverished nations, while other countries – again, South Korea is an illustration – with a skilled and educated labor force, apparently have been able to make the transition toward higher and more equitable levels of economic development?

These are the sorts of incongruities and conundrums – and the list could be extended quite easily – that both vex and excite those interested in the problems of development. Trying to formulate reasonable explanations for such observed disparities, and by extension, suggesting what might be done to overcome the barriers that retard economic, social and human development is what development economics is all about.

It is on this adventure into theory and reality that we are about to embark. There are no easy answers that apply always and everywhere. There is no magic, one-stop, cure-all solution that can be offered that apply to every country. Becoming more developed is a challenge that requires both vision and hard work by both the leaders of nations as well as their citizens. Nonetheless, there are patterns and lessons to be learned from successful as well as unsuccessful development experiences that can help those with the power and the will to move their nations forward.

It is to these patterns and regularities based upon the concrete historical experiences of both successful and failed development episodes that we shall turn repeatedly. We are looking for the critical signposts that mark the "process" of development, such that it will be possible to determine what, broadly speaking, needs to be done and what should be avoided if progress is to be made.

Many abstract theories of how to develop have been advanced by economists, and these will be considered in later chapters. Such theories are an integral part of development economics and provide an important historical window on how economists have thought and continue to think about development.

Also of importance for less-developed nations are the concrete, positive, historical experiences of successful developers. We shall be looking especially to the lessons that can be gleaned from the rapid growth of Japan, South Korea, Taiwan, and Hong Kong, as well as other nations of that region that the World Bank calls the "High-Performing Asian Economies" (HPAEs).[6] The analysis and recommendations for action in subsequent chapters often are based upon the lessons of the HPAEs and the now-developed nations, as well as contrasts with less productive cases of transformation, such as the Latin American economies where the growth process slowed dramatically in the 1980s after promising initial successes.

We do not fetishize the East Asian experience, however, or believe it is somehow *sui generis*. Each country wishing to develop must forge its own path using past experiences as guides as to what to do and what not to do. It is unlikely that any country can duplicate what other countries already have done in all the specifics. We do believe there are general patterns that characterize successful development experiences, and those patterns of change are what we try to highlight in this text.

Underlying our interest in development exists a definite moral dimension. For us, development is about realizing very fundamental human values and about finding the means to extend the fruits of these values to the greatest majority of the world's population. These human values include, but are not limited to:

> the opportunity for meaningful employment and the possibility to provide for one's self and family; sufficient food, shelter, and other amenities for a decent life above the poverty line; the opportunity for pursuing education and the

increased quality of life it promises; a reasonable level of health care; social security for old age; democracy and political participation in the life of the community and society; equal treatment under the law and in the economy for all, regardless of race, gender, religion, nationality, or other differences; and individual dignity.

This listing of development goals is not meant to be all-inclusive. It is meant, however, to touch upon at least some of the primary ingredients toward which development, and not just economic development, is directed.

For us, and we hope for you too, economic development is of the utmost interest and of the gravest consequence. It touches our shared humanity. The great economists of the eighteenth, nineteenth, and early twentieth centuries – Adam Smith, David Ricardo, John Stuart Mill, Karl Marx, Alfred Marshall – were inspired by a profound concern for understanding the roots of economic wealth and the reasons for poverty, as well as for discovering the mechanisms through which economic and social gains might best be increased and shared among the members of society.

These matters have captured the attention and hearts as well as the minds of many thinkers. They are the noble questions that often lead students to wish to study economics in the first instance. We shall inquire into what those in the less-developed nations must do if they are to improve their economic and social lot. Further, there will be reflection on how the developed world, including concerned citizens of those countries, might understand their role and responsibilities in our increasingly interdependent world of rich and poor. It is important to keep firmly in mind that everyone's economic interests are joined in a global economic system, sometimes positively, other times negatively, no matter how remotely connected we at times may seem to be.

Recent trends in economic growth

The 1980s and early 1990s were not particularly propitious for either economic growth or development (the differences between the "growth" and "development" are spelled out in greater detail in Chapter 2). Even the developed world suffered a slowdown in its rate of economic expansion, and some countries experienced a decline in living standards after years of relative prosperity following the Second World War, a trend that worsened with the new century. Unemployment rose in the European Union (EU) to levels that have been difficult to decrease. The greatest number of jobs being created in the developed nations seem to be concentrated heavily in segments of the relatively lower-paying, lower-productivity service sectors that often offer meagre benefits and other perquisites – from sick leave to health care to retirement packages – that have become integral to the rising living standards of the developed countries since the Great Depression of the 1930s.

In the United States, real wages fell for a broad spectrum of the work force after 1973. Family incomes barely edged upward, due primarily to the fact that more family members, particularly women, entered the labor force in record numbers in an effort to maintain their families' standard of living. For increasing numbers who do find work, it is often irregular and part-time, as permanent work forces are replaced by *contingent workers* with fewer rights, lower incomes and futures that are more precarious. Even the already-developed nations, apparently, can experience

Box 1.1 The Nobel Prize in Economic Science

In subsequent chapters you will learn of the development economists who have received the Nobel Prize in Economic Science. To that group two names have recently been added: Amartya Sen in 1998 and Joseph Stiglitz in 2001.

Amartya Sen's contributions to the advancement of economic thought are many, but there is no doubt that his analytical work on the relationship between famines and economic output has made him famous. Sen maintains that *"Malthusian optimism"* (see Chapter 4 for a discussion of Malthus) – evidence showing food output per capita continues to rise as fast or faster than population – "has been indirectly involved in millions of deaths which have resulted from inaction and misdirection of public policy" (Sen: 1998, 241). Such increases in food output, however, are periodically interrupted by famines in some nations, while some others have even experienced production declines on a per capita basis. Sen has stressed that famines can occur in nations where food is plentiful, but not available in the devastated area(s), or to impacted social strata of the nation. Yet, the famine is often presented to the public as "inevitable" due to "scarcity."

To addressing this crisis Sen adopted a *Basic Human Needs* approach, coupled with an *Entitlement approach*. In Sen's view even if human beings do not have the income needed to buy food in a famine – because their wage income (an entitlement based on the exchange value of wages) is too low to buy food, or because food is driven up in price due to hoarding, transportation failures, and speculation – they are *entitled* to food because it is a basic human need. In a famine the government must address the *acquirement problem*, either buying surplus food in one region and distributing it at no fee in the famine area, or providing income so that the famished may purchase food. A famine is often the result of a failed distribution system, not a production failure – suggesting the need for government intervention to buy (import) food.

Joseph Stiglitz, former Chief Economist of the World Bank, is a mainstream neoclassical economist whose research contributions to economics span several areas. In development economics he has written widely about market failures and market imperfections, particularly as they apply to the agricultural sector. Stiglitz may well be remembered for his dissent from prevailing views regarding development economics while at the World Bank (1997–2000). Stiglitz became a critic of the *Washington Consensus* – the view that developing nations would move ahead if they would simply adopt a "package" whereby state owned enterprises were privatized, all subsidies were eliminated, all tariffs and other restraints on foreign trade were eliminated and government policy was limited to budget balancing and the control of inflation. Stiglitz argued that this approach was too narrow. Development should focus on environmental sustainability, a push for democracy and some concern for income distribution to address extreme poverty. Stiglitz's concern for democratic participation blossomed into advocacy for a *Comprehensive Development Framework* which would shift the definition of "development" from such "hard" factors as per capita income growth or purchasing power parity to mass participation in the design and evaluation of development policy (*voice*), *transparency* in regards to government processes and *accountability* to the populace in the appraisal of development initiatives.

In development economics it is likely that Stiglitz will be remembered for his many innovations and for his occasional trenchant criticisms. Indeed, his exasperation with the *IMF's Austerity Programs* (Chapter 17) is well conveyed by his riposte, shortly after he left his World Bank position, that the IMF was full of "third rate students from first-rate universities" who were unknowledgeable regarding the nations over which they exercised vast control through their ability to give and withhold financial assistance.

Sources: Chang 2001; Sen 1998

problems of continued development, and these problems are often more complex today given the impact of global competition among nations and firms.[7]

The less-developed world, on average, fared even worse since the 1980s. Table 1.2 provides summary data on the levels of income in 2001 and growth rates of income since 1980 in different regions of the world. Although, as we shall learn in Chapter 2, income and income growth are not the whole of what development is about, these numbers, along with the data on poverty in Table 1.1 above, do shed some initial light on the wide disparities in living standards which continue to plague many regions and peoples of the world.

South Asia ranks as the poorest region in the world.[8] Annual income per capita averaged a little less than 2 percent of what was received in the developed world. Comparing regions within the less-developed world, South Asia received 44 percent of the average income in East Asia and the Pacific and only about 11 percent of what was received in Latin America and the Caribbean.

Sub-Saharan Africa fared only slightly better; it is the second poorest region in the world.[9] Annual income per person also averaged slightly less than 2 percent of what was received in the developed world.

Among the less-developed regions of the world, the Middle East and North Africa, Latin America and the Caribbean region are, on average, relatively better-off. Still, compared to the developed world, their average incomes were, respectively, about 8 percent and 15 percent of what was received in the developed nations. Clearly there exists a substantial gap in incomes between the less-developed and the developed worlds, a gap that closed not at all for the less-developed world over the 1990s. On average, incomes were not converging between poor and rich nations, as they must to some degree if there is to be true progress in the poorest regions.

Low- and middle-income less-developed nations

In our study of economic development, we shall be most concerned with the so-called low- and middle-income economies of the less-developed world. By the World Bank's categorization, 157 economies (out of a total of 207 nations and territories) fell into these two groupings in 1999. Of these, sixty-four nations were included in the World Bank's "low-income" sub-group, nineteen more than had been in that group in 1993. Another fifty-five fell into the "lower-middle-income" range.

Incomes ranged from the poorest nation in the world, Ethiopia, with a meagre $100 per capita yearly income, to Egypt, with an average annual income of $1,400 per person in 1999 to $8,490 for South Korea (which is classified as an "upper-middle-income" country and is well on its way to developed country status). Also among the low-income economies were China ($780 per capita income) and India ($450), the two largest countries by population in the world. The average annual income of the entire low-income sub-grouping in 1999 was $410 per person. For the middle-income less-developed nations, the average income was $2,000, with the "upper-middle-income" group averaging $4,900 (more complete data for other nations and analysis of the meaning of this data are presented in the next chapter).

The second column of Table 1.2 shows what was happening to the growth of real, inflation-adjusted income per person since the 1980s. For all regions except East Asia and the Pacific and South Asia, income per person declined over 1980s, as output contracted or as aggregate income and output growth relative to population growth was inadequate to prevent declines in income per person. Clearly for these less-developed regions, the income gap with the high-income nations, which on average experienced positive economic growth, widened in both absolute and relative terms over that decade.[10]

Over the 1990s, all the regions of the less-developed world returned to positive per capita income growth rates, with the exception of sub-Saharan Africa, which has suffered two decades of falling or zero growth of income per person. The per person income gap between the less-developed nations and the developed world has grown for all of the less-developed world since 1980, as is clear from the difference in the growth rates of average income compared to the developed world. However, East Asia and the Pacific and South Asia have been closing their income gap with the developed nations, and the reason why income convergence has occurred in those regions will be important to try to understand.

The lower growth rates observed in recent years is very different from the trends in the less-developed nations that prevailed in the period prior to the 1980s. During the United Nations' First Development Decade of the 1960s, the target rate of growth of aggregate income for the less-developed nations was 5 percent and for the Second Development Decade the target was 6 percent annual growth. Many countries met or exceeded these targets, so that real average income per person was rising in much of the less-developed world, though sub-Saharan Africa lagged behind. This explains why the slow-down, or even reversal, in growth rates after 1980 has been so disconcerting to policy-makers and development economists.

While Table 1.2 does highlight the enormous divergence in incomes separating the less-developed nations from the developed, and among the less-developed regions of the world themselves, even that data fails to underscore this disparity. Table 1.3 provides a more global and yet extraordinarily dramatic portrayal of the distance that continues to separate the developed "have" nations from the less-developed "have-not" countries.

The less-developed world, with more than four-fifths of the world's population in 2001, received slightly less than one-fifth of total world income. In a cruel symmetry, the developed world nations, with well less than one-fifth of the world's population,

Table 1.3 World income, world population and their distribution, 2001

	Share of world's income (%)	Share of world's population (%)
Less-developed world	19.8	84.4
Sub-Saharan Africa	1.0	11.0
East Asia and Pacific	5.3	29.8
South Asia	2.0	22.5
Middle East and North Africa	2.1	4.9
Latin America and the Caribbean	6.2	8.5
Developed world	80.2	15.6

Source: World Bank 2003: 235, Table 1, 239, Table 3.

Note
Missing data for Europe and Central Asia mean that subtotals do not add to totals for the less-developed world. The income shares are computed as a percentage of total world income as measured by GDP.

received four-fifths of total world income in 2001, a share that has remained virtually unchanged since the 1990s. Looked at slightly differently, the developed world received more than five times its "equality share" of total world income (80.2 percent of world income divided by 15.6 percent of world population).[11] The less-developed world received less than 25 percent of what its equality share of world income would have been.

Looked at from another angle, the richest 1 percent of the world's population in the mid-1990s received as much total income as the world's poorest 57 percent (UNDP 2001: 19).

Examining particular regions within the less-developed world, inequality was even more extreme and income more meagre. South Asia, with more than 22 percent of total world population, received but slightly more than 2 percent of world income. The relatively better-off Latin America and Caribbean region, by comparison, received more than 70 percent of what its hypothetical equality share of world income would have provided. Over the 1990s, sub-Saharan Africa's share of total world income fell slightly, even as its share of the world's population rose, which is why average income has been falling.

East Asia and the Pacific and South Asia increased their shares of total world income over the 1990s. Unfortunately, South Asia's share of total world population also rose over that same period, while East Asia and the Pacific's population share declined. However, even these figures fail to tell the whole story of income and income distribution, since they do not reveal how income actually was distributed to individuals and families *within* regions or within specific nations. This issue will be examined in detail in subsequent chapters.

The disparities between the less-developed nations vis-à-vis the developed nations shown in Tables 1.2 and 1.3 are not of recent origin. Worse, differences *within* the less-developed world itself have been growing, both between regions and within countries themselves. Since the 1960s, many of the poorest countries have suffered a relative decline, and in some instances, an absolute deterioration in their position on many significant measures of productivity and in their contribution to world output.

Between 1960 and 1990, for example, the share of total world output received by the poorest 20 percent of the world's population fell from 2.3 percent to 1.3 percent. Their share of world trade decreased from 1.3 percent to 0.9 percent, and their contribution to global domestic investment fell from 3.5 percent to 1.1 percent (UNDP 1993: 27, Table 2.1). The contributions of the poorest to production, to trade, and their share of world income declined relative to those of other groups in society, including better-off nations within the less-developed world.

It is a cliché, perhaps, to say that "the rich get rich and the poor get poorer." But in the 1980s and 1990s, cliché or not, that is what took place in some regions of the world, particularly in South Asia and sub-Saharan Africa. During the late-1990s some improvement in East Asia and Latin America could be noted, but the overall record of success in reducing the high incidence of poverty at the world level remains dreadfully inadequate by virtually any standard, as World Bank publications, such as the *World Development Report 2000/2001*, reflect.

Nonetheless, the gains that have been made in the less-developed world *despite* a weak record of economic growth and production since the late 1970s do provide reason for continued hope that positive and reasonably equitable progress remains possible if societies make the right choices. Advances in the human condition continue to be made, often in the direst circumstances. With the hope for a newly expanding world economy in the twenty-first century, the amelioration of poverty and further improvements in the standard of living of a greater part of the world's population must be one of the highest goals.

Why development, and why now?

Nations like Great Britain, the United States, Germany, Japan, France, and the Scandinavian countries that today can be considered developed by any standard did not attain that status overnight.[12] In fact, development in all its economic, political, and social dimensions took place quite slowly and proceeded unevenly over a very long period of time, centuries in fact.

The great majority of the countries now considered to be less developed have had significantly less time to become developed, at least as independent political entities. It is important to recall how many of the nations of Africa, Asia, and the Caribbean have achieved political independence only since the end of the Second World War in 1945 when the drive to de-colonize due to pressure from the newly created United Nations truly began in earnest. Since then, well over 120 newly independent countries have been established from the former colonial empires and, more recently, the collapse of the former Soviet bloc. It is in these new nations that the problematic of becoming developed and of making progress toward authentic human well-being is most pressing.

It is essential to keep this time dimension in mind, without finding in it an ultimate excuse for slow progress. Most of the less-developed nations have had, at best, only a few decades to work on the fundamental twin goals of post-colonial construction: nation-building and progress on the path toward higher levels of economic and social development. One can argue that it takes time to undo the ingrained patterns of production, social class and power inherited from the past. What we will call adverse *path dependence* in Chapter 3 weighs heavily on the present in many poor nations.

On the other hand, the means to realize development goals are closer to hand than at any time in history.[13] The range of available and potentially applicable knowledge would seem to make the conceivable diffusion of technological progress, of advances in medicine, of techniques of efficient business and government administration and so on easier to attain for today's less-developed nations than it was for earlier developers who had to painstakingly create that knowledge. If only this vast array of knowledge could be effectively transferred, harnessed and applied in the less-developed nations, the current state of poverty in most parts of the world could begin to be overcome.

It is thus necessary to try to balance the short time-frame that most countries have had in which to try to become more developed with the fact that the "know-how" for achieving development is available now as never before. Does that then mean that the less-developed nations are on the brink of becoming developed? Not necessarily. Whether the knowledge about *how* to increase economic growth and about *how* to become more developed can be applied in ways that succeed in taking the less-developed nations across the threshold to developed-world status depends upon how stubborn the barriers to development continue to be in each of those nations. Possibility still needs to be transformed into actuality, and the means to effect that transformation is central to the subject matter of development economics.

Economic growth and development requires structural change

Economics is often defined as the study of "how societies can best allocate scarce resources among alternative uses" so as to maximize something – usually the level of each individual's or household's satisfaction or utility – the presumption being (though it is often an unexamined proposition), that maximizing individual satisfaction also will maximize society's total well-being simultaneously. The allocation of society's resources is assumed to take place within a *given* institutional and organizational setting that is taken to be exogenous to the analysis done by the economist.

This operating framework of orthodox, or neoclassical, economics in which the allocation of existing resources occurs within a given and presumably immutable or slowly changing social and institutional structure has been the key to the robust analysis and the predictive capability of modern economic models. These are the theories studied in most beginning and intermediate economic theory courses. The presumption of given institutions and of *marginal* adjustments by economic actors to their environment is at the heart of neoclassical economics as taught around the world. So basic are these underlying presumptions that the great English economist Alfred Marshall was able to write on the title page of his *Principles of Economics*, first published in 1890, *"natura non facit saltum"*: nature makes no leaps.

The process of a country becoming more developed, of getting on the path to development and away from the ways of the past that have reinforced a lower level of growth and progress, is not however, simply about the efficient allocation of existing resources within a given institutional regime. It is not simply about maximizing utility or profits within the constraints of what is currently available to that society and inherited from the past. Rather, development is fundamentally about *regime change* and about the search for an optimal growth path, or at least one that is superior to the existing allocation of resources and current efficiency levels. Further, fomenting development typically requires new institutional patterns and organizational structures necessary to support such a dynamic process of change.

To get a country on the road to development, and contrary to many economic theories, very often does require a "leap" – often a quite substantial one – away from the past structures. Marginal modifications of the economy and society simply may be insufficient to propel an economy and society forward in the needed new direction and on to a higher path of progress for the future. For the less-developed nations, development compels them to undertake substantial *qualitative* structural change. The future cannot be just an extension of the past. The past and the path-dependent nature of its weight on the present are precisely what have made these nations poor and need to be transcended.

There are a number of major *structural changes* and patterns identified by development economists and economic historians that are believed to be characteristic of any successful development process. We shall be examining these in detail in later chapters. Here these structural changes are briefly introduced to suggest the nature of *qualitative* change required and to point out the direction we shall be taking in the chapters that follow.

1   **Growth of industrialization.** Economic growth and development are strongly associated with an increasing share of a nation's output and labor force involved in industrial, especially manufacturing, activities, at least initially, as we will see in Chapter 9. Over time, services become increasingly important too as the economy matures even further. Wages tend to rise in the industrial sector as the level and use of technology expands with increased production and as the fruits of this higher productivity are shared by workers and owners of enterprises as higher income. Production methods become relatively intensive in the use of knowledge – human capital – and of physical capital. As part of this unfolding process, the urban population tends to grow both relatively and absolutely compared to the rural population.

2   **A decrease in the role of agriculture.** Parallel to the expansion of the industrial sector of the economy is a decline in the share of agricultural output in total output, a reduction in the share of the total labor force employed in agriculture and a decrease in the share of the rural population to total population. The so-called "surplus labor" (i.e., low productivity labor) in agriculture migrates to urban areas in search of the promise of better-paid and higher productivity industrial employment. It is this shift of workers from low-productivity agricultural employment to higher-productivity industrial employment that contributes to the increase in national output. Technological progress and labor productivity tend to lag in the primary (agriculture, mining, and fishing) sector, but over time output per person approaches the level reached in the industrial, or secondary, sector as fewer workers in agriculture produce more output.

    One leading development expert has written that "economic development is a process of moving from a set of assets based on primary products, exploited by unskilled labor, to a set of assets based on knowledge, exploited by skilled labor" (Amsden 2001: 2). This description captures the nature of the first two fundamental structural changes required for long-term development progress.

3   **Changing trade patterns.** Successful development is almost always marked by a maturation in the structure of trade, as a limited range of primary exports – agriculture and fishing products, unprocessed mining and other extractive minerals, and forestry products – is replaced by both a greater diversity of export products and by an evolving export mix. Successful developers shift from a dependence on traditional, primary export products toward, first, simpler manufactured and non-traditional primary exports, and ultimately toward more complex commodity exports, from motorcars to computers to biotechnology products to information technology and other types of high-value added production. As a result of this evolutionary transformation, manufacturing exports typically come to dominate the export profile of more developed nations and the share of primary exports in total exports shrinks within the export profile.

4   **Increased application of human capital and knowledge to production.** Economic growth and development require increases in the productivity of labor in all sectors if incomes and the standard of living of the population is to rise. This is achieved partly, but quite importantly, through improvements in the training and education of the existing and future labor force through increases in what economists call *human capital accumulation*. This takes place via both the formal schooling process and because of "learning-by-doing" at the work place. Increased productivity is also the consequence of an expansion of the use of

more physical capital and increased rates of physical capital accumulation of machines and tools which typically embody more advanced technology and knowledge that can help to make a properly trained labor force even more efficient.

Human capital accumulation, physical capital accumulation and technology all increase the productivity of the labor force. At the same time, they contribute to the possibility of higher wages for labor and an easier, because less labor-intensive, work-place environment, both of which contribute to the potential well-being of the labor force. We shall stress again and again the essential *complementarity* of human and physical capital accumulation and the urgency for the less-developed nations to not only tap into the existing pool of technology available on the world level but also of developing over time an autonomous technological capacity based on indigenous labor skills (see Chapters 8 and 13).

5 **Undertaking essential institutional change.** Economic growth and development require fundamental institutional change. New organizations such as banks, stock and bond exchanges and insurance companies gain added importance. The role of the central government – the *state* – must change to facilitate and not thwart private initiatives. The social infrastructure of roads, ports, communications, the provision of electricity, water, and other power must be improved, and the state plays a central role in these areas, particularly during early stages of structural transformation.

The specific nature of the legal system and of property rights; the rules and regulations governing the emerging financial system of banks, stock and bond markets, and other financial intermediaries; the creation and operation of a civil service system; determining what will be taught in the schools and how success will be measured and so on all must be worked out and codified by government. Without changes in the fundamental rules of the game, without the specifics defining how new institutions will work and provide improved outcomes compared to existing institutions, many of the "big-picture" structural changes noted in the text will not have their full, desired effects. The state has a challenge in clearly defining and then enforcing the rule of law, including the defence of property rights, as one of its fundamental tasks. This means that the central government, which is itself an institution inherited from the past, must be greatly modified and made more efficient and streamlined if economic growth and development are to be advanced effectively.

Needed institutional change runs deep into basic values and motivations too. Businesses increasingly must be operated with more attention paid to efficiency and profitability in a more competitive and open atmosphere. Old ways of thinking and doing will undoubtedly be threatened by what will be an often unsettling attention to profit maximization by the "new" entrepreneurs in industry and agriculture. Even the family often is redefined during the process of development, as the extended family of the past is replaced by the nuclear family of more modern society, as individualism becomes more ingrained and as maximization behavior replaces the satisficing model of behavior of the past.

These institutional changes and many others will be considered in the following chapters. Economic growth and development, however, definitely require a break with the past. Some of the most cherished institutions of many societies today such as close family structures and interpersonal relations, religious traditions and the general pace of life will be altered over time, becoming more and more like those institutions in other societies on the path to development and more like those institutions and values already in place in developed nations.

These are not the only structural changes that less-developed nations must undertake if they wish to make progress toward development. Others, such as changes in macroeconomic policy to control inflation, for example, and the role of the state in a broader context that attend the process of becoming developed also will be considered in detail in later chapters.

Barriers to development

Throughout our study of economic development, we will confront repeatedly the perplexing problem as to why some countries are more developed than others. Why is Great Britain more developed than Angola or the United States than Colombia? The very simple answer, since it is basically a truism, is that the level and pace of economic development are lower the greater are the barriers to economic progress and transformation in a country and more rapid the fewer and less intractable are those obstacles. The challenge for the development analyst is thus to attempt to identify the most significant barriers to development in each country and to formulate effective measures, including public policy, that can begin to undo, remove, or at least minimize the effects of those obstacles to progress that slow or thwart the development process.

Barriers to change and development can be either *internal* or *external* to a country.

Potential internal barriers to development: Some examples of possible internal barriers that tend to block change and thus thwart economic growth and development are:

a   inequalities in the existing distribution of income and wealth, including the distribution of land ownership. For most countries, the wealth distribution is intimately related to the nature and power of class relations in society and to control over economic resources and the political sphere;

b   the level and efficiency of infrastructure development (roads, electricity, water, communication services, port facilities, and so on);

c   the role and level of development of organized banking and lending activities and of equity (stock) and other financial markets and financial intermediaries;

d   an ineffective or underdeveloped educational system, including both relatively low levels of general literacy and an imbalance between allocations of financing to lower and higher education;

e   prevailing ideological concepts and their impact on thinking and behavior, including the influence of religious thinking, the accepted role of women and ethnic or religious minorities, the prevailing economic orthodoxy and so on;

f   the initial endowment of natural resources of a nation;

g   the role of the state, that is, the power and nature of the influence of the central government, including the degree of political freedom and the strength of

democratic processes (included here is the macroeconomic environment that government at least partially controls, including the nature and definition of property rights and the functioning of the legal system);
h   the extent and importance of political corruption and patronage and the impact of these on public policies and on economic behavior of those governed;
i   the existence of substantial "market failures" such that market signals are not fully, completely, or accurately transmitted to economic agents, thus distorting resource allocation, production decisions, spending patterns, and so on.

Potential external barriers to development: Examples of possible external barriers to development include:

a   multinational or transnational corporations that control national resources;
b   the international division of labor and the prevailing patterns of international trade (e.g., primary commodity exporting countries versus manufactured-good exporting countries), including the operation of the organized institutional structure of the international trade system, the effects of the World Trade Organization's negotiations and of regional trade blocs, such as the European Union (EU) or the North American Free Trade Agreement (NAFTA);
c   the functioning of international financial institutions, including not only the international private commercial banks but also the World Bank and the International Monetary Fund (IMF);
d   the influence of the geopolitical and strategic interests of larger economic powers vis-à-vis smaller and weaker economic entities;
e   the economic policies of more developed nations on interest rates, for example, or on tariffs or non-tariff barriers in the global economic system, and so on.

This very general discussion of internal and external barriers is meant only to be suggestive in a general way of the types of barriers to progress that can confront individual countries; it could be extended and refined almost indefinitely. Throughout the book we shall be considering and analyzing these and other specific barriers to progress that many less-developed nations confront. For any specific nation, be it India or Thailand, Côte d'Ivoire or Somalia, Bolivia or Guyana, the list of possible internal and external obstacles can only be a guide toward the identification and detailed specification of the unique particulars of the barriers actually operating to thwart progress in that country. For every nation, the identification of the barriers to change, and then the specifics of how each obstacle acts as a restraint on progress, need to be clearly and analytically defined so that the nature of the remedy is also made more apparent.

The relative weight of external versus internal barriers should not be considered a constant in any particular situation.[14] The influence of internal and external barriers can and will alter in importance over time and because of unique situations particular to specific countries. The relative influence of internal and external barriers cannot be presumed a priori but must be understood in each specific and changing circumstance. What we can state with confidence is that where barriers to change, be they internal or external, are not terribly powerful, progress tends to be more rapid. On the other hand, development will be less vigorous where the barriers to change exert a more powerful adverse influence.

All countries, including developed nations, always face both internal and external barriers that act as obstacles to continued progress. What is central as to whether development in any particular nation will occur or not, and at what pace, is not whether there are obstacles to progress – for there *always are* – but rather how these existing barriers are to be overcome by that society. New obstacles to continued progress inevitably will arise as further growth and development take place, often as a consequence of overcoming an earlier barrier, and solutions to these new obstacles then must be devised. All countries thus confront forces – some active, others simply a consequence of lethargy – that tend to slow the pace of change and block the path of development.

The issue, then, is not why some countries face obstacles and others do not, since all nations constantly encounter barriers to further progress. The challenge is to try to discover how those nations that have been successful at fostering and sustaining economic growth and development by overcoming successive barriers have been able to do so and what might be learned from their histories.

Questions for review

1   Development tends to be slower the stronger are a nation's barriers to the necessary structural changes that are characteristic of successful development. Choose a less-developed nation in which you are interested and list three specific obstacles that you think may be acting to slow the pace of economic development. For each briefly explain how and why you think each obstacle retards economic progress. Indicate whether each obstacle is an internal or an external barrier to development. What suggestions for policy or action can you offer that might contribute to reducing the restraining influence of each of these barriers in the future?

2   Foreign multinational or transnational corporations (MNCs or TNCs) often are the target of criticism for their alleged detrimental impact on the economic welfare of less-developed nations. Their operations in the less-developed world are often controversial and evoke strong emotional responses. In fact, the operations of MNCs/TNCs, as is discussed in more detail in Chapter 14, can be either positive or negative in their consequences, and most likely will engender a mix of positive and negative contributions. List and explain two possible advantages that MNCs/TNCs might bring to the less-developed nations where they operate and two possible disadvantages that might result to those nations from the operations of MNCs/TNCs within their borders. Note that you are being asked only for *possible* or *potential* advantages and disadvantages; there is no presumption that either the advantages or disadvantages are necessarily realized. (In Chapter 14, we will consider how a country might go about attempting to maximize the net benefits from the location of foreign MNCs/TNCs within its borders; here you are being asked only to speculate about the effects of MNC/TNCs on the less-developed nations based upon your existing level of knowledge.)

3   Only a few broad indicators of well-being for the less-developed nations have been provided in the text, particularly income per person, life expectancy, infant mortality and so on, and these were considered only at a very aggregate level. Using data for a recent year from the World Bank (www.worldbank.org) and/or

United Nations sources (www.undp.org) choose *two* low- or middle-income less-developed countries of interest to you and *one* developed country for comparison purposes and make a table showing: (a) income per person; (b) total population and the population growth rate; (c) the percentage of the population active in agriculture (or, alternatively, the percentage of population that is rural); (c) the share of total production accounted for by industry; (d) the adult illiteracy rate; (e) life expectancy at birth; (f) the infant mortality rate; (g) population per physician; (h) the percentage of the population enrolled in secondary education; and (i) the percentage of the population with access to safe water. Briefly explain what information each indicator supplies about the level of economic development of the countries and about their future prospects; that is, what does each proxy measure indicate about either the level of development of the country and/or its chances for progress in the future? How do the two countries you have selected compare on each indicator with the developed nation you have selected? Speculate on the reasons for any differences.

4   How does the technology of agricultural production in, say, Somalia differ from that used in a more developed nation? Why do such differences exist and persist? Could Somalia use the same kinds of technology – tractors, harvesters, combines, fertilizers, irrigation and the know-how to effectively utilize these tools – on its lands? Why, or why not? (Hint: If you can utilize hypothetical production isoquants and isocost curves for Somalia and a more developed country, you might gain some additional insight. Think of differences in input prices, too, between Somalia and a more developed nation. Having done that, think about what possible *other* contributing factors, be they social, cultural or economic, might explain these differences in technology used.)

Resources for student use and suggestions for further reading

With every passing day, there are more resources available containing data and other information on the situation of nearly every country in the world. Of course, the Internet has opened up possibilities for research and data collection and analysis beyond what could have been imagined even a decade past. Every year the data become somewhat more comprehensive and reliable. It is possible to find information on everything from income to levels of education of women, to kilometers of roads, to the number of doctors and nurses, to the percentage of dwellings with indoor plumbing. Most college and university library collections are likely to have one or more of the publications listed below, and those with access to the Internet have a world of information at their fingertips – for free!

The statistical data included in this text are but an insignificant fraction of the data available from the available sources. You are encouraged to peruse the sources listed here and others in your library. We already encouraged you to begin to do that in Focus 1.2 at the beginning of this chapter. Learning how "to read" statistics, that is, attempting to determine the meaning and implications of data presented in statistical tables without reading the text accompanying such data, will vastly improve your powers of economic and social analysis.

The following sources should be of great help in studying the problems of economic development.

- World Bank, *World Development Report*, by year. Issued annually, this is an invaluable resource tool. Besides the statistical tables at the end of every volume, which, unfortunately have been reduced in recent volumes, each report has a "theme" that is explored in detail. For 2003, this has to do with "transforming institutions, growth, and quality of life"; for 2002, the focus was on institution-building for development; in 2001 the theme was poverty, and in 1999, it was on knowledge. In previous years, the focus has been on workers (1995), health (1993), poverty (1990), the environment (1992), and development strategies (1991). Every major university library should have copies of at least some of these volumes.

  Some of the data in the current *World Development* Report is available on-line at http://www.worldbank.org. This site has a large and varied quantity of data available for use. Many of the problems in this text invite you to access the World Bank data.

- United Nations Development Programme, *Human Development Report*, by year. Also issued annually, this report is complementary to the *World Development Report* in that it covers a broader range of development indicators and issues (available on-line at http://www.undp.org). The focus is more on people and the changes in economies that impact on "human development," as opposed to focusing on the economic side of the ledger. This is an important evolving source of information, having been published only since 1990. We will examine in more detail in the next chapter some specific information on human development published in the *Human Development Report*. Larger university libraries are also likely to have this publication in their international document section.

- The United Nations also publishes various kinds of data, mostly economic in nature, via its various regional Economic Commissions. One can find statistical and interpretive data published by: the UN Economic Commission for Asia and the Pacific; the UN Economic Commission for Africa and the Middle East; the UN Economic Commission for Latin America and the Caribbean; and the UN Economic Commission for Europe. If you can locate these volumes, interesting and often quite detailed statistical data can often be discovered, though it can be more difficult to work with than data from either of the above two sources, since different assumptions or definitions may be used in assembling the data.

- There are a number of scholarly journals related to the study of economic development that often have recent empirical research, as well as more "cutting-edge" theoretical articles. The most widely distributed are *World Development* (monthly), *Economic Development and Cultural Change* (quarterly), *Journal of Development Economics* (quarterly), and the *Journal of Development Studies* (quarterly). Also worth reading is the *World Bank Economic Review* (thrice annually) and a reading of the papers of the *Annual Bank Conference on Development Economics* available on the World Bank website.

- If you have not visited or lived in a less-developed country, it is often difficult to fully comprehend what it means to be extremely poor. To convey a sense of the deprivation which absolute poverty entails, Robert Heilbroner in *The Great Ascent*, Chapter 2, transforms a middle-class family in a developed country into an impoverished family in a "typical" less-developed nation. For gaining a sense of empathy short of traveling to a less-developed nation, this is an excellent resource. As an alternative, there also are three short vignettes about a poor family in Ghana, another in Peru, and a family in Bangladesh that provide some insight into the impact of poverty in the *World Development Report 1990*, pages 24–25.

Notes

1 Another way of looking at the statistics is that if children in the less-developed world faced the same mortality rates as children in the already-developed nations, the number of deaths would be reduced by more than 90 percent. That would have meant 1.1 million deaths of children, rather than the 12.4 million actually recorded.

2 Most often diarrhoea is the result of a lack of access to safe drinking water and inadequate sanitation. Young girls collect water for the family for the day from irrigation ditches or dirty well sources, and if this water is not properly handled – boiled for example – intestinal problems that can lead to diarrhoea can easily develop.

3 This is not to suggest that no progress has been made. Since 1945, the death rate of children under the age of five has dropped by half, but the growth in population since that time means the total number dying from poverty remains unacceptably high.

4 See Blackwood and Lynch (1994) for formal definitions of poverty, including alternative definitions, such as the Sen Index which attempts to combine a head count of the numbers in poverty, the poverty gap, and the distribution of income into one measure of poverty. Their article is an excellent primer on the differences in, and the variety of, poverty measures.

For more recent measures of the poverty gap, but for different years for most countries, see the World Bank's Global Poverty Monitoring site at http://www.worldbank.org/research/povmonitor. There they provide poverty gap measures for the $1 and $2 per day poverty thresholds. The poverty gap in Table 1.1 is for the $1 per day poverty line. For some Sub-Saharan African countries, such as Gambia, Lesotho, Mali and Niger, the poverty gap now exceeds 20 percent and in some cases, 30 percent for the $1 per day poverty line and is even higher for the $2 per day gap as the poverty situation in Africa worsened over the 1990s.

5 The term "Third World" was used to describe those nations and regions that were neither developed capitalist (i.e., "First World") nations and regions, like the United States, Canada, Europe and Japan, for example, nor part of the socialist (i.e., "Second World") bloc of China, the former Soviet Union and Eastern Europe. There was some blurring around the edges (Was Cuba part of the Third or Second World?), but in general, the Third World nations were considered to be the less-developed, poorer nations of Asia, Africa, and Latin America and the Caribbean. In gross numbers, some 140 countries might still be considered as coming within such a Third World classification.

With the collapse and fragmentation of the Soviet bloc after 1989, the continued usefulness of the First, Second and Third World categories has been called into question. The People's Republic of China remains as the sole major Second World nation, and many would have classified China as part of the Third World not the Second. Also in vogue for a time was the "North–South" terminology, with "North" being a shorthand for the already developed capitalist nations and the "South" denoting the less-developed countries. We have elected, for simplicity's sake, to use the terms "developed" and "less-developed" (or sometimes "underdeveloped" or "developing") to describe those nations which were considered part of, respectively, the First and Third Worlds.

6 The publication of a World Bank (1993b) study and responses to it by Asian economic specialists provides a growing body of knowledge that may be applicable to those nations that continue to be less-developed.

7 In fact, the emergence of the so-called new, or endogenous, economic growth theories in the 1980s can at least partly be traced to a concern with the stagnation of economic growth and the rise in unemployment rates in Europe and the United States. These theories and their important implications for economic development in the less-developed world are discussed in detail in Chapter 8.

8 Included in South Asia are Afghanistan, Bangladesh, Bhutan, India, Maldives, Nepal, Pakistan and Sri Lanka.

9 Included in Sub-Saharan Africa are Angola, Botswana, Burundi, Comoros, Democratic Republic on the Congo, Eritrea, Ethiopia, Kenya, Lesotho, Madagascar, Malawi, Mauritius, Mayotte, Mozambique, Namibia, Rwanda, Seychelles, Somalia, South Africa, Sudan, Swaziland, Tanzania, Uganda, Zambia and Zimbabwe in East and Southern Africa; and Benin, Burkina Faso, Cameroon, Cape Verde, Central African Republic, Chad, Republic of Congo, Côte d'Ivoire, Equatorial Guinea, The Gambia, Gabon, Ghana, Guinea, Guinea-Bissau, Liberia, Mali, Mauritania, Niger, Nigeria, São Tomé and Príncipe, Senegal, Sierra Leone, and Togo in West Africa.

10 The World Bank (1993a: 41–42) estimated that if economic growth rates had been as rapid in the 1980s as in the period 1960–1980 the number of infant deaths in the less-developed world would have been reduced by 6 percent (350,000 fewer deaths). In Latin America, which especially suffered from the slow-down in economic growth in the 1980s, infant deaths would have been 12 percent fewer, with a growth rate similar to the historical trend.

11 With 15.6 percent of world population, the equality share of world income for the developed world also would be 15.6 percent. Since, however, world income was not distributed equally, the developed world actually received 80.2 percent of total world income, more than five times its hypothetical equality share.

12 Of course, there are some who would argue that the crime, violence, drugs, lack of community, unemployment, pollution and environmental degradation, growing relative poverty, and homelessness in many of the developed nations, especially in their crowded urban areas, makes them unworthy of the name "developed." If "development" is the goal, some would argue, there is much about the already-developed economies that it is not particularly desirable to emulate. An economist might suggest that these are, perhaps, trade-offs that are the "price" of economic progress, that economic growth and development are not "costless," and that what each nation must do is to evaluate both the benefits and the costs associated in achieving a higher level of economic growth and development.

One must also question to what extent the problems of the developed nations are perhaps the result of particular patterns of unequally shared growth and development, rather than being necessarily inherent problems that accompany progress per se. Is it possible to achieve a higher level of economic growth and a higher level of development without incurring the problems mentioned above? That, too, is a challenge for the future.

13 See Gerschenkron (1962) for a fascinating study of so-called "late developers." Gerschenkron believed that late-developing economies had advantages in attempting to accelerate their pace of development by having access to the most recent technological advances, but that this was always a latent possibility. There was no guarantee that late-developing economies actually would utilize that knowledge to the best advantage. In other words, progress toward higher levels of economic and social development, though possible, was not predetermined simply by the availability of higher levels of world technological knowledge and know-how. It was still up to individual economies to find the means to effectively make use of such possibilities and to create the institutional structures capable of effecting such a transition. This theme, well captured by the endogenous growth theories and theories of technological progress, forms a large part of this book's understanding of the development process.

14 For example, it was common in the dependency literature on development in the 1960s and 1970s (see Chapter 6) to assume that the less-developed nations were poor primarily because of external forces. Whether these external barriers were the International Monetary Fund, the multinational corporations or simply "imperialism," the presumption was that it was the external barriers that kept the less-developed nations poor and that internal barriers if not insignificant, were primarily secondary to broader external forces. We make no such presumption about what the barriers to development are or of their relative weight in any particular country. Nor do we presume anything about the relative importance of internal and external obstacles to future progress.

References

Amsden, Alice H. 2001. *The Rise of "The Rest": Challenges to the West from Late-Industrializing Countries*. Oxford: Oxford University Press.

Blackwood, D.L. and R.G. Lynch. 1994. "The Measurement of Inequality and Poverty: A Policy-Maker's Guide to the Literature," *World Development* 22 (April): 567–578.

Chang, Ha-Joon (ed.). 2001. *The Rebel Within: Joseph Stiglitz and the World Bank*. London: Anthem Press.

Foster, Phillips Wayne. 1992. *The World Food Problem: Tackling the Causes of Undernutrition in the Third World*. Boulder, CO: Lynne Rienner Pubs.

Gerschenkron, Alexander. 1962. *Economic Backwardness in Historical Perspective*. Cambridge, MA: Harvard University Press.

McNamara, Robert S. 1976. *Address to the Board of Governors of the World Bank*, Manila, Philippines, 4 October. Washington, DC: World Bank.

Sen, Amartya. 1998. "Food, Economics, and Entitlements," in Carl Eicher and John Staatz (eds), *International Agricultural Development*, 3rd edn. Baltimore: Johns Hopkins Press.

UNDP (United Nations Development Programme). 1993. *Human Development Report 1993*. Oxford: Oxford University Press.

—— 2001. *Human Development Report 2001*. Oxford: Oxford University Press.

—— 1995. *Human Development Report 1995*. Oxford: Oxford University Press.

World Bank. 1990. *World Development Report 1990*. Oxford: Oxford University Press.

—— 1991. *World Development Report 1991*. Oxford: Oxford University Press.

—— 1993a. *World Development Report 1993*. Oxford: Oxford University Press.

—— 1993b. *The East Asian Miracle: Economic Growth and Public Policy*. NY: Oxford University Press.

—— 2000. *World Development Report 2000/2001*. Oxford: Oxford University Press.

—— 2001. *World Development Report 2001*. Oxford: Oxford University Press.

—— 2003. *World Development Report 2003*. Oxford: Oxford University Press.

WHO (World Health Organization). 1994. *The State of the World's Children 1994*. Geneva: WHO.

2 Measuring economic growth and development

After studying this chapter, you should understand:
- the difference between economic growth and development;
- the difference between gross national product (GNP) and gross domestic product (GDP), how to calculate each and the adjustments that can be made so that these measures are more useful for judging the level of development of economies;
- the implications of using either GNP or GDP per person as a measure of the well-being of a nation;
- how the purchasing power parity (PPP) definition of income differs from the usual GNP or GDP measure and why it may be a better measure for comparison;
- the importance of understanding income distribution, a Lorenz curve and the Gini coefficient when evaluating the level of development of a country;
- what the Human Development Index (HDI) is and how it can be used as a measure of development;
- the importance of sustainable development as a goal;
- the significance of the Kuznets' inverted-U hypothesis for the equity versus growth controversy and for understanding the process of development.

Introduction

What is meant by development? Though this may seem to be a deceptively simple question, the answer shapes how one judges different countries as to their respective levels of development. It affects what factors we consider as contributing to progress, and our answer to what development is will influence the public policies aimed at achieving a society's development goals. Knowing what is meant and what is not meant by development is thus a necessary first step if, as the British economist Joan Robinson once insisted, we are to ask the right questions.

We begin by considering how economists typically measure the level of development of a nation. There are two broad methodologies. One, the income per person or *economic growth*, criterion suggests that income levels are reasonably good approximate measures for comparing the level of development of nations and that income per person can serve as a logical surrogate for gauging overall social progress.

The competing view argues that development is such a complex, multi-faceted notion that it should be conceived from the outset as considerably broader than income and hence can only be measured by entirely different standards. Let us turn to a discussion of these two perspectives.

The economic growth/income criterion of development

Economists and other analysts often use a nation's per capita income as a proxy or substitute measure for evaluating the overall level of national development and welfare. The rate of growth of income per person can then be used to judge the progress a nation makes over time. Those who take this view are quite aware that the development of a nation actually encompasses much more than average income per person and the growth rate of that income. Development incorporates the diverse and broad aspirations of what might be called the "good life" in all its economic, social and political dimensions that each society sets, if only implicitly, for itself.

Societies may value, each somewhat differently of course, goals as diverse as:

a   equality of opportunity;
b   a rising income and standard of living, including a wider array of consumable goods and services over time;
c   equity in the distribution of income and wealth;
d   political democracy and wide-spread participation;
e   an expanded role for women, minorities and all social classes in economic, polit-
    ical, and social life;
f   increased opportunities for education and self-improvement irrespective of
    class, race, ethnicity, religion, or gender;
g   the expanded availability of, and improvements in, health care;
h   public and private safety nets to protect the most vulnerable – particularly the
    young, the old, the infirm, and the poorer – from extreme hardship;
i   a reasonably clean and healthy environment;
j   an efficient, competent, transparent, and fairly administered public sector;
k   a reasonable degree of competition in the private sector; and so on.

Each of us, as does each society, could add to or subtract from this list of goals (see Alkire 2002 for an overview of the issues involved in defining what encompasses human development). But there is no doubt that development encompasses a wide range of social and human goals that, while including the level of income and economic growth, goes well beyond this as well (see Focus 2.1 High-Quality Growth).

Development, being broader than income alone, typically requires fundamental structural change in the economy and society, as discussed at the end of Chapter 1. A higher level of development does not mean that a country needs to do more of what it already has been doing. Less-developed countries are less developed precisely because they produce and distribute a sub-optimal array of goods and services in inefficient ways. Development necessitates that these nations make changes that result in a substantially transformed future in which new values and ways of doing things, new institutions, and better functioning markets emerge.

The process of becoming more developed is without doubt often a process of

FOCUS 2.1   HIGH-QUALITY GROWTH

The International Monetary Fund (IMF) often has been taken to task for the "conditional-ity" it puts on borrowing countries, conditions that often have contributed to increases in poverty and lower average incomes (Chapter 17 considers this issue in depth). Over the 1990s, the IMF seemed slowly to be learning from the criticisms of its policies and from its own evaluations of past lending policies.

   Now, the IMF sees itself as promoting so called "high-quality growth," defined as

> growth that is sustainable, brings lasting gains in employment and living standards and reduces poverty. High-quality growth should promote greater equity and equal-ity of opportunity. It should respect human freedom and protect the environment. Obviously, growth cannot be high quality ... if it does not benefit fully, tangibly, and equitably a group that constitutes more than one half the population of the world and still bears the primary responsibility for the care, nutrition, and education of the world's children. Achieving high-quality growth depends, therefore, not only on pur-suing sound economic policies, but also on implementing a broad range of social policies.

Economic development is not just about economic growth, then, but about a *particular kind* of economic growth: high-quality growth in the IMF's terminology.

Source: IMF 1995: 286–288

wrenching social change. What is certain is that the legitimate and full range of development goals of any nation goes far beyond any simple concern with the level of income per person. *All* economists recognize this, including those who use a nation's income per person as an index for the broader development ambitions listed above.

Nonetheless, it is often convenient and simpler to use some measure of income per person as a substitute gauge for the broader goals of development that charac-terize the ultimate objectives of nations. Imagine how difficult it would be not just collecting data on the range of development goals listed above but then, with so many variables, trying to compare these for several countries. The complexity of comparing across a range of development variables with different values and inter-pretations is simply too daunting, even if each could be measured. Our brains, as complex as they are, still need some degree of simplification when many dimensions are being compared.

Fortunately, there is empirical evidence, some of which we shall examine below, to at least partially support the claim that income per person is highly correlated with key measures that attempt to capture the broader aspirations of economic, social, and political progress. Thus many economists, acknowledging that it would be wrong-headed to imply that higher income and economic growth are the same as development, firmly believe that it is reasonable to focus primarily on the factors that contribute to enhancing a nation's economic growth and income. This is because it is believed that the greatest number of the other dimensions of develop-ment that countries might wish to realize are more easily attained at and tend to accompany higher income levels. It is precisely from higher income over time that the means for reaching the broader goals of development are obtained.[1]

In this view, then, it is reasonable and informative to rank nations from highest to lowest by per capita income level as a measure of their relative development achievement.

Part of the attractiveness of using the per capita economic growth criterion is its very simplicity. All countries collect data on their level of economic activity, though with varying degrees of accuracy despite efforts by international institutions to unify the methods of data collection and to strive, to the degree feasible, for statistical comparability of the information collected.[2] The data for comparing income among countries, or for any particular country over time, are thus reasonably readily available and roughly comparable. We make use here of the annual data published by the World Bank in its *World Development Report*, a source which provides a consistent and reliable series of data available to researchers around the world. Thus in terms of facilitating comparisons as to the level of development of different nations, the income criterion has an undeniable attraction.

Measuring economic growth

Economic growth can be measured either by the growth of total output or of total income. In fact, the values of total final output and of income paid to all factors of production in an economy are equal to one another, by definition, as demonstrated in the simple circular flow diagram presented at the beginning of virtually every introductory economics text. The two most common measures used for international income and output comparisons, and hence for measuring economic growth, are GNP and GDP.

GNP is the total value of all income (= value of final output) accruing to residents of a country, regardless of the source of that income, that is, irrespective of whether such income is derived from sources within or outside the country. **GDP** is the total value (= value of final output) of all income created within the borders of a country, regardless of whether the ultimate recipient of that income resides within or outside the country.

How and why do the GNP and GDP measures of income differ? There will be no difference if an economy is completely "closed" to the rest of the world. Closed in this sense means that there is no migration of workers and no flows of investment between a country and the rest of the world. There may be exports and imports of goods, however, since trade flows do *not* affect the measurement of GNP or GDP and do not create any differences in the values of the two income measures.

If an economy were closed in this sense, then the only income that would be received by residents of the country would be derived from new productive activity taking place within the borders of that country. There would be no income received by residents inside the country originating from sources outside the country and no flows of income created within the borders of the country going to income recipients in other nations. In this case, GDP – the income produced within the borders of the country – would equal GNP – the income received by residents of that country.

However, in a world with multinational corporate investment moving across national boundaries and with financial capital and labor flows between nations, it is easy to see how a country's GNP might diverge from its GDP. For example, United States-based corporations had foreign direct investments outside the US equal to $468 billion in 1991. As a result of these investments in other countries, and taking into consideration US bank loans to other countries and other financial flows as well, a flow of profits, dividends, and interest income equal to $155.7 billion was returned to the US and was received as income by residents in the US. This income inflow *from outside the US* became part of the *GNP* of the United States. It was not part of the US GDP, of course, since it was not income created within the borders of the US. In fact, the value of this flow of profits, dividends, and interest to the US was included as part of the GDP of the *other* nations from which it originated. These income flows from other countries added, *ceteris paribus*, to US GNP, tending to make the income available to residents of the US greater than the income created within the borders of the US as measured by US GDP.

In the same year, 1991, just as US firms had investments in other countries, foreign firms had production facilities they had located in the US over the years. Total foreign direct investment in the US by other countries equalled $419 billion. These investments by foreigners in the US created income and output within the US borders that was included as part of US GDP. However, not all that income remained in the US to become part of US GNP. Profit, interest, and dividend income equal to $139.7 billion in 1991 belonged to investors in countries like the United Kingdom, Germany, and Japan that had made investments in the United States in the past. This income was created in the US (was part of US GDP), but it belonged to and flowed to income recipients outside the US, thus tending to reduce US GNP below the level of US GDP. The same effect was true of other income created in the US on investments owned by foreigners who then received income flows from the US.

In 1991, the *net* effect of the inflow of profits, interest, and dividends to the US from other nations **minus** the outflow of profits, interest, and dividends from the US to the rest of the world was equal to +$16 billion. Thus US GNP > US GDP by that amount, since more factor service payments flowed into the United States to pay for US investments and loans abroad than was paid to foreigners who had invested in or made loans to someone in the United States (US Department of Commerce 1994: 25; US Department of Commerce 1995: 58, 94). The same sorts of flows can create a divergence between GDP and GNP in other countries as well.

A second type of income flow between nations that can result in a divergence between GDP and GNP is due to worker remittances. As workers migrate from their home country to another in search of work, it is not uncommon that they leave some members of their families and other relatives behind. Frequently such workers send a portion of their income home. Such remittances by workers in one country to their families in their home country have the effect of tending to make GNP < GDP in the sending country where the migrating worker is located and GNP > GDP in the receiver nation where the family and relatives of the worker reside, all else being the same. For the US in 1991, such remittances (net) amounted to −$7.6 billion, indicating a net outflow of income earned in the US that was part of US GDP being sent to other countries to add to their GNP. Mexico, on the other hand, had a net inflow of income in the form of workers' remittances from other countries equal to +$1.9 billion (most of that from the US), helping to raise Mexico's GNP above its GDP, all else the same.

In general, then, whether a country's GDP < GNP or its GDP > GNP depends on the sum of the income inflows into the country from the rest of the world (ROW) less the sum of the income leakages leaving the country flowing to the ROW. Again, these are *income* flows; the level of exports and imports do not create any difference between the measured values of GNP and GDP. When the income inflows received by a country from the ROW exceed the income outflows of that country to the ROW, then that country's GNP>GDP. When the income inflows from the ROW are smaller than the income outflows to the ROW, then GDP>GNP for that country.

Table 2.1 provides some summary data on income and output for a number of countries for 1999.

The second and third columns of Table 2.1 provide information on total GDP and total GNP. The fourth column calculates the value of the GDP/GNP gap, that is, the difference measured by GDP − GNP. When the GDP/GNP gap is positive (GDP − GNP>0), the country had outflows of income to the ROW that exceeded inflows into the country from the ROW, and thus its GDP>GNP. When the GDP/GNP gap is negative (GDP − GNP<0), the country had inflows of income from the ROW that exceeded outflows to the ROW, and thus its GNP>GDP.

Table 2.1 GDP and GNP comparisons, selected nations, 1999

Country	Population (millions)	Total GDP[a]	Total GNP[a]	GDP/GNP gap[b]	GNP per capita ($)
Algeria	30.5	47.9	46.5	1.4	1,525
Argentina	36.6	283.2	277.9	5.3	7,593
Bangladesh	127.7	46.0	47.0	−1.0	368
Botswana	1.6	6.0	5.1	0.9	3,188
Brazil	168.1	751.5	742.8	8.7	4,419
Chile	15.0	67.5	71.1	−3.6	4,740
China	1,249.7	989.5	980.2	9.3	784
Côte d'Ivoire	14.7	11.2	10.4	0.8	703
Egypt	62.4	89.1	87.5	1.6	1,402
Ethiopia	62.8	6.4	6.6	−0.2	105
Ghana	18.9	7.8	7.4	0.4	392
Guatemala	11.1	18.2	18.4	−0.2	1,658
Haiti	7.8	4.3	3.6	0.7	462
India	997.5	447.3	442.2	5.1	443
Indonesia	207.0	142.5	119.5	23.0	577
Jamaica	2.6	6.0	6.0	0.0	2,308
Kenya	30.0	10.6	10.6	0.0	353
Malaysia	22.7	79.0	77.3	1.7	3,405
Mexico	97.4	483.7	428.8	54.9	4,402
Morocco	28.2	35.0	33.8	1.2	1,199
Mozambique	17.3	4.0	3.9	0.1	225
Pakistan	134.8	58.2	64.0	−5.8	475
Philippines	76.8	76.6	78.0	−1.4	1,016
Republic of Congo	2.9	2.2	1.9	0.3	655
Rwanda	8.3	2.0	2.1	−0.1	253
South Korea	46.8	406.9	397.9	9.0	8,502
Thailand	61.7	124.4	121.0	3.4	1,961
Venezuela	23.7	102.2	87.0	15.2	3,671
Vietnam	77.5	28.7	28.2	0.5	364

Source: World Bank 2001: 274–275, Table 1, 278–279, Table 3, 198–200, Table 4.2.

Notes
a Billions of US dollars.
b GDP/GNP gap = GDP − GNP, in billions of US dollars. A positive value means that GDP>GNP; a negative value indicates that GDP<GNP.

For example, China's total GDP was $989.5 billion and its total GNP was $980.2 billion in 1999. More income was created in China than was received by residents of China due to a net outflow of income from China to the ROW. In Chile, on the other hand, there was more income received by residents of the country (GNP) than was produced within the borders of the country (GDP), and thus there was a negative GDP/GNP gap reflecting this.

Adjustments to the total income measure

The values for both total GDP and total GNP shown in the second and third columns of Table 2.1 are **nominal** figures reflecting the *current dollar value* of total income and output of each country. There are a number of adjustments to these values that are desirable if income is to be used in a reliable manner as a surrogate measure suitable for ranking nations.

1 **Adjusting for population size** A first necessary correction to the total GNP and total GDP figures in Table 2.1 is to adjust them for the size of a country's population. Dividing GNP (or GDP) by the total population figures in the first column of the table provides a measure of per person income and output. It is a measure of a country's average income. The per capita GNP figures are shown in the last column of Table 2.1. If you wish, you can calculate per capita GDP from the data provided, but these are not shown in the table.

This population adjustment is essential for two reasons. First, using total GNP (or GDP) to compare different countries as to their level of development makes little sense. From Table 2.1, China had the highest total GNP, but it also had the largest population. To be able to compare countries as to their *relative* level of development, it is essential that we consider per capita income, as in the last column of the table, to account for differences in the size of countries. Otherwise, we would be trying to compare essentially non-comparable values.

A second reason for using per capita income is to determine if, over time, changes in the level of aggregate income of any particular country (a) are just sufficient to keep up with population growth, so that per capita GNP (or GDP) remains constant over time; (b) are more than sufficient to keep up with population growth, so that per capita GNP is rising over time; or (c) are insufficient to keep pace with population growth, such that per capita GNP is falling over time. Using per capita income figures allows us to measure, for any particular country, whether average income is growing or not.

Since GNP per capita is simply GNP ÷ population, the percentage change in GNP (or GDP) per capita can be determined as in equation 2.1. This tells us whether a country's total income is growing fast enough to provide for an increase in the income available per person.

$$\text{\% change GNP per capita} = \% \ \Delta(\text{total GNP/total population}) =$$
$$\% \ \Delta\text{total GNP} - \% \ \Delta\text{population} \tag{2.1}$$

The rate of growth of GNP per capita thus can easily be approximated as the difference between the rate of growth of total GNP and the rate of population expansion. GDP can be substituted for GNP in equation 2.1 to determine the rate of change of GDP per capita.

Equation 2.1 makes it clear why countries with high rates of population growth need to generate higher rates of growth in total income and output just to keep the level of per capita income constant compared to countries with lower population growth rates. If one country's population is growing at 2 percent per year, total GNP must increase by 2 percent per annum just to maintain a constant level of income per capita, which is a zero percentage change in per capita income in equation 2.1. Another country with 1 percent growth in population and 2 percent growth in total GNP would experience an increase in per capita GNP of 1 percent.

It would not be correct, however, to infer from equation 2.1 that slow population growth *causes* a faster rate of growth of income per person or that rapid population growth causes slower growth in income per person. Equation 2.1 is true by definition; it is a mathematical identity. It does not uncover the underlying reasons for rapid or slow income or population growth that result in rapid or slow per capita income growth. Equation 2.1 only indicates the *consequences* of specific rates of change of the two variables. This important issue of population growth and its precise relation to economic growth is examined in more detail in Chapter 12.

Having made this population adjustment to total income, countries with higher levels of income per capita may be said to be more developed than countries with lower levels of income per capita by the income criterion of development. Similarly, countries with faster growth rates of income per person as indicated by larger percentage increases in income per person may be said to be growing faster than countries with lower growth rates of per capita income by the income criterion of development.

2 **Accounting for income distribution** Looking at income per capita is an improvement over simply using the total income and output figures for determining how well any economy might be doing. However, this estimate is at best an imprecise measure of the *actual income* received by any particular person, since it is only a simple average derived by dividing total GNP or GDP by total population. The per capita income measure does not provide any information about the dispersion of actual incomes around this mean. It is thus helpful to also know something about the distribution of income in a country if one is to make reasonable sense of the per capita income figures. Table 2.2 provides some income distribution information on most of the countries in Table 2.1.

The table shows in the first two columns the shares of the total income (or consumption) received by the poorest 20 percent of the population (the lowest fifth or quintile of income earners) and for the richest 20 percent (the highest quintile) of the population. The number of persons or families in each quintile is the same within any nation, representing exactly one-fifth of all income recipients in that economy.

Also shown in the table in the third column is the ratio of the share of total income received by the richest 20 percent of the population divided by the share of total income received by the poorest 20 percent for each country. This tells us how many times larger the average income of the richest 20 percent of the population in each country is as a multiple of the average income of the poorest 20 percent of the population. The closer this number is to 1, the greater the degree of equality between the lowest and highest income receivers, and the further away is the ratio from 1, the greater the degree of relative inequality. In no country is this ratio very close to 1. In all countries, the richest 20 percent of income recipients receive more of the total income than do the poorest 20 percent in all nations, since no economy, not even communist China, has anything approaching complete equality of income. Thus, the average income of the richest 20 percent in all countries is higher, sometimes significantly so, than that of the poorest fifth of the population.

Of the countries shown in Table 2.2, Guatemala's richest 20 percent of the population receives an average income that is thirty times larger than the average income received by the poorest 20 percent. This is the greatest degree of inequality shown in the table. It is actually possible to estimate the average income of these two income groups separately using the data in Tables 2.1 and 2.2, as per the following.

Applying Guatemala's income distribution figures to its 1999 income values and given a total GNP in Guatemala of $18.4 billion in 1999 (from Table 2.1), the richest 20 percent of Guatemala's population (equal to 0.2×11.1 million total population = 2.22 million persons) received $11.6 billion (= $0.630 \times $18.4 billion total GNP) of the economy's total GNP, for a per capita income for the richest 20 percent equal to roughly $5,225 ($11.6 billion ÷ 2.22 million persons). The poorest

Table 2.2 Income (or consumption) distribution, selected economies

Country	Poorest 20%	Richest 20%	Richest 20% Poorest 20%[a]	Gini coefficient
Algeria (1995)	7.0	42.6	6.1	0.353
Bangladesh (1995–1996)	8.7	42.8	4.9	0.336
Botswana (1985–1986)	3.6	58.9	16.4	
Brazil (1996)	2.5	63.8	25.5	0.600
Chile (1994)	3.5	61.0	17.4	0.565
China (1998)	5.9	46.6	7.9	0.403
Côte d'Ivoire (1995)	7.1	44.3	6.2	0.367
Egypt (1995)	9.8	39.0	4.0	0.289
Ethiopia (1995)	7.1	47.7	6.7	0.400
Ghana (1997)	8.4	41.7	5.0	0.327
Guatemala (1989)	2.1	63.0	30.0	0.596
India (1997)	8.1	46.1	5.7	0.378
Indonesia (1996)	8.0	44.9	5.6	0.365
Jamaica (1996)	7.0	43.9	6.3	0.364
Kenya (1994)	5.0	50.2	10.0	0.445
Malaysia (1995)	4.5	53.8	12.0	0.485
Mexico (1995)	3.6	58.2	16.2	0.537
Morocco (1998–1999)	6.5	46.6	7.2	0.395
Mozambique (1996–1997)	6.5	46.5	7.2	0.396
Pakistan (1996–1997)	9.5	41.1	4.3	0.312
Philippines (1997)	5.4	52.3	9.7	0.462
Rwanda (1983–1985)	9.7	38.9	4.0	0.289
South Korea (1993)	7.5	39.3	5.2	0.316
Thailand (1998)	6.4	48.4	7.6	0.414
Venezuela (1996)	3.7	53.1	14.4	0.488
Vietnam (1998)	3.6	44.5	12.4	0.361
US (1997)	5.2	46.4	8.9	0.408
Japan (1993)	10.6	35.7	3.4	0.249

Source: World Bank 2001: 282–283, Table 5.

Note
a Share of income (or consumption) received by the richest 20 percent of the population divided by the share of total income (or consumption) received by the poorest 20 percent of the population.

20 percent of the Guatemalan population (also 2.22 million persons) received $0.3864 billion of the total income in 1999 ($0.021 \times$ $18.4 billion total GNP), for an estimated average per capita income for the poorest 20 percent of Guatemalans of about $174 ($0.3864 billion $\div$ 2.22 million persons) in 1999.[3]

Compare these two average income values for these two quintiles with the average per capita GNP value of $1,658 for Guatemala as a whole shown in the table. The richest 20 percent of income earners received an average income more than three times the level of GNP per capita reported in Table 2.1, while the poorest 20 percent of the Guatemalan population had an actual per capita income equal to about 10.5 percent of the reported average GNP per capita for the country as a whole. This clearly illustrates the importance of at least having some rough idea of the income distribution in a country if the per capita income figures are to have any meaning. When the gap between the richest and poorest is wide, as is the case in Guatemala, the average GNP values must be interpreted with some caution. This is especially true when we are using GNP per person as a measure of the well-being of a population.

Other countries have substantial deviations between the richest income recipients and the poorest, though none are so wide as found in Guatemala. Still, for any country, the percentage of income received by the richest 20 percent divided by the percentage of income received by the poorest 20 percent tells us by how many times the average income of the richest 20 percent of the population in a country exceeds the average income received by the poorest quintile of income earners in that economy. The larger this ratio in the penultimate column, the less meaningful is the average GNP per capita figure shown in Table 2.1 as a measure of the actual average income received and as a measure of the degree of average development of an economy.

Interestingly, the lowest such ratio shown in Table 2.2 is for Japan, which has the smallest gap – 3.4 times – between the average income of the richest and poorest. Why do you think there is so little inequality in Japan? Has this relatively low level of inequality been harmful or helpful to the Japanese growth and development experience?

Also shown in Table 2.2 are estimates of Gini coefficients for each country. The *Gini coefficient* is another method for attempting to capture in a simple form – as does the ratio of income of the richest 20 percent of income earners to the income of the poorest 20 percent – the degree of income inequality in a country, through the Gini coefficient is often a richer measure of the overall distribution of income. The value of the Gini coefficient can vary between 0 and 1. The closer the Gini coefficient is to 1, the greater the degree of income inequality in that country; the closer it is to 0, the lesser the degree of inequality. With some caveats, higher Gini coefficients tend to indicate greater inequality, while lower Gini coefficients imply lesser inequality. Similarly, over time, a rising Gini coefficient within an economy would indicate a worsening of income distribution, while a falling Gini coefficient suggests an improvement in the overall distribution of income (see Appendix 2A).[4]

With some caution, it would be possible to say that Bangladesh with a Gini coefficient of 0.353 has a more equal distribution of income (or consumption) than did Chile with a Gini coefficient of 0.565. More interesting and revealing, however, is to compare the evolution of an individual country's Gini coefficient over time. This would be an excellent mini-research project or class assignment.

3 **Adjusting nominal income (GNP or GDP) for price changes over time** The total and per capita GNP and GDP measures in Table 2.1 are shown for one year only. To obtain a measure of the pace of real economic growth, that is to know what is happening to income over time, it is necessary to examine how the level of GNP or GDP on a per capita basis is changing. To compare income levels for the same country for different years, it is necessary to convert *nominal* or *current* price GNP (or GDP) to *real* or *constant* price GNP (or GDP).

The GNP and GDP figures shown in Table 2.1 have been calculated at their nominal values, that is, they have been estimated by multiplying the current, or nominal, market price of each newly produced good and service by the number of units of new production of each of these goods and services and then summing across all goods and services. Prices act as a common unit of measure that allow us to add together physical quantities of different goods and services that otherwise would not be able to be totalled.

The economic wealth of society that economists wish to measure is comprised of what is produced in actual physical terms, for it is that material production which is available for use in consumption and investment and which can contribute to individual and social welfare. The nominal GNP or GDP measure of output permits us to compute the value of dissimilar physical outputs and services by measuring them with a comparable yardstick: a nation's own currency which is then converted into US dollars at the official exchange rate to allow comparisons among countries.

When it comes to comparing total output and income between years, however, it is obvious that unless prices in a country have remained constant, the nominal, or current, price measure of GNP (or GDP) will be a mix not only of changes in physical production but also of the variations in the prices of the goods and services produced.

Equation 2.2 shows how total nominal GDP is determined as the sum of all newly produced final goods and services created within a year, with: n being the number of such goods and services produced; P_i being the price of good or service i; and Q_i representing the physical quantity of good or service i produced.

$$\text{Total GDP} = \sum_{i=1}^{n} P_i Q_i \tag{2.2}$$

From this simple statement, it is clear that in different years the prices of goods and services – the P_is – can differ and that different prices will affect the nominal value of total GDP, even if total physical output – the Q_is – have not changed at all.

In comparing GDP (or GNP) in different years, we want to measure by how much real physical output, the Q_is, has changed, independent of any price changes that may have taken place between the years. To calculate real, or constant price, GDP (or real GNP), it is necessary to use the same prices, P_i, for all years compared. Once the base year vector of prices is chosen, these same P_is can be used in equation 2.2 to multiply the current Q_is measuring the output of all goods and services for all years to be compared. Thus we can write, for example,

$$2002 \text{ GDP}_{1987} = \sum_{i=1}^{n} P_{i,1987} Q_{i,2002} \tag{2.3}$$

Equation 2.3 shows how real GDP for 2002, calculated at 1987 prices (1987 has been selected as the *base year* for prices in this case), would be determined. Using the prices prevailing for each good and service in 1987 ($P_{i,1987}$), this price vector is multiplied by the physical quantities of all newly produced final goods and services actually produced in 2002 ($Q_{i,2002}$). The resulting sum is the real value of 2002 GDP stated in 1987 prices. Comparing 1987 and 2002 GDP, prices would be the same and any differences in GDP would be due to differences in the quantity of goods and services produced.

In practice, an equivalent approach for calculating 2002 GDP in 1987 prices is to deflate nominal 2002 GDP by the appropriate price index. For example, if the total nominal GDP of the fictional country of Luanda in 2002 was US$3,337 million, and the price index for 2002 was 331.7 (with 1987 = 100), then real 2002 GDP for Luanda, calculated in constant 1987 US dollars, would be equal to US$1,006 million, as shown in equation 2.4.

$$\frac{\text{2002 total GDP}}{\text{2002 Price Index Value}} \times 100 = \frac{\text{US\$3,337 million}}{331.7} \times 100$$

$$= \text{US\$1,006 million} \tag{2.4}$$

This calculation adjusts Luanda's 2002 GDP for the average price changes that occurred between 1987, the base year, and 2002. This operation is equivalent to the calculation in equation 2.3 where 1987 prices are multiplied by 2002 quantities.[5] After making this correction, which is absolutely necessary when comparing income between years, then real GDP or real GNP per capita can be calculated by making the population adjustment discussed above, if it was not done prior to the price adjustment.

4 **Other considerations when using the GNP or GDP measure** Both the GNP and GDP measures fail to include some new production that clearly adds to the level of well-being of individuals, while at the same time counting some production as income that does not contribute to human welfare.

One of the most significant omissions from the GNP and GDP measures is an estimate for the value of home-production. In particular, the value of the output from the labor services of women and children, and to a lesser degree, men, who cook and clean and tend children, who make and mend clothing, who toil in home gardens and who perform a variety of other unpaid tasks in the production of non-traded goods and services for their families' own consumption are not included in the traditional GNP or GDP estimates.

The value of this home production is excluded because such goods and services are not valued by or exchanged in the market. These are goods and services destined for the use of the household producing them. Without doubt, these productive activities contribute to the social well-being and to the social reproduction of these families (see Focus 2.2). In fact, for poor families, such non-market activities are likely to make a larger contribution to total income and consumption than is true for better-off families who receive more of their income from paid pursuits and purchase a larger proportion of their consumption. Thus, the estimates for full per capita income – from paid and unpaid sources – of poorer families are likely underestimated more than is the case for family's with higher incomes.

FOCUS 2.2   VALUING WOMEN'S WORK

A part of the work that women do is not counted as contributing to an economy's GNP or GDP. That is because the great bulk of work done by women is often done in the home – caring for and instructing children, preparing meals, drawing drinking and cooking water from wells, washing dishes, cleaning, and so on – and is not paid employment. The system of national accounts used to calculate the value of an economy's total GDP excludes such unpaid, non-market production, whether it is done by men or women, boys or girls. However, since it is women who are more likely to be involved in unpaid household production, much of women's work is said to be "invisible."

What is especially interesting is that women and girls everywhere put in more hours per week at paid and unpaid work than do men or boys. Of the total number of hours performed in all categories, women in less-developed countries account for 53 percent of the work done to men's 47 percent share. Rural women tend to carry an even larger burden of all work performed. For example, in rural Kenya, women were found to labor an average of 1.35 times more hours than men; in Bangladesh, the ratio was 1.1 times more.

However, though women work more in total than men in less-developed economies, more of women's effort is carried out in non-paid activities (66 percent) than in paid work, which accounted for 34 percent of women's total contribution of hours worked. For men, on the other hand, 76 percent of their labor contribution was in paid pursuits, while only 24 percent of men's total effort was performed in non-paid, non-market activities such as home food production or other unpaid activities.

For example, more than 15 hours per week were expended by women in Mozambique just to fetch water. Women in rural Kenya labor an average of 14 hours per week more than men and do ten times as much housework, none of which has a "value" in terms of total GDP. Obviously, though, such labor is essential to the living standard of their families and may often spell the difference between survival and perishing.

One estimate of the total contribution of women's unpaid, "invisible" activities was put at $11 trillion in 1993. Given that total global GDP was estimated at $23 trillion in that year, an adjusted measure of all production might result in a value for total global GDP that is as much as 50 percent higher than thought on the basis of the standard measure of total output and income. It's something to think about!

Source: UNDP 1995: ch. 4

On the other hand, the production of military goods, logging operations that cause environmental destruction of forests, and production processes that spew toxic wastes into the air and water and then force society to pay for their clean-up or which create health problems requiring remediation are counted as *positive* contributions to the measured level of GNP and GDP. Such activities do not add to the level of development or to society's welfare to the degree that their market-valued contributions would suggest, since social costs and private costs of such goods diverge, often dramatically, as a result of the negative externalities created by their production (see Focus 2.3).

Economists have devised alternative methods such as the measure of economic welfare (MEW) and more recently the Genuine Progress Indicator (GPI). These attempt to adjust the GNP and GDP measures both for the omissions from measured production that contribute to human welfare not included in the traditional methodology for determining GNP or GDP, as well as for those included values that adversely impact human welfare. While the specifics of making such adjustments are

FOCUS 2.3 SUSTAINABLE DEVELOPMENT: BALANCING ECONOMIC GROWTH AND THE ENVIRONMENT

Since the 1970s, at least, there has been a growing concern about the impact of economic growth on the natural environment. In 1971, a United Nations conference on the Environment and Development was held in Switzerland, followed in 1972 by the UN Conference on the Human Environment in Sweden. These and other gatherings of academics, politicians, activists, and NGOs (non-governmental organizations) culminated in the UN Conference on Environment and Development – the so-called "Earth Summit" – held in Rio de Janeiro, Brazil in 1992. The outcome of these various forums and of research has been a growing awareness of and interest in the issue of the *sustainability* of economic growth.

Sustainable development has been defined by the Brundtland Commission as "development that meets the needs of the present without compromising the ability of future generations to meet their own needs."

While there is still debate over precisely what this definition means, efforts to operationalize it to account for the impact of current economic activities on natural resource use and the carrying capacity of the environment to absorb adverse changes are evident in the creation of the Genuine Progress Indicator (GPI) and in other measures, such as the Environmentally-adjusted net Domestic Product (EDP), as well as other efforts to "green" the national accounts countries traditionally use to measure their economic progress.

The motivating conviction of sustainable development is that economic growth need not be in conflict with the natural environment if attention is paid in economic and public policy decisions to the goal of conserving and enhancing the natural resource base and in using technology in ways that value not only increased output but also consider their impact on the environment.

Part of the new way of looking at sustainability rests on the critical observation that there is pollution due to poverty, as well as perhaps the more familiar pollution arising from a society's affluence. Pollution due to poverty emerges in many less-developed nations from degradation of marginal farm lands by landless farmers, leading to the erosion of top-soil and desertification, and from the clear-cutting of forests, both of which lead to poorer water quality exacerbated by the lack of sanitation facilities. There also are toxic fumes generated from cooking with wood in badly ventilated areas.

But whatever the specific problem, these are the consequence of a lack of overall economic growth and of national systems of income and wealth distribution that lead desperately poor people to abuse their environment and their nation's stock of natural resources in their effort to simply survive.

Pollution due to poverty extends to the cities of less-developed countries in the slums and shanty towns where unclean water and a lack of sanitation create environmental hazards for the poor urban dwellers who crowd into areas that are too small and lacking in necessary services.

Pollution arising from affluence is the environmental damage resulting from increased industrial production and from higher-income consumption patterns, such as motor vehicles and non-recycled waste and refuse that contribute to air, land, and water degradation. This type of pollution tends to increase with economic growth, while pollution from poverty tends to decrease.

Both pollution arising from poverty and pollution due to affluence can have local and global effects. Pollution has been blamed for global warming, the depletion of the ozone layer, desertification, and species extinction (estimated in excess of 5,000 annually). The danger is that such pollution of the water, air and land has set in motion potentially irreversible processes, the effects of which, if unchecked, could have devastating consequences for future generations.

continued

Thus, there is a compelling need to find the means and the will to balance the press-ing need for continued economic growth and a better distribution of income and wealth in the poorest nations. Equally important is the necessity to *value* the world's natural and environmental resources more rationally, from a social point of view, so that the increased mass consumption that accompanies higher levels of GDP is not automatically counted as having value, while the environmental costs of increased production and con-sumption are ignored, with the environment essentially valued at a price of zero. This neglect of environmental costs has resulted in excesses in the pollution of affluence in the richer nations and in the urban areas of many less developed countries.

In discussions over the sustainability of economic growth, however, views often become polarized. The so-called "deep ecology" perspective tends to be anti-growth, valuing all of nature and all species and natural habitat equally. Humans, in this perspec-tive, have no special rights vis-à-vis other species or the environment. The deep ecology perspective exalts relatively simple living with limited material wants as a desirable objective.

Opposed to this viewpoint is that of those who promote economic growth as the means to best improve human development. In this traditional perspective, nature is there for the use of human beings. Not all species have equal value, and the expansion of consumption is one of the chief ends of economic life. Relatively little attention has been afforded to environmental concerns until quite recently for those holding to this per-spective.

The truth no doubt lies somewhere between these two extreme perspectives. The effort to define "sustainability" has been devoted to finding a middle ground between the view that all of nature is equally valuable and should be preserved as much as possible and the alternative view that nature is to be conquered for the benefit of human beings. Just as we shall find that developmental economists are taking a closer look at human capital inputs as being critical to progress, concern over sustainability can be seen as part of an effort to view environmental and resource capital as key inputs to potential national and global prosperity. Environmental and resource capital is now beginning to be valued, measured and thought about as a non-zero price input to production as important at least as are the more traditional inputs of labor and capital.

Increasingly, then, development economists are cognizant of the *"eco*-nomics" involved in the connection between ecology and development. This requires more than attention to the potential "negative externalities" of particular behavior, such as the dumping of toxic wastes in land fills, that has been the traditional way economics has incorporated environmental and resource concerns into its purview. New ways of meas-uring and valuing environmental and resource capital are called for, as are new institu-tions that can operationalize and internalize such calculations, including the nature of property rights to resources, land, and water.

The concept of the sustainability of economic growth and development need not be limited to considerations about the natural environment alone. It is also possible to con-ceive of the sustainability of social structures. The pace, level, and distribution of eco-nomic growth can be extended to quality of life issues, such as the impact of economic change on urban crime and violence, on illegal drug addiction, on racial and ethnic ten-sions, on religious conflict, on gender issues, and so on.

Sources: Bartelmus 1994: ch. 2; Elliott 1994; Redclift 1987; WCED 1987: 43

not examined here,[6] it is important to keep in mind that some of the goods and services included in the GNP and GDP measures may contribute negatively to a nation's development goals, while others, such as so-called "women's work" and much of home production in general are not included, although they represent activities that contribute positively to a nation's total production and to its potential for full human development.

GNP or GDP: is one income measure better than the other?

Which income measure of economic growth should one use: real GNP per capita or real GDP per capita? Does it make a difference?

The GNP measure provides some notion of what the residents of a nation have available to them for consumption and investment, including government spending. GNP thus furnishes a measure of the sum total of new final goods and services available to the residents of a country for their final use. In economic terms, the level of output and income measured by GNP is a proximate gauge of the material welfare or well-being of the residents of a nation. If one is going to use income and the economic growth criterion as the substitute measure for the broader goals of development for a nation, it probably makes sense to use real GNP per capita as the standard, since it measures what is available for contributing to the standard of living of the population, both now for current consumption and, in the future, as investment.

GDP, on the other hand, measures all the output or income produced within the borders of a country, even though not all of that income will necessarily be received by residents of the country. GDP is more purely an index of the value of all new production occurring within the frontiers of a nation rather than of the income and output available for use to the nation. Real GDP per capita is a less desirable measure to use if one is interested in a surrogate welfare measure for the broad range of development goals of nations. Real GDP per capita does give information on the pace of total production in a country, irrespective of who ultimately receives the income earned from such production. The GDP per capita measure, however, is not as closely connected to what remains in the hands of the residents of the nation for current and future consumption as is the GNP per capita measure, and thus GDP per person is a more imperfect measure of a nation's broader welfare targets.

Which measure is employed will be determined by the use to which the income criterion is to be put. If one is solely interested in the pace of economic growth and total production for a country, then the real GDP per capita measure will serve quite nicely. If, however, one wishes to use the income proxy that best measures what is available for use by a country's residents and which can concretely contribute to their level of well-being, it makes more sense to use the real GNP per capita measure as the surrogate yardstick.

International comparisons of income: purchasing power parity

There is a further issue to consider when using the income levels of countries as a basis of comparison and as proxy measures of their level of development. What exactly does a comparison of Cambodia's 1999 GNP per capita of $260 with Germany's 1999 GNP per capita of $25,350 mean? Of Malaysia's 1999 GNP per capita of $3,400 with Mexico's $4,400 GNP per capita the same year? Is it legitimate to infer from comparing these figures that one dollar of income in each country is worth the same? Does the local equivalent of one US dollar purchase an equivalent quantity of goods in every single country, so that one could say that the equivalent of US$1,500 of income provides the same standard of living in Germany, Malaysia, Mexico, and Cambodia?

The simple answer is, no, it is not the case that the equivalent of one US dollar purchases the same quantity of goods regardless of the country. A little introspection perhaps suggests why this is the case. Would you expect the price of housing, for example, to be the same in Cambodia with a lower level of income per person than Germany? Of a haircut? Of medical and dental services? It is likely that a country with a low per capita GNP will have lower prices for these items when these values are converted from the local currency to US dollars than will a country with a higher average GNP. In other words, the equivalent of US$1,500 will buy different quantities of goods and services in different economies since the prices of some goods and services will vary with the level of average income of an economy.

The GNP and GDP and the GNP per capita measures shown in Table 2.1 are shown in US dollar units, but these values are not precisely comparable, for the following reason. These values were calculated by converting each country's own GNP and GDP values, measured initially in each country's own currency units (pesos for Mexico, rupees for India), to a common US dollar measure. This is done using the *official exchange rate* between the currency of each country with the US dollar as the means to arrive at the US dollar values shown. This official exchange rate conversion, however, only makes comparable the prices of **traded goods**, that is, goods that are traded internationally, such as computers, motor cars, shoes, oranges, and wine. The presumption is that the prices of traded goods when converted at the official exchange rate to a common unit like the US dollar will be quite similar between countries due to the forces of international competition and the potential for arbitrage that large differences in prices between countries would offer on traded goods.[7]

However, for *non-traded goods* and *non-traded services*, which by definition do not enter into international trade between nations, prices between countries can vary quite substantially. These differences will depend upon conditions internal to each country, particularly the average level of income, but also local customs, regulations, the degree of competition, and so on. For non-traded goods and services, like housing, transportation, personal services, and prepared foods that are location-specific, there are no international forces of competition or the possibility of arbitrage to bring prices into line *between* economies. Significant price differentials for these goods and services between economies can make international GNP and GDP comparisons like those shown in Table 2.1 based on simply converting domestic currency measures to a common US dollar measure somewhat deceiving.

There, is however, another way to compare income between countries that attempts to overcome the shortcoming of the traditional exchange rate-converted GNP or GDP measure. This is known as the **purchasing power parity, or PPP, income measure**.

Table 2.3 provides a comparison between the values of GNP per capita calculated at the official exchange rate (the same as those shown in Table 2.1) and GNP per capita calculated at PPP values, both reckoned in US dollars. The PPP measure makes

Table 2.3 PPP measure of GNP per capita

Country	GNP per capita at official exchange rate, 1999	PPP GNP per capita, 1999
Algeria	1,550	4,753
Argentina	7,600	11,324
Bangladesh	370	1,475
Botswana	3,240	6,042
Brazil	4,420	6,317
Chile	4,740	8,370
China	780	3,291
Côte d'Ivoire	710	1,546
Egypt	1,400	3,303
Ethiopia	100	599
Ghana	390	1,793
Guatemala	1,660	3,517
Haiti	460	1,407
India	450	2,149
Indonesia	580	2,439
Jamaica	2,330	3,276
Kenya	360	975
Malaysia	3,400	7,963
Mexico	4,400	7,719
Morocco	1,200	3,190
Mozambique	230	797
Pakistan	470	1,757
Philippines	1,020	3,815
Republic of Congo	670	897
South Korea	8,490	14,637
Thailand	1,960	5,599
Venezuela	3,670	5,268
Vietnam	370	1,755
US	30,600	30,600
Ireland	19,160	19,180
Japan	32,230	24,041

Source: World Bank 2000: 274–275, Table 1.

an adjustment to GNP between countries similar to the adjustment made to determine real GNP or GDP discussed earlier. The prices of one country, in this case the United States, become the base prices for determining the PPP value of GNP per capita in other countries. Thus, Mozambique's PPP GNP per capita is determined as,

$$\text{PPP GNP per capita} = \frac{\sum_{i=1}^{n} P_{i,\text{US}} \times Q_{i,\text{M}}}{\text{Population}} \qquad (2.5)$$

Where $Q_{i,\text{M}}$ is the output vector of all newly produced final goods and services, i, in Mozambique and $P_{i,\text{US}}$ is the price vector for goods and services, i, in US prices. Effectively, then, what the PPP measure provides is the estimated value of Mozambique's physical output and income weighted by the prices for such goods and services prevailing in the United States. There is no need to use the exchange rate between the two countries to find the value of Mozambique's GNP per person. Mozambique's output is valued directly by multiplying production by US prices.

Obviously, large differences not only in the prices of non-traded goods and services between the two countries but of the mix of traded to non-traded goods in total national output will affect the PPP measure of GNP per capita compared to the value obtained from the official exchange rate conversion. From Table 2.3, for example, the 1999 per capita PPP value of income in Mozambique was about $797, which is more than three times greater than the exchange rate-converted GNP per capita value of $230. This PPP per capita income figure is more meaningful when comparing per capita income and the purchasing power of incomes in the United States and Mozambique. The PPP value of Mozambique's income can be interpreted as follows: $797 of income would be required in the US to buy what the equivalent of $230 is able to purchase in Mozambique with its lower prices for non-traded goods and services compared to the US. In other words, the equivalent of $230 in Mozambique can buy, roughly, what it would take $797 to buy in the US.

For the less-developed countries in the top part of Table 2.3, PPP GNP per capita > the exchange rate determined value of GNP per capita, with Rwanda having a PPP GNP per capita nearly six times as large as the exchange rate GNP per capita GNP value. For all the less-developed countries shown in Table 2.2, PPP GNP per capita exceeds the exchange rate GNP value by at least a third and most often by significantly more.

On the other hand, look at the comparison between Japan's PPP GNP per capita in 1999 and the value of GNP per person found by simply converting Japan's per capita GNP in yen to US dollars using the exchange rate. PPP GNP per capita is less. Why do you think that is? What does this say about the prices of non-traded goods and services in Japan compared to those prices in the US?

Typically, then, the actual purchasing power of income in lower-income countries tends to be *understated* by measures of per capita income converted at official exchange rates due to the relatively lower prices of non-traded goods and services, such as housing, retail services and local transportation in less-developed nations. These prices are lower due to the lower income of these countries that keeps the prices of local goods below what they are in more developed nations. The more developed economies tend to have PPP GNP per capita values closer to that calculated at the official exchange rate because of the greater openness to world trade, a mix of production with more traded goods relative to non-traded goods and due to their more modern structures of production which result in greater efficiency in production in both traded and non-traded goods and service sectors.

There is an increasing tendency for development analysts to prefer the PPP measure of income in making comparisons among countries over the exchange rate-converted GNP or GDP values. This is a move we applaud. In future, income comparisons used as a basis of determining relative levels of development will more and more use the PPP income measure and that will improve the quality of such comparisons and the meaning we attach to them.

The indicators criterion of development: the human development index

In the 1960s, there emerged from the International Labor Organization, from the World Bank and from independent researchers a growing backlash against the use per capita income and the rate of economic growth criterion as the exclusive measures of development. Whether what was proposed as an alternative to the GNP or GDP per capita measure was the basic needs approach or the physical quality of life index (PQLI), or some other composite measure, the objection to the use of the economic growth and income standard was the same: it was far too aggregate and did not capture the distributional inequalities all too common in many of the poor nations of the world.

The income per capita criterion gave a biased view, it was argued, of the level of progress achieved by many countries. Income per capita was, in and of itself, an insufficient target for ultimately achieving society's broader development goals listed earlier in this chapter. The link between the level of income per capita and the full range of development objectives was considered much too tenuous and unreliable, particularly in the poorest nations that needed to make the most progress and in those countries where democratic political processes were all but absent.

Neither the basic needs nor PQLI methodologies took hold, however; the former perhaps because of some undeniable theoretical and empirical ambiguity and the latter possibly for lack of a powerful institutional champion.[8] Beginning in 1990, a new measure of development, the Human Development Index (*HDI*), has been calculated and published each year by the United Nations Development Programme in its annual *Human Development Report.*

The HDI is a composite index using "longevity, knowledge, and a decent standard of living," as the representative indicators for development. The actual index uses estimates of life expectancy at birth, the adult literacy rate, and a school enrollment ratio and PPP GDP per capita to calculate an HDI value for each nation (see Appendix 2B).[9] The HDI measure of development is thus broader than the simple income per person yardstick, though income does enter into the calculation of the HDI, something not done in earlier efforts to create an alternative measure of development. At the same time, the HDI also gives direct value to those factors, particularly education, which help create opportunities for individuals to reach a higher and more fulfilling standard of living that may not be captured by the income measure alone. As the UN Development Programme (UNDP) described the issue:

> Human development is about much more than the rise and fall of national incomes. It is about creating an environment in which people can develop their full potential and lead productive, creative lives in accord with their needs and interests. People are the real wealth of nations.
>
> (UNDP 2001: 9)

That last sentence is extremely important. It is a nation's people that comprise the wealth of any society, and meeting the needs and desires of those people is the ultimate purpose of economic growth and development.

The HDI simplifies the comparison among countries by combining the achievement on the included variables into a single number. The value of the HDI can vary between 0 and 1, with an HDI score closer to 0 indicating greater distance from the maximum to be achieved on the aggregate of the factors entering the HDI. An HDI value closer to 1 indicates greater achievement relative to the highest attainable on the constituent elements of the index and thus a higher level of human development. Thus the HDI is measuring "relative deprivation," that is, it is measuring how far away a country is from the maximum achievable value of the components that make up the HDI. Roughly, since this is a deprivation index, one can interpret an HDI of 0.600 to indicate that the country has fallen 40 percent short of the maximum level of human development on the indicators in the HDI that could potentially be attained.

The HDI measure was created with the purpose of attempting to take into account the fact that countries, meaning both governments and individuals, make choices on their spending and use of resources among alternative uses. The use of these resources affects the range of choices open to people and their level of well being with results that may not always be captured in the income per person ranking of nations as to their relative level of development.

For example, among the less-developed nations, the UNDP found that though one-quarter of national income was spent via government, less than 10 percent of this share, on average, was dedicated to identifiable human development expenditures, such as education, health care, and social security. The largest area of government spending was on the military, the contribution of which to human development is, at best, controversial (UNDP 1993: 10). Of course, different nations will allocate their public expenditures in distinctive ways, both to achieve particular development goals, as well as to accomplish other priorities, such as defense, that are deemed significant. The impact of these choices, at least partly, will be captured by the variables included in the HDI.

Table 2.4 shows the value of the HDI and the HDI ranking for an even broader range of countries than was listed in Table 2.1.

The penultimate column of this table shows the difference between the PPP GDP per capita ranking and the HDI ranking in 1999 of each country. The values in this column do not vary systematically in any immediately obvious way, once again underscoring the point of those who have argued that the GNP (or GDP) per person measure alone is an incomplete index of development and that there is no automatic link between the level of income per capita and the level of development (at least as measured by the HDI).[10] What is the significance of these values in the penultimate column?

A positive value in that column of Table 2.4 indicates by how much a country's HDI ranking exceeded its PPP GDP per capita ranking since the column value is determined by taking the PPP GDP ranking – the HDI ranking (with a smaller number indicating a higher ranking among all countries, i.e., being ranked twentieth is better than being ranked twenty-fifth). Countries with a positive value in the next-to-last column were ranked higher among all the countries on the HDI than they were ranked on income alone. This means that for such countries the PPP GDP per capita ranking *understated* that country's level of development, as more broadly defined by the HDI.

For example, the Philippines (HDI = 0.749) had an HDI ranking that exceeded its per capita PPP GDP ranking by twenty-one places, since the PPP GDP ranking – HDI ranking difference was a positive 21. [What, then, was the Philippine's per capita PPP GDP ranking? We can infer its value from the table. Since the

Table 2.4 HDI and GDI, selected countries, 1999

	HDI value	HDI rank[a]	PPP GDP ranking – HDI ranking[b]	GDI[d]
High Human Development (HDI >0.800)				
Australia	0.936	2	10	0.935
United States	0.934	6	−4	0.932
Japan	0.928	9	2	0.921
United Kingdom	0.923	14	5	0.920
Singapore	0.876	26	−5	0.871
South Korea	0.875	27	5	0.868
Argentina	0.842	34	6	0.833
Chile	0.825	39	9	0.817
Costa Rica	0.821	41	8	0.813
United Arab Emirates	0.809	45	−19	0.798
Medium Human Development (0.500 <HDI <0.799)				
Mexico	0.790	51	0	0.782
Malaysia	0.774	56	−4	0.768
Venezuela	0.765	61	10	0.759
Thailand	0.757	66	−3	0.755
Saudi Arabia	0.754	68	−26	0.719
Brazil	0.750	69	−12	0.743
Philippines	0.749	70	21	0.746
Jamaica	0.738	78	17	0.736
Turkey	0.735	82	−21	0.726
Sri Lanka	0.735	81	19	0.732
China	0.718	87	7	0.715
South Africa	0.702	94	−49	0.695
Vietnam	0.682	101	19	0.680
Indonesia	0.677	102	3	0.671
Morocco	0.596	112	−14	0.579
Botswana	0.577	114	−55	0.571
India	0.571	115	0	0.553
Zimbabwe	0.554	117	−13	0.548
Kenya	0.514	123	18	0.512
Congo	0.502	126	29	0.495
Low Human Development (HDI <0.500)				
Pakistan	0.498	127	−5	0.466
Bangladesh	0.470	132	−4	0.459
Nigeria	0.455	136	11	0.443
Côte d'Ivoire	0.426	144	−20	0.409
Rwanda	0.395	152	−8	0.391
Mozambique	0.323	157	−11	0.309
Ethiopia	0.321	158	0	0.308
Sierra Leone	0.258	162	0	nd
High Income Economies[c]	0.926			
Middle Income Economies[c]	0.740			
Low Income Economies[c]	0.549			

Source: UNDP 2001: 141–144, Table 1, 210–213, Table 21.

Notes

a The highest, or best, ranking was 1 (Norway) in 1999; the lowest, or worst, ranking, was 162 in 1999.

b If positive, this indicates that the HDI ranking for the country is higher than the per capita PPP GDP ranking (PPP GDP rank − HDI rank >0); if negative, the HDI ranking for the country is lower than the per capita PPP GDP ranking (PPP GDP rank − HDI rank <0).

c High income: annual GNP per capita >$9,266; Middle income: annual GNP per capita $756–$9,265; Low income, annual GNP per capita <$755.

d Gender-related Development Index; adjust HDI for differences in achievement on the HDI variables between males and females.

PPP GDP ranking − HDI ranking = ? − 70 = 21, then the Philippines PPP GDP ranking must have been 91 in 1999, since 91 − 70 = 21.] In other words, the Philippines did substantially better on the HDI measure, ranking 21 countries higher among the 162 countries, at seventieth, than it had ranked on its PPP GDP, being ninety-first among the 162 countries. This was a better showing on the broader range of development indicators captured in the HDI than would have been expected from its per capita income ranking alone.

On the other hand, a negative value in the penultimate column of Table 2.4 indicates by how much a country's HDI ranking fell short of its PPP GDP per capita ranking among all countries since the PPP GDP ranking − HDI ranking can only be less than 0 if the PPP GDP ranking value < HDI ranking value. For those nations with a negative gap, their PPP GDP per person ranking tends to overstate the broader level of development as measured by the HDI.

For example, Botswana (HDI = 0.577) had a relative HDI ranking 55 places below its per capita PPP GDP ranking [PPP GDP ranking − HDI ranking = ? − 114 = −55 which means that the PPP GDP ranking had to be 59 since 59 − 114 = −55]. This strongly suggest that had we looked at income alone, it would have been reasonable to believe that Botswana's population had a higher level of development, ranking fifty-ninth among the 162 countries, than it actually does, at least as measured by the additional development indicators included in the HDI, where Botswana ranked a significantly lower one hundred and fourteenth among the 162 countries.

Adjustments to the HDI

Just as it is useful to adjust the per capita income figures so that they provide a more reliable standard of the level of development if one is to use that measure, so too are there some modifications that can be made to the HDI that refine the information it provides.

The Gender-related Development Index

The UNDP also calculates a gender-adjusted HDI, called the "gender-related development index" or GDI, which takes into account differences in the level of attainment of women and men on the values of the indicators that enter the HDI. The GDI values are shown in Table 2.4 in the last column. In making such a correction for gender differences in life expectancy, education and income, every country suffers a deterioration in the value of its gender-adjusted HDI, meaning in no country do women, on average, score higher than or equal to men on the HDI components. Thus, the GDI, which is simply a gender-adjusted HDI, is less than the average HDI reflecting the lower average level of attainment of women compared to men on the variables entering the HDI.

Some countries do better than others on gender-equality, however, so that the GDI ranking of countries is different than the HDI ranking, rising for those nations for which the average achievement of women is closer to that of men and falling for those nations where the achievement of women is more distant from that of men as a group. Still, no country had its GDI equal or greater than its HDI. Closing the gaps in education, health, income, and political participation between men and women is essential for full development of a nation, and the GDI gives us some indication of the success of countries in achieving gender equity.

The Human Poverty Index

Another weakness of the HDI is that it does not indicate what is happening to the poorest members of society, except to the extent that this is reflected in the overall HDI value via, say, the impact of poverty on average life expectancy. To attempt to capture the conditions of living of the poor more directly, the UNDP introduced in 1997 a human poverty index (HPI) that utilizes slightly different variables than either the HDI or the GDI and hence is not directly comparable. Instead of life expectancy as a variable, the HPI includes the probability at birth that a child will *not* survive to age 40; for education, adult *illiteracy* is included as a variable; and in place of an income variable, the HPI includes the "percentage of people not using improved water sources" and the "percentage of children under five who are underweight" as variables entering the index. All of these variables are stated in percentages and lower values for each is better than higher values since each variable is actually a "deprivation" indicator rather than an achievement indicator, as is the case of the HDI variables (for a sample calculation, see UNDP 2001: 241).

In 1999, for example, Costa Rica had an HPI of 4.2 percent, which means the combined probability of not living to age 40, of the incidence of illiteracy, of lack of access to improved water sources, and of underweight children is quite low. Pakistan's HPI was equal to 39.2 percent, meaning a worse performance on these deprivation indicators. Of the ninety less-developed countries with calculated HPI values, Niger was last, with an HPI = 63.6 percent, the result of having a 41.4 percent chance at birth of not living to age 40; of having 84.7 percent adult illiteracy; of 41 percent of the population lacking access to improved water sources; and of having half of all children less than age 5 being underweight. While this index is not as easy to use as the HDI, it does give some useful information about the levels of relative deprivation of different countries that can be used in conjunction with the HDI value.

The HDI is thus an imperfect measure of the well-being of a nation, just as is the income criterion. Neither measure is capable of capturing *all* the critical dimensions of development, but the HDI is broader in some important respects than is a simple income per person indicator.

For the future, it might be desirable to have an HDI that included some measure capable of quantifying environmental and sustainability issues. Such environmental matters are left out of the HDI, except to the extent they might indirectly affect life expectancy. With the growing awareness of the pressing need to understand the interrelation between biological and economic systems and the concern that an environmental threshold perhaps is being reached with continued global economic expansion, this is a glaring deficiency of the HDI, as it is in the GNP and GDP measures. So, too, is the absence of any weight in the gross HDI given to the degree of political democracy and participation. Other considerations and variables also might be important to include in an adjusted HDI on the lines that has been done with the GDI.

Comparing the income per capita and HDI measures

Is the effort to construct an HDI for each country worth the effort? Does the HDI provide information about the level of development of a country that is different from that which can be obtained from GDP or GNP per capita figures? Is it reasonable to use real GNP or GDP per capita as a proxy for the level of development, rather than the admittedly more-difficult-to-estimate HDI? As the UNDP writes (2001: 13):

> Rankings by HDI and by GDP per capita can be quite different, showing that countries do not have to wait for economic prosperity to make progress in human development.... Costa Rica and Korea have both made impressive human development gains, reflected in HDIs of more than 0.800, but Costa Rica has achieved this human outcome with only half the income of Korea. Pakistan and Vietnam have similar incomes, but Vietnam has done much more in translating that income into human development.... So, with the right policies, countries can advance faster in human development than in economic growth.

In a statistical study comparing GNP per capita (and not GDP) and the HDI as a means for ranking nations as to level of development, the question of a divergence between the HDI and income rankings was considered. It was found that there was a high correlation between the GNP per person ranking and the HDI ranking when the entire sample of countries was considered (Dietz and Gibson 1994; in that study there were 143 nations).[11] This tends to support the view of those who argue that per capita income is a reasonable proxy for ranking nations as to their relative and absolute level of development. However, when the sample was examined in more detail, this conclusion could be supported only weakly.

The study determined that using income per capita as a surrogate for development is most reliable both for the highest-income nations and for the lowest-income, least-developed nations, with some notable exceptions, like Sri Lanka, China, Guyana, and Indonesia in the latter category. For the seventy-two lower-middle- and upper-middle-income countries in the study, however, the level of income per capita turns out to be an unreliable indicator for the level of human development and an unreliable ranking methodology for relative human development among those nations.

The results of this study strongly suggest that considering both the level and relative position of a country using GNP per capita or GDP per capita (particularly if the PPP values are used) and the HDI score is, perhaps, the more prudent way to evaluate the level of development. Since the link between economic growth and development is neither direct nor constant for all countries, tracking progress over time using both indicators provides more information than either per capita income or the HDI value alone. Given that both income and HDI values now are readily available annually, there is a strong argument for making use of both, perhaps especially for the middle-income less-developed nations.

The HDI thus provides an alternative index to the income per person, economic growth criterion for evaluating the progress of a country in terms of achieving broadly accepted development goals. The HDI reminds us that though increased income is vital for the expanded choices it provides individuals and families, it is not the whole of what development is about. The unadjusted HDI partly captures the extent to which the spread effects of growing incomes is filtered through education, health, social security, and other areas of the economy and how incomes are distributed to expenditures that are both means to, and ends of, higher levels of development.

The search for any single indicator that will provide all the information that is important and relevant to development is elusive. Any indicator will be at best an imperfect measure of development. Awareness of the weaknesses of whatever indicator is used and an effort by the observer of the development process of any nation to "fill in the gaps" of coverage inevitable to any single index remains, nonetheless, an essential and somewhat subjective ingredient to evaluation and recommendation.

Economic growth and equity: goals at odds?

If a country places an emphasis on development and the targeting of objectives such as increased education and better health care that contribute to improvements on the HDI measure or to a reduction in the numbers of the poor, will this adversely affect economic growth? Conversely, if a country takes steps aimed at accelerating economic growth, what effect will this have on the goals of development, as measured by the HDI or GDI or by poverty reduction? In other words, are economic growth and development at odds or are they broadly complementary?

Underlying the insistence that some economists place on measuring development by income per capita and of targeting this as a proximate goal for development is a concern that if policy-makers place too much emphasis on achieving specific development goals this may slow the pace of economic growth by taking scarce resources away from investment and other uses. A slower pace of economic growth may actually make the achievement of these development goals all that much more difficult to attain by reducing the material resources available to be used to improve the level of human welfare. Is there, in fact, such a conflict between pursuing economic growth and pursuing development?

An influential study published in 1955 by the late Nobel Prize-winning economist Simon Kuznets examined the historical relationship between income per capita and income distribution, one broad indicator of equity. While trends in a country's income inequality are an imperfect indicator of what is happening to the broader goals of development, rising and high levels of income inequality, if persistent, may be indicators of some underlying weaknesses in achieving development for all. Further, the research Kuznets and others following in his footsteps have done has had a great influence on how many analysts think about the relation between economic growth, as measured by rising per capita income, and the achievement of the broader goals of development.

Kuznets' research suggested that at low income levels further economic growth tended to create more inequality, as measured by the Gini coefficient. As income per capita continued to increase, however, a critical threshold level of income was reached, and further economic growth and higher average per capita income tended to reduce a nation's overall income inequality. This relationship between the level of per capita income and income inequality is referred to as the Kuznets' inverted-U hypothesis, from the shape of the curve shown in Figure 2.1

The Kuznets' hypothesis is often interpreted to mean that there is a minimum

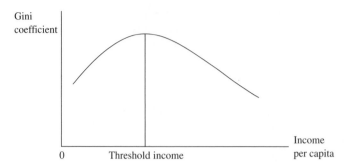

Figure 2.1 The Kuznets' curve.

level of income that a country must achieve before greater equity and higher levels of development can be attained. Once that threshold level of income is reached, further increases in income contribute to greater equity, as shown by the falling value of the Gini coefficient after the peak of the curve is reached at the threshold income level.

Prior to reaching the threshold level of income in Figure 2.1, however, rising income is associated with increasing inequality as shown by the rising Gini coefficient value associated with increasing income on the upward sloping portion of the curve. What the Kuznets' curve suggests is that the greater income inequality associated with rising income per capita prior to reaching the threshold level of income is necessary if the threshold level of income is ever to be reached, after which income inequality will be reduced through additional economic growth. In other words, poorer countries at an early stage of their economic development can expect a deterioration in income inequality until the threshold level of income is reached. Things must get worse before they can get better and a higher level of development is attained.

The Kuznets' inverted-U hypothesis sometimes has been interpreted as something of a law of economic growth and development. Nations wishing to promote equity and human development in the wider sense can best do so by increasing income per capita. Initially at income levels below the threshold level rising income per capita makes income inequality worse, that is the price that must be paid both to attain higher average income and to eventually reduce inequality. There is no apparent necessity to target development goals or poverty reduction per se if one accepts this view. The short-term loss in equity that accompanies economic growth before the threshold level of income is reached is the necessary cost of progress over the longer haul. From this interpretation of the Kuznets' curve, growth and development are not rival goals. Economic growth promotes development and equity in income over the longer term, even if there would seem to be a short-term trade-off (see Focus 2.4).[12]

The debate over the Kuznets' inverted-U hypothesis and whether it represents the "true" relation between rising average income and income inequality has generated a vast and often complicated literature. The relation Kuznets discovered between income and equity or development is not, in fact, a law of economics but rather a statistical relation.[13] What seems to happen is that once nations pass the

FOCUS 2.4 INEQUALITY AS A CONSTRAINT ON GROWTH

The conventional wisdom as expressed in the Kuznets' curve is that there is a trade-off between economic growth and reducing inequality. Thus an unequal distribution of income is sometimes believed necessary for rapid economic growth. If this is so, however, why do we find in Latin America relatively low rates of economic growth and high inequality and in East Asia low inequality and rapid growth?

Differences in the political economy and the policies of the two regions may be part of the explanation. In the period after 1945, governing elites in East Asia had their legitimacy threatened by domestic communist insurgents. They thus sought to widen their base of political support via policies such as land reform, public housing, investment in rural infrastructure and, most commonly, widespread high-quality education. In Latin America, governing elites acted as if they believed they could thrive irrespective of what happened to those with the lowest income since the tax, expenditure and trade policies that these political elites had legislated benefitted the poor relatively little.

The association of slow economic growth and high inequality in Latin America may in part be because high income inequality can be a constraint on growth that limits demand and the size of the market. Conversely, East Asia's low level of income inequality may have been a significant stimulus to economic growth by promoting demand and spending, for example. If this is the case, there is a strong argument that East Asia's investment in education has been a key difference in policies. Rising average levels of education have helped to sustain economic growth directly through their effects on productivity. Higher levels of education spread among the population have also meant better-educated workers who earn more, and this has reduced income inequality at the same time.

How important a constraint on growth is significant income inequality? It appears to be quite substantial. The results of recent research suggest that, *ceteris paribus*, after twenty-five years, GDP per capita would be 8.2 percent higher in a country with low inequality than in a country with income inequality one standard deviation higher.

The ratio of the income shares of the top 20 percent to the bottom 20 percent of income earners is 32 in Brazil and 6 in Korea. Simulation results suggest that if, in 1960, Brazil had had Korea's lower level of income inequality, Brazil's growth rate over the following twenty-five years would have been 0.66 percentage points higher each year. This implies that after twenty-five years GDP per capita in Brazil would have been 17.2 percent higher than it was with the higher degree of inequality, a substantial difference that could have contributed not only to a higher average standard of living but to the broader goals of development as well.

Source: Birdsall and Sabot 1994

threshold level of income, government expenditures in the areas of health, education, social security, and other social and human capital areas tend to rise relative to total expenditures in the economy. Thus, improvement in equity and on the HDI measure would be expected, as governments are able to focus on broader development goals, which leads to more economic growth in the future.[14]

More importantly, the Kuznets' hypothesis – which was found by looking at time series data for a number of countries – cannot be sustained as a "law" once the experience of individual nations is singled out. Some countries have experienced worsening equity along with economic growth, even after the threshold level of income has been reached (Brazil is a recent example), while other nations have been able to improve equity and score higher on the HDI measure at income levels well below Kuznets' threshold level of income (Sri Lanka, for example). The reason? Specific government policies on, for example, education and wealth distribution and other social policies can be aimed at targeting the broader development goals early on (Sri Lanka) or away from such goals (Brazil), somewhat independent of the level of current income. There is no hard and fast law that says that a country cannot have both rising income and more development at low income levels or vice versa.

What the Kuznets' inverted-U demonstrates, then, is historically what on average did happen for a group of nations. It does not imply that all countries, especially late developers, must necessarily tolerate or even promote increasing inequality to achieve economic growth. The particular path which any nation follows in terms of the relation between its economic growth rate and its success in reaching the broader goals of development is at least partly a consequence of conscious public policy. Such policy can be geared toward high economic growth and rapid development or high growth and slow development. Even slow economic growth paths can generate increasing or decreasing inequality, depending on government policies aimed at confronting inequality and development objectives.

The particular mix of economic growth and development is at least partly a public policy choice that a nation's leaders determine, with or without popular consent. This is not to say economic growth does not matter; it does. Over time, more economic growth and a higher average income level can contribute to greater development. The reverse is also true, since increased human development contributes to higher levels of labor productivity, particularly via increased education and better health care, which lead to higher economic growth and income.

Countries cannot ignore one side of the development equation – either economic growth or development – for very long without suffering the adverse consequences of a lop-sided policy. But as we shall see in later chapters, some East Asian countries recently have been able to achieve quite substantial progress on both the economic development and equity and development ledgers simultaneously, and that would seem to be a path worth emulating (see Focus 2.5).

The differences in the GDP and HDI rankings in Table 2.4 suggested the importance of policy decisions by government and society in achieving development goals at different levels of income, especially for the middle-income less-developed nations. The divergence in the rankings of countries on their income per person and on their HDI values also confirm that the Kuznets' curve is not strictly a law governing the relation between equity and development and the level of per capita income, or there would be no, or fewer, differences between the PPP GDP and the HDI rankings.

Depending on a nation's policies, greater equity and progress on development goals can be achieved even at relatively low levels of income. It is not necessary for countries to await the threshold level of per capita income shown in Figure 2.1 before progress toward greater equity can be accomplished. It is a matter of policy decisions, and even after attaining the threshold level of income there still is no guarantee of progress toward greater equity. Meeting development objectives depends on the nature of state and social policy aimed at attaining greater equity and a higher level of human development.

FOCUS 2.5   AN ENVIRONMENTAL KUZNETS' CURVE?

Some researchers have suggested there may be an environmental Kuznets' curve, similar to Figure 2.1, but with pollution levels measured on the vertical axis rather than income inequality. At relatively low income levels, increases in economic growth result in increased pollution and environmental destruction. However, after a threshold level of income per person is reached, pollution and adverse environmental effects will be reduced. Why might this be so?

Beginning from low income levels and given the relatively low value that society is likely to place on a clean environment compared to the value of a higher standard of living, little attention will be paid to environmental conditions. Increases in agricultural output might be expected to expand the volume of toxic wastes created, and if industrialization is just beginning it is quite likely that air and water pollution will accompany the growth of factories. Clean and safe technologies may not be available at a reasonable cost to poor countries. The alternative to paying for cleaner technologies is to absorb the damage caused by pollution and other environmental degradation as one of the "costs" of improvements in average living conditions.

A clean environment is often assumed to be a "luxury good" in the sense that its income elasticity is greater than one. If this is the case, only at higher income levels will a clean environment have a value worth preserving. If this is correct, then one would expect to see an environmental Kuznets' curve, at least for some kinds of pollution and environmental damage (e.g., sulfur dioxide, particulate matter) that accompany industrialization. Further, some types of environmental damages increase with higher income levels, e.g., carbon dioxide emissions from vehicles, groundwater contamination, and municipal waste and garbage, as the discussion of the pollution of affluence earlier in the chapter suggested.

However, much like the traditional Kuznets' curve for income growth, the observation of an environmental Kuznets' curve has been based on what has occurred in the past. Now there is better information, better environmental accounting methods, and greater awareness of the global significance of promoting a kind of economic growth that takes into consideration environmental effects, in poor and rich countries alike. Progress over time needs to be economically, politically, and environmentally sustainable. There is growing awareness of the desirability and the necessity of taking steps to flatten or even induce a downturn of the environmental Kuznets' curve. The real issue is whether it also is politically feasible. As the World Bank noted,

> The principles of sound environmental policy . . . are well understood. But they are difficult for national governments to introduce and are even more difficult to translate into international agreements. National governments may be reluctant to challenge those who cause environmental damage; they are likely to be rich and influential, while those who suffer most are often the poor and powerless.

In other words, it is not wise to leave the environment to chance and to purely market decisions. In many poor countries, it is not possible to simply wait until incomes rise and hope that the environment will be valued more. Environmental degradation is now a global problem and though its causes are often local, the international community needs to work to see that the age of an environmental Kuznets' curve is increasingly in the past.

Sources: Dasgupta and Mäler 1995: 2384–2388; World Bank 1992:
10–13, 18, 38–41, 43

Questions for review

1   Considering only the countries listed in Table 2.1, rank them from the "most developed" to the "least-developed" in terms of both GNP per capita and GDP per capita. Do these rankings differ substantially? Which is the better measure to use for determining the level of development?

2   (a) Over the period 1970–1980, Tanzania's total GDP grew at 3.0 percent per annum and by 3.6 percent from 1980–1993, while population expanded at 3.1 percent over the earlier period and by 3.2 percent during 1980–1993. What was the rate of growth of GDP per capita over both periods? (b) Botswana's population grew by 3.5 percent per year during 1970–1980 and by 3.4 percent during 1980–1993, while total GDP grew by 14.5 percent per year during 1970–1980 and by 9.6 percent per annum during 1980–1993. What was happening to Botswana's GDP per person over each period? (c) Does population growth "cause" slow or fast growth in GDP? What is the connection between population growth and the increase in income per person suggested by these two examples? (d) Can you derive a formula, similar to equation 2.1 in the text, for calculating the approximate rate of change of income per capita when you know the rate of change of total output and the rate of growth of population?

3   Determine the estimated *average* income of the poorest 20 percent and of the richest 20 percent of income earners in (a) Rwanda, (b) Malaysia, (c) South Korea, (d) Botswana, and (e) Kenya by applying the income distribution shares in Table 2.2 to total GNP in Table 2.1. Compare these estimated average incomes per capita for the richest and poorest 20 percent with the mean GNP values for the country as a whole shown in Table 2.1. For which, if any, of the countries does the overall average per capita GNP figure provide a reasonable measure of the actual income earned by the "average" income recipient?

4   Using one scatter diagram, with GNP per capita (column 5 of Table 2.1) on the horizontal axis and the ratio of income received by the richest 20 percent to the share received by the poorest 20 percent (column 3 of Table 2.2) on the vertical axis, (a) plot a point for each country. (b) Is there any systematic relation between GNP per capita and the degree of income inequality? Do countries with low levels of GNP per capita have more or less inequality than economies with higher levels of GNP per capita? (c) Now try plotting the income share of the poorest 20 percent and/or the richest 20 percent against GNP per capita. Do you find any systematic relationship, looking at the data in this way? (If you have access to Excel or Lotus 1–2–3 or some other spreadsheet program or a simple statistical analysis package, you could run a simple regression between the two variables to look for this relationship.)

5   In 1988, Pakistan's current (nominal) GDP was $34,050 million. Assume that in 1998 total GDP measured in current (nominal) US dollars had increased to $51,920 million. (a) What was the total percentage increase in nominal GDP over the period and what was the percentage change, on average, per year? (b) Now determine real (constant price) GDP in 1998 calculated at 1988 prices, given that the price index in 1988 = 100 and is assumed to be in 1998 = 215.9. (c) What was the percentage change in real GDP between 1988 and 1998, both in total and the per year average?

6   What might explain the fact that Japan's PPP level of GNP per capita is so

much lower than its GNP per capita calculated at the official exchange rate? What might that indicate about the prices of non-traded goods in Japan relative to world prices and also about the relative level of competition in the Japanese economy?

7　Explain why using the PPP measure of GNP per capita might be considered a better measure for comparing development levels between nations than is the exchange rate-converted GNP value.

8　Focus 2.5 discusses the possibility of an environmental Kuznets' curve and suggests that avoiding such an outcome is more of a political problem than one of know-how. In the quote in that focus, what does the World Bank mean that it tends to be the "rich and influential" who cause much of the pollution, and the poor who suffer from the effects? In what specific ways do the "rich and powerful" cause environmental damage? Why is it the poor who tend to bear many of the costs of such damage? In what ways do the poor bear such costs? Can you identify instances where it is the poor who contribute to environmental damage? (Hint: think of clear-cutting of forests for wood for charcoal or for grazing of animals, as one instance.)

Notes

1　Further, it is a strongly held belief of many economists that economic growth in capitalist societies occurs via a trickle-down process. With economic growth and an expansion of society's total income, there is assumed to exist an automatic dispersion of the benefits of this growth to all income classes of society. While it is admitted that the incomes of the wealthiest in society perhaps grow most rapidly as economic growth occurs, those at lower-income levels are presumed to benefit also from economic expansion as income "trickles down" the income pyramid. This may occur via the provision of new and better jobs that result from the increased investment undertaken by higher-income recipients who finance such ventures, given their higher disposable incomes. Thus, one view is that income inequality has a functional purpose in capitalist economies in that it is higher-income individuals who are likely to save a larger portion of their incomes relative to lower-income recipients. It is from this pool of savings that the loanable funds for investment arise. Much like a boat, all of whose passengers are lifted together on a rising tide, it is suggested that greater economic growth benefits all, or certainly the great majority, of the members of society via the automatic mechanism of trickle-down growth. This, of course, is only a theory; the important question is whether this process works as described in particular situations.

2　Poorer nations tend to have less dependable estimates of their national income for one obvious reason: collecting data is expensive and for economies already facing the constraint of limited financial and human resources, the collection and evaluation of economic data is likely to be done in a manner that is less desirable and certainly less than would be optimal. To develop strategies that contribute to development, however, there is a compelling need for reliable statistical data concerning the objective reality in less-developed nations. In fact, one is tempted to state that the effort put into collecting dependable and timely statistics, making such information available to the public and in analyzing such data is one measure of a country's commitment to doing something about its future development.

3　An equivalent and even easier method for calculating the average income of the lowest and highest quintiles is to remember that the $1,658 GNP per capita figure for Guatemala shown in Table 2.1 would be the actual income of all individuals in Guatemala only if income were perfectly equally distributed. However, the richest 20 percent in Guatemala actually received 3.15 times their equality share of total GNP (their 63 percent actual share of total income ÷ their 20 percent equality share). Thus the per capita income of the richest 20 percent in Guatemala can be calculated $3.15 \times \$1,658 = \$5,223$, very close to the figure in the text, the difference being due to rounding. For the poorest 20 percent, their per capita income is but 0.105 their equality share (the actual 2.1 percent of total income received ÷ a 20 percent equality share), for a per capita income of $0.105 \times \$1,658 = \$174$ for the poorest fifth of the population.

4 A Gini coefficient of 0 would indicate perfect equality of income. A Gini coefficient = 1 would indicate perfect inequality in the distribution of income.

5 There are some further caveats worth mentioning when calculating real GNP or real GDP and using these values to judge an economy's progress over time. The farther apart in time the comparisons of income are, the less meaningful they are likely to be. For example, some goods and services may no longer be produced in later years, while new goods and services can enter the production stream. Thus, price indices and the deflating technique become less reliable for comparing real output over long periods.

   The issue of the quality of the Q_is is not captured by the price index adjustment. Prices may rise with quality improvements over time (some couture clothing) or they may fall (as with computers), so some price changes reflect not inflation or deflation but rather differences in product quality. These differences will be lost in these adjustments for real income and such improvements in quality, when they occur, must be reintroduced via other methods. Still, while always being cognizant of these weaknesses in calculating real GDP or GNP figures, if the years being compared are not too far apart in time, calculations as in equations 2.3 and 2.4 can be taken as reasonable approximations for estimating the changes in real output over time

6 Any good macroeconomics book will have the details on this problem. On the GPI, for which calculations have been made for the United States, see Cobb and Halstead (1994).

7 Arbitrage is the process in which goods are purchased in one market to be resold in another market at a higher price and with a known and certain profit. For example, if the price of a bar of Nestle's chocolate in India sells for the equivalent of $1.50, while it sells for the equivalent of $2.50 in the Philippines, it would be to the advantage of profit-maximizing traders to purchase Nestle's bars in India and resell them in the Philippines, as long as the costs of doing so – transportation, tariffs, etc. – are less than $1 per bar of chocolate, since there would be profit to be made on such a transaction.

   This process of arbitrage itself for traded goods like Nestle's chocolate would tend to bring the prices of the two goods in line between the two countries, abstracting from transportation and other transactions costs. The price of Nestle's bars in India would tend to rise with the increased demand as traders bought in that market in pursuit of the profits of arbitrage, while the price of chocolate bars would tend to fall in the Philippines due to the increased supply as chocolate bars would be sold. Ultimately, an equilibrium price would exist in both countries at which all the opportunities for arbitrage and the making of a sure profit from trade would have been exhausted. For this reason, the prices of traded goods are expected to be very similar among nations, except for transportation and other transaction costs.

8 See Streeten (1979) and Streeten (1981) on the basic needs approach and Morris (1979) for the original contribution to the creation of the PQLI measure.

9 The actual calculation of the HDI for any country is based on the country's deviation from the defined targets for each component of the index: a maximum life expectancy of 85 years at birth; 100 percent literacy and 100 percent combined school enrollment at all levels; and a maximum PPP GDP income of $40,000. It is thus a measure of the relative position of a country compared with the maximum (and minimum) levels of achievement. In other words, the HDI is a measure of how far away a country is from the current maximum achievable values on the selected variables that enter the HDI (see any recent edition of the UNDP report).

10 Until 1994, the HDI was calculated and compared with GNP per capita evaluated at official exchange rates. Beginning in 1995, however, the HDI has been calculated using a PPP measure of GDP per capita within the index. It is thus not strictly correct to compare the HDI values calculated for years after 1992 (the HDI values in the 1995 *Human Development Report*), with the HDI values calculated for 1987–1991. Further changes in the methodology for calculating the HDI are possible in future.

11 This study was carried out prior to the UNDP's new methodology of using per capita PPP GDP as the income variable for ranking nations. Still, it is believed these results are worth considering.

12 It is perhaps worth remembering an important axiom of economic theory which states that there are an infinite number of efficient, i.e., Pareto optimal, outcomes for both the production and distribution of goods and services among the members of any society. As can easily be demonstrated with an Edgeworth-Bowley box diagram, any initial distribution of wealth will, under conditions of perfect competition and free exchange, generate a locally efficient level of production and distribution of society's goods and services, with trade resulting in the contract curve being attained. Thus the distribution of wealth and income among society's members is a choice variable open to economies, since the distribution issue is independent of the issue of efficiency. *Any* initial distribution can be efficient. For an excellent exposition of this issue, see Bator's (1957) classic article.

13 See Anand and Kanbur (1993) for a review of the literature. These authors argue that the best empirical relation between income growth and equity or development is actually the opposite of the Kuznets' hypothesis! This contradictory result illustrates one of the problems in studying economics. There often are competing models that purport to explain some particular phenomenon, frequently based on extremely complicated mathematical and statistical analyses, done by equally competent and respected investigators, that nonetheless come to diametrically opposed and often irreconcilable conclusions. How does one choose between such competing theories when compelling empirical evidence can be mustered supporting alternative theories? This is an excellent question for class discussion!

14 It is not just governments that today can affect the level of inequality and reduce poverty, even at lower income levels than in the past. There are also a growing number of nongovernmental organizations, or NGOs, which operate in the less-developed nations and which often have as their primary objective the alleviation of poverty. These range from large and relatively well-financed groups like Oxfam, the International Red Cross and Crescent, CARE, Caritas, World and Vision to small, regionally and often country-specific groups, such as the Voluntary Action Network India.

15 The 1995 *Human Development Report*, pp. 125–33, also provides a technical guide to the determination of the 'gender-related development index' (GDI) and the 'gender empowerment measure' (GEM) mentioned in the text above.

References

Alkire, Sabrina. 2002. "Dimension of Human Development," *World Development* 20: 181–205.

Anand, S. and S.M. Kanbur. 1993. "Inequality and Development: A Critique," *Journal of Development Economics* 41: 19–43.

Bartelmus, Peter. 1994. *Environment, Growth and Development.* London: Routledge.

Bator, Francis. 1957. "The Simple Analytics of Welfare Maximization," *American Economic Review* (March): 22–59.

Birdsall, Nancy and Richard Sabot. 1994. "Inequality as a Constraint on Growth in Latin America," *Development Policy*, Newsletter on Policy Research by the Inter-American Development Bank (September): 1–5.

Cobb, Clifford and Ted Halstead. 1994. *The Genuine Progress Indicator.* San Francisco, CA: Redefining Progress (September).

Dasgupta, Partha and Karl-Göran Mäler. 1995. "Poverty, Institutions, and the Environmental Resource-Base," Chapter 39 in Jere Behrman and T.N. Srinivasan (eds), *Handbook of Development Economics*, volume IIIA. Amsterdam: Elsevier Science.

Dietz, James L. and Louise Gibson. 1994. "What is Development?: The Human Development Index, A New Measure of Progress?", California State University, Fullerton.

Elliott, Jennifer A. 1994. *An Introduction to Sustainable Development.* London: Routledge.

IMF. 1995. "Gender Issues in Economic Adjustment Discussed at UN Conference on Women," *IMF Survey* (September 25): 286–288.

Morris, Morris D. 1979. *Measuring the Condition of the World's Poor: The Physical Quality of Life Index*. New York: Pergamon Press.

Redclift, Michael. 1987. *Sustainable Development: Exploring the Contradictions*. London: Routledge.

Streeten, Paul. 1979. "From Growth to Basic Needs," *Finance and Development* 16 (September).

—— (ed.). 1981. *First Things First*. Oxford: Oxford University Press.

UNDP (United Nations Development Programme). 1993. *Human Development Report 1993*. Oxford: Oxford University Press.

—— 1995. *Human Development Report 1995*. Oxford: Oxford University Press.

—— 2001. *Human Development Report 2001*. Oxford: Oxford University Press.

US Department of Commerce. 1994. *Survey of Current Business* 74 (July).

—— 1995. *Survey of Current Business* 75 (August).

WCED (World Commission on Environment and Development). 1987. *Our Common Future*. Oxford: Oxford University Press.

World Bank. 1992. *World Development Report 1992*. Oxford: Oxford University Press.

—— 2000. *World Development Report 2000/2001*. Oxford: Oxford University Press.

—— 2001. *2001 World Development Indicators*. Available at http://www.worldbank.org/data/databytopic/databytopic.html.

Appendix 2A: Calculating the Gini coefficient

To understand how the Gini coefficient is calculated, it is helpful to look at a Lorenz curve which provides a graphical representation of a nation's income distribution. Figure 2.1A shows a simple Lorenz curve drawn from the following hypothetical income distribution figures.

Income distribution, by quintiles, Country A

	Share of GNP	Cumulative percentage, total income
Poorest 20% of familes	4% of total GNP	4%
Second 20% of familes	8% of total GNP	12%
Third 20% of familes	11% of total GNP	23%
Fourth 20% of familes	18% of total GNP	41%
Richest 20% of familes	59% of total GNP	100%

Figure 2.1A plots the percentage of families on the horizontal axis against the percentage of income received on the vertical axis. The diagonal in Figure 2.1A is a reference "line of equality." Any point along it would mean that X percent of families received exactly X percent of total income (where X could be any value between 1 and 100). Along the line of equality, for example, 10 percent of the families would be receiving 10 percent of society's total income; 40 percent of the families would be receiving 40 percent of total income; and so on. The diagonal provides a referent for visually comparing and precisely measuring the dispersion of the *actual* income distribution of a nation with what would be a perfectly equal distribution of income among all members of society.

By plotting the hypothetical aggregate values of income received against the quintiles of population for our hypothetical example above, the bowed Lorenz curve in Figure 2.1A can be drawn. Very roughly, the further away the Lorenz curve is from the line of equality, the greater the degree of income inequality. From the

Total income

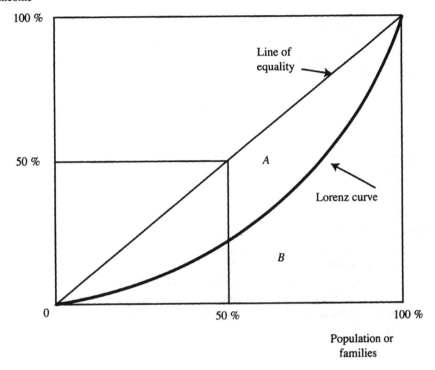

Figure 2.1A A Lorenz curve of income distribution.

Lorenz curve diagram, the Gini coefficient can be calculated. It is equal to the area *A* (the area between the Lorenz curve and the diagonal line of equality) divided by the total area $(A + B)$ of the triangle below the line of equality. Thus the Gini coefficient is equal to $A/(A + B)$.

Appendix 2B: Calculating the HDI index

With the 1995 issue of the *Human Development Report*, the HDI is calculated as a weighted average of educational attainment, life expectancy at birth and income. All components of the index measure the relative distance between a country's achievement and what is possible. Thus,

$$\text{index value} = \frac{\text{actual value of } x_i - \text{minimum value of } x_i}{\text{maximum value of } x_i - \text{minimum value of } x_i}$$

Educational attainment (E) is measured as a combination of two indices, one for adult literacy (minimum value = 0 percent; maximum value = 100 percent) and of the combined primary, secondary and tertiary enrollment ratios (minimum = 0 percent; maximum = 100 percent) with the following weight:

$$E = \tfrac{2}{3}\text{ adult literacy rate} + \tfrac{1}{3}\text{ combined enrollment ratio}$$

Life expectancy (L), for purposes of calculating the HDI index, has a minimum value of 25 years and a maximum value of 85 years.

Education (E) enters the HDI calculation as a combined index of adult literacy (A) and the combined enrolment in primary, secondary and tertiary education. Then these two indexes are combined with a weight of 2/3 given to adult literacy, A, and 1/3 to the combined enrolment ratio, C, to determine the education index, E, that ultimately enters the HDI calculation.

Income (Y) enters the HDI as a log value of the purchasing power parity (PPP) measure of GDP per capita. As the UN Development Programme writes (UNDP *Human Development Report 2003*: 341), "income serves as a surrogate for all the dimensions of human development not reflected in a long and healthy life and in knowledge." PPP GDP per capita income beyond $40,000 adds nothing further to the Y index.

The following shows how the HDI for 2001 was calculated for Albania. The basic data needed to calculate L, E and Y are: Albania's life expectancy was 73.4 years in 2001; the literacy rate was 85.3 per cent; the combined enrolment rate was 69 per cent; and PPP GDP per capita was $3,680.

The following HDI calculation for Albania is adapted from UNDP, *Human Development Report 2003*, p. 341.[15]

1. The *life expectancy index*, L, was determined as follows:

Using the first equation in the appendix above, and the minimum and maximum values for life expectancy, the life expectancy index, L, is equal to

$$L = \frac{73.4 - 25}{85 - 25} = 0.807$$

2. To determine the education index, E, a two-step procedure is necessary, again using the first equation in this appendix and the specific values for Albania for literacy and the combined enrolment ratio.

2a. First, the adult literacy index, A, component of educational attainment was computed as

$$A = \frac{85.3 - 0}{100 - 0} = 0.853$$

2b. Second, the combined enrolment index, C, the other component of education attainment, was determined as being

$$C = \frac{69 - 0}{100 - 0} = 0.690$$

Thus from 2a and 2b, the educational attainment index, E, was equal to

$$E = 2/3L + 1/3C = 2/3(0.853) + 1/3(0.690) = 0.798.$$

3. The income index, Y, for Albania and using Albania's PPP GDP per capita income shown above was equal to

$$Y = \frac{\log(3,680) - \log(100)}{\log(40,000) - \log(100)} = 0.602$$

The value of the HDI is then calculated as a weighted average of L, E, and Y, with each component having a value of 1/3. Since each of these is a "deprivation" measure, what is being calculated is the gap between a particular country's achievement level and what might be attained.

Thus, the HDI for Albania in 2001 is a simple weighted average of L, E, and Y, computed as

$$HDI = 1/3L + 1/3E + 1/3Y$$

$$= 1/3(0.807) + 1/3(0.798) + 1/3(0.602) = 0.735.$$

3 Development in historical perspective

After studying this chapter, you should understand:
- why and how colonialism left a lasting legacy in developing nations;
- the difference between semi-feudal/semi-capitalist social structures and capitalist social structures;
- the de-industrialization impact of colonialism and the biased nature of colonial infrastructure
- the new role credit played in the construction of neocolonial structures in the nineteenth century;
- the nature and importance of the terms of trade;
- economic dualism and its impact on colonial and post-colonial society;
- how to apply the concept of path dependency to post-colonial situations;
- the differential impact of early and mature colonialism; and
- the concept of colonial drain and the extent and significance of de-industrialization in colonial society

Introduction

Economic development demands and entails profound cultural change, including, often, transformation of the political system, of individual behavior norms, of the culture of work and production, and most fundamentally, modifications in the manner in which society confronts, moulds, propels, and adapts itself to the requirements of technological progress that are the font of economic growth and human development. Anyone studying the process of economic development must appreciate the wide-ranging cultural factors at work in any society. Failure to do so can result in a narrow and mechanistic interpretation of developing societies and the adoption of incomplete policy prescriptions which will, at best, diminish the effectiveness of efforts to achieve further progress.

At times, economists and others directly concerned with the process and problems of economic development have devoted too few of their efforts to understanding the historical conditions which have led to economic backwardness and underdevelopment. This failure may well arise from the fact that orthodox economists have generally been trained in the science of market behavior, with the assumption that human nature consists of, as Adam Smith maintained, a "natural propensity to truck, barter, and exchange." Taking such a perspective too literally, however, can lead to the view that the peculiarities and specificities of any country's history can be disregarded. The early development economists, to be discussed in Chapters 5 and 6, did not view history as insignificant, and we would argue that many of their insights as applied to the less-developed nations were richer as a consequence.

The social conditions under which production takes place often are significantly different in the developing world than in the advanced nations. Today the developing world incorporates, in shifting proportions, mixtures of neofeudal and peasant social and productive forces, combined with some of the most advanced components of early twenty-first-century capitalist production methods (this division is sometimes referred to as economic dualism). When development economics emerged as a separate discipline in the postwar period, the primary arena of its application was Western Europe and, to a much lesser degree, Japan. In both areas, economic policy had achieved tremendous success, as the Marshall Plan and US military assistance funds were pumped into Europe. Those economies responded rapidly to this stimulus, quickly regaining and then overtaking their past levels of development. In the early 1950s, then, fresh from this experience, the task of promoting economic development in the newly independent, less-developed nations did not appear daunting to policy-makers.

The relatively easy success in Europe and Japan in spurring output and employment formed the crucible for development thinking regarding the less-developed regions. One noted text of the 1950s, Benjamin Higgins' *Economic Development*, recounts an episode from the postwar period that seemed to justify such optimism. A small Pacific island community was overrun by US military personnel, resulting in the rapid transformation of their culture. Higgins drew a conclusion from this that was widely shared in the 1950s and early 1960s:

> This experience suggests that an almost complete transformation of a society can take place within *a few years* if the external "shock" to the society is powerful enough.
>
> (Higgins 1959: 312)

Higgins shared with most development economists of that time a strong presumption that whatever the nature or magnitude of the social, psychological, political, or historical obstacles inhibiting economic growth and human development, these barriers could be quickly overcome. The enduring structural distortions of economic dualism, deeply embedded in society due to historical factors which had given rise to economic retardation were not, however, adequately appreciated at the time.

The 1960s were cast as the First Development Decade by the United Nations, and already Higgins' "few years" for promoting development had been lengthened to ten, but the implication was essentially the same: economic backwardness would yield quickly to the expertise of the development specialists and to informed development advice.

Yet, after that first Development Decade had ended, the level of world poverty and despair had receded only marginally. In some nations, the standard of living had declined or remained roughly the same. In those nations where great leaps in overall economic performance had been achieved, such as Brazil, too often aggregate success had been accompanied by a *lower* standard of living for a significant portion of the population, as economic inequality worsened even as total output expanded. Few keen observers believed the Brazilian situation merely reflected the lead-up to the threshold income level suggested by Kuznets' inverted-U hypothesis, and time has proved them correct on this point. By the 1970s, much of the optimism about how quickly world poverty might be overcome had been muted, but development economists only rarely turned their attention to the study of historical and cultural factors to try to broaden their understanding of the stubborn persistence of world poverty. Let us briefly turn to a consideration of some of these issues as they relate to the less-developed nations, most of which, it is worth remembering again, reached political independence only after the Second World War.

The origins of economic development

Sustained increases in output and income per capita over time are of relatively recent historical origin. For much of known human history, population and total output tended to grow at about the same rate, so that per capita income remained roughly constant. Lloyd Reynolds has called this the period of extensive growth (Reynolds 1986: 7–9). What this meant was that for many centuries, until the early 1500s or so, the trend line of per capita production and income rose only very slowly, as shown in Figure 3.1. Most production was rurally based, there were few large urban settlements, and most people lived on and from the land, sometimes selling small surpluses in the village market-place for other goods. Small-scale

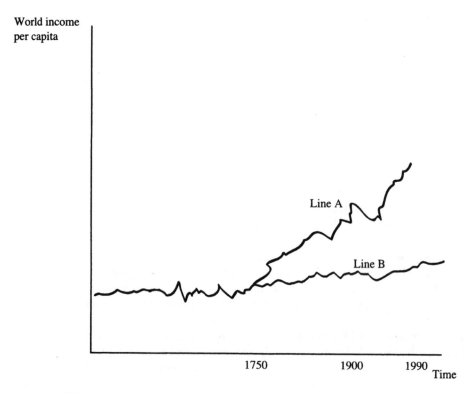

Figure 3.1 Historical growth trend of per capita income.

artisan and industrial-type products, such as textiles, and services, such as transportation, also were produced in the countryside, but on a very small scale. Besides agricultural production, families also produced non-agricultural goods, from clothing to cutlery to farm implements to soap and alcoholic beverages, primarily for family own-consumption.

Production methods were relatively simple during this extensive period of growth, and technology was very primitive. Such technology, as Reynolds (1986: ch. 1) argues, was not static, however. Technological methods were constantly adapting to the growing demands of population growth, to changing land conditions, and to new crops and strains of seeds. Such technological change tended to be sufficient to keep pace with population expansion and to maintain income per person roughly constant over long periods. Annual aggregate output during the period of extensive growth was subject to periodic ups and downs, but that was primarily due to exogenous factors, such as the weather, wars, and other crises.

The major "turning point" for world economic progress occurred with the transition from feudal production and social organization to the emergence of capitalist forms of production in Europe. Feudalism, an agricultural-based and hierarchical system of production organized around manors and based on the labor of serfs tied to the land, began to break down in the Middle Ages, especially in England, where the Industrial Revolution heralded the advent of the capitalist factory system as a new means of social and economic organization. With incipient capitalism, the purpose of production changed from survival and stasis to the pursuit of ever-increasing profit. Capitalist production was based fundamentally on the application of new knowledge and ever-greater quantities of physical capital that could produce more, at lower cost, with the same or fewer inputs to production. Industrial capitalism established the foundation for intensive production methods, which for the first time in history created the reasonable possibility of higher levels of output and income per person *without* increases in population or other resources. Output and income did not depend predominantly upon the availability of resources with intensive production and industrial capitalism, as they had in pre-capitalist forms of production, including feudalism. Now, the level of output depended upon the efficiency with which available resources were used and upon the application of technology to save on the use of such resources, so that more output and income could be produced from what was available. In Figure 3.1, the trend line of income per person (Line A) begins to rise after 1750 or so, when the capitalist system, with its factories and machines, began to triumph in some Western European countries. In those nations where capitalism did not become firmly planted, thus failing to displace traditional pre-capitalist methods of production, as in most of the less-developed world, the trend line of income per person (Line B) does not show the sharp upward trend that characterized income growth in the developed capitalist world along the path of Line A).[1]

It is important to keep in mind, then, that the possibility of sustained increases in income per person, that is, in economic growth and development, is a relatively recent historical phenomenon, dating back only some 250 years. Further, high levels of economic success have been, to date at any rate, strongly associated with the spread of capitalist methods of production and the displacement of pre-capitalist methods, in both agriculture and industry. Why have such methods of production, and the ways of thinking and doing that are associated with such production, developed so strongly in some regions of the world – the developed nations – and apparently so weakly in others – the less-developed countries?

Colonialism

As noted in the last chapter, most of the less-developed nations today were colonies of one or, sometimes, more than one, powerful capitalist country during their history. The period of imperial expansion after the "discovery" of the Americas by Columbus in the late 1400s led to a scramble by the European powers for land around the globe. Parts of Asia, Africa and the Americas fell into the hands of incipient capitalist nations bent on winning the competitive race by controlling as much of the world's resources as possible. Not only British colonies, on which, truly "the sun never set," but Dutch, French, Belgian, German, Spanish, Portuguese, and Italian colonial possessions multiplied, sometimes changing hands, but always attained and held in the interests of what, charmingly if inaccurately, was called the "mother country." The good of the native peoples of the colonies was of little concern to the colonizers, except as to how they might best serve to the advantage of the colonizer.[2]

As a consequence, during the long epoch of European colonialism, little thought was given to the question of economic development per se in the colonies. The colonizing powers repeatedly referred to their "civilizing" and often "Christianizing" missions in the colonial regions. Political leaders in the colonies occasionally commented upon their willingness to uplift natives through the introduction of Western education and modern science. It was almost taken as a truism by the colonizing powers that their presence in those "uncivilized" countries could not help but be beneficial to the natives, who so often seemed to be ungrateful for the sacrifices made by the colonizers. The colonial powers even defended European involvement in the nefarious slave trade on the grounds that slavery was widespread in Africa anyway, that Africa not Europe had invented it, and that life on a West Indian or Brazilian plantation often was preferable to death in an African tribal war or to a lifetime of slavery in Africa.

Even Karl Marx seemed to believe that the processes which European colonialism unleashed in the underdeveloped regions ultimately would be beneficial and were undoubtedly necessary if these regions were ever to make any substantial progress. For Marx, it was both inevitable and desirable, as part of his stages view of human progress (see Chapter 4), that pre-capitalist societies be swept away. The capitalism introduced by the colonial powers had a destructive and regenerative function to fulfill. Antiquated, backward cultures and patterns of behavior of the colonies needed to be eliminated if development was to occur, and the introduction of the capitalist, market society would lead to a higher standard of living and an all-round better life for the natives. As difficult and brutal as the colonial process might be, the inevitability of such progress was not called into question by Marx, as his writings on British colonialism in India clearly demonstrated. Nor did there seem to be any doubt that the destruction of the old societies brought on by colonialism, traumatic as that might be, was desirable in the final calculation.

Unlike the early apologists for European colonialism, or those who emphasized the destructive and regenerative nature of a process largely regarded as inevitable, many modern development economists, particularly in the 1950s, were careful to emphasize that the development process and development policy should be critically aware of the need to preserve and constructively alter elements of the post-colonial societies which were, in the view of the particular less-developed country, worthy of retention. Many Westerners, including perhaps surprisingly Marx, might have found this perspective incomprehensible. Yet in the areas of art, literature, handicrafts, music and dance, herbal medicine, the nurturing of children, cuisine, and attitudes toward mutual support among the family, the so-called backward cultures may be imbued with valuable social institutions worthy of preserving and adapting within more modern social and productive societies.

As developing societies evolve, a fusion of old but still functional societal elements with new forces and processes should be the goal; development does not have to mean the complete destruction of what makes any people and culture special and unique. In Latin America, the contradictions of pursuing modern development are sometimes summarized as follows: "Americans know how to work, and Latin Americans know how to play." The limits of a one-dimensional society are well-drawn in this saying. There are positive lessons that less-developed societies can learn from the already developed nations, but the obverse also is true.

The lasting effects of colonialism and path dependency

To some observers, the era of colonialism might seem, on first glance, to be merely a subject of historical import, devoid of any apparent immediacy as regards the problems of development in the less-developed nations today.[3] Colonialism, however, entailed more than the plundering of a militarily and economically weaker culture by a more powerful nation. Colonialism often resulted in severe demographic crises. This was particularly the case with the Spanish in Mexico and Peru, and with the British, Dutch, French, Portuguese, and Spanish in Africa.[4] Although demographers and anthropologists dispute the magnitude of the demographic crisis in Latin America between 1540 and 1640, there is no question that the indigenous population was drastically reduced due to a labor draft system which sent millions into the gold and silver mines to finance Spain's Siglo de Oro. Spain's forced labor system disrupted traditional Indian village systems of production, sent men and boys into the mines to toil without pay and then die, and left women and children to plant and harvest crops which had to support the males working in the mines.

In his fascinating account of the history of Spain in the New World, Eduardo Galeano (1973: 50) refers to research that suggests that Latin America's population declined from an estimated 70–90 million in 1540 to 3.5 million by 1690. Others question these figures, placing the original indigenous population figure at a lower level. But whatever the numbers, the sheer loss of life, whether from overwork, disease, or from struggle against better-armed adversaries, is stupefying. What consequences did this demographic crisis impose upon the Indians? To what degree was their culture decimated? What were the lasting effects upon the indigenous people who survived? How did these terrible events shape social attitudes in the region toward change in future generations? (See Focus 3.1.)

In Africa, a demographic crisis of similar proportions was spread over a period of nearly 400 years. The slave trade furnished one part of the colonial world with labor to fill the vast lands acquired by the colonial powers, at the cost of depopulating Africa. Between 1600 and 1900, approximately 12 million Africans were sold into

FOCUS 3.1   PATH DEPENDENCE AND COLONIAL STRUCTURES

The term "path dependence" has been used to describe the important role which historical events and historically formed institutions have in determining the future range of possibilities for a nation. Once institutions have been formed, they tend to lock-in a certain evolutionary path for the nation.

If the previously formed institutions are socially constructive, then the evolutionary path of the economy can be *virtuous*; the process of cumulative causation leads to an upward spiral of social progress. But if the institutional basis of a society has been formed through a long process whereby inhibiting institutions and social practices have become deeply entrenched, then it is more likely that the future evolutionary path will be one of *vicious circles* of cumulative causation leading to low levels of income and achievement.

Institutions may come into existence because they are desirable and superior to what has gone before. But retarding institutions may be imposed, if they serve the interests of powerful groups or nations. Even historians who are hesitant to fault colonial policies, such as David Fieldhouse, acknowledge that under colonialism only the ability to produce and export agricultural products or raw materials, such as minerals and forestry products, mattered. Colonial industry was ignored, as was any supporting matrix for industry, such as education, a financial system, or technical training.

With rare exceptions,

> colonial states constituted an arbitrary break in the historical process, sometimes splitting regions with some natural connection, elsewhere bringing together societies which had no capacity to cooperate; and in either case doing so at a speed that made it impossible for forces to operate satisfactorily. In this respect colonialism bequeathed an impossible heritage to the rulers of the new states.

History matters, then, according to path dependence theory. And, in the case of the underdeveloped nations, once free of colonialism, the weight of history continued to play a role in shaping the path of economic and social change of the future. This is not to argue that nations, once burdened by inhibiting institutions, are condemned mechanistically to repeat the processes and behavioral patterns established in the past. Rather, it is to argue that the past must be carefully understood, including the colonial past, in order to comprehend the nature of the challenges and limits which developing societies now confront. Path dependency helps us to understand why and where countries are today in their process of evolution. The concept is also helpful in beginning to grasp what is required to alter adverse path dependency by decisions that can lead to a higher level of growth and development in the future.

Sources: Acemoglu 2003; Acemoglu *et al.* 2001; Fieldhouse 1981: 15, 68

slavery and brought to the Western Hemisphere, with an additional 36 million dying as a result of constant warfare throughout Africa, or on the long march to the coast, or in the slave pens awaiting shipment across the Atlantic (Stavrianos 1981: 109). From 1650 to 1850, Africa's share of world population fell from 18 percent to 8 percent, due at least partly to the effects of the slave trade.

The slave trade had other effects that illustrate the lasting impact of colonialism: a new economic role for African chieftains was created, that of facilitator and regional beneficiary of the slave trade. Authoritarianism was strengthened and resistance to the status quo made more difficult by the new gains to be made from warfare on neighboring tribes. Furthermore, the constant wars encouraged by the slave traders, but perpetrated by the tribal chiefs in order to realize the potential gains of selling conquered tribes into slavery, tended to impede the emergence of inter-regional trade patterns, while at the same time it encouraged the importation of European manufactured products. Thus to the effects of depopulation through slavery, one should add the partial destruction of native manufactures and the hardening of authoritarian rule in Africa brought on by colonialism. Vertical trading patterns between Africa and Europe were often substituted for horizontal trade patterns across Africa, which could have contributed to the more robust development of linkages between the local economies. Such trade patterns might have acted as a check on tensions between tribes and regions in Africa which would have depended more on one another rather than on trade relations with Europe.

Forms of European colonialism

Spain: a case of absolute depredation

The earliest colonial empires, those of Spain and Portugal, while imposing devastating social and economic changes on the colonial regions, were, ironically, of no lasting benefit to the imperial powers either. As gold and, later, silver poured into Seville for roughly 200 years after 1500, Spain's quasi-feudal economy became steadily less cohesive. As these precious metals circulated as money, the rapid inflow of gold and silver resulted in severe inflation which undermined domestic Spanish industry, handicrafts, and agriculture. Conspicuous consumption among the Spanish elite, however, was enabled to reach new heights as a result of the flow of wealth emanating from the overseas colonies. Unproductive investments in government buildings and private villas and castles soared, and cheaper luxury goods and manufactures were increasingly imported from Holland and England rather than being produced in Spain. The tremendous economic surplus transferred from the mines of Mexico and Peru led to virtually no expansion of the productive capacities of Spain; technological development was restricted to addressing the most immediate necessities in mining and shipping, labor skills were not enhanced, corruption was not addressed, and authoritarian management techniques were never questioned.

A popular saying well-described the economic process which vitiated both Latin America and Spanish progress: "Spain held the cow, and the Dutch milked it." The "cow" was Latin America, and its wealth of gold and silver passed quickly to Holland and England from Spain to pay for the goods the Spanish elite coveted. But, when the last of the mining booms was exhausted in the 1700s, Spain's economy imploded, as did the economies of Mexico and Peru, now saddled with the backward institutions which Spain had imposed. However, the other economies of Europe, which had been providing the manufactured goods which the Spanish devoured, flush with plundered wealth, could only get gold and silver by *producing* things Spain wished to buy, so their economies flourished and continued to do so. Ironically, then, the wealth of Spain, based on colonial plunder, was illusory; the real "wealth" was that created by production, and that wealth was being built in the emerging and expanding factory system in an increasingly capitalist Europe which traded with Spain.

Merchant capital: from old colonialism to new colonialism

Spain's economy in the sixteenth century had been dominated by semi-feudal inter-ests, hence the emphasis on war, plunder, slavery, and short-term gain. Because there was as yet no capitalist logic of maximum profit at work, Spanish policies in the Western Hemisphere epitomized the old colonial system. While Spain and its colonies sunk into a morass of backwardness, European colonial policy continued to evolve. As new powers were drawn to colonial adventures, a complex half-way transition between feudalism and capitalism emerged. This transitionary period in Europe is sometimes known as the era of merchant capitalism, which gave rise to the new colonial system.[5]

The Dutch system, in particular, exhibited the characteristics of merchant capital-ism, beginning roughly in the mid-seventeenth century and spreading rapidly in the early eighteenth century. The Dutch established the first sugar plantation systems in Latin America and later in the East Indies. The plantation system sought to maxi-mize agricultural yields from a given amount of land, using slave labor, and the goal of production was clearly profit. The earliest plantation systems, prior to 1750, inten-tionally set such a demanding pace of work for the slaves that they survived, on average, perhaps no more than ten to fifteen years. (At that time, African slaves were cheap and readily available, since the drain on Africa's population was small relative to the late eighteenth and nineteenth centuries.) Thus the Dutch plantation system combined capitalist-type behavior, such as expanded production, as represented by the maintenance of a fixed investment in plantation lands, and the profit motive, with quasi-feudal attitudes toward labor.

The Dutch, and others who followed the Dutch plantation model, were quick to respond when slave prices soared in the mid-eighteenth century.[6] Labor conditions improved, the pace of work was made less arduous, and slaves lived longer. While the colonial powers under the sway of merchant capitalism took into account the necessity of maintaining the productive capacity of their colonial systems, the primary emphasis of merchant capitalism was on the *short-term* gains of trade and finance. The ethos of merchant capital was, above all, that of speculative gains. Adjustments toward economic rationality, including the introduction of technical change, were intermittent and limited to attempting to maintain the basis of social wealth for the colonizer. Extensive investments and training of workers were out of the question, as these would have absorbed current returns. The colonies were to be plundered at the lowest cost possible; they were not places in which to invest for the future.

British rule in India: the transition from merchant capital to industrial capital

Spain's and Holland's colonial legacy can be contrasted with that of the British in India. Britain, like many other powers, had gained access to coastal trading cities in India prior to the eighteenth century. In 1763, as a result of major military victories over France, Britain began to expand its sphere of control in India, eventually domi-nating much of the subcontinent in the course of the nineteenth century. Although British rule in India was without doubt harsh, the extent of British transgression in India never reached the depths attained by the Spanish in Latin America.

British policy toward India changed during the course of the late eighteenth and early nineteenth centuries, as merchant capital and mercantilist ideas steadily lost ground to industrial capital and capitalist views within England with the triumph of the Industrial Revolution and the steady rise of the factory system. Yet the process of pushing aside merchant capital and mercantilist policies was exceedingly complex. Even in the nineteenth century, British policy toward India clearly failed to conform to the axioms of free trade championed by the industrial capitalists and classical economists in Britain of the period. The precepts which underlay merchant capitalism, beliefs that basically assumed that the wealth of a nation depended upon its control over trade, were radically different from those of the classical economists like Adam Smith and David Ricardo (see Chapter 4).

Merchant capital, by contrast, emphasized the *relative terms* under which exchange took place. Controlling trade and controlling wages either through slavery or by decree meant that the relative terms of exchange would be extremely advantageous to Dutch and British merchants, and thus, it was assumed, the economic wealth and power of these nations would be augmented. By way of contrast, classical economists analyzed trade relationships upon the premise that each participant in a market, both buyer and seller, had sufficient resources to *withdraw* from the market if the price was not to their liking. Slaves, uprooted natives and colonial regions, by contrast, had no ability to withdraw from the colonial system, and merchant capitalists were not to be swayed by the logic of the classical economists. (See Focus 3.2.)

Britain developed a colonial system which combined elements of merchant and industrial capitalism. For some twentieth-century observers, such as the Austrian economist Joseph Schumpeter, this blending of the precepts of merchant capital and industrial capital in the British colonies was a glaring contradiction, an anomaly which could only be explained as a throwback to an earlier pre-capitalist era (Schumpeter 1951). The American economist Thorstein Veblen, by contrast, maintained that whatever the stage of capitalist development, residual elements of earlier economic eras tended to maintain a foothold, both physically and ideologically, and "recrudescences" were likely to arise, particularly during periods of prolonged economic stagnation or cyclical downturn (Hunt 1979: ch. 13).

Politically, the planters of the West Indies and the merchants operating in India were able to exercise a quotient of power, even when the industrial capitalists and their ideology dominated British policy-making. Merchant capital was able to maintain a certain limited autonomy regarding policy within the colonial system; policies that might have been increasingly anachronistic in England continued to coexist in the colonies, which lived a divided and incomplete existence, pulled in different and contradictory directions.

The functional role of colonialism

Merchant capital and industrial capital are indeed distinct forms. Yet, in the colonial system they could be complementary. In analyzing the history of the less-developed regions, it is important to understand that these regions played a notable, if sometimes overlooked, role in contributing to the British industrial revolution. For example, recent estimates place the mass of profits deriving from the British slave trade in the eighteenth century at £50 million. Profits from the British West Indian

---

FOCUS 3.2   WHAT DIFFERENCE INDEPENDENCE? THE UNITED STATES VERSUS MEXICO

Sometimes the following question is posed by those skeptical of the force of colonial rule: If colonialism imposed such a burden, why did some nations seem to shrug off the legacy of colonialism, while others languished after independence? A comparison of the United States and Mexico may help to answer this question.

Just prior to independence, the estimated *net burden* of colonial rule in the thirteen colonies of North America came to 0.3 percent of their national income. In contrast, the estimated annual burden of Spanish colonialism, measured in terms of the taxes paid to Madrid and the cost of being prevented from trading freely with other nations, has been estimated to be 7.2 percent of annual income during the last twenty-four years of Spanish rule over Mexico. Thus, in this method of measuring the net drain imposed by colonialism, the relative burden of Spanish rule was twenty-five times greater than that of British rule!

In 1800, Mexico's per capita income was 44 percent of that of the United States. By 1910, the gap had widened; Mexico's per capita income was a mere 13 percent of that of the US! Why did the gap widen so rapidly? John Coatsworth's comparative research points to two factors: first, the United States had a relatively good river system which allowed bulky goods to be transported cheaply. A similar transport system in Mexico would have reduced the difference between each nation's growth rate by about one-third.

The remaining differential Coatsworth attributes to Spanish feudalism. In theory, independence in Mexico in 1821 could have begun to dissolve the rigid institutions of Spanish rule. In fact, internal and international social and political conflicts left Mexico exhausted and directionless for more than fifty years. Reform of the colonial fiscal system was only completed in the 1890s, while new legislation regarding commerce, mining, foreign trade, and banking came into existence in the 1884–1908 period. These long-awaited reforms, unfortunately, largely served to facilitate an expansion of foreign ownership and control over the Mexican economy, rather than contributing to local development.

In the US, the institutions of British rule were only rarely feudal, such as the acceptance of slavery, the slave trade, and the plantation system. A costly civil war, which also stimulated industrialization in the North, had to be fought to rid the United States of its colonial legacy, and its neocolonial links with Great Britain.

Spanish colonialism of an essentially feudal nature thus lasted longer, penetrated deeper into the behavioral dynamics of Mexican society, and was more difficult to eradicate than British rule in the North American colonies. Elsewhere in the British Empire, however, the systematic colonialism of white-settler rule championed by John Stuart Mill was replaced by a more retarding blend of British institutions, such as the plantation economy of Jamaica. There and in India and other colonies under the Union Jack, the burden of British control was much heavier than in North America.

Sources: Coatsworth 1978: 84; Thomas 1965

---

sugar plantations were between £200 and £300 million in the same period (Crow and Thorpe 1988: 16). Between 1757 and 1812, the inflow of profits from India was estimated at between £500 million and £1 billion (Digby 1969: 33). Digby's estimate, originally published in 1901, has been viewed as an exaggeration by some, but a more recent analysis estimated that the British imposed a drain on India of the equivalent of 5–6 percent of GNP during the period (Bagchi 1984: 81; see Box 3.1).

While these capital flows from the colonies were exceedingly large, the fortunes

Box 3.1 The colonial drain

The Dutch ruled Indonesia for more than 300 years, beginning in the early 1600s, making substantial investments over this period. But Angus Maddison's research reveals that though "there had been a consistent and substantial trade surplus for 300 years, it is clear there was never any net transfer of funds from the metropole and that foreign claims on Indonesia arose from reinvested earnings of the colonists."

How does a colonizing nation assure a net outward transfer? In the 1700s, coffee was a major export crop. The Dutch guaranteed a net drain of income from their colony by forcing delivery of coffee from native cultivators and then "paying" the cultivators for only a fraction of the total. One practice was to receive delivery of 240 lb. of coffee but only pay the cultivator for 14 lb. The remainder the Dutch simply appropriated!

How much income did the Dutch drain off from Indonesia in a given year? Maddison calculated that the drain amounted to 15.6 percent of the net domestic product of Indonesia in 1930. That is, 15.6 percent of Indonesia's net output went to either Dutch corporations, Dutch nationals living in Indonesia, or to the Dutch government. In all, he estimates that the *total* income of the Dutch increased by 12.8 percent due to their ability to control Indonesia. What would have happened if Indonesia could have used much of the 15.6 percent of net income to increase its own productive base? Clearly, a drain of this magnitude would be sufficient to undermine the development prospects of any nation.

For comparison, Maddison calculated the drain from India to the British in 1931. India lost approximately 5 percent of its net income, while British incomes were increased by 3.3 percent. At this time, India was the "Jewel in the Crown" of the British Empire, but Britain was also in a position to drain colonial income from roughly 50 smaller colonies in 1931.

Had the Dutch in Indonesia, or the British in India, invested heavily in infrastructure, technology, and labor-training, and struggled to improve the social and economic organization of their colonies, this drain might not have been of fundamental, determining importance. This is so because the drain would have constituted a less significant net flow from an ever-expanding productive base. The expansion of the productive base would have benefitted the colonial region after Independence and might have altered the nature of path dependency.

But the evidence in the case of Indonesia, India, and many other colonies indicates that the colonial rulers, except in the rarest of instances, never made sufficient investments in infrastructure, industrial production, technologically sophisticated agriculture, or in any of the other areas which would have served to expand the productive base sufficiently to more than offset the drain resulting from colonial control.

The colonial drain constituted lost income, due to the institutions of colonialism. It quantified a national humiliation of major proportions, arising, in many instances, from land which had been appropriated and/or monopoly incomes attributable solely to the power of colonial domination.

Sources: Furnivall 1967: 40; Maddison 1990: 360, 364, 369

acquired in the British colonies were often squandered in conspicuous consumption in England. Nonetheless, there can be no doubt that a portion of these funds entered the British banking system thereby adding to liquidity, driving down interest rates and releasing a flow of investment funds which could be tapped by the early British industrialists for their industrialization projects. Colonialism also added to aggregate demand, without driving up British wage rates. An external market for ships and for traded goods in Africa, such as woollens, guns, iron and steel products, and a market for sugar refining equipment in the West Indies further stimulated British investments, production and employment. Such a chain of events had not occurred in Spain in the sixteenth century, because Spain had lacked an industrial base and industrialists, both destroyed by raging price inflation with the massive inflows of gold and silver from the colonies; Spain also lacked a sophisticated banking system which might have functioned as an efficient intermediary between savers and investors.

The colonial elite: the enduring significance of collaboration

At the same time that merchant capital and industrial capital were establishing a basis for complementary interaction in Britain, and to a lesser degree in Holland, merchant capitalism was consolidating its hold over the indigenous elite in the colonies which served as the medium of colonial dominion. Colonial rule was based upon a system of collaboration between the indigenous elite and the colonial power, as the case of India illustrates.

> British rule consolidated itself by creating new classes and vested interests who were tied up with that rule and whose privileges depended on its continuance. There were the landowners and the princes, and there were a large number of subordinate members of the services in various departments of the government, from the *patwari*, the village headman, upward. . . . To all these methods must be added the deliberate policy, pursued throughout the period of British rule, of creating divisions among Indians, of encouraging one group at the cost of the other.
>
> (Nehru 1960: 304)

Ronald Robinson sketched the pivotal role also played by the indigenous elite in Africa and Asia in the nineteenth century:

> Although potentially the power was there in Europe, in reality only a tiny fraction of it was ever committed to Africa or Asia. Europe's policy normally was that if empire could not be had on the cheap, it was not worth having at all. The financial sinew, the military and administrative muscle of imperialism was drawn through the mediation of an indigenous elite from the invaded countries themselves.
>   Its central mechanism, therefore, may be found in the systems of this collaboration set up in the pre-industrial societies, which succeeded (or failed) in meshing the incoming process of European expansion into indigenous social politics and in achieving some kind of evolving equilibrium between the two.
>
> (Robinson 1976: 131)

It is important to note that this process of elite formation was conditioned by the behavioral parameters and norms of merchant capital rather than industrial capital. Speculative behavior, monopoly practices, favoritism and patronage in employment, corruption within government, intermittent changes in technology, the absence of labor rights and labor norms, authoritarian governments, and profits based upon cunning trading of commodities and usurious banking practices, were all constituent elements of merchant capitalism. All were transplanted to the colonial regions where they thrived, grew and became entrenched, even as they were being surmounted in Europe by emerging capitalist methods. The new collaborative elite in the colonies became consummate masters of the artifices of merchant capital at the same time that their colonial masters were abandoning such systems at home.

De-industrialization in the colonies

Once this new indigenous elite was consolidated and corrupted by colonial rule, there were few social forces which could emerge within the social formation of the less-developed regions to challenge the sway of merchant capital and mercantilist ideas. Two case studies illustrate this point. In the late eighteenth century, Britain accelerated its expansion in India, which then had a thriving textile industry that had for centuries sold high-quality cotton products throughout India, in much of Africa, and in the Middle East. Large factory towns existed where skilled laborers were able to produce cloth so cheaply that the British East India company could buy from native industrialists, ship the product to England, and still sell their cargoes at a full 100 percent mark-up over cost. Thus, Indian manufacturing early on had the capability of successfully challenging the leading sector of the British economy at the very moment when the British "take-off" into industrialization was under way.

The British reacted to this potential challenge both economically and politically. The two reactions combined illustrate the political economy of British policy at a pivotal moment in both British and Indian history. On the purely economic terrain, British textile industrialists reacted to the challenge of Indian manufactures by increasing their investments in productive equipment, by raising the amount of capital that each worker utilized and by increasing the complexity and productivity of the production process by using ever more mechanized forms of production. These changes helped to drive down their unit costs of production, making them more competitive with Indian producers.

At the political level, British textile industrialists demanded and received protection from imported Indian textiles. By 1814, textile interests in Britain had placed a tariff of 70 to 80 percent on all imported Indian textiles, thereby pricing them out of the British market. At the same time, they forced open the Indian market to British-made textile exports. On the other hand, Britain accepted the import of raw cotton from India to be used in British production, without any tariffs being applied. The East India Company and British merchants in India then switched from textile exporting to the exporting of raw cotton to Britain. As a consequence, the Indian textile industry, which had exported to England in large part so that the British could re-export their products to the world market, lost one of its largest markets, and began to deteriorate.

At the same time, cheaper made *machino*-factured textiles from England were pouring into India, underselling the higher-cost *man*ufactured textiles of India. By the mid-nineteenth century, India's industrial base in textiles had been decimated, and India had been de-industrialized as a result of British policy. India no longer produced its own textiles, but now exported raw cotton to Britain only to import British-made cotton textiles, which soared from 1 million yards in 1814 to 53 million yards in 1844 (Stavrianos 1981: 247). As a result, the number of Indian textile workers (spinners and weavers) fell from an estimated 6.3 million to only 2.4 million from 1800 to 1913. While the spinners declined the handloom weavers sought to remain competitive through a precipitous drop in their wages. They "survived" by executing their own ruin, while their pauperization deprived the internal market of much needed purchasing power, driving down further the Indian economy (Amsden 2001: 34, 37, 50).

> India ceased to be a leading manufacturing country of the precapitalist era and was reduced to the position of a supplier of agricultural goods and raw materials to the industrializing economies of the West, particularly Britain.
>
> The long process of deindustrialization of India started with the catastrophic disappearance of cotton manufactures from the list of exports of India.... For more than seventy-five years up to 1913, India remained the major importer of cotton goods from Britain, often taking more than forty percent of the British exports.... Other rural or urban manufactures were ruined partly by the rise of alternative sources of supply and by government restrictions.
>
> (Bagchi 1984: 82)[7]

A somewhat similar situation occurred in Egypt between 1820 and 1840 under the leadership of Muhammed Ali. Ali sought to develop Egypt through industrialization. He borrowed extensively, developed a new strain of cotton called Egyptian long-staple, and advanced seeds to peasants to encourage cotton cultivation. Ali then constructed a series of textile factories and attempted to export high-quality textiles to the world market. The British, while championing modernization in the pre-capitalist regions, and officially wedded to a free-trade ideology, were appalled by this emerging challenge to their dominance in the global textile market.

Ali had other major enemies besides the British; his civil service worked against his dreams of a powerful and modern Egypt by appropriating whatever they could of an increasing national income through corruption and other means of skimming income. Meanwhile, Ali's plans to "hothouse" industrialization compelled the artisan class into the new factories where hours were long; extremely onerous working conditions led to theft, sabotage, and low morale. Peasants were forced to sell cotton to the government purchasing monopoly at a very low price, while Ali's state-owned factories sought the highest price on world markets for their excellent manufactured products. Internal forces of opposition and resistance certainly hindered the potential of Ali's experiment, but Ali also was undone when the British encouraged the Turks to make war on Egypt. The Turks were defeated, so the British intervened, and Ali was forced to grant free-trade access to British products, foreigners were granted free access to land, and Egypt became a typical raw material exporter rather than an industrial country, at least partly as a consequence of British opposition.

> Under the protection of the capitulatory treaties [of the war with Turkey and Britain] European speculators and adventurers were free to operate in Egypt outside the jurisdiction of the native courts and subject only to consular control. Many grew rich by smuggling opium and tobacco and invariably were protected by the foreign consuls.... These foreigners, who were completely exempt from

taxation, also served as agents in arranging for loans and contracts on extortionist terms. In 1873, for example, the [Egyptian Government] accepted a loan at face value of £32 million, but after heavy commissions and discounts received only £9 million. . . .

(Stavrianos 1981: 221)

Colonial industrialization?

Why not manufacture textiles in India or refine minerals and petroleum products in the less-developed nations where they originate? In analyzing international trade and production patterns, it is important to recognize that, the colonial powers encouraged the production of tropical products, and often contributed to increases in the efficiency of the processes of production in these goods. At the same time, they also actively discouraged the production of those goods in the colonies which might have competed with their own exports. This created patterns of distorted development, serving to internally disarticulate the less-developed economies, while contributing to the internal articulation and further development of the colonial power. Neighbouring nations, if they were dominated by different colonial powers, were deprived of whatever natural complementarities existed between them, as regional trade patterns were prevented from emerging. The colonies themselves had infrastructural systems which primarily served the interests of the colonial power (see Focus 3.3). Often major cities and regions within the colonies were not well connected with one another; what infrastructure there was had been designed to facilitate the movement of tropical commodities to the coast and onward to Europe to be consumed. In the course of the nineteenth century, an increasing number of colonies became mono-exporters, or exported, at best, a very limited range of primary products, such as agricultural goods and raw, unprocessed minerals, because that is what the colonial powers wanted, not because that was the optimal productive structure.

The process of internal disarticulation in the colonies could often be found in the disparate tendencies of peasant agriculture and export agriculture, the latter carefully stimulated by colonial policies. In India, commercial export agriculture benefitted via improved organization, mechanization, enhanced infrastructure, bank credits and ready access to the sophisticated talents of primarily British exporters. Peasant agriculture, by contrast, languished. Peasants were shunted off to poorer lands, where cultivation practices deteriorated, and where labor-intensive methods were unable to compensate for lower-quality land and the lack of financing and knowledge needed to increase worker productivity on the land. Table 3.1 records the divergent tendencies of agricultural production under colonial rule in India, reflecting the neglect of indigenous small producers and the benefits extended to exporters.

Table 3.1 Peasant versus commercial export agriculture in India, 1891–1941 (annual average growth)

	Peasant agriculture (food grains) %	Commercial export agriculture (cash crops) %
Output	−0.11	+0.67
Productivity	−0.18	+0.86

Source: Fieldhouse 1981: 89.

FOCUS 3.3 COLONIAL INFRASTRUCTURE

Huge outlays, often supported with forced labor, were necessary to build an infrastructure of highways, irrigation and flood control systems, communication systems and railroads in the colonies. But, as can be readily illustrated in Africa, this infrastructure lacked a developmental rationality for colonies. The purpose of colonial infrastructure was to facilitate the movement of tropical products and minerals from the colony to the ports and then on to Europe.

> [The railroads] were not laid down to facilitate the internal trade in African commodities. There were no roads connecting different colonies and different parts of the same colony in a manner that made sense with regard to Africa's needs and development. All roads and railroads led down to the sea. They were built to make business possible for the timber companies, trading companies, and agricultural concession firms, and for white settlers. . . . In Europe and America, railroad building required huge inputs of capital. Great wage bills were incurred during construction, and added bonus payments were made to workers to get the job done as quickly as possible. In most parts of Africa, the Europeans who wanted to see a railroad built offered lashes as the ordinary wage and more lashes for extra effort.

As a result of the Berlin Conference to partition Africa in 1884, Belgium's King Leopold II seized the vast territory of the Congo Free State in Central Africa. To draw out the coveted red mahogany, ivory, and rubber of the Congo, Leopold built a 241-mile railroad from the mouth of the Congo River to Stanley Pool, eliminating a three-week porterage. In the first two years of the construction project an estimated 3,600 of the 60,000 workers died.

> The railroad was a modest engineering success and a major human disaster. Men succumbed to accidents, dysentery, smallpox, beriberi, and malaria, all exacerbated by bad food and relentless floggings by the two-hundred-man railroad militia force. Engines ran off tracks; freight cars full of dynamite exploded, blowing workers to bits. . . . Sometimes there were no shelters for the people to sleep in, and recalcitrant laborers were led to work in chains. . . . When bugles sounded in the morning, crowds of angry laborers laid at the feet of European supervisors the bodies of their comrades who had died during the night.

On the use of forced labor, historian Walter Rodney wrote:

> The French got Africans to start building the Brazzaville to Point-Noire railway in 1921, and it was not completed until 1933. Every year of its construction, some ten thousand people were driven to the site − sometimes from more than a thousand kilometers away. At least 25 percent of the labor force died annually from starvation and disease, the worst period being from 1922 to 1929.

Sources: Hochschild 1999: 170–171; Rodney 1974: 209, 166

Measuring the impact of colonialism

Colonialism took an often bewildering number of forms, yielding various effects and outcomes difficult to gauge and combine. No one test, or set of quantitative tests, could measure the complex economic impact of colonialism. Nonetheless, a recent study sheds some light on an issue which has received less attention than it deserves. In his study "Colonialism, Decolonisation and Growth Rates," Alam (1994) measured the average annual growth rates of eleven politically independent nations, which he classified as either "sovereign lagging countries" or "dependencies." Sovereign lagging countries were those which were able to some degree to resist subordination to the Great Powers of Europe. Dependencies were either nations which were independent through history, or former colonial nations. These nations, while independent, operated with considerable constraints due to the influence of either disadvantageous trade treaties or the presence of foreign capital with a strong influence over trade and investment activities.

The sovereign nations were compared with a group of colonies or quasi-colonies (such as China). The test included the Group I countries (sovereign nations which had income per capita of less than half that of the United States in 1900), and the Group II colonies for which data were available. Together the sample included 59 percent of the world's population for 1980.[8] For the period 1900–1950, prior to the independence of all the Group II countries, the Group I countries had an average annual rate of growth of per capita income of 1.6 percent per year. The Group II countries had an average per capita growth rate of 0.0 percent per year (Alam 1994: 250). After colonial rule had ended for all the countries in the study, early in the 1950–1973 period, the Group I countries achieved a 3.5 percent annual growth rate of per capita income, while the Group II rate of growth rose to 2.8 percent. The results, then, tend to confirm that colonialism mattered in a negative way. First, the dramatic difference between absolute stagnation of the Group II colonial nations and the growth of the independent Group I economies is a notable result of the 1900–1950 period. Second, Group I nations grew at a 25 percent faster rate in the 1950–1973 period, which tends to confirm the idea that after formal independence the institutions and path dependence established by colonialism continued to exert an influence which constrained growth. Alam's thesis has recently been broadened and further strengthened with the publication of his book-length treatment of these issues (Alam 2000).

The terms of trade and comparative advantage

While colonialism and neocolonialism[9] played a dominant role in imposing a particular global pattern of production and trade on the less-developed nations in the course of the 100-year period 1780–1880, so too did global market forces. The result was an international division of labor in which the less-developed countries emerged as exporters of primary products to world markets and importers of manufactured goods; the more-developed nations exported manufactured goods and imported primary products. From the late eighteenth century to the 1880s, the terms of trade, measured as the quantity of imports which will exchange for a given quantity of exports, moved steadily in favor of the colonial regions as the prices of primary exports relative to manufactured imports rose, leading to an increase in the value of the terms of trade index for colonial exports.[10] This was the consequence of technological progress and competition among the powerful nations of Europe and the United States which pushed the prices of manufactured products downward, while the demand for tropical products and minerals rapidly expanded, but without commensurate increases in production efficiency in the less-developed regions producing these goods, leading to rising prices for these commodities in international exchange (Singer 1989; Spraos 1983). Increasing competition for raw materials and the relatively low level of technical change in agriculture meant that (over time) a given amount of exports from the colonial regions was able to purchase more imported manufactures from the more developed nations. On the other hand, Britain, whose terms of trade were moving in the opposite direction, had to export roughly two and a half times more manufactured products, on average, in 1880 than it had in 1800 in order to obtain the same quantity of tropical products and raw materials from the less-developed regions.

As a result of this upward movement of the terms of trade for tropical commodities, it appeared to many in the less-developed regions that a primary export economy was a viable vehicle for enhancing their nation's income and wealth. Little, if any, diversification of production for export was encouraged. Investment in primary production remained low, because of technological stasis in agro-export and mineral export activities and because high profits could be made by producing more using extensive techniques. At the same time, as wealth was acquired rapidly and easily in colonial agriculture and mining without the need for massive investments, any profits generated tended to be squandered in ostentatious displays of conspicuous consumption. The financing and distribution of imports and exports, in particular, became an active arena for quick profit-making. Argentina became a particularly notable example; the nation seemed to have mushroomed into a developed nation by the beginning of the twentieth century with virtually no additional effort. A small cadre of cattle ranchers, meat packers, grain growers, bankers, and traders dominated Argentine society. The ships transporting Argentine beef were made in Europe, however, as were the meat-packing facilities, the rails, freight cars, and engines which carried Argentine commodities to the ports for shipment to Europe, a pattern of external reliance that would not bode well for future development.

Argentina's economic miracle lasted somewhat longer than did the general commodities boom of the nineteenth century, but it too foundered when the terms of trade began to turn down sharply. From the 1880s onward, the terms of trade moved against commodity and mineral producers, with the exception of the periods of world war. The dangers and pitfalls of a global trading system and export production focused on a limited array of primary products became all too apparent, too late, to many in the less-developed nations. What had once appeared to be a successful process of natural selection, whereby the economy of a given colony tended to be centered on the basic production and export of one or two primary commodities, now was revealed to be a flawed strategy. With declining terms of trade, mono-exporters were on a treadmill and they had few means of getting off. They had to export more and more in order to buy the increasingly more expensive imported machinery and equipment if they were to maintain the production base of their agro-export or mineral-export economies and to sustain the consumption of the elites (see Focus 3.4).

FOCUS 3.4   TRENDS IN THE TERMS OF TRADE

There is a large literature which attempts to measure trends in the terms of trade, some of which we shall consider again in Chapter 6. However, the following estimates give some idea of the direction of change of the terms of trade for primary product producers.

	% change per year, primary export nations
(1) 1801–1881	+0.87
(2) 1882–1913	−0.42
(3) 1876–1938	−0.95
(4) 1900–1986	−0.52 to −0.84[a]
(5) 1979–1993	−4.00

Note

a The Grilli and Yang (1988) study breaks down the trend in the terms of trade for various sub-categories of primary product exports (for example, raw material; fuels; cereals; foodstuffs). They find a long-term downward trend for the terms of trade for all primary products in international trade with the exception of tropical drinks, which had a trend of 0.63.

Line (1) shows that over the early to late nineteenth century, the terms of trade for primary product producers were moving upward at the rate of 0.87 percent per annum. In effect, each unit of primary product export was able to purchase 0.87 percent more imports each year. Over the entire period, 1801–1881, the purchasing power of the average primary producer doubled in terms of ability to purchase imports with the same quantity of exports. This was the period over which it appeared that the primary product export focus of many of the now less-developed nations, and hence the productive structure created by colonial powers, was validated.

However, lines (2) to (5), based on estimates of the terms of trade of primary product exporters derived from different sources, tend to confirm that the longer-term, and certainly the modern, trend of the terms of trade for primary product producers is downward. Thus, the path dependency created by a primary product export focus turned out to be a long-term burden for economies which remained with such exports. (Note that the fall since 1979 [through 1993] was the most severe since the Great Depression, with real commodity prices 45 percent below their 1980 level by 1990!)

Sources: Grilli and Yang 1988; Maizels *et al.* 1998; Sarkar 1986; Spraos 1983

In thinking about the concept of comparative advantage (analyzed more fully in the next chapter), it is important to recall that in Britain, France, Germany, and the US, the leading trade sectors were forged through conscious state involvement such as subsidies, tariffs, selective construction of infrastructure, labor training, and prohibitive trade restrictions (Chang 2002). As we shall see in later chapters, this too has been at the base of the successful development experiences of South Korea, Taiwan, Japan, and a handful of other East Asian countries. In contrast, colonialism imposed a pattern of production and trade on the pre-capitalist, less-developed regions, a pattern that did not reflect the actual, potential, or conceivable dynamic comparative advantages of those nations. Their trade patterns reflected the needs, desires, and sometime whims of the colonizer. Later, as these patterns became ingrained, altering adverse path dependence was made more difficult even after political independence.

Credit and underdevelopment

In Latin America, once formal colonialism had been ended by the wars of independence in the 1820s, neocolonial mechanisms of credit allocation and debt financing replaced overt political domination, but they contributed no less to the distorted patterns of production and trade implanted several hundred years earlier by the Spanish and the Portuguese. In the nineteenth century, abundant credit became readily available to the colonial regions of Africa and Asia and to the neocolonial regions of Latin America for several interrelated reasons.[11]

1   As the scale of modern industry increased in the latter part of the nineteenth century, large US, German, British, and French manufacturers, working closely with major banks, often extended credit to finance the exportation of their products bought by elites in the less-developed regions. Financial markets increased both in size and sophistication, thereby enabling major banks to shift from regional and national markets to global markets.

2   The second industrial revolution, in the latter part of the nineteenth century, with the application of chemistry to the industrial process, the adaptation of steam power to ships and agricultural machinery, electricity, the telephone and telegraph, the internal combustion engine, time and motion studies in the factories, and so on, created new demands for tropical products and raw materials produced by less-developed nations and colonies. This was particularly true for rubber, for example, the demand for which grew rapidly for production and consumption purposes in the developed nations. Better and faster shipping meant that tropical commodities, such as bananas and pineapples, could become part of the diet in the developed nations. Increasing quantities of minerals were needed to furnish the demands of the industrial sectors of the great powers. Railroads penetrated deeper into the hinterlands of the less-developed regions as new geological discoveries were made, and cheaply produced mining products from the less-developed nations flooded the world market. In order to sustain these new activities, massive investments were typically necessary to build ports, railroad systems, communication systems, and roads. Credits were readily extended to private, often foreign, firms by colonial governments and the independent governments of Latin America to create such infrastructure.

3   Government entities in the less-developed regions often borrowed large sums in order to build needed infrastructure, loans that would presumably be paid from the increased output the country could expect from a more productive infrastructure. However, the borrowing entity, imbued as it was with the ethos of merchant capital, was rarely willing or capable of making a sound economic calculation of the costs, benefits, and risks of new loans. Such loans often were squandered by a corrupt governmental elite. But borrowing had another important function; it could mask economic downturns and extend a faltering boom period for the primary-product-exporting colonial or newly independent economy.

Borrowing from abroad was a seductive choice for many less-developed nations, in the past as now (see Chapter 16); it promised an immediate benefit, while the costs could be deferred. Lord Cromer, the British Consul-General in Egypt from

1883–1907, aptly sketched the attractions of credit, which often formed the basis for extended control by the European powers over the less-developed areas when loans could not be repaid.

> The maximum amount of harm is probably done when an Oriental ruler is for the first time brought in contact with the European system of credit. He thus finds that he can obtain large sums of money with the utmost apparent facility. His personal wishes can thus be easily gratified. He is dazzled by the ingenious and often fallacious schemes for developing his country which European adventurers will not fail to lay before him in the most attractive light. He is too wanting in foresight to appreciate the nature of the future difficulties which he is creating for himself. The temptation to avail himself to the full of the benefits which a reckless use of credit seems to offer to him are too strong to be resisted. He will rush into the gulf which lies open before him, and inflict injury on his country from which not only his contemporaries but future generations will suffer.
>
> (Cromer 1908: 58–59)

The growing sophistication of international banking extended the power of the advanced nations over the less-developed regions, even after the end of formal colonialism, often leading to new and more subtle forms of control and influence. "Tied loans" became commonplace; credits were extended to the less-developed areas on the condition that the bulk of the loan be used to purchase equipment from the lending nation. This often meant not only higher prices for the borrower, but possibly inferior equipment as a consequence. Tied loans also discouraged the development of indigenous suppliers of such products and other inputs. Even semi-skilled labor was normally imported to complete major projects. The economic stimulus from the construction stage provided by external borrowing thus was exceedingly limited, and it was usually restricted to a modest and brief tightening of the casual labor market. Meanwhile, much of the downstream benefit of the loan in terms of the increased future production of tropical commodities or minerals was forgone due to the drain of future interest payments and special loan fees attached to the loans.

The new imperialism: 1870–1914

The nineteenth century was fascinating not merely because new processes of control vis-à-vis the less-developed nations were being forged through the medium of credit. Much more startling was the revival of wars of conquest and seizure at the very time when virtually all the political leaders of the great powers were singing the virtues of free trade. Colonies multiplied at a stupefying rate during the so-called "Century of Free Trade." In 1800, the European powers effectively controlled 55 percent of the total global land mass, including former European colonies. By 1878, this control had increased to 67 percent, and by 1914, colonial holdings stood at 84.4 percent! As David Fieldhouse emphasized: "Expansion continued; by 1939 the only significant countries which had never been under European rule were Turkey, some parts of Arabia, Persia, China, Tibet, Mongolia and Siam. In addition to new colonies, there were new colonial powers: Italy, Belgium, USA, and Russia" (Fieldhouse 1967:

178). Table 3.2 records the magnitude of some of the major colonial systems hold-ings of the European powers and the United States at the outset of the First World War. The ranking is in terms of the population in the colonies. Of the total subju-gated population under the dominance of the Europeans and the US, some 530 million in 1914, nearly 100 million had been added over the period 1870–1914, when the scramble to take control of Africa peaked. Almost half of the territory con-trolled by the colonial powers in 1914 had been acquired in Africa after 1879.

How does one account for the widespread acceptance of the precepts of free trade between sovereign nations at the very moment when colonialism was reinvigo-rated? The answer, it seems, is that free trade theory was only to be applied to rela-tions between the powerful nations. As for the colonial regions, the most charitable interpretation, often utilized by supporters of colonialism, was that the less-developed nations were being readied for free trade, as enlightened colonial rule would "uplift" the colonial peoples and their economic system and prepare them for participation in the global economy.

Mature colonialism and progressive colonialism

Colonialism was an uneven institution; different colonial powers encountered differ-ent regions at different moments in history. The outcome, while perhaps never totally unique, was sufficiently varied, thereby making sweeping generalizations about colonialism difficult to establish and support. Throughout its long history, many came forward to sing the praises of the so-called colonizing mission. And, viewed carefully, there seems to be some support in two instances for the notion that colonialism could be somewhat benign, at least in some respects.

British and French colonialism in West Africa: 1945–1965

The European powers faced a new set of relationships after the Second World War, and this led to a fundamentally new approach to the issue of colonial rule. By then most of the colonial regions had engendered an emerging nationalist element which began to exert considerable pressure on the colonial powers. The nationalists'

Table 3.2 Selected colonial systems in 1914

Colonial power	Number of colonies	Population of colonies	Size (sq. miles)	Colonial pop./ National pop.	Colonial territory/ National territory
United Kingdom	55	391,583,000	12,044,000	8.52	99.20
France	29	62,350,000	4,111,000	1.57	19.90
The Netherlands	8	37,410,000	762,863	6.13	59.80
Belgium	1	15,000,000	910,000	1.98	79.80
Germany	10	13,075,000	1,231,000	0.20	5.90
US[a]	6	10,545,000	172,091	0.14	0.05
Portugal	8	9,680,000	804,440	1.12	22.70
Italy	4	1,397,000	591,250	0.04	5.30

Sources: Hobson 1965: 23; Stavrianos 1981: 264.

Note
a Data from 1905.

aspirations of political independence and national autonomy resonated in the capitals of Europe, where many of the new nationalist leaders in the colonies had lived, studied, and learned to aspire to ideals of political independence championed by a pantheon of European philosophers and political thinkers. The colonizers responded to this pressure by attempting to address issues which heretofore had been ignored.

First, money was poured into infrastructure, industry and, more generally, economic development projects. In many West African nations, the colonial governments formed marketing boards to purchase the production of native cultivators and ship their output to the world market. Additional funds came via governmental outlays derived from the colonial powers, with the bulk of these outlays being used to develop a system of paved roads. From 1945 to 1960, the paved road system of West Africa increased by a factor of ten (Hopkins 1973: 282). In the nine-year period 1947–1956, the French invested twice as much in West Africa as they had over the previous fifty years. Similarly, British expenditures for 1946–1960 exceeded those for 1900–1945 (Ibid.: 280).

During this period, sometimes known as "mature colonialism," colonial administrators practiced a new policy, known as "indigenization," which involved the hiring of Africans in the mining industry and on the staffs of the large trading companies which dominated economic activity in the colonies. Indigenization was aimed at generally involving colonial peoples in a wider range of economic activities. The policy extended to the promotion of export agriculture for native cultivators. At the same time, the colonial governments became alert to the need to diversify and balance the economic activity of the region. They thus commenced to promote some industrialization, and local firms were granted relief from taxes, provided with tariff protection from imports, were guaranteed state purchases of their output, and were extended bank loans at subsidized interest rates; occasionally outright grants were provided. As a result, many of the large trading companies began to produce a range of light consumer products. As impressive as this *volte face* may appear, the overall results were far from sufficient to reverse the structural biases and adverse path dependence created by colonialism. In 1955, for example, only 0.09 percent of Nigerians were employed in manufacturing; in the Gold Coast (Ghana), the figure stood at 0.44 percent; in Kenya, 0.7 percent; and in the Congo, 0.87 percent of the labor force was employed in manufacturing (Fieldhouse 1981: 102). Reviewing in some detail the period of mature colonialism in French West Africa, historian David Fieldhouse concluded:

> At the end of the colonial period French West Africa had hardly begun to industrialize and the great majority of even those industries that did exist were owned and run by expatriates. Such facts provide strong arguments for those who hold that colonialism was incompatible with "balanced" economic growth in the dependencies.
>
> (Fieldhouse 1981: p. 102)

Progressive colonialism

Could colonialism ever confer net benefits on a nation? It would be difficult to answer this question in the affirmative, because of the complex array of factors which would have to be considered and weighted to derive an answer. In most instances, it would appear that the list of advantages of being colonized would be quite short. However, it is common to accord some progressivity to Japanese colonial rule among all the colonial powers. The overall presence of the Japanese was greater in their occupation of Taiwan and Korea than was Dutch colonial power in Indonesia, but the Japanese brought technological improvement to agriculture in their colonies, and they injected a skilled technical labor force into Korean industry. Japan also invested heavily in colonial industry, and as a consequence skills were transferred to the colonies and their educational level was advanced. The colonial state left a legacy of "a rationalized currency system, banks and other institutions that the state controlled, long- and short-term economic plans, production oriented new technology and a variety of direct and indirect subsides" (Kohli 1999: 133). There was no drain on Korea's balance of payments, as was the norm for other colonies; in fact, Japan was a net provider of capital (Maddison 1990: 365). Over the period 1929–1938, the annual rate of real GDP growth in Taiwan and Korea was 1.8 percent and 3.5 percent, respectively. By comparison, the rate of growth of GDP in India over the same period was a mere 0.5 percent, and in Indonesia it was 1.6 percent (Maddison 1985: 19). In making this comparison, it is important to recognize that in India, at least, the British were then pursuing a "dual mandate," which entailed the idea that the purpose of colonial policy was to pursue economic development, including an attempt to industrialize India. It would appear that Japan's colonial policies, on the surface, were more successful in this regard.

While the contrast of the Japanese empire to other colonial powers is interesting, it is important to keep in mind that a larger portion of the growth in Taiwan and Korea in the period cited above was enjoyed by Japanese nationals, not the colonized subjects. And the loss of national identity and the imposition of alien and often arbitrary and cruel colonial practices by the Japanese raises serious questions regarding the extent to which colonialism was ever progressive in an overall sense anywhere.

Decolonization

Only in the closing years of the Second World War was it clear that the colonial regions, "readied" or not, would be released from their formal bonds of domination. Part of the impetus for this abrupt change came from the United States. Having won its independence from Britain via armed struggle, the United States had long declared its willingness to uphold the concept of national self-determination. President Woodrow Wilson had been particularly eager to impose this ideal on Europe's colonial system immediately after the First World War, but the United States had been too weak then to achieve this ideal.

In the closing days of the Second World War, the United States faced weakened European powers, unable to maintain their colonies without US financial assistance. In some instances, the United States was willing to prolong European dominance over colonial areas, particularly where Cold War considerations tipped the scales, but the basic thrust of US policy was clear: the colonial systems would have to be dismantled relatively quickly. Altruistic motives may have driven US policy to some degree. But the United States also was anxious to see the end of British dominance in much of the Middle East, where American oil companies were keen to extend their leases and exploratory activities. Likewise in Asia and Africa, US-owned mining companies expected to have equal access to resources, something the colonial powers had resisted granting their global economic competitors. Furthermore, the United States was haunted still by the image of the Great Depression; virtually every major American economist held that the end of the Second World War would mean the onset of economic stagnation or, worse, another depression. Hence there was a widespread appreciation of the possibilities of selling US products to former colonial regions, if only they could be opened to American products by being released from European colonial dominance.

Another part of the impetus toward the break-up of colonialism came from within the colonies themselves, particularly from India.[12] The Indian anti-colonial struggle was carefully observed, giving rise to new hopes and suggesting tactics to opposition leaders in other colonies. Indian nationalists had long struggled for independence prior to the Second World War, and during the war, the British were forced to borrow heavily from the Indian treasury. Indian military forces also were extensively used to aid the British war effort, fighting valiantly and nobly. The *quid pro quo* for such compliance, reluctantly agreed to by the British, was Indian independence after the war. India's example helped other colonial areas in their determined resistance to colonialism. Still, decolonization was far from an orderly or peaceful process. The French, in particular, bitterly resisted national independence in Algeria and Vietnam, with disastrous consequences and costs for the economic development prospects of the colonies.

Point Four Aid

From the end of the Second World War until 1949, the colonial regions were not the focus of attention of the great powers. For the US, in particular, the postwar economic breakdown of Europe, the presumed truculence of the Soviet Union, and the question of the future role of atomic weapons, crowded out the issue of colonialism. Rather than a depression or stagnation, after the war the United States actually enjoyed remarkable and rapid economic recovery.

In 1949, the less-developed regions were suddenly brought into the foreground again with President Harry S. Truman's inaugural address. Truman stated that he had "four points" to make; in the fourth point,

> He called for a "bold new program" for making the benefits of American science and industrial progress available to "underdeveloped" countries...
>
> The old imperialism – exploitation for profit – had no place in the plan, Truman said. Half the people in the world were living in conditions close to misery, and for the first time in history the knowledge and skill were available to relieve such suffering. The emphasis would be on the distribution of knowledge rather than money.
>
> (McCullough 1992: 730–731)

Truman's speech suggested that the United States could "supply the vitalizing force to stir the peoples of the world into triumphant action ... against ... hunger, misery and despair." The main thrust of US activity, however, placed "particular emphasis ... (on) the stimulation of a greatly expanded flow of private investment"

(US Department of State 1949: 4). The State Department, in articulating the policy initiatives which had given rise to Truman's speech, emphasized that the chief concern of the United States would not be private investment in general, but investment in resources:

> Location, development and economical processing of mineral and fuel resources is a major aspect of the program of a technical cooperation for economic development of underdeveloped countries.
>
> (US Department of State 1949: 20)

In the more sober, calculating terms of the State Department, the ostensible global struggle against misery appeared to be as much in the self-interest of the developed nations as it was an act of magnanimity on the part of a great power: "many underdeveloped mineral resources in the areas which will participate in the cooperative effort are of considerable importance to the more highly developed nations of the world including the United States" (US Department of State 1949: 20).

Whatever the conceptual and policy limits of Point Four Aid, the shift in US policy was of fundamental importance. It marked the beginning of a move away from an almost exclusive concern over European recovery after the Second World War. Not only were US funds and research now to be directed toward economic development in the less-developed world, but more importantly, the IMF and the World Bank (see Chapter 17 for a discussion of these institutions) began to restructure themselves in the early 1950s as a result of Point Four. From the early 1950s onward, these multinational institutions would grow in power and prestige, and their policies toward the underdeveloped regions would become of the utmost importance. Furthermore, the European powers followed the lead of Point Four, particularly in the policy formulations of the Organization for European Economic Cooperation. Economists who had been concerned with recovery in Europe now found new careers open to them as development economists within government, institutions such as the IMF and World Bank, with major foundations, and in the universities.

Economic dualism

There can be no doubt that colonialism fundamentally altered the economies of the underdeveloped areas. Having endured for centuries in many areas, the path dependence effects of colonialism were not to be swept away in a matter of years, or a Decade of Development. One of the worst features of colonialism, as it evolved in Africa, Asia, and Latin America, was the creation of what economists have termed the "dual economy." The Dutch economist, J.H. Boeke, was one of the earliest economists to make this distinction. Boeke, after decades of research in Asia, maintained that

> Social Dualism is the clashing of an imported social system with an indigenous social system of another style. Most frequently the imported social system is high capitalism.
>
> (Boeke 1953: 4)

Professor Boeke regarded dualism as a form of *disintegration*, which would last interminably and would undercut all prospects for development. Others have employed the concept without adopting either Boeke's pessimism or many of his assumptions regarding the impermeable nature of the pre-capitalist social system. After having subjected Boeke's general analysis to a withering critique, Benjamin Higgins stated:

> there can be no question about the phenomenon of dualism; it is one of the distinguishing features of underdeveloped countries. Virtually all of them have two clearly differentiated sectors: one confined mainly to peasant agriculture and handicrafts or very small industry, and the trading activities associated with them; the other consisting of plantations, mines, petroleum fields and refineries, large-scale industries, and the transport and trading activities associated with these operations. Levels of technique, productivity and income are low in the first sector and high in the second.
>
> (Higgins 1959: 281)

Thus dualism posited a "two-sector model" where a precapitalist, transitional form of production was juxtaposed to a modern, capitalist sector. These two sectors had nothing in common other than the fact that they existed side-by-side within one social formation, and that the pre-capitalist sector provided labor to the modern capitalist enterprises. The modern sector exists as a virtual enclave within the larger pre-capitalist and semi-capitalist sector, operating within the same overall social and economic structure, but also somewhat distanced from it.[13] The modern capitalist sector does not fully supplant this semi-capitalist sector; rather the pre-capitalist sector is slowly dissolved over an intermediate, and indeterminate, time period, as both the pre-capitalist and semi-capitalist sectors exhibit a determined capacity to resist the forces of change that capitalist methods of production attempt to implant. Peasants struggle to maintain their grip on marginal plots of land, mercilessly working themselves and their families to eke out an existence that is often near, or even below, subsistence. Landless agricultural workers struggle to acquire land, while those pushed into the cities often send a part of their meagre wages to their families in the countryside.

Governments in colonial dual societies often exhibited a profound urban bias (see Chapter 11 for further discussion). Taxes taken from throughout the social formation tended to be spent close to the capital city and on the highest cadre of "public servants," who often lived like potentates, and only then on the public facilities of the cities. The best infrastructure was and remains to be found in the major cities. The countryside remained starved for irrigation, roads, transportation, schools, and health clinics. Without roads, water, technical assistance, capital investment, manpower training, and education, the countryside atrophied, further sharpening the dualist nature of colonial society.

Everett Hagen was one of the early development economists who found the dualistic framework useful to analyze economic underdevelopment. For Hagen, the social–psychological distinctions to be made between the two sectors were profound: "In a psychological sense, the elite [i.e., the 'modern' sector] and the villagers of the peasant society live literally in different worlds and have extremely few interests in common" (Hagen 1957: 28). Hagen maintained that in the pre-capitalist and semi-capitalist sectors, one found the dominance of crude concepts of the physical world, primitive production methods, and extremely low literacy rates that affected the possibilities for future progress in these rural sectors.

Even in the modern sector, Hagen found fundamental weaknesses. In particular, he noted that the social elite tended to be self-reproducing and isolated. The lack of a "middle" class was notable and troubling: "In a technologically progressive society,... there is a more rapid circulation of the elite, more social mobility through economic success, and a substantial middle class" (Ibid.: 28). These were both missing in most less-developed nations. Hagen also noted that in both the modern and traditional sectors there was a pervasive disdain for both modern business practices and forms of labor which entailed physical effort.

Summarizing Hagen's conclusions regarding the necessary changes to be made for development to occur in less-developed nations, Higgins emphasized that "The individual's view of his relationship with the world must change radically, scientific knowledge and the scope of experience must widen, occupational values must undergo basic alteration, class relationships must alter in their social, economic and political aspects" (Higgins 1959: 306). Hagen emphasized that "drastic change in *any* one variable in the peasant society while the others remain at their peasant society level seem unlikely [to be able to foster development]" (Hagen 1957: 59). Yet, he nonetheless believed that, while quite difficult, a completion of the transition to a technologically dynamic society could be achieved in one generation.

In analyzing the modern or capitalist sector of the dual society, Paul Baran emphasized that it would be a grave mistake to believe that this sector always functioned precisely in the manner one might expect. The capitalist sector in less-developed nations continues to manifest distinct structural characteristics which revealed the continued influence of merchant capital and pre-capitalist ideas. For example, Baran noted that one would expect that large-scale investments in public goods such as railroads, highways, electrification projects and so on would generate external economies by lowering the cost of production of a variety of branches of the economy. Under pure capitalism such social investments create a virtuous-circle effect: more social investment → lower costs for private producers → greater incentive to invest → increases in construction activity → increases in employment → increases in consumption → increases in GDP → increases in tax revenues → increases in social investments, and so on. This fortuitous relationship, however, is not normally to be found in the dualist less-developed regions, given the weakness of the modern sector and the size of the pre-capitalist sector.

> it is not railways, roads, and power stations that give rise to industrial capitalism: it is the emergence of industrial capitalism that leads to the building of railways, to the construction of roads, and to the establishment of power stations. The identical sources of external economies, if appearing in a country going through the mercantile phase of capitalism, will provide, if anything, "external economies" to merchant capital. Thus the modern banks established by the British during the second half of the nineteenth century in India, in Egypt, in Latin America, and elsewhere in the underdeveloped world became not fountains of industrial credit but large-scale clearing houses of mercantile finance vying in their interest charges with the local usurers. In the same way, the harbors and cities that sprang up in many underdeveloped countries in connec-

tion with their briskly expanding exports did not turn into centers of industrial activity but snowballed into vast market places providing the necessary "living space" to wealthy compradors and crowded by a motley population of petty traders, agents and commissionmen. Nor did the railways, trunk roads, and canals built for the purpose of foreign enterprise evolve into pulsing arteries of productive activities; they merely accelerated the disintegration of the peasant economy and provided additional means for a more intensive and more thorough mercantile exploitation of rural interiors.

(Baran 1957: 193–194)

Baran's insight into the modern capitalist sector of the dual society serves to clarify the magnitude of the embedded distortions within the modern sector deriving from colonialism. This sector is modern or capitalist in relation to the pre-capitalist and semi-capitalist sector within the less-developed country, but it remains backward when compared to the advanced economies. One of the weakest and most debilitating components of the modern sector in the less-developed world is a continuing pervasiveness of merchant capital within the circuits of banking and finance. Rather than serving as a complementary force supporting industrialization and development, banking and finance are the locus of widespread speculative activities which absorb a large portion of the potentially loanable funds which could be used to support socially useful public and private investments.

Summary

For many former colonies, the lingering effects of colonial control are not quickly or even easily cast off. Colonization created productive structures designed not to exploit the potential comparative advantage of the dominated economy and its people. Rather, the colonizer organized production, particularly export production, around an extremely narrow array of tropical agricultural products, minerals, and other primary commodities to supply the colonizer's needs. Cost considerations were not particularly important, since production did not take place within a free-market context, but rather within a framework of domination and control. Thus, colonial regions acquired productive structures, skills, education systems, infrastructure, institutions, and organizations shaped to the interests of the colonizer. Created as mono-exporters of agricultural, mining, and other primary products, these path-dependent structures, including their embedded power structures, were carried over into independence.

One of the difficulties faced by former colonies, then, is that of altering past path dependence in ways that can lead to economic growth and human development. Countries, then, do not start as open books, as *tabulae rasae*. Rather, they begin with a complex past that has brought them to the present and will take them to the future. Making changes to the array of factors contributing to past path dependence, through proper policies, can establish new path dependence promising a better future.

Questions for review

1 How did merchant capitalism function to retard and distort the developmental potential in the colonial regions? How is it different from industrial capitalism?

2 How did the movement in the terms of trade in the nineteenth century lead to the widely held view that a primary product export economy was both desirable and, in some sense, good economics? What has happened to the terms of trade for tropical commodities in the twentieth century? How does this affect the conclusion that a primary product export focus can contribute to economic development?

3 Does it make sense for any country to have a majority of its export income derived from one or two exports, that is, to be a mono-exporter? Why or why not? Do developed countries have a limited array of exports? Why do most less-developed countries have such a limited array of exports?

4 Why and how were dualist structures fostered in the colonial regions, and how did they create barriers to further economic development?

5 In the era of industrial capitalism, how did institutions introduced under colonial rule act as a brake on economic development and constitute a schism with the historical pattern of evolution in the colonized areas? What role did de-industrialization play in this process? Why did the colonizers require de-industrialization in their colonies? Who benefitted and who lost?

6 All countries are subject to path dependence. This simply means that past decisions, and past history, affect the present conditions and possibilities for the future. What is meant by *adverse* path dependence? What role did colonialism play in creating adverse path dependence? How can countries that were former colonies overcome adverse path dependence? What specific changes would you suggest be undertaken by now-independent countries with economic structures shaped by colonialism?

Notes

1 In the developed capitalist and industrial nations, variations in income and output were increasingly the result of business cycles, that is, they were due to factors that affected the profits of producers and their willingness to produce. Variations in income and output due to purely exogenous forces, like the weather, became much less powerful as industrial production increasingly replaced agriculture as the motor force of society (as discussed in Chapter 9). Of course, some exogenous factors, such as wars and plagues, did from time to time adversely affect income levels, but the control exercised over the environment in which humans reproduced themselves via production was remarkable after the Industrial Revolution and the spread of the factory system of production.

2 Later, at and after the turn of the twentieth century, both the United States and Japan, relative late-comers to the capitalist revolution, also joined the ranks of the colonizers.

3 The wave of decolonization that created most of today's less-developed nations, with exceptions, like China, occurred after 1945. Many of today's independent nations in Africa and the Caribbean did not win freedom from colonialism until the 1960s and in some instances not until the 1970s.

4 There were notable exceptions. First, in relatively unpopulated areas such as the United States, Canada, Australia, and New Zealand virtual extermination of the native peoples was achieved quickly, and the subsequent "white settler" societies achieved self-governance and positive economic stimulus from the international economy. Second, Japan took control of Korea and Taiwan early in the twentieth century with results that, in many respects, diverge from that found throughout Africa, Asia, Latin America, and the Middle East.

5 Maddison (1982: 4, 13) dates the period of merchant capitalism from 1700 to 1820. It is during this period, he notes, that plunder is important to the progress of the colonizing nations.

6 In contrast, adaptation was never part of the old colonial system. Thus, the Spanish did not readily utilize the new plantation system, nor were there fundamental adjustments in colonial policy in light of the de-population of Mexico and Peru due to the liquidation of indigenous labor. Rather, as trade and commerce collapsed following the breakdown of the mining boom, the great *latifundio* system of the hacienda, which had been subordinate to the mining economy in the Spanish colonies, came to dominate the Latin American economy. As Francois Chevalier pointed out:

> The return to the soil helped revive in Mexico certain medieval institutions and customs recalling the patriarchal existence of Biblical times – the [hacendado's] peculiar mentality was not conducive to thinking in terms of efficient production. He acquired land, not to increase his earnings, but to eliminate rivals and hold sway over an entire region. His scorn for extra profits sometimes went to such lengths that he destroyed perfectly good equipment on land recently purchased.
>
> (Chevalier 1970: 307, 311)

John Coatsworth (1978: 86–93) has maintained that the generalizations of Chevalier, and many others, are not supported by a broad range of studies conducted in the 1970s which indicate that given the existing institutional structure of Latin America, the haciendas were economically rational. The institutional structure, however, was not.

7 Others, it must be noted, have argued that British rule regenerated India. Proponents of this perspective often stress the restoration of several canals and the renovation and expansion of major irrigation systems by the British, starting in the 1820s. Further, by 1914, India had obtained 34,000 miles of railroads, and 25 million acres of land, including Burma, were under irrigation. Moreover, the agrarian plantation economy was diversified in the course of the nineteenth century, with major investments in tea and coffee, indigo and sugar plantations, a sizeable jute mill industry, as well as coal and mica mines.

Commenting on this more favorable evaluation of British colonialism in India, Tom Kemp has argued that:

> although India was perhaps unique among underdeveloped countries in having an organized sector (factories) partly under native ownership, as well as railways, ports, banks and other attributes of a modern economy these remained localized in their influence. To put it another way, they had not initiated a genuine process of industrialization or fundamentally transformed the agrarian structure.
>
> Indeed, although part of agriculture production was hinged to the market, there was no shift of population out of agriculture; if anything the proportion of the population dependent on the land tended to rise. The existence of some advanced industries did little to raise per capita income or to initiate economic growth.
>
> (Kemp 1989: 93)

8 Group I countries were Finland, Italy, Norway, Sweden, Japan, Argentina, Brazil, Chile, Colombia, Mexico, and Peru. Group II countries were Bangladesh, China, India, Indonesia, Pakistan, the Philippines, South Korea, Taiwan, and Thailand.

9 Colonialism involves both political and economic domination. The colonial power administers the political structure of the economy. Neocolonialism is economic domination of one nation by another, without the necessity of direct, political control.

10 Technically, the terms of trade is a composite index defined by the ratio of two price indices. Taking P_M as the price index of imported goods and P_X as the price index of exported goods, then the terms of trade index (TOT) can be defined as $TOT = (P_X/P_M) \times 100$.

11 For an excellent account of the role of British finance in Latin America and India, see Cain and Hopkins (1993: Chapters 9 and 10).

12 The United Nations was also an important forum for the decolonization movement, and the growth in membership in that body is due to the end of colonization.
13 It is not unusual, however, to find home workers and small artisan-style workshops with a direct link to large national and even transnational corporations. It therefore may appear that there is little basis on which a strict separation can be made between the semi-capitalist sector and the capitalist sector.

It is important to realize that the distinction between two sectors in the dualistic models is based upon an interpretation of the motives and behavioral patterns characteristic of the distinct forms of production and not on formal interaction. A home worker or contract artisan workshop, while possibly linked to a world-straddling web of production and distribution, nonetheless may operate on a survival basis, using the labor of family members, with little mastery of technology, little or no access to credit, no power in dealing with the company it supplies, no strategy regarding cost minimization or production efficiency, and, most likely, little effective recourse to the legal system in the event that basic contract agreements are violated. While such producers may be an *appendage* of the capitalist system of production, they do not exist as capitalist producers themselves, but rather as semi-capitalist artisan workers. This is one of symbiosis, not a case of fusion between the two sectors.

References

Acemoglu, Daron. 2003. "Root Causes," *Finance and Development* 40, 2 (June): 27–30.

Acemoglu, Daron, Simon Johnson, and James Robinson. 2001. "Colonial Origins of Comparative Development: An Empirical Investigation," *American Economic Review* 91 (December): 1369–1401.

Alam, M.S. 1994. "Colonialism, Decolonisation and Growth Rates: Theory and Empirical Evidence," *Cambridge Journal of Economics* 18: 235–257.

—— 2000. *Poverty from the Wealth of Nations*. London: Macmillan.

Amsden, Alice. 2001. *The Rise of "the Rest."* Oxford: Oxford University Press.

Bagchi, Amiya. 1984. *The Political Economy of Underdevelopment*. Cambridge: Cambridge University Press.

Baran, Paul. 1957. *The Political Economy of Growth*. New York: Marzani & Munsell.

Boeke, J.H. 1953. *Economics and Economic Policy of Dual Societies*. New York: Institute of Pacific Relations.

Cain, P.J. and A.G. Hopkins. 1993. *British Imperialism: Innovation and Expansion, 1688–1914*. London: Longman.

Chang, Ha-Joon. 2002. *Kicking Away the Ladder: Development Strategy in Historical Perspective*. London: Anthem Press.

Chevalier, Francois. 1970. *Land and Society in Colonial Mexico*. Berkeley, CA: University of California Press.

Coatsworth, John. 1978. "Obstacles to Economic Growth in Nineteenth-Century Mexico," *American Historical Review* 83 (February): 80–110.

Cromer, Lord. 1908. *Modern Egypt*. London: Macmillan.

Crow, Ben and Mary Thorpe. 1988. *Survival and Change in the Third World*. New York: Oxford University Press.

Digby, William. 1969. *"Prosperous" India, A Revelation from Official Records*. New Delhi: Sagar Publications.

Fieldhouse, David. 1967. *The Colonial Empires*. New York: Delacorte Press.

—— 1981. *Colonialism 1870–1945*. New York: St. Martins Press.

Furnivall, J.S. 1967. *Netherlands India*. Cambridge: Cambridge University Press.

Galeano, Eduardo. 1973. *Open Veins of Latin America*. New York: Monthly Review Press.

Grilli, E. and H. Yang. 1988. "Primary Commodity Prices, Manufactured Goods Prices, and the Terms of Trade of Developing Countries: What the Long Run Shows," *The World Bank Economic Review* 2: 1–47.

Hagen, Everett. 1957. "The Process of Economic Development," *Economic Development and Cultural Change* (April): 193–215.

Higgins, Benjamin. 1959. *Economic Development*. New York: W.W. Norton & Co.

Hobson, John. 1965. *Imperialism*. Ann Arbor, MI: University of Michigan Press.

Hochschild, Adam. 1999. *King Leopold's Ghost: A Story of Greed, Terror, and Heroism in Colonial Africa*. New York: Mariner Books.

Hopkins, A.G. 1973. *An Economic History of West Africa*. New York: Columbia University Press.

Hunt, E.K. 1979. *History of Economic Thought*. Belmont, CA: Wadsworth Publishing Co.

Kemp, Tom. 1989. *Industrialization in the Non-Western World*. London: Longman Group Limited.

Kohli, Atul. 1999. "Where do High-Growth Political Economies Come From? The Japanese Lineage of Korea's 'Developmental State'," pp. 93–136 in Merideth Woo-Cumings (ed.), *The Developmental State*. Ithaca: Cornell University Press.

McCullough, David. 1992. *Truman*. New York: Simon & Schuster.

Maddison, Angus. 1982. *Phases of Capitalist Development*. Oxford: Oxford University Press.

—— 1985. *Two Crises: Latin America and Asia 1929–38 and 1973–83*. Paris: OECD.

—— 1990. "The Colonial Burden: A Comparative Perspective," pp. 361–376 in Maurice Scott and Deepak Lal (eds), *Public Policy and Economic Development*. Oxford: Clarendon Press.

Maizels, Alfred, Theodsios Palaskas, and Trevor Crowe. 1998. "The Prebisch-Singer Hypothesis Revisited," pp. 63–85 in David Sapsford and John-ren Chen (eds), *Development Economics and Policy*. London: Macmillan.

Nehru, Jawaharal. 1960. *The Discovery of India*. New York: Doubleday-Anchor.

Reynolds, Lloyd G. 1986. *Economic Growth in the Third World*. New Haven, CT: Yale University Press.

Robinson, Ronald. 1976. "Non-European Foundations of European Imperialism," pp. 117–142 in Roger Owen and Bob Sutcliffe (eds), *Studies in the Theory of Imperialism*. London: Longman Group Limited.

Rodney, Walter. 1974. *How Europe Underdeveloped Africa*. Washington, DC: Howard University Press.

Sarkar, P. 1986. "The Terms of Trade Experience of Britain Since the Nineteenth Century," *Journal of Development Studies* 23 (October): 20–39.

Schumpeter, Joseph. 1951. *Imperialism*. Oxford: Basil Blackwell.

Singer, Hans. 1989. "Terms of Trade," pp. 323–328 in John Eatwell *et al.* (eds), *The New Palgrave: Economic Development*. New York: W.W. Norton.

Spraos, J. 1983. *Inequalising Trade?* Oxford: Clarendon Press.

Stavrianos, L.S. 1981. *Global Rift*. New York: William Morrow & Co.

Thomas, Robert. 1965. "A Quantitative Approach to the Study of the Effects of British Imperial Policy upon Colonial Welfare," *Journal of Economic History* 25: 615–638.

US Department of State. 1949. *Point Four, Cooperative Program for Aid in the Development of the Economically Underdeveloped Areas*. Washington, DC: US Department of State.

Part 2

Theories of development and underdevelopment

4   Classical and neoclassical theories

After studying this chapter, you should understand:
- Adam Smith's contribution to understanding how a capitalist market economy operates, including the importance of the invisible hand, competition, specialization, and the law of capital accumulation and how these interact to affect the rate of economic growth;
- Thomas Malthus' theory of population, how and why he believed rapid population growth was so likely and the implications of rapid population growth for the living standards of the poor;
- David Ricardo's theories of diminishing returns, of comparative advantage, the argument in favor of free trade and how these relate to the pace of economic expansion;
- Karl Marx's critique of capitalism and the theory behind his belief in the ultimate collapse of that system;
- the logic behind a Solow-type neoclassical growth model, the importance of saving and investment in determining the level of per capita income and why the neoclassical model predicts "conditional convergence" of income levels among nations over time;
- the Harrod–Domar model's importance to subsequent growth theories and strategies.

Introduction

As we learned in the previous chapter, the pursuit of economic growth and development as a socially desirable goal is of relatively recent origin, being more-or-less contemporaneous with the rise of capitalism as an economic system. The Industrial Revolution in England in the mid-eighteenth century provides a convenient if somewhat arbitrary date for the emergence of systematic and intellectual interest in understanding how and why economic development occurs. It also marks the emergence of economics – or **political economy**, as it was called at that time – as a separate sphere of scholarly inquiry. Not at all coincidentally some of the earliest, most distinguished and most enduring thinking about economics and the process of economic development was produced in Great Britain during and following the transition from feudalism to capitalism when long-term economic expansion and rising income per capita first materialized on an extended scale (Maddison 1982).

Many of the great political economists whose ideas have shaped economic inquiry down to this day lived through the early changes brought on by the Industrial Revolution. These classical political economists attempted not only to explain the reasons for the rapid expansion of total economic wealth that accompanied industrialization. They also tackled the enigma of the extremes of wealth and poverty that attended this process and the lack of development affecting a large segment of the population. It was during this era that the still-acclaimed book, *An Inquiry into the Nature and Causes of the Wealth of Nations*, was composed by the Scottish philosopher and political economist, Adam Smith. *The Wealth of Nations*, published in 1776, provided a theoretical structure and explanation for the workings of the increasingly dominant market system at the center of the new capitalist industrial economy. It argued brilliantly for capitalism's superiority as a system of production compared to feudalism and its mercantilist tendencies. Smith's writings continue to provide the foundation for a good part of the optimism inherent to modern economic theory concerning the possibilities of progress in capitalist societies.

In the late eighteenth and early nineteenth centuries, Thomas Malthus' pessimistic musings on the future of capitalism, based on his famous theory of population, darkened enthusiasm for capitalism's future – but only temporarily. David Ricardo helped to make sense out of the changes in economic structure and institutions that emerged as a consequence of the spread of capitalism across Europe, and he added analytical tools to economic thinking that are central to economic analysis to this day.

And of course, there is Karl Marx. Though not a British subject, Marx spent many of his most productive years in England, much of it in the Reading Room of the British Library in Great Russell Street, writing both a theory and a critique of capitalism which appeared in the three volumes of *Capital*. Marx's analysis of the dynamics of capitalist development contain very important insights that have become central to both Marxist and, though many do not realize it or refuse to acknowledge it, to non-Marxist enquiry on economic growth and development.

In the first part of this chapter, the ideas and theories of these classical economists will be briefly summarized as they relate to economic and social progress. These political economists are called **classical** because they provided the framework and bedrock ideas of economics as a separate field of enquiry. Their ideas predate what is now labelled **neoclassical** economics which emerged after the 1870s in reaction particularly against the radical implications of Marx's version of classical theory.

Classical economists had an interest in the wider issues of the day, not only in how society produced its output and wealth but also in how it was distributed among competing groups with a claim on that income. The classicals were concerned with explaining how economic growth took place, while at the same time being concerned with reducing the numbers living in poverty. However, except for John Stuart Mill and Marx, the classicals were similar to the neoclassicals who followed them in assuming that the capitalist order that emerged from feudalism was not only a "natural order" but that it represented the highest achievement of human development.

Neoclassical economists shifted the emphasis of economics from the broader macroeconomics of growth and development to a narrower concern with the allocation of a fixed quantity of scarce resources to their best use with given institutions. This turn to *efficiency* as the focus of economics led to a more static and marginalist perspective for economics. Growth and development, which often require substantial qualitative change in society and not just small quantitative change, disappeared from view for quite some time.

In the latter part of this chapter, the influential neoclassical-type growth theories of Harrod and Domar and the Solow model are assessed. These theories have an affinity in form and assumptions, if not always in their conclusions, to the classical models discussed in the first part of the chapter. They focus on the requirements for achieving an equilibrium level of economic growth with a strong emphasis on the saving behavior of society as the determinant variable.

These models have been extremely influential in leading economists and policy-makers to concentrate their attention and strategies on specific critical variables and tools for accelerating economic development. Their models have focused public policies on how to best stimulate growth. No student can truly hope to understand how economists think about economic development without a rudimentary understanding of the simple foundational models reviewed in this chapter.

Adam Smith: a theory of competitive capitalism and growth

Adam Smith provided one of the earliest and most enduring metaphors for the operation of the capitalist market system: *the invisible hand*. What Smith called the "invisible hand" is simply what we now refer to as the forces of supply and demand working to attain equilibrium in a perfectly or nearly competitive economy. In such an environment, the individualistic desires of consumers for goods and services, combined with the self-interested drive to maximize profits by the producers of these goods and services, will tend toward determinant levels of production and prices. This is the equilibrium where the supply curve crosses the demand curve at which both consumers and producers gain from exchange. Smith's words continue to be worth recalling:

> As every individual, therefore, endeavours as much as he can both to employ his capital in the support of domestic industry, and so to direct that industry that its produce may be of the greatest value; every individual necessarily labours to render the annual revenue of society as great as he can. He generally, indeed, neither intends to promote the public interest, nor knows how much he is promoting it ... he intends only his own gain, and he is in this, as in many other cases, led by an *invisible hand* to promote an end which was no part of his intention.
>
> (Smith 1973: 423)

Smith believed there existed a harmony of interests among consumers and producers and among workers, landlords, and capitalists and other groups in society which the competitive market capitalist system mediates to the benefit of all. The purely self-interested, even selfish and greedy, behavior of consumers and producers of goods is not an evil to be despised or a lamentable flaw of the capitalist, market system. Such self-interested behavior is functional and virtuous and leads to higher levels of economic welfare.

It is not from the benevolence of the butcher, the brewer, or the baker, that we expect our dinner, but from their regard to their own interest. We address ourselves, not to their humanity, but to their self-love, and never talk to them of our own necessities but of their advantages.

(Ibid.: 14)

Smith's concept of the invisible hand is well-known by most first-year undergraduates. Often neglected, forgotten, or ignored is the equal importance Smith placed on *competition* within his philosophy of the gains expected from the market system. Competition acts as a *counterweight* to and a brake on the possible excesses that greedy and self-interested behavior might engender in its absence. An effective competitive environment is important in restraining the actions of producers and owners/capitalists who constantly are tempted to form cartels or monopolies or to take other action in an effort to increase their individual profits at the expense of both consumers and workers.

Smith's belief in the virtues of the capitalist market economy was thus not an uncritical view that only emphasized the market's harmonizing effects. In the absence of competition, Smith did not assume that "greed is good" and that all participants automatically would benefit from the capitalist order. Nor did Smith presume that private and societal interests were always identical. Smith was suspicious of the intentions of naturally acquisitive capitalists. He believed that, given the opportunity, they would eagerly monopolize markets for their own benefit at the expense of others.

For Adam Smith, the benefits to consumers of the market capitalist system thus rested on two, non-separable constituent components: selfish behavior kept in check and regulated by the forces of competition. When competition is threatened by the self-interested actions of producer/capitalists, it is one of the responsibilities of government to create the legal framework and to put in place the appropriate enforcement mechanisms to defend and maintain a competitive environment so that the potential benefits of the market system might be achieved for the largest number.

Smith's views on economic development

What is the relation of Smith's analysis of the functioning of the market system to his concept of the forces contributing to economic progress and development that are important for understanding how economic development takes place? In a broad sense, Smith saw in capitalism a productive system with the potential to vastly increase human well-being. In particular, he stressed the importance of the **division of labor** and the **law of capital accumulation** as the primary factors contributing to economic progress or, as he termed it, to the "wealth of nations."

The division of labor, or specialization, began to evolve rapidly with the spread of the factory system. Prior to the Industrial Revolution, the division of labor was relatively limited both between agriculture and industry and within the production of any particular product. From the spinning of the yarn obtained from the clippings of the sheep, to the weaving of the cloth from the yarn, to the cutting, sewing and finishing of the final garment, a single individual might have been involved in performing many, or even all, of the tasks of production. There was little or no specialization in such non-capitalist, non-exchange production. As might be expected, only a small quantity of output can be produced if one person must undertake all the steps required to produce a final product, and that was quite a typical situation prior to industrialization.

With the Industrial Revolution in Great Britain and the emergence of the factory system, the organization of production began to change, especially as peasants and farm laborers were pushed from the land and into the villages and cities by the Enclosure Movement. The factory system increasingly required that workers should come to designated locations to perform their tasks rather than producing at home.

Over time, the distinguishing characteristic of the factory system became the intensive use of machinery powered by water and steam. The pace of work was increasingly determined by the machinery with which employees toiled. With the expanded use of tools, the momentum toward specialization and the dividing of tasks into ever smaller and finer components was both accelerated and made more feasible. With specialization, the process of producing cloth changed. Some workers would be involved only in the spinning process, others in carding the wool, others in loading the yarn on to the machines, still others in moving the finished cloth to storage, in cutting cloth to patterns, and so on. Tasks would be divided and subdivided again and again, depending on the level of technology and the sophistication of the machinery available.

This division of labor and specialization of work within the factory, while often boring and repetitive for the workers involved, did unleash an extraordinary increase in the *productivity* of labor. More output could be obtained from the same number of workers than if they individually had produced a good from start to finish. Greater efficiency through specialization encouraged by the organization of production in factories thus contributed to increases in total national output and income and to an increase in the living standard for larger numbers of the population. This upward movement of average income per capita following the Industrial Revolution was shown in Figure 3.1.

In Smith's view, capitalism had a natural tendency toward this broadening and deepening of the division of labor, since doing so contributed to lower costs and increased output, thus enhancing the profit-making opportunities for producers. Smith's advocacy of free trade among nations also was based on this logic, for the larger the market of potential consumers – and what market was larger than the consumers of every country? – the greater were the possibilities for more specialization and for ever higher levels of output.[1] Capitalist owners of firms had a definite incentive to introduce into their production processes the latest and best machinery and the newest ways of producing things since doing so would tend to increase efficiency and hence profits by extending further the division of labor and by making workers even more productive. This "law of capital accumulation" was inherent to the competitive capitalist market economy and for Smith was a human characteristic.

In Smith's analysis, then, it is the accumulation of physical capital, technological progress, specialization of labor, and free trade that are the sources of expanding economic wealth. Economic growth will continue as long as capital is accumulated and new technology is introduced. Both competition and free trade contributed to making this process cumulative.

Smith was keenly aware that the institutional structure of a society played a crucial role in determining the likelihood of continued progress along such a path.

After all, his sustained criticism in *The Wealth of Nations* of England's mercantilist policies, the fettered trade relations it fostered, and the feudal remnants of production in the countryside had provided evidence for Smith's impassioned defense of capitalism, natural liberty and a smaller state as being essential to progress. *The Wealth of Nations* is essentially about how a transformed institutional environment unleashed the dynamic forces of growth in a competitive capitalist economy from which the greatest number might benefit. These constituent elements – capitalism, industrial capital accumulation, efficiency through specialization, free trade, and institutional innovation – continue to constitute essential elements in thinking about economic development to this day.

Malthus' theory of population and economic growth

Thomas Robert Malthus, educated at Cambridge University and a minister, is best known for his theory of population, the implications of which led Thomas Carlyle to utter his famous remark on economics as the "dismal science." Malthus published the first edition of his major work, *An Essay on the Principle of Population*, in 1798 when the effects of industrialization and the path of economic progress in England and Scotland looked quite different to him than they had to Adam Smith, the great optimist of classical political economy.

What observers of late eighteenth-century and early nineteenth-century England witnessed was not a world of a harmony of interests in which all gained, as Smith had postulated, but appalling conditions of degradation for a large part of the citizenry. Only a tiny minority of factory owners and some large rural landlords seemed to be benefitting from the spread of the industrial factory system. What had gone wrong in the last third of the eighteenth century to so alter the hopeful vision of the capitalist economy envisaged by Smith?

Malthus attempted to explain this disturbing state of affairs through his theory of population that argued that the poor were responsible for their own misery. At a time of rising class conflict and resentment, Malthus suggested that the rich were not the enemy of the poor, but rather the poor were the architects of their own fate. Worse, he argued there was not much anyone, including government, could do about this state of affairs. The existing division between the wealthy few and the impoverished many was the natural outcome of the capitalist system. Let's take a look at his thinking.

Malthus' theory of population

Malthus assumed population would grow whenever incomes rose above the level necessary for subsistence. Why? Because of the "animal nature" of human beings, specifically "the laboring poor," who Malthus viewed as morally inferior to the land- and property-owning rich. What's the connection between incomes and population growth?

If average income per person were to rise due to good weather and higher outputs that resulted, there would be more food and other necessities to go around. As incomes and food supplies rose above what was required for the subsistence of the existing population, additional children who were born now would survive. As a result, the effect of rising incomes and the "unquenchable sexual desires of the poor" (these are Malthus' words) meant population could be expected to double about every generation, or every twenty-five years, if there was no limit on such growth.

In Malthus' famous formulation, population increases in a "geometric progression," that is, the number of people tends to grow at the rate of 2, 4, 8, 16, 32, 64, 128, 256, 512, 1,024, 2,048, and so on. For Malthus, this principle of the tendency toward the doubling of population over every generation as wages rose above subsistence was the major factor for understanding why the poorer classes remained poor. How, though, does population growth per se lead to poverty?

Malthus posited that the ultimate limit on population expansion was the inability of the land to produce sufficient food to continue to sustain a population surge of such a magnitude. The production of basic foods could not keep up with population due to the natural tendency of the fertility of the soil to be lower as more land was brought under cultivation. Land best suited for food production already was in use. With a growing population and the need to increase food production, additional land brought under cultivation to try to meet this need would be of lower productivity than existing land. These new lands would produce less output per unit of land than more productive lands, so the growth in total food output would slow.

Malthus believed that agricultural output could only increase in "arithmetic progression," that is, at the rate of 1, 2, 3, 4, 5, 6, 7, 8, 9, 10, and so on, certainly more slowly than the geometric growth rate he assumed governed population growth. An increasing population would sooner or later bump up against the obstacle of the slower-growing production of basic foods and other goods required for subsistence. Income per person not only would not continue to increase, it actually would begin to fall if population growth continued, eventually falling *below* subsistence. Of course incomes below the minimum required for survival meant misery, starvation, death, and a declining rate of population expansion, maybe even a population decline. "Equilibrium" would be attained when population grew at a pace consistent with increases in food production.

Malthus did recognize that there were forces that could slow the natural rate of population growth before the ultimate barrier of incomes falling below subsistence was reached. Since the natural population growth rate depends upon the difference between the birth rate and the death rate, any forces that tended to reduce the birth rate and/or to increase the death rate would tend to slow the natural rate of population growth.[2] Malthus identified, first, what he called *preventive* (or *voluntary*) *checks* that tended to reduce the number of births through the means of human restraint, such as late marriage and sexual abstinence.

When these preventive checks to population growth on the birth rate side were absent or weak, as Malthus assumed them typically to be, particularly among the poor, a second restraint on population growth, the *positive checks*, came into play. These constraints affected the other side of the population growth rate equation by increasing death rates through war, filth, diseases, plagues, natural catastrophes, and the ultimate check, starvation. In fact, it was this "Malthusian spectre" of the apparent inevitability of poverty, squalor, disease, suffering, and death among the poorer classes that prompted Thomas Carlyle to voice his apprehension about economics as "the dismal science."

Malthus' vision of what seemed to be an inescapable dilemma flowing from economic growth to population explosion to misery for the poor led him to oppose all efforts at charity directed at the poorer classes, including better health care and hygiene, since they could only delay the unavoidable drift of living standards toward subsistence. Indeed, acts of charity, be they private or public, might even be expected to lead to a *decrease* in the willingness of the poor to work by diminishing their fear of starvation, hence reducing total national production and income and accelerating the pace of decline in society toward subsistence.[3]

Of course, we now know that Malthus made a critical error in his analysis. He ignored the importance of technological progress to increasing productivity and output, even from relatively fixed inputs, like land, over the long run (as discussed in Focus 4.1). Malthus assumed a constant productivity of any piece of land over time. To use modern terminology, Malthus envisaged a constant aggregate production function, as shown in Figure 4.1, which never shifted. Improvements in technology, however, are precisely what permit a shifting upward of a nation's production function such that more output from the same resources is possible (compare the level of output before and after changing technology at L^* units of labor). It is through increases in technology and higher productivity of society's inputs that a growing population can be accommodated. Further, with output growing rapidly enough, there is no necessary reason for income per capita to fall, and sufficient technological progress will raise total output and income per person.

What, then, might have accounted for the miserable living conditions among the poor that Malthus witnessed if they were not due to a fundamental imbalance between limited food production and rapidly growing population as he believed? Most likely they were due to transitional growing pains due to the radical structural changes taking place in Britain as feudal society became capitalist. The benefits of the Industrial Revolution to larger numbers of people awaited institutional changes and the further spread of technology that were still in the future.

One thing Malthus demonstrated was that there was no *automatic* mechanism by which all classes in society necessarily gained from the increased productivity of the new capitalist structure. Fundamental institutional changes – particularly central

---

FOCUS 4.1   WAS MALTHUS RIGHT?

Was Malthus right about the rate of growth of food production? What factor important for increasing the level of output, even on land that may not seen suitable for farming, did Malthus overlook?

If you guessed that Malthus was probably neglecting or not anticipating the advances in production that *technological change* in agriculture would permit, you are correct. Since the time of the Industrial Revolution, fewer and fewer persons working less and less land in the developed countries have been involved in producing more and more agricultural output. The reason is quite simple. Better technology in the form of machinery, seeds, fertilizers, pesticides and better-trained farmers have all contributed to a dramatic increase in agricultural output per unit of input. Fewer farmers in the rich countries feed ever larger numbers of persons around the globe by being able to produce with ever-greater efficiency on less land.

What the now developed nations experienced as they expanded their economies with the rise of capitalism was not only an industrial capitalist revolution. They also accomplished an **agricultural revolution** that increased food output and permitted higher living standards with less effort. At the time Malthus wrote, this great agricultural revolution was still in the future.

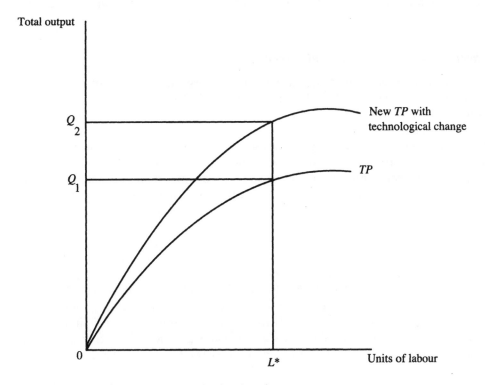

Figure 4.1 A classical aggregate production function.

government structures – that could contribute to the sharing of the fruits of increased productivity had yet to be devised. The new capitalist order which Smith had so praised did have its natural tendencies – greater aggregate productivity, efficiency, technological change – but the productive system existed within a social, human and institutional context which needed time and evolution to adapt to the new productive structures.

Ricardo's theories of diminishing returns and comparative advantage

David Ricardo, who became rich at a very young age from his investments on the stock exchange, was an English contemporary of Malthus. Indeed, they were good friends and intense intellectual rivals. While Ricardo accepted elements of Malthus' population theory, he parted ways with him over the dynamics of the capitalist system and, in particular, over the relative significance of landowners and capitalists. Ricardo believed industrialists to be at the dynamic center of the workings of the capitalist economy. With economic and population growth, landowners would receive higher, but economically unjustifiable, incomes. A shift of society's income toward landowners threatened the capacity of the capitalist system to continue to grow since this meant a reduction in profits of the industrial sector. What landowners gained in income with population growth, industrialists lost. Ricardo's views on this problem of growth in capitalist economies, or at least in England in the early 1800s, were based on his famous theory of diminishing returns.

The law of eventually diminishing returns

Every economics undergraduate early on encounters Ricardo's law of "eventually" diminishing returns. In Ricardo's (and Malthus') formulation, when economic growth occurs, land of progressively lower productivity is brought into use, the reasonable assumption being that farmers will make use of the best, most fertile lands first.[4] As marginal land is brought into use, the price of food will rise as it becomes more costly to produce additional food from this less productive land. For those producing the same product on land *more* productive than the marginal lands, however, the higher price that their output will now command – wheat is wheat and all will sell at the same price in a competitive market – is a *windfall* gain. Since the price of the wheat sold in a competitive market from more productive land is the same as that sold from less productive land but costs of production are lower on the farms with more fertile land, what economists call "economic profits" will be positive on all land more productive than the most marginal land.

In Ricardo's language, these windfall profits to landowners are called "rents." These rents increase as population grows and less and less of society's total income is available for wages and, significantly for Ricardo, for the profits of capitalists, who will be unable to continue to invest and expand production as in the past. As Ricardo wrote, "the interest of the landlord is always opposed to the interest of every other class in the community" (in Rogin 1956: 113).

It is from the law of eventually diminishing returns to agriculture that Ricardo deduced that every economy had a maximum level of income per person based on some optimum quantity of inputs. Any attempt to further expand production by adding more inputs would set off a decline in per capita income as food prices rose. Eventually, a stationary equilibrium state would be reached where, as was true in Malthus' analysis too, workers received only subsistence wages. This state of affairs was not absolutely binding for Ricardo, however. Economic growth in capitalist society thrived on cheap food according to Ricardo since that meant industrial wages could be lower, and lower wages meant higher profits for capitalists and greater possibilities for continued capital accumulation in industry. That meant more production and hence higher income levels for the economy as a whole.

Ricardo believed that it was the productivity of labor in agriculture, rather than in industry, which was the principal basis for sustaining economic growth. Only then would food, the indispensable and predominant component of the consumption of workers in industry, be produced at a lower cost thus permitting lower wages, higher profits, more capital accumulation and faster growth of industry. Ricardo believed greater productivity on existing land could be achieved over the long term from technological change. In the short term, however, it was overseas markets, especially the colonies, which could supply food to Europe to counteract rising food prices that the law of eventually diminishing returns implied at home. It is this perspective on how the dilemma of diminishing returns might be escaped that illuminates Ricardo's other contribution to economics, his emphasis on the advantages of *free trade*.

Ricardo favored the lifting of existing restrictions on imports of grains into England from the Continent and elsewhere. Opening the doors to free trade would flood the English market with imported grains, particularly wheat, a basic food item for workers at the time. This increase in supply would contribute to keeping wages lower by keeping the price of food down, though this would come at the expense of landowners at home who would see their economic rents dissipated by the lower prices they would now receive for their production due to increased competition.

For Ricardo, free trade and an *open economy* contributed to offsetting the adverse effects of the law of eventually diminishing returns from agriculture in the short term thus permitting industrial workers' real wages to continue to rise even with population growth. A subsistence income was not the necessary outcome provided that food prices could be kept sufficiently low. At the time Ricardo was writing that meant bringing down the barriers to imported food to England that the Corn Laws had erected.[5]

For countries today, achieving reasonable food prices and output in sufficient quantities may require the equivalent of an agricultural revolution. This would mean the adaptation of new technologies for farming, the use of new seed strains as with the Green Revolution, better pest control, irrigation, better training of farmers and a range of other strategies that can increase agricultural productivity and keep food prices, and hence basic wage costs, from increasing so rapidly that industrial production is made less profitable. Advances in agriculture are necessary if the rising wages and then the economic decline that follows are to be avoided. As in Ricardo's time, prices may be kept lower through freer trade, but the expanded possibilities from better use of technologies and training that did not exist in Ricardo's time to the extent they are today are also integral (these issues are discussed in more detail in Chapter 11).

The theory of comparative advantage

If there is one economic theory that the vast majority of economists accept as universally valid, it would be Ricardo's theory of comparative advantage. This suggests that unrestricted exchange between countries will increase total world output if each country tends to specialize in those goods that it can produce at *relatively* lower cost compared to its potential trading partners. Each country then will trade some of its lower-cost goods with other nations for goods that can be produced elsewhere more cheaply than at home. With free trade among nations, all countries will find that their *consumption possibilities* have been expanded by such specialization and trade beyond what would have been possible from domestic production possibilities alone, i.e., from **autarky**. Based on this compelling argument, economists tend to favor free trade since it is presumed to be "welfare enhancing" in that the aggregate level of national income is increased.

Using Ricardo's own numerical example (see Table 4.1) can demonstrate the logic behind the comparative advantage argument (Hunt 1979: 105). The first and second columns of the table show the number of hours it takes to produce one unit of cloth or one unit of wine in England and Portugal. Note, first, that Portugal actually is able to produce a unit of both wine and cloth with less labor than does England. Portugal thus has an *absolute advantage* over England in the production of both goods. Economists before Ricardo, including Adam Smith, often thought that a country with lower absolute costs should produce those goods and trade them to other countries for goods others could produce at less absolute cost.

Table 4.1 Number of hours required to produce one unit of cloth and one unit of wine in England and Portugal

| | *Cloth* | *Wine* | *Opportunity cost: one unit of cloth produced in terms of wine foregone* | *Opportunity cost: one unit of wine produced in terms of cloth foregone* |
	(1)	*(2)*	*(3)*	*(4)*
England	100	120	0.833	1.20
Portugal	90	80	1.125	0.888

Ricardo, by making use of the concept that we now call **opportunity cost**, showed that it was not absolute costs that really mattered. Ricardo focused on the *internal* trade-off in production of one good for the other, that is, on the *internal opportunity cost of production* within each country for one unit of each good in terms of how much of the other must be sacrificed. Ricardo's approach is based on *comparative* (or *relative*) *advantage*.

The third and fourth columns show the opportunity costs of producing one unit of each good in terms of the number of units of the other good that can no longer be produced once labor has been used up. For example, producing one unit of wine in England uses 120 hours of labor. Once that one unit of wine is produced, those 120 hours are not available for use in the production of cloth. How much cloth is forgone when one unit of wine is produced in England?

The 120 hours expended in the production of wine would have been able to produce 1.20 units of cloth (120 hours to produce one unit of wine/100 hours to produce one unit of cloth). For each unit of wine produced in England, the opportunity cost is 1.20 units of cloth that cannot be produced from the same labor once it has been expended in wine production.

Likewise, the opportunity cost of producing one unit of cloth in England is 0.833 units of wine that cannot be produced once the labor is allocated to producing cloth (100 hours expended to produce one unit of cloth/120 hours needed to produce one unit of wine). The same method applies to determining the opportunity costs of wine and cloth in terms of foregone production of the two goods in Portugal.

Ricardo recognized that what was important in determining what each country should produce for trade was the *relative cost* of producing each good within individual countries, not the absolute cost. Looking again at Table 4.1, it is clear that it is *relatively cheaper* to produce a unit of cloth in England, where the opportunity cost is 0.833 units of foregone wine, than it is to produce cloth in Portugal, where the opportunity cost is 1.125 units of wine foregone per unit of cloth produced. England sacrifices less wine to produce a unit of cloth than is the case in Portugal. Thus England is the lower cost producer of cloth.

Just the opposite is true for wine production. Portugal produces wine at relatively less cost (0.888 units of cloth foregone for each unit of wine produced) than does England (1.2 units of cloth foregone for each unit of wine produced.

With given supplies of labor in each country if England specializes in the production of cloth, the good for which it has comparative advantage, and Portugal specializes in wine production, the good in which it has comparative advantage, then world output can be increased above what it was when each country did not specialize. As a result, when countries specialize and then trade with one another, each country will be able to *consume outside its own production possibilities frontier*. The benefits of specialization do not require that each country completely forgo producing the good with the higher opportunity cost to gain from trade. It is only necessary to shift resources *toward* the good(s) that can be produced at relatively lower opportunity cost, that is, toward those goods with comparative advantage relative to potential trading partners.

Both countries will gain from specialization and trade in the example in Table 4.1 provided the international trade price between England and Portugal for cloth in terms of wine given up is between 0.888 and 1.20 or, to say the same thing, if the price of wine is between 0.833 and 1.125 units of cloth given up. The trade price between the countries needs to be somewhere between the **internal opportunity cost** trade-offs for the individual countries shown in the last two columns of Table 4.1. To see the benefits of specialization and trade more concretely, consider the following example.

If the trade price at which the two goods are traded is 1 cloth for 1 wine, then England would be able to produce one unit of cloth – the good in which it specializes – and trade it to Portugal for one unit of wine in exchange. How is that better for England? If England had instead produced that one unit of wine itself, it would have been necessary to have sacrificed the production of 1.2 units of cloth, since the production of one unit of wine in England requires 1.2 times as much labor as one unit of cloth. Clearly England, benefits by being able to trade one unit of cloth and get one unit of wine from Portugal rather than having to "pay" 1.2 units of cloth to produce one unit of wine itself.

Portugal also benefits from the exchange at this trade price. In return for the one unit of wine traded to England, Portugal obtains one unit of cloth. If Portugal produces cloth itself, it is necessary to give up 1.125 units of wine to release a sufficient number of workers (= 90 hours of labor) to produce that one unit of cloth (column 3 of Table 4.1). Portugal also benefits from the specialization and trade.

Ricardo's analysis of comparative advantage strongly suggests that specialization in production and free trade, that is, trade between countries with a minimum of tariff and non-tariff barriers, is the best policy for countries to follow.[6] Specialization and free trade increase world production and the consumption possibilities for each country by increasing the degree of internal efficiency in production in individual countries so that there is more available for all to consume, as shown in Figure 4.2.

The curve labelled PPF in Figure 4.2 is Portugal's production possibilities frontier.[7] When there is no trade between England and Portugal, the PPF is also equal to Portugal's consumption possibilities frontier since what is available for consumption depends exclusively upon domestic production. What Portugal produces is all that Portugal has available to consume in a world with no trade.

However, when Portugal specializes in the production of wine and then trades some with England for cloth at a mutually beneficial trade price, such as 1 cloth for 1 wine, Portugal's consumption possibilities frontier (CPF) will lie *outside* its PPF. With specialization and then trade, Portugal will be able to consume more of both goods, as shown by the line segment *AB* in Figure 4.2.

This is a truly remarkable result. By specializing and thus increasing world efficiency, trade can make every country better-off than if they had simply produced goods for themselves. It is little wonder, then, that Ricardo's theory of comparative advantage has had such a profound effect on economic policy and in providing an argument for more open trade among nations.

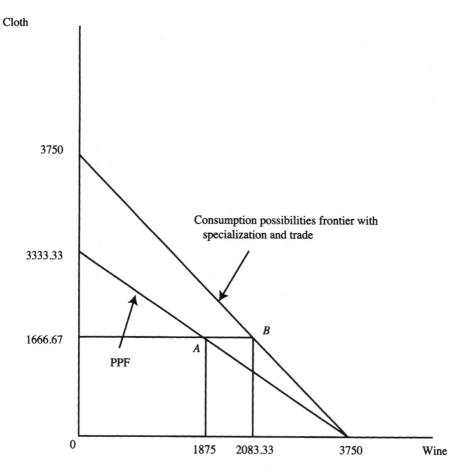

Figure 4.2 Production and consumption possibilities with and without trade.

An evaluation of Ricardo's theory of comparative advantage

There have been many criticisms of Ricardo's analysis of comparative advantage and the free trade conclusion to which it leads. It is important to remember some of the restrictions Ricardo applied to his theory. It was assumed that the factors of pro- duction – natural resources and land, labor and capital – were immobile and that both (all) countries had the capacity to produce both (or all) goods. Any imports are perfectly balanced by an equivalently valued export flow; thus no country incurs a trade deficit which must be financed.

Further, Ricardo assumed that perfect competition prevailed and that all resources in each country were fully employed. In fact, with less-than-fully employed resources, tariff or other protection to block imports and to increase domestic employment could well be the preferred policy, since the key allocative issue would be an internal mobilization of domestic resources to their full use rather than a reallocation among alternative uses.[8]

While these are important considerations having to do with the validity of assumptions, there are other concerns about a blanket endorsement of the comparative advantage argument and free trade recommendations that go beyond this. Economist Joan Robinson's comment on the real-time effect of following Ricardo's free trade advice and specialization, at least as far as Portugal was concerned, remains provocative:

> the imposition of free trade on Portugal killed off a promising textile industry and left her with a slow-growing export market for wine, while for England, exports of cotton cloth led to accumulation, mechanisation and the whole spiralling growth of the industrial revolution.
>
> (Robinson 1978: 103)

This is a potentially valuable historical lesson from the application of comparative advantage theory, and its corollary, the free trade doctrine, a conclusion supported by our discussion of path dependence and the effects of colonialization in Chapter 3. It is not just specialization that is important for a country, even if one grants all of Ricardo's assumptions. Specialization and free trade may not always and everywhere result in greater economic progress over time. Portugal specialized in a commodity that did not have the same growth potential as did cloth for England. Portugal's economy suffered consequently, as the productive structure and institutions were moulded in the direction of wine production. In fact, after trade was rapidly expanded following the Methuen Treaty in 1703, Portugal was left with a sizeable trade deficit as its exports to Britain fell short of its imports from Britain. The boom in Portuguese–British trade fortuitously coincided with a gold rush in Brazil, Portugal's colony, enabling the Portuguese to cover their deficit for a time with a colonial gold flow, but the benefits of specialization and trade over the longer term were illusive.[9]

It may not be specialization per se that is so important for a country's future as is the *choice of what to specialize in.* Some commodities are more likely to have expanding world demand over the future, as with England's cloth production. Other commodities may be more likely to benefit from the application of science and technology that reduce their production costs over time. It is this more dynamic way of understanding the theory of comparative advantage and the nature of the path dependence associated with any decision to produce particular goods which would seem to account for much of the success of the East Asian economies in recent years, as will be discussed in later chapters.

Such a forward-looking comparative advantage perspective presents the policy-maker with more problems – projecting demand, prices, technology, and other variables into an uncertain future – but also with more possibilities. Finding the right goods for specialization can contribute to a dynamically evolving economic system with a greater opportunity for contributing to sustained development, of overcoming the negative effects of past path dependence and which can shift production and society to higher and more efficacious paths toward development over the future.

As will be discussed in Chapters 9 and 10, Ricardo's theory of *static* comparative advantage is no substitute for a more future-oriented analysis of *dynamic* or *created comparative advantage.* The latter is a view of comparative advantage that looks to the future possibilities associated with the production of particular goods (dynamic comparative advantage) rather than to a consideration of what it is best to specialize in among the goods now produced (static comparative advantage). Nonetheless, among many economists, Ricardo's theory of static comparative advantage retains a particularly strong intellectual hold, one that often uncritically informs policy recommendations. We do not feel that the success of most late-developing economies is consistent, however, with the static version of comparative advantage theory but rather with a more dynamic understanding of that theory as suggested here based on a more robust understanding of Ricardo's theory.

A classical model of economic growth

Let us now consider a classical-type model of economic growth which builds upon Smith and Malthus but depends especially on Ricardo's formulation.

The aggregate production function for an economy, which shows how inputs are turned into outputs has land (N), labor (L), capital (K), and technology (T) as the inputs to production.

$$Y = f(N, L, K, T) \tag{4.1}$$

This production function is subject to the following restrictions: $f_N, f_L, f_K > 0$ and $f_{NN}, f_{LL}, f_{KK} < 0$, which simply states that the marginal product (f_i) of each input, i, is positive, but each also is subject to the law of diminishing returns ($f_{ii} < 0$). In other words, as additional units of each input, i, are added to production, all others held constant, output rises but it rises at a decreasing rate.

The rate of economic growth over time ($= dY/dt$) depends, then, on the productivity and the rate of expansion over time of the four inputs in the production function in equation 4.2.

$$dY/dt = f_N dN/dt + f_L dL/dt + f_K dK/dt + f_T dT/dt \tag{4.2}$$

It seems reasonable to take $dN/dt = 0$ since the available quantity of land, or more generally, natural resources, is given. The growth in the labor force, dL/dt, can be presumed to be proportional to the rate of capital accumulation, dK/dt, since greater capital accumulation requires more workers to operate the machines and tools of production. Thus we can write $dL/dt = q dK/dt$ ($q > 0$), where q is the number of workers required for each new unit of capital, K. If we also assume for simplicity that technology is given, or exogenous, in the short term, then $f_T = 0$.

Given the above conditions, equation 4.2 can be re-written as follows:

$$dY/dt = (q f_L + f_K) dK/dt \tag{4.3}$$

The rate of economic growth in the classical model depends essentially on the rate of physical capital accumulation, K. The more rapid the pace of capital accumulation, K, the faster the rate of economic growth. The rate of capital accumulation is determined by the rate of profit earned by capitalist investors. For Ricardo, the ultimate limit on the rate of capital accumulation, and hence on the rate of economic growth, was the binding nature of the law of diminishing returns. This can be seen from equation 4.3 since f_L, the marginal product of labor in the above statement, decreases as L rises, until eventually the point is reached when per capita income reaches a steady-state level (population growth performs the same function in Malthus' formulation of economic growth).

Marx's analysis of capitalist development

Unlike Smith, Malthus, and Ricardo, Karl Marx did not assume capitalism to be immutable or to be the natural order of society. Marx believed capitalism to be but one stage of a society's historical development that began with primitive communism and then evolved toward slavery, feudalism and eventually to capitalism, though this historical progression did not take place in all countries at the same time nor at the same speed.

Marx believed capitalism ultimately would break down and from it would be created a socialist economic system and, in due course, communism. Our interest here is not in Marx's historical–materialist philosophy, however, but rather in his analysis of the dynamics of capitalism, as traditional, feudal society was transformed and ultimately left behind. Chapter 3 touched upon some of Marx's ideas pertaining to the colonial regions, drawn largely from his observations of the effects of British policy in India. In this section, we shall explore in more detail Marx's analysis of the dynamics of the capitalist economy that most other classical economists, John Stuart Mill excepted, took for granted as the ultimate stage of human development.

Marx's great economic work was *Capital*, only the first volume of which was published in 1867 during his lifetime. Marx died in 1883, and the other two volumes of *Capital* were edited and published in 1885 and 1894 by Marx's close friend, collaborator, and benefactor, Frederick Engels, from notebooks Marx left. A further volume, *The Grundrisse*, which some have called the fourth volume of *Capital*, was not published in English until the 1970s. Marx's analysis of the broad dynamics of capitalism differs only slightly from the other classical economists in many respects. For example, in his study of the relentless drive toward capital accumulation that motivates capitalists and in the resulting division of labor there is little to distinguish Marx from Smith. It is in the *implications* of this process that Marx parted ways with the classicals.

Marx greatly admired the vast productive power of capitalism, a system that had succeeded, he noted, in creating more wealth in a hundred years than all other modes of production in previous human history. What appalled Marx was the human cost involved in producing such wealth and the extremely one-sided distribution that resulted from its production. Marx believed, and his analysis of the creation of surplus value attempted to demonstrate this, that it was only the working class, which he called the "proletariat," that created wealth through their labor power. Capitalists appropriated a disproportionate share of society's total income solely by their "virtue" of being the owners of the means of production, particularly of physical capital, required for producing society's commodities.

Marx argued that the uneven distribution of the ownership of society's means of production was the result of a historic process in which former peasants lost access to land for their own production and were forced into cities to become workers because of the Enclosure Movement in England. He thus argued that the ultimate distribution of income in capitalist society was unfair. He believed that, over time, workers, as they came to grasp the nature of their exploitation by capitalists, would seize political and economic power from the minority class of capitalists. Marx, however, did not think this transition toward socialism would be initiated until capitalism had reached a sufficiently high degree of development in its ability to produce and in its use of capital and technology. For Marx, a relatively high level of income per capita within a capitalist economic environment was a pre-condition for the future socialist and communist economic systems he believed would follow.

Neoclassical growth models

Interest among economists in examining the sources of economic growth and in understanding the trajectory of capitalist society disappeared from view for a time with the neoclassical, marginalist revolution in economic thinking after the 1870s, perhaps in reaction to the revolutionary implication of Marx's version of classical theory which predicted an overthrow of the capitalist order by disenfranchised workers. Neoclassical economic analysis was resolutely micro-oriented with a focus on the utility-maximizing behavior of individuals and the profit-maximizing actions of perfectly competitive firms. The macroeconomic perspective inherent in a concern for economic growth and in the distribution of income among classes that had motivated the classical economists gave way to a narrower interest in the conditions required for equilibrium prices and quantities in individual markets.

A Solow-type neoclassical growth model

One of the most influential neoclassical growth models, and one that has shaped much modern thinking about the process of economic growth, has been that of Nobel Prize-winning American economist, Robert Solow (1956). A Solow-type model can be depicted by a simple, aggregate production function like that shown in equation 4.4.

$$Y(t) = A(t)K(t)^{1-a}L(t)^a, \tag{4.4}$$

where $0 < a < 1$. Just as in the classical models, with which it shares strong similarities, the Solow-type growth model exhibits diminishing returns to both K and L in the short term, while there are constant returns to scale from changing all inputs by the same percentage over the longer term.[10]

$A(t)$ is *exogenous* technological progress which affects the production function's position but not its general shape. Exogenous technological change is assumed available to all economies at the same rate. Figure 4.3 shows a short-run neoclassical aggregate production function and the impact of exogenous technological change.

Just as in the classical production function shown in Figure 4.1, a change in $A(t)$ leads to an upward shift of the production function, $Y(t)$, such that more output can be produced with the same inputs. It is this *exogenous* technology which is basic to higher levels of income per capita over time. As Figure 4.3 shows, without technological change, the increased use of inputs in production, via more investment, K, has a limit in terms of total income and hence (assuming L constant) in terms of per capita income, as shown by K_{max}, Q_{max}.

If technology and the rate of increase of L, the labor force, are constant and assuming the labor force is always fully employed, a Solow-type growth function predicts that, for any given rate of savings and investment, there will be a constant,

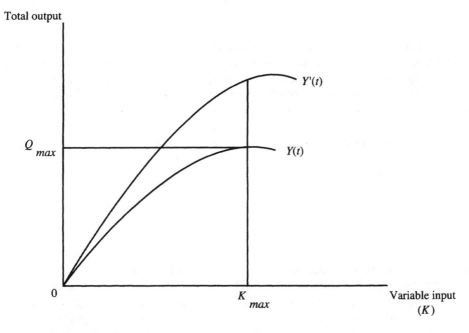

Figure 4.3 A Solow-type production function.

steady-state level of real per capita income achieved.[11] This result follows directly from the assumption of diminishing returns to K. Given a constant rate of saving (= investment, by definition), the return to capital for investors falls as the stock of capital rises[12] until, ultimately, the total amount of capital also reaches a steady-state level, and all new investment is just sufficient to replace old capital that has worn out. When that happens, the level of per capita income of a country will have reached its maximum level, given the rate of savings, population growth rate and assuming zero technical change, which is exogenous anyway.

An even more interesting and perhaps astounding implication of the Solow-type neoclassical model is that poorer nations will grow *faster* than richer nations, assuming equal rates of saving and investment and growth rates of population. In other words, the Solow model predicts the *convergence* of per capita income among different nations sharing similar "fundamentals." Two countries with the same rate of saving and the same population growth rate will tend to have, ultimately, the same real per capita income.[13]

However, according to the Solow formulation, and somewhat controversially, as we shall see in Chapter 8, it is *not* possible for a nation to increase its **rate** of economic growth by investing more of its income in accumulating more physical capital goods since the law of diminishing returns to capital means that more rapid accumulation will simply result in the country reaching its target level of per capita income more quickly. At this point, the steady-state (constant) level of income per person would be reached. Higher levels of saving and investing can contribute to a higher level of real per capita income so that nations that save and invest 25 percent of their output will have a higher steady-state level of per capita income than those which save and invest 15 percent of their income (assuming the same rate of population growth). But a higher level of saving and investment that adds physical capital machinery faster to the production process does *not* lead to a higher **rate** of growth of income that can persist over time. Regardless of the rate of saving and investment, there is a ceiling on the level of per capita income for that level of *S* and *I*. As an economy approaches that level of income, the rate of growth of per capita income decreases, eventually reaching zero as the steady-state income level is attained and the optimum level of physical capital is reached.

Without belaboring the mathematics of the Solow-type model, the level of per capita income of a country will be:

$$y = Y/L = (s/n)^{a/1-a}, \tag{4.5}$$

where *s* is the percentage of total income saved, *n* is the exogenous rate of growth of population and *a* and $1 - a$ are the income shares of labor and capital (Solow 1956: 76–77).

This formulation suggests that differences in income per person across countries are explained as the consequence of different rates of saving (which determine the level of physical capital accumulation) and population growth rates, assuming equal shares of income accruing to labor and capital across countries as expressed in the value for *a* and $1 - a$. This formulation clearly shows, too, that a higher rate of saving, *s*, will raise the steady-state level of per capita income, all else being the same, since that will increase the level of physical capital the economy has to be employed with its labor force.

Countries that are poor and not growing are thus poor, according to the Solow formulation, because they are not saving and investing a sufficiently high proportion of their gross income. Countries that wish to increase their standard of living whatever their growth rate of population can do so by increasing the rate at which national income is saved and invested, that is, by accumulating physical capital at a higher rate.

This recommendation to accumulate physical capital at a higher rate and hence to create higher levels of capital per person through increased saving has been a fundamental policy insight common to virtually all the strategies recommended by economists as the means to increase economic growth in less-developed nations.[14]

It's important to keep the basics of Solow's model in mind. It has been and continues to be an important starting point for many economists in theorizing about the underlying forces at work which influence the process of economic growth in real world economies. It is a theory which has had profound policy implications.

The Harrod–Domar model

The Solow-type, neoclassical growth model was developed originally not to try to explain income levels and differences in the standard of living among real-world economies, though such empirical work has been done and that has been the real importance of Solow's contribution to economic growth theory (Mankiw *et al.* 1992). Solow actually developed his theory in response to the troubling implications of the Harrod–Domar model. Sir Roy Harrod of Oxford and Evsey Domar of the Massachusetts Institute of Technology simultaneously, but quite independently, developed in the 1940s broadly similar explanations for the aggregate economic growth process.

The Harrod–Domar model makes the following assumptions about how economic growth occurs:

1   The labor force, L, grows at a constant rate $n = \Delta L/L$.
2   Net saving, S, and investment, $I = \Delta K$, are fixed proportions of total output, Q, such that $S = I = sQ$, where $0 < s < 1$. The usual Keynesian income multiplier relation is operative. $S = I$, *ex post,* as is typically assumed in most neoclassical models.
3   The two inputs to production, K and L, are used in fixed proportions. There is no substitution of K and L in production.[15] To produce any level of output Q, there is a minimum level of each of the inputs required, as given by the following: $L = bQ$ and $K = vQ$, where $0 < b$, $v < 1$, and b and v are the labor–output and the capital–output ratios, respectively.

Harrod and Domar introduced the concept of the *warranted rate of growth, g_w*, which is the rate of growth of output consistent with equilibrium in the input and output markets and turns out to be equal to s/v. If output, Q, also grows over time by this percentage value, s/v, which is the savings rate, s, divided by the capital–output ratio, v, the economy will be in steady-state equilibrium, such that Q, K, and K/L all grow at the same rate.

What was startling in the Harrod–Domar model, however, was that this equilibrium growth rate was found to be quite unstable. If output, Q, grows for some reason at a rate faster than s/v, then the growth rate of Q in the next period will be even larger, as investors react by investing and producing even more output. If the rate of growth of output is less than the warranted rate, s/v, the economy slows down even more in subsequent periods, as investors invest and produce less.

What the Harrod–Domar model suggested was that there was a *knife-edge* equilibrium. If the economy was not growing at *precisely* the rate required by current rate of saving, s, and given the current capital–output ratio, v, then the economy would veer further and further away from equilibrium, either growing too quickly, and eventually igniting inflationary pressures, or growing too slowly, leading to unused capacity and rising unemployment as the economy spiralled ever further downward away from equilibrium.[16]

It was but a small step from this startling deduction of the Harrod–Domar model – that equilibrium in most economies would be but a fluke – to the implication that government action, especially to affect the rate of saving, s, could be the means, perhaps the only recourse, for averting economic crisis. Otherwise, without the precisely right level of saving, s, the Harrod–Domar analysis predicted the alternative abysses of either self-perpetuating inflation or spiralling unemployment. While it would be perhaps too strong to insist that the Harrod–Domar instability problem suggested the importance of state planning of development in the less-developed world, it certainly is the case that the identification of key variables – the rate of saving and the capital–output ratio – that are amenable to public policy decisions eased the way for strategies to manipulate behavior and influence decisions to affect the pace of economic development by planners and economists influenced by the disquieting implications of the model.

The neoclassical response to Harrod–Domar instability

Solow's contribution to the economic growth literature was in response to the curious, unstable, and for neoclassical economists, worrying disequilibrium behavior of the Harrod–Domar model. Solow proved, however, that the Harrod–Domar result was the particular consequence of assuming that production required *fixed* ratios of the inputs to production ($L = bQ$ and $K = vQ$).

Solow made what is now the standard neoclassical assumption that the capital and labor inputs are infinitely substitutable in production, though such substitution was subject to the law of eventually diminishing returns. Rather than assuming that production isoquants for firms and for society formed right angles, implying no substitution of inputs as in the Harrod–Domar model, Solow assumed production isoquants to be smoothly convex to the origin as they typically are drawn in most economic theory texts. As a result, instead of running into the dilemma of requiring $g_w = s/v$ for steady-state equilibrium, an outcome that could only be fortuitous without, perhaps, some sort of manipulation of the variables by government, Solow's equilibrium, as shown in equation 4.5, did away with the problem of the knife-edge. For any rate of saving, s, there is a steady-state equilibrium level of income per person, and the disturbing instability of the Harrod–Domar model disappeared.

Still, Solow's model leaves the door open for public policy to impact the rate of growth and the level of per capita income, if not the long term rate of growth, via the saving rate, *s*, and the rate of population growth, *n*. In subsequent chapters we turn to such matters of development strategies to increase the pace of economic expansion.

Questions for review

1   For Adam Smith, the market capitalist system can yield benefits to both consumers and producers if two basic assumptions about the economic system are satisfied. (a) Explain these two conditions and why both are required if a "harmony of interests" among producers and consumers is to prevail. (b) Is it reasonable to presume that both of these conditions prevail today in most of the world's less-developed nations? Why, or why not? (c) If one or both of the stipulations upon which Smith's conclusion of a harmony of interests among consumers and producers in capitalist society is absent, what might be the effects on society and different groups of the unregulated operation of the market system? Who would be likely to gain? To lose?

2   How is "technology" defined? Is it only physical things, like machines, tools, and computers? Does it include ideas and knowledge? Does technology include human resources and their quality (what economists call "human capital")? What is the importance of technology to economic development? Can technology be imported from one country to another with the same expected outcomes in terms of the effects on total output? What are the preconditions that must be met for a country to make effective use of imported technology?

3   Adam Smith believed specialization or the division of labor to be one of the key factors in creating increased wealth for a nation. Give one example of (a) a commodity that is produced with very little specialization of labor and (b) one that is produced with a high degree of specialization. (c) How do the industries in which these goods are produced differ? (Hint: Consider differences in the use

of machinery, the profitability of the industry, the skill and education levels of the workers and the quality of the final product.)

4   Refer back to Table 4.1 on comparative advantage to answer this question. England has 500,000 labor hours available per day for production; Portugal has 450,000 labor hours available per day. (a) First, assume that England and Portugal do *not* trade with each other and that each currently devotes half of its available labor to the production of each good. How much output of each good will each country be able to produce? What is the total "world" output of both commodities without trade? Draw the production possibilities curve for both countries, being sure to indicate the maximum quantities of each good that can be produced in each country when the production of the other good is zero. (b) Now assume that England and Portugal both *completely specialize* in the commodity in which each has comparative advantage. How much output of each good will be produced by each country? What is the total "world" output of both commodities with specialization, but prior to trade? How do these totals compare to the "before specialization" level of world production? (c) Is it possible for both countries to benefit from trade, such that each has at least as much of one commodity and more of the other than was available for consumption prior to trade? How? At what range of prices in trade would both countries be better off with trade than without specialization and trade? Choose one such trade price and show your results in a table with the output of each good for each country and the consumption of each listed as well. What happens to total world trade? Can each country consume more of both goods than in the past? Include the consumption possibilities curve for each country on your graph of the production possibilities curve you drew in part (a).

5   Given your answer to question 4, what objections, if any, can one have to complete and open free trade between nations? What possible error is there in using Ricardo's theory of comparative advantage as a guide to policy? In what sense might the theory be correct at a point in time (the static view), but incorrect as a guide to what countries should do over time (the dynamic view of comparative advantage)?

6   To test your understanding of the theory of comparative advantage, make your own table similar to Table 4.1 but using different numbers. Determine which country has the comparative advantage in each good and then determine an acceptable trade price if the countries specialize and trade with one another.

Notes

1   The expansion of the market tended to decrease per unit costs of production as the benefits of economies of scale in production could be exploited at a higher level of output.

2   A detailed discussion of population growth and of birth and death rates and their determinants can be found in Chapter 12.

3   Implicit in Malthus' argument that poor relief would reduce the willingness to work is the assumption that the poor, unlike their more wealthy brethren, are not maximizers of their income and consumption opportunities. Apparently the poor were presumed to have relatively low "target" income and consumption levels which would satisfy their limited desires. In modern language, the poor were presumed to be "satisficers" rather than maximizers; they functioned with a different set of beliefs and motivations than capitalists and their presumed "betters."

4   Since Ricardo, the theory of diminishing returns has focused on the eventual decrease in the *marginal product* of a homogeneous variable input, as increasing quantities of that factor are added to production, all other inputs held constant. Ricardo's formulation had greater inputs of land of decreasing quality being added, that is, the input being added was actually heterogeneous, as successive units of land brought into use were of lower fertility.

5   Corn used to mean grains in general, but the Corn Laws were concerned primarily with wheat. The Corn Laws were amended in 1828 and 1842. By 1869, the last remnants of the restrictive Corn Laws on imported grains had been banished from the books.

6   There is one exception that Ricardo made to his argument that free trade was the best policy: "It is evident, then, that trade with a colony may be so regulated that it shall at the same time be less beneficial to the colony, and more beneficial to the mother country, than a perfectly free trade" (quoted in Hunt 1979: 109). Given this caveat, it perhaps seems reasonable to wonder if it is possible for a country to improve upon the free trade outcome with a colony by regulating trade, why would it not also, under some circumstances, be reasonable to suppose that the proper policy for a nation vis-à-vis nations other than colonies might also be other than free trade? We will consider the possibilities of how countries might be able to improve upon the free trade outcome in later chapters. This quote from Ricardo reinforces, too, the discussion of Chapter 3 on the role that colonies played in contributing to the well-being of the more advanced countries and the adverse impact that colonial policies had on the possibilities for economic progress in the colonies.

7   Normally, a PPF is assumed to be concave to the origin, indicating that inputs to production are specialized and that there are increasing marginal opportunity costs of production associated with producing more of one good. Here we make the simplifying assumption that it is possible to produce more of one good at a constant marginal opportunity cost of production in terms of the other good sacrificed at the constant trade-off shown in Table 4.1 and represented by the straight line PPF.

8   Modern analyses of the advantages of specialization and free trade, like the Heckscher–Ohlin theory, are based on Ricardo's original analysis, extending it to take into consideration differences in factor costs and other complications. The implications about specialization, however, remain essentially the same, especially as they relate to recommendations for indebted less-developed nations (Chapter 17) and as a basis for regional trade associations.

9   Between 1700 and 1770, more gold was mined in Brazil than the Spanish extracted from their colonies in the entire period from 1492–1800! Over 25 million pounds sterling of gold was transferred to Britain via Portugal between 1700 and 1770 (Fisher 1971: 128).

10 $dY/dK = (1-a)K^{-a} > 0$ and $dY/dL = aL^{a-1} > 0$; $d^2/(dK)^2 = -a(1-a)K^{-(1+a)} < 0$ and $d^2/(dL)^2 = a(a-1)L^{a-2} < 0$, which demonstrates the short-term existence of diminishing returns to each factor, holding the other constant. The aggregate production function 4.4 is also "linearly homogeneous," that is, multiplying both variable inputs by the same scalar, v, changes production by vY: $A(vK)^{1-a}(vL)^a = Av^{1-a}K^{1-a}v^aL^a = v(AK^{1-a}L^a)$, when $0 < a < 1$, i.e., the production function exhibits constant returns to scale. In this formulation of the production function, a, which is the elasticity of output with respect to a change in the labor, input, can be interpreted as the share of total output and income received by labor, and $1-a$ can be taken to be the share of total output and income received by capital (as profits, dividends, rents, and so on).

11 It is important to remember that saving and investment are in an accounting, or *ex post*, sense always equal. In a closed economy, and assuming no government for convenience, national income and output, Y, are equal to consumption by households, C, and investment by business, I. We thus can write $Y = C + I$. Rearranging, $Y - C = I$. By definition, any income not consumed is saving, S, thus, $Y - C = S = I$, showing that saving equals investment always, *ex post*. Further, $I = \Delta K$, that is, the change in the capital stock is the current level of investment, I, so $S = \Delta K$.

12 This is because each additional unit of capital produces less output than the previous unit due to the law of diminishing returns. Given a constant cost per unit of capital, costs of production will increase as more K is used, and thus the rate of return to all K will decline.

13 It is actually more accurate to state that the Solow-type neoclassical model predicts *conditional convergence* of per capita income. Poorer countries with the same savings rate as an

already richer country will, all else the same, tend to have a faster growth rate than the richer country, so that income per capita would tend to catch up with that of the richer nation. However, the poorer nation may have a higher rate of growth of population, n, that prevents per capita income from reaching the level of the richer nation. Convergence of per capita income levels, then, is conditional on the similarity of the so called "fundamentals," particularly the rate of saving and investment and secondarily, on the rate of population growth. Convergence of income among nations, then, depends on the rough equality in capital/labor ratios and savings behavior among such economies. See Mankiw *et al.* (1992) for a recent effort that suggests that an augmented Solow model provides a reasonable explanation for cross-country income differentials

14 In order to avoid drawing any inappropriate conclusions from the Solow model, it is important to keep in mind the assumptions of the model, one of which is that the society has an "efficient" institutional structure which will readily transpose increased savings into increased capital formation. In Chapters 5 and 6, we will encounter some of the embedded characteristics of many of the less-developed societies which often render inapplicable the assumption of an automatic, direct and smooth link between increased savings, increased investment, and income growth.

15 This means that all production isoquants form right angles and that there is a constant K/L ratio which is most efficient, that is, least cost, in production. This Harrod–Domar assumption also is known as a Leontief, or fixed-proportions, production function.

16 Consider the following simple example. If $s = 0.2$ and $v = K/Q = 2$, then $g_w = s/v = 0.2/2 = 0.1$, or 10 percent. A rate of growth of 10 percent would mean that if $Q_{t-1} = 90$, then $Q_t = 100$ (measuring growth as a proportion of Q_t). If investors expect $Q_t = 100$, then $\Delta K_t = I_t = v\Delta Q_t = 20$. Given a savings (or marginal propensity to consume) of 0.2, the Keynesian income multiplier will be equal to 5, so $Q_t = $ multiplier $\times \Delta$spending $= 5 \times 20 = 100$, so expectations are realized ($S_t = I_t = 20$) and steady-state equilibrium is attained and maintained, as long as expectations remain the same.

However, imagine that investors *expect* $Q_t = 101$, so that $\Delta Q_t = 22$. Then, $\Delta K_t = I_t = v\Delta Q_t = 22$. By the multiplier formula, the *actual* $Q_t = 5 \times 22 = 110$. Investors will feel they have under-invested by anticipating too low a level of Q_t and in the next period will invest more, thus pushing the economy further away from equilibrium.

If the labor market is also added to the model, such that the labor force grows yearly by the rate n ($= \Delta L/L$), then the trick of reaching and maintaining equilibrium in the Harrod–Domar model is exacerbated. Then, to avoid rising unemployment, even when $\Delta Q/Q = s/v$, this warranted rate, g_w, must equal the natural rate of growth, g_L, of the labor force, n. Thus a steady-state equilibrium requires $g_w = s/v = n = g_L$. The knife-edge equilibrium problem is even more exacting and the possibility of steady-state equilibrium even more remote when a growing labor force is introduced into the model.

References

Fisher, H.E.S. 1971. *The Portugal Trade*. London: Methuen.

Hunt, E.K. 1979. *History of Economic Thought: A Critical Perspective*. Belmont, CA: Wadsworth.

Maddison, Angus. 1982. *Phases of Capitalist Development*. Oxford: Oxford University Press.

Mankiw, N. Gregory, David Romer, and David N. Weil. 1992. "A Contribution to the Empirics of Economic Growth," *Quarterly Journal of Economics* 107 (May): 407–437.

Robinson, Joan. 1978. *Aspects of Development and Underdevelopment*. Cambridge: Cambridge University Press.

Rogin, Leo. 1956. *The Meaning and Validity of Economic Theory*. New York: Harper & Bros. Publishers.

Smith, Adam. 1973. *An Inquiry into the Nature and Causes of the Wealth of Nations*. New York: The Modern Library.

Solow, Robert. 1956. "A Contribution to the Theory of Economic Growth," *Quarterly Journal of Economics* 70 (February): 65–94.

5 Developmentalist theories of economic development

After studying this chapter, you should understand:
- the concept of hidden development potential in less-developed nations;
- the possibility of market failure and the role of positive externalities in creating virtuous circle effects;
- the importance of social overhead capital and a nation's augmentable initial endowments to growth;
- balanced versus unbalanced growth strategies and their shared paradigmatic perspective;
- the theory of export pessimism;
- backward and forward linkage effects and their key role in development;
- the idea of hidden comparative advantage;
- the potential role of surplus labor as a stimulant to growth in Lewis's dualist framework for transition; and
- Rostow's stages of growth theory, particularly the "take-off" stage.

Introduction

After the Second World War, and particularly after the quick success of the United States-financed Marshall Plan in helping to rebuild the European economies, several economists who had been directly involved either in the Marshall Plan or with institutions such as the United Nations and the World Bank, turned their attention to the question of economic development of less-developed regions. Among these early pioneers of development thinking were the Finnish economist Ragnar Nurkse, the Austrian economist Paul Rosenstein-Rodan, the German-born economist Albert Hirschman, the West Indian and later Nobel Laureate economist, Sir Arthur Lewis, and the American economic historian Walt Whitman Rostow. Only Lewis remained outside of the policy-making institutions in the late 1940s and early 1950s, but by 1957 he too was employed by the UN.

In a broad sense, the ideas of these early development economists were mutually supportive. They formed a loose school of thought on the issue of economic development, emphasizing a less theoretical and more historical and practical approach to the question of how to develop – particularly in relation to those who stressed the applicability of neoclassical models, such as the Solow model discussed in the last chapter. Like any such school of analysis, there were differences of emphasis and interpretation between these theorists. These differences are particularly striking in the work of W.W. Rostow, who stressed a descriptive approach while emphasizing the near inevitability and predictability of economic development, based on the premise that the industrial past of Europe presents a rough picture of the approaching future of the developing nations. The others emphasized analytical constructs and were not striving to construct a mega-theory of economic history. Yet they shared many fundamental propositions. Above all, they coincided in believing, in Rostow's words, that "the tricks of growth are not that difficult" (Rostow 1960: 166). They also felt that the time period necessary for achieving economic development in the less-developed world would be relatively short, a matter of a decade or perhaps a generation, rarely more.

Furthermore, all these economists shared, to different degrees, an affinity for the work of English economist John Maynard Keynes, whose views on macroeconomics had swept the economics profession in the late 1930s and 1940s. Thus, they emphasized *aggregate* phenomena, such as the rate of saving, measured by the share of income not consumed in gross national product (S/Y), and the rate of investment (I/Y), as fundamental variables, a perspective which fits well, too, with the Solow-type model of the previous chapter. They agreed with the Keynesian assumption that poor economic performance reflected a lack of aggregate demand, rather than from a shortage of, or limits to, resources, though Keynes had come to this conclusion based on his knowledge of the advanced capitalist nations, not from studying the dualistic, less-developed economies to which this insight would be applied.

These early development economists also manifested a notable preference for industrialization as the driving force of economic growth, believing industrialization would release a tide of prosperity lifting all other sectors of the economy. Finally, while these **developmentalists** had a profound respect for market forces, they were not hesitant to advocate large-scale, short-term governmental intervention into the economy, very much after the Keynesian manner, if that might be expected to force economic growth. Markets were perceived as a *means* to realizing the end of economic development; they were not an end in themselves. Markets could achieve some objectives rather well, but there were other spheres in which the market worked less well. Under certain conditions, an assertive, and even a leading, role for government was to be encouraged and was perhaps necessary. In the long term, however, the developmentalists expected that an economy would achieve its best results with a competitive market interacting with a responsive and efficient governmental apparatus, and thus the interventionist role of government in development would be reduced to its stabilizing function as in the already developed nations. In this sense, the developmentalists had very conventional economic ideas, but only in the very long term.

In this chapter, some of the leading theories of the developmentalists are examined. Their theories and recommendations are more pragmatic and operational than the neoclassical or classical formulations. The theories were devised with an eye to directly affecting public policy in the less-developed countries. We shall see that their influence on the thinking of many economists remains strong, though there have been, and need to be, further refinement of their analyses.

The theory of the big push

One of the early theories about how a country might create the conditions for economic progress, where growth and development had not already arisen spontaneously, was formulated by Paul Rosenstein-Rodan based upon research he had conducted during the Second World War. After analyzing the economic structures of a number of poor Eastern and South-East European nations, Rosenstein-Rodan drew several conclusions which became basic building blocks for the field of development economics emerging after the war.[1]

Rosenstein-Rodan was noted for his effort to call attention to the **hidden potential** for economic development in less-developed regions. Much of his work centered on taking advantage of the *increasing returns* that could be realized from large-scale planned industrialization projects that encompassed several major sectors of the economy simultaneously. A "big push" of concurrent industrial investments could launch a chain reaction of virtuous circles and complementary investments that would then ripple in many directions through the economic system. Large-scale investments in several branches of industry would lead to a favorable synergistic interaction between these branches and across sectors. If economic development was to get a start in the now less-developed nations, Rosenstein-Rodan argued, it would have to come from a concerted and substantial "push" from government to create, effectively, an entire industrial structure in one huge and interlocked undertaking (see Box 5.1).

While concentrating on the hidden potential of large-scale future investments, with each successive increment to investment having an increasingly strong impact as output expanded at a rising rate,[2] Rosenstein-Rodan simultaneously maintained that these potential gains could not be realized within a purely market frame of reference. Individual entrepreneurs would be unlikely to invest enough to "push" the less-developed economy forward at its maximum potential rate, because under the profit-and-loss calculations of private entrepreneurs, their frame of reference would be too limited. Profit-maximizing steel producers are not concerned about whether their own private investments, if sufficiently large, will induce other investments and technical change in metallurgy which will then make that industry more profitable. Backward linkage effects which may be provoked by the investment actions of the steel industry are not taken into consideration by private decision-makers in the steel industry, because those firms cannot profit from these spin-off industries or even calculate the likelihood of the emergence and success of such linked firms.

Using Rosenstein-Rodan's terms, the steel industry cannot "appropriate" the future potential benefits to be gained in other sectors that are external to their business and hence they do not take these effects into account in making their private investment decisions. Because of this information and appropriation failure, market decisions will lead to a sub-optimal level of investment from the standpoint of society as a whole.[3] Rosenstein-Rodan was convinced that there were many such hidden potentialities for expanded production in less-developed economies that went unexploited because of the inability of the market economy to coordinate the multitude of simultaneous investment decisions that needed to be made.

Insufficient economic development would occur, because the private sector mechanisms in place in less-developed societies lead to economic decision-making which is sub-optimal. More investment was needed, and in many places at one time,

> **Box 5.1 Virtuous circles**
>
> Although Rosenstein-Rodan does not detail this point, one can sketch such virtuous circle effects: large-scale investments in steel-making could lead to research in metallurgy which would have "positive external" effects on companies which use metal products. Perhaps stronger alloys could be found that could then be used in the metal fabricating industries, reducing wear and fatigue and downtime for the machines in this sector. All this could reduce costs to another branch of industry, perhaps in railroad equipment manufacturing. Lower costs in the rail equipment could then be passed on to farmers, in the form of lower transport costs. Farmers, in turn, would now be able to invest in better mechanical equipment from the metal-manufacturing industry, creating a further surge of positive ripple effects. Each branch of industry, or at least many branches of industry, would be caught in a web of interacting and mutually complementary activities. The more efficient are supply conditions, the lower costs of production will be, and the greater the demand for the product. Cross-sector positive externalities will also be transmitted, for example, from industry to agriculture. In recent years interest in Rosenstein-Rodan's big-push theory has grown. His ideas were formalized by Kevin Murphy, Andrei Shleifer and Robert Vishney (1989) and his views are increasingly evoked by proponents of **endogenous growth theory** (see Chapter 8). This more recent work tends to highlight the role of demand **spillover effects** which, like the examples above, stress the virtuous circle effects which occur when an expanding manufacturing sector that raises productivity then stimulates income growth that, in turn, leads to increasing demand for the products of the expanding manufacturing sector. Increasing growth in this manufacturing sector could lead to increasing demand for inputs that – because they are produced on a larger scale – lead to economies of scale in the production of these inputs. This virtuous circle will then lower the costs of production for the manufacturing sector, which could lead to increasing demand and growth – another virtuous circle!
>
> Source: Hoff and Stiglitz 2001: 4401–4413

in order to shift the economy away from its low-level equilibrium trap and toward rapid and sustainable growth. Of particular importance to this process is the provision of social overhead capital or infrastructure: roads, bridges, docks, communications systems, hospitals, schools, utilities, irrigation and flood control projects, and so on, which also generate substantial positive external benefits to society as a whole.

> The market mechanism alone will not lead to the creation of social overhead capital, which normally accounts for 30 to 35 percent of total investment. That must be sponsored, planned, or programmed (usually by public investment). To take advantage of external economies (due to indivisibilities) requires an "optimum size" of enterprise to be brought about by a simultaneous planning of several complementary industries.
>
> (Rosenstein-Rodan 1984: 209)[4]

For example, if schools are built and operated under the profit motive, then they will be available only for the child whose parents can pay. Bright and ambitious children of poor parents will be less likely to gain needed skills, and society's labor force will be under-skilled and operating below its potential as a consequence. The hidden potential of the future labor force may never be realized if the market is left to provide social overhead capital, such as schools. This is the framework that Rosenstein-Rodan and others utilized when they argued that the market mechanism will not adequately create social overhead capital.[5]

In terms of the sequencing of investment decisions, Rosenstein-Rodan prioritized social overhead capital as an essential initial endowment, albeit one that nations have to actually create. Social overhead capital is not an initial endowment in the same sense that, say, land is.

> Because of indivisibilities and because services of social overhead capital cannot be imported, a high initial investment in social overhead capital must either precede or be known to be certainly available in order to pave the way for additional more quickly yielding directly productive investments.
>
> (Rosenstein-Rodan 1976: 635)

Rosenstein-Rodan's idea of the need for creating a "big push" of investment simultaneously in a number of branches of industry, and his emphasis on social overhead capital as fundamental to the success of the development project in less-developed nations, are his best-known contributions to the literature, but they are not the whole of what he had to say about the development process. Summing up his own contributions in the area of development economics, Rosenstein-Rodan claimed that he had made four innovations.

First, he had stressed **disguised unemployment**, that is, those workers, particularly in agriculture, who receive very low or no pay and whose work effort results in relatively little increase in total output. Their labor could be tapped to create the vast public works of social overhead capital which would be necessary for development, without reducing output in the economy.[6]

Second, by emphasizing the complementarity, and the external economies, of distinct investments, Rosenstein-Rodan demonstrated that large-scale investments could have an impact on overall economic growth greater than might be expected based on the calculations of individual entrepreneurs alone. It is necessary to take into account the positive externalities of one investment on others and on the possibility of increasing returns from successive units of investment. In order to achieve these serendipitous effects, however, economic planning of a limited nature would be necessary. Key industries or branches of industry would have to be targeted for expansion, and their initial investments would need to be subsidized if they were to occur at all.

Rosenstein-Rodan's third innovation was his emphasis on social overhead capital. Such investments, he argued, should precede the expansion of consumer-goods manufacturing investment if the latter is to be successful. As we shall discover in Chapter 8, this is a view supported by recent research on endogenous growth models.

And fourth, a "big push" of investment through the economy could result in **technological external economies**. These effects he defined in terms of work force training. Large-scale industrialization could contribute to a socially beneficial level of labor training that would have spread effects to other sectors throughout the economy, whereas incremental, market-driven development would not have the same impact, or at least dependence on the market would result in sub-optimal social quantities of such training. Private businesses would not invest in the socially optimal level of labor training, again because any individual employer will be unable to appropriate the increases in income created by the new skill, especially if a worker moves on to another employer, who would not need to make any investment to benefit from the worker's increased skill level. However, under the big-push approach, labor training could be funded as part of a more general development plan. A broader time and planning horizon could be entertained by government, which could determine the training needs of an entire industrial complex and which could calculate the social profitability of any investment of additional educational expenditures and labor training. As we shall see in Chapter 8 in the discussion of endogenous growth theories, Rosenstein-Rodan was ahead of his time in maintaining that appropriate labor training was of equal, or perhaps even greater, importance than capital accumulation in the process of industrialization and economic development.

A theory of balanced growth

Ragnar Nurkse, like Rosenstein-Rodan, emphasized above all the need for a coordinated increase in the amount of capital utilized in a wide range of industries if the critical threshold level of industrialization was to have a chance of being achieved. Nurkse agreed that a massive injection of new technology, new machines, and new production processes spread across a broad range of industrial sectors held the key to igniting the development process in less-developed nations.[7]

Export pessimism and the need for domestic industrialization

This perspective of how to initiate rapid economic growth needs to be contrasted with what was, in the 1940s, a received doctrine in trade theory: to foster economic progress, less-developed regions were counseled to concentrate on increasing their exports of tropical products and raw materials, products in which, it was suggested, such countries had a comparative advantage. In Nurkse's view, this rather standard prescription for accelerating economic growth in less-developed countries was likely to yield meagre results for two basic reasons. First, Nurkse maintained that in future the world demand for tropical products and raw materials would be relatively limited and slow to expand. An increase in supply under such conditions would result in a decrease in the market price. The reduction in price could be of such a magnitude that the total revenue received ($=$ unit price $\times$ quantity of the product sold on the world market) after an increase in supply could be less than the export income that was received prior to the drive to increase such exports.[8]

Nurkse did not devote himself to proving this point; rather he seems to have utilized this insight more as a working assumption based upon the weak pattern of prices for traditional primary exports from the less-developed nations he observed in the first half of the twentieth century. Because of this break with the orthodox view that the colonial and post-colonial regions had a comparative advantage in tropical products and raw material exports which could be further exploited through even more ambitious and pragmatic economic policy to expand such exports, Nurkse was branded an "export pessimist" (see Focus 3.4 for details).

The second reason for his rejection of the export-led road to development was based on Nurkse's interpretation of the propensity to import.[9] In orthodox trade theory, it was assumed that a less-developed nation with the ability to export either tropical products and/or raw materials would use the income earned to import machinery, equipment, and manufactured consumer goods for domestic consumption. Trade would balance, that is, the value of exports would equal the value of imports, at least over an intermediate period of time. To challenge orthodox assumptions, Nurkse utilized a socio-psychological theory which explains why consumption continues to rise as income rises. This theory assumes that some "wants" are not innate, but rather are socially created. In this framework, some new goods are "demonstrated" to be desirable, because they are consumed by higher-income recipients in society. These goods confer social status and are therefore sought by others with less income.[10] Nurkse believed that the less-developed regions would be very vulnerable to the pernicious affects of this international demonstration effect. High-income consumers would spend inordinately on imported luxury products to "keep up with the Joneses" of the richer nations. Not only would there be an upward bias toward imports, especially of consumer goods, but the already limited potential supply of savings in the less-developed nation that might have been directed toward much needed domestic capital formation would be drawn down, as consumption as a share of total national income rose. Furthermore, the drive to show status through the importation of luxury commodities would conceivably cut into the ability of the economy to purchase imported machinery for industry, as the two forms of demand for foreign exchange competed for a limited stock of foreign exchange earned from primary product exports.

Less-developed regions were poor, according to Nurkse, because productivity per worker was low, and productivity, in turn, was low because savings were low, just as in the Solow model. With a low capacity for savings, the level of investment would, by necessity, be low, and consequently with only a modest amount of capital equipment available to each worker, the end result had to be a low level of per capita income because output per workers would be low. Small, incremental increases in capital formation would not solve the problem, in Nurkse's view. The market-based approach would more than likely fail, because as an individual business or a single industry alone attempted to raise its output level by increasing its individual capital investment, it ran the risk of not finding a market for its product due to the low level of overall average income. Alternatively, Nurkse emphasized that by attempting to solve the problem of underdevelopment via an expansion on the supply side alone, that is, through the expansion of production capacity, one ran the risk that the lack of demand for new output would short-circuit the attempt to move the economy forward.

The only solution that Nurkse foresaw, as had Rosenstein-Rodan, was via balanced growth. Large-scale increases in supply sweeping across a large number of industrial sectors would, at the same time, be met by a large-scale increase in demand created by the same expansion.[11] The essential demand-side stimulus would come from industries that were expanding as a result of the overall, balanced investment program; they would need more inputs of raw materials, intermediate or semi-processed products, and labor, and their act of buying inputs would create income for their suppliers. This income would then be transposed into a further expansion of demand by other firms and by workers in those firms buying the increased array of domestic goods available. But this widespread expansion could only happen if the initial effort at development was "balanced," that is, only if supply increases were coordinated with simultaneous demand increases across the economy.

Although Nurkse's theory of balanced growth is very similar in many respects to the big-push formulation of Paul Rosenstein-Rodan, Nurkse's work was not merely a repetition. He did not advocate planning, as did Rosenstein-Rodan, nor was his approach open to the charge of being statist or of being dependent on the dominance of the public sector, a criticism that might be leveled at Rosenstein-Rodan. Rather, Nurkse felt that dynamic *fiscal policies* could have a very positive effect on the prospects for development without large-scale government involvement in production decisions or large-scale planning projects. Specifically, Nurkse advocated **forced savings** through an increase in taxes on upper-income recipients. The government, then, could repress the level of consumption out of national income, thereby increasing the level of overall savings. Then, the increased investment funds generated could be allocated to the most promising industrial sectors, possibly via government-operated development banks designed to identify and promote industrialization in the private sector or via private sector banks.

Industries would be encouraged to increase their capital formation and to raise their productivity, both because of the availability of loans from the development banks and because of the effects of infant industry protection, in which government would raise tariffs against cheaply manufactured imports from the advanced nations that might compete with the production of the new enterprises. Thus, both supply and demand factors would be addressed. The supply of savings would be expanded, leading to an increase in the supply of available domestic output via enhanced capital formation. At the same time, a market for domestically produced goods would be created, because potentially competing imports would be deflected via tariffs to the purchase of lower-priced domestically produced goods, a strategy which, later, became known as **import substitution industrialization** (discussed in detail in Chapters 9 and 10).

Like Rosenstein-Rodan, Nurkse felt strongly that less-developed regions possessed the hidden potential for greater progress; the resources and talents of society simply needed to be coordinated and released.

Unbalanced growth

Not all developmentalist economists believed, however, that the resources needed for implementing a big-push or a balanced growth strategy actually were available, though ideally this might be the optimum path in some abstract sense. One who voiced such concern was Albert O. Hirschman. Like most of the pioneers in the field of economic development, Hirschman was involved in the postwar economic reconstruction of Europe. However, this experience was followed by a four-year stint in Colombia, where his role as adviser to the National Economic Planning Board arose as a result of the recommendation of the World Bank (Hirschman 1984: 90). Hirschman's experiences in Colombia were formative; he would draw on a fund of experiences within this less-developed country to provide specificity to his emerging ideas on development. His work since that time has continued to convey a sense of immediacy and applicability that was at times lacking in the abstract and aggregative approaches employed by Rosenstein-Rodan, Nurkse, and other developmentalists.

Because Hirschman employed the term unbalanced growth in his major work

(1958) on economic development, and because his seminal work came considerably later than the ideas expressed by Rosenstein-Rodan and Nurkse, it has been commonly assumed that Hirschman's work was to be interpreted as an attack on the theory of big-push or balanced growth. It is important, therefore, to note that Hirschman agreed with the vast bulk of the ideas expressed by both Rosenstein-Rodan and Nurkse. He supported an "industrialization first" strategy, and he firmly believed that the key to rapid industrialization was to be found in large-scale capital formation in several industries and sectors. Hirschman also shared the optimistic opinion that less-developed nations harbored significant hidden reserves of talent, that potentially complementary relationships were waiting to be released, and that there were major potential externalities which would be instrumental in speeding the thrust toward industrialization. Hirschman's own interpretation of the relationship of his work to that of Rosenstein-Rodan and Nurkse was that he was a dissenter *within* the framework of the big-push/balanced growth paradigm.

The less-developed economies did indeed need a big push; without it, there would be either a snail's-pace rate of economic and societal change, or perhaps no discernible progress at all. But Hirschman advocated a big push for only a limited range of industries, with the idea that by inducing development in key sectors first, overcapacity would be created in these sectors, while supply bottlenecks would simultaneously increase production difficulties elsewhere in the economic structure. These bottlenecks would create pressures for new investments to resolve the supply inadequacies. In other words, Hirschman deliberately advocated the unbalancing of the economy, creating disequilibrium situations, for two basic reasons.

First, he maintained that there were resource limits in the less-developed regions and that this would necessitate prioritizing some areas of industry over others for the use of limited investment funds. It was impossible to move forward on a "broad front" in all industries at the same time as was envisioned in the big-push and balanced growth theories. Second, in deliberately unbalancing the economy and in creating excess capacity in some areas and intensifying shortages in other areas, he believed that the pressures created would result in subsequent reactions that would speed the development process by opening up opportunities for profit for new entrepreneurs.

In industries where overcapacity was generated, the output of these sectors would be made cheaper than previously, due to economies of scale; as output grew, unit costs of production would decrease as the firm moved down the average total cost curve. Hirschman believed this decrease in costs, assuming these were passed on to the final consumer, would then contribute to stimulating **upstream investments**. Hirschman's theory might be illustrated with the following example: by deliberately oversupplying electrical power, and thus lowering its price to users, sectors of the economy which used large amounts of electrical power as an input into their production process could be stimulated by this lowering of their marginal and average costs. Hirschman argued that in conditions of limited resources, as applied in the less-developed world, where it would be impossible to simultaneously increase electrical power-generating facilities and still have sufficient investment funds to stimulate industries that were intensive users of electrical power, it was the task of economic development economists to prioritize one of these two possible areas of growth, and then rely upon the positive effect of disequilibrium imbalances to push the economy forward as private entrepreneurs responded to the possibilities created by bottlenecks via the market.

The priority sector could be the upstream or the downstream industry. Excess capacity in social overhead capital could lead to the rapid expansion of private sector investments which would then subsequently utilize the excess capacity generated in the public sector, thus justifying its initial creation. On the other hand, were private sector investments to be prioritized, the need for a rapid increase in social overhead capital would subsequently manifest itself as the demand for electricity outstripped the supply; the profitability of more social investment would be made manifest. Bottlenecks and shortages of some inputs would create opportunities for profits for private entrepreneurs to fill in the gaps. These profits would attract other investors in search of profit windfalls created by such bottlenecks. Investments would flow into under-supplied sectors where prices and profits were rising. Perhaps this response would overshoot the needs of the market, thereby creating downstream opportunities for other businesses that could turn the new excess capacity and falling prices to their advantage.

Imbalances, or disequilibrium situations, would be conducive to further change; doing things "the wrong way around" could provide greater benefit than any other strategy in Hirschman's view. Basically, what Hirschman was explaining was how a market system responds to shortages and surpluses, but his contribution was to suggest how development planners might utilize market disequilibriums to stimulate economic progress.

Backward and forward linkages

One of Hirschman's best known and most creative ideas was that of **industrial linkages**. When one industry expands, it requires inputs from other industries to be able to produce. These are called **backward linkages**, that is, they are induced effects on the output of supplying industries. For example, coal mining and iron ore mining constitute backward linkages from a steel mill. On the other hand, when an industry sells and transports its production to other firms and sectors in the economy, these are the **forward linkages** of the original producer, that is, the induced effects of the output of the first industry in the direction of the final consumer. The metal fabrication industry and the chemical and paint manufacturing industry which use the output of the steel industry as their inputs would be forward linkages to the steel industry, and these industries might have further forward linkages to, say, the production of household stoves. Railroads or alternative forms of transport would enter the example as both backward and forward linkages to steel production and at each stage of production.

Thus, the production of one firm in one industry has a multiplicity of backward and forward linkages with firms in other industries in the domestic economy and, perhaps, abroad as well. In communicating the induced effects from one sector of the economy to another via shortages and excess capacity in Hirschman's unbalanced growth process, the size of potential backward and forward linkages were of paramount importance in evaluating where to locate the initial investment. Development strategies could be built around the maximization of the estimated stimulus of promoted industries in generating domestic backward and forward linkages.

Hirschman argued that the case could be made for large-scale capital-using projects, such as steel mills, if these investments could stimulate significant backward and forward linkages. Indeed, such investments could spark the creation of whole new industries, providing not only increased output, but also increased employment, and with rising levels of production, lower costs and lower prices to consumers as the benefits of economies of scale were reaped. Nor would such large-scale capital-intensive investments necessarily displace workers, as sometimes is alleged. In an empirical study which analyzed the relationship between industrial structures and employment in Latin America, Hirschman found that

> once the indirect employment effects (via backward and forward linkages) are taken into account, investment in large-scale (capital-intensive) industry turns out to be just as employment-creating as investment in small-scale (labour intensive) industry for the industrially advanced countries of Latin America.
>
> (Hirschman 1984: 97)

How might such linkages be measured? Even at the time Hirschman was writing, **input–output** analysis of national economies was being elaborated, based on the pioneering work of Wassily Leontief at Harvard. Using input–output tables, it is possible to calculate the impact of a change in the output of one industry on supplying backward-linked producers and simultaneously on the production of forward-linked industries that use the originating output as inputs. An input–output table is a matrix showing the multiplier effects of the impact on other industries per unit change of output in another industry, as well as on labor use, imports, and final demand. For any country seriously thinking about stimulating development, at least a simple input–output table and the required calculations are almost essential for effective decision-making and monitoring of effects.

Changing the social organization of the labor process

Hirschman advanced an additional reason for promoting a capital-intensive, unbalanced industrialization program in less-developed nations. Many social scientists had argued that an attitude of "achievement" needed as a precondition for industrialization was missing in both the labor force and in management in less-developed nations. It had been suggested that standards in the work place were exceedingly lax in less-developed countries, and that neither workers nor managers were willing to take responsibility for errors in production. Slack management techniques often made it impossible to assign culpability when tasks were left uncompleted or were not completed within the time-norm set for a particular task. Hirschman did not take issue with this characterization of the work place in the less-developed nations. Rather, he noted that with the introduction of more advanced, machine-paced techniques, it would become easier both to calculate reasonable work-norms and to evaluate both success and failure in completing tasks (see Box 5.2).

Hirschman thus advocated new forms of production on the shop floor that might "hot-house" the completion of the less productive handicraft and manufacture stages of industrialization and allow the less-developed countries to move quickly to the machino-facture stage and its higher level of productivity. Under simple, relatively labor-intensive manufacture, the human operative has a great deal of control over the pacing of and output of a machine, since the worker chooses how quickly to

---

Box 5.2 Achievement orientation in the work place

A study of Mexican corporations conducted by the international consulting company, Vertex, may illustrate the significance of achievement attitudes. In comparing output per worker in Mexico with similar firms in advanced nations, Vertex found that productivity was 50 percent below international work-norms. In the most complex operations relating to production and maintenance, productivity was only 40 percent of what might be anticipated elsewhere.

Only 55 percent of the work day was devoted to work; 17 percent of time was spent in office gossip and coffee drinking, and 28 percent of the day was lost to (1) inefficiency of personnel, (2) communication problems, (3) repeating work due to errors, and (4) repeating instructions to employees. Among the difficulties cited by Vertex were the lack of motivation of workers due to the unwillingness of management to delegate authority, the lack of communication skills and proper training of workers, and the high turnover of workers with minimum loyalty to the firm. These conditions, they stated, tended to create apathy and negligence and an "it can't be done" mentality in the work force.

Source: Crevoshay 1994: 11

---

work and how much effort to put into the production process. Under machinofacture, or more capital-intensive production techniques, however, norms and rates of production are pre-determined to a great extent by the pace at which the machines are engineered to operate. Workers and managers are faced with a situation that is much more "all or nothing": maintain the pace of work and the quality of output determined by the machines, or risk losing employment. This situation, argued Hirschman, forces a change in the labor process which could lead to a rapid rise in productivity and could force institutional and behavioral changes that would be conducive to further economic development. This is another example of a Hirschmanian "pressure point," or disequilibrium process, designed to disrupt the production process and society in a way that promotes a positive outcome.

New attitudes and expectations regarding the labor process, both at the level of the shop floor and in management, could be inculcated as a by-product, or positive externality, of this more capital-intensive industrialization as the pace of work is increasingly dictated by machines. Both traditional labor practices and often ritual management responses would be made untenable with the new rules of the game, and a new cadre of workers and managers would be created as a complementary effect of industrialization, with positive and cumulative spin-off effects for other industries. Hirschman felt that innovative attitudes toward efficiency and responsibility on the job would also be transmitted to society at large. A system built upon merit and performance eventually would threaten the outmoded social structure built upon privilege and ceremony, a system which far too often remains a source of inefficiency in the less-developed world.

Antagonistic growth

Like all the developmentalist pioneers, Hirschman was extremely optimistic about the possibility for progress in the less-developed world in the 1950s. In his *Strategy of Economic Development* (1958: 5), he stated that development depends not so much on finding optimal combinations for given resources and factors of production as on calling forth and enlisting for development purposes resources and abilities that are hidden, scattered, or badly utilized.

In a self-review of his own work in the 1980s, Hirschman struck a more sobering note. He defended his argument that development via excess capacity, or unbalanced growth, could be a viable strategy, while acknowledging that problems arising from resource scarcity also need to be given a more central role in conceptualizing the development process. Under conditions of resource scarcity – and all less-developed nations face scarcity, be it of investment funds or of skilled labor – an over-emphasis on a certain sector, such as industry, can mean that another sector, especially agriculture, fails to receive the inputs and support it needs to progress at a reasonable or desirable pace. Thus unbalancing development in one sector can leave another sector worse off, leading to what Hirschman termed an antagonistic growth process. In such a situation, Hirschman warned, further economic growth along the same lines will serve only to exacerbate existing levels of economic inequality. And this, of course, can lead to difficult if not explosive political struggles. So, both efficient allocation and effective reallocation of resources must be considered at the same time. It is not one or another that is most important for development.

Growth with unlimited supplies of labor

Another of the most important pioneers of early development economics is Sir Arthur W. Lewis who, along with Gunnar Myrdal, is one of only four development economists to have been awarded the Nobel Memorial Prize in Economic Science. Lewis's most cited work, and one of the best-known models in development economics, is his classic article on unlimited supplies of labor (1954). From 1970 to 1974, Lewis, who was born on St. Lucia in the Caribbean, was President of the Caribbean Development Bank, having previously held high-level positions at the United Nations in the area of development policy.

Like the other developmentalists discussed in this chapter, Lewis was quite optimistic that hidden reserves of strength could be tapped in the less-developed nations, and that by doing so, economic development could rapidly be promoted. He also shared their conviction that industrialization was the route the less-developed nations needed to pursue to escape poverty and reach a higher level of economic and social progress. Lewis's reasons for supporting industrialization, however, were quite distinct. He was not an "export pessimist." In fact, Lewis produced a major research work (Lewis 1969), the purpose of which was to demonstrate that tropical products and raw materials exports, the traditional primary exports of less-developed nations, were *not* subject to falling international prices resulting from supposed limits of the advanced nations to absorb these products. On the contrary, he drew the conclusion that rising incomes and rising levels of production in the already developed nations would call forth a stronger demand for tropical products and raw materials. Thus, the promotion of such exports promised higher levels of export income in future.

Despite this latent potential, Lewis nonetheless insisted that the wage level of the less-developed nations was moving upward at much too slow a pace; workers' incomes in the less-developed nations were falling further behind that of their counterparts in the developed nations. Lewis believed this growing disparity was the result of differences in the productive structures existing between the two areas. The already-developed nations had large industrial and manufacturing sectors, where many workers were employed, and relatively small agricultural sectors, using a relatively small proportion of the labor force. Just the reverse structure prevailed in the less-developed nations, where most of the labor force was occupied in rural areas, with agricultural production their primary activity.

Higher wages were paid to workers in the manufacturing sector compared to agriculture in both the developed and less-developed nations, though the gap was smaller in the already-developed nations, because productivity per worker was higher in both the industrial and agricultural sectors. Especially low incomes prevailed in the agricultural sector of the less-developed countries, where most of the population lived and worked, since output per worker also was quite low, primarily because of the lack of capital and the relatively primitive technologies in use. Thus the higher average income in the already-developed nations was a structural function of having more workers in the higher-productivity, higher-wage industrial sector relative to the less-developed regions.

While the less-developed nations often were portrayed by economists and policymakers as having a comparative advantage in the production of tropical agricultural goods and raw materials for export that should continue to be exploited, Lewis suggested that they also had a potential, hidden, dynamic comparative advantage in some types of manufacturing. At the time, this was still a somewhat unconventional view as applied to the promotion of manufacturing. It arose from his observation that wages in the manufacturing sector in less-developed nations were relatively low compared to those of the advanced nations. Since wages were an important component of costs in labor-intensive manufacturing processes, such as textile production, if the less-developed regions could restructure their economies toward this type of manufacturing, they could perhaps create comparative advantage based on their relatively lower wage costs.[12] Lewis actually was an "export optimist," believing that the small net addition to global manufacturing exports coming from less-developed regions would be easily absorbed by a growing world market. Thus a higher level of manufactured exports from the less-developed nations need not spark a defensive reaction in the advanced nations in terms of new tariffs and other barriers, because Lewis believed that the increases in labor-intensive manufacturing exports added by the less-developed nations to total exports would be dispersed throughout the global economy. He thus did not believe that any developed country would face a serious threat from manufactured export competition coming from the less-developed regions. Consequently, the developed nations would not resort to protectionism to stop the flow of new manufacturing exports.

Lewis wanted to advocate shifting labor away from agriculture and into industry. But, as a well-trained orthodox economist, he had been taught that switching labor from agriculture to industry would mean that agricultural production must surely decline with such a reallocation, assuming the marginal product of labor in agriculture to be greater than zero. Consequently, food prices might be expected to rise, as fewer farmers would be producing less output for a growing number of non-agricultural workers.[13] With rising food prices, industrial wages would need to rise to ensure at least a subsistence wage, and the potential comparative advantage of the less-developed country in producing labor-intensive manufacturing goods for export would disappear with the rising wages. Was there no way out?

Surplus labor

It was at this point that Lewis brought into development economics an important construct which had been widely utilized by Keynesian economists in analyzing the Great Depression (1929–1939) within the industrial countries in writing about disguised unemployment. What if labor in the agricultural sector was being utilized in an extremely inefficient manner, to the degree that, by taking agricultural workers out of this sector and employing them in industry, agricultural production would not decline at all, while industrial output was increased with the influx of greater employment? What if there were actually a *surplus* of agricultural workers, such that by transferring some labor from agriculture to industry the remaining workers could work longer hours, or more efficiently, and total agricultural production could remain constant or even rise?[14] Or, alternatively, agricultural producers who had been selling to the export market could replant their fields with an eye to the potential profits created by the growing domestic market resulting from the process of industrialization. In any event, Lewis reasoned, if there was surplus labor in agriculture, then that "hidden reserve" could be tapped for industrialization, and development perhaps would not prove to be so difficult to attain after all.

If industrialists were to pay a wage somewhat, say 30 percent, above the average wage prevailing in agriculture to cover the costs and discomforts of migrating to industrial areas and to compensate for the higher cost of urban living, then industrialists could hire all the labor they might want at a constant wage, as long as surplus labor conditions prevailed in agriculture. Industrialists could look forward to a double advantage. First, the absolute level of wages would be above but close to subsistence, yet domestic wages would be far below the wage prevailing in the advanced nations. Second, as industry shifted to higher and higher levels of production over time, more and more surplus agricultural laborers would be brought into the industrial sector. But wages in that sector would not have to rise at all, because the cost of food, the basic determinant of the wage level, would remain constant until the labor surplus was exhausted.

The Lewis surplus labor model

We can formalize the Lewis model along the following lines. Lewis presumed that the typical less-developed nation was **dualistic**, not only in having two key sectors, but in the sense that these sectors had little interconnection. There was a traditional, low-productivity rural and predominantly agriculture sector, where the great bulk of the population worked and produced what it consumed. But there also existed (or there could be created) an incipient modern capitalist sector, where production was more technologically driven and, accordingly, worker productivity was higher than in the traditional sector. The modern sector bought food, and perhaps other inputs, from the traditional sector for use in the production process, and the traditional sector provided labor to industry in the cities, but otherwise the links between the two sectors were weak.

It was in the labor supply link between the two sectors that Lewis found a transformation dynamic. His model can be explained by examining Figure 5.1(a) and (b). Figure 5.1(a) shows the marginal product (MP_L) and average product (AP_L) of labor curves in agriculture. Since Lewis assumes a surplus of labor in agriculture, it can be presumed that the $MP_L = 0$, so that L_A workers are employed in that sector. However, unlike the usual neoclassical assumption that workers are paid their marginal product, which, in this case, would mean agricultural workers would be paid nothing – clearly an impossibility – workers actually receive a wage, w_A, equal to their average product when L_A workers are employed. Why? In the traditional sector, it is presumed income is shared by the members of extended families. One can think of the production process being organized around the household, rather than by and for individual decision-makers. Work often is done collectively on family farms, where the marginal product calculation of the optimal use of labor inputs would be a wholly alien concept.[15] All family members may contribute to production in their own fashion; and all share in the fruits of the labor process more or less equally, regardless of the individual contribution to production.

If the industrial sector pays a wage w_I that is above w_A, then labor will be attracted from agriculture to industry (Figure 5.1(b)). Industrial capitalists, who are presumed to be profit-maximizers, will hire L_n workers: additional labor will be used until the industrial wage is equal to the MP_{L1} in the industrial sector.

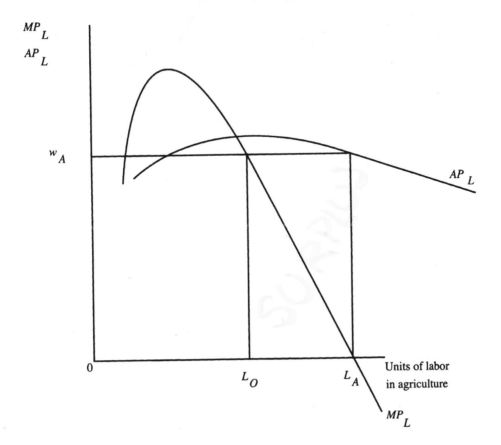

Figure 5.1(a) Lewis's surplus labor model: agriculture.

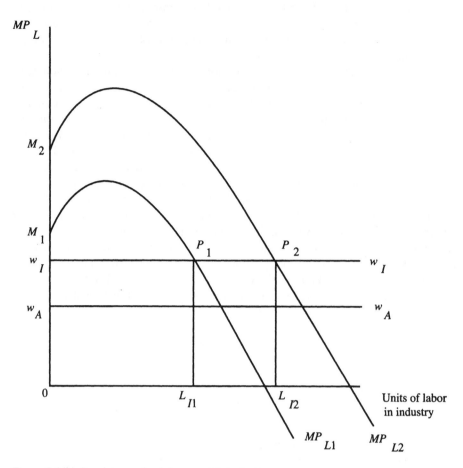

Figure 5.1(b) Lewis's surplus labor model: industry.

The industrial sector's total output is equal to area $OM_1P_1L_{I1}$; the workers' share of that income is equal to area $Ow_IP_1L_{I1}$, while the capitalists' share is area $w_IM_1P_1$.

When this profit or surplus is reinvested, in whole or in part, depending on other costs and considerations, the addition of new physical capital, and the technology embodied in that capital, will shift labor's marginal product curve in the industrial sector upward and outward, since the effect of more capital and more technology is to increase the productivity of labor. With increased investment, and hence the new MP_L curve, M_2P_{L2}, and given the labor surplus which keeps the industrial wage at w_I, L_{I2} workers now will be employed in the industrial sector. Thus, with continuing reinvestment from the profits of the modern sector, the transfer of labor from agriculture to industry is accomplished in the Lewis model, especially if the capital–labor ratio in industry does not rise very much – that is, as long as production remains labor-intensive. Employment in industry will rise, along with total national output.

The process of transferring labor from agriculture to industry will slow and eventually come to an end, of course. As labor leaves agriculture, the marginal product of labor, and its average product, must eventually rise as the labor surplus is exhausted. In Lewis's view, the upward pressure this puts on wages in agriculture will force producers in that sector to become more productive via the adoption of better technologies, thus forcing the "modernization" of the primary sector as well. Of course, this process happens gradually, rather than discreetly, as some agricultural producers embrace modern methods of production earlier than others, but the effect of a growing scarcity of labor in agriculture will require the use of greater amounts of capital and technology to save on labor. In the process, productivity and incomes in agriculture also will rise.

To keep this "virtuous circle" of labor transfer going once started, there would have to be more and more capital formation in manufacturing capacity, which would necessitate a higher level of savings which then could be transformed into investment. In Lewis's view, only the fledgling capitalist sector would save. Large landowners, monopoly bankers, mine owners, and other wealthy strata of traditional society, including the political elite, would be more likely to squander their economic surplus in ostentatious consumption and/or capital flight out of the country. Only by increasing the share of national income which accrued to industrial capitalists, Lewis reasoned, could the less-developed regions move forward, and this would be accomplished by the transfer of labor from agriculture to industry, shown in Figure 5.1(b).

The distribution of income

As Lewis defined the problem, his surplus labor model suggested a very rapid dynamic process would unfold. A significant and rapidly rising share of national income would be shifted to the national, industrial capitalist strata. As this class increased its productive investments by ploughing back its profits into new investments in pursuit of ever-greater profit, total national output would rise. But since wages would not rise as long as the labor surplus remained, a growing share of a growing total national income would accrue to the capitalist class. They, in turn, motivated only to increase production and profits further, would reinvest at an accelerated rate, thereby ensuring that national income would rise further. A perpetual-motion machine would be put into play, moving faster as time went on.

What would happen, though, when the unlimited supply of laborers was finally depleted? Lewis was unconcerned. At that point, the objective of the transformation of the economy would have been achieved. Wages for workers would rise, the standard of living would improve, and the gap between the poor and rich nations would have closed considerably. This Lewis saw as the inevitable and desirable end of the process he envisioned.

Lewis often has been accused of advocating a worsening of the distribution of income as a means to promote development. In his model, the share of income going to relatively well-off capitalists rises over time, as can be seen in Figure 5.1(b). Meanwhile, a small gap opens between the average wage in the agricultural sector and that of the industrial sector, to the disadvantage of agricultural workers, whose income remained relatively stagnant as long as there was surplus labor. Lewis was well aware of this criticism, but he felt that it missed the mark. Painful as it might be to contemplate, Lewis found no other way to foster growth. He pointed out that he was not advocating a worsening of the distribution of income. What he was advocating was economic development and a general rise in the standard of living, and he could see no other way to exploit the "hidden surplus" of disguised unemployment in agriculture without such an adverse, but temporary, increase in inequality between agriculture and industry (see Box 5.3).[16]

Joan Robinson put the matter well in another context: "The misery of being exploited by capitalists is nothing compared to the misery of not being exploited at all" (Robinson 1966: 46). In other words, the wage of the industrial worker is likely to be higher, and the standard of living better, than for the rural peasant or rural worker. The transition from agricultural poverty to a higher standard of living in industrial production was desirable, even if it engendered temporary inequality. One suspects that Lewis would have agreed with Robinson's pithy comment.

Box 5.3 Other dualist models of structural transformation

The Lewis model of unlimited supplies of labor is but one, though perhaps the best known, of a number of dualist models examining the transfer of labor from agriculture to industry.

The Fei–Ranis model   This was an extension and elaboration of the basic Lewis model, a major distinction being an upward-sloping labor supply curve after some amount of labor has been extracted from agriculture to industry. The Lewis model also envisages such a tendency, though it is not formalized as it is in the Fei–Ranis model. This was a theoretical contribution, and it does not detract from the basic Lewis conclusion that labor will be attracted from rural areas to urban industrial centers by a wage higher than that paid in agriculture, and that it is that transfer which contributes to the desired structural transformation of production (which will be examined in Chapter 9).

The idea that total national output and income per person could be increased by such a strategy of labor transfer, where the marginal product of labor in industry exceeded the marginal product of labor in agriculture, is the key insight of both the Lewis and Fei–Ranis models.

The Harris–Todaro model   Though traditionally the Harris–Todaro model is not categorized as a dual economy model, but rather one explaining rural–urban migration and urban unemployment and underemployment, it is in the tradition and spirit of the Lewis model. The Harris–Todaro model envisages workers in agriculture rationally choosing to migrate to urban, industrial centers in the pursuit of wages that, with some probability, are expected to be higher than in rural areas. Urban wages are higher due to many forces: higher productivity of workers, higher living costs of cities, and, perhaps, the "wedge" of unionization pushing wages above the market-clearing level.

As a consequence of a "too"-high differential between urban and rural wages, too many migrants continue to be attracted to urban areas relative to the number of urban, industrial jobs available in the formal sector. As a consequence, many migrants are forced into informal sector employment in low-productivity, low-income jobs: domestics, street vendors, beggars, jugglers, newspaper vendors, day laborers, and so on.

Further, urban slums emerge and grow, as the urban formal sector wage wedge relative to agricultural wages continues to draw migrants hoping to find formal sector employment. Thus the disguised unemployment or underemployment of some rural migrants becomes open unemployment, or the disguised underemployment of the urban informal sector.

Sources: Fei and Ranis 1964; Harris and Todaro 1970

Lewis subsequently broadened his definition of what contributed to a labor surplus, or disguised unemployment, to include:

1   individuals unemployed due to technical change in agriculture and industry;
2   the underemployed in rural areas;
3   the movement of women from the household to the labor force;
4   the surplus labor generated by rapid increases in population.

Of these factors, he considered the last the most powerful force for creating a labor surplus (Lewis 1984: 133).[17]

Utilizing the economic surplus

Although Lewis is best known for his article on unlimited supplies of labor, he later took a somewhat different approach to the development problem. He felt that more attention should be paid to the inordinately high level of consumption as a share of total income in the less-developed regions. Much of the income generated in less-developed countries was squandered in conspicuous consumption, and not just by capitalists, who were too small in number to have much of an impact and who, in any case, were presumed to save and invest much of their income in pursuit of future profit. Rather, it was residual classes, like landowners and plantation barons, as well as new groups such as financial manipulators and a political elite who were skimming-off part of aggregate income that could have been used for investment, who engaged in superfluous consumption (Lewis 1976: 257).

In order to reduce this waste, Lewis advocated raising the tax burden on the top 10, or perhaps the top 20 percent of income recipients to the point that government would receive 20 percent of national income. The state, in turn, would devote roughly 60 percent of those revenues, or 12 percent of national income, to basic public services, such as schools, hospitals, social security, and so on, and 40 percent of tax revenues (8 percent of national income) to public capital formation or social overhead capital. Thus, the mature version of the Lewis model should include *two* forms of investment that would be promoted: private-sector investment in manufacturing and industry deriving from the private capitalist, and public investment in social overhead capital, such as roads, communications systems, energy and so on, deriving from government decisions as to priorities. Of the two, Lewis felt that the role to be played by the state in taxing the unproductive elite and allocating national income to socially productive purposes to be far more important in future.

By 1984, Lewis had determined that political and economic matters could not be separated. Development was as much a matter of "getting public policy right," as of providing a constructive environment for the private sector, a view with a strong Keynesian resonance. Achieving development, Lewis seemed to say, was as much a question of political will as it was in finding the technical means. Sir Arthur continued to advocate a large increase in savings and investment, but he also emphasized that the only way to achieve this was to reduce the unproductive and wasteful consumption levels at the top of the income pyramid, especially of unproductive classes who continued to control significant economic and political resources.

Nowadays in most underdeveloped countries people know what economic growth requires; the difficulty is to make available the quarter of the national income which it costs. Personal consumption which should only be 75 per cent of the national income is nearer 85 per cent, leaving for the public services and for capital formation together only about 15 per cent instead of the 25 per cent they need.

(Lewis 1984: 256)

The legacy of the Lewis model

The Lewis model has continued to have an important influence in development economics (we shall use it again in Chapter 9). Subject as it was to a great deal of critical scrutiny, it is not surprising that many objections were raised. Most telling were two. First, the model ignored institutional factors which influence the level of wage determination in the industrial sector. Governmental labor standards, including minimum wages, and unions are absent from the model. In fact, many less-developed nations have introduced relatively advanced labor legislation, and unions often have been able to negotiate a wage far above that determined by the free play of market forces. Many of these institutional factors were introduced by, or were a reaction to, foreign transnational firms in mining and agriculture. These firms could easily afford the increase in their costs which would improve working conditions. However, via "target bargaining," such improved conditions can quickly become the bargaining norm for unions and workers in other industrial sectors not linked to the transnationals. The end result often has been to ratchet up wages for those workers in the industrial sector who have permanent jobs (i.e., who are not hired on a day-by-day or per-job basis). Thus rather than a constant industrial wage with some premium above the agricultural wage, industrial workers in some countries have been able to achieve substantial increases in wages, thereby eroding the potential comparative advantage in wage costs and undercutting Lewis projections for economic development by reducing the absorptive capacity of the industrial sector.

A second major objection concerned the socially virtuous behavior which Lewis assumed the capitalist strata would engage in, that is, the continued reinvestment of earnings in new production. Some have argued that the native capitalist strata may short-circuit the growth process through capital flight, rather than ploughing profits back into production; of course that possibility certainly exists. Lewis assumed that capitalists would have a high propensity to reinvest and that their earnings would not leak out of the country via capital flight or via the conspicuous consumption of luxury imports. Whether capital flight or reinvestment takes place, however, is not something that can be assumed. As we shall see in Chapter 15, governments interested in promoting economic and social development can help to create an internal economic environment attractive to domestic investors, particularly by keeping the inflation rate relatively low and stable. There are other aspects of the internal balance that are important, as we shall see, but there is no guarantee that capitalist profits will be reinvested, especially in an increasingly global capitalist economy.

There can be no question that capital flight played a major role in many less-developed nations in the 1980s, often contributing to an external debt crisis. However, to criticize the Lewis model in this context would appear to be inappropriate, for two reasons. First, Lewis's model was developed in the early 1950s when international currency and financial markets were in a shambles, and most nations maintained strict currency controls. Second, given Lewis's strong advocacy of governmental intervention in order to tap the economic surplus of high income recipients, it is doubtful that Lewis would oppose the reinstitution of currency controls to block capital flight. Nations, such as Brazil, that imposed currency controls in the 1980s suffered relatively little capital flight.

Stages of growth theory

The last developmentalist theory to be examined in this chapter is Walt Whitman Rostow's stages of growth analysis (1960). Rostow's writing on the economics of what he called the "take-off" into sustained growth quickly became influential, in large part because of his remarkable ability to use metaphors, such as the take-off, and his deft compaction of European economic history. Like Marx before him, Rostow sought a *universal* interpretation of history, and this he provided in his stage model. He argued that all nations pass through five phases: the traditional society, the pre-conditions for take-off, the take-off, the drive to maturity, and the age of mass consumption. Rostow built his theoretical analysis upon the history of Britain, as had Marx. In doing so, he utilized a framework that most economists and other social scientists knew quite well. The plausibility of his argument seemed to many to be well-anchored in historical dynamics, both because it seemed to fit quite well the British experience, which had long been the basis for countless generalizations in economics, and because many economists did not have a ready grasp of the economic history of the less-developed regions. Thus, the model projected by Rostow seemed to generally conform to what many economists knew, or at least believed, to be true.

Stage 1: traditional society

In defining his first stage of historical and economic development, Rostow was rather vague. He likened traditional society to that of medieval Europe, and more broadly to any society that was pre-Newtonian. That is, traditional society was pre-scientific. Scientific progress might occur from time-to-time, but there was no *systematic* mechanism which led to the introduction of scientific knowledge into the production process on a continual basis. Traditional society was dominated by a perspective which Rostow defined as "long-term fatalism." According to his formulation, traditional society was predominantly agricultural, with landholders playing a dominant role in the determination of political and economic power.

Although Rostow attempted to demonstrate a general theory of historical stages, it would seem his sketch of traditional society best fits Europe prior to the sixteenth century during its feudal period. He made virtually no effort to extend his analysis to the Third World. Were these vast regions, from 1500 to 1800 similar in any meaningful way to Europe, *ca.* 1400? Certainly the information surveyed in Chapter 3 on Colonialism demonstrates that this vast region was not traditional or unchanging – on the contrary the changes imposed by colonialism were revolutionary. Rostow neglected to forge the link between traditional (European) society and the societies in the Third World – because non exists.

Stage 2: the pre-conditions for take-off

After his brief sketch of traditional society, Rostow moved forward to the second stage, the pre-conditions for take-off. Here, under one stage category, we find two processes at work: the beginnings of a sweeping destruction of traditional society, and the gathering of societal forces which will propel it forward into the subsequent take-off stage. But in his emphasis on the destruction of traditional society, usually through an outside source, probably colonialism according to Rostow, he blurred the line between a nation which becomes colonized and the colonizing nation itself. The presumption is that both colonizer and colonized are swept forward through this stage, both benefitting from events which stimulate development. But, in the case of the colonized nations, Rostow fails to entertain the likelihood that the process of destruction will be so thorough that the colonized society will be set on a path that does not lead to take-off, but to stagnation.

Thus the processes of both entering and leaving a major transformational epoch is commingled in the same stage, without a detailed analysis as to how these two processes unfold. Rather than doing so, Rostow presents a shopping list of changes which he expects to arise during this stage, without much apparent regard to either causality or sequence. He states that new types of entrepreneurs and managers will appear in the private and public sector, banks will appear and investment will increase, particularly in infrastructure. Modern businesses will be created which will make use of new and sophisticated methods of production. As this process unfolds in the colonial or post-colonial regions, "reactive nationalism" sets the less-developed region on a new course, the drive for modernization (see Box 5.4).

Stage 3: the take-off into sustained growth

Our brief review of Latin America in the nineteenth century in Box 5.4 suggests that neither the role of "reactive nationalism" nor the existence of the profit motive appeared to be sufficient conditions to launch Latin America into its take-off stage. Rostow does not explain the movement from one stage to the next, and since he does not provide his reader with an interpretation of the nineteenth-century economic history of Latin America that would support his views, the Rostovian framework may be less universal than Rostow had hoped. Nonetheless, given the importance of Rostow's work in the field of development economics, it is useful to briefly analyze what he considers to be the key stage in the development process: the take-off. This stage is defined as emerging under the following simultaneous conditions.

> (1) a rise in the rate of productive investment from, say, 5 percent or less to over 10 percent of national income; (2) the development of one or more substantial manufacturing sectors with a high rate of growth; (and) (3) the existence or quick emergence of a political, social and institutional framework which exploits the impulses to expansion.
>
> (Rostow 1960: 39)

Furthermore, Rostow states that there must be a sweeping reallocation of resources devoted now to

Box 5.4 Testing Rostow's concept of reactive nationalism: the case of Latin America after independence

In attempting to test Rostow's hypotheses regarding the pre-conditions stage, the situation in Latin America in the early nineteenth century would appear to be an important case. Here we find, however, that the breaking of the colonial bonds did not lead to a full rupture with the past. Factions within the new nationalist elite fought among themselves for political control for another half-century, and then split into independent nations that mirrored the separated colonial vice-royalties that had kept the colonies divided from each other prior to independence. Moreover, the new nationalist elite classes were not interested in, or were not capable of, transforming their newly independent countries along the path that had been followed in Europe and the United States, that is, following a dynamic capitalist and industrial revolution. Rather, the goals of these new elite classes were relatively limited. They wished to gain the class privileges Spanish colonial policy had for so long reserved exclusively for pure-blooded European immigrants. Such a backward-looking elite was content to continue the pattern of exporting primary commodities begun under Spanish rule. This new dominant class of large landowners, merchants, and politicians, was certain to enrich itself through the expansion of such exports.

As we have noted in Chapter 3, throughout nearly the entire nineteenth century, raw material prices soared and the terms of trade moved, perhaps fortuitously, in favor of such products. Trade with the advanced industrial nations permitted the nationalist leaders to import the manufactured luxury goods to which they aspired as emblems of their social status. With easy access to vast reaches of land, much of it expropriated from the Catholic church and native Indians, the new nationalist elite was able to prosper by producing in the same technologically backward manner while utilizing more land, that is, using *extensive* forms of production.

Thus the Latin American elite by-passed one of the prime defining characteristics of the Rostovian second, pre-conditions, stage; they were not forced to utilize the latest technological advances in an effort to make each unit of land more productive, that is, they did not pursue *intensive* production methods. Contrary to Rostow, there was an obvious lag in the development of Latin America's essential infrastructure, such as banks, communications systems, and roads. And this, in turn, tended to reinforce the lag in the modernization of the productive apparatus, that is, a delay in the introduction and use of machinery, equipment, knowledge, and managerial strategies in tropical agriculture, mining, farming and ranching, let alone in industry. It was in the period after 1870 that Latin America's pernicious pattern of limited export diversity was consolidated. In some countries this was manifested by mono-export production.

Source: Dietz 1995: ch. 1

building up and modernizing the three non-industrial sectors required as the matrix for industrial growth: social overhead capital; agriculture and foreign-exchange earning sectors, rooted in the improved exploitation of natural resources. In addition, they must begin to find areas where the application of modern technique are likely to permit rapid growth rates, with a high rate of plow-back of profits.

(Ibid.: 193)

The take-off is to occur in the space of roughly twenty to twenty-five years. According to Rostow's dating, India began its "take-off" in 1952. Thus India, with a per capita income in 2000 of only $460, ranked thirty-sixth in terms of the poorest country in the world, should in fact have had by then a relatively strong economy. Yet in the period 1980–1991, decades past the presumed take-off stage, India's per capita growth rate was a disappointing 0.7 percent per year (per capita growth rose to an impressive 4.2 percent per year in the 1990s). Following the take-off, growth at rates well above the population growth rate was expected to be the normal condition. The take-off into sustained growth had faltered in India, apparently – an event that the stage model cannot even consider.

Critical responses to the concept of the take-off

As intuitively appealing as Rostow's list of conditions for take-off may be, it is disconcerting to note that a number of development economists who have reviewed the historical record have found that the concept does not accord with the history of most of the nations which have purportedly moved beyond take-off into "self-sustained growth." For example, Albert Fishlow argues that, in the now advanced nations, there was no major abrupt jump in either the rate of investment or the rate of growth of output for most nations (Stage 3 above). Rather, there was a gradual speed-up in the rate of investment and growth in most countries, and a sharp rise in investment and growth only in some (Fishlow 1976: 84–85). Simon Kuznets also argued (1971a) that a review of the economic history of the now developed nations showed no sudden significant rise in the rate of savings during what might be considered their take-off stage. Kuznets further pointed out that when the now developed nations moved into the take-off stage, they did so at per capita income levels much higher than those prevailing in the less-developed world currently (Kuznets 1971b: 224).

Gerald Meier elaborated on this point by concentrating his analysis on the agricultural sector. He drew a contrast between the robust agricultural sector of the nations which went through a take-off in the eighteenth, nineteenth and early twentieth centuries, such as Britain, France, Germany, the United States, Canada, and Australia, with the weak agricultural sectors generally prevailing in the less-developed regions.

> It is fairly conclusive that productivity is lower in the agricultural sector of underdeveloped countries than it was in the pre-industrialization phase of the presently developed countries. Although direct evidence of this is unavailable, it is indirectly confirmed by data suggesting that the supply of agricultural land per capita is much lower in most underdeveloped countries today than it was in presently developed countries during their take-off, and that there is a wider difference between per worker income in agriculture and nonagricultural sectors in the underdeveloped countries today than there was in the pre-industrial phase of presently developed countries.
>
> (Meier 1976: 95)

Meier pointed to another important difference between the conditions prevailing in the present-day less-developed regions compared to those that prevailed when the now developed nations entered into their initial period of rapid development: population pressures were relatively moderate in the past, whereas today an annual population rate of growth of 1.5–3 percent necessitates a much higher level of investment in order to move the economy forward fast enough just to keep per capita income constant. That is, what would have been considered a remarkably fast rate of aggregate economic growth during Britain's industrial revolution, 3 percent per year, is often the minimum rate of aggregate growth that must be attained in many less-developed nations today in order simply to maintain the existing, low standard of living per capita.

Furthermore, migration played a tremendous role in the economic performance of the now advanced nations during their early industrial period. For some nations, like the United States, Canada, and Australia, the influx of trained, ambitious, young immigrants was a clear economic boon. At the same time, the out-migration of young workers from Europe tended to eliminate both potential unemployment and social problems that might have arisen from structural unemployment. Lacking surpluses of labor, many of the now developed nations had a strong incentive to adapt new machinery and equipment which would dynamize the productive process.

Criticism of the takeoff have continued to be published. Nicolas Crafts' research confirmed the analysis of Fishlow and Kuznets. Based on more recent work he suggests that we "discard Rostow's linear model":

> Rostow's notion of the takeoff seems to be completely discredited. GDP growth [in England from 1780–1830] exhibited a steady acceleration over perhaps half a century … and there is no sign of the rapid doubling of the investment rate postulated by Rostow. The notion of a leading sector has also faired badly.
>
> (Crafts 2001: 312)

Stages 4 and 5: maturity and high mass consumption

Rostow's last two stages, maturity and high mass consumption, are defined sequentially as:

- A period wherein growth is sufficiently high so that there is significant increase in per capita income. The economy becomes diversified and technologically sophisticated, such that the society can now produce anything, but not everything, it chooses;
- A subsequent period where production is largely for the purpose of consumption, with relatively little concern for the need to further build production capabilities. Society is now devoted to the pleasures of consumer choice, the pursuit of security, and the enjoyments of the arts and leisure.

Rostow's legacy

In spite of the fact that it has been his fate to serve as a lightning-rod for criticisms from virtually all schools of thought in development economics, Rostow clearly made a powerful contribution. He forced other economists to review the experiences of the now-developed nations and to demonstrate the tremendous gulf that exists between the historical conditions which gave rise to the developmental success stories of the eighteenth, nineteenth and twentieth centuries and the experiences with patterns of distorted development, stagnation and economic decay that prevail in the less-developed world today. Rostow also opened the debate to another question in development economics. Did colonialism lead to the entrenchment of backward socio-economic forces and processes in less-developed nations which could not be displaced easily once political independence was achieved? A full exploration of this matter will be left for the following chapter, where we will review the work of a number of analysts who clearly argue that Rostow's main analytical error was to be found in his failure to incorporate the retarding and inhibiting forces of colonialism into his model.

While today little remains of Rostow's analysis which is of general use in the field of development economics, Rostow was clearly a pioneer in opening up new areas for study, debate, and analysis. Without his "big-picture" approach, many major issues might not have received a critical airing. Furthermore, Rostow's willingness to express his ideas within the difficult terrain of political economy forced those who would refute him to consider a broad range of factors at the analytical points of intersection of historical dynamics, political processes, and economic forces.

Questions for review

1 Contrast Nurkse's "export pessimism" with Lewis's views on development. In what respects do their apparently contrasting views on exports actually coincide, and where do differences remain?
2 In what sense would you argue that the economists discussed in this chapter formed a school of thought? What ideas did they tend to share?
3 How can a fair test of Rostow's stages model be formulated? Analyze the history of a specific economy to see if such a test can be made.
4 Why and how did Hirschman argue that by putting things the wrong way around, by actually creating disequilibrium, economic development could be promoted?
5 Why might unbalanced growth be easier, and less costly, for a poor economy to follow than a balanced growth strategy?
6 Briefly explain the ideas of virtuous circles. Can you give two different examples of virtuous circles that might affect a less-developed economy? Summarize the various forms of positive external effects and virtuous hidden effects which Rosenstein-Rodan utilized to argue that development could be achieved quicker than one might expect. Can you speculate on what a "vicious circle" might be?
7 What did Lewis mean when he wrote that there was a surplus of labor in agriculture? How does one measure that surplus? To what standard is labor in surplus, that is, in surplus relative to what?

Notes

1 Rosenstein-Rodan became an influential policy-maker after the war. He held a top-level post within the World Bank from 1947 until 1953, and from 1962 to 1966 he served on a key directive committee of the United States-sponsored development program for Latin America, known as the Alliance for Progress.
2 This is the situation of increasing returns to successive inputs of investment, so that if investment increases by x percent, output rises by more than x percent. For an aggregate production function of the form $Q = f(K, L)$, where Q is total output, K is capital and L is

labor, this means that both $f_K, f_L > 0$, but also that $f_{KK}, f_{LL} > 0$, that is, diminishing returns to the inputs to production have not yet been reached. If one draws the aggregate production function, it will have both a positive and increasing slope. Interestingly, the possibility of increasing returns, which seems to go against the grain of so much of both classical and neoclassical economic thinking and the law of eventually diminishing marginal return, is one of the pillars of the new, endogenous theories of growth considered in Chapter 8 that have become increasingly influential since the late 1980s.

3 Rosenstein-Rodan's argument illustrates an important example of a larger phenomenon in economics, called **market failure**. Whenever there is a divergence between private and social benefits, as in this instance, and/or private and social costs, an unfettered market economy may fail to produce the socially optimal level of output. What is desirable is to have the marginal social benefits of any action equal to the marginal social costs, but private calculations of benefits and costs may, and often do, differ from the social values. Basically, Rosenstein-Rodan was arguing that the inability of any single private entrepreneur to appropriate all the social benefits – in this case profits – of an action will result in an under-estimation of the total value of any private action. One entrepreneur's private investment decision, such as that of the steel firm, creates positive externalities that accrue to other potential entrepreneurs, such as the metallurgy industry, and/or, society in the form of increased opportunities, higher demand, and lower costs that resulted from the decision of another. Government intervention may be required in such circumstances, particularly when many persons or firms are involved, if the social and private benefits and costs are to be equated, and if the optimal and socially desirable level of output is to be reached.

4 The term "indivisibilities" was another of Rosenstein-Rodan's favorites. Unlike neoclassical economic analysis, which assumes that capital can be combined with labor in precisely optimal amounts on the assumption that there is an infinitely divisible set of combinations of capital and labor available, the concept of indivisibility is intended to illustrate production situations where fixed, minimum amounts of capital (or labor) are necessary. A little less, and the product cannot be produced. For example, in building a steel bridge, one cannot simply and infinitely substitute labor for capital inputs and still produce the bridge; obviously labor cannot completely substitute for capital and other inputs, like steel or bolts. The bridge will be engineered in such a way that a specific amount of structural steel will be needed; an amount somewhat less and there will be no bridge at all. Likewise in oil drilling, the drilling company either buys *all* of a drilling rig, or none. It is not a divisible item. In general, social overhead capital tends to be of this nature. Often Rosenstein-Rodan referred to the "lumpiness" of capital in this context.

5 Of course, government-sponsored projects can lead to over-investment or under-investment in social overhead capital. The developmentalists did not naively believe that every action of government was per se justified. If government does not employ *transparent* methods whereby officials can be held accountable for their actions and their spending of public funds, then the government itself can become one of the primary sources of social inefficiency. Without an efficient government bureaucracy, the state itself often becomes an arena where individual fortunes are amassed through the manipulation of public funds. Unfortunately in many less-developed nations, the most promising avenue for upward social mobility lies within the governmental apparatus where accountability is nearly non-existent and corruption is rife. This barrier to progress is one we shall have occasion to comment on again later in discussing "economic rents" and the relative economic success of the East Asian nations in recent decades.

6 This theme of "surplus" labor in agriculture is one that recurs again and again in the development literature. One of the leading theories of development, that of Sir Arthur Lewis, considered below, makes this basic assumption central to the structural transformation required for economic development.

7 Nurkse is best known for his book, *Problems of Capital Formation in Underdeveloped Countries* (1953). His remarkable essay "Patterns of Trade and Development" (Nurkse 1962), which constituted an attack on the idea of trade as the "engine of growth," was finished only a month prior to his untimely death in 1959.

8 This adverse effect of a lower price and greater quantity will occur, assuming demand to

be constant, as supply increases if the demand for the good is price inelastic. In such cases, the larger quantity of export sales will be insufficient to compensate for the lower price, and hence total export revenues will decline.

9   The **propensity to import** is technically defined from the statement, $M = mY$, where M is the value of imports purchased, Y is national income (GNP or GDP), and, m, which has a value $0 < m < 1$, is the "marginal propensity to import," that is, it is the proportion of income that society chooses to spend on imported goods and services. This proportion depends upon the level of average income, the income distribution of society, and social and cultural factors.

10 In modern economic analysis, such consumption items are referred to as **positional goods**.

11 It is not sufficient to simply produce more to have economic growth; if the increase in output is to be sustainable, it must find a market and be sold, or capitalist enterprises will stop producing.

12 This is simply an extension of the insight that was formalized early in the 1920s in the Heckscher–Ohlin theory of trade, which suggested that countries with an abundance of one factor of production over another, would, with free trade, tend to export those goods using the abundant, that is, relatively cheaper, input because that is where their comparative advantage would exist vis-à-vis other nations. Thus less-developed economies, with their abundant labor and scarce capital, could be expected to export those goods, be they agricultural or industrial, that were labor-intensive in their production and, by the Stolper–Samuelson theorem of international trade, this would be expected, over time, to lead to the equalization of income for the different factors of production within and among nations, assuming free mobility of capital and labor and perfect competition.

13 In effect, as labor left agriculture, the supply of agricultural output might be expected to decrease as the quantity of labor, L, in agriculture falls, while the demand for agricultural goods would, at best, stay the same, and might even be expected to rise if workers in industry have rising incomes. Thus, from simple supply and demand analysis, if the supply of agricultural output decreases (the supply curve shifts inward), while the demand rises (an outward shift), the equilibrium price of agricultural products must increase, given the assumptions.

14 In effect, what if the marginal product of labor, MP_L, in agriculture, at the current level of labor usage, is such that $MP_L = 0$? In such a case, extracting L from agriculture will not reduce agricultural output, if $MP_L = 0$, and will result in an increase in agricultural output if $MP_L < 0$. As long as the MP_L in manufacturing $> MP_L$ in agriculture, a shift of labor from agriculture to manufacturing will increase aggregate output.

15 In this instance, given w_A, which can be interpreted as the subsistence wage, the optimal quantity of labor to be employed in agriculture would be L_O, which is clearly less than L_A, the actual level of employment with the household calculation of labor usage in which income is shared and average income is distributed among family members.

16 Such an outcome in the transition from a surplus labor economy might be one explanation for the Kuznets' inverted U-hypothesis considered in Chapter 2, which also prognosticated a worsening of income distribution with economic growth, up to a threshold level of per capita income, after which the income distribution might be expected to improve.

17 Two very important theoretical models related to the Lewis model are the Fei–Ranis and the Todaro models. These are briefly explained in Box 5.3.

References

Crevoshay, Fay. 1994. "Complejos, Confusiones y Autoritarismo, Barreras para la Aplicación de la Calidad Total en México," *El Financiero* (21 abril): 11.

Crafts, Nicholas. 2001. "Historical Perspectives on Development," pp. 301–334 in Gerald Meier and Joseph Stiglitz (eds), *Frontiers of Development Economics.* Oxford: Oxford University Press.

Dietz, James L. (ed.). 1995. *Latin America's Economic Development*, 2nd edn London and Boulder, CO: Lynne Rienner Publishers.

Fei, John C.H. and Gustav Ranis. 1964. *Development of the Labour Surplus Economy*. New Haven, CT: Yale University Press.

Fishlow, Albert. 1976. "Empty Economic Stages?," pp. 82–89 in Gerald Meier (ed.), *Leading Issues in Economic Development*, 3rd edn Oxford: Oxford University Press.

Harris, J.R. and M.P. Todaro. 1970. "Migration, Unemployment, and Development: A Two-Sector Analysis," *American Economic Review* 60 (March): 126–142.

Hirschman, Albert O. 1958. *The Strategy of Economic Development*. New Haven, CT: Yale University Press.

—— 1984. "A Dissenter's Confession," pp. 87–111 in Gerald Meier and Dudley Seers (eds), *Pioneers in Development*. Oxford: Oxford University Press.

Hoff, Karla and Joseph Stiglitz. 2001. "Modern Economic Theory and Development," pp. 389–459 in Gerald Meier and Joseph Stiglitz (eds), *Frontiers of Development Economics*. Oxford: Oxford University Press.

Kuznets, Simon. 1971a. *Economic Growth of Nations*. Cambridge: Harvard University Press.

—— 1971b. "Notes on Stage of Economic Growth as a System Determinant," pp. 243–268 in Alexander Eckstein (ed.), *Comparison of Economic Systems*. Berkeley, CA: University of California Press.

Lewis, W.A. 1954. "Economic Development with Unlimited Supplies of Labour," *Manchester School of Economic and Social Studies* 22 (May): 139–191.

—— 1969. *Aspects of Tropical Trade*. Stockholm: Almqvist and Wiksell.

—— 1976. "The Cost of Capital Accumulation," pp. 256–257 in Gerald Meier (ed.), *Leading Issues in Economic Development*, 3rd edn Oxford: Oxford University Press.

—— 1984. "Development Economics in the 1950s," pp. 121–137 in Gerald Meier (ed.), *Pioneers in Development*. Oxford: Oxford University Press.

Meier, Gerald. 1976. "Future Development in Historical Perspective," pp. 93–99 in Gerald Meier (ed.), *Leading Issues in Economic Development*, 3rd edn Oxford: Oxford University Press.

Murphy, Kevin, Andrei Shleifer and Robert Vishny. 1989. "Industrialization and the Big Push," *Journal of Political Economy* 97 (October): 1003–1026.

Nurkse, Ragnar. 1953. *Problems of Capital Formation in Underdeveloped Countries*. New York: Oxford University Press.

—— 1962. "Patterns of Trade and Development," pp. 282–336 in Gottfried Haberler and Robert Stern (eds), *Equilibrium and Growth in the World Economy*. Cambridge, MA: Harvard University Press.

Robinson, Joan. 1966. *Economic Philosophy*. Harmondsworth: Penguin.

Rosenstein-Rodan, Paul. 1976. "The Theory of the 'Big Push,'" pp. 632–636 in Gerald Meier (ed.), *Leading Issues in Economic Development*, 3rd edn Oxford: Oxford University Press.

—— 1984. "Natura Facit Saltum," pp. 207–221 in Gerald Meier and Dudley Seers (eds), *Pioneers in Development*. Oxford: Oxford University Press.

Rostow, Walt. 1960. *The Stages of Economic Growth: A Non-Communist Manifesto*. Cambridge: Cambridge University Press.

6 Heterodox theories of economic development

After studying this chapter, you should understand:

- the importance of the distinction between the center and the periphery in structuralist theory;
- the Prebisch–Singer hypothesis on declining terms of trade for primary product exporters and the debate surrounding it;
- the role of import substitution industrialization according to the economists of the Economic Commission for Latin America and their subsequent critique of this policy;
- Ayres' concept of inhibiting institutions and the importance of education and technology to the institutionalist perspective;
- Gunnar Myrdal's seminal ideas about spread effects and backwash effects as examples of cumulative causation;
- the distinction between associated dependent development and the dependency perspective of underdevelopment;
- Baran's view of the equilibrium trap of underdevelopment; and
- the distinction between stagnationist dependency analysis and the classical progressive Marxist view of development as presented by Bill Warren.

Introduction

This chapter discusses and analyzes the ideas of economists and social scientists who have broken with economic orthodoxy and also have moved beyond the framework of the developmentalist economists considered in the previous chapter. These heterodox economists do not believe that relatively minor changes in economic conditions, such as an increase in foreign aid or a sudden increase in investment, will be sufficient to create the "big push" or the "take-off" into sustained growth, as did the developmentalists. In fact, many of the heterodox economists would argue that such limited changes, within the context of the existing structures and institutions prevailing in less-developed societies, might result in a strengthening of backward socioeconomic framework, consolidating adverse path dependence. For the heterodox economists, the changes required to propel the development process forward are more fundamental, more sweeping, and more profound.

Included among the heterodox grouping are a number of thinkers who hold no more in common than the fact that they vigorously dissented from the general premises and propositions of the developmentalist economists, and of orthodox economists, as well. In this chapter, then, we will trace the ideas of the Latin American structuralists, represented by Raúl Prebisch and Hans Singer; the institutionalists, represented by Clarence Ayres and Gunnar Myrdal; the dependency school, represented by Paul Baran and Fernando Henrique Cardoso; and the classical Marxist approach in its more modern form, represented by Bill Warren.

The heterodox thinkers reached their maximum point of influence within the field of development economics in the late 1960s and early 1970s.[1] Indeed, the impact of some of their views was so profound that their ideas exerted some indirect impact on the leading development institutions, most notably the World Bank. In the 1970s, these institutions embraced the basic needs (BN) approach, as is discussed in Chapter 17. As we shall see, the heterodox thinkers had much more ambitious hopes for change than those embodied in the limited goals of the basic needs approach.[2]

The Latin American structuralists

In 1948, as the result of a Chilean initiative, the United Nations agreed to form the Economic Commission for Latin America, known best by its acronym as ECLA. Unlike the UN's more technically oriented Economic Commission for Asia and the Far East, created in 1947, or the Economic Commission for Africa (1958), the ECLA was destined to become a center of advocacy for a distinct Third World perspective, and a hotbed of controversy. It was in and around the work of the ECLA that a Latin American school of structuralist economics was forged. The structuralists argued that the less-developed countries of the periphery were structurally and institutionally different from the developed nations of the center in ways that made some aspects of both orthodox economic theory and developmentalist theory inapplicable. In particular, the Latin American structuralists were quite suspicious of the Ricardian theory of comparative advantage and the alleged benefits of free trade among nations that supposedly derive from specialization and trade. In introducing the possibility of conflictive or adversial relations in trade, the Latin American structuralists challenged the "harmony of interests" assumption in market transactions that had been a cornerstone of economic thinking since Adam Smith (see Chapter 4). As Gabriel Palma explains, structuralism is concerned with the *totality* of a social system and the many forms of interaction of the component elements within that system.

> The principal characteristic of structuralism is that it takes as its object of investigation a "system", that is, the reciprocal relations among parts of a whole, rather than the study of the different parts in isolation. In a more specific sense this concept is used by those theories that hold that there are a set of social and economic structures that are unobservable but which generate observable social and economic phenomena.
>
> (Palma 1989: 316)

The structuralism of Raúl Prebisch

Perhaps the best-known Latin American structuralist economist was Raúl Prebisch (1901–1986). As a young man finishing his MA degree in economics at the University of Buenos Aires, he already had published six articles on economics, and his views and analysis were impeccably mainstream, orthodox, and neoclassical. During Prebisch's formative years, at least to the early 1920s, Argentina seemed to symbolize an outstanding example of the validity of the theory of comparative advantage, with producers having a cost advantage in producing beef and wheat for the world market. From the 1860s through to the second decade of the twentieth century, the Argentine economy grew at a rate that can only be described as spectacular, and the country's standard of living rivalled that of the great European powers. It certainly seemed that specializing in the export of a limited range of primary products to the world market was successfully contributing to the overall development of the country.

In the 1920s, Argentina began to experience difficulties with its primary trade partner, Britain, as the prices for its main exports began to fall. As the country incurred a growing foreign debt burden, trained observers, including Prebisch, viewed Argentina's troubles as transitory. By the 1930s, however, Argentina faced both the adverse effects of the Great Depression and the growing dominance of the world economy by the United States. Unlike the late nineteenth century, when Britain's thirst for Argentina's exports had seemed unquenchable, now Argentina had to confront the troubling reality that the United States had a relatively modest propensity to import, compared to Britain. Even worse, the United States had a surfeit of domestically produced beef and wheat and did not want or need Argentinian exports to the same degree that Britain had.[3]

Like most Argentinians who had experienced the favorable conditions of the late nineteenth and early twentieth century, Prebisch was extremely reluctant to revise his views on the Ricardian doctrine of comparative advantage (see Chapter 4). None the less, he eventually did so, with consequences which were particularly far-reaching. Much of Prebisch's work on questions of development policy pivoted on his willingness to draw a distinction between the timeless constructs of neoclassical economic theory and what he saw as the dynamic effects of real economic forces, particularly those existing between the already developed center nations, such as the European powers and the United States, and the less-developed **periphery nations** of Latin America, Asia, and Africa. Prebisch began to learn and grapple with the fact that behind the laws of demand and supply there often lurked power relations and quite dissimilar forms of production between nations.

In particular, Prebisch noted that during the Great Depression, the export prices of agricultural and other primary products fell much further and faster than did the prices of manufactured, or secondary, products. At that point, in 1934, Prebisch did not as yet have a theory as to *why* this asymmetry in the behavior of the export prices of primary and secondary products might be occurring, but he did begin to develop a critical perspective on neoclassical economic theory. According to Prebisch's calculations, in 1933, Argentina had to sell 73 percent more of its primary agricultural products into the world market in order to import the same amount of imported manufactured products as it had in the mid- to late-1920s, as a result of the asymmetric behavior of world export prices.

By 1937, Prebisch and his colleagues at the Argentine central bank had begun to develop a theory which would explain the relative collapse of the agricultural markets. In manufacturing, they reasoned, the supply of output was relatively price elastic; thus as demand decreased (from D_0 to D_1), so did the quantity supplied. The equilibrium price would fall, of course, but in a somewhat more limited manner, depending on the value of the supply elasticity, as shown in Figure 6.1, along supply curve S_M. In the extreme case, as with supply curve S_E, which is perfectly elastic, the decrease in demand has no effect on price, but only on the quantity traded in the market.

On the other hand, in the agricultural markets, supply conditions are dramatically different; suppliers, many of whom were small farmers with limited land, tended to plant or grow as much as possible, year-in and year-out. Supply was therefore relatively price inelastic. When demand decreased, the quantity supplied did not fall by much, but prices quickly and dramatically decreased, as shown along supply curve S_A in Figure 6.1. In the extreme case, which might be somewhat more common in agriculture than in manufacturing, the momentary supply curve would be perfectly inelastic, as for supply curve S_I, and all the decrease in demand would be transmitted as a lower equilibrium price for the agricultural good.

What might account for these differences in the supply response of primary product prices and for manufacturing good prices? Prebisch's early explanation was somewhat vague. Industrial producers of manufacturing goods could control supply, at least to some degree, whereas in agriculture, producers had failed to organize their production and control their output. In 1933, Prebisch became active in the

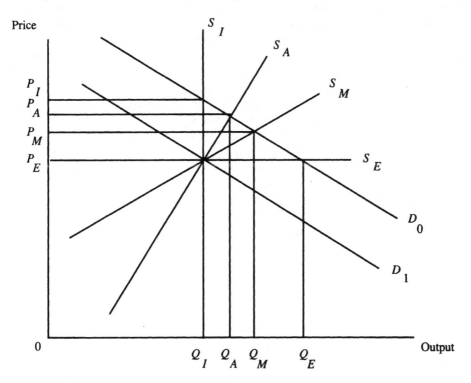

Figure 6.1 Elasticity of supply and equilibrium price adjustment.

attempt to form an agreement among the major wheat-growing nations of Argentina, Australia, Canada, and the United States to try to stabilize the world market price. Unfortunately, all the participants had violated the terms of the agreement by late 1933. This experience undoubtedly helped form Prebisch's perspective on the meager possibilities of coordinated actions undertaken among nations with the goal of controlling global agricultural output. But, at this point in time, Prebisch's explanation for the differences in the supply behavior of primary agricultural products and secondary manufactured goods in the face of changes in demand was mostly incipient.

The terms of trade

In mid-1948 Prebisch joined ECLA, having been asked to be its first director. At ECLA, Prebisch made a major and lasting breakthrough with his study *The Economic Development of Latin America and Its Principal Problems* (Prebisch 1950). This study was largely made possible by a UN report entitled *Relative Prices of Exports and Imports of Underdeveloped Countries*, which provided an empirical basis for a thesis that soon would become associated with Prebisch: given the existing international division of labor, in which the developed center countries produced manufactured goods for export to the periphery and the less-developed peripheral countries produced primary products for export to the center, *all* the benefits of trade would accrue to the center and none to the periphery. The periphery would have to produce more and more agricultural or raw material products simply to obtain the same quantity of imported manufactured products. Technically, this result was the outcome of a long-term deterioration of the terms of trade for the primary exporting peripheral countries.[4] Based on the years from the late nineteenth century to the late 1930s, the UN study had concluded that "On the average, a given quantity of primary exports would pay, at the end of this period, for only 60 percent of the quantity of manufactured goods which it could buy at the beginning of the period" (UN 1949: 7), and it was this data Prebisch used in reaching his conclusion on the detrimental effect of the existing trade patterns on the periphery.

Prebisch was soon to be the target of a number of attacks by those who argued that the methodology of the UN study was flawed. Unfortunately, the study was flawed, particularly in the sense that the prices used were not really comparable. The study measured British manufactured exports in terms of "freight on board" (F.O.B.) values, while British raw material imports were measured in terms of "cost including freight" (C.I.F.) values. The prices of exports at F.O.B. prices did not include shipping charges, while those of imports did. During the later part of the nineteenth century, rail and steamship charges dropped rapidly due to improvements in technology. Thus, by capturing the price benefits of technological change on only one side of the equation, British imports of raw materials, and excluding such changes on the other side, British exports of manufactured goods, the method utilized by the UN biased the results.

Was the conclusion Prebisch reached therefore incorrect? Controversy has stirred over this matter for over fifty years. Correcting for changes in both shipping costs and the changing quality of traded goods, studies conducted by J. Spraos have continued to support the basic hypothesis of Prebisch, as has research conducted by Prabijit Sarkar (Sarkar 1986; Spraos 1983). Spraos, for example, found that from 1950 to 1970, the terms of trade for primary products (in relation to manufactured products) decreased by 25 percent (Spraos 1980: 121–126). In a more recent study, D. Sapsford found a 1.2 percent decline per year in the net barter terms of trade (NBTT) from 1900 to 1982 (Sapsford 1985). Perhaps most startling is the recent confirmation of Prebisch's view by A. Maizels, T. Palaskas and T. Crowe, who show a decline of the NBTT of roughly 4 percent per year from 1979 through 1993 (Maizels *et al.* 1998: 74). More generally, Sapsford and J. Chen demonstrate that since Prebisch's ECLA study *none of the 10 major published empirical studies has refuted the Prebisch findings* – although two found no trend, perhaps due to the time period under analysis (Sapsford and Chen 1998: 28–29). When we examine the contribution to this debate made by Hans Singer, below, we shall elaborate on the mechanisms by which such a deterioration in international purchasing power might be explained.

If Prebisch was correct in believing that the terms of trade would move against the developing nations, then a successful development program would, of necessity, force a nation to either:

- adopt a program that emphasized *internal* changes which would restructure the peripheral economies more toward the domestic market and away from exports, or
- develop a new export strategy which would emphasize manufacturing and processing and other secondary production activities, rather than the export of raw materials, foodstuffs, and other primary products.

Abandoning raw materials exports, or de-emphasizing them, was viewed as a radical and theoretically unfounded step by the more orthodox within the economics profession, who continued to insist that it was in these goods that the less-developed nations had comparative advantage.

Import substitution industrialization as a response to declining terms of trade

At ECLA, Prebisch became known as the chief advocate of the "development from within" approach, a strategy that is often associated with **import substitution industrialization**, or ISI.[5] With ISI, a country begins to manufacture the simple, consumer non-durable goods that are being imported. As we shall examine in more detail in Chapter 9, this stage of industrialization involves relatively simple production and does not require either large physical or financial capital outlays or the use of sophisticated technology. If, in fact, the terms of trade were tending to shift against the periphery due to the structure of export production, an argument could be made for industrializing the peripheral economy so that it became more like the center nations in terms of its productive and export structure.[6]

Furthermore, even if the declining terms of trade argument proved to have no validity or were weaker than Prebisch had supposed, no one contested the fact that over the course of a normal business cycle, primary product prices tended to rise much faster during an expansion and to fall to a much greater degree during a contraction. Thus, there was a second argument for industrialization: greater overall economic stability could be maintained if the degree of industrialization was increased. Third, an industrial base might facilitate the transmission of technological advances from industry to agriculture – that is, a growing manufacturing base could create technological externalities in agriculture which would increase productivity and income.

The success of ISI required that governments restrict imports of goods that might compete with the new ISI industries through the imposition of effective tariff barriers. ISI also entailed an activist governmental policy in providing and allocating public expenditures to those areas where the highest rate of return could be anticipated. In Prebisch's words:

> The structural changes inherent in industrialization require rationality and foresight in government policy and investment in infrastructure to accelerate growth, to obtain the proper relation of industry with agriculture and other activities, and to reduce the external vulnerability of the economy. These (are) strong reasons for planning.... International financial resources (are) to complement and enhance a country's capacity to save, while changes in the structure of trade (are) necessary to use these savings for capital goods imports. Planning should help obtain these resources and accomplish the latter objective. Planning (is) compatible with the market and private initiative. It (is) needed to establish certain basic conditions for the adequate functioning of the market in the context of a dynamic economy. But it [does] not necessarily require state investment, except in infrastructure and development promotion.
>
> (Prebisch 1984: 180)

Prebisch did have some reservations regarding ISI. First, in order to promote industrialization, it would be necessary to import a considerable amount of technology embedded in machinery and equipment, or to obtain it under licensing agreements. Thus a new drain on already scarce foreign exchange earnings would be created. Furthermore, some of this technology would be more capital-intensive than previous production methods, meaning that expansion in the industrial sector would absorb a relatively modest amount of labor unless the level of investment increased substantially. There was thus a danger of structural unemployment, as young workers entered the labor force and migrants from rural areas entered the cities in search of industrial jobs at a rate faster than they could be absorbed. Finally, the domestic market was too narrow to permit the most efficient use of imported machinery and equipment. The economies of scale to be anticipated from large-scale industry would only be achieved if equipment was utilized at its peak rate, and given the relatively low incomes of much of the population, the demand for industrial output would quite likely fall short of what was required to move to the most efficient level of production. In spite of such reservations, Prebisch maintained that the anticipated benefits of leaving the treadmill of the agro-mineral peripheral export economy clearly outweighed the costs of industrialization.

Prebisch's advocacy of ISI did not initiate such policies in Latin America. ISI had been adopted in a number of Latin American nations since the 1920s, and in some as far back as the 1890s. For the most part, these ISI programs were extremely successful in their initial or "easy" stage in spurring growth in the Latin American economies. By the 1960s, however, the easy ISI stage had ended. As Prebisch moved on to head the UN Conference on Trade and Development (UNCTAD) in 1963,

ECLA itself became the source of increasingly strident attacks on ISI, as the optimism for what such a strategy might achieve, which ECLA had projected in the early 1950s, disappeared. ECLA's structuralist critique of ECLA's ISI concluded that these policies had resulted in:

1 a failure to diversify exports and a continued reliance on one or a few raw materials or agricultural products for export;
2 a shortage of foreign exchange earnings;
3 an increase in foreign debt;
4 a weak domestic agricultural sector, leading to major food imports; and
5 increasing foreign ownership of the economy by transnational corporations, leading to a drain on scarce foreign exchange as profits were repatriated

(Kay 1989: 39–46; Sunkel 1990: 137–139)

Thus ECLA, originally the crucible for initiatives which were based upon optimistic projections, became one source of critical analysis known as dependency theory. Dependency theory, to be discussed below, nearly inverted the early optimism of ECLA; development came to be viewed either as an impossible task, or one that demanded a major reorientation of the policies originally pursued by ECLA. We will argue in Chapter 10 that what was necessary was to go beyond ISI, something ECLA had promoted, but which governments in their policies failed to do, in Latin America at any rate. It was not so much ISI which had failed, but the deficiency of policy follow-up.

The contribution of Hans Singer to the terms of trade debate

Hans Singer, a German-born economist, received a PhD from Cambridge University in 1936, precisely during the period when J.M. Keynes' influence was reaching its zenith. In 1947 Singer, an ardent Keynesian, went to the United Nations as one of the first three economists to be employed in the newly created Economics Department. He remained there until 1969, when he became associated with the influential Institute for Development Studies at the University of Sussex in England.

Singer is perhaps best known for a widely cited research paper, the argument of which closely paralleled Prebisch's theory of the tendency of the terms of trade to fall for the periphery. Thus, in development economics, the theory that the terms of trade tend to move against raw materials and agricultural and primary producers is known as the Prebisch–Singer (P–S) hypothesis.

The Prebisch–Singer hypothesis

Prebisch had analyzed the relations between nations at unequal levels of development using the spatial imagery of the center and periphery. In this perspective, the more advanced center countries tend to reap the gains from international trade and investment at the expense of the less-developed periphery. Indeed, trade relations between the center and periphery reinforce higher levels of development in the center countries, while maintaining a relatively lower level of development and poverty in the periphery. In Prebisch's and Singer's analysis, then, free trade can actually be harmful to the peripheral, less-developed nations. This view, of course, is in diametric opposition to the very basic orthodox economic contention, from the time of David Ricardo at least, that the pursuit of comparative advantage in international trade will benefit all participating nations and that, in time, income levels between different regions of the world should tend toward equality as a consequence of the equalizing tendencies set in motion by the movement of goods and factors of production with free trade.

The reasoning behind the P–S hypothesis, that the relations between the center and the periphery are antagonistic and detrimental, rather than complementary and harmonious, is derived from three bases. In essence, the existing economic, productive, and labor market structures of the center and the periphery are sufficiently different to the degree that engaging in trade can be detrimental to the periphery, for the following reasons.

The application of technology to traded goods, predominantly manufactured goods for the center and primary products from the periphery, has quite different consequences. The advanced center countries are dominated by oligopolistic industries with a substantial degree of control over the prices of their final products; in other words, they are "price-makers." Further, unions and widely accepted social convention dictate that rising worker productivity from technological change be rewarded with higher incomes. In the periphery, on the other hand, most primary products, that is, agricultural goods and many minerals, face substantial domestic and, especially, international competition in trade, so the supply price is difficult to control by individual producers, who are classic, competitive "price-takers." Labor, particularly unskilled labor, is generally in some degree of surplus in the periphery, and this puts downward pressure on wages. Unions and pro-labor social attitudes, particularly in the primary sector, are not as strong in the periphery, so the institutional mechanism present in the center for raising wages with increased productivity as a result of advances in technology is lacking.

Given these structural differences, the application of new, cost-saving technology in the center would contribute to greater worker productivity and hence higher wages. However, there would be little tendency for output prices to reflect falling unit costs due to oligopolistic pricing by firms. Corporations would thus see their profits rise, as they shared with workers the fruits of technological progress in higher incomes. In the periphery, however, where something closer to the competitive "ideal" is common in many primary product lines, the introduction of new technology results in falling output prices, as the industry supply curve shifts out and downward with technological progress. Stagnant, and perhaps even declining, wages for workers is the result, given the labor surplus conditions characteristic of the rural sector and the lack of social mechanisms for demanding higher incomes with greater productivity.

Thus, according to the P–S hypothesis, the center nations gain doubly from new technology and trade with the periphery, while the periphery becomes worse off as a result of a deterioration in their terms of trade that results from the price movements on center exports and periphery exports. In effect, with the constant spread of new production technologies in the world economy, the P–S hypothesis predicts that the prices of what the periphery sells on the world market will decline, while the import prices of what the periphery purchases from the center remain about the same. Just the reverse is true for the center nations, which find their terms of trade, and hence the purchasing power of their exports, rising.

As a result, the center nations are able to buy the periphery's cheaper imported primary products with their own higher-profit manufacturing exports and with higher wages for workers, while the periphery nations find that new technology only forces the prices of their exports down on the world market, thus requiring more to be exported just to be able to purchase the same quantity of manufactured imports from the center. All the benefits of new technology, which is constantly advancing, thus accrue to the already-developed nations, as their incomes rise and the prices of what is imported from the periphery fall.

The center realizes all the benefits from trade over time; the periphery gains nothing. Any benefits from comparative advantage were realized long in the past in the first period of specialization, when a shift of production in the direction of the lowest relative opportunity cost (as discussed in Chapter 4) result in a one-time gain in world efficiency. Since that one-time gain, however, the P–S hypothesis argues that the declining terms of trade for the particular goods in which the periphery has specialized have made primary product specialization by those nations a source of impoverishment, rather than a means to increase income and welfare.

Embedded in this critique of trade is an obvious policy recommendation. To avoid declining terms of trade for its exports, the periphery should become more like the center, particularly through greater industrialization. With time, imports of manufactured goods would become less necessary. Basically, the escape from the Prebisch–Singer dilemma requires the periphery to follow a path of structural change similar to that traced by the center nations before them; as we shall see in Chapter 9, that is what import substitution industrialization as an initial strategy for development was at least partly about.

According to the P–S hypothesis, then, less-developed countries that continue to follow traditional comparative advantage by persisting with primary products exports will not benefit from trade, due to the tendency for their terms of trade to deteriorate. The theory of comparative advantage may provide a one-off boost to world production such that all countries gain, but over time, primary product exporters will not profit from staying with that static comparative advantage. Singer believed that he and Prebisch had been quite successful in alerting the developing countries to their dilemma, and that these countries had, in many instances, responded correctly by either diversifying their exports or developing their own internal markets via ISI policies. "We do not know what the data would have been without such action – the deterioration in terms of trade would presumably have been even sharper than it was" (Singer 1984: 283).

Additional factors contributing to declining terms of trade

Besides the tendency for the ever-changing impact of technology to result in declining terms of trade for the primary product, given the existing domestic and international structures of production and trade, Prebisch and Singer identified two additional forces at work in the world economy that tend to move in the same direction and which reinforced the Prebisch–Singer effect.

First, differences in the income elasticities of manufactured versus primary commodities, especially agricultural goods, work over time to the detriment of the periphery.[7] In essence, as world income grows, the demand for manufactured goods, which have an income elasticity >1, rises faster than the demand for agricultural products, with an income elasticity that is positive, but <1 (this is the essence of **Engel's Law**), thus contributing to the secular, or long-term, deterioration of the terms of trade for the periphery. The differences in income elasticities for the exports of the center and periphery simply reinforces the need for peripheral industrialization, as suggested by the P–S hypothesis, along with the need for international commodity agreements to stabilize primary product prices, and regional integration to expand existing markets and increase competitive pressures on firms.

The second contributing factor to declining terms of trade for many peripheral countries, and certainly those in Latin America, was the lower level of the import coefficient in the United States than in Great Britain, already mentioned. As the United States replaced Great Britain as the world's major economic power, it became more difficult for some countries to expand traditional exports to be able to earn the foreign exchange required to purchase the desired manufactured imports, again supporting the argument for expanded industrialization in the periphery.

There is by now a substantial body of research over the P–S hypothesis, evidence that generally supports the Prebisch–Singer prediction of the long-term evolution of primary product export prices and the deterioration of the terms of trade facing nations that specialize in the export of these commodities. Oil, of course, has been a partial exception to this tendency in some decades, and a limited number of other primary-based goods (e.g., tropical drinks) show a long-term tendency toward rising prices. And even a few countries in the region, at least since the Second World War, have had rising terms of trade over some periods, but the overall trend would seem to be downward for primary product exports (see Focus 6.1 and Figure 6.2).

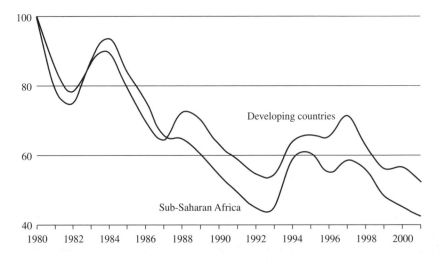

Figure 6.2 Declining real commodity prices: 1980–2001[a] (1980 = 100).

Source: World Bank Economic Policy and Prospects Group, World Bank, *Global Development Finance*, www.worldbank.org/prospects/gdf2002/.

Note
a Excluding petroleum products.

FOCUS 6.1 THE TERMS OF TRADE DEBATE

Debate over the terms of trade of primary product producers has raged since Prebisch and Singer published their hypothesis of a long-run downward trend. Recently, support for the Prebisch–Singer hypothesis came from an unexpected quarter: the IMF.

Prices of commodities other than energy products are near their lowest levels this century in real terms. And given that prices have been trending downward over most of the past 95 years, nonenergy commodity exporters should be studying how to accommodate the drift in prices and not how to resist it, . . . [M]ost of the commodity price declines have been too persistent to be cyclical and, for purposes of policy design, can be assumed to be permanent.

The following data illustrate the nature of the deterioration of the terms of trade for developing countries.

	average % change/year
Raw materials, 1957–1987	−0.78
Raw materials, 1968–1987	−1.52
33 Commodities, 1979–1993	−3.6 to 4.2

Changes in demand in developed countries, better technology, which saves on the use of primary products in manufacturing production, and substitutes for some primary products (such as rubber) mean smaller markets for primary product producers and more difficult demand conditions.

What can primary product exporting countries do, according to the IMF report, to reduce the impact of declining terms of trade for their exports? Economies which evolve away from depending upon primary product exports and begin to substitute manufactured goods exports, such as has occurred among some of the East Asian economies, have a chance to transform themselves into economies structurally more similar to the center developed economies, just as Prebisch had recommended. Becoming an exporter of manufactured goods is the best protection against declining terms of trade.

At the same time, the IMF study notes the importance of improving the productivity of the agricultural sector which does remain. The transformation toward a diversified range of exports, in which manufactures dominate, cannot ignore the need to transform traditional agriculture into a modern, productive sector as well.

Sources: IMF 1994: 350–352, based on Borensztein *et al.* 1994; Maizels *et al.* 1998: 74; Ocampo 1995: 134

Structural characteristics and the terms of trade

In a recent work, Singer has taken pains to clarify a point that neither he nor Prebisch had adequately emphasized in their early work; it may be more important to analyze the *structure* of a nation than it is to simply distinguish between the nature of exports. That is, economic structure may be a more important explanation of the direction of the terms of trade than whether a country is a raw materials or manufactured goods exporter.

It will be noted that some of the ... explanations for a deteriorating trend in terms of trade of developing countries relate as much or more to the characteristics of different types of *countries* – their different level of technological capacity, different organization of labor markets, presence or absence of surplus labor, etc. – as to the characteristics of different *commodities*. This indicates a general shift in the terms of trade discussion away from primary commodities *versus* manufactures and more towards exports of developing countries – whether primary commodities or simpler manufactures – versus the export products of industrial countries – largely sophisticated manufactures and capital goods as well as skill-intensive services including technological know-how itself.

(Singer 1989: 326)

There is a growing body of evidence that supports this insight that declining terms of trade may be associated not so much with the structure of exports, as with the institutional and economic structure of the less-developed countries per se. Thus, even as the periphery diversifies exports and adds manufactured exports to its tradables, the deterioration in the terms of trade may still be observed (see Focus 6.2).

Not only did relative price conditions continue to move against the poorest nations in recent years, Singer also emphasized that relative changes in the volume of trade had also cast the poorest nations in a disadvantageous position:

FOCUS 6.2   ARE THERE ADVERSE TERMS OF TRADE FOR SOME MANUFACTURED GOODS?

Using official IMF and UN data, the results on manufacturing terms of trade are conflicting. For the period 1960–1980, UN data show a 0.77 percent per year increase in the terms of trade of manufactured exports from less-developed countries. Covering a slightly different period, IMF data reveal a −0.88 percent per annum *decrease* in less-developed country manufactured goods terms of trade.

If the latter figure is correct, it may suggest that, at this point in time, less-developed countries tend to produce and export manufactured products in highly competitive international markets, for example, for textiles, shoes, and toys. The same pressures on prices when there is technological change would be likely to be working on these commodities as on primary products and agricultural products, just as the P–S hypothesis suggested. This downward tendency of the terms of trade for manufactured exports would fit Singer's concern that it is not the products, per se, being exported by the less-developed economies, as it is the structural characteristics of the countries (surplus labor) and of the markets where the exports are sold (highly competitive) that is important. In a study of the terms of trade for manufactured products between developing nations and the EU, Maziels, Palaskas and Crowe found an annual decline of −0.30 1960–1994, with the decline accelerating after 1980. They note that the volume of manufactured products exported to the EU has risen faster than the fall in prices. East Asian high-technology exports faired better in terms of their terms of trade than did any other region.

If Singer and other observers are correct, then countries need to look to produce commodities, be they agricultural or manufactured, for which the demand is more income elastic and for which competition is perhaps not so fierce. For example, one agricultural export that has been successful for Chile has been wine. Wine is a **non-traditional** primary product export, and it is one for which demand is quite income elastic. Further, competition is not perfect, so countries with outstanding or niche products have a chance to experience increasing terms of trade.

Sources: Maziels *et al.* 1998: 75–83; Ocampo 1995

in overall terms, and in spite of the group of fast-growing LDC [less-developed countries] exporters of manufactures, the volume lag of LDCs is clear. Between 1948 and 1970, world trade volume (excluding the socialist countries) increased by 7.3 per cent a year, but the export volume of LDCs by only 5.3 per cent. In the decade 1970–80, the figures are 5.8 per cent and 3.1 per cent respectively. For the least developed countries, typically primary exporters, the respective growth rates were only 4.4 per cent [for the 1948–70 period] and a dismal −0.4 per cent for 1960–70. At least in this relative sense, volume changes have increased any gap created by the worsening terms of trade and in that sense trade pessimism has not been proven wrong.

(Singer 1984: 295)

Like Prebisch, Singer remained a strident critic of neoclassical policy-making and of the effects which unmediated market forces tend to impose on the poor nations.

The role of foreign aid

Convinced as he clearly was of the unequal effects of market outcomes for the poor relative to the advanced nations, it is hardly surprising that Singer advocated non-market offsets to compensate for the effects of *laissez faire*. Singer was, indeed, perhaps the most outspoken and relentless advocate of foreign aid among the heterodox economists. He maintained that aid could take many forms, such as buffer stock purchasing programs for primary products to temporarily offset falling raw materials prices, and "soft loans," that is, lending made at below the market rate of interest to the poorer nations to permit them to build up their infrastructure and/or make other long-term social investments. Such projects, Singer believed, would very rarely, if ever, find private-sector backing. Singer devoted much of a decade to an attempt to create a soft-loan fund at the UN to be known as SUNFED, the Special United Nations Fund for Economic Development. Because the UN expected to control this fund and to distribute much-needed credits on a multilateral basis, and without regard to the foreign policy priorities of either the United States or the United Kingdom, these nations systematically blocked attempts led by Singer to operationalize this fund.

The institutionalists

Institutionalists believe that the institutions of an economy, that is, the forms of production, ownership, work processes, and ideologies which combine to create an economy and society, are the proper subjects for economic analysis. Since, furthermore, such institutions are subject to evolutionary change, the process of studying economics should also properly be evolutionary. This is clearly not the case for those who postulate that economics is the science of choice and that the function of economics is to discover the laws of the economy, just as a physicist might attempt to understand the laws of physics. While institutionalists have not made development economics their primary focus, there have been notable contributions. We shall consider but two, the American economist Clarence Ayres, and the Swedish Nobel Prize winner in economics, Gunnar Myrdal.[8]

The Ayresian view of development

Clarence Ayres (1891–1972) was one of the leading proponents of an American school of institutional economics, centered from the 1930s to the 1960s at the University of Texas, Austin. Ayres was dismissive of much of mainstream economics, and his references to development economics occur within a much broader framework. Ayres was interested in a "megatheory" of development, which would have application to both the advanced and the poor nations alike. At the center of Ayres' theoretical structure on the "how" of economic development are two fundamental forces: technology and ceremonialism.

Technology

Ayres placed more emphasis on technology than on any other factor which contributed to economic development. Technology, to Ayres, arose from a combination of tools and human beings, with the latter actually defined as "tool-users." Past tools lead to future tools, because human beings are so constituted as to be endowed with "the inveterate restlessness of human hands and brains" (Ayres 1991/95):

> the technological process can be understood only by recognizing that human skills and the tools by which and on which they are exercised are logically inseparable. Skills *always* employ tools, and tools are such *always* by virtue of being employed in acts of skill by human beings. Once the dual character of the technological process is understood, the explanation of its dynamism is obvious. Technology advances by virtue of inventions and discoveries being made.... But all inventions and discoveries result from the combining of hitherto separate tools, instruments, materials, and the like. These are capable of combination by virtue of their physical existence ... no one ever made a combination without there being something to combine. Furthermore, the more there is to combine in any given situation the more likely inventions and discoveries become.
>
> (Ibid.: 90–91)

For Ayres, technological progress and economic development were virtually synonymous.

Ceremonialism

Unfortunately, this "restlessness" which speeds forward the technological process can be curbed or limited by **ceremonialism**, the dichotomous opposite of technological dynamism. Ceremonialism imposes a curb on human creativity; in its essence, it is any past-binding behavior that tends to thwart the forward progress that technology imparts. There are five ways in which ceremonialism intrudes on any society, according to Ayres:

1   the nature of social stratification or class structures;
2   via social mores or conventions of what is acceptable behavior;
3   ideology which justifies the existing social stratification and mores and which

further attempts to emphasize the negative consequences of changing either the social strata or the mores;

4 a social system of indoctrination which emotionally conditions individuals to accept the dominant ideology, mores and class and social stratification; and

5 social patterns of ceremonial behavior designed to reinforce the first four factors.

Which of the two elements – past-binding ceremonialism that tends to retard the pace of change, or technological dynamism which expands human potentiality – is dominant at any point in time is the determining factor in establishing a country's pace and level of development. For Ayres, all societies, developed and less-developed, have ceremonial and technological forces at work in them at the same time, often within the same organizations and institutions. Ayres insisted that economic development is the consequence of the successful triumph of technology over ceremonial behavior. Ceremonial structures assign privileges to some classes, while they condition the population to resist social and economic change. Successful development, in the Ayresian view, thus requires a revamping of those institutions, and the behavioral patterns that accompany them, which continue to be detrimental to the creation of an indigenous technological capacity (this need is discussed more fully in Chapter 13).

The central role of education

In Ayres' view, the means to diminish the negative effects of ceremonialism on technological progress was via expanded education, which he defined as the diffusion of knowledge and skills. Of course, organized educational institutions can be hostile to "educating" and be a determined element in society's efforts to inculcate and perpetuate the prevailing ceremonial structures. Indeed, this is often the case with educational institutions in poorer nations, even through the university level. Still, Ayres felt strongly that expanded educational opportunities for larger numbers, or what we will later call **human capital accumulation**, was the surest means for any society to promote economic and social progress:

> [T]he most important factor in the economic life of any people is the educational level ... of the community. A technically sophisticated community can and will equip itself with the instrumentalities of an industrial economy. There is no instance of any such community having failed to do so.
>
> (Ayres 1995: 94)

Economic development in the Ayresian perspective is thus indistinguishable from technological progress, and without continuing technological change economic development falters.

Technological change is the result of scientific discovery, experiment and innovation. The successful introduction of technology into the domestic production process in any country, what can be called domestic innovation, requires a scientific establishment capable first of adopting and adapting foreign-produced technological knowledge to local conditions and, later, of conducting its own research, designing its own experiments and recognizing the potential and sometimes actual dangers of its own discoveries when applied to the domestic economy. In short, a developing nation must attain an independent technology learning capacity. This is the first step toward greater technological self-sufficiency.

While Ayres' work does not address the particularities of any developing society, and while it is difficult to link his unique form of analysis to that of the other hetero-dox thinkers, he addressed issues of crucial importance which complement the other perspectives presented in this chapter. And while Ayres had no major influence on mainstream thinking, his views on the importance of technology, the significance of education and other human capital creation, and the need for creating an appropri-ate institutional structure that is supportive of sustainable economic and human progress is one that is quite compatible with the viewpoint of the endogenous growth theories to be examined in Chapter 8. Thus, by isolating issues stressed by Ayres, one can explain a very significant proportion of the successes of the East Asian economies in recent decades. (We consider such matters directly in Chapters 8, 9, 10, and elsewhere in the remainder of this text.) So although Ayres' own writ-ings perhaps exerted little influence at the time, the thrust of his approach and his insights into the sources of growth and of the barriers to progress are substantially the same as the perspective behind much of the recent scholarship on the growth process.

The institutionalism of Gunnar Myrdal

Gunnar Myrdal's contribution to the social sciences has been remarkable, particu-larly for its breadth. A Swedish-educated economist, Myrdal (1898–1987) won the Nobel award in economics in 1974, ironically sharing it that year with one of the most fervent supporters of the free market, Frederick von Hayek. G.L.S. Shackle, a noted Cambridge economist, maintained that had Keynes not achieved renown for his revolutionary innovations in macroeconomic theory, the early work of Myrdal indicated that he would have supplied the same theory. Myrdal and his wife, Alva, made fundamental contributions to the development of the welfare state in Sweden, and Myrdal's study of American racism (1944) has remained a classic study of race relations. His massive work, *Asian Drama* (1968), established his reputation as a development specialist, which began in earnest in 1957 with his *Economic Theory and Underdeveloped Regions*.

In his later book, Myrdal drew three main conclusions which he sought to further support and demonstrate in his subsequent research.

1   "In the absence of counteracting policies inequalities would tend to increase, both internationally and within a country" (Myrdal 1984: 152).
2   International trade theory was biased against the poor regions, particularly in the contention that trade in commodities would tend to equalize factor prices, especially wages.
3   Greater income equality, rather than inequality, was the correct basis to achieve enhanced economic growth.

We shall examine briefly the significance of each of these three propositions.

Cumulative causation and backwash effects

Each of these three propositions was, in Myrdal's view, directly linked to the others, and all could be understood through an appreciation of what Myrdal termed **cumulative causation**. This concept sought to account for dynamic economic effects which progressively moved a society away from equilibrium. Myrdal assumed that there were notable inequalities between the regions of poor nations – that is, there was "dualism," as discussed earlier. What happens when a less-developed nation receives a stimulus to growth? If, as is likely, this stimulus is experienced in the more prosperous region of the economy, then that region will surge even further ahead, leaving the more economically deprived regions of the economy lagging behind.

This cumulative causation will occur for many reasons, only a few of which can be summarized here, but all of the reasons lead to a movement in society away from equalization among regions and sectors and toward increasing inequality. First, more ambitious and better-trained workers will migrate from the poorer regions to the growing regions. This will leave behind a bifurcated population of the young and the old in the poorer areas, a population largely composed of dependents and low-productivity workers compared to those who leave. At the same time, in backward rural areas, there is likely to be a higher rate of fertility, leading to a more rapid rate of population growth that puts increasing demand on a smaller number of the least productive workers, pushing down income per person in these poorer rural regions. Thus movements in any one direction tend to be cumulative, exacerbating poverty and sustaining low levels of development where they exist and favoring and expanding upon economic development and progress where they already exist. The cumulative movements which tend to economically weaken a region were termed **backwash effects**.

Secondary backwash effect also might be anticipated. If the economic stimulus took the form of the expansion of industry in the economically more advanced region of a country, the output of the new firms might well compete with the peasant and artisan production methods prevalent in the poorest region. Artisan production might then be undercut by the economies of scale realized by manufacturers in the more advanced region of the country, slowly disrupting and then displacing artisan and small manufacturing industry in poor, rural regions. Such effects could be accelerated if the more economically advanced region of the country became more involved in international markets.

The **spread effects**, or positive externalities, of such a new growth stimulus might induce other, linked domestic manufacturing needed to support an expanded export sector, à la Nurkse's "balanced growth" or Hirschman's "linkage" models considered in the previous chapter. One might think that such effects would be a plus for development. Myrdal, however, cautioned that proper analysis demanded an understanding of both the positive impact of spread effects and the negative impact of backwash effects. Benjamin Higgins neatly summarized this aspect of Myrdal's thinking:

> The spread effects could outweigh the backwash effects only if income and employment in the leading sectors grew relative to that of the laggard sectors, as they did in the now advanced countries. In underdeveloped countries, however, the historical pattern of growth has been weak. The rural sector did not produce

the raw materials for the expanding industrial sector, nor did the expanding industrial sector rely heavily on the rural sector for foodstuffs. Thus the growth of the industrial sector did not much expand the market for cash crops of the rural sector.

(Higgins 1959: 351)

The pattern of production in most less-developed countries reflected the legacy of colonialism and neocolonialism. The structure of the economy was one wherein a predominance of backwash effects arose because of past institutional arrangements, rather than on the workings of the laws of comparative advantage. The failure of investments in the export sector to generate multiplier effects sufficient to swamp the backwash effects arose from the lingering effects of colonial policies and adverse path dependence. In the advanced nations, investments in the raw material sector created new opportunities for manufacturing and processing, as well as for banking and shipping. But Myrdal argued that in most Asian and African countries, colonial policy was concerned only with advancing the key sectors owned or controlled by the advanced nations. Therefore, the stimulus to banking and insurance, shipping, processing, and manufacturing occurred primarily in the advanced nations, rather than in the colonial or post-colonial regions. The very weakness of the spread effects, coupled with the strong backwash effects, virtually guaranteed that the latter would dominate the former in the poor nations.

The state

For Myrdal, a crucial difference between the advanced nations and the poor nations was to be found in the strong state in the former and the weak (or soft) state in the latter (Myrdal 1970: ch. 7). With a strong state, the advanced nations could develop a coherent national policy which could address the question of the manner in which the benefits of economic growth might be spread through the economy. This was due to the fact that, to some degree, the state has some power to influence and direct the growth process. On the other hand, in the poor nations the state lacks effective policies to either ensure that there is a movement toward national economic integration or to address the impact of backwash effects.

Myrdal noted that one of the major weaknesses of the state in the less-developed nation is that it is an institution of, and for, the top social strata. He did not believe it likely that redistribution of wealth and income could be achieved via income and wealth taxes. The rich would only evade these, since they effectively controlled the taxing authorities through their political power. The elites thus did not fear state power. On this point, Myrdal noted that in Singapore, economic development proceeded to a certain degree, because it was "one of the few States in the underdeveloped world which actively fought against corruption" (Myrdal 1984: 158).

Myrdal's institutionalism

Myrdal utilized an institutional approach, but in a manner largely distinct from Ayres. Myrdal believed that one could not understand the sources of economic underdevelopment nor address the problems of underdevelopment as long as analysis was restricted to the intellectual constructs of orthodox economics, such as the theory of comparative advantage.

> The institutional approach meant enlarging the study to include what in a summary way I referred to as "attitudes and institutions". They were found to be largely responsible for those countries' underdevelopment and would have to be changed in order to speed up development.
>
> (Myrdal 1984: 153)

Only radical institutional reforms would allow for development. Some examples of such changes needed might be land reform, a campaign against corruption, and displacement of the elite from the commanding heights of state policy. In short, the causes of underdevelopment and the cure for poverty were to be found in the study of and changes in the "attitudes and institutions" of the less-developed nations. Economic theories about saving and investment, "big push," "balanced" or "unbalanced" strategies were hardly enough.

Dependency analysis

Dependency analysis became extremely fashionable, particularly in Latin America, and later in Africa, in the late 1960s. Dependency analysis built on the ideas of the structuralists, specifically Prebisch's distinction between the center and the periphery. The center was viewed as *cause* and the periphery as *effect*. According to dependency writers, the less-developed nations had to be understood as part of a global process. Their fate was merely to provide the inputs to the advanced nations or to receive their cast-off, low-wage manufacturing processes under trading conditions which were likely to worsen. Dependency theory found the causes for the lack of development to be *external* to the socio-economic formations of the less-developed nations. Thus, alleged internal backward or dysfunctional institutions of the less-developed nations were not treated seriously by dependency writers as a subject of analysis, or were seen as extensions of external domination. Internal institutional structures, such as the role of state corruption, large and unproductive land holdings, the extreme concentration of wealth, unresponsive political institutions, and so on, were played down. Instead, the negative influence of transnational corporations, multilateral institutions like the World Bank and the IMF, and the extensive influence of foreign governments in the internal affairs of less-developed nations were highlighted.

Several factors contributed to the rise of dependency analysis. Of utmost importance was the sway of "modernization" theory on social science analysis and policy, which promised quick and sweeping development, as suggested in the developmentalist theories considered in Chapter 5. As was noted there, Rosenstein-Rodan, Nurkse, Hirschman, Rostow, and others had maintained that the attainment of development for the less-developed countries was only a matter of time. Since most nations had already reached the "pre-take-off" stage, using Rostow's stage categorization, spectacular results were to be anticipated in little more than a decade. Yet, in the 1950s and 1960s in most of the less-developed nations, growth was only modest. Population growth had slowed gains in per capita income. Furthermore, confirming Myrdal's work, a process of cumulative causation leading to greater dualism could be observed. Economic growth had created poles of prosperity in a sea of despair. Shanty-towns and slums ringed the new and fashionable city centers. Water quality was abysmal, state schools were pathetically incapable of offering an adequate education, for most people health care remained either non-existent or minimal, transportation was a daily nightmare, and the average diet remained rudimentary and inadequate. New woes arose, or were first analyzed, in these decades: environmental pollution and degradation accelerated, while work-place hazards mounted, as new chemicals and substances were introduced into the production process.

True, a new techno-bureaucracy of government functionaries, applied scientists and engineers, financial operatives, and managerial cadres now shared some of the income with the agro-export elite in some nations. A skilled middle class had formed, and they had experienced tangible social mobility. But for the working classes and small farmers who made up the bulk of the population, the changes wrought in the 1940s through to the 1960s were both traumatic and cruel.

It is not possible to find one dependency writer who could serve as an exemplar of this school of thought. Indeed, in what may well stand as the classic attempt to summarize and detail the ideas of the Latin American dependency writers, Cristóbal Kay referred to their works as a "Tower of Babel" (Kay 1989). While the gradations and subtleties of positions defy condensation, we have, following Kay, utilized a logical division: Marxist dependency analysis and non-Marxist dependency thought. Even this distinction, unfortunately, is less crisp than it might appear at first glance. The dependency writers were nothing if not eclectic, and borrowing from Marxism and employing Marx's categories and concepts was never treated as "trespassing," even by the non-Marxist theorists.

Marxist dependency analysis

Paul Baran was, at the high-water mark of McCarthyism in the 1950s, the only known Marxist economist to hold a tenured professorship at a major US university, Stanford. Unlike Marx, who believed that capitalism had a dual role of "destruction and regeneration" to play in the colonial regions, Baran emphasized the destructive side of capitalism in less-developed regions, but could find scarce evidence of "regeneration." Rather, twentieth century **monopoly capitalism**, unlike the earlier form of competitive capitalism which Marx had scrutinized, had, according to Baran, a vested interest in maintaining backwardness and dependence in the periphery.

It might be argued that Baran initiated the analytical process which later led to the flowering of the pessimistic and stagnationist dependency school in Latin America and Africa. Baran's favorite example of the destructive effects of capitalism was that of India. He found that many Indian social scientists had discussed and developed concepts very similar to those employed by the dependency writers, but that they had done so as early as the late nineteenth century, having experienced the full force of British imperialism (see Chapter 3).

Baran's theoretical point of departure was an analysis of what he termed the **economic surplus**. This is defined as the mass of resources, actual and potential, which a society could have at its disposal in order to facilitate economic growth; it is the amount that might be reinvested in productive ways to increase the future level of social output. This "surplus" is that residual left over out of total income after a society's basic needs have been met for food, clothing, shelter, and human companionship. But this surplus may be grossly misused. It may be utilized to erect sumptuous and multiple residences for the rich, or it might be wasted through a variety of other forms of conspicuous consumption. The military or the church may make tremendous demands on the surplus, or it may be drained away by a foreign power via plunder or simple profit repatriation, as a result of foreign control over a less-developed economy's most important industries. Baran's study of the history of the less-developed regions under colonialism led him to argue that the source of their poverty was to be found in the extraction of this surplus. Had this surplus, or a large portion of it, been used for investment rather than for waste, then the poor regions would have been transformed.

Colonialism, however, blocked the potential for change. Baran summarized in one short paragraph the broad history of colonialism, condensing in the process a tremendous amount of material, striking at the very essence of the colonial legacy:

> To oppression by their feudal lords, ruthless but tempered by tradition, was added domination by foreign and domestic capitalists, callous and limited only by what the traffic would bear. The obscurantism and arbitrary violence inherited from their feudal past was combined with the rationality and sharply calculating rapacity of their capitalist present. Their exploitation was multiplied, yet its fruits were not to increase their productive wealth; these went abroad or served to support a parasitic bourgeoisie at home. They lived in abysmal misery, yet they had no prospect of a better tomorrow. They existed under capitalism, yet there was no accumulation of capital. They lost their time-honored means of livelihood, their arts and crafts, yet there was no modern industry to provide new ones in their place. They were thrust into extensive contact with the advanced science of the West, yet remained in a state of the darkest backwardness.
>
> (Baran 1957: 144)

Reviewing the history of colonialism, Baran drew an extremely powerful conclusion.

> Thus the peoples who came into the orbit of Western capitalist expansion found themselves in the twilight of feudalism and capitalism, enduring the worst features of both worlds.
>
> (Ibid.: 144)

National capital, foreign capital, and the state

Potentially, Baran argued, there were three forces which could both increase the economic surplus and harness it for economic development. These three potential sources for socio-economic change were national capital, foreign capital, and the state.

Regarding the first, Baran acknowledged that in some of the poor nations ISI had changed the structure of the economy. But he also maintained that ISI had failed to go far enough, and that, in fact, the end result of ISI would be the perpetuation of a fragmented and disarticulated national economy dominated by pervasive monopoly and oligopoly firms.

> The new firms, rapidly attaining exclusive control over their markets and fencing them in by protective tariffs and/or government concessions of all kinds, blocked further industrial growth while their monopolistic price and output policies mini-mized the expansion of their own enterprises. Completing swiftly the entire journey from a progressive to a regressive role in the economic system, they became at an early stage barriers to economic development rather similar in their effect to the semi-feudal landownership prevailing in underdeveloped countries. Not only not promoting further division of labor and growth of productivity, they actually cause a movement in the opposite direction. Monopolistic industry on one hand extends the merchant phase of capitalism by obstructing the transition of capital and men from the sphere of circulation to the sphere of industrial pro-duction. On the other hand, providing neither a market for agricultural produce nor outlets for agricultural surplus labor and not supplying agriculture with cheap manufactured consumer goods and implements, it forces agriculture back toward self-sufficiency, perpetuates the idleness of the structurally unemployed, and fosters further mushrooming of petty traders, cottage industries, and the like.
>
> (Baran 1957: 176)[9]

As to the second potential source of change, Baran agreed with Hans Singer, whom he cited in this regard, that foreign investment, while clearly a *potential* source of development, actually failed to have an impact on more than a narrow, isolated portion of the national economy. Not only did he emphasize the enclave effect of foreign investment, Baran took the analysis one step deeper, arguing that foreign capital diminished the possibilities of economic development. This was so, Baran argued, because in order for the foreign mining and agro-export capitalists to gain a foothold in the less-developed areas, it was necessary to form an alliance with the merchant capitalists who dominated politically and economically within these regions. These relatively backward elements, with semi-feudal and semi-capitalist ideologies and behavioral traits at one and the same time, were actually strength-ened by foreign investment. And, in turn, the institutions which they sought to per-petuate, Ayresian-type ceremonial or retarding institutions, also were bolstered by the enhanced revenues which flowed into the possession of the national strata of bankers, speculators, semi-feudal landlords, and political operatives.

In Baran's view, foreign investors in mining, oil and gas, and agro-export firms learned quickly to become hostile to genuine economic development as promoted through ISI. He listed four reasons for such opposition.

1   higher wages and tolerance of unionization meant lower profit margins;
2   foreign capital would become a targeted source for increasing state revenues, meaning that higher taxes and royalty payments would be imposed;
3   foreign exchange controls limiting the amount of funds which could be taken out of the country as repatriated profits would be imposed; and
4   tariffs on imported wage goods would be utilized to protect domestic manufac-turing, thereby raising the likelihood that workers would demand higher wages to maintain their living standard, thus cutting into profits.

As to the third potential source of the surplus, in theory the state could break this deadlock by opting for new programs which would make ISI ever more dynamic and successful. In fact, however, the state in the less-developed regions seemed incapable of performing the crucial role or in making the decisions needed to move forward on any front that would advance development.

For Baran, following the capitalist road in the less-developed regions was to steer a course which would eventually lead not to Rostow's society based on mass consumption, but rather to an economic and social graveyard. Only by turning to socialism could the less-developed countries reasonably expect any relief from their poverty.[10]

Associated dependent development: non-Marxist dependency theory

One of the most noted non-Marxist dependency writers was Fernando Henrique Cardoso, who has had an active career as a Brazilian sociologist/economist with a worldwide reputation, and also as a powerful Brazilian politician, rising to be President of Brazil from 1994–2002. While most dependency economists argued that the nations of the periphery were capitalist, they suggested it was a particular kind of *peripheral* capitalism. One of the defining characteristics of this mutation was economic stagnation, or "the development of underdevelopment," in the catchy rhetoric of Andre Gunder Frank, another of the eminent dependency writers.

Cardoso, however, did not embrace this stagnationist perspective. Rather, he maintained that the economies and societies of the periphery had evolved and could continue to do so (Cardoso and Faletto 1979). There had been three major stages in the economic history of the less-developed countries. First was the agro-export stage of the colonial period, when economic dualism was prevalent. During this stage, the pre-capitalist sector of artisans, petty producers, and peasant producers had accounted for the bulk of all economic activity. Some sectors of the economy were integrated into the world economy, particularly the production of precious metals, minerals, and tropical products which were exported to the world markets. Production of these export products often took place in a modern semi-capitalist enclave.

Second, after the First World War, a major transformation in some of the less-developed economies, especially those of Latin America, had occurred with the creation of what Cardoso called the "developmentalist alliance." The strategic locus of this transformation was ISI. A new social structure of accumulation had been formed on the basis of common or cooperating interests of industrial workers, industrialists, governmental workers, and some powerful individuals in shipping, banking, and the agro-export sector who had made the change from the agro-export model of accumulation to that of ISI.

Eventually, however, the developmentalist alliance had been replaced by an authoritarian-corporatist regime. In this third stage, the populist orientation of the state, which had been characteristic of much of the ISI stage, had given way to drastic curbs on democracy, unions, the universities, and other areas of society where dissent might be encountered and tolerated. The weak welfare state developed in the ISI stage, in which social security and minimum wage legislation, public health care, and public education had been expanded for at least some part of the population, gave way to drastic cuts in the public service aspect of the state's budget. Above all, in this stage, the transnational corporations (TNC) were welcomed and accommodated in the less-developed nations. In fact, the TNCs became pivotal in the new process of accumulation and were central to the growth process.

Although this new capitalist model was extremely accommodating to the interests of the TNCs, Cardoso argued, the TNCs were not all-powerful. The nations of the periphery needed the TNCs due to their ability to control and reproduce technology and complex capital goods. But the TNCs also needed the nations of the periphery, as their middle- and upper-income consumers had become an important source for final TNC sales. The peripheral labor force, kept docile and cheap by the authoritarian state, was necessary to keep costs down in an era of global competition.

Under this new regime, in which the authoritarian state and TNCs cooperate, some economic growth and development does occur. GDP rises; even the standard of living for the masses may improve. The continued stagnation that some dependency writers, like Frank, argued was the fate of the less-developed nations was neither theoretically plausible nor, even more importantly, argued Cardoso, was it empirically founded. One should not anticipate economic stagnation, or be surprised at a certain degree of economic progress in less-developed nations. Nor should one view the peripheral nations as powerless to shape their destiny, simply buffeted about by outside forces. Rather, a new form of capitalist accumulation was at work, which Cardoso termed **associated dependent development**.

Cardoso did not view this new stage, or its particular characteristics, as immutable. The poor nations had a certain capacity to bargain with the TNCs and the advanced nations and they had certain, but limited, opportunities to develop their own technological capabilities. The question was how, within this new structure, the poor nations were to respond. Innovation could have certain rewards. On the other hand, Cardoso found that the yearnings for a revolutionary rupture with the world system, as voiced by many dependency writers, was unfounded. By attempting to portray a situation of submissive dependency and stagnation, many intellectuals had hoped to stimulate a political shift toward revolution. Cardoso disagreed with the thrust of this analysis; the economic situation of most less-developed nations no doubt was difficult, the state had ceased to attempt to combat some of the most noxious problems in their nations, but the growth created by the new alliance between domestic capital and the transnationals under dependent development opened up some new possibilities for elements of the working class, the techno-bureaucracy, and the state to progress. At least for some less-developed nations, there was reasonable hope for modest reform and some limited autonomy, within the context of a new, more globalized, system of production. Less-developed nations may "depend" upon outside technology and finance via TNCs, but Cardoso believed that good state policy would permit less-developed nations to take advantage of the reciprocal needs of the TNCs in the less-developed countries, so that the poorer countries could obtain some of the positive effects of TNC investment and some of the benefits of economic growth would be shared within the poorer countries (see Focus 6.3).

Cardoso did not see dependency as necessarily a "zero-sum" game, in which the periphery lost and the center nations gained, as the stagnationist dependency writers believed. Rather, the current world economy provided opportunities for "positive-sum" games in which both the developed and less-developed nations could "exploit" each other. Growth in the periphery was possible, but achieving it depended on having the appropriate internal policies to gain advantage vis-à-vis the TNCs.

FOCUS 6.3   DEPENDENCE AND THE SEMI-PERIPHERY

By the late 1970s a chorus of voices dissented from the simple center–periphery dichotomy of many dependency writers. The periphery, as destined to stagnation without a break with the world capitalist system, was increasingly seen as an incomplete, and inaccurate, description of the socio-economic conditions and the dynamic of change at work in some parts of the less-developed world, as Cardoso also argued.

It was true that some nations seemed caught in a post-colonial torpor, continuing to specialize in one or a few raw material exports. These non-industrializing nations, it was suggested, could best be described by what did not exist, but needed to be in place, if they were to develop. These nations were thus described as the **dependent economies**, stuck on the periphery of progress. They seemed incapable of autonomously altering their economic structures, stuck with adverse path dependence born of colonial structures carried over into independence.

Some less-developed nations, however, were growing and industrializing rapidly. For these economies, the term **dependent development** was applied by those who accepted this new way of looking at center–periphery relations. These were countries in the periphery, but which seemed to be changing their economic structures. Economic growth, often quite rapid growth, was taking place. These countries (Mexico and Brazil often were singled out), did not fit the stagnationist perspective of the original dependency analysis, but neither did they fit the pattern of independently developing nations.

In another path-breaking attempt to present an alternative to the stagnationist dependency perspective, Peter Evans defined "dependent development" as a situation which included:

> both the accumulation of capital and some degree of industrialization on the periphery. Dependent development is a special instance of dependency, characterized by the association or alliance of international and local capital. The state also joins the alliance as an active partner, and the resulting triple alliance is a fundamental factor in the emergence of dependent development.

Although economic growth is achieved, countries engaged in a process of dependent development suffer a variety of ills:

> a regressive profile of income distribution, (an emphasis on) luxury consumer goods as opposed to basic necessities ... underutilization and exploitation of manpower resources ... [and the] frequent reliance of foreign firms on capital-intensive technologies [which] increases rather than solves the unemployment problem.

Politically, a nation at the stage of dependent development is categorized as being in the **semi-periphery**, neither in the periphery nor in the center. Could nations undergoing dependent development ever graduate to the status of "core" nations? Dependent development theorists, such as Evans and Cardoso, did not rule out the possibility.

Sources: Evans 1979: 32; Evans and Gereffi 1982: 113

Classical Marxism

While the dependency and other heterodox perspectives discussed in this chapter were under heavy attack from more orthodox development economists, an attack was also mounted from the political left.

Bill Warren, a former lecturer in Economics at the University of London, provided a cutting and intelligent critique of both non-Marxist and Marxist dependency analyses. His ideas were extremely controversial, and his untimely death in 1978 foreclosed the possibility of a meaningful dialogue with his many critics.

Warren's position was that capitalism continued to be a progressive force for change wherever it operated. The capitalism sweeping into the less-developed regions of the world at a rapid rate may manifest signs of social pathology, but they were of a transitory nature, similar to the problems of early capitalism in England after the Industrial Revolution. Capitalism, Warren argued, had brought trauma and social dislocation in its wake wherever it had been established. But, he maintained, it had also brought an incomparably higher standard of living to the masses than any previous socio-economic system (you will recognize this, from Chapters 3 and 4, as Marx's view too). Furthermore, as the less-developed regions industrialized at a rapid rate, their industrial work force expanded. This social class would eventually bring socialism to those countries, but only after the initial triumph of capitalism, which was a necessary stage of social and economic development.

Holding aside Warren's prediction of a shift toward socialism somewhere in the undefined future of the less-developed regions, what is one to make of Warren's claims of the progressiveness of capitalism in the periphery? He made use of statistical data to show that in the 1950s and 1960s overall annual per capita growth in the poor regions had been relatively high: 2.4 percent in the 1950s and 2.6 percent in the 1960s. He implied that the pace was improving over time, noting that in the early 1970s, the average rate of growth of per capita income reached 3.8 percent.

Warren maintained that overcrowding, slums, and chronic unemployment arose from population growth, but that this growth itself was a fundamental indicator of an improvement in living standards. For Warren, all institutions within the less-developed nations which were ceremonial or dysfunctional from the standpoint of economic development were by-products of the colonial era and earlier modes of production. That era had ended after the Second World War, according to Warren, and a new era had dawned with political independence. And this, he argued, was sufficient to thwart whatever impediments to social and economic progress which could be attributed to either the policies of transnational corporations, the multilateral institutions, or the governments of the advanced nations. The spread of capitalist methods of production would sweep away outmoded institutions and structures, and the now less-developed nations would be brought into the modern era, just as England was, by the imperative forces of capitalist progress.

In the heady era of the early 1970s, Warren's thesis had a ring of plausibility; there can be no doubt that, like the developmentalists with whom he quarrelled, he shared a fundamental optimism about the possibility, even inevitability, of progress. However, the aggregate data utilized by Warren need to be carefully analyzed in terms of their representative nature. Warren's results were strongly influenced by the performance of the East Asian miracle economies. Without detracting from the great strides made in these nations, which are discussed beginning in Chapter 8, it should be noted that there has been a significant decline in their rate of growth in recent years. Thus, the Asian miracle economies had a tendency to skew the aggregate data after the 1950s and through the early 1970s. Warren, and others who use similar forms of analysis, should have presented disaggregated data, showing the overall growth of less-developed nations both with and without the miracle Asian economies. This would have been a more reasonable basis for attempting to evaluate the thesis that "Capitalism has struck deep roots [in the less developed regions] and developed its own increasingly vigorous dynamic" (Warren 1980: 9).

Events would seem to have overtaken Warren's brash analysis. The durability of the retarding factors which disturbed the heterodox development economists have, if anything, became more significant for most developing nations in the 1990s. Ayres, Baran, Myrdal, Prebisch, and Singer would, we suspect, not have been surprised by the difficult conditions faced by many less-developed nations since 1980, nor by the anaemic responses to these conditions from so many of these economies. It is not that progress is impossible; it is just that, contrary to Warren, it is unlikely that it is *inevitable*. Becoming developed requires the right decisions and the proper policies; it does not just happen to all countries like manna from heaven, just as a consequence of the spread of capitalism.

Questions for review

1   Using the definition in note 4 for the terms of trade, (a) calculate what happens to the terms of trade index for some country between 1995 and 2000, if, in 1995, the price index for its exports was 110 and the price index for its imports was 108; and in 2000, the price index of exports was 105 and the price index of imports was 112. Has there been an increase or a decrease in this country's terms of trade? If the country wishes to buy exactly the same physical quantity of imports in 2000 which it purchased in 1995, how much more, or how much less, will it have to export, in physical terms, in 2000 compared to 1995? Now, (b), examine what has happened to the terms of trade for two countries of your choice over a period of at least five years, using data in either the *World Development Report* or the *Human Development Report*. Does the trend you discover tend to support or refute the P–S hypothesis? Explain.

2   What is meant by the "international division of labor"? What function does the periphery play vis-à-vis the center countries in this division of labor? Who benefits from it?

3   Why do you think Raúl Prebisch's use of the terms "center" and "periphery," and the idea that relations between them were antagonistic, was such a challenge to orthodox economists?

4   Imagine you are an adviser to your government and that your economy faces a problem of declining terms of trade for its exports. Discuss the possible policy changes for the economy and any other strategies you would recommend to avoid declining terms of trade in the future.

5   What are the problems faced by primary product exporters? Are there primary products that countries might export which would, perhaps, not be subject to the same difficulties? Can you give some examples of so-called non-traditional primary products which it might be desirable to export? In general, what makes one export a "good" export and another less desirable?

6   Distinguish between backwash effects and spread effects. Are these the same as vicious circles and virtuous circles? How do these two ideas of Myrdal's relate to the concept of cumulative causation?

7   What similarities are there between the classical Marxist view of Bill Warren and the views of the developmentalist economists reviewed in Chapter 5? What differences are there?

8   Contrast the institutionalist approach to development with the dependency approach? Are there strong similarities, as well as differences?

Notes

1   As we shall see in Chapter 8, however, the ideas of the institutionalists concerning the central role of education, technology, institutions, and path dependency have been "rediscovered" by the new development theorists, though without attribution.

2   The basic needs approach to development issues was a retreat from the optimism of the 1950s and 1960s, which had anticipated that within a decade or two the poor nations, or many of them, could achieve sustained growth and development. By the 1970s, such optimism had been shaken for many reasons. Among these reasons was the unexpected durability of social institutions which were to have been swept away by the forces unleashed via the developmentalist path. In lieu of the high hopes projected by the developmentalist perspective, the basic needs approach substituted a more modest and immediate agenda: some significant part of development funds were to be expended on projects that had a direct and tangible effect on the well-being of the poor, for example, self-help housing projects, water treatment projects, health clinics, schools, and so on. Much of the BN approach attempted to address an uncontrolled result of economic change in the less-developed world: the phenomenal growth of urban slums and blighted mega-urban areas.

3   The propensity to import is defined in Note 9, Chapter 5. For the United States, this ratio was much smaller than was true for Britain, meaning that imports were less important for the United States economy and that exporters to the United States would have less bargaining leverage on prices as a consequence.

4   Specialists in the area of international trade have used at least four separate concepts under the heading of "terms of trade." We will utilize the most basic concept, which is the ratio of the price of exports to the price of imports in a given period compared to some earlier (base year) period. The terms of trade is an index number. Thus $(P_{x,i}/P_{m,i}) \times 100$ where $P_{x,i}$ is an average price index of exports in year i and $P_{m,i}$ is the average price index of imports in year i. This measure of the terms of trade is sometimes referred to as the **net barter terms of trade**.

   Another measure of the terms of trade that captures changes in productivity between nations is called the **double factorial terms of trade**. We will not attempt to consider this or any of the other terms of trade measures which might be used. Students wishing to do so should turn to any text in international trade.

   The *Human Development Report* includes data on the terms of trade for all countries covered.

5   The "development from within" approach, correctly understood, encompasses more than ISI, however. It is an evolutionary strategy of development that depends upon domestic sources of finance, domestic entrepreneurship, and domestic innovation to produce for both export and the domestic market. However, sometimes in practice, "development from within" has been too focused only on the domestic market, so that it has become "inward-oriented" development. This, however, was not Prebisch's own view, though it has incorrectly been attributed to him (see Sunkel (1993), for a finely detailed look at development from within).

6   Certainly, complete industrialization in all sectors would not be urged on all of the national economies of the periphery. Prebisch's experience with industrialization programs was primarily with relatively large economies, like Argentina, Brazil, Mexico, Peru, and Venezuela. The smaller economies, such as Costa Rica, Sri Lanka, the Caribbean countries, and some African countries, could not hope to have large and diversified industrial sectors. For smaller economies, Prebisch advocated enhanced common market-type arrangements so that sharing of markets could accomplish what was possible internally in large economies. The development problems facing small nations may sometimes be a bit more difficult, but as the successes of Singapore and Hong Kong in recent decades suggest, the situation is far from hopeless. Size, per se, does not seem to be a particularly powerful explanatory variable.

7 Income elasticity measures the change in consumption resulting from a change in income. Technically, it may be written as

$$E_Y = \frac{\%\Delta Q}{\%\Delta Y}$$

Where E_Y is the income elasticity, Q is the level of consumption of some good or service, and Y is income.

8 There are two newer branches of institutionalism besides the dominant strain discussed in this section. One is European institutionalism, organized around the efforts of the European Evolutionary Economics Association. The other, grounded in the work of another Nobel winner in economics, Douglass North, is called the "new institutional economics." For recent applications of the latter view, and a number of critical evaluations, see Harriss *et al.* (1995).

9 In Marx's writings, a major distinction was made between economic activities which took place in the "sphere of circulation" and those which took place in the "sphere of industrial production." In the former, activities such as banking, insurance, stock, and bond markets, were to be found "circulating" funds from various groups within a social strata, for example, savers and investors. In the sphere of production were to be found workers and capitalists, investment activity, production of manufactures and raw materials and, most importantly, technological development. The sphere of circulation was viewed as unproductive, although to some degree necessary for the economy to function, while the sphere of production was viewed as productive. Hence, an expansion of the sphere of circulation indicated that the surplus was being diverted and development opportunities thwarted.

10 Recall that when Baran died, in the mid-1960s, the Cuban revolution was viewed quite positively by many, and China seemed to be making forward strides in many areas as well. We will not attempt to speculate on how Baran might have viewed the issue of capitalism versus socialism from the perspective of the twenty-first century. He greatly admired the Cuban revolution and seemingly agreed with his close associate Paul Sweezy that the Soviet Union had became a "state-capitalist" society dominated by a bureaucratic strata of state-managers, and that progress would be only for a narrow elite.

References

Ayres, Clarence. 1995. "Economic Development: An Institutionalist Perspective," pp. 89–97 in James Dietz (ed.), *Latin America's Economic Development*, 2nd edn London and Boulder, CO: Lynne Rienner Publishers.

Baran, Paul. 1957. *The Political Economy of Growth*. New York: Monthly Review Press.

Borensztein, Eduardo, Mohsin S. Khan, Carmen M. Reinhart, and Peter Wickham. 1994. *The Behavior of Non-Oil Commodity Prices*. Occasional Paper no. 112. Washington, DC: IMF.

Cardoso, Fernando Henrique and Enzo Faletto. 1979. *Dependency and Development in Latin America*. Berkeley, CA: University of California Press.

Harriss, John, Janet Hunter, and Colin M. Lewis. 1995. *The New Institutional Economics and Third World Development*. London: Routledge.

Higgins, Benjamin. 1959. *Economic Development*. New York: Norton.

IMF (International Monetary Fund). 1994. "Adjustment, Not Resistance, the Key to Dealing with Low Commodity Prices," *IMF Survey* 23 (October 31): 350–352.

Kay, Cristóbal. 1989. *Latin American Theories of Development and Underdevelopment*. London: Routledge.

Maizels, Alfred, Theodsios Palaskas, and Trevor Crowe. 1998. "The Prebisch–Singer Hypothesis Revisited," pp. 63–85 in David Sapsford and John-ren Chen (eds), *Development Economics and Policy*. London: Macmillan.

Myrdal, Gunnar. 1944. *An American Dilemma*, 2 vols. New York: Harper & Row.

Myrdal, Gunnar. 1957. *Economic Theory and Underdeveloped Regions*. London: Duckworth.
—— 1968. *Asian Drama*, 3 vols. New York: Pantheon.
—— 1970. *The Challenge of World Poverty*. New York: Vintage Books.
—— 1984. "International Inequality and Foreign Aid in Retrospect," pp. 151–165 in Gerald Meier and Dudley Seers (eds), *Pioneers in Development*. Oxford: Oxford University Press.
Ocampo, José Antonio. 1995. "Terms of Trade and Center–Periphery Relations," pp. 121–142 in James Dietz (ed.), *Latin America's Economic Development*, 2nd edn London and Boulder, CO: Lynne Rienner Publishers.
Palma, Gabriel. 1989. "Structuralism," pp. 316–322 in John Eatwell *et al.*, *The New Palgrave: Economic Development*. New York: W.W. Norton.
Prebisch, Raúl. 1950. *The Economic Development of Latin America and Its Principal Problems*. New York: United Nations.
—— 1984. "Five Stages in My Thinking," pp. 175–191 in Gerald Meier and Dudley Seers (eds), *Pioneers in Development*. Oxford: Oxford University Press.
Sapsford, D. 1985. "The Statistical Debate on the Net Barter Terms of Trade: A Comment," *Economic Journal* 95 (September): 781–788.
Sapsford, D. and J. Chen. 1998. "The Prebisch–Singer Terms of Trade Hypothesis," pp. 27–34 in David Sapsford and John-ren Chen (eds), *Development Economics and Policy*. London: Macmillan.
Sarkar, Prabijit. 1986. "The Singer–Prebisch Hypothesis," *The Cambridge Journal of Economics* 10 (December): 355–372.
—— 1984. "The Terms of Trade Controversy," pp. 275–303 in Gerald Meier and Dudley Seers (eds), *Pioneers in Development*. Oxford: Oxford University Press.
—— 1989. "Terms of Trade and Economic Development," pp. 323–328 in John Eatwell *et al.*, *The New Palgrave: Economic Development*. New York: W.W. Norton.
Spraos, J. 1980. "The Statistical Debate on the Net Barter Terms of Trade," *Economic Journal* 90 (March): 107–128.
—— 1983. *Inequalising Trade?* Oxford: Oxford University Press.
Sunkel, Osvaldo. 1990. "Reflections on Latin American Development," pp. 133–158 in James Dietz and Dilmus James (eds), *Progress Toward Development in Latin America*. Boulder, CO: Lynne Rienner Publishers.
—— (ed.). 1993. *Development From Within*. Boulder, CO: Lynne Rienner Publishers.
UN (United Nations). 1949. *Relative Prices of Exports and Imports of Underdeveloped Countries*. New York: United Nations.
Warren, Bill. 1980. *Imperialism: Pioneer of Capitalism*. London: Verso.

Part 3

The structural transformation

7 The state as a potential agent of transformation

From neoliberalism to embedded autonomy

After studying this chapter, you should understand:

- the neoclassical perspective on the role and nature of the state in the economy;
- P.T. Bauer's critique of developmentalist theories and his case for spontaneous development;
- the origins and importance of market failure versus government failure;
- the nature of the so-called New Political Economy and DUP activities;
- the importance of government leadership versus government followership;
- how state activities can result in crowding-out or crowding-in of private investment;
- the crucial role of a meritocracy of state employees to successful development;
- the characteristics of the predatory, the intermediate, and the developmental state;
- the meaning and significance of embedded autonomy; and
- the four roles of the developmental state.

Introduction

This chapter concentrates on one of the most disputed areas of development studies, the role of the state in the process of economic transformation. It begins by framing the discussion within the context of major socioeconomic realignments of the 1980s which set the stage for a renewed debate over the role of the state. It concludes with recent research which attempts to reaffirm the potential of the state as an agent of economic growth, a view widely held by the early developmentalists as well as the heterodox thinkers discussed in the previous two chapters.

While England was passing through the agonies and ecstasies of the Industrial Revolution (1750–1840), a group of industrialists, pundits, and economists urged unrestrained *laissez faire* as the best means to advance the wealth of the nation, and they made an impression in national political–economic debates of the period. Because many were located in the thriving industrial town of Manchester, they became known as the "Manchester Liberals." In their view, if the British government would only eliminate almost all regulations and constraints on market behavior, then England would forge ahead even faster.[1]

Economic liberalism receded into the background in the latter part of the nineteenth century, however, and it seemed to have all but disappeared by the time that Keynesian economics dominated policy-making and economic theory, from the 1940s to the mid-1970s, except among economists associated with the Austrian school and monetarist doctrines. As Keynesianism appeared unable to cope with the turmoil of inflation, instability in global commodity markets, and recurrent business cycles that swept the advanced nations in the 1970s, a counter-revolution in economics began to emerge. At first this new liberalism appeared to be restricted to the economic policies of the United Kingdom under the prime ministership of Margaret Thatcher (1979–1990) and of the United States under President Reagan (1980–1988), but the political changes in those countries opened the door widely to a rethinking of many economic concepts.

Very quickly, this counter-revolution in economic thinking found its way into development issues. Perhaps most telling was the Cancún Conference in Mexico in 1981, when the Mexican President José López Portillo (1976–1982) hosted the assembled dignitaries of the "North" and "South" in what was to have been the first in a series of global conferences designed to establish a **New International Economic Order** (NIEO). The NIEO concept had arisen in the course of the 1970s; at best, it constituted a hazy vision of a revised global economy wherein the needs and aspirations of the developing nations were to be given new and greater consideration by the already developed nations. The NIEO concept reflected the fact that in the 1970s in many less-developed nations a new optimism and assertiveness had replaced the caution and uncertainty of the 1960s vis-à-vis the developed nations. The Organization of Petroleum Exporting Countries, OPEC, above all, had made great strides in its bid to confront the transnational oil companies of the advanced nations by pushing up oil prices via a classical cartel arrangement. The funds earned by OPEC were to a large degree deposited in private banks in the major financial centers of London, New York, Frankfurt, and Tokyo. Dubbed "petro-dollars," these funds subsequently were recycled back to the less-developed nations, where they became an important means of financing new, often grandiose, development projects and, just as often, conspicuous consumption contributing to the debt crisis which overwhelmed many less-developed nations in the 1980s (see Chapter 16). Privately owned corporations in many less-developed nations also had been courted assiduously by investment bankers from Europe, Japan and the United States, who sought to offer loans without serious investigation of these firms' repayment capacities.

At the Cancún Conference, both Prime Minister Thatcher and President Reagan attacked the NIEO concept, expressing their distaste for the stabilization of raw material export prices and the enhancement of foreign aid spending from the developed nations that formed two key planks of the NIEO proposal. At the same time, though, Mrs Thatcher's and President Reagan's call for a greater reliance on the free market as the vehicle for promoting economic development seemed to fall on deaf ears. But not for long.

By late 1982, the debt crisis was in full swing, and as a result of a recession in the advanced nations which had begun in 1981, oil prices fell rapidly and the terms of trade began to move strongly against the less-developed nations. Economic crisis spread through the world economy, hitting many less-developed nations particularly hard, especially the Latin American and African nations which had accumulated huge, and unsustainable, external debts. Not all the less-developed nations had borrowed heavily, however: or if they had, some apparently had used their loans more productively. Nor did all the less-developed economies have their economic dynamic closely tied to the export of raw materials, which especially suffered from the world recession. A small number of East Asian nations, South Korea and Taiwan in particular, seemed able to adjust to the changing economic circumstances of the 1970s and 1980s with a minimum of distortion to their economic and social growth. Most less-developed nations, however, were not so fortunate. With the global economic environment so drastically changed, the basis for the hopeful assertiveness of the less-developed nations apparent at the beginning of the 1970s, which had been based on a growing world economy, quickly evaporated. The ideas and policies advocated by Mrs Thatcher and President Reagan soon became central to the new economics of the late 1970s and beyond. And there was to be no subsequent North–South conference to give voice to the concerns of the less-developed nations. Brief and never very productive, even the idea of a "North–South" dialogue seemed moribund.

Giving initial shape to the new economic policies advocated by Thatcher and Reagan were a group of economists known as **monetarists**. Like the Manchester Liberals before them, monetarists abhorred government regulation, advocated a minimalist role for the state to enforce property rights, to maintain order and social stability, and to provide for the public defense. They interpreted the economic turmoil of the 1970s as largely the result of too much governmental intervention in private markets. It was not long before the monetarists became known as **neoliberals**, since the new policies they would recommend went beyond the old monetarist formulations. The neoliberal program was broader and more fundamental in advising novel policies in all spheres of the economy, compared to the earlier monetarist policy package which centered on limiting the rate of growth of the money supply to control inflation and spur growth. By the mid-1980s, the term neoliberal had supplanted monetarism as a label to describe the predominantly *laissez faire*, market-driven economic policies sweeping across the globe from advanced countries to less-developed nations and to the newly formed republics emerging after the collapse of the Soviet bloc in 1989.

Origins of the neoliberal paradigm

P.T. (Lord) Bauer, a Hungarian-born economist whose research work in England elevated him to the peerage in 1983, was an early pioneer in development economics, with a strikingly different perspective from any discussed in previous chapters. Lord Bauer attributed his distinctive insights to reasonably long stints in the tropics, first studying colonial rubber production in Malaysia and later examining the role of traders in West Africa who provided both inputs to the production of cocoa, peanuts, cotton, and kola nuts and then, later, acted as intermediaries when they bought the cash crops for sale on the world market.

Based on his field experience and his interpretation of cause–effect relationships, Bauer boldly rejected many of the most widely used concepts that had become central to the emerging field of development economics. For example, he denied that there was any evidence of vicious circles of poverty in less-developed nations or "cumulative causation," as Gunnar Myrdal had called these mechanisms which exacerbate poverty where it already exists. At the same time, in observing key export crops such as rubber, cotton, and cocoa, he maintained that the benefits of expanded production of these crops spread down to even the very small farmers; there were no "enclaves" in the export-oriented economy that did not gain from export expansion. Thus, Bauer returned to the Smithian idea that the market "harmonizes" the interests of all participants; everyone gains. Even major investments in infrastructure by government, he claimed, were not necessary to start off, accelerate, or push the process of development forward, a view distinctly contrary to what other development economists had claimed, as we read in Chapter 5.

Bauer's criticism of traditional development economic ideas is so sweeping that it is worth citing him at length, to capture the breadth and intensity of his views.

> The historical experience I have noted was not the result of conscription of people or the forced mobilization of their resources. Nor was it the result of forcible modernization of attitudes and behavior, nor of large-scale state-sponsored industrialization, nor of any other form of big push. And it was not brought about by the achievement of political independence, or by the inculcation in the minds of the local people of the notion of national identity, or by the stirring-up of mass enthusiasm for the abstract notion of economic development, or by any other form of political or cultural revolution. It was not the result of conscious efforts at nation building or the adoption by governments of economic development as a formal policy goal or commitment. What happened was in very large measure the result of the individual responses of millions of people to emerging or expanding opportunities created largely by external contacts and brought to their notice in a variety of ways, primarily through the operation of the market. These developments were made possible by firm but limited government, without large expenditures of public funds and without the receipt of large external [aid].
>
> (Bauer 1984: 30–31)

For Bauer, then, it was not government intervention, a driving vision of the future, a desire for development, infrastructure creation, a "big push" of industrialization, or anything other than the pursuit of individual gain by individual members of society, mediated by the market, that resulted in economic growth and development. Bauer's view, then, is little more than a restatement of Adam Smith's praise of the invisible hand as a coordinating mechanism and of how the decisions of individuals to accumulate capital in the pursuit of profit lead to social progress. But it is important to draw the distinction between Lord Bauer having *concluded* this is how development was taking place in the less-developed nations and his providing any evidence as to whether, in fact, this is what was actually happening.

The free market, exports, and the nature of colonial rule: a case study of British West Africa

How is one to assess Bauer's view that development is really a very simple process that results from allowing unimpeded market forces to work, thus permitting individuals to freely pursue their self-interest in a free market setting? This is an important question to pursue. A complete answer would take us into a complex study of

British West Africa and Malaysia, subjects far afield from the theme of this chapter. Nonetheless, a brief discussion is in order, and our comments will be limited to the situation in West Africa.

To begin, it is necessary to restate the obvious: in Ghana (known as the Gold Coast in the colonial era) and Nigeria, it was British colonial policy in the era described as "mature colonialism" in Chapter 3, rather than unregulated and impersonal free market forces, which determined economic results. Furthermore, in the case of tropical West Africa, it is important to understand that the leading theorists of colonial rule were committed to the concept of **native paramountcy**; they sought to preserve indigenous cultural patterns and structures of production. Foremost in taking this position was F.D. Lugard, who was born in India and made a career in the British military and as an administrator of the British Empire.[2] (In pointed contrast, in East Africa the British sought to introduce large plantations and turned over the bulk of the economically desirable resources to British subjects. The case of land settlement in Kenya is described in Chapter 11.) In West Africa there were few large mineral deposits which could form the basis for a mining enclave economy.

Many West African peasants had established skills in the cultivation of export products. After the elimination of the slave trade in the nineteenth century, many small farmers, through the intercession of traders, maintained centuries-old trade links with the global economy. Peasant agriculture, geared to the rapidly expanding global market, became the new motor-force of the West African economy. When the British expanded their colonial empire into West Africa in the late nineteenth century, Lugard's new principles of colonial rule were easily adapted to fit the West African situation. This created a modicum of stability, permitting the British to operate profitably within an established economy based on peasant production for the global market:

> [The] first principle was that African colonies should be supervised by strong central British governments, but that actual administration should be left to "native authorities", preferably hereditary chiefs, who must be both "unfettered" and yet "subordinate". "Unfettered" meant that they were largely autonomous, with their own treasuries, courts, laws, etc. "Subordinate" implied that they lost control over foreign relations, obeyed laws made by the colonial government and the order of the British officials, and contributed part of their revenues to the colonial treasury. Thus the system tried to balance native autonomy and imperial authority, enabling non-Europeans to take an active part in their own government without weakening British control.
>
> (Fieldhouse 1967: 299)

What quickly becomes obvious, then, is that whatever the merits of Bauer's observations, he managed to conduct his research in an area of the British Empire which was extremely atypical, even in relation to the rest of Africa, where plantation-based or and/or mining enclave economies were the rule, not the peasant-based export-oriented structures found in West Africa.

The British sought to press their advantage in West Africa via their control of inputs and outputs, leaving direct cultivation of crops to native cultivators. By all accounts the peasant cultivators did respond to market (or price) incentives. Yet, it is important to recognize that while small farmers were free to respond to price changes, they did not own the land they farmed. Villages and tribes owned this land and determined individuals' access to it. Custom, therefore, served as a barrier to the emergence of a landed aristocracy. Consequently, one of the basic elements of a market economy, a free market in land, did not exist.

Perhaps the greatest stimulus to increased export production arose from strategic government investments in infrastructure. For example, between 1898 and 1932 the colonial government built 2,100 miles of railroad and 6,000 miles of roads in West Africa. The new transportation system permitted peasants to deliver their crops more easily from the hinterlands to the global markets. Previously, cultivators had been restricted to transporting marketable surpluses via small river canoes and human porterage over crude trails where no draught animals were used.

Furthermore, the native crops proved to be atypical, in that prices generally rose over time, with the terms of trade either working to the advantage of West African commodities, or at least not moving strongly to the disadvantage of such commodities (Kemp 1989: 180–181). Nigeria was atypical too, in that it sold a small but diversified range of commodities, such as cotton, peanuts, palm oil, rubber, and cocoa, which generally maintained their value in the global market. Therefore, it was not dependent on merely one cash export crop. Moreover, the absence of mineral resources encouraged the development of indigenous cultivators.[3] Thus, based upon native cultivation and strong prices, an indigenous middle class began to emerge, composed of prosperous peasants, small tradesmen and shopkeepers, astute middlemen traders, and well-trained African employees of the colonial administration.

But the West African situation left the indigenous population dependent on foreign manufactured goods, since colonial rule had precluded industrialization. Meanwhile, large, usually British-owned trading companies eventually bought the commodities produced in Africa and made profits on shipping, insurance, and finance. A division of labor imposed by colonial rule, not by the market, permitted the West African middle class to share in the economic prosperity, though this was not wholly of the market's making. And, although Bauer dwelt upon the individual initiative of the native cultivators, major changes in agricultural technique were, in fact, brought about by the government's Agricultural Department in the 1920s and 1930s, not by small-scale decision-makers in the fields (Kemp 1989: 179).

The Depression of the 1930s and the turmoil of the Second World War ushered in a fifteen-year period of debate and experimentation, leading to an attempt by the British to foster economic development in West Africa via an activist role for government. Bauer, writing in the early 1950s, deemed this experiment a failure. His critique concentrated on the role of Marketing Boards which, beginning in Ghana in 1939, began to buy up all the main export crops, ostensibly in order to maintain and stabilize prices. Under this scheme, individual West African middlemen buyers could still negotiate with peasant cultivators, but they were forced to sell to the government at a fixed price. Rather than actually benefitting the peasants, the marketing boards were a disguised means to help finance Britain's war effort. To understand the size of the wedge which the government had driven into the export market, immediately after the war the Marketing Boards were absorbing 42 percent of the value of the Nigerian cotton crop, 40 percent of the peanut crop, and 39 percent of the cocoa crop (Kemp 1989: 182). Compounding difficulties was the fact that prices commenced to fall in the 1950s, and the terms of trade began to turn against West African primary producers. Meanwhile, the Marketing Boards used their vast surpluses to finance colonial rule and to subsidize a range of infrastructural investments and development programs (Helleiner 1966: 32–33). As one result, British-financed public investment flowing into British West Africa was greater in the period 1946–1960 than it had been in the previous forty-five years (Hopkins 1973: 280).

Examining the role played by the Marketing Boards, long after Bauer had chronicled their failure to either stabilize prices or help the small producers, Gerald Helleiner argued that Bauer had misrepresented the changing objectives of colonial rule. For Helleiner, the Boards were to be judged not as instruments to protect the interests of the small cultivators, but as devices to facilitate the economic development of Nigeria. He concluded that, on the whole, the Marketing Boards had used their surpluses wisely, investing in agricultural research, road construction, and local industry (Helleiner 1966: ch. 10). In doing so, hypothesized Helleiner, the Marketing Boards had successfully forced the prosperous peasantry to save and invest a portion of output that would have otherwise been spent on imported consumer goods. The Marketing Boards, then, were instrumental in helping to break the vicious circle of the open economy, whereby the lack of a balanced infrastructure and industry, had forced West Africa to depend upon and perpetuate a primary commodity-based development strategy, which had reached its limits by the early 1950s, if not earlier.[4]

No one seems to question the entrepreneurialism and market responsiveness of the peasant cultivators of Ghana and Nigeria. Yet those characteristics alone have been insufficient to lift West Africa from economic backwardness, Lord Bauer's analysis notwithstanding. By all accounts, West Africa's relative success with an open economy based upon the supposed comparative advantage in commodities such as cotton, palm oil, peanuts, coffee, and cocoa had been exhausted by the early 1950s, when the terms of trade moved against West Africa, as they tend to do for most primary products.

Today, Nigeria, despite its good fortune in having discovered massive petroleum reserves since Bauer conducted his research, is one of the poorest nations in the world. In the World Bank's listing of 133 nations, Nigeria is thirteenth from the bottom, with a per capita average income of $260 per year in 2000 ($790 in PPP). For the period 1990–2000, average per capita income *decreased* by 1.0 percent per year. On the human development index, Nigeria ranked 152nd out of 175 countries, with an HDI value of 0.46. Life expectancy at birth in 1999 was 51.5 years, only 57 percent of the population had access to safe (potable) water. Ghana had a slightly higher per capita income of $350 in 2000, ranking twenty-first from the bottom in the World Bank's listing. Ghana, enjoyed modest per capita growth of 1.7 percent per year, 1990–2000, but its per capita income peaked in 1978. On the HDI Ghana was 134th, with an HDI value of 0.57, life expectancy at birth in 1999 was 56.6 years, and 36 percent of the population lacked access to safe water (UN Development Program 2003).

To what degree have forces totally beyond the control of these nations been instrumental in their development experience? How much of what has occurred, or has not occurred, since the 1940s in terms of development can be accounted for by factors stressed by the developmentalist and/or the heterodox economists discussed in the previous two chapters? In order for Bauer's view to be accepted, he would have to address these issues with care. This he has never done, as John Toye has argued (Toye 1987: ch. 3).

Did Bauer actually uncover through his studies evidence that the market and *laissez faire* are key to economic development, or did he merely observe an unusual series of virtuous circles operating at a point in time that led him to be unduly optimistic about what the market might achieve on its own? Michael Lipton has maintained that Bauer observed situations that were extreme and atypical, and that it would be inaccurate to draw broad conclusions from such research.

> Export-crop production and trade in Dutch and British colonies in some areas received significant inflows of private foreign capital from 1900 to 1940. The local farmers and traders in a few such areas – having much spare land and enjoying population growth well beyond present rates in poor countries – built significant growth, quite widely shared, upon these inflows. Because rubber (and tin) and, in the early stages, cocoa and robusta coffee faced promising markets, international commodity cartels – or even agreements – were nuisances, not necessities. But were these realities too specific and temporary to allow us to transfer the lessons to other situations?
>
> (Lipton 1984: 48)

Lipton is of the opinion that Bauer failed to demonstrate the generality of his examples. As a counter example, Lipton offered the case of Bangladesh, where the two main exports are jute and tea; both faced a price-inelastic world market demand. Bangladesh failed to attract foreign capital inflows, unlike Ghana and Malaysia, there is little spare land, and the population has a low capacity to save and invest that could allow them to shift production to other crops that might be more advantageous or to industrialize (Lipton 1984: 49–50). Lacking the fortuitous inflows of foreign capital may account, at least partly, for the extremely low level of per capita income of $380 in Bangladesh in 2000, the thirty-fourth lowest among the 133 larger countries the World Bank lists, with an HDI value of 0.50, 139th out of 175 in ranking.

Ethnicity and race

For Bauer, growth is due to both reliance on the free market and intangible characteristics which he believes are "natural" to certain ethnic groups. For example, Bauer made the following comparison:

> Indians have many valuable economic qualities, especially when they are not hampered by a very restrictive social environment, they are nevertheless generally less ingenious, energetic, resourceful and industrious than the Chinese, as is suggested by the relative performance of Chinese and Indian emigrants.
>
> (Srinivasan 1984: 52–53)

T.N. Srinivasan cites a study conducted by an Australian expert invited by the Japanese to analyze their economy in 1915 that offered similar "cultural" observations to those of Bauer:

> My impression as to your cheap labour was soon disillusioned when I saw your people at work. No doubt they are lowly paid, but the return is equally so; to see

your men at work made me feel that you are a very satisfied easy-going race who reckon time no object. When I spoke to some managers they informed me that it was impossible to change the habits of national heritage.

(Srinivasan 1984: 53)

No development specialist would agree with such a characterization of the Japanese today (or of the Indians and Chinese). For institutional economists, such as Ayres (see Chapter 6), the great change in the Japanese work force arose due to evolutionary change in the institutions of Japanese society and economy that brought on changes in attitudes and work behavior. The "nature" of the Japanese was not immutable for all time, assuming that the characterization in the above quote was ever reasonable. And, one would presume, had evolutionary changes identical or similar to those in Japan taken place in other nations, or were they to take place in the future, they too would exhibit a history of emerging economic development, as the "traits" of the population changed to fit the evolving social and productive structure's needs. Racial and ethnic theories of development have been dismissed by careful empirical research, yet they seem to resurface in subtle ways in some scholarly circles again and again for those looking for easy explanations for differences in levels of development among nations.

Government in the process of development

Bauer's perspectives have been applied selectively by the advocates of neoliberal economics. For example, race and ethnicity do not play an explicit explanatory role in neoliberal thinking. Yet, one of Bauer's major themes has become the pivotal point of neoliberal analysis: the essentially negative role of government. If one were to express in a sentence the essence of the neoliberal approach to development issues, it would be the following: "Nations are not poor because they are poor, that is, because of vicious circles; rather they are poor because of too much government interference." Bauer and others have constructed their criticism of the state on three pillars:

1   The public sector has become over-extended in the economy.
2   The public sector has over-emphasized capital formation and mega-investment projects.
3   The public sector has caused the proliferation of economically distorting controls in the economy that create incentives for inefficient production and ineffective economic structures.

One difficulty with the first proposition is that Bauer and others fail to demonstrate an operational definition of the proper size of the public sector; thus "overextended" becomes little more than an ideological construct, sometimes supported by anecdotes of government inefficiency suggesting the need for a smaller state.[5] Regarding the second statement, Bauer has maintained that relatively little initial capital investment is needed to foster more rapid development, and consequently foreign aid is unimportant, as is any "big push" to kick-start the economy. On this detail, Bauer is very much the exception within the neoliberal school. Neoliberals typically regard foreign aid and technical assistance as extremely important instruments of influence which can be utilized to impose their policies on less-developed nations or risk forgoing such assistance. In the 1980s and 1990s, the World Bank and the IMF became extremely influential in curbing the public sector in the less-developed world, and in the transitional economies of the former Soviet bloc, by using the threat of withholding aid and loans as their prime instrument for gaining policy agreements with less-developed nations that were consistent with neoliberal precepts.

Furthermore, Bauer's position suggesting but a modest role for capital formation in the process of economic growth has not received much theoretical or empirical support (remember the neoclassical growth model of Chapter 4; see Chapter 8 on endogenous growth theories). Clearly, however, there have been instances when mega-projects, such as a huge irrigation complex of dams and canals, have been poorly thought through and executed and where, alternatively, small sums spent on large numbers of individuals, small farmers for example, ultimately could have benefitted society more than the mega-project. At the same time, one can find instances when funds spent on small businesses and micro-industries were squandered or poorly conceived from a social point of view. Such anecdotal information, however, proves nothing (see Box 7.1).

In many instances, the size of government is determined by the degree of market failure in society, that is, by the extent to which unregulated market outcomes are

---

Box 7.1 Governmental inefficiency and growth

The World Bank's *World Development Report* for 1983 argued that governmental policies led to large price distortions and that such distortions negatively affected the growth process. The study was based on thirty-one less-developed nations, and it did show that governmental controls over the foreign trade sector, such as over- or under-valued exchange rates, tariffs, and subsidies, which introduced large price distortions were, in fact, correlated with slower growth rates.

However, such large distortions could explain only 25 to 34 percent of the variance in growth between nations. The World Bank could not account for the most important factors which determined differences in the growth process between nations. At least part of the remaining two-thirds to three-quarters of the determinants of growth divergences may be due to positive effects associated with government spending on infrastructure, education, public health, and other government-induced forms of expenditure. Analyzing the World Bank's conclusions, John Toye noted "[The World Bank study] cannot be expanded into a justification for ... the unrestricted play of market forces and government non-intervention in economic life."

Recently, based upon a close study of the East Asian economies (see Chapter 8 for more details), the World Bank now suggests the extreme importance of human capital formation to economic development. And government action in this arena is a fundamental source of such investment, which so positively influences future growth rates and the level of per capita income. Government intervention of this type is a kind of "policy distortion" that is favorable. As we shall see, there is no doubt government polices *can* adversely affect growth and development. However, there is nothing about the experiences of the successful developers to suggest that this must be the outcome. There is good state policy and there is bad state policy creating "good" distortions and "bad" distortions.

Sources: Toye 1987: 86; World Bank 1993

inefficient or by situations when the market does not perform the desired function at all. In societies where there are pervasive monopoly and oligopoly forces, government action is clearly called for to reconstitute competitive forces. Likewise, if there is widespread hunger and malnutrition, subsidized food programs targeted at the needy poor may be both a social and political necessity, as well as being economically sound, since healthy and adequately fed workers are likely to be more productive as well. If employers are few and powerful, that is, if there is monopsony in the labor market, a government policy of minimum wages and protection for unions may be called for. Many essential infrastructure and social overhead capital projects, including the provision of universal public education, will not be provided via the free market, because the *private* rate of return is too low, and the payout period too long, to interest private investors, though the *social* rate of return can be quite high and the benefits to future economic and social growth large. The list of possible situations wherein there may be a need for corrective or complementary government action in the private sector could easily be extended, but the point is that due to the failure of the market system to deliver results that are either economically efficient or socially acceptable, there is a legitimate role for government that most economists accept as necessary to improve the operation of the entire economy, including the private capitalist sector.

Where to draw the line between legitimate and illegitimate public sector activity cannot be determined without a careful examination of the needs and situation of each nation. Should a government own the railroad, or a bicycle factory, subsidize health care, provide subsidies to export businesses, tax imports, provide low-cost loans, or control the price of life-saving pharmaceuticals? There is no a priori answer that is correct for all time and all circumstances. For neoliberals, however, the answer to these questions is almost invariably, no. Government should do as little as possible and never should it favor one sector of the economy over another, what neoliberals call trying to "pick the winners." Commenting on this, John Toye draws the contrast between the neoliberal interest in proving "government failure" and their corresponding disinterest in studying, or sometimes even acknowledging, market failure.

All the well-known causes of market failure – including various types of monopoly – are brushed aside as insignificant, while "government failure", in the form of corruption, centralization of power and loss of individual liberty is brought to center stage. But the ploy of using government failure to outweigh that of market failure is a shallow one. Apart from the fact that the methods for balancing one kind of failure against another cannot be specified, the underlying assumption that the two types of failure are separate and unconnected is false. All markets are made within some legal, social and political framework of institutions. One of the most familiar causes of market failure, for example, public goods externalities, is precisely an explanation of why this must be so. . . .

But just as importantly, the causal link also works in the other direction, from market failure to government failure. Technical externalities are a source of monopolistic behavior and oligopolistic behavior. Monopoly or oligopoly firms which are also large can usually exercise considerable political power and influence. This is not just a matter of contributing to political parties' funds. It extends more subtly to other forms of patronage . . . [e.g., good jobs to former state employees].

(Toye 1987: 67)

The above citation reveals another cornerstone of neoliberal analysis: the market is presumed to be the repository of efficiency. Government, on the other hand, is the root of inefficiency. The two sectors of the social economy are treated as autonomous, as if there were a firewall between them. What if, however, government inefficiency arises, at times, due to powerful economic interests, such as an agro-export-financial elite, who exercise determinant power over government policy in certain areas? Shrinking the size of government under these conditions actually might increase the latitude of power of these private sector groups which are unconstrained by competitive markets. This result is assumed not to occur, however, because neoliberal economists make the critical, if typically unspoken, assumption that less-developed nations operate within a framework that essentially is a competitive market system. What happens if one drops the competitive assumption? Then, as Adam Smith understood (see Chapter 4), much of the supposed efficiency of markets disappears as more powerful interests can manipulate the market system in their favor. The need for government and public sector action as a counterweight becomes more compelling.

The neoliberalism of Deepak Lal

Deepak Lal was professor of political economy at University College, London, is now at the University of California, Los Angeles, and has conducted a great deal of research under the auspices of the World Bank. He is perhaps best-known for his 1985 book *The Poverty of Development Economics*. He had earlier assisted in an influential compendium under the editorship of Ian Little which was critical, but not dismissive, of the role of the state in development (Little *et al.* 1970).

In his 1985 book, Lal attempted to dismiss virtually the entire body of thinking, analysis, and research conducted by the developmentalist and the heterodox thinkers discussed in the previous two chapters. Utilizing a polemical style, Lal maintained that heretofore development economics has been subject to what he termed a "dirigiste dogma," that is, a preference for state-led development strategies. He suggested that development economists had embraced instinctively the notion that the price and market system should be "supplanted (and not just supplemented) by various forms of direct government control ... to promote economic development" (Lal 1985: 5). Lal, however, offers not a single example of such thinking. One might reasonably ask, exactly where in their writings have the major contributors to development economics advocated the elimination of market processes? Certainly there were some who strongly advocated development planning to propel forward certain projects and sectors. But this, in itself, falls far short of "supplanting" markets throughout an economy and replacing them with "direct government control."

Within the broad spectrum of development ideas there is, as already noted in earlier chapters, a healthy skepticism regarding the degree of efficiency of many markets in less-developed nations. This skepticism has not arisen, however, due to a "dogmatic" rejection of markets, nor due to any lack of knowledge as to what markets can accomplish when they function well. Rather, it is due to an understanding that markets often do not function properly in a society that is in transition from a pre-capitalist, dualistic social formation to a fully articulated capitalist society. The need to supplement the market process in many areas has been vigorously advocated, but supplanting the market has not been a major or even a minor theme of development economics. Virtually *no* economist would deny the importance of the information and coordination functions of properly functioning markets. Markets are an essential component of any well-functioning economy, and the more efficient such markets are, the better. The role of government will likely be less when markets work well, but every society needs some degree of state intervention to have a well-functioning social system, of which the economy is only a part, albeit an important part.[6]

Lal further attacks development economics for its emphasis on macroeconomic considerations, such as growth, industrialization, investment, and employment, rather than on micro-efficiency. This, of course, is a valid observation. But the corrective is not to be found in the direction which Lal advocates: emphasizing micro-efficiency, while assuming that the "big picture" macro issues will somehow take care of themselves as a result of the focus on the microeconomic matters. Refutation of Lal's microeconomic perspective has come from various respectable quarters, for example the eminent development economist Gerald Meier and, more recently, the World Bank. The Bank has shown that the successful less-developed economies, such as South Korea and Taiwan, owe their success not to "getting prices right" (i.e., micro-efficiency) so much as to finding the right dynamic strategies at the macro level and the micro level that can accelerate growth and improve productivity (World Bank 1993). Meier shows that the arguments made in favor of import substitution industrialization, emphasizing the dynamic effects of policies while devoting relatively little attention to micro-inefficiencies which may either arise or be exacerbated by such policies, actually have their application in the so-called export-led success cases (Meier 1990: 155–169). Hla Myint, another admirer of the neoliberal school, makes a similar observation:

> Is it really true that the export-oriented countries are free from trade distortions in the neoclassical sense?... the export-oriented countries, such as Korea, appear "to have intervened virtually as much and as 'chaotically' on the side of export promotion as others have done on the side of import-substitution" and their success cannot be attributed to "the presence of a neoclassically efficient allocating mechanism *in toto* in the system."
>
> (Myint 1987: 117)

What is most interesting here is that the study cited by Myint in support of government intervention (Bhagwati and Krueger 1973) was written by two of the most prolific and influential contributors to the modern neoliberal school! In looking at some countries, the least successful less-developed nations, neoliberals argue that government intervention has slowed economic growth. In other cases, such as Japan and East Asia, they suggest that government intervention has *not* slowed growth and may even have accelerated it. So even from their own observations it would seem that it is not *whether* there is government intervention into the economy or not, but rather the *nature* of such intervention. Again, policy can be either good, enhancing growth and human development, or it can be bad, consistent with stagnation.

A third component of Lal's critique of development economics concerned the abandonment of the theory of comparative advantage, as a result of export pessimism (declining terms of trade). He maintains that the East Asian "miracle economies" have employed a policy of virtual free trade (Lal 1985: 47–48), by which he seems to mean that the Asian economies tampered just enough with market outcomes, and that a little fudging against the doctrine of *laissez faire* is permissible if one ends up promoting exports. An observer might reasonably ask, "Why is it wrong to promote industrialization policies designed to expand the internal market (ISI), but correct to utilize the same degree of government policy guidance to promote the external market?" Why term one approach "dirigiste dogma" and the other "virtual free trade"? Cannot both be equally effective?

Such questions are not adequately addressed by Lal. However, in much neo-liberal analysis it is argued that the state can, and perhaps should promote exports, but only as long as the domestic economy is "open" to the world market. The need for openness arises from the desire to achieve micro-efficiency. It is argued that if domestic producers are cut loose from all price supports, tariffs, and subsidies they will be *forced* by the market to either become competitive with imports, or die.[7] This "do-or-die" imperative can have unfortunate collateral effects, however. It can flood an economy with imports, thereby creating a balance of payments crisis. It can also produce a general business slump. In other words, the search for micro-efficiency via the neoliberal shock treatment may create macroeconomic instability. Furthermore, the idea of both promoting exports and forcing a *laissez faire* regime on domestic producers is logically flawed. Countries on the receiving end of export promotion policies may wish to retaliate, for good reason, when such policies affect their domestic production and employment. Furthermore, an extensive econometric study by Dani Rodrik points to the conclusion that "there is no economic argument for government policies that favour export activities" (Rodrik 1999: 37).

> The claims made by the boosters of economic integration ... are frequently inflated or downright false. Countries that have done well in the postwar period are those that have been able to formulate a domestic investment strategy to kick-start growth and those that have had the appropriate institutions to handle external shocks, not those that have relied on reduced barriers to trade and capital flows. Policymakers therefore have to focus on the fundamentals of economic growth – investment, macroeconomic stability, human resources, and good governance – and not let international economic integration dominate their thinking on development.
>
> (Rodrik 1999: 13)

Other difficulties with Lal's analysis arise when he seems to simultaneously decry all government interventions, and hold up government policy as the chief source of economic growth:

> It can be argued that the very large increase in infrastructure investment, coupled with higher savings rates provides the major explanation of the marked expansion in the economic growth rates of most Third World countries during the postwar period, compared with their own previous performance and that of today's developed countries during their emergence from underdevelopment.
>
> (Lal 1985: 72)

This would seem to be a justification of government intervention, at least as it extends to the provision of infrastructure. But, only a few pages onward, government seems to again have become the root of all evil!

> Most of the more serious distortions in the current working of the price mechanism in the Third World countries are due not to the inherent imperfections of the market mechanism but to irrational government interventions, of which foreign trade controls, industrial licensing and various forms of price control are the most important. In seeking to improve upon the outcomes of an imperfect market economy, the *dirigisme* to which numerous development economists have lent intellectual support has lead to so-called "policy-induced" distortions which are more serious than any of the supposed distortions of the imperfect market economy it was designed to cure.
>
> (Ibid.: 77)

Why, one might ask, if governments were so astute as to create the proper amount of infrastructure, were they so incapacitated in pursuing policy elsewhere? Lal's all-out attack on earlier development economists has provoked a strong response, particularly from John Toye, who has analyzed the propositions and analytical constructs of the neoliberal school:

> The idea that development economists approve all forms of economic controls, whatever their defects, and whatever their costs, is a total misrepresentation of other people's views.... It can easily be shown that, for example, Gunnar Myrdal, who is named by Lal as an arch *dirigiste*, published his criticisms of economic controls in India *before* the publication of the OECD volume [Little *et al.* 1970] and that the details of the criticism are very similar.
>
> (Toye 1987: 77)

The new political economy

From 1982 to 1987, Anne Krueger was the chief economist of the World Bank, the largest economic research organization in the world. During that period, the World Bank's shift toward neoliberalism was consolidated. In 2001 Krueger was appointed First Deputy Director of the IMF, the second-ranked position in that vastly influential organization. Professor Krueger has authored numerous books and articles on development policy, and she is one of the most renowned advocates of the neoliberal perspective. Although Krueger draws extensively on the work of Bauer, Little, and Lal, her own research lacks the stridency of tone and/or the broad sweep of much of the work of the other major contributors to the neoliberal perspective. Professor Krueger has concentrated on the economic waste and social distrust and instability which occur when the state has the capacity to redistribute income to selected elements of society. For example, import licenses create monopolies and permit the earning of economic profits for those who receive the licenses. If the price of the license is less than the economic advantage of owning such a license, the fortunate importer is in a position to receive revenues that have not been earned. Such revenues are "windfalls" which constitute unearned sources of income, or **rents**. Krueger has argued that the large state sector in many less-developed nations creates widespread opportunities for such rents and under such conditions one should expect a pathological result: the **rent-seeking society**.[8]

The factional state and rent-seeking behavior

In Krueger's interpretation, the state is a ready source of rents via subsidies, tax exemptions, tariffs, and a wide range of government policies. Once such rents have been captured by certain interests, those groups have a vested interest in maintaining such policies in place. The implication seems to be that state activities drain the economy of its dynamism. Wrong-headed policies are maintained, because groups with an interest in the rents to be derived from such policies exert pressure on the state to maintain those policies. As a consequence, consumers end up paying unnecessarily high prices, production costs are too high, and tax revenues are squandered, as state functionaries fail to pursue the general welfare in deference to vested interests.

The above is a description of what Krueger depicts as the "factional state" (Krueger 1993: 66). The factional state can be either democratic or authoritarian. In either case, such a state can be riddled with corrupt and inefficient behavior. Under such conditions, what can be done? Krueger and neoliberal thinkers advocate the shrinking of the state to a minimum by selling off government-owned firms via privatization programs, the elimination of tariffs and import licenses, the end to special subsidies, and the elimination of any policy that might create gains for special interests.

An assessment of the neoliberal theory of the state

This school of thought has made a contribution to mainstream economic theory by arguing that the state should not be treated as *exogenous* and given in constructing economy theory and analysis. Rather, the state should be seen as *endogenous* to the economic system. This insight, hardly a path-breaking advance for heterodox theorists who have taken such a position from the outset, could be the building block for a much more powerful understanding of the development process. How this can be achieved will be the subject of the remaining sections of this chapter.

Development economics needs a detailed theory of the state, and it also needs a body of research which reveals the extent to which rent-seeking prevails both within the structure of the state and within the private sector. Since by definition rent-seeking is socially wasteful and usually regarded as parasitic, it is often a difficult task to conduct research on such a topic. How can reliable research be conducted when those who receive rents and those who permit such rents to occur are determined to hide their activities?

The assumption that rents arise uniquely in the state sector is unwarranted. It is presumed that within the private sector there is either perfect competition or enough "workable" competition to eliminate rents. Throughout the developing world, however, there is scarce evidence to support such a proposition. One of the conditions for perfect competition is that all participants in the market have equal access to knowledge of the conditions of the market – the perfect, or symmetrical, knowledge assumption. Knowledge is a scarce commodity, however, often closely guarded. This is part of the problem. Also, there is often an absence of knowledge or information. In a society that has not reached a certain level of development, the mechanisms to produce and diffuse knowledge such as journals, professional associations, and their congresses, often do not exist, or do not exist to a sufficient degree. Public records may be either incomplete or very difficult to obtain. The difficulty in obtaining information means that there is a greater cost involved, compared to more developed nations, in terms of time required to search out relevant information, and even though the value of time may be lower in poorer nations, inaccessible information is just that – inaccessible, at least to some. Participants in the market will have different access to knowledge (asymmetric information), at least partly because of their varying ability to pay in terms of time devoted to the search for accurate information.

Of course, perfect competition entails much more than symmetric knowledge. The definition of free competitive markets is so restricted that even in the advanced nations there are few sectors that come close to this "norm" of orthodox economics. To make the assumption that the less-developed nations have efficient competitive markets, and are merely saddled by a corrupt state, as do the neoliberals, serves only to undermine the neoliberals. At minimum, the burden of proof is on those who boldly assert the existence of competitive markets. The literature which we have reviewed in this chapter does not present such a proof, nor does it explore this all-important theme.

Has neoliberalism run its course, to be replaced by yet another major focus in the early twenty-first century? There is strong reason for thinking this to be the case. First, the countries which have received the strongest inducements to shift toward neoliberalism have fared rather poorly, with the possible exception of Chile. The largest social experiment with neoliberalism has been conducted in Mexico. The neoliberals strongly believe in using aid from World Bank funds, IMF funds, and bilateral institutions to induce a shift toward neoliberal policies. Mexico has received more assistance from such sources than any other nation in the late 1980s and early 1990s. The shift toward neoliberalism seemingly succeeded in bringing inflation under control. But, since 1987, the primary device used to control inflation has been a tripartite agreement between the government, business, and organized labor, such that major prices have been set by decree, exactly the opposite mechanism from that advocated by neoliberals. The government's deficit was eliminated, but this was due in large part to the massive one-time sell-off of most of the government-owned firms. Where will the government find revenues once the funds from privatization have been spent?

While the neoliberals are anxious to point out their victory over inflation and their taming of the government's deficit, the Mexican economy has been plagued by modest growth, declining or stagnant living standards, massive migration into the United States, and the near-elimination of much of the small-business sector. As the Mexican economy slid into recession in 1995, neoliberals seemed to lose interest. Yet, the lessons are there to be learned. Neoliberalism did not revive the Mexican economy (Cypher 2001a). And, given the magnitude of the effort and the willingness of the Mexican policy-makers to introduce neoliberal policies, it is doubtful that a better case study of neoliberalism can be found (Cypher 2001b).

Neoliberalism faces a deeper difficulty than the failed experiment in Mexico, however; it falsely claims that the Asian miracles of Taiwan, South Korea, Singapore, and Hong Kong were models of free market economies which successfully developed. In the following chapters, we discuss the process of development in these nations. And, we will show how this process radically diverged from the market-driven interpretation of the neoliberals. For the moment we cite only the conclusions of an important study of the industrialization policies of Taiwan and South Korea. Here Robert Wade poses the question: "Did government policies lead the industrialization process, or did government policy *follow* where the free market would have taken these nations?" If the first part of Wade's inquiry is answered in the affirmative, then Taiwan and South Korea would be seen as successful examples of state-led development. If the latter part of his question is answered in the positive, they would be seen as having received a modest boost from the government, arriving at the same destination as they would have without any government intervention. Here are his major findings:

> We began with the mainstream interpretation of East Asian success within economics, which I called the self-adjusting market theory. It gives government an important but background role as regulator and provider of public goods. Whatever else we conclude from the present evidence, we can surely say that the governments of Taiwan and South Korea have gone well beyond this theory – beyond the role described for them in neoclassical accounts, and beyond both the practice of Anglo-American governments and the neoclassical principles of good economic management.
>
> The second conclusion is that much of this intervention has been of a leadership rather than just a followership type. It has done more than assist private producers to go where they have gone anyway.
>
> (Wade 1990: 260)

As a result of the critical scrutiny of the state that the neoliberals undertook in the 1980s, a new and more robust conception of the role of the state in the development process has begun to emerge. By forcing such a reassessment, the neoliberals have made a positive contribution to our understanding of the process of development. This reassessment is based upon the concept of the endogenous nature of the state. It is increasingly understood that *all* successful development has depended on an activist state (Adelman 2001; Chang 2002; Morris and Adelman 1988). In a recent study, which is extremely critical of the neoliberal stance, Helen Shapiro and Lance Taylor point out:

> During the industrialization push in all now-rich nations public interventions were rife.... [The] US courts restricted individuals' control over property; decisions came to favor community property over absolute domain.... US state legislatures controlled exports and granted monopoly power to public corporations. At the Federal level, industrial interventions in the United States during the nineteenth century were huge. The government targeted railroads and farmers with land give-aways and was highly protectionist until after World War II. Following the Meiji Restoration, the Japanese state set itself up as an entrepreneur, financier, and manager in several manufacturing lines. Its activist role continued throughout the militarist period and after World War II in the famous industrial programing of MITI [Ministry of International Trade and Industry].
>
> (Shapiro and Taylor 1990: 866)

Working with a set of studies conducted by the World Institute for Development Economics Research (WIDER), Shapiro and Taylor demonstrate that "getting prices right," the neoliberal recommendation for the ills of less-developed nations, is not enough. They find that only if attempts at price reform are coupled with large-scale state interventions, such as aggregate demand manipulation, export subsidies, public investment, and barter trade deals, can countries improve their economic performance.

The neoliberal school often cites Turkey as an example of a successful development path based on free market principles. Shapiro and Taylor point, however, to a WIDER study which discovered the following set of relationships almost the reverse of the account offered by the neoliberals.

> Turkey's export "miracle" in the first part of the 1980s rested upon a preexisting industrial base created by ISI, policies leading to contraction of domestic demand for manufactures, attempts at general price reform, subsidies of up to one-third of export sales plus related incentives, and rapid growth in the demand for the products the country could produce by culturally compatible buyers in the region (the Gulf countries and both sides in the Iran–Iraq war). Had any one of these factors been missing, the boom probably would not have occurred.
>
> (Ibid.: 866)

Research conducted by WIDER also shows that public investment tends to stimulate private capital formation; this is in direct opposition to the presumed relationship postulated by the neoliberal school. For them, public investment crowds-out private investment. A large body of research suggests that this is simply not true. Indeed, these studies suggest that on average every dollar of public investment *induces* one dollar or more of private investment. In other words, public spending results in the **crowding-in** of private investment.

The practitioners of the "New Political Economy" believe that the state should be a maximizer, rationally finding the right combination of minimalist policies which free the "natural" development forces in an economy. According to their view, nations such as South Korea owe their success to their willingness to follow the guidelines of neoclassical economic theory. Writing on the Asian miracles, Gottfried Haberler flatly stated: "These economies pursue, on the whole liberal market-oriented policies.... Their success is fully explained by, and confirms, the neo-classical paradigm" (Haberler 1987: 62). Such a perspective is totally alien to specialists who have studied these economies. Tun-jen Chung notes that factors never mentioned by neoliberals, particularly colonialism, transnational firms and the World Bank, had much to do in shaping development strategies which were spearheaded by the state (Cheng 1990: 141).

As the logical critiques mounted and as the empirical research proliferated, those who continued to favor the neoliberal theory of the state faced deepening skepticism within the field of development economics. Major theoreticians and researchers, particularly the Nobel Prize award recipient Joseph Stiglitz have sought to advance the discussion of the role of the state. By the late 1990s Stiglitz was urging the creation of a "Post Washington Consensus" that would refocus the entire discussion of the state toward (1) concepts and policies originally advocated by the

Developmentalists (see Chapter 5) and (2) a detailed emphasis on lessons to be learned from the experience with successful forms of state intervention in selected developing nations (Amsden 2001; Evans 1998; Stiglitz 2001). It is to that discussion that we now turn in the closing sections of this chapter.

Embedded autonomy

Peter Evans has made great strides in the development of a robust theory of the state in less-developed nations. Evans maintains that it is possible to identify three archetypes of the state: The Predatory State, the Intermediate State, and the Developmental State (Evans 1995). In his conceptualization, states can vary, depending on the historical evolution of specific societies. States are the result of complex historical forces and relationships, but they are also actors or agents potentially capable of shaping and influencing the ongoing process of historical evolution:

> States are the historical products of their societies, but that does not make them pawns in the social games of other actors. They must be dealt with as institutions and social actors in their own right, influencing the course of economic and social change even as they are shaped by it.
>
> (Evans 1995: 18)

In Evans' richly detailed study one finds a thorough depiction of both intermediate and developmental states. These are states where the structures and capacities deployed by the state serve as *agents* of societal transformation and growth. In these states and societies, there exists a viable joint project, wherein civil society (the private sector) and the state managers are able to constructively and dynamically interact to engage in societal transformation.

While Evans offers a theoretical conceptualization of states, he does not present a dynamic analysis of why and how his three archetypical states come into existence, how they are perpetuated, or how they metamorphose from one archetype to another. In this dynamic sense, he does not offer a complete theory. And, clearly, much work needs to be done to construct such a theory. But, Evans' research will provide an important foundation for subsequent work in the field of economic development. We now turn to a discussion of Evans' depiction of state forms.

The predatory state

The predatory state is one wherein the appropriation of unearned income via rent-seeking has become endemic and structural. Everything is for sale: the courts, the legislature, the military, the taxing authority, etc. Government employees use their authority to maximize, in the shortest possible time, their accumulation of wealth. Political offices are held not for the reason of providing service to a nation, but for the purpose of individual gain in a society which may offer few alternative avenues to wealth accumulation. With corruption endemic, "rational" individuals may prepare for their own demise by establishing secret bank accounts in Switzerland or other havens for flight capital.

Evans does not devote much of his research to the predatory state, and a critical review of this construct has stressed the fact that he here neglects the possible causal

FOCUS 7.1   PERFORMANCE STANDARDS AND STATE STIMULUS IN THAILAND

Thailand adopted meritocracy as its civil service employment standard in 1932. Many of the best-trained university students were attracted to government employment – particularly with the Board of Investment (BOI) – the key institution that oversees the promotion of industry in Thailand. The BOI was created in 1960 as the result of the "Promotion of Industrial Investment Act."

"A very large number of investment projects grew up under the BOI's wing.... According to the BOI's own estimates it was involved in roughly 90 percent of Thailand's major manufacturing projects covering both the private and public sectors and foreign and local firms." As the BOI's influence rose after 1960, the average annual rate of growth of manufacturing production rose 60 percent in the 1960s – to 9.1 percent – and then to 10.1 percent in the 1970s. As the share of manufacturing climbed the BOI used a variety of forms of industrial stimulus – but only to the degree that *reciprocity* occurred in the form of *performance.*

Below many of the forms of stimulus and the performance standards devised by the BOI are simply listed in order to put in a more concrete form how both *Intermediate* and *Developmental States* might proceed to both encourage and influence the process of industrialization.

Stimulus policies	*Performance standards*
Tax exemptions	Export targets
Local-content standards	Tariff protection
Subsidized credit (loans)	Debt/equity ceilings
Developmental banks	National ownership floors
Entry restrictions	Operating scale minima
Special benefits to	Hiring local managers
foreign firms	Technology transfers
Import duties on luxuries	Investment time tables
Duty exemptions on machinery	Regional location requirements
(not made in Thailand)	Product-quality specifications

The BOI has been viewed as "daring" and innovative, but also, at times, as indiscriminate in its support. Thus, while the rules of "micro" efficiency may have been violated, the growth achieved by the BOI's policy of tying programs of economic stimulus to tailor-made performance standards – as a firm condition for such stimulus – has been considered insignificant in light of the rapid surge of economic growth achieved by Thailand. While Thailand's growth was interrupted by the Asian Crisis of 1997, nonetheless annual per capita income growth in the 1990s was a strong 3.3 percent.

Source: Amsden 2001: 20–24

linkages between a predatory private sector and the state as the two collude (Kohli 1999: 99). He does show, nonetheless, that this formulation closely fits the Congolese state, and probably aptly describes many other states in Africa, Latin America, and the Middle East. In the predatory state, we find a vitriolic mixture of traditionalism and arbitrariness characteristic of pre-capitalist societies. There is a scarcity of trained bureaucrats, and an absence of both a meritocracy and rule-governed behavior throughout the state apparatus. The state operates under the whims of a strong president or leader who functions in the "patrimonial tradition" of an absolutist ruler. Around the president is clustered the "presidential clique" of perhaps fifty people who control the state apparatus and use it for their own ends, due to their personal and perhaps familial ties to the leader. Beyond the inner circle lies the "presidential brotherhood," the second circle of power where state managers seek to both plunder society and continue to pledge their allegiance to the inner circle of power. Some of the most notorious features and results of the predatory state are (Evans 1995: 12, 248):

- "Predatory states extract at the expense of society, undercutting development even in the narrow sense of capital accumulation."
- "Predatory states lack the ability to prevent individual incumbents from pursuing their own goals."
- "Personal ties are the only source of cohesion, and individual maximization takes precedent over pursuit of collective goals."
- "The predatory state deliberately disorganizes civil society."[9]

The intermediate state

Fortunately, in Evans' view, most states need not be, and in fact are not, typified by the archetype of the predatory state. Rather, most states are *intermediate* states where inconsistencies reign. Such states do, at times and within specific sectors, exhibit the loathsome features of the predatory archetype. But they also exhibit a complex range of attributes which cannot be explained within the neoliberal paradigm which accepts the predatory state as an inevitability. The intermediate state exhibits "pockets of efficiency," where state managers demonstrate both their professionalism and competence in designing, promoting, and completing imaginative and important projects, either jointly with the private sector, or on their own through state-owned enterprises (SOEs). A particularly good example of this is to be found in Alice Amsden's careful treatment of the very successful Brazilian development bank BNDES (Amsden 2001: 141–145). But, the state apparatus is not built on a pure meritocracy. Intermediate states fall victim to "bureaucratic fragmentation," where professionalism dominates in some sectors and agencies while personal ties and/or corruption form the basis for decision-making and authority in other parts of the state apparatus.

Such a state fails to confirm the neoliberal portrayal of utterly futile and unproductive state intervention. Yet, intermediate states lack the means to consistently transform society, even as they are able to engineer successful sectoral transformations.

Such societies do not suffer from too many bureaucrats, but too few, according to Evans. For Evans, evoking the concepts of Max Weber, a fully formed and fully functioning bureaucracy entails merit-based recruitment, long-term career rewards for state managers, social status for government employees, and a coherent institutional structure which can form a constructive counterpart to private-sector institutions. Intermediate states demonstrate some of these Weberian attributes, some of the time, in some sectors of society. But pervasive imbalance is endemic.[10]

These concepts can be employed to understand both Brazil and India (Schneider 1999; Herring 1999). But to really understand his use of the term "intermediate," it is necessary to view this type of state in relation to Evans' third possible state form, the *developmental state*. Understanding this third archetype will sharpen our conceptions of the other two state forms, and it will allow us to introduce a concept which will become an integral component of the development process as described in Chapters 8–11.

The developmental state

The key characteristic of the developmental state is **embedded autonomy**. An embedded state possesses a variety of institutionalized channels wherein the state apparatus and the private sector continually interact in a constructive manner via a "joint project" of fostering economic development. The developmental state is clearly *endogenous*; it is broadly embedded in civil society via a dense web of networks. Some parts of the state apparatus may be tightly linked to specific sectors. These broad and dense institutionalized channels of communication and interaction provide the links whereby the state is continually in the process of constructive negotiation and renegotiation of policies and goals intended to move a society toward a higher and higher level of economic and social development (Pempel 1999: 141–160). "Embeddedness ... implies a concrete set of connections that link the state intimately and aggressively to particular social groups with whom the state shares a joint project of transformation" (Evans 1995: 59).

But, embeddedness alone is not enough, for there is always the danger that the state apparatus can be "captured" by the very interests and sectors it seeks to guide, promote, and control. In order to guard against the risk of capture, the state apparatus must have integrity, loyalty, and cohesiveness. In short, the state must also exhibit the characteristics of *autonomy*. Autonomy implies that the state can stand alone, above the fray and beyond the controlling reach of vested interests which would seek to capture the power of the state and turn that power to their very specific, short-term advantage. An autonomous state has to be able to draw on its own vision of economic transformation, and this vision has to be the result of a highly competent group of state managers who have achieved their power via proven performance and professional competence which undergird the merit-based hierarchy of state employees. State managers cannot be mere visionaries; they must develop their own capability to deliver technological entrepreneurship to selected sectors of the economy (see Box 7.2).

Obviously, the pure concept of embeddedness logically leads to the capture of state policy-making by the sectors which the government seeks to guide and promote. The pure concept of autonomy leads to the problem often exhibited by the Indian state; a merit-based state management which is culturally cut-off from the wider society and which lacks the ability to find the common ground for "joint projects" leading to economic transformation. Each concept alone is an insufficient, though necessary, characteristic of the successful state. Combining the two enables the state to overcome the risk of "capture" while avoiding the trap of pure autonomy whereby there is no effective means of constructively interacting with the private sector (Evans 1998).

The four roles of the developmental state

Developmental states, such as those in South Korea and Taiwan, have the discretionary power to adopt several roles, depending on the needs and demands of

---

Box 7.2 Advanced electronics and embeddedness in Korea

In the 1970s, the Korean government isolated the electronics industry as a key sector for promotion. For the two previous decades, South Korea had developed a robust electronics assembly industry. Now it was to make the leap into the production of high value-added products, commodities demanding advanced technologies in both production and design. To enable the electronics industry to make such a change, the Korean government took many steps to assist the growth of the industry. Among these was the creation of the government-funded and run Electronics and Telecommunication Research Institute (ETRI).

By the mid-1980s, ETRI employed 1,200 highly skilled technicians and research personnel. ETRI was then deeply involved with industrial giants Samsung and Goldstar, and many other firms, to develop the technology for the production of large-scale computer chips. The objective was for South Korea to match the pace of technological advance in the semi-conductor industry set by Japan. Cooperative research conducted by the industry and the government, and careful monitoring of technical progress by ETRI, was one major component of the process. Selective prodding by the government, along with the allocation of generous loans, was the other major component for achieving success. All the companies eventually involved in the project acknowledge the constructive and crucial role of government cooperation with the private sector. Korea achieved its goal of shifting from low value-added assembly electronics to technology-intensive, high-value added electronics production over the planned period. As a result, workers' wages were able to rise, too.

Sources: Amsden 1989: 81–83; Evans 1995: 141

---

society in general and the specific needs of sectors of the economy. Autonomy allows the developmental state to switch roles in specific sectors, as conditions dictate. Here we review the four roles described by Evans, utilizing his sometimes colourful terminology.

The custodian role

All states must have the ability to formulate and enforce rules and regulations. This role embodies the functions of the minimalist state, or the state conducting its "watchman/caretaker" activities.

The producer role

Even a minimalist state must produce adequate social overhead capital, or infrastructure, wherever and whenever there is a need for collective goods of this type. Beyond this relatively passive role, accepted as legitimate even by neoliberal critics of the state, there may be a need for the **demiurge** function. Here the state shifts to creating certain types of goods via state-owned enterprises or via joint venture schemes which link state investment funds with private-sector investors.

> When the state decides to play demiurge, it becomes involved in directly productive activities, not only in ways that complement private investments but also in ways that replace or compete with private producers. . . .

Playing the demiurge implies strong assumptions about the inadequacies of private capital. Local capital is presumed incapable of becoming a "transformative bourgeoisie," of initiating new industries and sectors. Transnational capital is presumed uninterested in local development. If local capital is indeed unable, and transnational capital is in fact unwilling, to develop a new sector, then taking the role of demiurge may be the only way to move industrial development forward.

(Evans 1995: 79)[11]

But, Evans cautions, the demiurge role is potentially dangerous, because it may create a climate wherein the state is tempted to expand beyond a point where it can effectively marshall its limited capabilities to act as an agent of economic transformation. Further, organizational problems may surface when state managers seek to expand or diversify an SOE into an area where it performs poorly and where the motivation to expand arises from the organizational structure of the SOE, rather than from the imperatives of transformational development. Finally, Evans points out that both the custodial role and the demiurge role arise from essentially negative conceptions of the private sector and of market structures.

The midwife role: a "greenhouse" policy

Here the developmental state acts as a facilitator by steering, assisting, and inducing the private firms to attempt new production challenges in areas which are of high priority. The state can lower risks, or increase the rate of return on investment, by allocating credit, limiting import competition, or even by providing subsidies. Essentially, midwifery entails the shifting of production activities into new areas which are believed to be conducive to development and which would not be areas where private capital would venture if left to market forces alone.

The role of husbandry: a policy of prodding and supporting

Husbandry tends to accompany and complement the role of midwifery. Often, in creating a new industry, there are related tasks which the state can undertake in order to help ensure the successful emergence of a new industry. Such activity will vary greatly with circumstance. Examples might be the state setting up research and development facilities or laboratories which undertake research which is complementary to a new industry. It might entail the establishment of state-owned facilities to produce the most technologically challenging inputs into an industry which the developmental state seeks to foster.

Depicting state forms

In Figures 7.1(a) and (b), we sketch the outlines of the Brazilian and South Korean states to exemplify the archetypes of the intermediate and developmental state. In both instances, the state essentially arises from two interrelated foundational pillars. Supporting the state on one side is its internal organization. Here one finds the characteristics which serve to define the cadre of the state employees. In Brazil (Figure 7.1(a)), one finds pockets of efficiency, but in general there is endemic

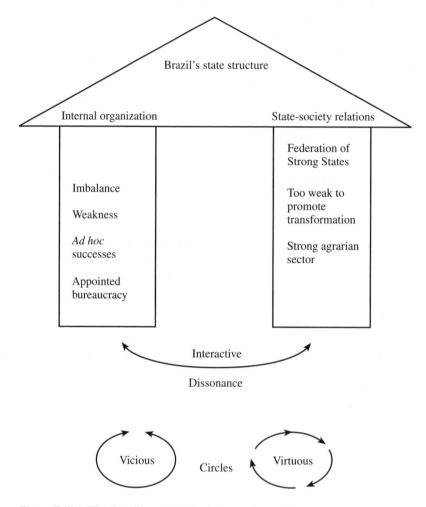

Figure 7.1(a) The Brazilian state: the intermediate state.

organizational weakness – particularly because the 60,000 state workers who gain positions with each election are an *appointive* bureaucracy that is not embedded.

> Officials in an appointive bureaucracy rarely have the time to develop the long-term relations of trust and reciprocity with business that characterize developmental states in Asia because officials move to another job in another area of the State or the private sector whenever . . . presidents change.
>
> (Schneider 1999: 304)

Imbalance reigns between the competent and cohesive portions of the state apparatus, and the wider areas where professionalism is in short supply. This gives state policy its *ad hoc* and irregular character. The state lurches toward viable projects, only to slide toward a morass of futility. But it does not stay mired. It demonstrates integrity *and* incompetence. It cannot generalize its successes, however.

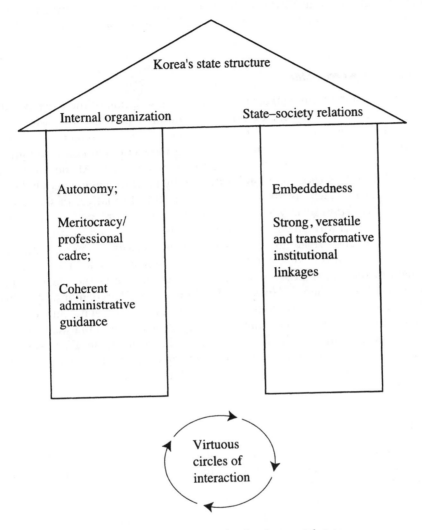

Figure 7.1(b) The South Korean state: the developmental state.

The second foundational pillar undergirding the state is the state–society relation. Here, argues Evans, the Brazilian state has been unable to achieve embeddedness with industrial interests, because of the continuance of a strong agrarian sector of huge landowners who seek to utilize the power of the state to further their own interests. To a degree, because of its lack of autonomy from backward-looking agrarian interests, the Brazilian state is unable to pursue industrialization with all of its resources and capabilities. It has divided loyalties. It is partially captured by the agro-export interests, and therefore only intermittently does it exercise its transformational potential by establishing and nurturing a strategic industrial sector. Thus connecting the two foundational pillars is problematic. The state is "shaky" because at the foundational level there is some "interactive dissonance." Adding to this tension, the regional states exercise some autonomy as they are not fully subordinated to the Federal State. At the crucial point of linkage between the two foundational pillars, we find both vicious circles of dissonance *and* virtuous circles of interaction.

A *depiction of the Korean state*

Our last consideration in this chapter is to turn to a description of the Korean state. Figure 7.1(b) depicts the concept of embedded autonomy. Notice that within the pillar of internal organization we find that employment is based on merit. Therefore a professional, coherent state bureaucracy is able to exercise autonomy *and* utilize its power to deliver administrative guidance to the civil society. At the same time the second pillar, state–society relations, is defined by institutional linkages between the state and society which are strong, versatile and transformative. In short, state autonomy is *embedded* in society. Consequently, the South Korean state constitutes a developmental state, with an endogenous basis of transformation capable of channelling both public and private investment to strategic sectors. Numerous attempts have been made to distort or discredit the record of the Korean state, particularly in the aftermath of the Asian Crisis of 1997, because it constitutes the greatest challenge to the neoliberal theory. However, Ha-Joon Chang has demonstrated that the Asian Crisis did not arise from any endemic failings of state intervention. Rather, it was the turn *away* from industrial policy after 1993 and the weakening of the state apparatus which facilitated duplicative investments in the 1993–1997 period (Chang 2000). As we will see in the following chapters, the concepts of the state developed here have wide application and profound implications for the process of development.

Conclusion

Our journey through the debate over the role of the state in the developmental process has led to the insights offered by Peter Evans, whose archetype constructions of the predatory, intermediate and developmental states will be of use in understanding the role states play in given societies. Can intermediate states become developmental states? Evans argues that such a metamorphosis can be a daunting, but not an impossible, endeavor.

> existing public bureaucracies, certainly in Latin America and even to some degree in Africa, are not the irredeemable cesspools of incompetence that they are sometimes painted by neoliberal rhetoric. There are dedicated individuals working in public service in almost all countries ... Most state bureaucracies, at least in Latin America, contain key agencies that at least in certain periods have displayed many of the institutional traits of "Weberian bureaucracies". Such agencies have performed with levels of efficiency comparable to those [of] their East Asian counterparts, despite being surrounded by a public sector that is much less effectual overall.
>
> (Evans 1998: 80)

He warns that: "The concept of embedded autonomy is a useful analytical guidepost, not an engineering formula that can be applied, with a few easy adjustments"

(Evans 1995: 244). The goal of state policy must be to induce private investment and to channel such investment to strategic sectors. But embeddedness is easier to describe than attain. "Connecting state and society is the more difficult problem. Capacity without connection will not do the job" (Ibid.: 244). Evans also warns us that the state-led successes in East Asia will not be easy to follow, because of the fact that state and society were well connected there due to what may be rather unique historical circumstances. Still, Evans illuminates a path to follow, while showing there is no simple road map to development.

Questions for review

1. Using Peter Evans' categories of predatory, intermediate, and developmental states, review the discussion of the critique of state policies and practices offered by the neoliberals. How do these categories help you better understand the role of the state and the dangers of generalizing too broadly on the weakness of state intervention from specific instances?
2. Evans emphasizes that states have to play specific roles in order to promote development. Review the discussion of Deepak Lal and determine if the issues raised by Lal can be understood with greater precision with the use of Evans' categories. Why, or why not?
3. Review the case of Nigeria and Lord Bauer's analysis of West Africa, as presented in this chapter. What are the lessons to be learned regarding the role of the state versus the role of the market in this instance?
4. Professor Krueger has maintained that the solution to rent-seeking on the part of state functionaries is the shrinkage of the state. Peter Evans' perspective is quite different. Compare their contrasting approaches to rent-seeking. Where do they agree, and when and why do they disagree?
5. Under what social and economic conditions are markets likely to fail? When is there likely to be government failure? Is macroeconomic inefficiency (for example, a high level of unemployment and underemployment) due to market failure or government failure?

Notes

1. The classic study of the term "liberalism" is Girvetz (1963).
2. Lugard was an administrator of great renown and influence. He served as High Commissioner of Northern Nigeria from 1900 to 1906, and then as Governor of Nigeria from 1912 to 1919. After retirement he published a landmark work on colonial administration, *The Dual Mandate*. According to P.J. Cain and A.G. Hopkins, those who followed Lugard into colonial careers "were inclined to idealize rural Africa, to identify with 'natural' pastoralists and cultivators, and to view urbanized and supposedly 'detribalized' Africans with a mixture of disdain and alarm" (Cain and Hopkins 1993: 218).
3. Some mining occurred. Tin accounted for about 10 percent of Nigeria's exports before the Second World War.
4. Independence in 1960, unfortunately, did not carry with it a deep and profound consolidation of hopeful trends and forces which had surfaced in the mid-1950s. From 1954 to 1960, Nigeria experienced a very modest increase in annual per capita income of 0.32 percent. From 1960 to 1966, there was an annual decline of 0.72 percent in per capita income. In his interesting discussion of the Nigerian case, Tom Kemp argued that the Nigerian elite could not capture the momentum of the developmental strategy which was colonial rule's last effort in Nigeria. Nigeria's leaders had sprung from the prosperous peasantry, and

their largely positive historical experience with market forces led them to adopt a relatively uncritical and passive posture regarding the limitations of markets. Thus, while the elite dabbled in developmental projects, their lack of determination and commitment to a strategy of "governing the market," as it is now termed, led to a downward spiral of dependence and decay:

> Already privileged economically and in the possession of educational advantages, they accepted personal advancement and enrichment as valid goals, modelling their expectations very much upon the life-style of expatriate Europeans in colonial times. The way was thus open for cooperation and collusion between politicians and civil servants on the one hand and indigenous entrepreneurs, of whom there were no lack of aspirants, and foreign businessmen on the other. Speculation and corruption became endemic in the new state, intertwined with regional and ethnic rivalries and favoritism which were to plague the country, bringing instability and a tragic war within less than a decade.
>
> (Kemp 1989: 184)

5 One particular target has been state-owned industries, or para-statals. The hypothesis of the neoliberals is that any activity which conceivably could be undertaken in a market environment will be more efficient if it is operated on a "for profit" basis. (Implicitly this approach assumes that the less-developed country has an efficient set of markets already in place.) Thus, in order to cut the state to its "proper" size, the neoliberals have strongly advocated privatization of state-owned industries.

Research into the issue of efficiency of state-owned industries is limited. However, one summary of the literature for Mexico, which has carried out the largest wave of privatizations in the less-developed world, indicates that many of the state-owned industries were no more inefficient than private-sector firms, while other state firms were operated "inefficiently" on purpose in order to subsidize private sector accumulation and/or to achieve other broad political goals. In other words, even though the employees and managers of these firms were government employees, that fact alone did not suffice to explain the efficiency level of the firm (Cypher 1990: ch. 5).

6 The entire theme of the dynamic relationship between the state and the market has been brilliantly explored in a twentieth century classic, Karl Polanyi's *The Great Transformation* (Boston: Beacon Press, 1957).

7 We will discuss the impact of openness on the domestic economy further in subsequent chapters, especially 9 and 10. Some neoliberals have emphasized the possibility of accelerating technical change under the "do-or-die" imperative, while others have suggested that under such pressures indigenous entrepreneurial capabilities might blossom.

8 Rent-seeking is often subsumed under the more general category of "directly unproductive profit-seeking" (DUP) activities, such as lobbying, smuggling, bribery, monopoly, or any other activity which generates profits, but produces no goods or services directly.

9 Notice that the predatory state describes some of the features noted by Krueger, earlier in this chapter. Here, in contrast to Krueger, the dysfunctional state is viewed as an outgrowth of a specific historical condition. It is the "traditional," or pre-capitalist (semi-feudal/semi-capitalist) society, perhaps imbued with the ethos of merchant capital which results. Krueger assumes that by shrinking the state the society will be strengthened, because there is assumed to exist an ordered, structured, market-based economy. Evans avoids the dichotomous assumption "bad state/good civil society." Here a chaotic socioeconomic system is complemented by a predatory state apparatus. Destroying such a state while leaving the socioeconomic system untouched would not solve the basic underlying problems.

10 Notice the surface similarities between Evans' intermediate state and Krueger's factional state. Krueger finds rent-seeking, which distorts the intention of government policy by locking in place subsidies and other forms of vested interests. Her solution is shrinking the state.

For Evans, rents arise not from too much intervention, but from too little effective intervention, because of a lack of an adequately trained, professional civil service.

While far from the ideal, the intermediate state exhibits "pockets of efficiency" in the state sector, something Krueger rules out by assumption. Such "pockets" are hardly trivial; they form the basis for the creation of whole new industries. They redefine the production base, creating new forms of comparative advantage. Krueger's approach cannot accommodate such activities, which Evans presents in some detail. And, therefore, the new political economy approach has difficulty explaining the economic development of such nations as Brazil, India, or Mexico, all important instances of the intermediate state.

11 The concept of demiurge is not the same as what Lal called "dirigiste dogma." Lal refers to a situation wherein the government seeks to supplant the market, rather than supplement it. The demiurge function is limited to the creation of state-owned enterprises, or what are sometimes known as para-state firms.

References

Adelman, Irma. 2001. "Fallacies in Development Theory," pp. 103–134 in Gerald Meier and Joseph Stiglitz (eds), *Frontiers of Development Economics*. Oxford: Oxford University Press.

Amsden, Alice. 1989. *Asia's Next Giant*. Oxford: Oxford University Press.

—— 2001. *The Rise of "the Rest."* Oxford: Oxford University Press.

Bauer, P.T. 1984. "Remembrance of Studies Past," pp. 27–43 in Gerald Meier and Dudley Seers (eds), *Pioneers in Development*. Oxford: Oxford University Press.

Bhagwati, Jagdish and Anne Krueger. 1973. "Exchange Control Liberalization and Development," *American Economic Review* 63 (June): 419–427.

Cain, P.J. and A.G. Hopkins. 1993. *British Imperialism: Crisis and Deconstruction 1914–1990*. London: Longman.

Chang, Ha-Joon. 2000. "The Hazard of Moral Hazard: Untangling the Asian Crisis," *World Development* 28: 775–788.

—— 2002. *Kicking Away the Ladder: Development Strategy in Historical Perspective*. London: Anthem Press.

Cheng, Tun-jen. 1990. "Political Regimes and Development Strategies," pp. 139–178 in Gary Gereffi and Donald Wyman (eds), *Manufacturing Miracles*. Princeton, NJ: Princeton University Press.

Cypher, James. 1990. *State and Capital in Mexico*. London and Boulder, CO: Westview Press.

—— 2001a. "Developing Disarticulation within the Mexican Economy," *Latin American Perspectives* 28 (May) 11–37.

—— 2001b. "NAFTA's Lessons: From Economic Mythology to Current Realities," *Labour Studies Journal* 26 (Spring) 5–21.

Evans, Peter. 1995. *Embedded Autonomy: States and Industrial Transformation*. Princeton, NJ: Princeton University Press.

—— 1998. "Transferable Lesson?: Re-examining the Institutional Prerequisites of East Asian Economic Policies," *Journal of Development Studies* 34 (August) 66–86.

Fieldhouse, David K. 1967. *The Colonial Empires*. New York: Delacorte Press.

Girvetz, Harry K. 1963. *The Evolution of Liberalism*. New York: Collier Books.

Haberler, Gottfried. 1987. "Liberal and Illiberal Development Policy," in Gerald Meier (ed.), *Pioneers in Development*, 2nd series. Oxford: Oxford University Press.

Helleiner, Gerald. 1966. *Peasant Agriculture, Government, and Economic Growth in Nigeria*. Homewood, IL: Irwin.

Herring, Ronald. 1999. "Embedded Particularism: India's Failed Developmental State," pp. 306–334 in Merideth Woo-Cumings (ed.), *The Developmental State*. Ithaca: Cornell University Press.

Hopkins, A.G. 1973. *An Economic History of West Africa*. London: Longman.

Kemp, Tom. 1989. *Industrialization in the Non-Western World*. London: Longman.

Kohli, Atul. 1999. "Where do High-Growth Political Economies Come From? The Japanese Lineage of Korea's 'Developmental State,'" pp. 93–136 in Merideth Woo-Cumings (ed.), *The Developmental State*. Ithaca: Cornell University Press.

Krueger, Anne. 1993. *Political Economy of Policy Reform in Developing Countries*. Cambridge, MA: MIT Press.

Lal, Deepak. 1985. *The Poverty of Development Economics*. Cambridge, MA: Harvard University Press.

Lipton, Michael. 1984. "Comment [on Bauer]," in Gerald Meier and Dudley Seers (eds), *Pioneers in Development*. Oxford: Oxford University Press.

Little, Ian, Tibor Scitovsky and Maurice Scott. 1970. *Industry and Trade in Some Developing Countries*. Oxford: Oxford University Press.

Meier, Gerald. 1990. "Trade Policy and Development," pp. 155–169 in Maurice Scott and Ian Little (eds), *Public Policy and Economic Development*. Oxford: Oxford University Press.

Myint, Hla. 1987. "Neoclassical Development Analysis: Its Strengths and Limitations," in Gerald Meier (ed.), *Pioneers in Development*, 2nd series. Oxford: Oxford University Press.

Morris, Cynthia and Irma Adelman. 1988. *Comparative Patterns of Economic Development: 1850–1910*. Baltimore: Johns Hopkins Press.

Pempel, T.J. 1999. "The Developmental Regime In a Changing World Economy," pp. 137–181 in Merideth Woo-Cumings (ed.), *The Developmental State*. Ithaca: Cornell University Press.

Rodrik, Dani. 1999. *The New Global Economy and Developing Countries: Making Openness Work*. Baltimore: Johns Hopkins Press.

Schneider, Ben Ross. 1999. "The *Desarrollista* State in Brazil and Mexico," pp. 276–305 in Merideth Woo-Cumings (ed.), *The Developmental State*. Ithaca: Cornell University Press.

Shapiro, Helen and Lance Taylor. 1990. "The State and Industrial Strategy," *World Development* 18 (June): 861–878.

Srinivasan, T.N. 1984. "Comment [on Bauer]," in Gerald Meier and Dudley Seers (eds), *Pioneers in Development*. Oxford: Oxford University Press.

Stiglitz, Joseph. 2001. "More Instruments and Broader Goals: Moving Toward the Post-Washington Consensus," pp. 17–56 in Ha-Joon Chang (ed.), *The Rebel Within: Joseph Stiglitz and the World Bank*. London: Anthem Press.

Toye, John. 1987. *Dilemmas of Development*. Oxford: Basil Blackwell.

UN Development Program. 2003. *Human Development Report 2003*. New York: Oxford University Press.

Wade, Robert. 1990. "Industrial Policy in East Asia: Does it Lead or Follow the Market?," in Gary Gereffi and Donald Wyman (eds), *Manufacturing Miracles*. Princeton, NJ: Princeton University Press.

World Bank. 1993. *The East Asian Miracle*. Oxford: Oxford University Press.

8 Endogenous growth theories and new strategies for development

After studying this chapter, you should understand:

- the difference between "conditional" and "unconditional" income convergence;
- the basic structure of endogenous growth models and how they differ from both the classical and neoclassical growth theories;
- the importance of human capital, learning-by-doing and other positive externalities to sustaining economic growth;
- the significance of constant and increasing returns in the endogenous growth models;
- the effects of inequality of income and land distribution on the rate of economic growth;
- the importance of social infrastructure and other alterable initial endowments to the rate of economic growth;
- the significance of "technical efficiency change" and "total factor productivity" to economic growth; and
- the role that social institutions can play in contributing to or thwarting economic progress.

Introduction

Near the end of Chapter 4, the Solow neoclassical growth theory was introduced. It has been interpreted as predicting that the per capita incomes of economies will tend to converge to the same level over time as lower income nations grow faster than higher income nations, assuming they all have access to the same technology and share similar savings and investment rates.[1] Solow's theoretical structure lent credence to and validated the policy recommendations of many of the early developmentalist economists and their policy-oriented theories, like the "big push," "balanced growth" and "unbalanced growth" strategies considered in Chapter 5. You will remember that these were strategies that focused on the expansion of the industrial capital stock and the rate of savings as the means to promote economic growth and higher income per capita.

The primacy of physical capital accumulation, the K variable in the Solow-type aggregate production function, has continued to draw the attention of development economists. In this traditional view, to develop, countries need to save and invest so as to augment the total capital stock of the nation. A larger physical capital stock per worker will boost the attainable level of income by increasing the productivity of each worker who will have more physical capital with which to work. Of course, it was recognized that many poor nations would have trouble in accumulating this capital, as their low level of income meant limited savings to finance new investments. Because of low incomes and savings, the level of capital accumulation might remain insufficient to achieve higher levels of per capita income in such countries.[2]

However, as Chapter 5 discussed, flush with the success of post-Second World War reconstruction in Europe and Japan, most early development economists believed that domestic saving and investment could be complemented by external financing. Total saving and investment, and hence aggregate economic growth, were not constrained in some absolute sense by a shortage of domestic resources in less-developed nations. Rather, total saving was equal to $S = S_D + S_F$, where S is total saving, S_D is domestic saving by households, business, and government and S_F is foreign saving in the form of loans, aid, and direct foreign investment. The level of investment of a country was not believed to be rigidly determined by the country's own limited ability to save, thus breaking the link between low income and low savings that seemed to constrain the possibilities of the poorest of the less-developed nations to a vicious cycle of poverty. External resources could add to, and complement, domestic financing for investment and thus spur economic growth and development.

The income convergence controversy

The 1950s and 1960s were periods of relative optimism among development economists and policy-makers alike. The economic models of the day strongly suggested that economic growth was essentially a technical problem to be solved through larger injections of physical capital and secondarily through measures to slow population expansion. Development economists had no shortage of recommendations as to the strategic means for adding to that stock of capital, as we learned in Chapter 5.[3] Further, the convergence of world income levels predicted by Solow-type neo-classical growth models, with which the economics literature abounds, reassured economists and policy-makers alike that within the not-too-distant future, world poverty could perhaps reasonably be expected to be eradicated. The relatively rapid rates of growth of many countries in the less-developed world compared to the already-developed nations in the period after the Second World War seemed to corroborate these hopeful prognostications, at least for a time.

As Table 8.1 shows, there did seem to be data to support such optimism concerning the future of the less-developed world and of the prospects for income convergence. Comparing the "low- and middle-income economies" with the "high-income economies" over the period 1965–1980, the rate of per capita income growth of the former exceeded that of the latter, providing support for the income convergence hypothesis. But, from 1980 onward through 2001 the convergence hypothesis is unsupported – except in Asia.

When the data are looked at more closely and disaggregated by regions, there is much greater variability in the results. Over some periods, some regions outperform the high-income economies (for example, Latin America from 1965–1980), while in other periods they do not (again, Latin America underperformed over the period 1980–2001).

Table 8.1 Comparative growth rates

	2001 GNP	Average annual rate of growth of income per capita[a] (%)			
		1965–1973[a]	*1973–1980*[a]	*1980–1990*[b]	*1990–2001*[b]
Low- and middle-income economies	1,160	4.3	2.7	1.2	1.9
Low-income	430	2.5	2.6	2.0	1.4
Middle-income	1,850	–	–	1.3	2.2
Sub-Saharan Africa	470	1.7	0.9	−1.3	0.0
East Asia and Pacific	900	5.0	4.8	5.9	6.3
South Asia	450	1.2	1.7	3.4	3.6
Latin America	3,560	4.6	2.2	−0.3	1.6
Middle East and North Africa	2,000	6.0	1.7	−1.7	0.9
High-income economies	26,710	3.7	2.1	2.6	1.8

Sources: World Bank 1993b: 199, Table A-2; 1995: 162–163, Table 1; 2003a: 235, Table 1; World Bank 2003b: 187, Table 4.1.

Notes
a GNP; the World Bank now calls GNP *gross national income* or GNI.
b GDP.

Two regions, however, stand out for their consistency. Sub-Saharan Africa's growth rates have been lower than those of the high-income economies in every period, while East Asia and the Pacific, which includes South Korea and Taiwan, have unfailingly had growth rates of income per person greater than those in the high-income economies.

Disaggregating the economic growth data, then, provides us with what some take to be contradictory evidence for income convergence and for the neoclassical hypothesis that one should expect faster growth *rates* for countries with lower incomes. In some cases, for example, East Asia and the Pacific, the neoclassical theory would seem to fit. For other regions, like sub-Saharan Africa, just the opposite appears true. Virtually the poorest region, sub-Saharan Africa has had the worst overall growth performance. The neoclassical model would have predicted that it would have been precisely these lower-income economies that would have the greatest opportunities for profits from increased capital accumulation. Their growth rates would have been expected to be the highest, not the lowest as they actually were.

This way of looking at the data in Table 8.1 might be termed the crude neoclassical prediction and would be consistent with an expectation of unconditional income convergence over time. It is an interpretation based on the belief that in a relatively open international economy, where both physical and financial capital are relatively mobile, if in some regions or countries capital is scarce, as in sub-Saharan Africa, then the lower quantity of capital will correspond to a higher expected rate of return to investors.[4] It would be expected that international capital flows would be toward such capital-scarce nations, thus increasing their rate of investment relative to total output and to their level of GNP, and contributing, over time, to the convergence of incomes among nations as the stock of capital rose in the less-developed nations.

As discussed in Chapter 4 and in note 1, however, the Solow-type neoclassical model actually anticipates income convergence *only* when countries have similar savings rates and similar population growth rates – that is, income convergence is "conditional" on countries sharing the same *fundamentals*. It is not dependent upon international capital flows to productive investment, the magnitude of which could never achieve convergence (see Chapter 14 on the size of such flows). Sub-Saharan Africa has the lowest level of investment and savings as a share of GDP of any region, as can be seen from Table 8.2. Thus, even if population growth rates were similar between this region and the higher income economies (which they are not; see Chapter 12), we should *not* expect to see a convergence of income per capita between Sub-Saharan Africa and the high-income economies, due to the large differential in the rate of investment and saving. In other words, the necessary conditions for income convergence to occur are absent.

On the other hand, East Asia and the Pacific have experienced a dramatic increase in investment and saving rates, so that investment equals 30 percent or more of output. Growth rates of per capita income in East Asia increased more rapidly over the period, as shown in Table 8.1, so the gap between East Asian incomes and incomes in more-developed nations was closing. In fact, as the Solow-model would predict (refer back to equation 4.5), if East Asian saving and investment rates were to remain as high as they are for a sufficiently long period of time, per capita income in the region would eventually be even higher than those of all other regions, when the steady-state equilibrium level of income was reached, since the region's level of investment and saving is the highest in the world!

However, there is something slightly disconcerting about the statistics contained in Tables 8.1 and 8.2. The differences in investment and savings rates and in the aggregate size of the capital stock in different nations do not seem to be able to explain the persistence of the large absolute income differentials which persist between regions. Why, even though sub-Saharan Africa saves and invests less than the high-income regions, is the *absolute* level of income so low relative to the high-income areas, given that the differences in savings and investment rates shown in

Table 8.2 Saving and investment by region (as a percentage of GDP)

	1965		1989		2000	
	S	I	S	I	S	I
Low- and middle-income economies	20	20	27	26	26	23
Low-income	18	19	26	28	20	20
Middle-income	21	22	27	25	26	24
Sub-Saharan Africa	14	14	13	15	17	17
East Asia and Pacific	23	22	35	34	35	30
South Asia	14	17	18	22	20	23
Latin America	21	20	24	20	19	20
High-income economies	17	17	22	22	22[a]	22[a]

Sources: World Bank 1991: 220–221, Table 9; 1995: 178–179, Table 9; 2002 World Development Indicators data set.

Note
a 1999.

Table 8.2 are not that dramatic and that new investment there should be more effective in raising incomes compared to higher income economies?[5] What other forces are at work besides the level and rate of saving and investment that might be affecting both growth rates and the absolute levels of income?

Income convergence and path dependence

Lloyd Reynolds found what seemed to be path-dependent patterns of growth rates for regions in his study of "turning points" in economic development. Some countries with certain shared characteristics invariably performed better over time in terms of their income per capita growth rates than other economies with different characteristics (Reynolds 1986: 79–80). If there is path dependence resulting from specific growth-inhibiting characteristics that are cumulative in their effects, then catch-up by the poorest countries, which have had the lowest average growth rates, obviously would be impossible. What seems to be clear is that countries which already have attained a higher level of income and output and are embarked on a high growth path tend to continue to grow faster in the future, for reasons which are considered below. Those countries with low absolute incomes and which find themselves on a lower growth path tend to grow slower in future, so that the income gap is widening among poor and rich nations rather than shrinking. All this is contrary to the predictions of the neoclassical models and the hopes of so many development economists. How well countries are performing today seems to be the best predictor of how they will perform in the future.

Yet, the past does not have an absolute stranglehold on the future. There remain anomalies among the less-developed nations. Some have apparently altered the character of their path dependence. They have found the means to jump to a higher standard of living and more rapid economic growth. The faster growth rates and rapidly rising incomes observed in some countries or regions that had been relatively low-income in the not-too-distant past, like South Korea in East Asia, and their ability to sustain these high rates of growth over time are reminiscent of the "virtuous circles" and "cumulative causation" effects that many developmentalists and heterodox economists observed at work in their earlier historical studies of other nations (Chapters 5 and 6). Further, one might argue that the negative impact of Myrdal-type "backwash effects," or "vicious circles," might account for the consistent lack of progress in sub-Saharan Africa and South Asia, despite investment and savings rates that would have led one to believe that incomes should be rising more rapidly than they are.

The lingering repercussions of path dependence, then, as discussed in Chapters 3 and 5, thus seem to be at work in many instances. Once started on the road to development – the high path – a virtuous circle of rewards in the form of continued growth follows. For countries which are poor, being poor puts them on a low-growth path, a vicious circle leading to low incomes in the future. The conundrum remains, however, of how nations on a low path might switch to a high path, so that a prior debilitating path dependence is overcome and replaced by a qualitatively new, growth-augmenting style of path dependence, with greater promise for economic and human development over the future. What is important to realize is that the possibility exists of changing the nature of path dependence, for good or bad, via the decisions which governments and their citizens take in the present.

Such incongruities in what economists thought should be happening to growth rates of different nations and regions based on the neoclassical model, coupled with concerns over the widening, rather than shrinking, income gap among some countries, led in the mid-1980s to a re-examination of growth theory. The causal factors in the economic growth process were reassessed with greater attention to the effects of path dependence and vicious and virtuous circles as propagating mechanisms.[6]

Endogenous growth models

The relatively slow progress of many African and South Asian economies have caused quite a number of economists to question the validity of any growth model which predicts eventual income convergence, conditional or unconditional. This has led to a critical examination of the policy recommendation to accumulate ever more physical capital, that is, to save or borrow more, that flowed from the neoclassical economic formulations. As one economist recently put it:

> The idea that capital investment is essential to the long-run state of growth of a nation is a common, if somewhat vague, axiom of most policy discussions of economic growth and development. Yet for the better part of a generation the preeminent theory of economic growth developed by the Nobel Prize winning economist Robert Solow and the data summarized by the important contributions of Edward Denison, John Kendrick, Solow, and others have provided us with virtually no basis for making such claims. Perhaps even more striking was the fact that theory seemed unable to explain the extreme and persistent differences in living standards or growth rates across countries.
>
> (Plosser 1993: 57)

The empirical research on growth using the neoclassical framework typically found that a significant portion of the growth rate of a country, often well over 50 percent and more, could *not* be accounted for by changes in the use of capital and labor, leaving the unexplained Solow residual as the major determinant explaining growth rates. All the diverse factors and influences that might reasonably be attributed to this residual – such as the effects of education, technology, business organization, research and development efforts, culture, growing international trade, local politics, and so on – invited much speculation, but empirical models that might have helped to untangle, classify, and identify these possible influences on economic growth rates were slow to appear.

Then, in the late 1980s, a spate of endogenous growth models began to emerge in the economics literature. Endogenous growth theories do not assume, nor do they find, physical capital accumulation to be the dominant determining factor in spurring economic growth nor in explaining differences in income levels among nations. Perhaps most importantly and controversially, these models jettison the neoclassical and classical assumption of diminishing returns as applying to any of the reproducible inputs to production, particularly capital and labor, but also technology, effectively turning a nation's short-run production function into a long-run, dynamic relationship that can be constantly evolving. And, lastly, the rate of growth of long-run per capita income is not constrained or explained by exogenous technological change.[7]

In the endogenous growth models, a higher level of investment, properly defined, not only can increase per capita income, as in the neoclassical view, but higher investment rates, again properly understood, also can *sustain* greater rates of growth of per capita income in the future. This is something not possible within the traditional neoclassical growth model, which finds that a steady-state income level, determined by the rate of saving and the population growth rate, is the equilibrium outcome of the growth process. If we take population growth as a constant, higher levels of income simply are not attainable in the neoclassical view *without* either an increase in the rate of saving or an exogenous boost to the level of technology. This is not the case in the endogenous growth models; it is possible for countries to continue to grow quickly for long periods, even when they already have achieved relatively high incomes. This sustaining of growth rates can occur *without* an increase in the rate of saving, an astonishing result. By breaking the link between the rate of economic growth and the law of diminishing returns and by removing the ceiling on income per person for any particular rate of savings and investment, endogenous growth models can quite easily account for a widening gap in income between poorer and richer nations, and they are able to do so in a manner reminiscent of our discussion of "cumulative causation" and consistent with recent theorizing about the power of path dependence in determining future growth trends.

In most endogenous growth models, one of the most important factors of production contributing to higher and sustained growth has been found to be both the rate of accumulation, as well as the initial stock, of human capital.[8] While these models share some similarities with the capital- and saving-centered neoclassical growth models in their form, the endogenous growth models do not predict the convergence of income levels, even among countries with similar rates of saving, investment and population growth rates. Indeed, these models reveal just how it is possible for some countries to continue to grow faster than others far into the future, with both the absolute and relative income gap growing. Endogenous growth models also place a quite different emphasis on what is required to boost a country's economic growth and development possibilities compared to the recommendations derived from the capital- and saving-centered neoclassical-type models. Today, the endogenous growth model structure is shaping the way many economists think about policy and how they identify the most severe barriers to development.[9]

A key document both contributing to and signalling this shift in emphasis was the World Bank study, *The East Asian Miracle* (World Bank 1993a).[10] This study of the "high-performance Asian economies" – the HPAEs – of Japan, Hong Kong, South Korea, Singapore, Taiwan, Indonesia, Malaysia, and Thailand is built around the insights flowing from the endogenous growth theory's methodology for identifying the crucial policy variables that might be manipulated in the growth process. These models also help to explain the power of path dependence on growth rates, as well as suggesting what is needed if countries are to jump from lower paths of growth and development to higher paths.

A simple endogenous growth model with externalities

The major conceptual difference between the Solow-type neoclassical growth models and the endogenous growth models is the presumption in the endogenous models that there are not necessarily diminishing returns to the reproducible factors of production, K, the stock of physical capital, to H, the stock of human capital nor to technology. Rather it is assumed that constant, or perhaps even increasing, marginal returns are possible.[11] How is this possibility explained?

What the endogenous growth models assume is that there are likely to be substantial positive externalities to human capital accumulation and, perhaps, to some physical capital accumulation to the extent that new capital embodies new technology, so that the classical and neoclassical result of diminishing returns to K and H are avoided through such society-wide spill-over effects. When the social benefits from human capital accumulation exceed the private benefits, there will be positive secondary and tertiary effects from, say, an increase in a country's average education level or enrollment ratios that reverberate through the economy. More educated and presumably more productive workers not only produce more at their own tasks, but they also interact synergistically with their workmates so that the productivity of other workers also rises, even though their level of education may have remained unchanged.[12]

Higher average levels of education among a population also can contribute to learning-by-doing effects, that is, the capacity of labor to build upon its past education and training, so that the same level of human capital input actually is able to improve its productivity over time in the process of producing goods and services on the shop floor, or wherever production takes place. Learning-by-doing contributes to increases in the potential level of total output without the need for an increase in any additional inputs and with no increase in investment. Learning-by-doing effects increase the productivity and effectiveness of labor. The presumption is that the higher the level of human capital accumulation in an economy, the stronger will be such effects, again breaking the link between growth in labor and human capital accumulation and diminishing returns.[13] In the endogenous growth theory view, the ability to use technology, the ability to develop it and the skills of the labor force available to complement technological knowledge are all formed in and shaped by each particular economy. In other words, growth is an endogenous process, coming from within each particular economy, with each having a different production function reflecting different quantities and qualities of its inputs.

A very general aggregate production function in the endogenous growth model form for a representative economy would look like (Romer 1994: 16):

$$Y = F(R, K, H) \tag{8.1}$$

where Y is total output, R is research and development (R&D) done by all firms in the economy, K is the accumulated capital stock and H is the accumulated stock of human capital. For analytical purposes, this formulation has at times been operationalized as a particular linear aggregate production function, often called an "AK" production function, for obvious reasons, shown in equation 8.2.

$$Y_t = aK_t \tag{8.2}$$

where K is redefined as a measure of the combined stock of human, physical, and research capital and a is a constant multiplier.[14] In this very simple formulation, there are constant returns to scale to K in production (since $xY_t = axK_t$, where x is any finite number), as well as constant marginal returns in the short-term, since

$dY/dK = a > 0$ and $d^2Y/dK^2 = 0$, so that the marginal product curve, MP_K, is a horizontal line with a constant value a. Since increased increments of K are not less effective than prior additions to K, both a rising per capita income and a non-decreasing rate of growth of per capita income are possible.

In a slightly more complex formulation that captures a bit more of the "endogeneity" of the growth process, we can write the aggregate production function as

$$Y_t = A(K)_t K_t \tag{8.3}$$

where $A(K)_t$ is the "induced or endogenous technological change" imparted to the economy by the stock of physical, human, and research capital particular to that country. In the production function shown in equation 8.3, different economies will have distinct $A(K)$ values, depending on the feedback mechanisms affecting technological adaptation and technological change specific to that economy. This reflects differences in human capital accumulation, micro and macro policies of business and government organization, social and physical infrastructure capacity, and so on. In the original Solow-neoclassical formulation, by comparison, technology, A, was "exogenous" to all economies, affecting them identically like manna from heaven. Technology was assumed to grow at the same rate for all countries, regardless of their own resources, policies, or actions.

In the endogenous growth models, technological progress as represented by $A(K)$ is dependent on the functioning of the particular economy. Specifically, it is dependent on the rate of capital formation, broadly defined. This includes physical, human and research capital, and *it also includes the organizational and institutional structures of that economy.* Such structures affect an economy's capacity to effectively utilize the world pool of knowledge in production, to adapt it, and eventually to add to that knowledge.

Thus, in the endogenous growth formulation, the level of technology and the rate of its application are not determined externally to the operation of that particular economy. The pace of technological change and the nature of the technology *in use* is endogenous, that is, it is internal to the specific functioning of any particular economy. Given this formulation, countries that accumulate more K and more H and undertake more R&D, R, may be able to continue to grow, and even to accelerate their economic growth rates over time compared to nations which accumulate these inputs at slower rates. Indeed, the pace of any individual country's technological progress is conditional on:

1 the level and type of education of the labor force and on the level and types of investment the society makes in R&D;
2 certain government policies, for example, tax credits for R&D, worker training and education, patent and copyright laws, and so on;
3 the economy's and society's organizational and institutional capabilities formed over time in both the private and *public* sectors.

Technology is not the A of the Solow-model available equally and identically to all countries as if it were a costless public good. In the endogenous growth models, technological change is country-specific. Moreover, it is, at least in part, a private good that is costly to produce for each country. The profits of such technology can be appropriated, to a degree, by the creator of the technology, which is typically assumed to be a private firm operating in an environment of imperfect competition.

Figure 8.1 shows an endogenous-growth production function implied by equation 8.3. Also shown for comparison is a typical, Solow-type neoclassical production function which exhibits diminishing returns to K. The neoclassical production function will shift upward for all economies when there are changes in exogenous technology, but along any given production function there are diminishing returns to the variable input shown on the horizontal axis (be it capital, K, or labor, L) as can be seen by the smaller slope of the production function at higher levels of K. However, for the endogenous growth function, $A(K)_t K_t$, there are no diminishing returns to the variable and reproducible factors of production (be they K, or human capital, H, or research and development, R).

Thus, while further investment cannot increase total output and hence output per person, Y_N/L, above Y_N given the neoclassical production function and its assumption of diminishing returns, additional investment in K, H and R in the endogenous growth formulation *can* increase output beyond Y_E along the $A(K)$ production function. As shown in Figure 8.1, there are constant returns to the reproducible inputs to production along $A(K)_t K_t$.

Given the embedded constant returns to each factor that endogenous growth models allow, convergence of income levels will not occur automatically via the law

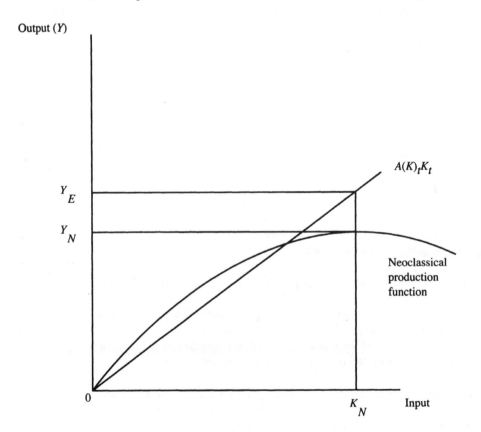

Figure 8.1 An endogenous growth production function.

of eventually diminishing returns to the variable inputs, since higher initial stocks of "augmented" K (physical, human, and research capital) contribute to even higher rates of growth in future. This occurs not because the world pool of "best practice" technological knowledge has expanded exogenously but as a consequence of the interaction of the reproducible inputs with each other in ways that positively contribute to greater efficiency in a given economy.

This, once again, is the result of past and current capital accumulation of all types which contribute to positive externalities and other spin-off effects from using the ever more high-powered and augmented inputs. More of some of the inputs to production, especially more human capital and research effort, permit the country to access and make use of the world pool of knowledge with greater facility. For example, a higher average level of education among the population today tends to promote better and more efficient human capital in the future so that the rate of economic growth need not decline, so long as such accumulation continues and so long as learning-by-doing and other production externalities persist. Similarly, expenditures by business and government directed toward facilitating research and development can contribute to long-term growth without such investment necessarily facing diminishing returns. Technological progress thus can be generated internally, at a pace that can prevent diminishing returns to the variable inputs from occurring.[15]

In the endogenous growth theory perspective, the key inputs to production are not perfect substitutes for one another. Physical capital, human capital and technology are, in fact, complementary inputs to production. This "means the higher the capital stock, the more technology can increase productivity. Instead of a one-time boost to productivity, higher rates of saving and capital investment increase the rate at which productivity rises. *There is no steady state of growth . . .* the key inputs of growth – skilled labour, sophisticated capital, new forms of technology – are not independent of each other but are positively interdependent" (Landau *et al.* 1996: 6; also see Lau 1996).

Endogenous growth models suggest that government policies can affect the rate of accumulation of both physical and human capital, as well as the level of research and development expenditures. Such policies are extremely important in boosting the long-run rate of growth for an economy by shaping future path dependence. Markets for saving and borrowing are often absent or less-than-perfect in many less-developed economies. Consequently, a purely market-based development strategy will *fail* to adequately tap a society's potential to the extent that investment is financed by private savings and investment decisions. Further, since firms that invest in labor training and in research and development often create positive externalities in production that spread to other producers, not all the profits from their investment activities will accrue to the firms making such investments. Therefore, left to their own devices, private firms are likely to invest less than would be socially desirable in labor training, in research and development and other such nonfully appropriable investments, since the private and social benefits of such expenditures diverge. Consequently, government action may be necessary to subsidize or otherwise directly augment such investment activities by private firms if the socially desired level of augmented capital accumulation is to be attained. (The theory of positive externalities, and the case for government action in the face of this type of market failure, are explored in detail in Chapter 12.) At the very least, the endogenous growth models and their insistence on the existence of pervasive positive externalities suggest a wider arena for public policy action than is immediately evident from the simple Solow model.

Key inputs to growth in endogenous growth models

The work on endogenous growth has been primarily empirical and econometric in nature. Robert J. Barro's research has been especially influential in this regard, but there are many other contributions, including some useful review essays (Barro 1991, 1993; Romer 1994; World Bank 1993a: ch. 1). The endogenous growth research measures the impact of various inputs on aggregate production. Table 8.3 presents the results of some of this research drawing on the World Bank's study (1993a) of the HPAEs (based on Barro's methodology) and a follow-up study by Rodrik (1994) incorporating additional factors affecting economic growth.

The regression coefficients in Table 8.3 show the contribution of the various factors in production to per capita income growth. They can be interpreted as follows. For the first variable, "Relative GDP," the World Bank's negative coefficient suggests, as the Solow-type neoclassical models predict, that countries with lower incomes will grow faster, holding all other factors constant. For example, for a country with a 1960 GDP only 40 percent of 1960 US GDP, it would be predicted that the poorer country would be expected to grow 1.28 percent (-40×-0.0320) faster per year than the United States over the period 1960–1985, *ceteris paribus*.

This "other factors remaining the same" assumption is quite important; it is an "as if" assumption used in interpreting each variable independently. It assumes when we look at the first coefficient that the only difference between a poor nation and a rich nation is the level of relative income, itself a reflection of the mass of physical capital employed, with this stock lower in poorer nations and higher in richer nations. All other possible differences between nations on all other variables are assumed away. Over time, then, the income per capita of poorer nations would be expected to converge to that of richer nations, provided the only difference

Table 8.3 Estimates of input contributions to per capita economic growth

Variable	World Bank coefficient	Rodrik coefficient
1 Relative GDP, 1960	-0.0320^b	-0.38^b
2 Primary school enrollment, 1960	0.0272^b	2.66^a
3 Secondary school enrollment, 1960	0.0069	
4 Population growth, 1960–1985	0.0998	
5 Average investment/GDP, 1960–1985	0.0285	
6 HPAEs	0.0171^b	
7 Latin America	-0.0131^b	
8 Sub-Saharan Africa	-0.0099^a	
9 Gini coefficient for land, around 1960		-5.22^b
10 Gini coefficient for income, around 1960		-3.47
Adjusted R^2	0.4821	0.53

Sources: World Bank 1993a: 51, Table 1.8; Rodrik 1994: 20, Table 3.

Notes
a Statistically significant at the 0.05 level.
b Statistically significant at the 0.01 level.

between countries *is* this initial difference in incomes due to differences in the initial stock of physical capital. Thus **conditional convergence** is confirmed in the World Bank model, since the first coefficient shows that being poor relative to the rich countries does tend to raise growth rates of output, all else constant.

However, actual convergence of income among countries is not presumed to occur in the endogenous growth models simply because of initial income differentials. Even among nations with identical rates of savings and investment, there are other inputs to production, especially the level and type of human capital in the World Bank model, that can and do result in quite different rates of economic expansion. In fact, as we shall see from examining the remainder of the coefficients in the first column of Table 8.3, income convergence is predicted to occur in the World Bank endogenous growth models only if a poorer country has a higher than average stock of human capital which will allow it to make ever better use of the world pool of technological knowledge and to take advantage of the positive externalities which result from higher human capital investments.

Income convergence is thus conditional on other factors at work internal to individual economies which can promote, permit, and support, or alternatively discourage, block and hinder, income convergence. The initial level of income and the pace of physical investment are insufficient factors in and of themselves in the endogenous growth framework to generate income convergence.

The second statistically significant variable in the World Bank model in Table 8.3 is the initial stock of accumulated human capital, as measured by primary school enrollment rates in 1960.[16] An increase of 10 percent in the primary school enrollment rate could potentially increase the annual predicted rate of growth of the average country by 0.27 percent (10×0.0272). Thus Peru, with a primary school enrollment rate in 1960 of 83 percent, would have been expected to have grown 0.95 percent faster each year than Mozambique, which had a 1960 primary school enrollment rate of 48 percent, again assuming all other variables are the same (World Bank 1993a: Table 25, pp. 196–197).

Variables 3, 4, and 5 in Table 8.3 were not found to be statistically significant in the World Bank model, that is, their coefficient values were not able to be confirmed as being different from zero, though the investment variable is statistically significant when variables 6, 7, and 8 are not included in the estimates.[17] Thus, the endogenous growth model suggests the unimportance, *by itself*, of the level of physical investment.

What variable 6 tells us is that if a country is one of the HPAEs,[18] that status added 1.7 percent per year to the growth of real per capita GDP. Unfortunately, exactly *why* HPAE status has this impact is unexplained by the variable itself: it is actually a *residual*, or dummy, variable that captures all the intangible factors that affect economic growth but which themselves are not measured in the World Bank model. These might include: good public administration; better organization of production at the firm level; appropriate macroeconomic policies; more efficient use of the world pool of technological knowledge; more and better R&D expenditures; education appropriate to modern economic growth; effective institutional and financial organizations; and so on. In a general sense, the reason for the better performance of the HPAEs is likely due to a more appropriate and facilitating institutional environment that has been conducive in recent decades to rapid economic growth and development at both the micro and macro levels. The East Asian economies have had weak *ceremonial* structures since the 1950s that do not impede, and in some cases may have promoted, the growth process.[19]

When one compares the values for variables 7 and 8 (also dummy variables) in the World Bank model, these estimates tell quite a different story than the HPAE dummy coefficient did. Being a Latin American country actually reduced the predicted growth rate by −1.31 percent per year over the 1960–1985 period, all else constant. For countries in sub-Saharan Africa, their growth rates were predicted to be lower by −0.99 percent per year, all else constant. Thus if a country in Latin America (or sub-Saharan Africa) were to be compared with one of the HPAE countries, even if each were identical with respect to all other variables, the Latin American (or sub-Saharan) economy would be predicted to have an annual growth rate per capita of 3.02 percent (2.70 percent) *lower* per year than the comparable HPAE economy.

Returning again, then, to the interpretation of variable 5, average investment as a share of GDP, the interpretation of this coefficient as statistically insignificant should be understood with care: this result does *not* prove that new capital formation in an economy is unimportant. Rather, the investment coefficient suggests that capital formation per se is a necessary, but not sufficient, condition for strong economic growth. In the case of the high-growth Asian economies, the necessary and sufficient conditions have been met. There, a given physical mass of capital equipment is more productively utilized than in Latin America and Africa. This is due to higher educational levels and other organizational and institutional factors not isolated by the World Bank study but rather captured in the dummy variables. When the World Bank compared the Asian economies with Latin America, it still found that 34 percent of the predicted differences in the growth rates between the regions could be explained by the higher physical investment levels in the HPAEs. Clearly, then, capital formation is important, but in the Bank study, relative educational levels explained more, 38 percent, of the predicted differences in growth rates between the two regions (World Bank 1993a: 53).

Note, too, from the value of the adjusted R^2 that the variables shown in Table 8.3 for the World Bank's model can explain only about 48 percent of the growth rate of per capita income of the average economy. That still leaves quite a lot out of the picture, in fact more than half of what determines growth remains unexplained, much as the Solow-residual left about half of the growth rate unexplained.

This unexplained difference in growth rates between regions or nations unaccounted for by differences in relative income levels, human capital or investment is, of course, of extreme importance. This variation in performance tells us that some countries perform better with the same endowments of labor, physical capital, and human capital than do other economies. They are more efficient in producing output than other economies that are seemingly identical in the so-called fundamental economic variables, that is, initial physical and human capital stocks. Thus simply accumulating capital, be it physical or human, is not the whole story of what promotes a higher level of economic development in the World Bank's version of the endogenous growth model. It is but part of what is necessary to stimulate economic growth and to qualitatively change the nature of path dependence.

Accumulating human capital may be necessary for achieving higher rates of economic growth, but it surely is not sufficient or more of the variation in income would be explained by the World Bank model. There are other factors, such as the entire macroeconomic environment of the economy, the types of human capital accumulated and their effectiveness in using technology and physical capital, and other positive externalities associated with the production process and the creation of technology that interact to contribute to aggregate growth. And surely, there are both micro and macro organizational and institutional forces at work. But none of these additional factors is identified explicitly in the World Bank estimation. They are implicit only.

Other empirical models have included more explanatory variables. For example, Barro (1991) uses the number of revolutions per year as a proxy measure of political stability; it has the expected negative effect on growth. So, too, do fertility rates, though weakly. Other estimates add R&D expenditures as an explanatory variable, and this raises the explanatory power of the model. There is a danger of adding too many different variables to the endogenous growth models. One wants a theory with some generality, not a grab bag of everything that might affect growth, since virtually anything can conceivably do so. What is important is to identify those factors that are *most* significant in influencing growth and for affecting the nature of path dependence. For endogenous growth theory in the World Bank-type endogenous growth format, these have been found to be human capital accumulation, capital accumulation (if only weakly supported), R&D expenditures, political stability, and openness to international trade.

Other endogenous factors: income and wealth distribution again

Dani Rodrik, of Harvard University and the National Bureau of Economic Research (NBER), redid the World Bank study, altering slightly the endogenous variables, but otherwise following the structure of the World Bank model (Rodrik 1994). By excluding the investment rate (see note 17), secondary education, and the population growth rate (which were not significant in the World Bank model shown in Table 8.3), and by including Gini coefficient measures for the degree of inequality in land and in income distribution, Rodrik was able to explain more of the growth rate in per capita income – between 53 and 67 percent, as opposed to 48 percent for the World Bank estimate.[20] Since data on land and income distribution were available for only forty countries, fewer than the sample used by the World Bank, Rodrik's study is somewhat less comprehensive. Nonetheless, these findings do contribute to the current research on the factors determining growth rates.

Taking the Asian nations as a group, one does find a significantly lower degree of inequality in land and in income distribution than in most other less-developed nations (see Focus 8.1). Rodrik's findings suggest that the lesser the degree of inequality in land distribution, the higher the level of economic performance. For example, a reduction in the Gini coefficient for land distribution from 0.5 to 0.4, implying less inequality, would be predicted, from coefficient 9, to increase the rate of growth of per capita income by 0.52 percent per year, a not insignificant amount.

From Chapter 2, Focus 2.4, we have already seen that too much inequality can be a substantial burden on economic growth rates, so it is valuable to have Rodrik's independent confirmation of precisely how adverse the effects of inequality are. Even though the Gini coefficient for income was significant only at the 10 percent confidence level (variable 10), its negative value, like the statistically significant negative value for land distribution, does imply an inverse relation

---

FOCUS 8.1   INEQUALITY AND GROWTH

There is no doubting that the East Asian HPAEs individually and as a group have had substantially less inequality in both their income and land distribution patterns than is the case for other less-developed nations, as the following table, from Rodrik (1994: 18) clearly shows. All Gini coefficient values are for the year closest to 1960.

	Gini coefficient for land	income
Hong Kong	–	0.49
Japan	0.47	0.40
South Korea	0.39	0.34
Malaysia	0.47	0.42
Taiwan	0.46	0.31
Thailand	0.46	0.41
Average, all eight HPAEs	*0.45*	*0.39*
Argentina	0.87	0.44
Brazil	0.85	0.53
India	0.52	0.42
Kenya	0.69	0.64
Mexico	0.69	0.53
The Philippines	0.53	0.45
Average, selected others	*0.68*	*0.50*

It will be remembered from Chapter 2 that Gini coefficients closer to 1 imply greater inequality while values closer to 0 suggest greater equality of the respective distribution. It is quite impressive to note the substantially greater degree of equality in both land and income distribution in the HPAE economies compared to other less-developed nations. It is certainly relevant to examine, as Rodrik does, the significance of these differences on the rate of growth and development. Rodrik finds that too much inequality is harmful to the level and to the pace of economic growth.

---

between inequality and per capita income that is very suggestive for policy. Since both of these Gini coefficient measures were for 1960 (or close to that year), lesser inequality may be a significant initial condition, just as the stock of human capital is, which countries need to achieve as a threshold instrumental variable fundamental for future success in economic and human development. Rodrik also found, as did the World Bank, that the level of accumulated human capital, coefficient 2 in Table 8.3, to be very significant for growth.

Thus part of the reason for the lower growth rates of income for non-HPAEs such as economies in Latin America and in Sub-Saharan Africa may be due to the greater degree of inequality in those economies. While Rodrik's work still leaves other reasons for differences in income levels among economies as unexplained, as evidenced by the adjusted R^2 value, the inclusion of the degree of inequality would appear to add a further insight of importance for nations that remain relatively poor.[21] Further, as Rodrik (1994: 22) argues,

> once initial levels of schooling and equality are taken into account, there appears to be nothing miraculous about the HPAE's growth experience ... Around 90 percent or more of the growth of Korea, Taiwan, Malaysia, and Thailand can be accounted for by these economies' exceptionally high levels of primary school enrollment and equality around 1960.

In other words, Rodrik does not believe that the East Asian economies have resorted to any "miracle" strategies, as the title of the World Bank study might suggest, in shifting from a less-developed path to one taking them toward a more developed status. What the East Asian economies achieved and what contributed to their economic growth is tangible and reproducible and was "by design." No miracles were required. Attention was directed and public policies devised to forge the key "fundamentals" that provided the essential initial conditions conducive to future progress. In the case of primary and secondary education and increased equality, these are examples of **social infrastructure** or social capital. They are just as important to economic growth, and to human development, as are physical infrastructure, such as ports, roads, water and power, and communications systems. Too often, perhaps, social infrastructure has not been accorded sufficient attention by policy-makers in less-developed economies. The evidence now seems clear, and more will be adduced later, in support of more productive public policies for economic growth.

Technical efficiency change

Part of the story told by the endogenous growth theories has to do with the effectiveness with which the endowments – human capital, physical capital, other resources, knowledge, etc. – which an economy has available are utilized in the production process. This effectiveness can be measured by what the World Bank calls **technical efficiency change**. The idea behind this concept is illustrated in Figure 8.2, which shows a standard production possibilities frontier. Technological change, which we might think of as a change in the aggregate of technical knowledge at the world level irrespective of whether any particular country can make use of it, can be represented by an outward shift of the frontier from FF_1 to FF_2.[22] If an economy had originally been producing at A on FF_1 and then, after the technological advance, moves to B on FF_2, it would be exactly keeping pace with the current rate of technological advance and of international "best practice." For this country, its rate of economic growth will be determined by the rate of world technological advance. In doing so the country itself may even be contributing as an innovator via its own research and development efforts (World Bank 1993a: 49–50, 68–69).

Consider an economy beginning at a position like C, inside of FF_1, which moves toward D, inside FF_2. By approaching closer to the new production possibilities frontier compared to its position relative to the former production possibilities frontier, it will be experiencing *positive* technical efficiency change. The level of international best practice is being approached as the nation's productive resources are better able to capture the advantages of increases in world knowledge. For such countries, their rate of economic growth will exceed the average rate of world technological change as measured by the shift outward of the PPF. Such economies are better able to make use of their current resource endowments in ways that enhance the overall rate of economic expansion. This permits growth rates that exceed the pace of overall, world best-practice technological change. In other words, such countries are able to combine their existing resources in more efficient combinations by being better able to utilize and perhaps create technological change. This may be due to improvements in the stock of human capital accumulated, learning-by-doing, continued improvements in the macroeconomic or microeconomic

Capital goods

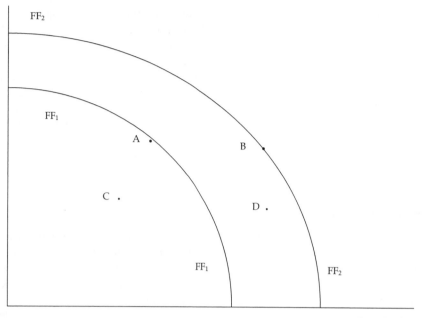

Consumption goods

Figure 8.2 Technological change versus technical efficiency change.

management of the economy, or to any of a number of possible causes, internal and external.

Table 8.4 summarizes the World Bank's estimates of how various countries and regions did relative to international "best practice" technology, that is, in terms of technological efficiency change and their progress toward reaching the ever-moving optimal production possibilities frontier resulting from constant technological change at the international level.

Of the HPAEs, Hong Kong, Japan, Taiwan, and Thailand were making progress toward using, and using more effectively, the best available technology.[23] This happened, the World Bank suggests (and Chapter 12 will consider this reasoning in detail) because these countries had accumulated an appropriate stock of human capital that permitted them to learn from, adapt and use new technologies, new ideas, and new production processes discovered elsewhere, perhaps even adding to best practice methods adapted to their own economies as a consequence of trial-and-error. Singapore, Malaysia, Indonesia, and even apparently South Korea, however, were slipping behind world best practice. Graphically this would mean that their relative position compared to the outward-shifting production possibilities frontier in Figure 8.2 was to be further inside the outward shifting frontier, that is,

Table 8.4 Estimates of technical efficiency change, 1960–1989

	Technical efficiency change
Latin America	−1.4217
Sub-Saharan Africa	−3.4539
HPAEs	
Hong Kong	1.9714
Japan	0.9876
Taiwan	0.8431
Thailand	0.1067
Indonesia	−1.2352
Malaysia	−1.7767
South Korea	−0.2044
Singapore	−3.4510

Source: World Bank 1993a: 69.

further away from the expanding pool of technological knowledge and its application to the production process.[24]

For Latin America and sub-Saharan Africa, there also was a growing shortfall from the most efficient production methods. This situation was most severe in the case of sub-Saharan Africa, which, effectively was falling further and further behind in the ability to use its resources in ways that could positively augment production and human development. This reflects a weakness in the creation of human capital and in R&D expenditures, and perhaps also is a consequence of the inequalities in land and income distribution that render the sub-Saharan economies unable to use, adopt or even adapt very effectively what the world pool of technology has to offer. Additionally, the productivity gap between sub-Saharan Africa and Latin America and the HPAEs was widening due to these differences in technological capacity, making even relative, unconditional convergence of incomes impossible without a substantial turn-around in the level of technical efficiency change. That will require changes in the factors that the new growth theories see as fundamental to stimulating growth. More saving or investment alone are not sufficient. There must be appropriate human capital accumulation and sufficient research and development funds so that a critical threshold of domestic technological competency is reached, better macroeconomic policies, changes in industrial organization and business practices, and, following Rodrik, amelioration of severe inequality even may be a prerequisite. These are themes we will touch on in the remaining chapters, building on the endogenous growth theories and the identification of some of the fundamental policy variables.

Questions for review

1 Distinguish between "conditional convergence" and "unconditional convergence" of per capita income. On what does "conditional" convergence of income depend in the neoclassical model? Do either the Solow-type growth model or the endogenous growth model predict *unconditional* convergence of incomes among nations? What would unconditional convergence of incomes imply for the future?

2   As economies become more developed, a larger share of output tends to be produced first by the industrial sector and then by the services sector, including government, as the movement of labor from agriculture is completed. Historically, growth rates of mature economies like the United States, Great Britain, and Germany have slowed as the service sector grows in importance, compared to their growth rates during their industrial phase. Discuss the possibility of what might be called the *structural convergence* of income among countries if the transition to service economies is reached by more developed countries, while more less-developed countries industrialize and accelerate their growth rates.

3   How can increased human capital accumulation, say to a higher average number of years of education for a population, contribute to sustaining the rate of economic growth over time? What *specific* positive externalities might be expected from workers with more education interacting with other workers with education? Can you see how two (or more) such workers might be more productive together than they would be if they did not interact? Can you give some concrete examples of how and when such interaction has resulted in such positive externalities? (One example: Have you ever studied with someone else? Can both learn more by such sharing than by studying alone? Is this a positive externality effect?)

4   How can a country try to improve its pace of "technical efficiency change"? What public policies might be required? Are there "initial conditions" important if an economy is to have a positive rate of technical efficiency change? Such as? Is "technology" something that all economies can use with the same effectiveness? Why, or why not?

5   What does it mean to say technological change is *endogenous* to an economy? How is this different from viewing technological change as *exogenous*? How does the idea that technology is country-specific fit into this view? Can technological change be both exogenous and endogenous at the same time? Which view makes most sense to you?

6   Looking back at Table 8.1, how many years will it take the low- and middle-income countries to double their per capita income, assuming they continue to grow at the average annual rate which prevailed during 1990–2001? How many years will it take for the high-income economies to double their per capita income, using their average annual growth rate for 1990–2001? How long would it take sub-Saharan Africa to double its income per person if it grew at the average annual rate which prevailed from 1990–2001? (Hint: If you do not know the Rule of 70, look forward to Chapter 12, where it is reviewed.)

7   Consider Table 8.4 on "technical efficiency change." What might be some reasons explaining the negative value for South Korea? Does negative technical efficiency change necessarily mean an economy is inefficient or becoming more so? What does negative technical efficiency mean, then?

Notes

1 In Solow-type neoclassical models, technology is treated as if it were a pure public good available to all countries and firms freely and with the same effect on productivity when applied to the production process, regardless of any differences in organizational or institutional structures or in the levels of education or skill levels of the work force.

Income convergence among nations will not occur in the Solow model, however, if a poor country does not save and invest at the same rate as higher-income countries, that is, there is not unconditional convergence predicted by the neoclassical model. Being a model where growth is based primarily on capital accumulation, that is, on additional investment, which is equal to saving in the neoclassical formulation, the Solow model only predicts convergence of poor nations to rich nations if the poor nations save and invest a proportion of their GDP which is similar to that of the richer nations, assuming comparable rates of population growth. Income convergence is thus conditional on the similarity of the fundamental variables affecting the level of income per capita shown in equation 4.5.

2 The level of savings in period t, S_t, is related to the level of aggregate income. In simple models, this relation is often stated as $S_t = a + sY_t$, where Y_t is income in period t, $a > 0$ is some constant amount saved out of income each period t, and $0 < s < 1$, is the marginal propensity to save (MPS), that is, the fraction of each additional unit of income which is saved rather than spent. It is easy to see that if the constant, a, the marginal propensity to save, s, and income, Y_t, are small, then so too will be S_t. To the extent that saving is required for investment, then a low level of aggregate savings contributes to a low level of aggregate investment and a lower rate of economic growth in future. Other, more complex, and perhaps more realistic, theories of savings, such as the "permanent income hypothesis" and the "relative income hypothesis" can be read about in any intermediate macroeconomics text, but the "low income–low saving" relation remains in force within these more complex formulations.

Also of interest are the Kaleckian or Kaldorian-type savings functions which disaggregate savings behavior by classes, usually the working and the capitalist class, each of which is presumed to have a different propensity to save. In such models, the higher income, capitalist class is assumed to save more than workers, and thus income inequality is presumed to functionally contribute to a higher level of investment and greater economic growth. In many developing nations, however, this may be an unwarranted assumption. To the degree that conspicuous consumption plays an important role among the remnants of the agro-export and financial elites, the rate of domestic saving may be driven down, as will the rate of capital formation, by a high degree of income inequality. This possibility is considered later in this chapter.

3 The literature is vast and often quite challenging. For a useful collection of original readings, see Stiglitz and Uzawa (1969).

4 This is due to the assumption of diminishing returns to capital. As the amount of capital, K, in use increases, its marginal product, $MP_K = df(K)/dK$, decreases. If we use the shorthand of assuming profit, r, to be the return to capital paid in units of production, then the return to capital when there are K_0 units of capital, r_0, is greater than where there are K_1 units of capital in use, if $K_0 < K_1$. Graphically, the slope of the production function gets flatter, and r decreases as K increases.

5 Plosser (1993: 63–64), for example, notes that recent estimates of the Solow model show that if physical capital differences were to account for the fact that per capita income in the United States is about twenty times that of Kenya, the United States capital stock per person would have to be of the order of 8,000 times greater than in Kenya, when in fact it is "only" about twenty-six times larger. This leads to the suggestion that there must be factors other than the stock of physical capital and of rates of investment which can account for wide income differentials between developed and less-developed nations.

6 The slow-down in economic growth rates and in the pace of job creation in Europe and the United States since the early 1980s also exerted a strong influence on the re-evaluation of the sources of economic growth. Economists have been pushed into service to discover the reasons for the lags in productivity beginning to haunt some of the leading Western economies. The recent concern over long-run growth by the economics profession thus has not been aimed solely at understanding why most less-developed nations have remained poor while others, particularly the East Asian economies, have been able to make progress. Rather, they have been concerned with why Europe and the United States were stagnating relative to Japan and other emerging economic powers.

7 In fact, the Solow-type model might be called an *exogenous* growth model, in the sense

that once a nation reaches its "steady state" level of income per capita as determined in equation 4.5, income per capita will *only* grow in future at a pace determined by the rate of exogenous, that is, externally determined, technological change taking place at the world level. On the other hand, in the *endogenous* growth models, the rate of change of both short- and long-term income per capita are internal, that is endogenous, to the workings of that specific economy, its organizational structure, labor types and skills, institutions, and an entire range of factors we shall be discussing below which interact to "determine" the pace of technological process specific to that economy.

8 Human capital creation is defined as any improvement in the quality of labor, be that the result of increased education, on-the-job learning, better health care, interaction with other workers with accumulated human capital, or other influences which improve labor's productivity without adding more physical capital to production.

9 However, controversy over superiority of the endogenous growth models versus the neo-classical model continues. The endogenous growth theories ask economists to let go of the concept of diminishing returns in the short-term for some variable inputs, especially human capital, a large theoretical leap given the power of neoclassical theory. For a taste of the strength of the passions, and perhaps egos, involved on both sides of this debate, see the mostly non-technical symposium on endogenous growth in the *Journal of Economic Perspectives*, Winter 1994. Leading proponents of the endogenous model, such as Paul Romer, square off against skeptics, like Robert Solow, who defends a revised neo-classical model.

10 It is perhaps worth noting that the World Bank study was initiated at the insistence of, and financed by, the government of Japan as a result of "a determination on Japan's part to get the World Bank to pay greater attention to the distinctive features of the East Asian development experience, which stood in marked contrast to development approaches the Bank was then advocating" (Fishlow and Gwin 1994: 3). As many commentators have noted, there is much in the Bank's report that would seem to reflect a criticism of past World Bank policy and an acceptance of at least some aspects of a more activist approach for certain kinds of state involvement in the support of more rapid economic growth and human development.

11 Solow (1994: 49–51) has argued, however, that the jettisoning of diminishing returns to the variable inputs is one of the weakest links in the endogenous growth models. He shows that if marginal returns are increasing, then the theoretical endogenous growth model would predict an infinite level of per capita income in the finite future, a clear impossibility. Typical of Solow, known for his humorous side, he comments on this "knife-edge" instability of the increasing returns assumption: "It is one thing to say that [income] will eventually exceed any bound. It is quite another to say that it will exceed any stated bound before Christmas." So, if there are increasing returns to any factor, the theoretical model explodes to infinity. If there are diminishing returns, on the other hand, the endogenous model is reduced to the Solow model, and there will be a finite, steady-state income level. Only when there are constant returns to the variable factors does the possibility of sustained increases in long-term per capita income make theoretical sense in the endogenous growth model. Solow, however, does not think that the real world is likely to be so precise.

Lau (1996: 90), however, finds increasing returns to scale on the order of 1.6 for developing economies and approximately constant returns for more mature economies, suggesting sustained growth is possible and that, perhaps, the real world is more precise than Solow would give it credit and that it may be possible to have "constant" increasing returns.

12 As Lucas (1988) observed, individuals who have accumulated human capital tend to gravitate toward locations where human capital is abundant not toward where it is scarce. Thus individuals in rural areas with more education migrate to cities, and highly educated persons in less-developed nations often migrate from the cities of their own country to the cities of more-developed nations – the so-called brain drain – to associate with others with abundant human capital.

This is strong, if casual, evidence for the positive externality effect of human capital; the productivity of one individual's human capital is increased, not decreased, when it is combined with more human capital inputs similar or higher in quality. That is, this is evidence for an absence of diminishing returns to human capital accumulation and, via positive externalities, for increasing returns to such inputs. Myrdal, of course, made much the same point in discussing "virtuous circles" (see Chapter 6).

One estimate of the social rate of return to an additional year of secondary schooling is 13 percent, while another finds that each additional year of schooling above three to four years added to the average years per person contributes about 5 percent to total output (Rowen 1996: 103).

13   Learning-by-doing effects are not limited to industrial and manufacturing pursuits or even to the productivity of those doing the learning-by-doing. In a study of the introduction of high-yield seed varieties in agriculture, Foster and Rosenzweig (1995: 1205) found that "farmers with experienced neighbors are significantly more profitable than those with inexperienced neighbors," as they benefitted positive learning-by-doing spill-over benefits. Such spill-over learning effects to other farmers suggest that subsidies to early users of new technologies may help to not only increase total output and efficiency, but also to contribute to the attainment of the social optimum.

14   The constant, a, can be interpreted as the output–capital ratio, that is, Y/K, which indicates, on average, how much additional output can be produced from each additional unit of physical capital. The value, a, may also be interpreted as the incremental output–capital ratio, that is, even though a is a constant at any point in time, it is not necessarily fixed through time. As the economy evolves and grows, the value of a can change, rising with increasing returns, falling with decreasing returns, though at any point in time, it can be taken as a constant value.

15   On technological models of endogenous growth which are quite consistent with the Ayresian approach or Myrdal's "cumulative causation" considered in Chapter 6, see the very suggestive work of Grossman and Helpman (1991, 1994). This theoretical work puts the technological process at the forefront of the development process, a view we argue is essential (in Chapter 13).

16   The primary school enrollment rate is defined as the number of all students enrolled in primary school as a percentage of primary-school aged children. The ratio can exceed 100 percent due to the presence of students older or younger than the normal primary-school age. For example, in Zimbabwe in 1990, the primary enrollment rate was 116 percent, indicating that there were students younger and/or older than the primary school age enrolled in primary school (UNDP 1994: 15).

17   There is a good reason to exclude the share of output going to investment as a variable explaining the rate of economic growth, however. There is a feedback from economic growth to investment and back to income and output growth that makes these two variables interdependent rather than independent. This is Rodrik's rationale for not including the investment rate as an independent variable in his re-estimation of the World Bank model (Rodrik 1994: 19–20).

18   Again, the HPAEs are the eight high-performance Asian economies of Japan, Hong Kong, South Korea, Singapore, Taiwan, Indonesia, Malaysia, and Thailand.

19   Recall, from our discussion in Chapter 6, Ayres' emphasis on ceremonialism as a retarding factor that can obstruct the creation, the spread, and the adaptation of new technology. In Latin America, on the other hand, ceremonial institutional structures would include the extreme concentration of land ownership and income, monopoly power in certain industries, military dictatorships, and pseudo-democratic authoritarian structures, many of which have been quite detrimental to economic growth.

20   The adjusted $R^2 = 0.67$ was obtained by Rodrik when the investment/GDP ratio coefficient is included as an explanatory variable, but since Rodrik feels that it is inappropriate to include investment as a separate explanatory factor for economic growth given the feedback between the two, we have reported is regression 3 results only (Rodrik 1994: 20).

21   Why should land and income inequality play such a strong role in growth performance? Rodrik acknowledges that research on this question should be extended. Nonetheless, two responses have been forthcoming; one concentrates on aggregate demand. Studies of Japan and Taiwan have indicated that robust demand by farmers for domestic manufactured goods contributed strongly to economic growth during the formative stages of the industrialization process. The second focus on the link between inequality and economic

growth has been on social stability; societies with a greater degree of equality are likely to be more politically stable. When political instability is a recurring event, investment of all types, and hence economic growth, is reduced. Rodrik's study does point out that the World Bank *did* recognize that income distribution and land distribution were important factors in the HPAEs success, but noted that the Bank's study "[lacked] a serious discussion of equity as a precondition of growth" (Rodrik 1994: 26).

22 In this example, technological change is neutral. Assuming equal units on both axes, production possibilities frontier FF_2 shows that technology has had a similar impact on the production of capital goods, K, relative to the impact on consumption goods, C. **Hicks-neutral technical change** means an equi-proportional outward shift of the production possibilities frontier for both goods, so the capital–output ratio in production would be unchanged.

23 It is not enough to simply have access to the best technologies or the most modern capital equipment if greater efficiency is to be attained. Technology transfer or technology purchases do not guarantee that a country has the capacity to make effective use of such technology. As Nelson and Winter's analogy suggests, buying the best and most advanced tennis racket available is not the same thing as having mastered the skills necessary to play the game. This is where human capital accumulation, R&D expenditures, industrial organization, and a whole range of "inputs" to production enter into determining success or failure of the development effort.

24 It may be that the very rapid economic transformation of South Korea, particularly the "compressed" nature of the industrialization process compared to the already developed countries, has meant that the ability to keep up with international best practice has been difficult. On the other hand, it may be that the measures of technical efficiency change for countries with rapid growth do not accurately measure such advances toward best practice. With very rapid physical capital accumulation, new machines typically will embody the latest technology, so some of what might be counted as technical efficiency in slower growing economies is imputed to increases in physical capital in rapidly growing economies.

References

Barro, Robert J. 1991. "Economic Growth in a Cross Section of Countries," *Quarterly Journal of Economics* 106 (May): 407–443.

—— 1993. "Human Capital and Economic Growth," pp. 199–216 in Federal Reserve Bank of Kansas City, *Policies for Long-Run Economic Growth*. Kansas City: Federal Reserve Bank.

Fishlow, Albert and Catherine Gwin. 1994. "Lessons from the East Asian Experience," pp. 1–12 in Albert Fishlow *et al.*, *Miracle or Design?: Lessons From the East Asian Experience*. Washington, DC: Overseas Development Council.

Foster, Andrew D. and Mark R. Rosenzweig. 1995. "Learning by Doing and Learning from Others: Human Capital and Technical Change in Agriculture," *Journal of Political Economy* 103 (December): 1176–1209.

Grossman, Gene M. and Elhanan Helpman. 1991. *Innovation and Growth in the Global Economy*. Cambridge, MA: MIT Press.

—— 1994. "Endogenous Innovation in the Theory of Growth," *Journal of Economic Perspectives* 8 (Winter): 23–44.

Landau, Ralph, Timothy Taylor, and Gavin Wright. 1996. "Introduction," pp. 1–18 in Ralph Landau, Timothy Taylor, and Gavin Wright (eds), *The Mosaic of Economic Growth*. Stanford: Stanford University Press.

Lau, Lawrence J. 1996. "The Sources of Long-Term Economic Growth: Observations from the Experience of Developed and Developing Countries," pp. 63–91 in Ralph Landau, Timothy Taylor, and Gavin Wright (eds), *The Mosaic of Economic Growth*. Stanford: Stanford University Press.

Lucas, Robert E. 1988. "On the Mechanics of Economic Development," *Journal of Monetary Economics* 22 (July): 3–42.

Plosser, Charles I. 1993. "The Search for Growth," pp. 57–86 in Federal Reserve Bank of Kansas City, *Policies for Long-Run Economic Growth*. Kansas City: Federal Reserve Bank.

Reynolds, Lloyd G. 1986. *Economic Growth in the Third World: An Introduction*. New Haven, CT: Yale University Press.

Rodrik, Dani. 1994. "King Kong Meets Godzilla: The World Bank and 'The East Asian Miracle,'" pp. 13–53 in Albert Fishlow *et al.*, *Miracle or Design?: Lessons From the East Asian Experience*. Washington, DC: Overseas Development Council.

Romer, Paul M. 1994. "The Origins of Endogenous Growth," *Journal of Economic Perspectives* 8 (Winter): 3–22.

Rowen, Henry S. 1996. "World Wealth Expanding: Why a Rich, Democratic, and (Perhaps) Peaceful Era Is Ahead," pp. 92–125 in Ralph Landau, Timothy Taylor, and Gavin Wright (eds), *The Mosaic of Economic Growth*. Stanford: Stanford University Press.

Solow, Robert M. 1994. "Perspectives on Growth Theory," *Journal of Economic Perspectives* 8 (Winter): 45–54.

Stiglitz, Joseph E. and Hirofumi Uzawa (eds). 1969. *Readings in the Modern Theory of Economic Growth*. Cambridge, MA: MIT Press.

UNDP (UN Development Programme). 1994. *Human Development Report 1994*. Oxford: Oxford University Press.

World Bank. 1991. *World Development Report 1991*. Oxford: Oxford University Press.

—— 1993a. *The East Asian Miracle*. Oxford: Oxford University Press.

—— 1993b. *World Development Report 1993*. Oxford: Oxford University Press.

—— 1995. *World Development Report 1995*. Oxford: Oxford University Press.

—— 2003. *World Development Report 2003*. Oxford: Oxford University Press.

9 The initial structural transformation

Initiating the industrialization process

After studying this chapter, you should understand:
- the need for industrialization as a means to accelerate the pace of economic development;
- the nature of the structural transformation from primary production to secondary and tertiary production;
- the structural changes which easy import substitution industrialization can help to initiate as the first stage of industrialization and which are part of the structural transformation aimed at altering future path dependence;
- the static and potential dynamic welfare effects of infant industry tariffs;
- the role that development banks, financing, and other government initiatives can play in supporting the first efforts at industrialization; and
- the potential benefits and potential dangers of pursuing an import substitution industrialization strategy.

Introduction: an industrialization imperative?

Achieving an adequate level of economic growth and development appears to be inextricably intertwined with the level of industrialization of an economy. One chronicler of the nature of structural change in the development process has written that the issue is not whether industrialization is necessary for development but only "when and in what manner it will take place" (Syrquin 1988: 218).

The structural transformation that accompanies the process of industrialization alters not only the physical landscape of nations via urbanization, internal labor migration and the establishment of a complex of, typically, urban business enterprises. It also alters many of the cultural, social, and other institutional arrangements that have stamped a particular society and made it what it is to that point in time. With industrialization, nations become more homogeneous in terms of what is consumed, what is read, what is seen on the television and at the cinema, and what is learned in schools and in universities. Of course, many cultural differences remain even after industrialization since they arise from distinct historical experiences woven into the fabric of individual societies in their language, literature, law, folklore, music, cuisine, and a variety of embedded and shared attitudes, perspectives and practices.

Industrialization and development provide unmistakable benefits to society, but sacrifices also are required, as is true whenever choices must be made. One inevitable cost is a wrenching change in social values and the everyday rhythms of life of less-developed nations. Industrialization induces adjustments that often are disruptive of ancient patterns of life and ways of doing things. Frequently, opposition to industrialization arises from powerful groups who benefit from the status quo and feel threatened by the possibility of a new order. In other circumstances, opposition to industrialization and the changes it sets in motion comes from religious or cultural institutions which see a way of spiritual life threatened by the material concerns of a business society and the private acquisitiveness and individualism on which it thrives.

Opposition to industrialization is natural and expected, and the debate over how to develop, how fast and who is to benefit are important issues for any nation to consider and evaluate. There is no a priori reason why all nations must follow the same industrialization path or must make the same sacrifices on the road to a higher living standard and an improvement in their level of human development. Since many decisions about development can have irreversible effects on the local environment or on social structures, it is wise for societies to engage in an ongoing dialogue over the future. Too often, in evaluating the expected effects of development, economic, and business concerns – perhaps because they are more amenable to measurement – are treated as if they are more important than are spiritual, cultural, environmental, or religious interests, which are intrinsically more subjective and hence more difficult to quantify. That should not make them less important to consider, however.

Reconciling conflicting interests may slow progress, but each society must evaluate as objectively as possible to what extent trade-offs made to sustain traditional dimensions of social, political, and cultural life are worth the sacrifice. In some cases, caution in balancing growth and development versus other interests is justified. In other circumstances, an unnecessary slow-down in progress for the majority can follow from catering to narrow special interests.

Nonetheless, all nations are linked and interdependent to varying degrees, making the general forces and pressures of the global capitalist economy difficult, perhaps increasingly impossible, for nations to circumvent. Given these economic bonds and the real need for less-developed nations to make progress along both economic growth and human development dimensions, higher levels of industrialization – even with its attendant costs – would seem to be absolutely necessary.

Table 9.1 suggests the close relation between the rate growth of industry and the

Table 9.1 Industrialization and economic growth (percentage annual growth)

	Industry		GDP	
	1980–1990	*1990–2000*	*1980–1990*	*1990–2000*
Sub-Saharan Africa	1.2	1.6	1.6	2.5
East Asia and Pacific	9.3	9.3	7.9	7.2
South Asia	6.8	6.2	5.6	5.6
Middle East/North Africa	0.3	0.9	2.0	3.0
Latin America and the Caribbean	1.4	3.3	1.7	3.3
China	11.1	13.7	10.1	10.3
South Korea	11.4	6.3	8.9	5.7

Source: World Bank 2002: 406, Table 4.1.

rate of growth of total national output for different regions.[1] There would seem to be a positive correlation between the rate of growth of total output (measured here by gross domestic product, GDP) and the pace of manufacturing growth, though the direction of causation is certainly not proven by this data.

If one disaggregates further to look at the link between industrial growth and the growth of total GDP for specific countries, it is easy to identify industry as the leading sector. This would seem to be the case, for example, for China and South Korea, shown in the last lines of the table. More rapid industrial growth tends to be associated with more robust GDP growth. A speed-up in industrial growth, as in China over the 1990–2000 period, goes with more robust GDP growth.

Besides the apparent positive association between industrial expansion and economic growth, there is a further reason for pursuing industrialization. As considered in Chapter 6 in the discussion of the Presbisch–Singer hypothesis, countries which predominantly produce and export primary products and import the bulk of their manufactured goods are apt to experience instability in their terms of trade, that is, in the purchasing power of their exports in being able to buy imports. In fact, there has been a long-term deterioration in the purchasing power of these exports relative to the manufactured goods these countries import. Industrialization is therefore a means to create not only a more productive domestic economic structure which raises domestic incomes, but it also helps to create the possibility for an import and export pattern more similar to that of the already-developed nations, one that tends to be more stable in terms of export purchasing power.

There is thus a two-fold industrial imperative: first, higher levels of industrialization contribute to higher rates of economic growth, and second, industrialization sets the stage for a desired transformation of import and export patterns.

Structural change and economic growth and development

It is not simply the expansion of the industrial and manufacturing sectors that is critical to the pace and path of development. The process of growth and development is the unfolding consequence of a quantitative and qualitative reorientation of the entire economic and social structure of a nation, of basic changes in the education level of the population, in what they know and can do, in business organization and in the population's way of thinking about their relation to the world around them.

The size of the agricultural (*primary*) sector tends to shrink with economic growth as rural workers move into the industrial (*secondary*) and services (*tertiary*) sectors. This transformation entails the internal migration of labor from the rural countryside to urban areas where former rural workers become urban workers available to run the machinery of industry and to work in all the supporting firms and institutions, including government, that an expanding economy requires.

During successful industrial transformations, agricultural production becomes more efficient and intensive in its use of capital, both physical and human, and in the use of technology which increases worker productivity. As we saw in Chapter 8, a revolution in agriculture and land distribution patterns in which there is greater equality of ownership and of income seems to be associated with more rapid progress, as well. As an economy proceeds to ever higher paths of development, there is a further structural transformation as even more workers shift from the secondary sector toward the service sector to work in industries such as commerce, transportation, trade, government, finance, and so on.

Over time, then, more modern and more developed economies tend to have the majority of the labor force employed in, and the greatest part of total income generated in, the modern industrial and service sectors as the importance of agriculture and rural industries shrinks. All sectors of production show a tendency toward converging levels of worker productivity over time if development efforts are successful. The spread of technology and human capital accumulation generates a trend toward homogeneity among the primary, secondary, and tertiary sectors in terms of the level of output per worker (Chenery 1979: 18–21; also see Kuznets 1971, on structural change patterns that induce and accompany economic growth and development).

Table 9.2 clearly shows how at higher levels of development there has occurred a structural shift of labor usage from primary production toward secondary and tertiary activities. Regardless of which of the three parts of Table 9.2 one considers, a strong inverse relation between the share of the labor force in agriculture and the level of per capita income and the level of human development is quite evident. The larger the share of the total labor force engaged in agriculture, the lower the level of development. At higher levels of development, the share of the labor force engaged in agriculture is relatively small.

Likewise, there is an equally strong positive relation between the share of the labor force in industry and in services and the level of development. The smaller the share of the labor force in industry and services, the lower the level of income and development of the country or region. The larger that share, the higher the level of aggregate income and development.

The slow pace of both agrarian transformation and of industrialization in the

Table 9.2 Labor force distribution, by sector[a]

	Agriculture[b]		*Industry*[b]		*Services*[b]	
I.						
Developed nations	10		32		58	
Developing nations	58		15		27	
II.						
Level of human development[c]	*Agriculture*		*Industry*		*Services*	
	1965	*1990–1992*	*1965*	*1990–1992*	*1965*	*1990–1992*
High	49	26	20	26	32	48
Medium[d]	62	44	15	19	24	37
Low	75	66	8	10	14	24
III.						
Least developed nations	83	74	6	8	11	18

Source: UNDP 1995: 176–177, Table 1.

Notes
a As percentage of total labor force.
b 1990–1992.
c Less-developed countries only.
d Excluding China.

"least developed nations" in Part III of Table 9.2 and in the "low" human development achievement of countries in Part II provide strong evidence of the compelling *correlation* between the agricultural and industrial transformations that contribute to greater development as measured by income or by the human development index (HDI).

Development, then, involves both an industrial revolution and reorganization of the agrarian sector, as well as the additions to human and physical capital and the attention to endogenous technological change considered in the previous chapters. Development is at least partly about indispensable structural changes in production and in labor usage, with a profound shift from agriculture toward industry and services as higher levels of productivity of labor in all sectors are attained.[2]

An industrial transformation aimed at raising a nation's level of development that fails to foment an effective agrarian transformation eventually will falter and fail, just as it will be less effective without the attention to technology and to the quality of inputs that have been identified in endogenous growth theories as central to sustained growth in income per capita.[3] All sectors of the economy must become progressively more technological and more productive as the shift in labor from primary to secondary to tertiary uses moves forward. This typically involves a slow, then accelerating, reduction in the significance of primary production within the economy. One development economist, Benjamin Higgins, has referred to this structural transformation from agricultural dominance to industrial and service production as the strategy of "getting rid of farmers" (Higgins and Higgins 1979).[4]

The Lewis dual-economy model of structural transformation

How does this structural evolution that shifts labor from agriculture to industry come about in practice? What sets this labor migration process in motion? A classic description, already presented in Chapter 5, was provided by Nobel Prize-winning economist Sir W. Arthur Lewis. Here we only briefly review the main points of his argument.

If there is surplus labor in agriculture, that is, if the productivity of labor in agriculture is lower than in industry, as is most likely to be the case in most LDCs, then it is possible for a more productive and higher-wage industrial sector to attract labor from the rural countryside to urban industrial areas by paying wages slightly above rural wages. Shifting workers from lower productivity activities in agriculture to higher productivity industrial jobs will result in an increase in total national output.[5]

Lewis observed that the typical less-developed nation was dualistic, not only in the sense of having two key sectors, agriculture and industry, but also in the more fundamental sense that these sectors had little interconnection. There was a traditional low-productivity, low-technology rural agriculture sector where the great bulk of the population lived, worked, and produced most of what they consumed. There also existed, or there could be created, an industrial sector where production was profit-oriented, more capital-using, and technologically-driven and where worker productivity was higher than in the traditional sector. Those working in the modern sector bought food and perhaps some other inputs from the traditional sector. But the most important link between the traditional and modern sector is via the provision of labor from the primary sector to industry via labor migration from the countryside to the cities where industry is located.

It was in this labor supply link between the two sectors that Lewis found the transformation dynamic that could contribute to greater growth and development via expanded industrialization. Lewis argued that continuing reinvestment of profits of the modern sector could facilitate the transfer of surplus labor from agriculture to industry, especially if the capital–labor ratio did not rise very much in industry (for details review the discussion around Figures 5.1(a) and 5.1(b)).

The Lewis model has been a powerful theory for understanding how the structural transformation from an agriculture society to a more industrial system might be accomplished. If all works more or less as Lewis envisaged, the labor migration process is cumulative once begun as the higher wages of industry attract rural workers until an equilibrium is reached when the productivity of workers is more or less equalized between sectors. Now, we shall consider how countries might foment such a migration of labor from agriculture to industry if it has not begun on its own or how to speed it up if it has begun. Remember, it is the belief that economic development requires a structural transition from a primary product-producing economy to an industrial (and service) economy that motivates our interest in understanding how to get industrialization going.

Initiating the structural transformation toward industrialization

Is there a particular development strategy that less-developed nations can follow that can help to initiate or accelerate the transition of labor from agriculture to industry and contribute to the positive transformation of the productive structure of the economy from an agricultural to an industrial base?

Historically, import substitution industrialization (ISI) has been the means by which governments have encouraged this structural revolution. In this chapter, we consider in some detail how ISI can propel an agriculture-based economy into a more modern, industrially-based economy. We will also note the pitfalls to be avoided if the potential transformative benefits of this instrumental strategy are to be reaped.

The first stage of industrialization: easy ISI

With the exception of Great Britain, the first modern industrializing nation, all subsequent successful efforts by nations to modernize have involved elements of ISI as a means to promote the expansion of a domestic industrial sector. ISI involves the establishment of, typically, domestically-owned firms within the less-developed economy that begin to produce for domestic consumption some of the manufactured goods currently being imported. With ISI, domestic production replaces – *substitutes for* – some imported goods.

Which commodities are the most likely candidates for new or expanded domestic production when beginning ISI?

Typically, ISI begins with the production of relatively simple *non-durable consumer goods* such as clothing, beverages (soft drinks, beer, canned and bottled juices), furniture, shoes, cloth diapers, building materials, and so on. These are goods with pre-existing market demands that are currently being met predominantly by imports. The technology and know-how for producing these products tends to be relatively rudimentary, of low cost and frequently available "off-the-shelf" on the world market with few or no restrictions on use, as for example, for sewing machines or bottling equipment. The demands on the skills of the labor force are moderate, which is important since many industrial workers will be recent entrants from rural areas with but modest levels of education and other training, certainly in factory settings.

A focus on producing non-durable consumer goods is also consistent with the Lewis model. The labor surplus coming from agriculture will be absorbed more easily if industrial production is concentrated in labor-intensive processes. This focus on labor-intensive production can help to avoid problems of urban unemployment and underemployment. It is precisely consumer non-durable production that tends to be labor-using, conserving on scarce physical and financial capital by making use of the less-developed economy's most abundant factor of production, its abundant labor.

Concentrating on producing goods similar to those being imported removes some of the risk for both local entrepreneurs and for government policy-makers undertaking these projects since there is a pre-existing demand for, say, tee shirts or children's sandals. Given a known import demand, local producers will be more likely to be able to make reasonable calculations as to the probability of the profits that can be expected from initiating or expanding production. These profits will depend upon local wage and cost conditions, the level of technology and human capital accumulation, and the expertise level of local workers, managers, and entrepreneurs. This first stage of ISI with the focus on producing simple consumer non-durable goods for the domestic market has been called *easy*, *primary*, or *horizontal* ISI.[6]

It is not necessarily desirable nor recommended that ISI be initiated for all non-durable consumer goods products being imported. Nor does ISI need to take place simultaneously via a "big push" in all sectors. Some industries may be better candidates for easy ISI than others. Some imports may present better opportunities for substitution later rather than sooner. Factors that need to be considered in determining the pace and reach of ISI include:

1   the size of the domestic market including population size, average income, and the income distribution;
2   the size and skills of the existing pool of potential entrepreneurs who would operate the new enterprises;
3   the educational attainment and available skills of the labor force and the speed of migration of labor from agriculture to industry;
4   the availability of finance for the purchase of technology, needed physical capital and other inputs and for the needed training of managers and workers;
5   the potential for growth of demand over the future for each import substitution good and the learning-by-doing potential from the production of each; and
6   possible linkage and spin-off and spill-over effects (*positive externalities in production*) that might stimulate production in other industries as the consequence of initiating production in any particular easy ISI industry.

Whether a "balanced" or "unbalanced" ISI strategy in the sense discussed in Chapter 5 is followed will depend on the evaluation in each country of the feasibility and of the expected gains and costs accruing to either "blanket" versus more "selective" ISI promotion of non-durable consumer goods production. If selective ISI is chosen, as will be the case in most instances, then the timing of the promotion and expansion of particular industries and firms can be decided taking into consideration the factors listed above.

Japan, India, and the larger countries in Latin America (Brazil, Mexico, Argentina, Chile, and Colombia) followed an easy ISI strategy of industrial transformation beginning as far back as the mid-1800s in the case of Mexico and by the last third of the century for the others (Amsden 2001: 43). In Japan, the conscious decision to industrialize via ISI was part and parcel of the Meiji restoration after 1868, and "all modern industries were started as import substitutes" (Amsden 2001: 174).

ISI in Latin America was to some degree forced upon the countries by the breakdown in normal trade patterns as a result of the successive crises of the First World War, the Great Depression and then the Second World War. As a result of these disruptions, it was difficult to purchase imported consumer goods due to supply interruptions. It was equally difficult to sell agricultural and other primary exports to traditional markets to earn the foreign exchange required to purchase imports. As a result of these interruptions to trade, local manufacturing firms were able to emerge and expand by producing for the domestic market behind the artificial barrier of these external international crises that shielded them from the normal competition they would face from imports (see the discussion around the structuralists in Chapter 6).

For the ISI strategy to work so that LDCs are less likely to be subject to long-term declining terms of trade as primary product exporters, it is necessary that both the pattern of domestic production *and* exports be altered. A reorganization of the internal structure of production toward a higher degree of industrialization is insufficient for long-term progress *without* a fundamental reorientation of what less-developed nations export to the world market. It is very important to keep this qualification in mind as we continue through the following discussion. Industrialization must go beyond just being internally oriented so that it ultimately reaches out to world markets if long-term success is to be attained (see Focus 9.1).

It is incorrect for countries to accept the existing export structure as immutable and definitive or as reflecting an optimal outcome of international specialization in production, as described by Ricardo's theory of comparative advantage for example. Rather, the existing patterns of trade relations might better be viewed as a single frame of a motion picture, a static snapshot. It is not the whole of the movie. Initiating easy ISI is a means to begin to create *new comparative advantage* in more dynamic product lines that promise greater gains in productivity and income growth over the future in both domestic and, if successful, international markets. To advance the metaphor, ISI is not a rapid "jump-cut" to a more efficient productive structure compared to foreign producers. It is more akin to a scene within the whole of a movie that ultimately advances toward the desired conclusion: an evolving industrial structure, alterations in the sectoral use of labor and changing patterns of imports and exports that can instrumentally contribute to a progressively higher standard of living.

The array of inputs any society possesses at any particular moment is its resource endowment. However, every nation is capable of modifying and making more productive its *reproducible* inputs to production, particularly human capital,

FOCUS 9.1   THE EXPORT STRUCTURE

A fundamental characteristic of the typical less-developed country is the predominance of primary product exports as a percentage of total exports. Poorer countries typically have only a small proportion of manufactured goods as a percentage of their total exports.

Successful structural transformation not only changes what is produced domestically as the agriculture focus of the economy shifts toward an emphasis on industrial goods and services. Long-term development also requires a change in the export and import profiles of an economy. To avoid the problem of declining terms of trade, what is exported must be modified so that traditional primary product exports are replaced by manufactured good exports and/or non-traditional primary product exports less likely to be subject to declining relative prices.

The following table reminds us of the often heavy concentration of primary product exports in total exports for many less-developed nations.

| | Primary product exports as percentage of merchandise exports | | | |
	1970	1993	1999	GNP[a]
Bolivia	97	81	59	1,010
Brazil	86	40	44	4,419
Chile	95	81	81	4,740
Colombia	92	60	69	2,250
Costa Rica	81	67	32	2,740
Côte d'Ivoire	94	83	–	707
Ghana	99	77	79	392
Indonesia	98	47	43	577
Malaysia	93	35	19	3,405
Mexico	68	47	15	4,402
Mozambique	90	80	–	225
Nicaragua	84	93	91	430
Nigeria	98	98	99	310
Pakistan	43	15	16	475
South Korea	24	7	8	8,502
Thailand	92	28	23	1,961
Venezuela	99	86	88	3,671
Canada	48	34	27	19,320
UK	17	19	14	22,640
US	30	18	13	32,230

Note
a 1999 per capita income, US$.

Examining the above figures carefully, it is possible to detect some correlation between the percentage of primary exports to manufactured exports and the level of per capita income in 1999. A larger percentage of primary exports to total exports tends to be associated with a lower per capita income in 1999.[7]

The correlation is not perfect, however. There are countries like Venezuela with a large share of primary exports and yet income per capita is not as low as one might expect from that fact alone. Why? Venezuela's major export is oil. Some primary product exports, particularly oil, may not be as associated with low average incomes as is the case for other primary product exports.

Pakistan also stands out as an exception, too, having both relatively low per capita income and a small share of primary product exports. The bulk of Pakistan's exports are concentrated in manufactured goods, but the majority of these were textile fibers, textiles and clothing which tend to be generally low value-added, low income-generating exports. Clearly, then, having manufactured exports alone is not the whole of the story for becoming more developed. The concentration of exports and their diversity and type also are important. There are "good" manufacturing exports and not-so-good, just as there are "good" primary exports (like oil, for example) and others that are not so valuable.

Sources: World Bank 1995: 190–191, Table 15; 2000: 74–75, Table 1; UNDP 2001: 186–189, Table 13; Table 2.1 of Chapter 2 (above)

technology and physical capital. Growth of the stock of these assets helps to increase the pace of economic expansion. In effect, each economy has a *constantly changing* resource endowment on which it can build for the future. It is always changing as population grows, as education takes place, as research and development occurs leading to technology advances, and so on.

It is clear, then, that public policy has an impact, for good or bad, in affecting the evolution of a nation's potential resource endowment. In fact, for development to continue a society must alter and make more productive its resource base so as to keep pace with the maturation of the world economy and its changing demand patterns. In this process, governments have a fundamental responsibility. The products and services in which a nation has a comparative advantage are, from this perspective, subject to a substantial degree of control and design through the particular policies chosen regarding investments in human capital, technology, better organizational methods and improved public sector decisions which are under the full or partial control of government policy-makers, as the endogenous growth theories of Chapter 8 suggested.

Why is government-sponsored ISI needed?

In an industry where no, or only a few, local firms currently are producing products similar to imported goods, stimulating domestic production most likely will require some sort of government intervention that can provide insulation to local producers from foreign competition. This is necessary because in most less-developed nations there are likely to be no, or few, local firms that will be able to efficiently produce and compete with imported goods, at least initially. As relative late-comers to industrialization, less-developed nations are likely to be at a substantial competitive disadvantage vis-à-vis existing foreign firms which already produce for the international market. Even with political independence, many less-developed nations did not move quickly toward industrialization. A lack of financing for projects, few trained entrepreneurs, low skill levels of workers and foreign competition from imports all worked against the expansion of the manufacturing sector in most LDCs.

Without an industrialization strategy supported by government, a thriving domestic industrial sector may continue to be an impossibility, particularly in this era of very open international markets with few barriers to trade among nations. This is because new firms face start-up difficulties that tend to make their costs higher than for comparable firms in other countries that already supply goods to the international market. One specific difficulty prospective manufacturers encounter is in attempting to borrow funds for projects in less-developed economies with very imperfect markets in banking and finance (see Focus 9.2). Thus without a government-sponsored industrial initiative, the high probability of market failure

FOCUS 9.2   CREDIT MARKETS AND MARKET FAILURE

Some economists have argued that if there were sufficient future expected profits to justify the creation of an ISI firm, potential private firms and entrepreneurs would recognize such opportunities and borrow against future earnings to establish such enterprises. If that were the case, there would be no need for government intervention to initiate industrialization. The private sector would act on its own. And this is true, in the abstract.

However, even if such a profit calculation is made by private entrepreneurs, any *market failure* problem in the financial capital markets due to a weak or poorly functioning banking and financial intermediation system or due to the lack of an equity capital or bond market may make the realization of such projects unlikely by rendering borrowing difficult or even impossible. This is an example of *institutional inadequacy* quite common in less-developed economies that results from incomplete or poorly functioning markets. The result of such market failure will be an inefficient allocation of society's resources, both currently and into the future via thwarted investment, and a sub-optimal level of economic and human development. Under such conditions, there is a strong case to be made for government remediation to compensate for this market failure.

A further complication enters the picture when it is asked whether it is reasonable to expect prospective entrepreneurs to even be able to make the future expected profitability calculations for establishing new enterprises. This is an issue concerning the availability of information. Joseph Stiglitz and Kenneth Arrow, both Nobel Prize-winning economists, have written extensively on the economics of information and the issues it raises.

They have argued convincingly that information is not free; it is a "good" much like any other. There is a cost to both producing information and to obtaining it. In less-developed nations with only a rudimentary industrial structure, is it reasonable to expect that potential individual private entrepreneurs will be able to identify the expected future profit stream of an investment that no one else in the economy has yet made?

If the economy currently lacks the required social and physical infrastructure, appropriate human capital resources, existing supplying enterprises, sources of financing, and so on, is such an estimate a reasonable possibility? If not, there is a valid economic rationale for government action that corrects for market failure and for information costs that distort the private calculation of future benefits. The ISI strategy can be one part of this overall thrust toward structural transformation that compensates for the market failure and contributes to overcoming these in the future.

Source: Stiglitz 1992

due to institutional inadequacy will result in a sub-optimal level of industrialization and a sacrifice of overall economic welfare.

Transitional inefficiencies

New firms anywhere, but especially those in less-developed economies, are likely to incur higher production costs for some time compared to firms already successfully producing for the international market in the same product line. These higher costs are the consequence of what can be called *transitional inefficiencies*. Such inefficiencies can result from:

* inexperienced management and labor training concerning modern industrial marketing, accounting, financial, management and other techniques;

- a lower level of technological development and technological effectiveness in the LDC;
- a lower level of human capital accumulation and educational attainment; and, among other reasons that could be listed,
- less efficient financial markets and initially low output levels that prevent the attainment of economies of scale.

What is not in doubt is the effect of transitional inefficiencies: they raise the costs of production for new firms relative to established producers in other countries which export to markets around the world.

Transitional inefficiencies can only be reduced and overcome through "learning-by-doing," a real-time process that requires the initiating of production so that workers, managers, and entrepreneurs have the opportunity to improve their efficiency level in the process of actually producing. Transitional inefficiencies also can be addressed via more formal processes such as technology acquisition and licensing, improvements in managerial and worker education to increase the quantity and quality of the stock of human capital, and through organizational innovations like equity and bond markets and an expansion in financial intermediation via banks and other such institutions that reduce the costs of borrowing.

Figure 9.1 shows the real effect of transitional inefficiencies in production:

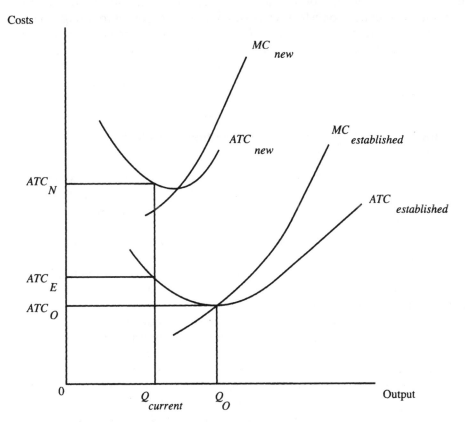

Figure 9.1 Average costs of production, new versus established firms.

average total costs (ATC) and marginal costs (MC) are higher for new domestic producers compared to established foreign producers. Particularly for production at less than the optimal level where unit costs of production are minimized at the bottom of the average total cost curve, average and marginal costs of producing are higher than they otherwise might be due to the effects of transitional inefficiencies.

At relatively low levels of production like $Q_{current}$ for an easy ISI firm just beginning production, unit costs of production along ATC_N are higher than they would be at the same level of output for established producers on ATC_E. Compared to the per unit costs of production ATC_O at the optimal level of production, Q_O, the combination of transitional inefficiencies and low production levels (i.e., unexploited economies of scale) when beginning ISI result in higher costs of production per unit of output of the ISI goods. These higher per unit costs translate into higher prices for new domestic producers compared to foreign firms with experience in producing.

For many small nations, the limited size of the domestic market due to a small population, low average incomes and/or substantial income inequality may continue to be a barrier to fully attaining the cost reductions consistent with optimal production levels even after the sources of the transitional inefficiencies have been removed (that is, output still may be less than Q_O in Figure 9.1).[8] However, the domestic market is not the only potential outlet for the output of ISI producers. There is no inherent reason why such goods cannot be exported to foreign markets which would contribute to the expansion in demand that could help producers achieve lower costs per unit through scale economies *once and if* transitional inefficiencies are overcome. This is an important factor to keep in mind. Efficient domestic producers can become exporters to the world market, thus reaching beyond the always limited domestic market.

Infant industry tariffs: government intervention to protect domestic industry

The higher per unit costs of production for new domestic producers compared to established foreign producers shown in Figure 9.1 mean higher prices will be charged to consumers. Given the choice between a higher priced (and probably, initially, lower quality) domestically-produced good and the foreign imported good at a lower price, there is little question as to which most consumers will choose. In the face of such external competition and given the inevitability of transitional inefficiencies for new firms, new domestic producers can hardly be expected to be able to compete head-to-head at the beginning of ISI. They may choose to not even initiate production under such circumstances.

It is the difference in average and marginal costs of production between potential domestic producers and established foreign firms and the price differential to consumers it entails that lies behind the argument for the placing of *infant industry tariffs* on imported goods if domestic industrialization is to be stimulated. Raising the price of imported goods to final consumers by imposing an appropriate import tax will make the prices of domestically-produced import substitutes more attractive to consumers in the home market.[9] The need for protection from imports at the beginning of the industrialization process is rooted in the difficulty for new producers to acquire the knowledge associated with the technology of production that results in the transitional inefficiencies discussed above (also see Amsden 2001: 5–6).

> The fundamental rationale for protection is found in the tacitness of technology, which implies that internationally competitive levels of productivity cannot be reached without experience-based learning which entails comparatively high costs that must in some way be financed.[10]
>
> (Evenson and Westphal 1995: 2284)

A protective tariff is one way to finance this learning process. As a tax on a specific import, it raises the average cost of the imported good thus making the higher-cost domestic output better able to compete, assuming no substantial consumer bias in favor of foreign goods. The final price of the imported good to the consumer may even be pushed above that of the domestic import-substitute. This will augment the demand for the domestic good as substitution by consumers takes place away from imports and toward the ISI product, thus permitting the domestic producer to slide down the average cost curve (ATC_N in Figure 9.1) with higher rates of domestic production. From this perspective, an infant industry tariff may best be looked at as simply another form of social investment in industrialization. For future growth possibilities, past and present "manufacturing experience matters" in permitting countries to learn to produce. There is no alternative if the beneficial path dependence of an industrial-based economy is to be forged (Amsden 2001: ch. 5). All paths toward development involve both costs and benefits. The infant industry tariff and the higher prices for ISI goods it generates is one of those costs. The only way a new firm can begin to produce more cheaply is by initiating production and, with experience, producing more output at a lower per unit cost.

An alternative to a tariff on imports is a subsidy provided to ISI firms. A subsidy would lower the average costs of production of new domestic enterprises and could provide the same degree of protection from imported goods as a tariff without increasing the price of the good to the final consumer as a tariff will do. However, a subsidy creates a drain on public resources, already likely to be in short supply in most less-developed nations. For this reason, infant industry tariff protection is a universal feature of ISI programs.

Tariff protection is but one instrument to promote easy ISI. Undervalued exchange rates, low interest rates extended to particular borrowers, directed credit allocation via state-owned investment banks (see Focus 9.3), technology and R&D assistance, planned government purchases of private firm output, tax incentives for training and investment and the creation of parastate firms are but a few of the alternatives available to public policy-makers to initiate, sustain and stimulate the industrialization process. The goal is to create the desired structural transformation from an agriculturally-based economy to an industrial and service economy. Successful developing countries use a combination of these instruments to promote industrialization.

FOCUS 9.3   DEVELOPMENT BANKS AND ISI

Development banks, which are state-owned and state-directed non-commercial banks, have been an important tool for directing a nation's savings and borrowed funds toward higher-risk projects which can help jump-start development.

One of the most successful development banks has been Mexico's Nafinsa. In 1940, Nafinsa was directed by the Mexican government to pursue the following objectives: (1) promote industrialization, (2) promote the production of intermediate and capital goods, (3) invest in infrastructure, (4) help stimulate and develop indigenous entrepreneurial talent, (5) build confidence within the Mexican private sector, and (6) reduce the role of direct foreign investment in industry.

Nafinsa went through two major stages: aggressive promotion of industrialization from 1940 to 1947, and then promotion of infrastructure and heavy industry from 1947 to the early 1960s. In making its investments, Nafinsa emphasized potential linkage effects. An emphasis on linkages is well-known today, but in the early 1940s, Nafinsa engaged in innovative policy-making. In a classic study of Nafinsa, Calvin Blair emphasized the "systematic" nature of Nafinsa's investments.

> Nafinsa established in 1941 a department of promotion and began to make systematic studies of industrial development projects. With a predilection for manufacturing, it promoted enterprise in practically every sector of the Mexican economy over the course of the next several years. The roster of firms aided by loan, guarantee, or purchase of stocks and bonds reads like a "who's who" of Mexican business.

In addition to promoting parastate firms, Nafinsa engaged extensively in lending long-term capital to the private sector and in forming partnership investments with both the private sector and international firms. By 1961, Nafinsa's investments were supporting 533 industrial firms, and its long-term investments were twice as large as the sum of such loans from the private banking system. Between 1940 and 1980, the Mexican economy grew at an average annual rate of 6 percent, after adjusting for inflation. Nafinsa's role was a major ingredient in what was then known as the "Mexican Miracle."

Nafinsa continued to be a prominent development agency through the 1980s, but its "golden age" was in the 1940s and 1950s, when the private sector's reluctance to commit funds to industry was particularly acute.

By the early 1990s, all but thirteen of the hundreds of state-owned firms which Nafinsa had helped to create had been privatized, merged, or liquidated. Nafinsa still continues to play a vital role, now channelling funds into the export sector to promote the expansion of manufactured products.

Source: Blair 1964: 213

The contribution of an infant industry tariff to industrialization

The effect of an infant industry tariff on the domestic market price, consumption, domestic output, and on total social welfare is shown in Figure 9.2. It is assumed that currently the imported good enters the domestic market with a zero tariff.

The current (or potential) domestic supply curve of clothing is S_D. S_W is the world supply curve of clothing, which is drawn as perfectly elastic, reflecting the assumption that with free trade the less-developed country can purchase any quantity of clothing it wishes at a fixed free-trade price, P_F. In other words, the less-developed economy is a price-taker on the international market.

D_D is the domestic demand for clothing. Demand depends on per capita income,

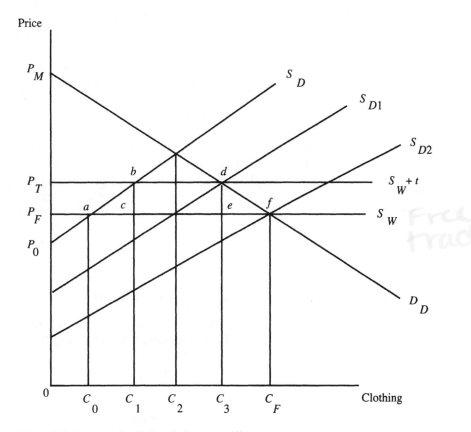

Figure 9.2 Impact of an infant industry tariff.

the income distribution, population size and preferences of consumers for the good. Given the premise of free trade prior to initiating the ISI program, the price to domestic consumers for clothing in the less-developed country would be equal to the world market price, P_F. The total quantity of clothing demanded and supplied would be C_F, determined by the intersection of the world supply curve, S_W, and the domestic demand curve, D_D.

At the world market price P_F, local firms would produce quantity C_0 of the good, determined by where P_F crosses the domestic supply curve, S_D.[11] The quantity of imported clothing in Figure 9.2 is equal to $C_F - C_0$, that is, total quantity demanded minus domestic production. This quantity also represents the potential market for import substitution for this good.

If the less-developed economy imposes an infant industry tariff of a fixed amount, t, this will shift the world supply curve of clothing to $S_W + t$.[12] With the tariff, the price of the imported good to consumers in the country imposing the tariff would be pushed upward to the new equilibrium price P_T, where supply equals demand at $S_W + t = D_D$.

Domestic producers would now be willing to supply more to the domestic market at the higher price, potentially up to quantity C_1. The price of the clothing produced by domestic clothing firms, assuming it is of equal quality and in that sense a perfect substitute for the foreign good, could be as high as P_T. However, it is possible that some clothing, equal to any quantity less than C_1 in Figure 9.2, might be sold by domestic producers at a price below P_T but above P_0. This price-cutting behavior by domestic producers would reduce their profit, but it may be necessary in those cases where the domestically produced good is not a perfect substitute for the foreign import due to quality differences or due to a strong bias in favor of imported goods by consumers. As shown in Figure 9.2, there still may be imports of foreign clothing even with the tariff, in this case equal to the quantity $C_3 - C_1$, depending on the level of the tariff and actual domestic production.

What the imposition of the tariff does is to provide space for domestic firms to expand production for the domestic market. Higher levels of output provide more employment for rural workers migrating to the urban industrial sector and is the training ground for learning how to become more efficient. "Another way of looking at this cost [of infant economy protection] is possible: the reduced availability of goods and services can be considered an investment" (Bruton 1989: 1607). It may in fact be an essential investment in the future human and economic development of late-developing economies.

Static and dynamic welfare effects of an infant industry tariff

In analyzing the impact of a tariff, economists typically measure the so-called *welfare loss* to society from imposing a tariff, t, by looking at the impact of the tax on consumer surplus.

Prior to imposing the tariff, *consumer surplus* is equal to the large triangle $P_F f P_M$ in Figure 9.2. It measures the additional amount consumers would have been willing to pay to buy quantity C_F of the good but did not have to pay due to the fact that all units of the good could be bought for price P_F. The consumer surplus is the triangle-shaped area above the prevailing price of the good and below the demand curve.

The imposition of the tariff results in a reduction in the domestic consumption of clothing equal to the quantity $C_F - C_3$. After the tariff, the consumer surplus is equal to the triangle $P_T d P_M$. It is easy to see that there has been a loss in consumer surplus due to the tariff equal to the area $P_F P_T df$, which is the difference between the large triangle of consumer surplus and the smaller triangle. Domestic consumers clearly have been made worse off by the tariff. They are paying a higher price for the good, are consuming less and now have less consumer surplus than at the free market price that prevailed prior to the imposition of the tariff.

Who gains, if anyone, from the tariff? How can an infant industry tariff be justified if consumers, many of whom are poor, are made worse off?

Not all of what consumers lose is a pure loss to society. Part of the lost consumer surplus due to the tariff is received by the government as tariff revenues. These revenues are equal to the area of the rectangle $bcde$, which is equal to the tariff, t, times the quantity of imports remaining after the imposition of the tariff, $C_3 - C_1$.

Domestic firms producing the import substitute also gain from the tariff. After all, the purpose of imposing an infant industry tariff in the first instance is to make it possible for domestic firms to compete with foreign producers. With the tariff and the higher price of imports, domestic producers are able to increase their level of production from C_0 to C_1. As a consequence, they receive additional *producer surplus* equal to $P_F P_T ab$.[13]

Looking at the lost consumer surplus area in Figure 9.2 and comparing it with the tariff revenues and the producer surplus, it is clear that some of the lost consumer surplus goes to no one. There is a portion of the lost consumer surplus that is a pure loss since no one else in the local economy gains. The infant industry tariff results in what economists call a (static) *deadweight loss*. It is equal to the lost consumer surplus that is not transferred either to domestic firms as producer surplus or to government as increased tariff revenues. The deadweight loss is equal to the sum of the areas of the two small triangles, $abc + def$.[14] There is thus a net loss in total social welfare from the imposition of the infant industry tariff compared to the free trade situation.

What, then, can be the justification for the infant industry tariff except as a means to increase tariff revenues or to augment the producer surplus of local firms? Consumers are worse off by having to pay higher prices for less clothing. How can such a tariff (or other market-distorting policies – see Focus 9.4) be defensible?

Remember, the motivating purpose of the infant industry tariff is to assist ISI firms in getting started and to give them time to overcome their transitional inefficiencies. If these firms succeed in becoming more efficient over time, then the domestic supply curve, S_D, will shift outward and downward toward S_{D1}. If the domestic clothing industry becomes internationally competitive the supply curve will shift all the way to S_{D2} in Figure 9.2 (in other words, curve S_D will move outward and downward to this new position at S_{D2}).

What would cause the domestic supply curve to shift in this fashion? First, an increase in the number of domestic producers who would be able to emerge and succeed behind the protective wall provided by the tariff would shift the supply curve outward. Second, and of greater importance, the domestic supply curve would be shifted outward as a consequence of:

1   increased efficiency of domestic enterprises through the use of "cutting-edge" or "best-practice" technology;
2   the more effective application of whatever technology already is in use, that is, via "technical efficiency change";

FOCUS 9.4   TAIWAN'S EXPERIENCE WITH ISI IN TEXTILES

In the early 1950s the Taiwanese government paid particular attention to the textile industry as part of the core of a loosely formulated plan for industrial development. The first textile entrepreneurs were mostly relocated mainlanders, so the industry did not arise *de novo*. Nevertheless, a whole battery of market-distorting and even market-replacing methods was used to establish the industry quickly. The market-distorting methods included tariffs and quantitative restrictions on imports of yarn and finished products, restrictions on the entry of new producers to prevent "excessive" competition, and controlled access to raw materials. From 1951 to 1953, a government agency, with help from a US mission, replaced market allocation altogether. It supplied raw cotton directly to the spinning mills, advanced all working capital requirements, and bought up all the production – and did basically the same at the weaving stage.

The supply response was dramatic. Between 1951 and 1954 production of cotton yarn went up by over 200 percent and woollen yarn by over 400 percent. By mid-1953 Taiwan was more than self-sufficient in yarn and cloth.

Source: Wade 1990: 79

3   better training of managers and workers in schools or special institutes;
4   "learning-by-doing" on the job, whereby both workers and managers becoming more efficient with practice, adaptation and even trial-and-error while they work;
5   the application of more effective management and financial techniques and quality control;
6   improvements in banking and financial institutions to facilitate financing of production;
7   the improvement of infrastructure, such as roads, communications, ports, power, and so on.

All of these factors, and others could be added, would contribute to reducing marginal and average costs of production with the outcome being an outward shift in the domestic clothing industry's total supply curve toward S_{D2}.

It is easy to see from the graph that with the full elimination of transitional inefficiencies so that S_{D2} intersects D_D at C_F, the consumer surplus will be equal to what it was prior to the imposition of the tariff (area P_FP_Mf) *if* the domestic price is again at P_F. Now, however, the *domestic producer surplus* would be larger than in the pre-ISI free trade regime as the supply curve has shifted outward allowing domestic firms to capture revenues previously received by foreign firms.

With domestic production at C_F there would be both more industrial employment and a higher level of GDP and GNP produced by the country than was the case when the free trade regime prevailed. What the imposition of the tariff, t, can facilitate, then, is the attainment of *dynamic welfare gains* for society that, accruing over time, can quite easily exceed the static welfare losses that the tariff initially imposed on the economy. In other words, as a means to promote the transformation of the structure of an economy from agriculture to industry and to shift workers from lower to higher productivity employment, infant industry ISI tariffs can foster important dynamic social welfare gains that can easily outweigh any short-term deadweight loss due to any uncompensated consumer surplus. With industrialization, a country can realize higher income per person that exceeds what would have been attained without having begun ISI.

The use of an infant industry tariff is one example of how "getting prices wrong," in this case, raising prices above the international market level with a tariff, can sometimes yield positive development outcomes. Rather than abdicating control over the economy to past adverse path dependence and to market forces, the conscious forging of an ISI sector, as in South Korea, Taiwan, Brazil, Mexico, and many other large less-developed nations, can be a means to bend domestic resource allocation, production, and labor usage in more productive directions.

Such "governing" of the market, as Wade (1990) calls it, does lead to market-distorting and perhaps even market-replacing policies, at least for a time. But when such policies are carried out with care and monitored for results and where vested interests have difficulty in influencing state actions, the practice of "getting prices wrong" by governing the market rather than the neoclassical and orthodox policy of "getting prices right" and accepting existing market forces as optimal, can result in substantial gains in output, income, and human development by accelerating the pace of industrialization.

The elimination of infant industry protection: when is enough, enough?

How long should infant industry protection from lower-cost imports be extended to new domestic firms? How long should it reasonably be expected to take before ISI firms facing transitional inefficiencies are able to compete head-to-head with foreign-supplied imports without the artificial benefit of tariff protection?

Obviously, from Figure 9.2, once transitional inefficiencies are overcome and the domestic supply curve has increased to S_{D2}, tariff protection becomes redundant and unnecessary. In that case, domestic industries can compete with foreign imports and at world prices since domestic firms will have attained the same level of efficiency at output C_F as is the case for producers elsewhere.

In fact, as firms begin to achieve more efficiency through learning-by-doing, the need for a tariff at the original level, t, is diminished. It is perilous, perhaps, to put a number to this, but in the non-durable consumer goods industries in which ISI begins, five to seven years would seem to be a reasonable target date for ending protection and for expecting domestic producers to have overcome the basic transitional inefficiencies encountered at the beginning of easy ISI.[15] For more complicated products with longer learning curves or where technology is more complex, somewhat longer transition periods may be warranted. For some goods, the transitional period may be even less. In instances where a society's overall level of human capital accumulation and its technological and R&D capacity needs to be improved through relatively large social investments in education and health care, the period of tariff protection may need to be lengthened to permit the needed investment in these areas to bear fruit so that the necessary "initial endowments" are in place to provide domestic firms a reasonable opportunity to become competitive with international enterprises.

> Case study research on infant industries reveals that significant increases in productivity, where they occur, come initially from technological efforts related to raw material control, product and process quality control, production scheduling, repair and maintenance, changes in product mix, as well as others including episodic trouble-shooting to overcome problems encountered in the course of operations.... Infant industries rarely achieve international competitiveness without having realized productivity gains from such technological efforts.
>
> (Evenson and Westphal 1995: 2249)

Whatever the specific time frame for the termination of infant-industry protection, what is critical is that a timetable for the eventual phasing-out of tariff protection should be part of the government's policy. When ISI is begun, government should reveal this schedule to the new firms so that they anticipate with *certainty* the end of infant industry tariff protection.[16] In this way, domestic producers do not become complacent, thinking and acting as if protection is a permanent fixture of the economic landscape that permits higher-cost, less-efficient domestic producers to prosper, permanently immune from outside competition. Domestic producers must expect that protective tariffs will end at a determinate date. At that time they must either be competitive with imports by having overcome any transitional inefficiencies (as on supply curve S_{D2} in Figure 9.2) or suffer the consequences when imports are permitted to re-enter the domestic market at world market prices once tariff protection is fully removed.[17]

If tariffs on ISI industries are not phased out, then the tariff itself can become a substantial internal barrier to progress. Retaining infant industry tariffs beyond the time when they should be unnecessary not only is a threat to further industrialization but also to the higher levels of growth, development, and social and human welfare that are the motivating forces for initiating easy ISI and the transfer of labor from agriculture to industry via ISI in the first instance. If tariff protection is not withdrawn from domestic producers, there is a strong likelihood that static dead-weight losses will persist as permanent deadweight losses, thus sacrificing the potential dynamic welfare gains shown in Figure 9.2 when the supply curve increases. No one can be in favor of such an outcome.

The importance of embedded state autonomy to successful ISI

One of the concerns many economists have about countries that pursue an easy ISI strategy is precisely that this stage will become virtually permanent, so that tariff protection is never fully withdrawn.[18] And that has happened. In India and many Latin American countries as well as in other economies, high levels of protection continued far longer than can be justified by the infant industry argument and by appeals to transitional inefficiencies of local firms. Producing behind a highly protective tariff wall, domestic producers gain a quasi-captive market which can return substantial above-normal profits, with minimal attention being paid to efficiency, to improvements in technology or training, to product quality or to consumer complaints. Industrialists in an ISI sector where tariffs are not progressively removed may be able to reap substantial economic rents, that is, to earn profits higher than are necessary for calling forth the current level of production, since the tariff prevents the full-force of foreign competition from being felt by domestic producers.

When tariff protection is prolonged rather than phased out, this typically is the consequence of close links forged by entrepreneurial elites in the ISI sector with administrators in government having responsibility for the industrialization program, connections that can diminish the independence of state decision-makers to act on broader social interests. Such links may be quite informal. Industrialists and government officials may belong to the same clubs. They quite likely operate in the same social circles, meeting at restaurants, the theatre, social gathering, weddings, and so on. The contact between protected industrialists and government bureaucrats can involve substantial degrees of corruption and bribery. When governments lack relative autonomy from strong vested interests, they often respond to the private concerns of those groups which have the power, money, influence, and access to government to make their voice heard. In the process, more general interests of society for more efficient, more technological, more productive, more equitable, and higher-paying and expanding domestic industry are sacrificed, as the ability of the majority segment of the economy to voice its interests is circumscribed by relatively closed and exclusive political processes that respond to powerful interests first and public concerns later, if at all.

This problem of a captured state is not, however, one inherent to countries which initiate an ISI strategy. It is rather due to the nature of the political process and the privileged of access to some groups to state decision-making which create a barrier to the desired reduction of tariff protection on ISI industries. These elites are able to turn state economic policy in their direction for their own profit at a cost to the domestic economy and to domestic consumer interests, thus making it more likely that the static welfare losses measured by the deadweight loss shown in Figure 9.2 will persist. Whenever the state is to some degree *captured* by special interests who can create and maintain laws and regulations that allow them to earn a larger producer surplus and economic rents without becoming more efficient, economic policy is likely to be distorted in the direction of those elites' interests at the expense of overall economic efficiency and social welfare.[19]

Such distortions and interference by predatory elites with state policy can arise regardless of the particular economic strategy an economy pursues. It is not a necessary consequence of the ISI stage, as the experience of the East Asian economies, reviewed in the next chapter, clearly demonstrates. The experiences of South Korea, Taiwan, and other LDCs do not support the conclusion that this is a necessary outcome of the ISI stage of industrialization either (Amsden 2001).

The problem of continued protectionism during ISI, then, is one of politics and is not due to the particular economic strategy in force. It is purely coincidental that such "captured" states are most evident during ISI, but that is because ISI is most often the natural and logical first stage of industrialization and of the structural transformation process required for development.[20] A large number of LDCs are relatively new nations emerging from a colonial past with weak states in which small elites dominate the political process. Captured states have too often been the outcome in such circumstances.

In such circumstance, ISI is more likely to become stuck in the first transition stage and tariff protection is more likely to be maintained long beyond its justifiable usefulness for infant industry protection. But it is not the ISI strategy that is to blame. It is the nature of the political process and its captured status in relatively new nations without a history of democratic experience that leads to the detrimental over-extension of tariff protection. The barrier of a weak, captured state needs to be overcome by appropriate institutional reform, culminating in the creation of a developmental state, as described in Chapter 7.

Potential gains from the easy ISI stage of industrialization

What are the expected gains to countries from initiating easy ISI industrialization? Given the nature of the production methods for the manufactured goods produced as import substitutes, this stage of industrialization tends to be relatively labor-intensive. As the sector grows, the easy ISI stage can provide increasing employment opportunities for an expanding proportion of the labor force. This will be especially important if the increasing numbers of migrants exiting the agricultural sector who are attracted to industrial jobs by the pull of higher wages in the ISI sector are to be absorbed in productive employment.

During the easy ISI phase, the industrial labor force develops both *specific and general human capital skills* as a result of learning-by-doing as they work with modern machines and technology. These skills will be at least partially transferable to other firms thus shortening the lag time required for other firms to overcome transitional inefficiencies in the future. There is thus an acceleration of the learning process that is likely to accompany the expansion of the ISI sector as new production linkages are created.

As the endogenous growth theories of Chapter 8 suggest, such positive technological and human capital externalities can accelerate the pace of economic expansion, even with the same level of other productive resources in use. Through their interaction with technology and the learning which accompanies such activity, the ability of augmented labor to better utilize existing technology is improved and the growth and development prospects of the economy are enhanced. Further, management and other essential entrepreneurial skills will be acquired and improved during the easy ISI stage. These are skills that are integral to successful and sustained industrialization over the long term, especially in the post-easy ISI stages of industrialization considered in the next chapter.

Another characteristic of easy ISI is that it is a training ground for entry-level local industrialists who have an opportunity to mature and learn how to produce. Over time, with successful ISI, the initial disparity between the management skills and information levels of domestic managers and capitalists and those of foreign industrialists will be progressively narrowed. This stage of industrialization for late industrializers thus facilitates the establishment, extension and solidification of a domestic class of private entrepreneurs who are essential to the continuation of the process of development in the future.

In the easy ISI stage, the rise of the modern capitalist business ethic is encouraged and reinforced. The attention to detail and quality, to financial and accounting costs, to time schedules and to contracts that are characteristic of production in the already developed nations have a chance to begin to seep into the thinking and behavior of businesspeople. Where corruption and cheating of the customer might have been the norm of behavior by sellers in the past, the progressive elimination of tariff protection can contribute to the alteration in entrepreneurial behavior toward levels of efficiency, stability and responsibility to the consumer that modern industrialization demands (Gerschenkron 1962: 47–48).

Seen in this light, easy ISI is imperative, though not by itself sufficient, to the continued prosperity of the development process. It is the first step, then, on a journey toward industrialization and development. It is not in any way the final stopping point.

Parastate firms and social capital[21]

In many instances, private-sector development in less-developed economies will require assistance from state-owned firms, perhaps especially during the initial ISI transformation. Infrastructure investments such as heating oil and natural gas, electricity, ports and telecommunications are all industrial activities that require enormous start-up costs in terms of physical and financial capital outlays. These are enterprises that also demand a mastery of intermediate levels of technology that may be beyond the capacity of local private entrepreneurs to provide in the early stages of industrialization.[22] The state, however, may be able to supply the necessary capital resources, the organization of production, and contribute to the shaping of a cadre of engineers and state-managers capable of providing the infrastructural base and other key inputs to the industrialization process that are required for the efficient operation of the private sector of the economy.

There are those who argue strongly against the expansion of state-owned firms, even in the early ISI stage. It is most commonly alleged that state enterprises are prone to be less efficient than if they were to be privately operated. It is asserted that the prices charged by state-owned firms are set too low, that is, below what the unfettered market price would be. State-owned enterprises thus often fail to recover all of their costs of production or to make a reasonable rate of return on the initial public investment in them. Any losses incurred by state enterprises are funded out of the national budget, thus creating a drain on scarce government revenues that cannot then be used for other purposes.

While it is true that state enterprises often do operate at a loss, that is not always the case. Even in those instances in which a state enterprise does not recover its full costs, it is not accurate to claim that the mere existence of an *accounting* loss implies a *social* loss from the operation of the parastate firm. To the extent that a state enterprise's operations promote the production of positive externalities accruing to private producers in the economy in the form of increased private returns, it is entirely possible that a subsidized state enterprise selling its output at a price below what unsubsidized private producers would charge will contribute to reaching the socially optimal level of production better than if the enterprise were to be in private hands with the firm's output priced at the private profit-maximizing level.

The theory of positive externalities is quite unambiguous in asserting that, in the presence of high transactions costs such as are involved in any large-scale infrastructure investment, producers of positive externalities must be subsidized if they are to produce the optimal level of production where marginal social benefits are equated to marginal social costs. Unsubsidized producers of positive externalities most certainly will under-produce.[23] Mustering evidence of state enterprises with accounting losses falls short of providing evidence of their relative inefficiency compared to private firms. Such state enterprises may, in fact, be contributing quite effectively to *social* efficiency by producing the socially optimal level of electricity, water, transportation, or gas and contributing the attendant positive externalities helping to make the private sector more productive, to increasing incomes and to raising employment in the private industrial sector. Is there any evidence to support this point of view?

In Taiwan in the 1950s during that nation's phase of easy ISI, state enterprises of all types produced well over half of all of Taiwanese industrial output. Parastatals overshadowed private firms in "fuels, chemicals, mining and metal working, fertilizer and food processing, textiles, and utilities" (Wade 1990: 78). In the glass, plastics, steel, and cement industries, state enterprises initiated production, removing the initial investment barrier, and then, after they were up and running, these firms were turned over to entrepreneurs in the private sector to be run for profit.

The parastate solution is, however, only one among many possibilities for providing essential inputs, especially infrastructure, to the emerging industrial sector. Depending on the circumstances, joint-ventures of combined ownership and control by national entrepreneurs, foreign owners and the state in various combinations can substitute for a parastatal. In other situations, for example where technology is very expensive and well-trained domestic management and maintenance personnel are scarce, the most reasonable solution for obtaining the production and positive externalities from needed infrastructure investment may well best be provided via the intervention of a wholly-owned transnational firm. In any case, all successful ISI programs have incorporated parastates to one degree or another, and these enterprises often were catalytic forces in the industrial transformation. Parastatals are not, by definition, purveyors of inefficiency.

Measuring the success of easy ISI

A successful easy ISI stage of industrialization shifts a country's production possibilities frontier (PPF) outward both along the agricultural axis, if agricultural productivity is raised simultaneously, and along the manufactured goods axis, as shown in Figure 9.3.

The curve PPF$_1$ is the original production possibilities frontier prior to the initiation of easy ISI when the country remains predominantly an agricultural producer and a primary product exporter. The country initially operates at a mix of production like that at *A*, which lies inside the frontier, recognizing the misallocation of resources that characterizes less-developed, agriculture-based economies where some labor has a low or even zero marginal product for at least part of the year. The entire production structure is organized primarily around agricultural production.

With the start of easy ISI and the transfer of labor from agriculture to industry

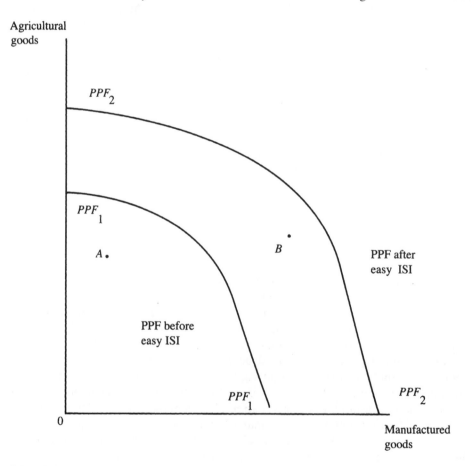

Figure 9.3 Impact of easy ISI on the production possibilities frontier.

and the introduction of new technology into both agriculture and industry, a new production possibilities curve, PPF$_2$, emerges that lies outside PPF$_1$. The new mix of production involves a movement toward both the industry axis and toward the PPF frontier, to a mix like *B*, as resources are better utilized, especially labor which is shifted from low marginal productivity uses in agriculture to higher productivity occupations in manufacturing. Both the share of total production and of total employment originating in manufacturing rises over the transition.[24]

Conclusions

Easy ISI is only a first step on the path of industrialization. But it is an essential first step if countries are to move to a higher level of economic development. It is true that some nations have become stuck at this stage due to internal barriers to transforming productive and social structures. It is also the case that for those nations that have successfully transitioned through this stage it has been fundamental in creating new initial conditions for future progress.

In the next chapter we shall consider the possible stages of structural transformation that different economies have followed *after* the easy ISI stage. We shall see that there appears to be a bifurcation in possible transitions. One path leads toward greater opportunities to realize the dynamic effects of particular forms of physical and human capital accumulation, as discussed in the endogenous growth theories. The other path after ISI reduces the opportunities for continued progress and slows the pace of human development.

Questions for review

1 Table 9.1 suggests a strong positive correlation between the rate of growth of the manufacturing sector and the rate of growth of total GDP, but this is shown only for regions. Select five low- and middle-income countries and draw a graph with the manufacturing growth rate on one axis and the growth rate of GDP on the other. For each country, graph its specific manufacturing growth rate and its growth rate of GDP as one point on your graph. Do you see any relationship between the two variables? Draw a straight line through the points you have graphed. Does it have a positive or a negative slope? What does that positive or negative slope tell you? (If you have access to Excel or some simple regression program, you might try to estimate a simple one-variable regression equation.)

2 Table 9.2 provides evidence for a strong relation between a decrease in the share of the labor force engaged in agriculture (the primary sector) and an increase in the share of the labor force employed in industry (the secondary sector) and services (the tertiary sector). Draw two graphs. On one, put the "level of development" (measured by income per person or by the HDI indicator) on one axis and the "share of the labor force employed in agriculture" on the other. Plot the data from Table 9.2 and, using the same five countries considered in Problem 1 above, plot the data for these countries. On a second graph, with the "level of development" on one axis and the "share of the labor force employed in industry" on the other, plot the data from Table 9.2 and for your selected countries. Draw a straight line through the points which best fits the data. What relationship do you find in each graph as determined by the

slope (positive or negative) of the "regression" line you have drawn? (Again, a simple regression could be estimated here.)

3   What is the economic rationale for imposing an infant industry tariff? Are there any alternative ways for a country to encourage firms in a less-developed country to initiate production in competition with imports without such tariff protection?

4   A few possible sources of transitional inefficiencies were noted in the text. List two or three other possible sources of such inefficiencies in less-developed economies.

5   Using Figure 9.2, show that if transitional inefficiencies are overcome and domestic ISI producers approach the level of international competitiveness, there is a *dynamic welfare gain* to society from promoting ISI with protectionist measures that is greater than the free trade welfare benefit. (Hint: measure the change in domestic consumer *and* domestic producer surplus with free trade and after the forging of a competitive ISI sector when the domestic supply curve has now shifted to S_{D2}.) Is the economists' argument that free trade is beneficial for all countries incorrect? Is it true in the short term but perhaps not true for the longer term? Explain by considering the possible advantages to a country that successfully completes ISI.

6   What is the importance of gradually removing infant industry tariffs if easy ISI has any hope of being successful? As infant industry tariffs are removed, what does this imply about the quality and prices of the goods produced by domestic ISI firms compared to imported goods? What is the danger of leaving tariffs on too long?

7   Using a graph, show that the level of production of a producer of positive externalities to other firms will under-produce compared to the socially optimum level of production. (Hint: assume that social marginal costs = private marginal costs and that the social marginal benefit curve lies outside the private marginal benefit curve.) Then show that an appropriate subsidy provided to the producer of the positive externality can lead to the "internalization" of the externality, thus leading to a larger level of output and a lower price for the good creating the positive externality.

8   Explain how the accounting profits (or losses) of an unsubsidized public enterprise, the output of which creates positive externalities for other firms, will understate (overstate) the true level of profits (losses) of that firm. Is it possible for a parastatal firm which creates positive externalities to private-sector enterprises to have an accounting loss but still be "socially profitable"? Explain.

9   Focus 9.1 shows the share of primary exports in total exports for a limited range of countries. Choose three low-income less-developed nations not listed in the table. Does the primary product export pattern dominate in each of these as well (you can find data at http://www.cia.gov/cia/publications/factbook/index.html)? What potential problems do countries face if their export profile is dominated by primary exports? Why is it "better" to have a larger percentage of manufactured goods exports as a share of total exports?

10   Define the following terms: market failure; easy ISI; non-traditional exports; transitional efficiency; positive externality; parastatal; primary sector; secondary sector; tertiary sector.

11   Some economists claim that import substitution industrialization is a mistaken

policy for countries to follow because of the inward-oriented focus of production it encourages. However, other economists insist that ISI, and certainly easy ISI, is a necessary stage of industrialization. a) Taking the position of the latter economists, carefully explain why easy ISI is an important step for countries to take (*i.e., discuss the possible benefits to be gained from a well-executed easy ISI program*). b) What must be done by the state to help ensure that the easy ISI stage of industrialization is successful in contributing to a nation's future development prospects? Be specific.

Internet exercise

Choose a less developed country for the following exercise: *find*

a the share of total output (GDP) produced in agriculture and industry and services for 1999 from http://www.worldbank.org/poverty/wdrpoverty/report/tab12.pdf the share (i.e., percentage) of the labor force working in agriculture and industry and services http://www.worldbank.org/data/wdi2002/pdfs/table%202-3.pdf. You may have to average the M and F rates if both are given. Calculate the productivity of each 1 percent of the labor force in these two sectors by dividing the share of GDP by the share of labor in each sector.

b If you reduce the labor force working in agriculture by 10 percent and add 10 percent to the labor force working in industry for this country, what is the effect on total GDP?

c Is the labor force in your country distributed optimally, that is, could total GDP be increased by shifting labor from one sector to another? Explain.

Notes

1 The industrial sector includes the manufacturing sector. Within the industrial sector, but not classified as manufacturing industries, are electrical power generation, communications, gas and water generation, mining, transportation, and other non-manufacturing enterprises.

2 It is perhaps worth remembering Alexander Gerschenkron's insight that there is the possibility of "substitution" in how any particular country becomes developed. Becoming developed is not a process of simply copying what other successful countries have done before in all aspects. There are patterns, of course, or there would be no purpose in teaching about development. Still, each country must forge its own particular path within the patterns of structural change identified. Kuznets wrote in this regard,

> there is a connection between the high rate of growth associated with modern economic development and a variety of structural changes, not only economic but also social; not only in institutions but also in ideology. This does not mean that all the historically associated shifts in economic and social structure and ideology are requirements, and that none of them could be avoided or substituted for. It does mean that some structural changes, not only in economic but also in social institutions and beliefs, are required, without which modern economic growth would be impossible.
>
> (Kuznets 1971: 348)

Further, as the endogenous growth models examined in Chapter 8 suggest, it is not just structural change that is the key to successful growth. Efforts at structural change alone – for example, the transfer of labor from agriculture to industry – that lack the required changes in the quality of inputs to production via human capital accumulation, funding for R&D and technology acquisition and additions of more productive physical capital are likely to be substantially less effective. Further, as we shall consider in subsequent chapters, there are fundamental macroeconomic concerns that must also be a part of any successful development strategy.

3　Industrialization involves the transfer of what is often called surplus labor from agriculture to the emerging factory system, as is reviewed in the section on the Lewis model below. If that movement of labor is not to result in a decrease in basic food production, higher food prices and the need for expanding food imports, domestic agricultural production must become more efficient at the same time.

　　One important additional and non-economic reason to transform agriculture is to remove a potential political obstacle, that is, an Ayresian ceremonial barrier, to further industrialization and development. If large and politically powerful landowners derive a portion of their wealth from their primary product exports, they are likely to oppose the desired evolution of the industrialization process into diversified exporting, particularly when the aim of such a transformation is to change the export profile of the nation by progressively replacing agricultural and other primary exports with the manufactured outputs of the emerging industrial sector.

4　It is typically the case that the benefits of primary product specialization, that is, of an economic structure dominated by agricultural and natural resource extraction, tend to accrue to only a relatively small elite in the country. Industrialization opens the door to a wider distribution of the gains of production and an increase in total social welfare not as easily attained if a nation remains in the primary product producer category (Chenery 1979: 35). Thus, industrialization increases the opportunities for greater income dispersion, as well as higher incomes per capita, that can contribute to improvements along the HDI dimension as well, particularly as universal primary and secondary education become the norm. To the extent that income distribution is improved as a consequence of such an evolution in the productive structure and in the accumulation of human capital, and to the extent that an improved income distribution contributes to a higher level of development, this transformation is "growth-enhancing," that is, it contributes to faster economic progress.

5　This can be demonstrated relatively easily by determining the productivity of 1 percent of the labor force in producing GDP in agriculture, industry, and services. In most less-developed economies, the productivity of the agricultural sector is less than 1 and substantially less than the productivity of labor in industry. Shifting workers from lower productivity agriculture to higher productivity industry will thus increase total GDP. The Internet exercise at the end of the questions challenges you to do this.

6　It is "easy" ISI in two senses. First, since the demand for a particular manufactured good already is known from the quantity of imports, the potential size of the market for that good also is known. All local producers need do is produce to service that demand. And second, this stage is "easy," because the technology used in production is relatively simple; often standardized, off-the-shelf machinery can be purchased on the world market. The term "primary ISI" recognizes this stage as a first phase of ISI, not its endpoint. The term "horizontal" ISI recognizes that the first stage of ISI is taking place within particular industries; during this stage, industrialization does not extend backward into the other, supplier industries, a phase which will be termed vertical ISI, and which involves a deepening of the industrialization process.

7　As one of the poorest regions among the LDCs, sub-Saharan Africa's exports – more than 80 percent – remain dominated by unprocessed primary products (Wood and Mayer 2001: 376).

8　This may be a further reason why too much income and wealth inequality can limit the pace of economic growth, as Rodrik's study suggested in Chapter 8. Excessive inequality limits the size of the domestic market, thus impeding the pace of domestic industrialization and growth and development by restricting total demand. This may be the case for large economies too, not just small ones.

9　Bruton (1989) prefers the term "infant economy" protection, which perhaps better conveys that, for the less-developed economies, the transformations in production, organization, education, public policy, and so on that are required to overcome the transitional inefficiencies go far beyond any particular industry and reach deep into the entire social, political, and economic fabric of society.

10 Evenson and Westphal (1995: 2284–2285) argue that protection is only a second-best policy. The first-best policy would be to have efficiently functioning capital and financial markets, as discussed in Focus 9.2, such that protection would be unnecessary. However, in poor nations, the option of forgoing tariffs may not be open. It is not just because waiting for the maturation of financial markets may be costly in terms of long-term growth which is sacrificed. It is also because, for poor countries lacking government revenues, tariff revenues obtained from infant industry protection provide an often important share of total government revenues. And given, as Evenson and Westphal note, that no program of protection of infant industry which has lacked needed investments in technological capacity has been successful, those tariff revenues provide a potential source of funding for precisely the technological development required for long-term progress, from research and development to the training of human capital, if they are put to good use. These issues are considered in detail in Chapters 12 and 13.

11 This quantity could be zero if the domestic supply curve begins at a reservation price, or minimum supply price, greater than P_F.

12 Adding a fixed tariff amount to each unit of a good imported, say $3 per unit, is to impose a specific tariff. Alternatively, if a tariff is imposed as a percentage of the value of the imported good, say, a 30 percent tax, then this is an ad valorem tariff. In this example, with a fixed international price, either an ad valorem or specific tax will have the same effect of causing a parallel shift upward of the world supply curve, S_W. However, if the world supply curve were to be drawn as upward sloping, then an ad valorem tax would result in a non-parallel upward shift of the world supply curve for the country imposing the tariff. As the price of the imported good rose, the gap between the original world supply curve and the world supply curve plus the ad valorem tariff would widen, since the price to which the percentage tariff was being applied would be greater.

13 Producer surplus measures the extra revenues domestic firms receive above and beyond what is necessary for them to be willing to supply a particular level of output. It is equal to the area above the domestic supply curve and below the prevailing market price.

14 The deadweight loss equals the loss of consumer surplus minus the increase in producer surplus minus the increase in government tariff revenues. Graphically it is: $P_F P_T df - P_F P_T ab - cbde = abc + def$.

15 Most countries levy some minimum tariff on a large array of imports for reasons other than infant industry protection. Such tariffs, particularly when they are uniform (say, 4 percent or 6 percent) and do not discriminate against any particular good, are often assessed as a means to raise revenues to help cover the costs of customs and other border operations, such as immigration. Thus, with the end of ISI protection, tariffs do not necessarily, and most likely will not, decline to zero.

16 The phase-out of tariffs can be uniform over the protected period or accelerating. For example, if the domestic beverage industry initially is provided a 25 percent protective tariff, to be phased out over five years, then 5 percent of tariff protection could be removed at the end of year 1, a further 5 percent at the end of year 2, and so on until all compensatory protection has been lifted (note there still might be a minimal tariff on beverages after the protective tariff is removed to cover the administrative costs of the customs service). Alternative schemes might leave the full 25 percent protection for two years; remove 5 percent at the end of year 3; remove 10 percent at the end of year 4; and at the end of year 5 remove the final 10 percent of protection. Whatever the phase-out pattern, it should be clear to enterprises that it is non-negotiable after start-up and that the end period for eliminating tariff protection is final.

17 There may be some exceptions where tariff protection is not fully removed, for example, in the case of certain industries deemed to be critical for national security. However, even in such industries (motor vehicle production may be one such industry), there are likely to be better means to guarantee the survival of firms when full tariff protection is withdrawn, e.g., low-cost loans and government procurement programs, that help to push enterprises to be more competitive and efficient.

278   *The structural transformation*

18 For a critique of ISI policies in general, see Balassa 1982.

19 This effort to capture economic rents is referred to as DUP or "directly unproductive profit-seeking" activity. In the process of attempting to retain tariff protection, ISI firms expend resources for lobbying and perhaps graft for dishonest politicians and other public servants to convince them to maintain high tariffs. Such expenditures are clearly unproductive uses of society's resources, as they do not contribute to increased output or efficiency, thus increasing the net loss of a tariff to society (see Colander 1984). For a recent analysis of state structures, see Evans (1995: ch. 7), who describes a "captured" state as a predatory state.

20 One need only think back to David Ricardo's analysis of the advantages of free trade and of the struggles over the Corn Laws in England discussed in Chapter 4 to realize that the search for economic rents by those with privileged access to political power is neither new nor confined to countries making use of ISI development strategies. Large English landowners struggled hard to keep European grains from entering British shores through the implementation of restrictive trade measures which kept their "rents," or incomes, artificially and unnecessarily high, at the expense of others, particularly low-income British consumers.

21 Parastate firms, or parastatals, are government-owned and operated enterprises.

22 Further, there is the usual market failure dilemma arguing for government provision of such goods and services. Infrastructure production tends to generate substantial positive externalities. Not only does such production tend to lower costs of essential inputs, like electricity, to third-party private industrialists, thus increasing their profits without a private cost outlay, the mere existence of sufficient electrical generation capacity creates opportunities for new production to emerge. Private entrepreneurs in infrastructure cannot appropriate as private profits any of the higher returns to third parties made possible by the provision of infrastructure, and there is thus likely to be under-investment in such essential inputs if the market is left to provide such output. The state, as the representative of society, can, however, factor in and calculate the private returns of all parties in making an infrastructure investment decision, thus raising the benefits of such investment relative to the cost. Of course, a state enterprise will not realize all the benefits, so the social profitability of the infrastructure investment will always be larger than its accounting profitability. Taxes on private corporate profits, however, can be used to capture at least part of the profits due to the state-provided inputs and might be added to the infrastructure provider's revenues to get a fuller concept of the state firm's true revenues, costs and profits.

23 Unsubsidized private producers of positive externalities have no way of appropriating any of the additional profits that their production process creates for other firms. Concerned only about their own private benefits of production, which, when there are positive externalities, are less than the social benefits of production, the private level of (unsubsidized) production will be less than the social optimum. This is because the marginal private benefit curve intersects the marginal social cost curve at a lower level of output than the marginal social benefit curve intersects the marginal social cost curve. Thus, the private prices of firms affected by the positive externality will be higher than the socially optimum price and their output levels will be lower than would be desirable due to under-provision of the positive externality by private firms.

24 For those who argue that ISI breeds inefficiencies, the issue still remains whether the level of production with ISI, even if taking place inside PPF_2, results in a higher growth path than the mix of production associated with the original PPF_1 with the output mix at A. It is not transitional, static inefficiency of ISI versus an ideal ISI that is crucial as industrialization is initiated, but rather the impact of growth and development associated with pursuing the ISI strategy versus staying on the status quo path. Of course continued ISI inefficiency is not desirable, but that is contained in the concept of "transitional" inefficiencies which can be reduced as tariff protection (or subsidization) is removed and competition encouraged.

References

Amsden, Alice. 2001. *The Rise of "The Rest": Challenges to the West from Late-Industrializing Economies*. Oxford: Oxford University Press.

Balassa, Bela. 1982. *Development Strategies in Semi-Industrializing Economies*. Baltimore, MD: The Johns Hopkins University Press.

Blair, Calvin. 1964. "Nacional Financiera," pp. 193–238 in Raymond Vernon (ed.), *Public Policy and Private Enterprise in Mexico*. Cambridge, MA: Harvard University Press.

Bruton, Harry. 1989. "Import Substitution," ch. 30 in Hollis Chenery and T.N. Srinivasan (eds), *Handbook of Development Economics*, volume II. Amsterdam: North-Holland.

Chenery, Hollis. 1979. *Structural Change and Development Policy*. New York: Oxford University Press.

Colander, David C. (ed.). 1984. *Neoclassical Political Economy: The Analysis of Rent-Seeking and DUP Activities*. Cambridge, MA: Ballinger.

Evans, Peter. 1995. *Embedded Autonomy*. Princeton, NJ: Princeton University Press.

Evenson, Robert E. and Larry E. Westphal. 1995. "Technological Change and Technology Strategy," ch. 37 in Jere Behrman and T.N. Srinivasan (eds), *Handbook of Development Economics*, volume IIIA. Amsterdam: Elsevier Science.

Gerschenkron, Alexander. 1962. *Economic Backwardness in Historical Perspective*. Cambridge, MA: Harvard University Press.

Higgins, Benjamin and Jean Downing Higgins. 1979. *Economic Development of a Small Planet*. New York: W.W. Norton Co.

Kuznets, Simon. 1971. *The Economic Growth of Nations*. Cambridge, MA: Harvard University Press.

Stiglitz, Joseph. 1992. "Alternative Tactics and Strategies for Economic Development," in A.K. Dutt and Kenneth P. Jameson (eds), *New Directions in Development Economics*. Notre Dame, IN: University of Notre Dame Press.

Syrquin, Moshe. 1988. "Patterns of Structural Change," ch. 7 in Hollis B. Chenery and T.N. Srinivasan (eds), *Handbook of Development Economics*, volume I. Amsterdam: North Holland Publishers.

UNDP (United Nations Development Programme). 1995. *Human Development Report 1995*. Oxford: Oxford University Press.

—— 2001. *Human Development Report 2001*. Oxford: Oxford University Press.

Wade, Robert. 1990. *Governing the Market: Economic Theory and the Role of Government in East Asian Industrialization*. Princeton, NJ: Princeton University Press.

Wood, Adrian and Jörg Mayer. 2001. "Africa's Export Structure in Comparative Perspective," *Cambridge Journal of Economics* 25 (May): 369–394.

World Bank. 1995. *World Development Report 1995*. Oxford: Oxford University Press.

—— 2000. *World Development Report 2000/2001*. Oxford: Oxford University Press.

—— 2001. *World Development Indicators*. Washington, DC: World Bank.

—— 2002. *World Development Report 2002*. Oxford: Oxford University Press.

10 Strategy switching and industrial transformation

After studying this chapter, you should understand:
- the limits to easy import substitution as the motor of industrialization and to overall economic development;
- the importance of strategy sequencing and timely strategy switches to successful development programs;
- the importance of export substitution as a fundamental phase on the path to industrialization;
- the costs associated with premature secondary or difficult import substitution;
- the importance of trade as a promoter of increased productivity and of more efficient technology use;
- the importance of public policy to augmenting resource endowments appropriate for future progress;
- the need to search for and promote dynamic comparative advantage and the role of "contests" in achieving this objective; and
- the key role of appropriate institutions in supporting warranted strategy switches.

Continuing structural change

In the previous chapter, we saw that the initial impulse toward a higher level of development comes with the movement of labor from agriculture toward industrial production and that this typically is achieved via easy import substitution industrialization (ISI) as relatively simple, non-durable manufactured goods are produced for the domestic market. This structural shift in the production process and of labor usage toward import substitution is common to virtually all successful and to many unsuccessful development experiences.

ISI is only the *first* step along a complex path of structural change that makes further progress possible but without guaranteeing success. No single development strategy is likely to be sufficient over time if economic growth and progress are to be sustained. Decision-makers, including those in government, need to be prepared to make changes in the prevailing strategy of development when it no longer provides the base for continued growth. The marks of good policy-making and of relatively long and stable periods of sustained expansion are the ability to recognize the need for and to quickly and effectively make such **strategy switches**.

Industrial sequencing: beyond easy ISI

The stage of easy ISI examined in Chapter 9 has a natural limit as a contributor to sustained growth and development. Once all the potentially viable non-durable consumer good imports have been replaced by domestic production, then industrial growth in the domestic market will be limited to population growth plus any aggregate income expansion.[1] Then, the pace of economic growth is likely to slow as the ability of the manufacturing sector to **lead** the growth of the rest of the economy will have been reduced. In fact, *diminishing returns* to the easy ISI strategy will be apparent long before all the import substitution possibilities for non-durable consumption goods have been exhausted. Countries thus face a dilemma. What can be done to ensure continuing economic growth and development and the shift of labor from agriculture to industry? What measures might facilitate strategy switches in the design of a country's process of structural change to further the desired structural transformation?

The changing composition of imports

Complicating matters, during the easy ISI stage, there is a change in the composition and, often, the total volume of imports. The share of non-durable consumer good imports as a percentage of total imports obviously declines as these are replaced by domestic production. In their place, a country pursuing an easy ISI strategy begins to import more expensive and more complex manufactured goods. These include a rising share of total imports as *intermediate inputs*, such as, for example, needles, bobbins, dyes, and thread for the textile industry and physical *capital goods*, such as sewing machines, destined for the easy ISI sector. To the extent that easy ISI is fairly generalized and not limited to a restricted range of consumer goods, the percentage of total imports accounted for by non-durable consumer goods will continue to shrink as ISI proceeds.[2] As the limit to easy ISI is reached continued progress in terms of both expanded rates of industrialization and of aggregate income growth sooner or later will require a redirection of economic policy.

It was at one time thought that an easy ISI strategy actually might reduce the dependence of less-developed countries on the world market and especially on the developed nation or nations that are their major trading partners. By reducing the demand for non-durable consumer imports, it was thought less-developed countries would be producing more of the goods the country consumed, which was partly true, and hence would be more self-reliant, which turned out to be not *always* true. Easy ISI replaced the demand for imported consumer non-durables with the necessity of importing many of the inputs required in the newly promoted import substitution industries, since these inputs, especially physical capital, often were only available from the more developed nations. The urgency to continue to maintain a sufficient level of export earnings thus remained compelling, perhaps even more so, if the inputs to the ISI industries were to be purchased. Dependence on the external market simply changed its form. Imports now had become indispensable to the domestic industrial production process, to economic growth and to continued employment within the expanding easy ISI sector.

In an important sense, then, dependence on the external market continues and probably even is intensified after initiating an easy ISI strategy, even though the overall *import coefficient* declines for most countries.[3] This continued external dependence is evident from the importance imported machinery and transport equipment inputs assume as a share of total imports during the periods in which many less-developed economies were still in their easy ISI phase of expansion as shown in Table 10.1. The shift toward intermediate and capital goods imports is most pronounced in the regions where industrialization has been most rapid, particularly East Asia and Latin America. It is this "import imperative" that has forced nations to make changes to their development strategies as the easy ISI grew and then began to reach its natural limit of expansion.

Foreign exchange shortages

Most countries that have initiated the easy ISI stage find that, as the strategy continues, recurrent balance of payments problems (discussed more fully in Chapter 15) threaten economic stability.[4] Quite simply, earning the foreign exchange required to import the manufactured inputs to keep the easy ISI industries operating and the economy growing becomes a constant struggle. This is due to the fact that the bulk of foreign exchange earnings needed to purchase imported industrial inputs and capital continue to be derived from the same limited array of primary product exports the country has long been selling to the international market, often since colonial days. Easy ISI does not relieve this constraint on the balance of payments.

Whether because of instability in commodity prices or due to declining terms of trade or as a consequence of inefficiencies in primary product production or a combination of all these effects, the level of export income derived from primary exports tends to fall short of what is needed to pay for the imported inputs required

Table 10.1 Composition of imports (as a percentage of total imports)

	Primary goods[a]		Machinery and transport equipment		Other manufactured goods		M/GDP
	1970	1992	1970	1992	1970	1992	1992
Sub-Saharan Africa	15	16	38	39	42	37	22
East Asia and Pacific	23	15	33	39	37	36	23
South Asia	33	21	24	22	31	39	13
Middle East and North Africa	26	21	32	35	39	39	25
Latin America and the Caribbean	18	16	35	40	36	35	10[b]
High-income economies	32	16	25	35	33	41	16

Source: World Bank 1994: 189.

Notes
a Includes food but excludes fuels, so components do not sum to 100 percent.
b 1991.

by the easy ISI industries. The lack of dynamism in traditional primary product export markets limits the growth of foreign exchange earnings at the same time the need for such income to finance the purchase of industrial inputs is ever more pressing.[5]

There are two paths or sequences of industrialization that nations have followed after the easy ISI stage in an attempt to ease this foreign exchange constraint: *easy export substitution* and *difficult or secondary ISI*. Each takes a country in a different direction in terms of its industrial structure, export and import patterns, and the impact on the balance of payments, as well as long-term economic growth and human development possibilities.

From examining the historical experience, there would seem to be a "superior" and a "sub-optimal" strategy switch for ordering industrial growth and for further-ing the structural transition.[6] The choice is not, however, between import substitu-tion **or** exporting as overall strategies, as the neoliberal economists often frame the issue. The policy choice is rather between the *sequencing of import and export sub-stitution stages* and the nature of what is exported and at what stage in the cycle of industrialization. Proper "strategy sequencing" involves the appropriate combina-tion of exporting *and* ISI; it is not a choice between one or the other. No less-developed country has successfully made the transition to a higher stage of economic growth and development without passing through **both** ISI and the stage of exporting manufactures to the world market.

Easy export substitution

If infant industry tariffs have been progressively eliminated during the easy ISI phase, as is indispensable to future economic progress as seen in Chapter 9, then those ISI firms that have learned to compete on price and quality with imported goods have a further option beyond the domestic market for expanding their pro-duction, sales, and profits: they can export these same non-durable consumer goods to the international market.[7] Having been forced to become competitive with imports on the world market to survive within the domestic market as tariffs and other forms of protection were reduced, and not all the original ISI firms will necessarily weather the challenge, domestic firms with the requisite expertise can begin to export.

Warranted government policy can support this process of improving competit-iveness of domestic producers via: international marketing assistance; an exchange rate that is not artificially over-valued and is, perhaps, mildly under-valued; low but positive, real interest rates for borrowing for productive investment ("financial repression"); education subsidies; and so on.[8] The point is that for those easy ISI firms able to meet foreign competition, their potential market extends far beyond the local consumer to regional and world markets. For smaller nations with rela-tively limited domestic markets and few firms in each industry, the ability to compete at all with foreign firms may require the *early* intervention of government to assist in pushing production into export markets so that economies of scale and technological maturity can more rapidly be realized than would be possible from depending on the domestic market size alone.[9] In fact, for small nations with rela-tively small domestic markets, this imperative may be even more compelling if future progress is to be attained.

The advantages for countries entering export markets are many, and not solely and most obviously for the individual firms which expect to earn higher profits. From the national or social viewpoint, an expansion of total exports by selling easy ISI manufactured goods in international markets provides for the possibility of financing a higher level of total imported goods, a faster pace of economic growth and development, and a continued increase in employment for rural migrants into the still relatively labor-intensive easy ISI industrial sector. These exports of simple manufactured goods contribute to the foreign earnings needed to import the necessary intermediate and capital inputs required by the ISI industry itself, thus helping to self-finance the export expansion.

Further, and of great importance, to the extent that the exports of ISI firms begin to *replace and substitute for traditional primary exports*, the economy's export structure will begin to become more like that of the developed nations, thus reducing the pressures arising from the Prebisch–Singer declining terms of trade dilemma (considered in Chapter 6) that in part had contributed to weakened export earnings and to recurring foreign exchange problems in the past.[10] Manufactured and other non-traditional exports will increase in significance in the export mix as export substitution proceeds, since the essence of export substitution is to extend the production of easy ISI goods, further shifting labor out of agriculture and into industry, and reducing the significance of the prior pattern of primary exports in both relative and absolute terms within the export profile. In other words, within the export profile of a nation pursuing easy export substitution, manufactured exports are more than just an addition to the primary product export base. Over time, easy ISI manufactured exports *take the place of* primary product exports, hence the name, export substitution. Old exports are being replaced by new exports.

Gustav Ranis (1981) has suggested that *export substitution* is the logical and recommended next stage of evolution in the industrialization strategy. It is this stage which was followed by the East Asian nations of South Korea, Taiwan, Hong Kong, Japan, and other HPAEs ("high performance Asian economies") after completing their phase of easy ISI. And it is one that economic policy-makers in nations still in the easy ISI phase of transformation, or taking steps to deepen ISI, should be planning to implement in a relatively open international economy. Exporting simple consumer non-durables allows less-developed countries to penetrate the international market at a low level in the so-called "life cycle" of manufactured good exports. This is a natural, evolutionary niche for most less-developed countries in that such production tends to be labor intensive and hence relatively low-cost, due to low wages and the continuing labor surplus and its use of simple technology.

The gains from export substitution

During the export substitution stage, labor-intensive production methods continue to be used, since it is simple non-durable consumer goods that are being produced for both domestic and, now, for foreign consumption. Export substitution deepens the industrialization process and allows for the continued growth of employment in the domestic manufacturing sector. Rising exports can help to maintain a higher rate of economic growth.[11] By increasing total production to meet domestic and export demand, scale economies in production may be attained which can reduce per unit costs of production. Of particular importance too will be the management, financial, marketing, technological, and other essential capacities that can be learned from operating successfully in the international marketplace. Such skills often are transferable to other domestic industries as spill-over effects multiply and as the nation's pool of domestic talent is enlarged and extended to new arenas.

This prospect of *backward* and *forward linkages* in new areas of production emerging through a process of entrepreneurial-deepening is one of the prime benefits of moving into the export-substitution phase. This stage provides continuity in the industrialization process and helps to augment the training of the domestic entrepreneurial and professional class, as well as upgrading the skills of the labor force on the job. Local entrepreneurs are allowed to flourish, albeit with substantial government assistance.

What is important is that the local entrepreneurial class is permitted to come to maturity in this phase by being forced to become internationally competitive on price and quality and via the continuous up grading of technological skills and training. It is precisely these sorts of positive externalities that endogenous growth theories envisage as fundamental to sustained growth over time, and it seems that *the capacity to export* helps to endogenize such behavior within the domestic economy. Foreign capital and foreign technology have a role to play in this stage of the transformation, but at least in the East Asian economies, foreign interests and foreign capital were subordinated to local interests, local capital, and local entrepreneurs (see Focus 10.1 Foreign Capital and Technology in South Korea).

It has become an article of faith in recent years among many economists that an export orientation, as opposed to an inward-oriented ISI policy, is essential for economic success in less-developed nations. Exports are perceived as an *engine of growth* for the economy as a whole. Sometimes the successes of the HPAEs and Japan have been put forward as exemplars of the efficacy of this strategy. However,

FOCUS 10.1   FOREIGN CAPITAL AND TECHNOLOGY IN SOUTH KOREA

South Korea has utilized foreign investment as a strategic means to gain access to technology and skills at a lower cost than might otherwise be possible. But the state's approach to such investment from abroad has been anything but *laissez faire*, taking what has been called the "eye of the needle" approach, making certain that any foreign investment met South Korea's needs.

In one study, it was found that only 29.7 percent of foreign direct investment (FDI) in South Korea took the form of wholly-owned subsidiaries of multinational companies. This compares with 33.1 percent for Japan at the same time (1976), and an average 69.1 percent ratio for the 66 countries in the study. In fact, South Korea's ratio was the lowest in the sample. "Foreign investors were expected by their partners and by the Korean government to make a continuing contribution to Korean development, one which was complementary to, rather than at the expense of domestic manufacturing interests."

In terms of technology transfers, the government usually approves these through the Economic Planning Board or the Ministry of Finance, with input from the Ministry of Science and Technology. Technical assistance contracts are typically limited to no more than three years, except in complex processes, with the intent of forcing domestic firms to learn how to do technology themselves rather than depending on foreign consultants.

Foreign technology in South Korea was viewed as a teaching tool to encourage local adaptation; it was not a fundamental cog in the development project.

Source: Luedde-Neurath 1988: 84–85, 90–93

more recent research suggests that it is not just exporting, but export substitution and before that ISI, that were essential to these accomplishments. And even then, export substitution is *not sufficient* for successful economic development, even if it would appear to be a *necessary* stage of industrial transformation. As we know from the endogenous growth models of Chapter 8, higher and sustained rates of economic growth require improvements in the stock of human capital and in the adaptation and use of new technologies in production. Countries which fail to accumulate human capital at a sufficiently high rate and to sustain technology acquisition ultimately will face lower growth rates than comparable countries with more human capital accumulation, even if both have identical levels of manufactured exports.

Further, countries which fail to accumulate human capital forego some of the potential technological gains available from the world pool of "best practice" production knowledge, and sacrifice economic efficiency, even if they are exporting manufactured goods on a relatively large, or increasing, scale.[12]

It is important that countries search for goods to export to the world market that have a reasonable prospect for having an expanding demand over time and with substantial **value-added** to the local economy. A greater volume of exporting per se is no panacea for less-developed nations or the colonies would have become developed long ago.

On balance, the search for dynamic created comparative advantage dictates an export mix dominated by goods with *income elasticities* that are not just positive, but preferably greater than one and which promise significant opportunities for growth in export earnings over time.[13] Manufactured goods, such as most electronics products, computer software, recreational and sports equipment, plumbing supplies, and so on, fall into this category. Some of these may even be produced during the easy ISI stage. Goods with high-value added are those which require more labor time and more machinery, technology, and knowledge to produce. Value-added in production is equivalent to the income created at each stage of production of a good, so the greater the value-added in production of a good the more income that is created for the local economy. Countries want to increase the production of goods with higher-value added accruing to domestically-owned resources, since it is the production of these goods for the domestic market and for export which will add most to a country's total income.

In a study of thirty developing economies over the period 1970–1982, Sebastian Edwards (1992) demonstrates that trade and openness to the international economy are important not solely because exports are a contributor to growth, but that, combined with the appropriate human capital base and with supporting government policies, openness is a significant *transmission mechanism for technological learning* by firms operating in the global economy. This also is the view of the World Bank's study (1993) of the HPAEs. It is not trade per se and exporting and openness to the international economy via reduced tariffs and restrictions on the movement of goods internationally that is so beneficial over the long term. It is the accrual of new vital knowledge in the domestic economy and the interaction with the proper human capital resources that is the pay-off from increased involvement in international trade in manufactured goods. The World Bank writes:

> The HPAEs' rapid export growth has often generated positive interaction between human capital, physical capital, and knowledge. The externalities

generated by manufactured exports ... in the form of cheaper and more effect-ive knowledge transfers would have undoubtedly been less productive had there been fewer skilled workers to facilitate their absorption.

(World Bank 1993: 321)

The success of not only Taiwan and South Korea in recent decades, but of Japan before them, would seem to strongly suggest that the *sequencing of industrialization* from easy ISI and then transitioning to easy export substitution is a design that not only builds upon the *created comparative advantage* forged during the easy ISI stage but also furthers the goal of augmenting and revealing new dynamic comparative advantage in the future.[14] Comparative advantage changes, sometimes quite rapidly, as the result of increases in education and in the skill levels of workers and man-agers, with the pace of technological change and its domestic adaptation, and as a consequence of rising incomes and the changing structure of domestic demand that accompanies an expanding urban, industrial society. The economy's domestic pro-ductive base, as well as its export structure, must be evolving in concert with, or perhaps even leading, these changes.

Table 10.2 provides some information on the evolution of export structures over time for the major regions and for various countries.

East Asia, dominated by the HPAEs, such as South Korea and Taiwan, and South Asia show the greatest movement toward manufactured exports within the regional export profile. Latin America and the Caribbean, despite a relatively high

Table 10.2 Export structure

	Manufactured good exports (percentage of merchandise exports)		
	1970	*1990*	*2000*
Regions			
East Asia and Pacific	32	68	83
Latin America and the Caribbean	16	34	48
Middle East and North Africa	5	15	14
South Asia	48	71[a]	80[b]
Sub-Saharan Africa	19	24	36
[High-income Economies	72	79	82]
Countries			
Argentina	14	29	32
Bangladesh	65	81[a]	91[c]
Brazil	13	52	59
Cameroon	8	9	5[b]
Côte d'Ivoire	6	11	14
Kenya	12	29	21
Malaysia	7	54	80
Mexico	32	43	83
South Korea	77	94	91

Source: World Bank 2002.

Notes
a Predominately textiles and clothing.
b 1999.
c 1998.

level of industrialization by some measures (for example, the share of the labor force), has not shown as strong a movement toward manufactured exports within its merchandise exports even by 1990, though the share by 2000 had reached near half. South Korea's share of manufactured exports in merchandise exports reflects the effects of the government's conscious efforts to promote export substitution as easy ISI's gains began to diminish.

The growth in the manufactured goods exports of the East Asian countries shows up, too, in the evolution of the region's share of all manufactured goods exports. Considering only Hong Kong, Taiwan, South Korea, and Singapore, their share of manufactured goods exports as a proportion of the manufactured goods exports of **all** less-developed countries has grown steadily, from 13.2 percent in 1965 to an astounding 61.5 percent of the total in 1990 (World Bank 1993: 38). Latin America's share of less-developed country manufactured goods exports has declined over the same period. This shift is not surprising when it is realized that East Asia's exports grew at an annual rate of 10.5 percent over the period 1980–1992, led by manufactured exports, so that total exports increased more than three-fold. Over the same period, Latin America's total exports grew by 2.9 percent per annum, increasing little more than 40 percent over the same period. Though East Asia's total exports had been less than Latin America's in 1980, by 1992 East Asia's total exports were about double Latin America's exports. Income levels of the HPAEs, though they started off in the 1950s substantially lower, now rival those in Latin America, where both industrialization and ISI have had a longer history.

What accounts for the relatively poor performance of Latin America's manufactured goods exports relative to the HPAEs? How have the HPAEs been able to "leap over" the level of development of the larger Latin American countries, like Brazil and Mexico, and begin to approach the threshold of developed country status at a more rapid pace than the Latin American countries which had a head start? And, by extension, what can other late-developing nations in Africa and South Asia perhaps learn from the two experiences?

Difficult or secondary ISI

One explanation for the growing gap between the HPAEs and the rest of the less-developed world is found *partially* in the fact that an alternative sequencing of the path of industrialization can be followed after exhausting the possibilities of easy ISI.[15] The larger Latin American nations proceeded from easy ISI directly to *difficult, secondary* or *vertical ISI* in the 1950s, foregoing and skipping the easy export-substitution phase that was followed by the East Asian economies.[16] It will be recalled that with easy ISI the structure of imports is transformed toward a growing proportion of intermediate and capital goods, as non-durable consumer good imports are progressively replaced by domestic production. Secondary ISI *deepens* the domestic industrialization process by *extending* import substitution *backward* into the domestic production of durable consumption goods (like motor cars), intermediate goods (such as tires and batteries), and capital goods (like body stamping machines), the imports of which contribute to balance-of-payments difficulties on the spending side.

The shift toward secondary ISI is motivated by two parallel concerns. First, the exhaustion of easy ISI growth possibilities means that continued economic expansion fueled by manufacturing growth is impossible without new production for new markets. One possibility is to create these markets through *domestic vertical integration*, pushing production backward into intermediate and capital goods sectors and consumer durables now being imported. This creates the possibility for renewed growth based on local demand, since investment and production in these new industries can contribute to economic expansion via the usual macroeconomic *income and employment multiplier* effects and the *crowding-in* of tertiary production that emerges to service the new industries.[17]

Second, balance-of-payments difficulties caused by persistent trade deficits that are the result of having $M > X$ can motivate a decision to "strategy switch" toward secondary ISI. Balance-of-trade problems result from the need to import and pay for industrial inputs for the easy ISI firms in a situation where there is a problem of generating sufficient export income from the existing primary product export base, the prices of which are often unstable and subject to falling terms of trade. Thus, the decision to reduce the *import bill* even further via additional ISI does seem a logical alternative to increasing foreign exchange export earnings via export substitution, which is the alternative means for attempting to resolve the balance-of-payments disequilibrium and the exhaustion of easy ISI growth prospects. The thinking behind such a decision is based on the assumption that an additional unit of foreign exchange *saved* by a deepening of ISI is equivalent to an additional unit of foreign exchange *earned* by exporting via export substitution.

However, this static and purely mathematical view obscures longer-term tendencies and effects that suggest that a one unit savings in foreign exchange from *overextended or premature* secondary import substitution is actually worth less over time than a one unit increase in foreign exchange earnings that results from switching to an export substituting strategy. The Latin American economies prematurely entered secondary ISI, for reasons to be explored, and they thereby short-circuited the potential for more dynamic growth and structural transformation that the easy ISI phase had initiated. As a result, the period of ISI-led industrialization in Latin America was distorted and over-extended, lasting in some larger countries from the 1890s, and in others from the 1930s, to the 1950s in the easy ISI phase, followed by the stage of secondary ISI from the 1950s to the 1970s or so.

By contrast, the easy stage of ISI as a *central* component of the structural transformation in the East Asian economies lasted only about a decade, from roughly 1953–1963 (though there was some isolated ISI before), and then the strategy switch was to export substitution and a more dynamic export pattern, dominated by manufactured goods.

The costs of premature secondary ISI in Latin America

1 Viable entrepreneurial skills

The production of intermediate and capital goods and consumer non-durables characteristic of secondary ISI tends to be more capital- and knowledge-intensive than is true of easy ISI production. The technology for secondary ISI production is not only more difficult to master, it often is based upon proprietary knowledge lodged in transnational corporations. Countries, and this has been particularly true in Latin America and India, that enter the secondary phase of ISI directly following the easy

ISI stage have done so primarily by promoting transnational investment within their borders. It is these companies which control the technology and expertise, from management to engineering to quality control, required to produce the more complex products involved in secondary ISI.

This has resulted in a shift in the locus of power in the economy *away from* the still emerging class of domestic entrepreneurs who had been nurtured by the easy ISI strategy. Easy ISI had helped to create, protect and promote the growth of an indigenous capitalist class with the potential to be world-class competitors. The strategy switch in the larger Latin American countries in the direction of secondary ISI stunted and even reversed the growth of the local capitalist class, particularly as it came at a stage of development when this emerging class was not fully prepared to produce the more complex array of products characteristic of the secondary ISI phase. They had but limited contact with the international economy and lacked the higher levels of technological proficiency demanded if they were to compete with foreign imports since they had not been forced to become efficient and competitive via facing foreign competition in export markets.[18]

This cutting-short the development of the local entrepreneurial class is a crucial cost of shifting prematurely toward secondary ISI strategy rather than transitioning to easy export substitution strategy after easy ISI. Easy export substitution allows the local entrepreneurial class to continue to mature by becoming more efficient producers able to weather international competition. In Latin America and India, the shift toward favoring transnational investment as the agents of premature secondary ISI has made the technological learning process more difficult for local producers, who found themselves increasingly closed out of the productive circle.

2 Labor absorption

Even worse, since secondary ISI is more capital-intensive than easy ISI or easy export substitution, this strategy tends to slow the rate of labor absorption in the industrial sector, unless the level of overall investment rate is extraordinarily high, which it has not been in the nations that skipped export substitution and jumped to secondary ISI. As labor continues to migrate from the rural areas to the cities attracted by the hope of higher wages, the labor surplus that had characterized the rural agricultural economy is now transferred to an urban setting. However, with the premature implementation of secondary ISI many migrants fail to find work in the factories, and they often are forced to enter the **informal urban sector**, where productivity and incomes are extremely low. There they labor as artisans, petty traders, taxi drivers, day laborers, domestics, and so on, with the hope of formal sector employment in manufacturing at best a distant possibility. The relatively few workers employed in the secondary ISI firms often earn higher incomes than those employed in domestically-owned easy ISI firms.[19] The growth of employment in the secondary ISI sector tends to be very limited, thus a bifurcation of income classes among workers tends to emerge in the urban areas, with an adverse impact on the income distribution (see Box 5.3 on the Harris–Todaro model's predictions of precisely this sort of evolution if the wage wedge between the industry and agriculture was not closed over time).

Just the opposite happened in South Korea and Taiwan and other HPAEs. By continuing labor-intensive production of consumer non-durables in the easy ISI sector, pushing production outward into the international market via export substitution policies, the domestic capitalist class continued to be able to thrive and to hone their skills, knowledge and their management and production expertise in an ever more open environment in which not only domestic entrepreneurs but also the domestic labor force learned to be more efficient. The flow of workers from the countryside was more easily absorbed by the labor-intensive production characteristic of easy ISI firms now exporting to world markets with greater demand, employment in the modern sector expanded rapidly. Urban unemployment rates remained low and the substitute of informal sector employment required in economies skipping export substitution stage was minimal. Workers and entrepreneurs upgraded their productivity and efficiency levels, though for some time this did not appear as any substantial income growth for workers, as gains from productivity growth were plowed back into further investment, much as the Lewis model had predicted (see the discussion in Chapter 5).

In Latin America, India and a few other areas, premature secondary ISI meant the continuance of infant industry protection to block foreign imports from entering the domestic market, as protection was maintained on easy ISI goods and now extended to intermediate goods production as well. Thus, operating behind relatively high tariff walls, domestic producers did not confront the same external pressures as did East Asian entrepreneurs to become more technologically knowledgeable. Worker education or training on the job was not emphasized to the same degree, as these investments in productivity were not necessary given the high tariff levels maintained.[20] The result has been negative technical efficiency change, such that many economies were moving away from "best practice" technology and away from their potential production possibilities, given the inputs to production (refer back to Table 8.4).

Latin American and Indian manufacturers have suffered from the "*reluctant exporter syndrome*," meaning that they actively have pursued the export market during times of economic slump in their domestic economies, only to return to a focus on the internal market when domestic recovery returns. The export market thus has been viewed as little more than a safety valve for excess capacity in bad times, with the preference always being on the domestic market where profits are higher and where the producers know much more about the competition, the consumer and the social framework under which they produce and sell. The export market has not been seen as a means of advancing and improving the domestic market in such economies, with the adverse impact on technological adaptation and productivity that one would expect.

Endowments and policies: explaining strategy switches

It is not enough to know that the East Asian economies followed an industrial path that contributed to further economic expansion, while the Latin American and a few other economies, such as India, failed to initiate an export substitution strategy following easy ISI.[21] It is necessary to try to determine the underlying reasons for the distinct paths leading some countries to pursue export substitution and others to shift to secondary ISI following easy ISI, if other countries are to learn from these experiences.

Differing Endowments: The Resource Curse

One might think that having relatively abundant natural resources would be a blessing. However, Ranis (1981: 180–183) argues that for the Latin American countries, and by extension for other large countries with ample natural resources, the apparent resource base "cushion" of this *initial endowment* actually allowed those economies to continue along the same path of exporting primary commodities to earn foreign exchange and to continue their highly protected easy ISI phase, even extending it into premature secondary ISI. Exports could be increased by simply producing more sugar or coffee or beef by using more of the abundant land via extensive production methods, rather than having to resort to becoming more efficient as would have been required if land had been less abundant. Further, there was the continuing influence and economic and political power of an agricultural elite who profited from the existing primary export structure. Given that the benefits of the protected ISI sector provided both profits and relatively high wages for a small urban elite, the "many decades of import substitution growth have led to encrusted habits and strong vested interest groups able to resist reforms or even marginal policy changes" (Ranis 1981: 180). Thus a large natural resource base, given particular institutional barriers to change as prevailed in Latin America and India, actually *hindered* the transition to the more optimal path of export substitution. An apparent resource blessing turned into its opposite, a so-called "resource curse."

> The availability of amply natural resources and/or foreign capital can thus be viewed as permitting the system to continue on its old tracks, thus avoiding the political and, at least short-term, economic pain of having to move to a different policy package. Growth rates can in this way be maintained – just by adding more fuel to the engine – and difficult decision postponed.... While additional resources, in theory, should be able to ease the actual and psychological adjustment pains, they can be used, and in the real world are often used, to put off – or entirely avoid – difficult decisions.
>
> (Ranis 1981: 180)

In the East Asian economies, however, land was at a premium. It was not possible to simply increase the quantity of primary product exports to compensate for the declining terms of trade and continue to do easy import substitution. ISI industries required a steady inflow of imported inputs and capital equipment that could only be paid for by expanding the quantity of exports. Sufficient foreign exchange earnings simply could not continue to be generated by the primary product export sector to avoid recurring balance-of-payments crises. Lacking a natural resource base, the East Asian economies were forced to confront the urgency of maintaining and increasing foreign exchange earnings, if the growth of domestic industry was to be sustained. It seemed that the only means for doing so was to find new exports, specifically manufactured exports, given the limited natural resource base.

There is another factor, however, that helps to explain the different responses to the natural resource endowment. While land distribution and ownership patterns have changed very little in this century in most Latin American countries and in much of South Asia, in East Asia, particularly in South Korea and Taiwan, fundamental *agrarian land reforms* were imposed after the Second World War (see Chapter 11). Thus, East Asian policy-makers did not have to concern themselves with the "encrusted habits and strong vested interest groups" who might oppose the replacement and substitution of primary product commodity exports with manufactured good exports from the easy ISI industries. The former landed class had been forcibly stripped of its position, power, and prestige, and thus resistance to industrialization and industrial exports at the expense of primary product exports did not materialize. No elite group with political power was threatened by the transition to a changed export mix dominated by manufactured goods. Agrarian reform in those countries made it feasible for those remaining in agriculture, now typically small farmers created after the agricultural revolutions, to increase the productivity of the land they worked. Without any substantial agrarian reform, any shift in the export structure away from agriculture in Latin America and India would have encountered fierce resistance from the landed elite. This is another *institutional difference* of importance that made initial endowments and their distribution act as barriers to effective industrial transformation in Latin America and other countries with similar structures.

Policy choices and institutional appropriateness

But there is another dimension to the differences in the strategies of development followed by the East Asians and the Latin Americans and other countries that followed a similar development trajectory. East Asian policy-makers, on the whole, made *better* decisions, implemented policies *better*, monitored policies *better* and were willing and able to alter quickly any decisions and policies if they did not provide the desired results. Governments in East Asia and Latin America and India both actively intervened in ways that affected the operation of their economies and the nature of path dependence. In East Asia,

> the government intervened – systematically and through multiple channels – to foster development, and in some cases the development of specific industries. Policy interventions took many forms: targeting and subsidizing credit to selected industries, keeping deposit rates low and maintaining ceilings on borrowing rates to increase profits and retained earnings, protecting domestic import substitutes, subsidizing declining industries establishing and financially supporting government banks, making public investments in applied research, establishing firm- and industry-specific export targets, developing export marketing institutions, and sharing information widely between public and private sectors. Some industries were promoted while others were not.
>
> (World Bank 1993: 5–6)

This quote from the World Bank's study of the HPAEs makes clear that policy intervention to shape the East Asian economies was pervasive. In South Korea and Taiwan, the banking system was, until recently, entirely publicly owned. "Financial repression," in which interest rates were reduced and loans provided to firms that could meet the desired social, economic, and development goals, helped to speed investment, technological change and growth. The East Asian economies do not exemplify what a "market-based" approach to development can attain, but rather just the opposite, what a "governed" market can do. They clearly represent the possibilities of vigorous and competent policy-making with well-defined goals. In the East Asian economies that goal was to raise the level of efficiency and technological capabilities of those economies to new levels that would permit a higher standard of living and the prospect of greater human development for a larger proportion of the population. They did this through a policy of *shared growth*, in which all classes gained from progress, and by *development from within*, that is, by depending predominantly on local capital and local capitalists to operate industry, based on expanded human capital accumulation and an augmented technological capacity.

Critics often have charged, however, that the South Korean economy was able to grow rapidly because of severe labor repression and a long period of non-democratic rule, only recently ended. And there is some truth to that. But, with time and economic expansion, and given the relatively high levels of education among the population, there have been substantial spread effects accompanying the structural transformation of the economy and society, so that average incomes have risen rapidly with a relatively low degree of inequality and with substantial progress on the key human development indicators. In South Korea in 1993, the share of total income received by the richest 20 percent of income earners as a ratio of the share of income received by the poorest 20 percent was 5.2 ($=39.3$ percent/7.5 percent). In Mexico, for 1998, the ratio was 13.6, and in Brazil, the ratio of income of the richest to the poorest income earners was 29.1 (64.1 percent/2.2 percent) for 1998 (UNDP 2002: Table 194–195).[22] Incomes are certainly not equal in South Korea, but the degree of inequality between the rich and the poor is much lower than in any of the Latin American countries. Given the higher rates of growth and higher income in South Korea, it would seem that economic expansion over time has tended to promote, or at a minimum sustain, equity. This trend toward greater equity also has been strengthened by the spread effects of greater human capital accumulation reaching a broader spectrum of the population, especially through education, as we shall see in Chapter 12. Shared growth has been a fundamental component of the Korean state's strategy for sustaining economic growth and for legitimizing its policies.

The South Korean and East Asian states can certainly be faulted for certain excesses, but there also have been undeniable accomplishments that could, if emulated, help other countries poorer than the HPAEs to make substantial progress out of extreme poverty.[23] One does not have to go too far back into time to when South Korean and Taiwanese per capita income levels were well below those of Mexico or Brazil; today the relation is reversed. And even though we know quite well that per capita income is not all of what development is about, it is an important part of what development is about.

Subsequent strategy switches

Since the 1970s, both the East Asian economies and the larger Latin American economies have altered their development strategies, again going in slightly different directions that have altered the nature of their path dependence, but with important and distinct consequences.

Secondary ISI/secondary export substitution

Even before the export substitution boom in consumer non-durables produced by the first era of ISI industries began to slow, South Korea and Taiwan (and Japan before) entered a stage of state-promoted *secondary ISI accompanied by secondary export substitution* (Ranis 1981; World Bank 1993: 123–155). In selected industries like chemicals and machinery or automobiles, the state assisted in the formation of industries with *backward linkages* to the existing industrial sectors. These new vertical ISI industries operated behind substantial infant industry tariff and non-tariff barriers that shielded them from international competition as they initiated production. But the state also required that these industries be prepared to export at an increasing rate over time *as a condition* of obtaining loans or subsidies to finance domestic production.

Over time, these new more sophisticated exports with their higher value-added and higher wages began to replace – substitute for – some of the non-durable exports of the previous phase of easy export-substitution industrialization. Once again, the East Asian economies consciously worked to alter their export profile, replacing simpler manufactured good exports with more complex manufactured exports. These exports also tended to have higher income elasticity values. Thus with growth in the international economy, the demand for these goods could be expected to rise rapidly, contributing to the expansion of export income and national incomes (see Focus 10.2).

The East Asian state provided constant guidance and assistance to the private sector throughout these transformations, though with a *quid pro quo* attached. Firms receiving state subsidies or privileged access to credit or special training or whatever cost-saving advantage which might be extended to them through special state programs were expected to meet specific *performance standards*, particularly exporting targets, if they hoped to be beneficiaries of special state assistance in

---

FOCUS 10.2 CREATING COMPARATIVE ADVANTAGE

Korean manufacturing giant Samsung Industries began making microwave ovens in the early 1970s in a cramped old laboratory, turning out a few hundred overpriced ovens annually for the heavily protected domestic market. By the 1990s, Samsung was making 80,000 microwave ovens a week and ranked as the world's biggest producer. How did a Korean company with almost no experience manufacturing complex ovens beat better financed and more experienced US and Japanese companies?

The government's Economic Development Board was a key player in Samsung's success. Government officials were keenly aware that the Republic of Korea could not rely forever on low-wage manufacturing. Just as the United States had lost countless textile industry jobs to Korea, they reasoned, so Korea would one day find it could no longer compete for labor-intensive manufacturing jobs with lower-wage neighbors such as China and Indonesia. To prepare for that day, government officials, working in consultation with the private sector, developed incentives for new knowledge- and capital-intensive industries. Incentives varied widely and included the government building industrial parks, subsidizing utilities, giving tax rebates for exports, and making cheap loans for investment in new products. By 1980, urged forward by subsidies and incentives, Korean industry had moved into steel, ships, and even cars and was about to leap into world-class electronics.

Sources: World Bank 1993: 130, Focus 3.3

future. Unproductive rent-seeking by the private sector thus was kept to a minimum, particularly given that most government bureaucrats were relatively honest and above being bribed, unlike in other countries. Firms could and did earn economic profits or rents, but they were permitted and assisted in doing so by government policy on the condition that the firm continued to meet the performance standards set by the state. When firms failed that test, they lost access to subsidized credit, marketing outlets, bank loans and so on, usually wiping out their economic profit or worse. Thus the pressures to conform to government policy by the private sector were strong, and at the same time, this persuasion by government ensured that private decision-makers' goals tended to be consistent with those of the overall development strategy.

Contests: rules, rewards, and referees

MIT economist Alice Amsden (1989, 1994, 2001) identified the importance of East Asia's use of a "performance-based allocation" system as central to their aggregate economic success. What Japan, South Korea, and Taiwan did was to create a **reciprocal structure** wherein there are *rules*, *rewards*, and *referees* for private firms wishing to gain access to, say, credit or a license to open a branch bank. To "win" a contest, a firm must meet the performance standards set by government (the "rules") if there is any hope for the reward of above-normal profits (World Bank 1993: 93–102). Typically, one of the rules of the contests has been sustained export performance, so that firms have been forced, as a condition of obtaining credit or exclusive licenses to produce, to become and remain internationally competitive.

This has required firms to pay constant attention to learning about and utilizing best practice technology, to the upgrading of their labor and management skills and generally to increasing efficiency and decreasing costs per unit of output via the utilization of superior technology, the best physical capital and highly trained human capital. Contest-based competition among firms has meant that the tendency toward excessive rents and monopoly profits earned via bribery and unproductive activities were substantially reduced, that is, unproductive activity in search of economic profits was dramatically reduced. Instead, the ability to reap economic rents was the reward to efficient performance, thus forcing productive activities to dominate. East Asian policy-makers chose to take the *high path* of improving the quality of production methods and of its factor inputs as the means to reduce costs, rather than relying on the *low path* of holding costs down by keeping wages low as other less-developed countries have so often tried to do (Amsden 1994: 635).

Key to the success of the contests has been the integrity of the referees. These might be banks that provide credit or other government bureaucrats in charge of economic development in the issuance of licenses, subsidies, or other special privileges. The creation of an honest, professional and dedicated civil service seems absolutely essential to good policy-making. A corrupt and incompetent cadre of bureaucrats will result in poor quality policy, to no one's surprise. If this outcome is not to occur, it is important that civil servants be relatively well-paid compared to what could be earned in comparable jobs in the private sector. The lower the relative income paid to members of the civil service, the lower is likely to be the average level of competence and the higher the probability that "informal" income, that is, bribery and corruption, will permeate the system as a substitute for income earned on the job.

Any prestige and employment security that comes with a government job cannot fully compensate for incomes that are too low. In Taiwan, public sector salaries average about 60 to 65 percent of comparable private sector income; in South Korea, public sector income averages 82 to 99 percent of private sector salaries; and in Singapore, where the civil service is highly regarded, public sector salaries exceed comparable private sector earnings. The relatively high incomes of the East Asian civil service at least partly accounts for the higher average quality of its activities. On the other hand, Argentina's public sector workers, at every level, earn between 25 and 30 percent of what could be earned in the private sector, and in Somalia, the pay is less than 15 percent of private sector incomes (World Bank 1993: 177). Can countries that pay their civil servants at these levels expect to recruit and retain the best workers into the public sector? Should bad policy decisions, and perhaps endemic corruption, emanating from such civil servants be unexpected?

Of course, if less-developed countries have bloated public sectors and if public employment is being used to provide posts for urban workers with few other alternatives for employment, it is difficult to pay higher salaries. But the reason for over-staffing in public employment in such circumstances is a failure of the existing development program to generate sufficient employment in the private sector for those migrating from the rural areas to the cities. What is required, then, is a strategy shift along the lines followed in East Asia. The need for a shift toward a labor-using easy export substitution strategy and the efficiency it promotes cannot be overstated. Then, there can be a phase-out of excess government employment as the industrial strategy begins to pay dividends in increased industrial employment.

With the ability to shrink public sector employment rationally rather than through wholesale lay-offs, there can be a turn toward the recruitment to the public sector at comparable pay with the private sector of competent and dependable civil servants who can rise within a *merit-based employment system*. It is this core of government bureaucrats who can, with some integrity and relatively insulated from the private sector, oversee the policies and programs that the state in late-developing economies must implement to assist the private sector in reaching maturity, with higher efficiency, greater private sector employment, and shared growth the goals.

If one thinks of a competent and honest civil service as part of the essential social infrastructure required to develop, it is obvious that this is another area of potential public investment which promises a very high pay-off in terms of the positive externalities which can be expected to accrue to society at large. The relatively high pay commanded by workers in key public administration sectors, such as budgeting, economic planning, oversight and so on, will be well worth the expenditure if economic growth is accelerated, for it will at least partly be the result of their efforts, ideas, and monitoring of the progress of the economy.

Export promotion

When the larger Latin American economies shifted from easy ISI to secondary ISI, part of the rationale had been to try to reduce imports so as to improve the trade balance and to relieve the constant problem of insufficient foreign exchange earnings from exports relative to import expenditures. However, to the extent that the state contributed to sustaining the pace of overall economic growth, the demand for imported goods also expanded, not only for the remaining imported industrial inputs required, but also because of the demand for manufactured goods and services the economy did not produce at all, or did not produce in the right quantities, or with the desired qualities: televisions, radios, computers, sporting goods, movies, insurance, wines and liquors, designer clothing, foreign travel, and a whole range of products. Unfortunately, the ability to purchase the increased volume of imports desired by Latin American consumers was threatened because of the importance of the primary product export base which grew only very slowly and typically only by increasing the volume of exports. The premature secondary ISI strategy in Latin America did not solve the balance of trade problem by reducing imports. The basic problem of foreign exchange inadequacy increasingly revealed itself to be a *failure to export* and to *earn foreign exchange*. Saving foreign exchange was not a sufficient solution to the balance of trade dilemma.

The countries which prematurely initiated secondary ISI faced the realization that the possibility of further reducing imports via a deepening of the import substitution process designed to conserve foreign exchange could never generate sufficient foreign exchange savings relative to the foreign exchange that might be earned by *expanding* manufactured goods exports. It was at this point that the larger Latin American economies, such as Brazil, Mexico, Chile and Argentina, perceived that saving a unit of foreign exchange via import substitution was not always equivalent to the earning of a unit of foreign exchange via exporting. Saving foreign exchange generated a *one-time benefit* that could not overcome the problem of declining terms of trade that continued to afflict their traditional primary product exports. On the other hand, creating additional export capacity could, period after period, provide *cumulative returns* in terms of foreign exchange earnings, particularly if the new exports were income elastic.

What the Latin American economies turned toward with this realization, however, was not easy export substitution or even secondary export substitution, as had happened in the East Asian economies. Instead, they began to practice what Ranis (1981) calls *export promotion*. The Latin American countries began adding-on to the existing export structure some specially-promoted manufactured goods exports, but without the intention of reducing the importance of the primary product export base within the overall export structure. In other words, export promotion was not export substitution. There was not a fundamental *underlying* change in the structure of production that put less emphasis on traditional agriculture and more on labor-using manufacturing that might absorb the surplus labor accumulating in the urban centers.

Nor was the export of manufactured goods the natural consequence of the maturing of a *domestic* entrepreneurial elite that had learned to be more efficient and internationally competitive over a period of time, as it was with the East Asian export-substitution experience. Export promotion was rather the consequence of special subsidies extended to, often, transnational corporations operating in Latin America to export some of their output to the world market.[24] The residual strength of the agriculture and mineral elite class contributed to the difficulty of fundamentally modifying the structure of both production and exports and moving toward a more dynamic and productive economy on a higher sustained path of growth and development. Neither the export profile, nor the productive structure, of the Latin American countries has been fundamentally altered to reduce, over time, the significance of primary products within the productive structure, though manufactured exports have been added-on in some countries, such as Brazil.

Continuing change

Figure 10.1 includes a fifth phase of transformation for the East Asian economies. They have begun to move toward even higher value-added production both for the domestic market and for export in knowledge- and technology-intensive industries, such as electronics, computer technology, software, biotechnology, communications equipment, precision instruments, and so on. These are "cutting-edge" industries with rapidly rising demands and good possibilities for future growth. They build upon the existing human capital base, and at the same time contribute to additional human capital accumulation through best practice learning-by-doing. There may even be a Phase 6 to be added in the future to Figure 10.1. What the East Asian economies have done, as have successful developers in the past, is to climb the product cycle from simple produced goods to more complicated manufactured goods via timely "strategy switches" promoted by innovative and flexible state policy which encourages and allows the private sector to continue to innovate. As proficiency is gained at each level of production, ascending to the next level has been made easier by past policies. At the base of the East Asian success is a series of past good policy decisions: expanding educational opportunities; creating a competent civil service; creating mechanisms ("contests") to promote technological adaptation and efficiency; and supportive government spending, advice, and policies to increase profitability in the private sector.[25]

	Optimal (East Asia-type)	*Sub-optimal (Latin American/India-type)*
Phase 1	Primary production, pre-industrial (*agriculture-based*)	Primary production, pre-industrial (*agriculture-based*)
Phase 2	Easy ISI (*1st industrial stage*)	Easy ISI (*1st industrial stage*)
Phase 3	Easy export substitution (*opening of economy begins*)	Pre-mature secondary ISI (*infant industry protection continued*)
Phase 4	Secondary ISI with, secondary export substitution; high value-added production (*reduced significance of primary product exports*)	Export promotion (*some opening to trade; primary product exports remain basic*)
Phase 5	Knowledge-intensive production, both ISI and export substituting continue in new, dynamic industries	??

Figure 10.1 Phases of structural transformation.

Sources: Based on Ranis 1981; World Bank 1993: ch. 3.

What can other less-developed nations learn?

Many nations of Africa and South Asia have yet to proceed as far in their structural transformations as have the East Asian or the larger Latin American economies or India, which provide our recent historical insight. Without being over simplistic (If becoming developed is so easy would not every country be doing it?), following a path similar to the general outlines of the optimal East Asian strategy in Figure 10.1 promises the best outcome in a relatively open, growing world economy. Even small economies can use this as a guide to structural transformation, focusing on a limited range of ISI products and then expanding into exporting as efficiency levels are improved. For small economies, regional trade arrangements that allow a sharing of regional markets for attaining economies of scale, to gain the benefits of learning-by-doing and to permit other transitional inefficiencies to be overcome could precede wider exporting to the world market. Larger economies with a higher level of domestic demand have more opportunities for both import substitution and exporting, but they also potentially face more pitfalls, especially if they are land or natural resource rich.

As Gerschenkron (1962) stressed in his famous book, *Economic Backwardness in Historical Perspective*, no nation can or should attempt to duplicate the success story of any other. Nations have been able to *build* on the accomplishments of other nations, often skipping over, and learning from, the arduous steps taken by path breaking nations. Thus, Table 10.1 is not a blueprint for "how to develop," so much as it offers guidance for thinking about the sequence of structural change that has been most beneficial in a growing, relatively open international economy.

Institutions matter

What a close study of the differences between the more successful East Asian economies and the less-prosperous larger Latin American economies reveals is how important sound policy-making by government and the private sector is to creating virtuous change. The institutions of society matter profoundly, from the civil service, to banks, to educational institutions, to professional organizations, like accounting societies, to the importance placed on honesty in business and personal relations, and so on. As Amsden puts it,

> Since East Asia has had some of the highest growth rates of output and productivity in the world, and since East Asia provides no evidence that any other set of policies is as good or better than its own set, why not advise developing countries the world over to adopt a variant of the East Asian model?... why not use the [World] Bank's awesome powers of conditionality to help other countries to build the institutions and skills necessary to adopt, modify and effectively implement East Asia's approach to suit their own needs?
>
> (Amsden 1994: 632)

In other words, what other late-developers would be advised to do is to create the building blocks of the proper institutional structures that can allow them, using their human capital, physical capital, and financial resources, to replicate a variant of the East Asian experience. These institutions are pre-conditions or co-requisites of more rapid development, and what Amsden is suggesting is that the international community, especially the World Bank, assist countries to restructure these building blocks. This can be done with the "stick" of withholding aid when institutions are not reconstructed and the "carrot" of lower interest rates, easier repayment schedules, marketing assistance, technological sharing mechanisms, and other perquisites extended to the private sector which can lead, as the East Asian economies have shown, to rapid "performance-based" results.

Where we are headed

Figure 10.2 schematically shows how institutions, policies, and endowments interact to contribute to the structural transformations that are aimed at achieving a society's goals of development.

To read Figure 10.2, begin from the right-hand side, Goals. These were enumerated in Chapter 2; they are the ends toward which society is directed. Moving to the left in the figure, we see that achieving these goals requires fundamental structural transformation in the productive and export structure of an economy. This structural transformation is affected both by the policies of the state and by the initial and augmented endowments of the economy and society (with augmented endowments contributing to changing comparative advantage via state policy and as

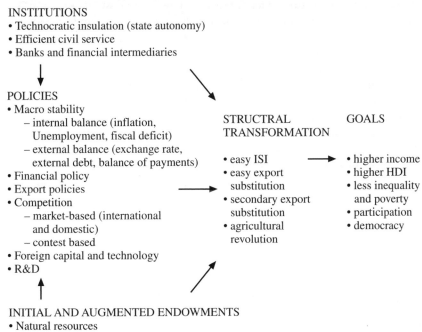

INSTITUTIONS
• Technocratic insulation (state autonomy)
• Efficient civil service
• Banks and financial intermediaries

POLICIES
• Macro stability
  – internal balance (inflation, Unemployment, fiscal deficit)
  – external balance (exchange rate, external debt, balance of payments)
• Financial policy
• Export policies
• Competition
  – market-based (international and domestic)
  – contest based
• Foreign capital and technology
• R&D

INITIAL AND AUGMENTED ENDOWMENTS
• Natural resources
• Physical capital
• Human capital
• Saving and investment
• Efficiency and productivity growth

STRUCTRAL TRANSFORMATION
• easy ISI
• easy export substitution
• secondary export substitution
• agricultural revolution

GOALS
• higher income
• higher HDI
• less inequality and poverty
• participation
• democracy

Figure 10.2 The transition of development.

Source: Adapted from World Bank 1993: 88, Figure 2.1.

a consequence of individual decisions). Society's institutions, only three of which are listed here, affect the efficiency of policy-making and hence the nature of the structural transformation. In Chapters 9 and 10, we have considered the industrial side of the structural transformation. In Chapter 11, the agricultural aspect will be examined. Chapter 8 considered the importance of endowments such as human capital accumulation, technology, and research and development (R&D) to the overall development process, themes which are examined in more detail in Chapters 12 and 13. The issues surrounding macroeconomic policy, the role of transnational corporations, financial policies and aid are examined in Chapters 14–17. Figure 10.2 serves to remind us that the goals of development are only attained through a complex web of institutions, policies, and endowments interacting, and at times conflicting, which impact on the structural transformation leading to the desired ends.

Questions for review

1   Determine from World Bank or other data, the import coefficient in 1970 and in 1995 for the following countries: Brazil, Kenya, India, Mexico, South Korea, Singapore, Botswana, and Nigeria. What might account for the changes, if any, in each country's import coefficient over time? How do you interpret Singapore's coefficient? Would you expect the import coefficient of larger economies to differ from that of smaller economies? Why?

2   If one examines the ratio of income received by the richest 20 percent of income earners to that received by the poorest 20 percent, one finds a value of 4.7 (= 41.3 percent/8.8 percent) for India in 1988–1989, a *greater* degree of equality than in South Korea. In Pakistan, the ratio also was equal to 4.7 for 1991. Both Pakistan and India had per capita income levels equal to less than 10 percent of the level in South Korea. Does this suggest that being a poor country contributes to greater equality? How does this information fit with what you learned about Kuznets' inverted-U hypothesis in Chapter 2? What might explain the greater equality observed in India and Pakistan than in higher income Mexico and Brazil? Do other very poor nations also have relatively more equal income distributions than richer countries? Are there very poor nations with very unequal income distributions? How does South Korea fit the pattern?

3   Explain why a country that is currently a primary commodity exporter and that also has a relatively large land area and abundant natural resources might be more likely to remain a primary product exporter compared to another country, which is also now a primary product exporter, but which lacks abundant land and other natural resources. Do abundant resources necessarily act as a brake (this is sometimes called a *resource curse*) on the evolution of the economic structure? Under what conditions might natural resources and abundant land be a blessing for future growth possibilities? Might there be a difference in terms of the "resource curse" between countries which have abundant *but unowned* natural resources and those with abundant but *unequally* owned resources?

4   Explain the importance of the easy export substitution stage of industrial transformation as a means to absorb labor from less productive sectors, particularly agriculture. Why is it that this stage is able to absorb more labor than the sec-

ondary ISI stage? What other benefits are there to easy export substitution compared to secondary ISI as a follow-up phase of industrialization to easy ISI?

5 How were the East Asian economies able to avoid unproductive rent-seeking by industrialists interested in earning above-normal profits, perhaps by over-extending infant industry protection, while the Latin American economies seemed unable to avoid such costs? What role do "contests" play in reducing unproductive rents?

6 Some critics of the East Asian strategy as a model for other countries argue that the success of their export strategy depended upon a rapidly growing international economy able and willing to absorb additional exports. It is suggested that in a world economy which is growing only slowly that the export substitution strategy is not one that can be copied by other countries as a strategic means to become more developed. Evaluate this view. If possible, use statistical data on growth rates of the world economy in the 1960s, 1970s, 1980s, and 1990s, along with growth rates of manufactured goods exports in each of these decades, to bolster your argument, one way of the other.

7 What is meant by "strategy switching"? Why are such switches an important component of good policy-making?

8 A competent, merit-based civil service system seems indispensable for making good policy. What steps can governments take to implement such a civil service system if one is not in place? What obstacles might be expected to be encountered in overhauling the existing civil service system?

9 Define premature secondary ISI. What potential problems are there for countries which follow up easy ISI with secondary ISI, thus skipping the export substitution stage (define this, too) of transformation?

10 Some observers believe that the East Asian countries have succeeded because they have followed a policy sometimes called "shared growth." Explain what shared growth is, how countries might achieve it, and why shared growth might be expected to contribute to a more rapid pace of economic growth.

Notes

1 For any particular commodity, the impact of aggregate income growth on demand for that good will depend on the income elasticity of that individual good, as well as any changes in the distribution of income affecting consumption patterns.

2 Consumer goods imports, even of non-durables, are unlikely to ever be fully replaced by domestic production. There will always be some goods, say, for example, scotch whisky, that are not produced domestically. Further, more expensive consumer non-durables, including brand names not licensed for production in the local economy, will continue to be imported for the consumption of those with higher incomes willing and able to pay both higher prices and any tariffs imposed on such items. Durable consumer goods – like home appliances, autos, computers – will also be part of total imports.

3 The *import coefficient* is equal to M/GDP, where *M* is the value of total imports. It is the share of total income spent on imports.

4 You will remember from the previous chapter and the discussion in Chapter 6 around the Prebisch–Singer hypothesis that balance of payments problems due to the difficulties in importing and exporting during war and economic crisis had pushed the larger Latin American economies on the road to easy ISI by the 1930s. In fact, it has been balance of payment crises that most often force countries to rethink and alter their strategies of economic development. This is another example of how imbalances and disequilibriums can be functional in identifying problem areas in an economy that need attention. At times,

for example, with an imbalance between the quantity demanded and the quantity supplied of laundry soap, the market can most easily, efficiently and rapidly resolve the disequilibrium. In other instances, as when the complex of economic policies guiding an economy are creating imbalances, the state will have to take some sort of action to change the direction of path dependence. This functional change undertaken by means of government policy we refer to as a *strategy switch*.

5   Very simply, the problem is that export income (X) is insufficient to pay for desired imports (M). Thus, the inequality, $X < M$, expresses the basic problem of the "foreign exchange constraint." Countries exporting primary products to pay for the imports needed for their ISI industries find that their income begins to fall short of their expenditures, creating the need to borrow or take other steps to finance the expenditure excess. Such an imbalance between income and expenditures that requires continual external borrowing cannot be sustained by countries forever, just as it cannot be sustained by individuals or families over the long term. Sooner or later, countries must achieve a balance between exports and imports, or, have $X > M$.

6   Alternatively, we could say that each strategy creates new forms of path dependence, with one a progressive and transformative path and the other much less so. We say this realizing that the optimal path depends upon the existence of a growing world economy and relatively open trade among countries. The first condition is met over the longer term, if not always in the short term. Relatively open and free trade among nations has been institutionalized only since the end of the Second World War, especially via the various "rounds" of talks of the General Agreement on Tariffs and Trade (GATT), which have reduced border restrictions on trade by slashing tariffs and, to a lesser degree, non-tariff barriers. If, in future, the open trade system closes, a new optimum strategy of development will need to be implemented.

The GATT was replaced in 1996 by the World Trade Organization (WTO), a more formal and ostensibly more powerful, institutional structure for maintaining an open international trade system. The WTO (and the GATT before it) is the trade "leg" of the tripartite international institutional structure for overseeing international economic relations among nations forged at Bretton Woods in 1944. The other two "legs" are the IMF, concerned with exchange rates and balance of payments issues, and the International Bank for Reconstruction and Development (the World Bank), responsible for issues related to economic development. There is more about this division of labor among international agencies in Chapter 17.

7   Imports will be able to re-enter the domestic market as tariffs are reduced over time, so domestic producers will need to be competitive on price and quality with these goods, or consumers will substitute toward imports and away from less-desirable domestic goods as tariffs fall. It will be remembered from the last chapter that it is important that infant industry tariffs are a temporary means to allow domestic producers to overcome transitional inefficiencies common to new enterprises. At some point, and sooner rather than later is best, these tariffs should be eliminated.

8   Such selective interventions by government are considered "market friendly" by the World Bank (1991, 1993) in that they assist the market in doing what it would do if there were not market imperfections. The World Bank has cautiously recommended such stimuli but recognizes that to be effective the preconditions for their success must be in place, including an effective and relatively incorruptible government bureaucracy and constant monitoring of the results of such selective intervention in meeting the goals of structural transformation and development.

In the opinion of some area specialists, like Wade (1990) and Amsden (1989), however, such interventions by government in East Asia have been more than simply market friendly. Wade terms the East Asian development strategy as one of *governing the market* through a variety of practices, some of which are discussed in the latter parts of this and other chapters. Such practices, it is suggested, have allowed the East Asian economies to improve upon what even a perfectly functioning competitive economy would have achieved by *bending* the allocation of productive resources in more dynamic directions than would have been achieved by the market alone. By governing the market, it may be possible to outperform what a perfectly functioning market would achieve.

9 Nations with large domestic markets have more room for maneuver. A large domestic market means, assuming there are a number of firms in each ISI industry, that the forces of domestic competition for market share can complement the external threat of eventual foreign competition as infant industry protection is withdrawn. In such economies, such as Brazil, domestic competition also can be a spur to greater productivity (Pazos 1985–1986). Even in such economies, however, a reduction of tariff and other protection would still seem to be warranted.

10 There are three developed countries with a high level of primary product exports rather than manufactured goods exports: Australia, New Zealand, and Norway. However, production in these economies is quite diversified, and there has been an evolution over time in the particular primary products exported. In other words, these developed countries did not remain with static comparative advantage in one or a few primary product exports but rather the exported primary products changed with changing external circumstances and evolving domestic comparative advantage (Lewis 1989: 1596). It may be the case that some less-developed countries can follow such a path of non-traditional primary product exporting. One such example may be Chile, which has had rising income per capita with a continued high level of primary, but diversified and changing, exports (see Focus 9.1 in the previous chapter).

11 Exports, X, are a component of the total output and income of an economy, since $Y = C + I + G + (X - M)$. Thus, increasing X, all else constant, will increase an economy's total GDP and aggregate income level.

12 We emphasize the role of the foreign trade sector, because nations must have some strategy to overcome foreign exchange deficits which arise with easy ISI. The imbalance between imports and exports needs to be resolved or foreign exchange shortages will lead to increased external indebtedness and, eventually, a cessation of economic growth. Nonetheless, for any nation with a sizeable population, production for the *domestic market* will remain an important factor for economic growth. In South Korea, for example, roughly 70 percent of all economic activity takes place within the national economy.

Although the idea that South Korea's rapid economic growth has been the consequence of its success in foreign trade has now reached the status of conventional wisdom, it is important to keep in mind that a relatively large and growing domestic economy can generate economies of scale in industry and that a viable export capability *typically follows from and builds upon* successful performance in the domestic economy. Actually, causality runs both ways: exports can stimulate the growth of the local economy, and the growth of the domestic economy can strengthen a nation's capacity to export via higher levels of investment, technology and research, training, education, and so on, which improve productivity and increase competitiveness on the international market. Domestic and international forces are complementary to one another.

13 *Income elasticity* measures the relative change in consumption of a good resulting from a change in income. Technically, the income elasticity, E_Y, of good Z, is

$$E_Y = (\% \, \Delta Q_Z) \div (\% \, \Delta Y),$$

where ΔQ_Z is the change in the consumption of good Z and ΔY is the change in income. If $E_Y > 0$, Z is a "normal good," meaning as income increases, consumption of good Z also increases. If $E_Y < 0$, Z is an "inferior good," meaning as income increases, the consumption of good Z decreases.

For normal goods, if $0 < E_Y < 1$, as income increases the consumption of the good rises, but by less, in percentage terms, than income rises. If $E_Y > 1$, the consumption of good Z increases faster, in percentage terms, than income increases. It is this category of "superior or luxury normal goods" that, over time, a country would like to increase within its overall export mix. Actually, a country would like to have the sum of the weighted average of the income elasticity of its exports to exceed one. Then, as world income increases, spending on that country's exports will rise.

14 Based on an econometric study, William Cline has issued a cautionary warning about the generality of this process. He argues that the East Asian export strategy cannot be

universalized for all less-developed nations. His results suggest that increasing manufactured exports in a manner similar to that achieved in the East Asian nations would require the industrial nations to import about 60 percent of their manufactured products from the developing nations. Cline argued that the less-developed nations had, by the early 1980s, reached a threshold level with their manufactures and that further incursions into the world market for manufactures would call forth a protectionist response from the more-developed economies (Cline 1988).

Given the possibility that Cline suggests, and assuming that it is possible in future that other less-developed nations may find the export substitution path less rewarding than did the Asian "pioneers," it is doubly important that the easy export substitution stage be merely a part of a *flexible* overall development strategy and that the domestic market not be regarded as secondary to the world market. The evidence for this more cautious approach? From 1950–1973, the volume of the world's exports rose by 8.6 percent per year; in the period 1973–1979, this growth rate slowed to 4.8 percent and more recently to 4.6 percent, 1979–2002 (Maddison 1982: 60, Table 3.7; IMF 1995: 3; WTO 2002: 33). Of course, the later growth figures are applied to a growing volume of trade, so the cautionary note of Cline, though worth keeping in mind, may not be so binding, especially as the absolute volume of world trade expands.

15 We say "partially explain," since we know from the studies of endogenous growth in Chapter 8 that the East Asian economies have a higher average level of human capital accumulation than other regions (this is considered again in Chapter 12). They also have had lower average inflation rates; have not had seriously over-valued exchange rates (Chapter 15); have a lesser degree of income inequality (Chapter 8); and policy-makers have generally been more adept at designing appropriate policies for growth and development, in implementing and monitoring them, and in changing policies when required to maintain the pace of both growth and development.

16 Recalling our discussion in Chapter 1 of external *barriers* to growth, it is important to recognize that *timing* can be a major determinant in the choice of a development strategy. In the early 1950s, when the Latin American economies faced balance-of-payments crises and foreign exchange shortages requiring a change in economic strategy, the global economy was relatively closed, with Europe and Japan still recovering from the Second World War. Consequently, the *absorption capacity* for additional manufactured products from the less-developed economies in the international economy was highly constrained.

By the early 1960s, however, due to the success of international efforts to reduce tariff barriers between nations and other efforts to achieve greater openness, the East Asian economies were able to ride the crest of a new wave of trade expansion when they faced the need to alter their economic strategy to handle balance-of-payments crises. At this *turning point*, however, the Latin American nations failed to take advantage of an historical opportunity in which they too might have advanced their economic strategy by shifting to an export substitution phase of industrialization in certain sectors.

17 From basic macroeconomics, the *income multiplier* determines the maximum change in total output and income in domestic economy from a one unit change in total investment (or any autonomous spending). In the simplest formulation, the income multiplier = $1/(1 - MPC) = 1/MPS$, where MPC is the marginal propensity to consume and MPS is the marginal propensity to save. Thus, if the MPC = 0.95 (95 percent of an additional £1 will be spent on consumption), then the maximum income multiplier = $1/(1 - 0.95) = 1/(0.05) = 20$. An increase of £5 million of investment would have a maximum effect of increasing total output and income by £100 million. In more realistic, but similar, calculations, the income multiplier's maximum value will be reduced by any "leakages" from the domestic spending stream, for example, for imports or for taxes.

The *employment multiplier* measures the change in employment resulting from a change in income. The size of the employment multiplier depends upon the capital-labor ratio of the economy, the *incremental capital output ratio* (ICOR) and the pace of change in total output. Thus,

$$\Delta L = \frac{\Delta L}{\Delta K} \times \frac{\Delta K}{\Delta Y} \times \Delta Y$$

which says that the change in employment, ΔL, is equal to the inverse of the incremental capital–labor ratio *times* the incremental capital–output ratio *times* the change in output.

    Crowding-in refers to the stimulus to additional investment following from some initial investment. For example, investment in the production of motor cars may stimulate other investment in battery production or glass production to supply the motor car industry. This description of how an industrial structure evolves should sound familiar; it is the linkage, or strategic disequilibrium, perspective associated with Albert Hirschman's unbalanced growth theory considered in Chapter 5.

18 This shift in control over production was especially evident where TNCs tended to enter the local market through the purchase of existing production facilities, thus "denationalizing" the production process and replacing domestic capitalists with foreign capitalists (see Chapter 14).

19 These often are the economy's most skilled workers, with a higher than average level of training and education. They work in more capital-intensive facilities, and their level of productivity and income tend to be higher. On the other hand, being capital-intensive, such industries cannot absorb the continued growth of the labor force arriving in the cities at a pace greater than the absorption capacity of these industries.

20 And even in the larger economies, such as Brazil and India, with large internal markets, the forces of internal competition among enterprises in the same industry was not always sufficient to assure a high level of technological competency.

21 The record of many Latin American nations following an easy ISI strategy was nonetheless impressive, at least for a time. Indeed, just as today it is fashionable to discuss the East Asian miracles, it was once in vogue to cite the Mexican miracle and the Brazilian miracle or the Puerto Rican miracle. For example, from 1940–1980, Mexico maintained a real annual average growth rate of 6 percent, no modest achievement. Unfortunately, however, in the 1970s, when Mexico might have changed its development strategy and looked to the export market, it plunged ahead with secondary ISI, a decision fueled to a great extent by easy access to external debt (see Chapter 16).

22 Income distribution worsened substantially in the overwhelming majority of Latin American nations in the 1980s. In Mexico, between 1984 and 1992 the ratio slipped considerably. By 1992, the ratio of the top 20 percent to the poorest 20 percent reached 14.6 (54.2/4.4) (Banamex 1994: 176). In 1984 it was 13.6.

23 Again, South Korea repressed labor by banning labor unions and strike activity that helped to keep wages lower and contributed to the extended period of labor-intensive production in the easy ISI and easy export substitution stages. And there is abundant evidence of high-level corruption of government officials that no one can condone. Still, neither direct labor repression (as opposed to wage restraint) nor corruption were central to the success of South Korea's economy over the past four decades.

24 For a discussion of Mexico's troubled export promotion program and its reliance on TNCs, see Cypher (1994).

25 It would take an entire book, or various books, to detail all the different microeconomic policies a country might implement in pursuit of its development goals. A careful reading of the World Bank's study (1993) of the HPAEs can provide a wealth of specifics on policies that have worked and on others which have been less successful. Policy-makers truly interested in taking positive strides toward better decisions could do worse than to *carefully* study that volume, as well as Amsden's bench-mark book (2001).

References

Amsden, Alice. 1989. *Asia's Next Giant: South Korea and Late Industrialization.* NY: Oxford University Press.

—— 1994. "Why Isn't the Whole World Experimenting with the East Asian Model to Develop?: Review of *The East Asian Miracle,*" *World Development* 22 (April): 627–635.

—— 2001. *The Rise of "The Rest."* Oxford: Oxford University Press.

Banamex. 1994. "Income Distribution," *Review of the Economic Situation in Mexico.* (April): 170–190.

Cline, William R. 1988. "Can the East Asian Model of Development be Generalized?," pp. 282–297 in Charles Wilber and Keith Jameson (eds), *The Political Economy of Development and Underdevelopment*, 4th edn NY: Random House.

Cypher, James. 1994. "Mexico's Export Promotion Policies," in Paul Ganster (ed.), *Changes in US-Mexican Economic Relations*. Mexico City: UAM-Profmex-Anuies.

Edwards, Sebastian. 1992. "Trade Orientation, Distortions and Growth in Developing Countries," *Journal of Development Economics* 39: 31–57.

Gerschenkron, Alexander. 1962. *Economic Backwardness in Historical Perspective*. Cambridge, MA: Harvard University Press.

IMF (International Monetary Fund). 1995. *World Economic Outlook* (May). Washington, DC: IMF.

Lewis, Jr., Stephen R. 1989. "Primary Exporting Countries," ch. 29 in Hollis B. Chenery and T.N. Srinivasan (eds), *Handbook of Development Economics*, volume 2. Amsterdam: North Holland Publishers.

Luedde-Neurath, Richard. 1988. "State Intervention and Export-oriented Development in South Korea," ch. 3 in Gordon White (ed.), *Developmental States in East Asia*. NY: St. Martin's Press.

Maddison, Angus. 1982. *Phases of Capitalist Development*. Oxford: Oxford University Press.

Pazos, Felipe. 1985–1986. "Have Import Substitution Policies Either Precipitated or Aggravated the Debt Crisis?," *Journal of Interamerican Studies and World Affairs* 27 (Winter): 7324

Ranis, Gustav. 1981. "Challenges and Opportunities Posed by Asia's Superexporters: Implications for Manufactured Exports from Latin America," *The Quarterly Review of Economic and Business* 21 (Summer).

Wade, Robert. 1990. *Governing the Market: Economic Theory and the Role of Government in East Asian Industrialization*. Princeton, NJ: Princeton University Press.

World Bank. 1991. *World Development Report 1991*. Oxford: Oxford University Press.

—— 1993. *The East Asian Miracle*. Oxford: Oxford University Press.

—— 1994. *World Development Report 1994*. Oxford: Oxford University Press.

—— 2002. *World Development Indicators 2002*. Washington, DC: World Bank.

WTO (World Trade Organization). 2002. *International Trade Statistics 2002*. Geneva: World Trade Organization.

UNDP (United Nations Development Program). 2002. *Human Development Report, 2002*. Oxford: Oxford University Press.

11 Agriculture and development

After studying this chapter, you should understand:
- the significance of the dual biases confronting agriculture: urban bias and gender bias;
- why agricultural development is crucially dependent on governmental infrastructure investments;
- the extent and nature of the difficulties faced by mono-exporters of primary products;
- the special conditions and behavioral responses to economic variables of peasant cultivators;
- the nature of environmental problems in the agricultural sector, including issues of erosion and deforestation, the "circle of poison" effect, and the dispute over property rights and resource depletion;
- the structural barriers created by historically defined land tenure systems;
- the Green Revolution's achievements and limitations;
- the nature of large-scale agricultural enterprises;
- the promise and limits of transnational agribusiness; and
- the elements of successful land reform and its role in undergirding development strategies.

Introduction

Most people in the developing regions are either cultivators, farm laborers, or relatively small-scale producers of services or manufactured goods in the countryside. In 1970, 75 percent of the population of low- and middle-income countries lived in rural areas; by 1999, this share had fallen somewhat to 61 percent. In the low-income countries, the share of the rural population in 1999 was still 74 percent (UNDP: 2001: 157; World Bank 1994: 222–223, Table 31). In 1993 there were over 2.2 billion people involved in agriculture as producers, while another 800 million lived in rural areas. As we know, there is a strong inverse relationship between a nation's level of per capita income and the size of the rural population: 78 percent of the population in nations with per capita income below US$400 per year were located in the rural sector, whereas in the "upper-middle income countries" with per capita income above $1,601 per year, the rural population accounted for only 35 percent of the total population.

Despite the large proportion of the population living and working in rural areas, mostly in farming activities, agriculture contributes a relatively small share of total gross domestic product. This is why incomes are low for countries with large rural populations; agriculture tends to be a sector which generates low value-added in production. For example, among the "low-income countries," only 23 percent of total GDP was produced by agriculture in 2000, despite the fact that 69 percent of the population lived in rural areas – most involved in agricultural production (UNDP 2001: 157; World Bank 2002: 237). This relationship clearly highlights one of the major issues in development: the pervasiveness of low agricultural productivity. Despite this obvious problem, agricultural development is rarely the central focus of most development strategies. Why? In studies of the development patterns of what are today the more developed nations, as was discussed in Chapter 9, it has been demonstrated that agriculture has shrunk dramatically both in terms of the percentage of the labor force occupied in this sector and of the contribution of the sector to total output. In this context agriculture has been viewed primarily as a provider of labor to industry, to the government sector, and to the service sector of the economy during the structural transformation process. Such a perspective was dramatically reinforced by the Lewis model, where agricultural labor was treated as redundant, having a very low, or even zero, marginal product. The general tendency in development economics to overlook the significance of agriculture has been of major concern to many agricultural specialist. John Mellor has noted that "it is surprising that the principle broad conceptualizations in development economics have not articulated a central place for agriculture" (Mellor 1998a: 136).

During the 1990s the rate of growth of agricultural production dropped dramatically in relation to the 1980s, yet the consequences of this decline were partially mitigated by strong reductions in population growth rates. For the 2.4 billion people living in "low-income countries" (per capita GNP averaging only $410 in 1999) annual agricultural growth fell from 3 percent per year in the 1980s to 2.5 percent in the 1990s – a drop in the growth rate of 17 percent. The population growth rate fell by slightly less (13 percent) leaving the food situation, on the whole, somewhat more critical (World Bank 2000/2001: 275, 279, 295). This discouraging trend should be considered in context – some 840 million people suffered from chronic malnutrition in 1996, and many (perhaps most) lived in rural areas (Eichner and Staatz 1998: 8). More disturbing has been the trend of the 1990s for "middle-income countries" (nations with an average per capita income of $2,000 in 1999). In these nations – comprising 2.7 billion people – while population growth rates fell by an impressive 29 percent in the 1990s compared to the 1980s, the growth of agricultural output slowed more dramatically – from 3.5 percent per year in the 1980s to 2.0 percent in the 1990s (a staggering 43 percent drop in the growth rate). Nonetheless, these nations retained a strong edge over their population growth rates, as food output continued to grow at a rate that was 40 percent faster than population growth (Table 11.1).

As the world's population continues to shift out of agriculture in the coming years the need to increase food output at a rate faster than the rate of population growth will continue. It is currently anticipated that the food needs of developing nations will increase by nearly 100 percent from 1994–2025, primarily because it is

Table 11.1 Declining growth rate in agricultural output

	Low-income nations	Middle-income nations
GNP per capita (1999)	$410[a]	$2,000
Population (1999)	2.4 billion	2.7 billion
Annual population growth		
1980–1990	2.3%	1.7%
1990–1999	2.0%	1.2%
Agricultural output growth		
1980–1990	3.0%	3.5%
1990–1999	2.5%	2.0%

Source: World Bank 2000/2001: 275, 279, 295.

Note
a US dollars.

thought that the urban population will rise from 1 billion in 1985 to 4 billion by 2025, with total global population rising by 2.5 billion (McCalla 1998: 39).

Urban bias

The relative neglect of agriculture may be partly explained by the theory of **urban bias**. This perspective, pioneered by Michael Lipton (1977), argues that agriculture receives relatively little attention in the implementation of most development strategies, due to a complex of social forces and processes operating both in the developing and in the developed nations. As a rule, the leading economic strategists and policy-makers in less-developed nations live in the capital city or some other major urban area. They have relatively little contact with, and little knowledge of day-to-day activities in the rural sector. Not only are they physically divorced from the rural areas, they are also intellectually trained in a Western academic paradigm which has little concern with or understanding of backward agricultural regions. Development is equated with industrialization, and industrialization has been predominantly an urban phenomenon. Hence, this urban bias leads to a neglect of the rural agricultural sector. Urban bias can be and has been quantified: Maurice Schiff and Alberto Valdés found that for a sample of 18 developing nations, had the governments of these nations *not* imposed policies that were adverse to the interests of the countryside (but supportive of urban interests) the domestic terms of trade (the price of agricultural products over time measured against the price of urban produced goods and services) would have been 43 percent higher in the 1960–1985 period (Schiff and Valdés 1998: 228). In spite of the fact that the research of Schiff and Valdés shows clearly that nations with a low bias against agriculture have (1) lower rates of migration from agriculture – into the belts of urban misery, (2) increased investment by cultivators, (3) greater technological adaptation, and (4) *higher economic growth*, the bias against adequate support for agriculture remains.

Culture and caste

The relative neglect of agriculture is often traceable to the quite strong sense of a cultural divide prevalent in many poor nations. Small cultivators are often depicted pejoratively as "peasants," "tribal peoples," indigenous people, or lower-level caste groups; they often are the "others" who speak a different language or dialect, wear traditional clothing, and live in a milieu that is to a very great degree seen as primitive and beneath those who occupy positions of political, social, and economic power both in the advanced industrial nations and in the poor developing nations themselves. Wide disparities in income between ethnic groups and those of the dominant group often reflect the pervasiveness and depth of urban bias, as well as cultural and class differences (see Box 11.1). For example, male Bolivian Indians have an average earning level that is only 40 percent of that of non-indigenous employees.

This disparity reflects differences in schooling and training, that are often a reflection of the lack of schools in the countryside, and outright discrimination. In India, one in every seven of the population is lower caste, for whom agricultural employment is one of the few occupational opportunities available. In Malaysia, until late in the twentieth century, ethnic Malays were confined to traditional small-scale agriculture, with the higher-income-generating activities in industry and finance controlled by the ethnic Chinese. Only recently have governmental policies specifically

---

Box 11.1 Gender bias: women in agriculture

In poor nations, women typically play a major role in agricultural activities. In Africa, women work both as farm laborers and as farmers on family plots. Women account for 60 percent of all cultivators and produce an estimated 80 percent of the food. In India, 48 percent of self-employed cultivators are women.

Total work time for women in the rural areas is about 20 percent more than for men. Relative to adult males, women shoulder the heaviest burden: 55 percent of all labor time. Women in agricultural regions divide their time between unpaid household duties and paid activities, which can include direct farming and marketing, handicraft production, garment making, and brewing. In Nepal, women spend an average of nearly three hours per day in direct farm work, and nearly four hours per day gathering fuel wood and scavenging. Another three hours per day is committed to food preparation and related household activities. Rural women throughout the developing world can be seen spending long hours on the mundane task of acquiring water. In Senegal, for example, women devote an average of 2.5 hours per day on water collection alone; in Mozambique, it is over two hours per day.

Women often cannot acquire legal title to land ownership, or as in the case of Africa, maintain their customary rights to communal lands. Women cultivators have generally been ignored in land reform programs. Lacking title to land, women face high barriers when they need credit. In Africa, women receive only 10 percent of the bank loans to small farmers, a mere 1 percent of all agricultural credits, despite the disproportionate numbers of women involved in agricultural activities. Even the multilateral lending banks (discussed in Chapter 17) ignore women farmers' credit needs, extending 95 percent of their loans to men.

Women farmers also receive unequal support from agricultural extension services. In India, most women farmers are excluded from the benefits of extension services completely. In Africa, women receive 33 percent fewer visits from farm advisers than do men cultivators. Indeed, if women farmers had the same level of education and inputs as men, their farm yields would increase by as much as 20 percent according to studies conducted in Kenya and Burkina-Faso.

Sources: Tomich *et al.* 1995: 29; UNDP 1995: 38, 93; World Bank 2001: 119

been targeted to improve the educational and training opportunities of the ethnic Malays. In Thailand, the earnings of the northern hill people in the 1990s were more than 75 percent below the national average, and schools were attended by fewer than 30 percent of the population, so that some 85 percent of the population could not read or write (World Bank 1995: 44–46). In South Africa in 1994 the average amount of land held per-person on black-owned farms was only 1.3 hectares, while whites held 1,570 hectares (Deininger 1999: 664).

Inadequate infrastructural investment

Whatever the cause or causes, agriculture is either neglected or relegated to a subordinate position in development strategies, too often an afterthought to industrialization. This relative disinterest takes many forms, but of paramount importance to rural cultivators, both large and small, is the inadequate provision of infrastructure and social overhead capital: schools and health clinics, roads, dams and irrigation canals, crop storage facilities, farm extension services, agricultural research, and farm credit programs are inadequate, if they exist at all. Roads and water resources are fundamental to agriculture. Small cultivators in particular confront tremendous difficulties in bringing their output to urban areas for marketing, due to substandard road systems. At their best, rural roads often are unpaved, and trucks are forced to crawl along, lest a breakdown occurs. This means long hours on the road, in quite small trucks, it raises the costs of transportation inordinately and makes it more difficult for small producers to compete with larger ones. This also means more spoilage, with a smaller share of output reaching its final destination in usable form. Bad weather results in the wash-out of poorly constructed bridges, or as is more likely, streams that cannot be forded as they rise to cover and muddy roads. The lack of irrigation means that levels of production are less predictable due to the need to depend on the irregularities of rain, and growing seasons are shorter than they might be if there were more control over nature that irrigation provides. In many tropical regions, irrigation would permit near year-round cultivation.

To a great degree, many of the infrastructural projects mentioned on page 314 are of an all-or-none nature. This means that for the agricultural sector, and most particularly small-scale agriculture, it is the **state** which must finance these large-scale investment programs if productivity in agriculture is to be raised. Given urban bias, given the general lack of investment funds available to most poor nations, and given that the pay-off from investments in agriculture and in rural areas often require decades of concentrated effort to show success, it is perhaps not too surprising that examples of successful agricultural programs in less-developed nations are few and far between. Because such programs would have to take place over a relatively long period of time, and because governments in most poor nations are extremely insecure and often lack adequate financial resources, the state rarely can afford to take the long-term view. Thus public funds tend to be allocated to areas where more short-term, and more limited, objectives, including political support, can be achieved, and this has typically meant stimulating industry and urban development.

In addition to physical infrastructural outlays which could directly raise agricultural productivity, other basic public expenditures are usually desperately needed in the countryside. Here we refer in particular to the urgent need for educational

---

Box 11.2 Agriculture and the environment: deforestation and soil erosion

Improvements in infrastructure in agriculture must be accompanied by a strategy to sustain the resource base. Without adequate training, adequate investment, and adequate regulation in the maintenance of forests, however, deforestation has become a major problem in much of the developing world. in Latin America in the course of the 1980s alone, over eight million hectares were deforested annually, as trees were felled for new farms, for grazing land, for firewood, or for the wood itself. In Asia, roughly 3.5 million hectares suffered deforestation, while in Sub-Saharan Africa, approximately two million hectares of forest were lost per year. For the decade as a whole, then, some 165 million hectares of forest were destroyed in the poor regions of the world. From 1900 to 1990, one-fifth of all tropical forests were destroyed, and the rate of deforestation has accelerated in recent years.

Soil erosion and soil degradation are also, unfortunately, widespread. The World Bank estimates that in many poor nations soil depletion due to run-off and improper use of land reduces annual growth rates by between 0.5 and 1.5 percent. Clearly, the cumulative, long-term effect can be very large. In addition to the measured impact of erosion on agricultural output, soil erosion also undermines and damages the fragile infrastructure of roads, bridges, canals, and dams, while reducing water quality and adversely affecting freshwater fish and animal habitats.

Some studies indicate that relatively simple and inexpensive measures can effectively combat soil erosion. Mulching, for example, could reduce erosion by 70 percent or more. Contour cultivation could reduce erosion by 50 to 85 percent, while grass contour hedges can also be extremely effective. Unfortunately, such measures are too rarely employed, both because they are an additional expense and because the dissemination of knowledge regarding ecologically sensitive and sustainable agriculture is poor. It is not that poor farmers wish to destroy the land and the natural resource base. They simply lack the tools, including the knowledge, to be able to do different. Further, given their low incomes, the choice is often between starvation and overuse or misuse of the land.

Erosion and deforestation can have dramatic effects: in Mexico, for example, soil erosion reduces the amount of cultivable land by 371,000 acres per year. In addition, deforestation robs the country of 1.5 million acres per year. One result of these processes is **desertification**, which expands the deserts of Mexico at an annual rate of 556,000 acres. Deforestation is caused both by ecologically insensitive forestry practices and by the drive to introduce cattle ranching. As alarming as these figures may seem, the extent of deforestation which exists in Mexico is exceeded in other nations. In fact, annual deforestation throughout the developing nations averaged 113,000 sq. kilometers in 1990–1995. (Impacting an area equal to the size of the nation of Honduras.)

Sources: Barry 1992: 264–268; Doolette and Smyle 1990;
World Bank 1992: 6, 2001: 291

---

programs and health care, both of which contribute to enriching the human capabilities of the rural population and contribute to growth. The educational demands of rural areas may well pose special difficulties for decision-makers compared to those in urban schools. In many nations, much of the rural population may have only the most rudimentary knowledge of the dominant or official language. Adult literacy and second-language programs may be of the utmost necessity, yet the lack of trained personnel to provide such services may make it difficult to move forward in these areas. Still, these are investments which are desperately required and for which the returns, both individual and social, are likely to be quite high (see Chapter 12).

Health care, primarily through rural public health clinics, could immediately help to reduce high rural infant mortality rates and contribute to raising productivity by damping-down the widespread exposure to intestinal parasites which sap the energy of small cultivators. Public health programs to create and then maintain sanitary water supplies and to treat waste water are essential for these goals, but they too demand sizeable public outlays, and the competition with urban areas for funds has most often been lost.

Agrarian dualism

Nearly every poor nation was once a colony of one developed nation or another at one time, as discussed in Chapter 3. Even some independent nations fell under the indirect sway of the colonizing powers. Although the first wave of colonization and control in the sixteenth century was concerned with extracting precious metals and controlling trade routes and trading stations, the focus of colonization quickly turned to agricultural commodities which could be marketed in the international markets as the flow of precious metals ultimately slowed in the mid-1700s. The production of "King Sugar," or "white gold," became of paramount importance as early as the nineteenth century. A host of other primary commodities played key roles in the determination of the agrarian structure of the less-developed nations between 1500 and 1960, when colonial rule finally ended in most nations. Tobacco, indigo, rice, tea, jute, henequen, bananas, coffee, chocolate, sugar, cotton, and spices were some of the major commodities produced through the centuries of colonial rule to meet the demands, usually of the elites, of the more-developed nations. Even items which were not driven by the logic of tropical production, such as beef and wheat, were often leading commodities exported from the colonial and post-colonial nations to the more-advanced industrial nations.

The vast trade in tropical commodities, including some such as rubber used as inputs into industrial production, carried with it a massive structural change in rural landholdings in colonial and post-colonial society. With rare exceptions, the colonial powers sought to turn over vast tracts of land to a new planter aristocracy. Often this new elite survived only due to the sophisticated slave trade which brought captive laborers to the new plantation regions. Thus, whatever the nature of landholding prior to colonialism, the indigenous population generally was forcefully relegated to the most marginally productive and, often, the most distant lands. The truly optimal tracts of fertile land were claimed by well-positioned members of the colonial powers or by colonial-born creoles, and by a select few members of the colonized society who had become instrumental in maintaining colonial rule. Thus a fundamental characteristic of colonial agriculture, one which persists to the present, emerged, creating a dichotomous production structure wherein a relatively few planters controlled vast expanses of the most productive land, while a large mass of cultivators clung tenaciously to small plots of marginally productive land at considerable distances from urban areas with the worst communication network of roads linking them.

This pattern, while established in the somewhat distant past, continued into the twentieth century. In Mexico, for example, between 1877 and 1910, under the infamous rule of Porfirio Díaz, seventy-two million hectares of land were appropriated from indigenous peoples and turned over to large landowners, domestic and foreign (Smith 1972: 3). In Kenya, during the course of 1903, British colonial administrators sold immense areas of the land to British growers at less than one US cent per hectare. Some of the estates acquired that year included Lord Delamere's acquisition of 311,615 acres; Lord Francis Scott's purchase of 89,032 acres; and sales to two companies known as East Africa Estates and East Africa Syndicates of 311,615 and 89,032 acres, respectively (Dixon 1990: 43). The British even divided Kenya into two areas: the "scheduled areas," where the colonial settlers were allowed to hold land, and the "native reserves," to which the indigenous population was relegated. Prior to the end of the colonial era, colonial settlers in scheduled areas had acquired 36,260 square kilometers of land, where 3,500 colonial farms and estates were established on the best soil. The four million "native" farms were crowded on to 134,670 square kilometers. Foreign colonial settlers thus owned farms averaging 10.4 square kilometers of land each, that is, more than 2,500 acres (or 1,000 hectares), while indigenous smallholders held an average of only 0.034 square kilometers, or less than 9 acres ($3\frac{1}{3}$ hectares).

There was little change in land concentration after independence. In the 1980s, 2.4 percent of the cultivators controlled 32 percent of the cultivated land, and most of the cash crop came from this land of the highest quality (Dixon 1990: 46). Throughout most less-developed countries, this concentrated pattern of land ownership characteristic of Kenya and Mexico is repeated, and neither Kenya's nor Mexico's inequality is the most extreme. While Kenya had a Gini coefficient for landholding inequality of 0.77 in 1981, the figure for Colombia in 1990 was 0.84, for Saudi Arabia 0.83 in 1983, while Brazil's was 0.86 (Deininger 1999: 655; UNDP 1993). Translating the Gini coefficient in the case of Colombia, the top 1.7 percent of landowners controlled 42 percent of the farmland, while the minifundistas with less than 5 hectares (57 percent of all farmers) held a miniscule 4.2 percent of the farmland.

In virtually all less-developed countries, with the exception of those relatively few where meaningful land reform has been consolidated, this dualism and inequality is evident. Large numbers of peasant cultivators control extremely small parcels of land, while a few large landholders, who constitute the landed oligarchy, own and vie with agribusiness transnationals to control vast quantities of land. One study, published in the 1970s, analyzed six Latin American nations and found that an average of 52 percent of all the farmland was controlled by the largest landholders, though they constituted less than 1 percent of all the agrarian households in these nations. Small farms, employing no more than four family members, held approximately 25 percent of the land, while accounting for the vast bulk of the agrarian households. Counting landless peasants, they and small cultivators accounted for 94 percent of all rural households (Barraclough 1973: 326–327, 331–332).

With smallholders crowded on to the poorest and less productive land, a serious problem of overgrazing and overuse occurs, both on the land itself and in forests and wooded areas where firewood and fence materials are collected (see Box 11.2). The inadequacy of fallowing, that is, of leaving land idle for a period of time so that it can regain its nutrients, is a result of small farm size, where families are forced into practices which abuse the natural resource base. This, combined with relatively high population growth rates in rural areas, sets up a vicious circle of excessive land use leading to greater degradation of soils via erosion, soil exhaustion, leaching of minerals and loss of water sources, which results in declining productivity of the land and falling output levels, which, in turn, leads to even greater use of increasingly marginal land at a too-intensive rate. This is an example of the "pollution of poverty" introduced before (see Focus 2.3).

This destructive and non-sustainable cycle already could be noted in Mexico and in the Andean highlands nearly 500 years ago, as villagers were pushed up onto ever higher mountain slopes, operating on more difficult lands, receiving lower yields, reducing the nutritional content and reliability of their diet. Among the less-developed nations, only in those where successful land reform has been implemented has there been a noticeable shift from the dichotomous nature of agriculture and the overuse or misuse of land resources due to the need for survival brought on by small farm size. High-yield varieties of wheat, rice, corn, and some other staples, discussed later in this chapter, have brought some relief from this vicious circle for smallholders in the past thirty years. In the least-developed economies, however, land yields have remained low, and the rate of growth of population has greatly exceeded overall agricultural growth, pushing down the per capita level of food production, so that in 1991 food production per person was 92 percent of what it was in 1979–1981. In Sub-Saharan Africa, 1991 production per capita was 96 percent of 1979–1981 production. This pattern continued (with the exception of Angola and Nigeria – Africa's most populated nation) through the 1990s, as Table 11.2 shows.[1] Also note from the table the spectacular eighteen year achievement (1979–1997) of China, with a population of 1.25 billion in 1999, managing to raise food output by a total of 69 percent!

Primary product mono-exporters

One further structural aspect of agriculture in less-developed nations is important to note. In most nations, primary product food and fiber exports account for a very high percentage of total exports. This, again, reflects the legacy of colonial rule when, in many instances, the single strongest motivator for acquiring colonial territories had been to gain access to the production of tropical commodities so desired in the more temperate center economies. In many economies, then, unprocessed agricultural exports constitute the pivot on which not only export income depends, but on which the entire economy turns. A shortfall in production and/or a decline in the world price for one or two commodities can force a less-developed nation into an economic tailspin as the terms of trade deteriorate. When a nation is largely dependent on the export of one or a very limited number of exports, the term mono-exporter is generally applied.[2] Table 11.3 provides some representative data for several mono-export nations. Most oil exporting nations, particularly throughout the Middle East, are reliant on oil and gas exports – Venezuela is representative, with 80 percent of exports coming from petroleum in 2002. No developed economy depends upon only one or a few exports. There is an obvious value to producing a diversified array of exports; this reduces the risk to total export income, and hence to the ability to import, of any downturn in the price of any one exported good.

Table 11.2 Changes in per capita food production

	Food production index	
	1991 (1979–1981 = 100)	*1997 (1989–1991) = 100)*
Least-developed economies	92	NC[d]
Low human development[a]	109	NC
Angola	79	104
Gambia	90	64
Congo (Democratic Republic of)	94	71
Nigeria	124	121
Medium human development[b]	118	NC
Kenya	103	84
India	119	107
Pakistan	106	118
Honduras	92	91
South Africa	82	86
Jamaica	96	119
Malaysia	159	106
China	138	131
Botswana	68	81
High human development[c]	99	NC
Mexico	96	107
Chile	117	119
South Korea	95	115
Argentina	95	116

Sources: UNDP 1994: 154–155, Table 13; World Bank 2000/2001: 278–279, Table 3, 288–289, Table 8.

Notes
a (HDI < 0.500).
b 0.500 < HDI < 0.750.
c HDI ≥ 0.750.
d Not calculated.

Table 11.3 Degree of export dependency, 1985

Nation	*Commodity*	*% of export earnings*
Burundi	Coffee	85
Colombia	Coffee	65
Cuba	Sugar	86
Ethiopia	Coffee	77
Ghana	Cocoa	75
Malawi	Tobacco	57
Seychelles	Oilseeds	65
Somalia	Livestock	87
Uganda	Coffee	86

Source: UNCTAD 1987.

Dutch disease and boom-and-bust cycles

Because the prices of agricultural exports, particularly tropical exports, are prone to very wide swings in price from year to year as a result of supply variations due to weather, disease, and other factors, a special feature of mono-export economies is their tendency toward macroeconomic instability. This can result in boom–bust cycles, which bring about speculation on the upswing of the business cycle that, if not moderated, can result in over-borrowing and a large inflow of foreign exchange earnings as higher export prices result in growing export earnings. The widespread, but fortuitous, availability of foreign exchange earnings due to higher prices following a bad crop elsewhere in the world can lead to distortions in the internal structure of an economy, as imported commodities temporarily are rendered cheaper than many which are locally produced. This occurs when the exchange rate of the local currency increases in value, as will happen if exchange rates are not fixed but are determined at least in part by the market, and there is an increase in total export income due to the higher export price (see Chapter 15 for a full discussion of exchange rates).

Ironically, then, the increase in the value of the exchange rate brought on by the increased purchases of a higher-priced export makes that export, and any other exports from that country, more expensive on the international market, leading to a reduction in purchases and employment in those sectors. At the same time, the increased imports of foreign goods, made possible by the same increase in the value of the currency, can cause a downturn in production for import substitution industries whose prices are undercut by cheaper imports due to the exchange rate overvaluation. In addition, the greater income created as a consequence of increased export revenues can set off inflation in the domestic economy. This further exacerbates the tendencies for exports to become more expensive and imports cheaper. Particularly impacted will be the prices of those goods, like transportation and local food products, that are not traded on the world market, so that both the "tradable" and "non-tradable" goods sectors of the local economy are affected. Thus, perhaps paradoxically, the higher international price of the commodity export sets in motion a series of events that tend ultimately to slow economic activity in the less-developed nation. This phenomenon has been dubbed Dutch disease, because its effect was first noticed following discoveries of natural gas reserves by the Netherlands in the 1960s and 1970s.[3]

When the price of the commodity export turns down in future, then export revenues will decrease, and due to both lower domestic income and the decrease in the exchange rate of the currency, imports will become more expensive. Thus domestic producers of import substitutes will once again find a market, as the decrease in income and in the value of the currency leads domestic consumers to be able and willing to import less. However, some firms are likely to have been priced out of the market on the upside of the "boom-and-bust" cycle, and they may not be able to swing back into production, perhaps because their businesses have been bankrupted and sold off. Machinery and equipment may now be dispersed into other parts of the economy, or have fallen into disrepair. Worse, the labor force formerly used to produce for the local market in the import substitution industries may no longer be available, even if a firm wished to expand or re-start production. Thus the domestic economy is weakened and its productive base reduced as a result of the twists and

FOCUS 11.1   AN AGRICULTURAL-LED DEVELOPMENT STRATEGY?

Can agriculture be a leading sector rather than a follower? Until the era of the **Green Revolution of the 1950s and 1960s** (discussed below) there seemed to be no reason to entertain such a notion. And – as we have seen in earlier chapters – no development theorist ever suggested an "Ag-led" development strategy. Yet, Robert Fogel's research on British economic growth demonstrates that from 1790–1980 a truly impressive 30 percent of all economic growth arose from better nutrition and increased human capability arising from the improved ability of the labor force given greater energy from their food consumption (Fogel 1994). Rising productivity in agriculture, then, appears to induce rising productivity in the remainder of the labor force as food prices fall – this is an important **externality** – engendering a virtuous circle. In addition, a booming agricultural sector can be an important source of domestic industrial demand both for consumer goods which farmers will buy and industrial inputs which can create economies of scale in the production of manufacturing products.

An "Ag-led" strategy can also be appealing because of the daunting needs for infrastructure in agriculture. Dams, irrigation canals, water storage facilities, roads, bridges etc., can all be produced under very labor-intensive methods – more so than easy import substitution activities such as the textile industry. At the same time, with agricultural output growing rapidly, the demand for landless workers in the countryside will grow – thus, an "Ag-led" strategy will target some of the poorest people. Developing nations, particularly when they seek to industrialize, find that they need foreign exchange to fund needed imports. But agriculture is less import-intensive.

Research shows that if the "Ag-led" strategy is concentrated on small landowners there is a high degree of stimulus to the remainder of the economy – the "multiplier effect" of increasing agricultural output by $100 is to create an additional $80 of total output due to the need for both more consumer goods and farming inputs. But, agriculture cannot move ahead without a serious commitment to rural education, and, many argue, a sustained effort to "reform" the agricultural sector with policies that enable smallholders and especially the landless to gain access to land by breaking up large estates – which are known to be less productive per unit of land.

Using a "food first" strategy, Indonesia was able to shift from being the world's biggest importer of rice to food self-sufficiency in only sixteen years! While there seems to be a growing interest among agricultural specialists in the possibilities of an "Ag-led" policy (at least for some nations) the major aid institutions, such as the World Bank, have shifted away from supporting agriculture. Through 1980 the World Bank had devoted 23 percent of its loans and grants to agriculture, but by 1999 this sector received less than 10 percent of total funding.

> The decline in attention to agriculture in foreign aid has the greatest impact on countries that are lagging developmentally, currently the bulk of Africa and a few Asian countries. The front runners in development have already benefitted from the period when agriculture was uppermost in technical assistance. In Asia, for example, agriculture is moving, and now rapid industrial growth is providing a demand pull to agriculture. The laggard countries are still largely agricultural, with weak institutional structures for agricultural growth and limited human resources.

Peter Trimmer credits Indonesia's development success in the 1970s and 1980s to an "Ag-led" strategy which used the rural economy as the motor force for growth. Noting that the poverty rate fell from 50 percent of the population in the 1960s to only 20 percent in 1990, he found that 40 percent of the new jobs acquired by the growing labor force between 1969–1994 occurred due to agricultural development. Indonesia's success combined adoption of the **Green Revolution** in the 1960s with support for the agricultural sector that centered on the needs of small landholders.

Sources: Mellor 1998b: 62; Trimmer 1998; UN, Department of Economic and Social Affairs 2000: 131–155

turns of the boom–bust cycle and the phenomenon of Dutch disease, and these effects are strongest for countries that are mono-exporters. But, with the strategy of export diversification, the risk of Dutch disease can normally be reduced or eliminated.[4]

Peasant agriculture and small-scale cultivators

It is commonplace to find reference to "peasants" as a principal category of cultivators in the less-developed world who operate in a milieu of traditional agriculture. Exactly what these two terms – peasant agriculture and traditional agriculture – are intended to convey is too often left unstated. Unlike the peasants of medieval and feudal times in Europe, small cultivators in the less-developed nations are not tied to any particular landowner as serfs were bound to feudal manors. It is rare to find compulsory labor imposed on particular days or in particular seasons on small cultivators by large landholders. Nor do large landholders have "reciprocal obligations" to peasants as was the case in feudal Europe (for example, to provide protection).

Rather, what the terms are meant to convey is an emphasis on the self-sufficiency of the peasant farming operation; production for family consumption is thought to dominate decision-making. "Traditional" appears to be utilized to suggest a certain timelessness in the production process. In one telling phrase, Walt W. Rostow maintained that traditional agriculture was "pre-Newtonian" (Rostow 1960). He meant, apparently, that small cultivators farmed without regard to trial-and-error methods of cultivation, harvesting, irrigation, and seed selection. He also used the term to imply that there was a ceiling on the peasant production function, meaning, apparently, that farmers quickly encountered diminishing returns, and even absolutely diminishing returns, when they sought to raise output by working their land harder or longer. In any case, the image of traditional agriculture conveyed was one wherein productivity was abysmally low and did not rise over time, except in the most intermittent and unpredictable manner where pure chance might bring an improvement in cultivation techniques. The application of science and technology to improving productivity or of investments in human capital were presumed to be absent from peasant or traditional farming.

Is this a realistic portrayal of the poorest and most numerous cultivators in the less-developed nations? Probably not, certainly as a generalization. First, peasants and other small-scale cultivators do not produce solely for family consumption, selling only any surplus that might remain. Peasant farms typically combine both non-market and market production. Small cultivators also often maintain modest numbers of animals and a vegetable garden for their own use to supplement what can be earned by marketing their cash crops. Since small cultivators are almost without exception very poor, and since they are very poor in large part due to the fact that they are small cultivators without access to large areas of productive land, they do not need to spend all of their time cultivating the crops cultivated on their land. Maintaining animals and gardening usually occurs in an environment in which there are few other claims on the time of the cultivator. To the degree that peasants can find work elsewhere as day laborers on public works projects or larger farms at harvest or planting time, alternative employment is often sought, while other members of the cultivator's family, particularly women, maintain the family's non-cash production. While non-market activities are an important source of real income to the small cultivator, it is very rare to find small cultivators consuming all of what they produce, or having all their consumption limited only to what they themselves produce.

Thus, the concept of "self-sufficiency" has a relatively limited meaning in describing agriculture in most less-developed nations today. As a defining characteristic, it would be more accurate to emphasize the relatively low degree of specialization of small cultivators. They often combine the roles of small market producer with that of family production, artisan producer, day laborer, and migratory worker, and in this categorization should be included the labor activities of most, if not all, the family members.

Traditional agriculture has virtually no applicability today if it is intended to suggest the image of a rigidly set pattern of cultivation determined by custom and impervious to change, even when a change in the method of cultivation has clearly been demonstrated to be more efficient. Anyone traveling in the less-developed world today certainly can encounter cultivators utilizing some methods of cultivation which have been employed for centuries, if not a millennium. Wooden plows drawn by oxen, for example, abound. Cultivators often use a "digging stick" to plant, pushing soil over the indentation in the earth with their feet after planting a seed. Machetes are ubiquitous. Yet, these same cultivators, seen with digging sticks and machetes, may return to their crops a few weeks after planting to douse them with synthetic fertilizers produced by one of a handful of giant transnational oil companies. They may, and often do, use herbicides and insecticides on their crops, often indiscriminately and with little apparent regard to their own health or that of the ultimate consumer (see Box 11.3). Today the seeds in use by peasants quite often come from giant agro-industrial corporations which have spent millions of dollars to create new strains of crops to increase agricultural productivity.

If traditional agriculture means anything, then, perhaps we can take it to mean farming activities that combine the marketing of a modest-sized cash crop and some self-consumption of production, all organized around family labor. These are operations which are small and quite labor- and land-intensive in their production methods; they lack much capital, and the land in use is often marginal at best. Traditional agriculture tends to be low-productivity, low-value added, certainly as measured by output per worker, but it would be incorrect to suggest that there is no innovation or no capital in use, or that peasant farmers cannot learn-by-doing or by observing, or that they will not undertake change which can be demonstrated to be worth the risk involved.

Attitudes toward risk and change

With regard to production methods used by peasant farms, then, what is to be noted is the *unevenness* of production techniques. Combinations of some quite advanced methods with techniques which are ancient are not unusual or unexpected. Yet cultivators rarely cling to ancient methods simply due to some desire to maintain customs and traditions. The degree of resistance to change often may be noticeably higher in less-developed nations, but this observation is different from an assertion that cultivators are mired in unchanging techniques of production which are hopelessly out of date. Change often is slow to come in peasant agriculture for three very important reasons.

Box 11.3 Agriculture and the environment: pesticides and the circle of poison

Pesticides are used moderately in Sub-Saharan Africa, but elsewhere in the less-developed world their use is widespread, commonplace, and subject to rapid growth. For example, in the period 1980–1985, the rate of growth of pesticide application exceeded 10 percent per year in Indonesia, Pakistan, the Philippines, and Sri Lanka. Often pesticide use has been stimulated by government subsidies which, along with technical assistance in applying these chemicals, have been extended to large- and medium-sized farm operations. Pesticide use often is problematic, because it can poison groundwater supplies, disrupt ecosystems and cause serious harm to humans and animal life. Alternatives to widespread pesticide use do, however, exist: **Integrated pest management** calls for carefully timed spraying of pesticides, combined with the introduction of natural predators, pest-resistant crop varieties, and crop rotation, measures which are more environmentally friendly and which can contribute to sustainability of fragile ecosystems.

One study of farming in Guatemala indicated that peasants used three times the amount of pesticides per hectare as did large- and medium-sized cultivators. And they applied pesticides as a precaution, without regard to specific pest infestation. Furthermore, they generally failed to leave an adequate interval between spraying pesticides and harvesting. As a result, their crops often were unacceptable for export due to high concentrations of toxic agents; such commodities were sold, however, in the local market. Other agricultural products from the less-developed countries with lower levels of contamination, however, continue to be exported.

This so-called **circle of poison** occurs when industrial nations prohibit the domestic use of certain pesticides, but continue to allow their chemical corporations to produce and export these banned poisons to other countries. The United States, for example, controls 25 percent of international trade in pesticides, but approximately one-quarter of this output cannot be sold in the United States. Many of these pesticides re-enter the United States, however, via food exports from the developing nations which utilize the banned pesticides. The US imports as much as half of certain fresh fruits and vegetables from Mexico between December and March each year. Less than 1 percent of these items are tested for pesticide contamination. Mexico, however, continues to use DDT and BHC, more than twenty years after their patents were revoked due to the health dangers associated with their use. Other dangerous herbicides and pesticides such as paraquat, parathion, and ethylmercuric substances are regularly utilized to dust crops.

Indiscriminate and widespread use of insecticides and herbicides is creating new, complex and expensive public health problems, which poor nations are ill-equipped to remedy. For example, in some of the cotton-growing regions of Central America, DDT residuals in breast milk are the highest ever recorded in humans. These are passed on to young children, with potentially devastating consequences.

Sources: Barry 1992: 269; Pingali 1998; Russell 1994: 252; World Bank 1992: 140

First, there is cultural resistance, as there is in any society, to change; these are the Ayresian "ceremonial" structures and institutions that are backward-looking but which exist in any society (see Chapter 6). The pace of change is likely to be slower than in the more developed, industrial nations, but peasant society is far from static.

Second, given the fact that small cultivators are very poor, they often are extremely risk averse. Unproven changes in production methods or the introduction of new seed strains or new crops may mean the taking of risks that, if the gamble is successful, can increase a family's income and perhaps take them out of poverty. On the other hand, risky changes can result in decreases in income, when the risk does not pay off, which takes the family from near-subsistence to below subsistence income.

The possibility of the down-side of the risk, with its devastating consequences, may for the rationally calculating peasant simply outweigh the potential gains of the projected change.[5] Consequently, prudence often leads small cultivators to hesitate in innovating, not because they cannot envision the conceivable benefits of change, or because they are irrational, but rather because they can only too well balance the costs and benefits of change and must do so carefully; that is, near-subsistence peasant producers may not change, thus sticking to "traditional" methods, precisely because they are rational and because they have evaluated the risks involved in changing production. However, even within the classification of "small cultivators," one finds peasants with somewhat more land and other means of economic survival, who, given their somewhat greater access to resources, are more likely to accept new innovations, because failure is less likely to result in destitution.

Third, many small cultivators remain mired in production techniques which are clearly obsolete, not out of any choice they make, but because they have little or no access to cash or credit which would enable them to finance more advanced tech-nologies, even though it is clear these could increase productivity. Or, even if financ-ing were to be available, farm technologies appropriate to small-scale farming operations may not be available because of a paucity of demand for such techno-logy. With only a limited number of small cultivators able to make such purchases, forms of "appropriate technologies," such as small tractors, may be unavailable because it is not profitable to provide them via the market. On the other hand, large- and medium-scale capitalist cultivators find a wide spectrum of farming tech-nologies, and financing, more readily available on the market.

Are peasants efficient producers?

Development economists have expressed great interest in the question of the effi-ciency of small cultivators. The issue has been approached from three distinct per-spectives. First, several of the early developmentalist economists took the position that a lack of efficiency in agriculture actually reflected another area in which less-developed nations had "hidden potential" which could be quickly and easily tapped to propel the nation onto the path of greater development. Their potential produc-tivity simply needs to be released through proper policies. Second, one encounters the argument that peasants are, in fact, true maximizers in the neoclassical sense, who behave no differently than any other market participant. And, third, one encounters the position that peasants endure even though they are inefficient by the standards of neoclassical economics, because there is a special logic to peasant culti-vation. Below we consider each of these three positions.

The hidden potential of peasant producers

The argument that there is hidden potential within the agricultural sector due to the inefficiency of peasant cultivation is rather straightforward, though the inefficiency of the peasantry is often assumed, rather than demonstrated. This was not always the case. Gunnar Myrdal, particularly in *Asian Drama*, took great pains to discuss a multiplicity of factors which he felt led to inefficient production in small-scale agriculture. If agriculture is inefficient, then there are structural changes which could lead to a rapid increase in output without any increase in inputs. Once these blockages or bottlenecks in agricultural production are identified and corrected, output should rise steadily, at least until maximum efficiency is attained.

The Lewis model is one such theory with this underlying perspective. Recall that Lewis asserted that the marginal product of labor in agriculture was zero and was certainly less than the marginal product of labor in industry (Chapter 5). Consequently, shifting labor from agriculture to the industrial sector would not reduce farm output, while industrial output would rise. Thus agriculture was viewed as a hidden reserve for development. The structural inadequacy, or bottleneck, was the surplus of labor in agriculture, and thus transferring labor from agriculture to industry was the means to overcome the barrier to progress. Quite a large number of cultivators could be withdrawn from the agricultural sector, and the remaining farmers could work a bit harder and a bit better to generate a food surplus to feed the growing number of workers in the industrial sector. Clearly, this process could not go on and on; there were limits to Lewis's virtuous circle. But such limits were not Lewis's main concern or focus. He understood quite well that agriculture would reach its limits somewhere in the not too distant future, but in the meantime he envisioned a successful transition to a semi-industrialized economy which would have much greater possibilities to improve the long-term productivity of agriculture, releasing its hidden potential.

The Chicago School approach: efficiency attained

In 1964, Theodore Schultz published *Transforming Traditional Agriculture* to challenge the idea that small-scale farmers were inefficient at all, particularly in their use of labor (Schultz 1964). Schultz took the position that small farmers were efficient; given their knowledge and access to information, and given their income levels and stocks of tools, implements, and draft animals, and given their command over labor power (primarily the family unit), one could not recombine the inputs which peasants controlled so as to increase output. Nor could one reduce inputs and maintain output at the same level, as Lewis had argued. Furthermore, according to Schultz, if prices for agricultural products were increased, peasants would respond by increasing their inputs to production for those goods, just as neoclassical market analysis would predict. Consequently, Schultz concluded, small-scale agriculture was efficient.

This interpretation essentially argues that there is nothing which is unique about small-scale agricultural production in the less-developed nations. Small farmers are assumed to be quite poor, but through no fault of their own. Nor is their poverty due to any particular cultural impediments which might be linked to a pre-capitalist or pre-modern ideology or to land ownership patterns. Rather, small farmers are poor due to governmental policies which either inhibit the workings of a free market in agriculture, such as price-setting for crops, or they are poor due to government policies which insufficiently assist in the workings of the market. Although this approach generally tends to emphasize the negative impact of government, Schultz also highlighted the neglect of government-provided agricultural extension and agricultural research, and the need for rural schools which would improve the managerial abilities of small-scale producers. How, then, in this view, is the low level of productivity in agriculture to be improved? New and better inputs, such as high-yield varieties, will raise output per hectare. The elimination of price ceilings and other governmentally imposed policies which reduce the rate of return to farmers will serve to eradicate rural poverty by removing the sources of low productivity behavior in response to the "wrong" price signals.

Schultz's interpretation has been challenged on several grounds. Most directly, the economic anthropologist, Polly Hill, who spent long periods of time painstakingly observing peasant cultivators in Africa and Asia, rejects Schultz's analysis as being based on second-hand studies which fail to prove his argument. Hill (1986) notes that Schultz relied on only two empirical studies: one conducted on Guatemalan peasants and the other on an Indian village. She rejects the finding of the Guatemalan study due to the fact that the village observed was a trading village, not a village of commodity producers. Traders, she maintained, would surely have acutely attuned responses to market incentives or they could not survive, but this proves nothing regarding the behavior of producers such as peasants who do not survive solely on the basis of trade. Further, she states that the absence of disguised unemployment or underemployment in this particular village was unrepresentative of Guatemala and of less-developed economies in general.

Second, she rejects the study of Indian farmers, because it failed to differentiate between the behavior of rich and poor small farmers. Based on her research in India, and the work of others, Hill maintains that the poorest farmers are inefficient in relation to relatively richer farmers. Rich farmers and poor farmers are not equally motivated, equally skilled, or equally informed. Hill points out that, in India, the poorest farmers are inefficient from the standpoint of the village's standards, since they cannot afford to buy manure, thus reducing their yield per acre and engendering soil exhaustion. And, even in the case of the rich small farmers, who come closest to fitting Schultz's ideas, Hill rejects the notion of the ubiquity of profit-maximizing responses. She mentions, for example, the stability of rural wages for farm laborers in spite of the seasonality of agricultural labor. Using a hypothesis based upon the universality of market-driven behavior, such as that espoused by Schultz, one might predict that wages would rise and fall with the changing demand for that labor (Hill 1986: 22). She also noted the general lack of a properly functioning market in credit and land. Hill quotes the work of two economists who had sought to demonstrate the validity of Schultz's generalizations in Palanpur, India.

> We are unable to confirm that neoclassical economics is alive and well and residing in Palanpur.... Farmers were not doing the best that they could do given their resources.
>
> (Bliss and Stern 1982: 291, 293)

Peasant agriculture as a special category

According to modernization theory, particularly as presented by Rostow, the agricultural sector should move rapidly forward with the dissolution and consolidation of traditional or backward agriculture, as inefficient, small-scale farming is phased out with structural transformation. Small farmers should be found migrating, en masse, to the industrial and service sectors. This has not been the case, thus far, in most of the Third World, despite the rapid growth of urban centers. Rather, large numbers of peasant cultivators have clung tenaciously to their landholdings. Once landless, many have continued to reside in the countryside. Small cultivators may migrate to urban areas, or they may migrate internationally, for one or more seasons per year. Yet, their base often remains in the agricultural regions of the countries where they originated. Without doubt, the number of small cultivators is declining, and the realm of purely capitalist farmers is expanding, as is the extent of urbanization. But the pace of this change has been relatively slow. To try to explain the tenacious hold land has on small cultivators, a large body of literature has emerged, some of which is summarized here.

In one study of the phenomenon, Alexander Schejtman defines "peasant economy" in the following manner.

> The concept of the peasant economy encompasses that sector of domestic agriculture activity in which family-type units engage in the process of production with the aim of ensuring, from one cycle to another, the reproduction of the living and working conditions, or, to put it another way, the reproduction of the producers and the unit of production itself. Achieving this objective generally means generating, first, the means of subsistence (biological and cultural) of all members of the family, active or not, and second – a fund designed to pay for the replacement of the means of production used in the production cycle and to deal with the various eventualities which may affect the existence of the group.
>
> (Schejtman 1992: 278)

Peasants, then, seek to attain survival or to sustain themselves. In commercial agriculture, on the other hand, the objective is to maximize profits, or to leave the agricultural sector if the market rate of return is higher in other pursuits. Peasants do not utilize the pure logic of profit maximization. Nor do they concern themselves with the "opportunity cost" of farming, exiting the agricultural sector if the wage to be obtained in the industrial or service sector is higher, as in the Lewis, Fei–Ranis and Harris–Todaro models, or if the rate of return in the non-agricultural sectors of the economy is higher.

Exactly how widespread this behavior may be is not specified. Yet the imputation is clear; family-size farms are most likely to be part of the peasant economy. Table 11.4 provides some idea of the division of land ownership on the basis of farm size in the 1970s. For Latin America, smallholdings were defined as less than ten hectares, while large holdings were above 100 hectares. For the Near East, the division between these two categories was taken to be less than five hectares and greater than twenty hectares. For Africa and the Far East, the division was less than two hectares and more than ten hectares. In all regions, small-sized peasant farms dominate the total number of farms.

Some researchers who have studied the peasantry have defined these cultivators as either subsistence or semi-subsistence producers. In the later category, it is assumed that only agricultural surpluses are sold in the market. Thus, there is an attempt to define the peasantry not merely in terms of its behavioral patterns, which fail to fit the model of standard market participants, but also as producers who generally operate outside a market context. There are such economic entities, but

Table 11.4 Land tenure relations[a]

	Smallholdings			Large holdings		
	Average Number	Area	Size	Average Number	Area	Size
	%	%	ha	%	%	ha
Latin America	66.0	3.7	2.7	7.9	80.3	514
Africa	66.0	22.4	1.0	3.6	34.0	28
Near East	50.0	11.2	1.6	10.3	54.7	50
Far East	71.1	21.7	0.7	4.0	31.1	17

Source: Dixon 1990: 71.

Note
a Medium-sized holdings not included in the table.

Hill believes "such communities are statistically so rare in the world that they (can) be ignored" (Hill 1986: 19). In general, a very high quotient of total production will be marketed, not merely some residual which is not consumed, and this marketing usually takes place at the peak harvest time when prices descend to their lowest point. The need to make payment on borrowed money and/or the inability to store crops for sale at a more opportune time, if the crops so permit, typically forces the smallest cultivators to sell at the worst moment.

While peasants do draw on unpaid family labor which can allow them to devote a large mass of labor power to their small plots, it is not always true that small cultivators are the most efficient in terms of yield per acre or hectare, as is sometimes supposed. For the poorest of the small cultivators, it appears that management of family labor is weak; poverty and duress force many family members to seek outside employment to support a fragile existence. This employment can come at the very moment when the family's land needs the most attention. Furthermore, since peasant farmers generally sell at peak harvest time, their return has to be balanced against the fact that the price earned on the quantity produced typically will be less than that of the richer small farmers. This is because more well-to-do small farmers are able to manage their family labor with an eye toward pushing their yield upward, while being able to afford manure and other inputs which will tend to enhance yield. Moreover, they may well be in a position to store some of their cash crop in order to await a rise in the market prices as seasonal surpluses dwindle.

High-yield varieties and rural productivity

Concern for the precarious economic position of small cultivators, combined with the fear that they might become a politically active group if their living standard was not improved as they gradually lost land ownership, led to attempts to improve seed varieties which could be employed in the less-developed economies on small plots to increase productivity. Such seeds, of course, were not limited to usage by or for smallholders. Nevertheless, there was widespread hope that such seeds, termed high-yield varieties, would contribute to reducing rural poverty. Research on new wheat seeds conducted in the 1940s and 1950s in Mexico provided the basis for a breakthrough in scientific plant breeding. Later, the revolution spread to rice and has more recently been extended to corn, millet, and sorghum production. Widespread application of these new plant varieties did not occur until the 1960s, however. In 1968, the term Green Revolution was first applied to these efforts. This term constituted not only the recognition of a major technological change undergoing rapid diffusion, but most importantly a strategy wherein it was hoped that seed technologies could be substituted for missing land reform and for more radical "red revolutions" of the socialist variety threatening to sweep across the globe at the time. In the view of those who advocated the Green Revolution, the absence of high-yield varieties, coupled with growing population pressures in rural areas, would eventually result in a situation wherein the pressures and burdens of the small cultivators would be released in a political explosion. Poor peasants with few alternatives and little hope, it was feared, would seize plantation and estate lands, as well as those lands held by agribusiness conglomerates and transnationals.

Critics of the Green Revolution strategy predicted that the diffusion of high-yield varieties would, however, further exacerbate rural poverty and accelerate the tendency toward the concentration of landholdings. They foresaw peasants driven out of rural areas by falling prices for their crops as supplies rose as a result of better technology and higher levels of production. In this view, only rich peasants, mid-size capitalist farmers and larger landholders would be able to take advantage of the Green Revolution's promise. Critics took this position because the cultivation of these new varieties usually required irrigation and the intensive use of fertilizers. Thus the necessary complements to high-yield cultivation were thought to be beyond the reach of the mass of poorer peasants. Furthermore, such new varieties were prone to pests and plant disease, which might destroy most or all of a crop. Under the theory that poorer peasants are most likely to resist change, since they can least afford the risk involved if there is a crop failure, it was argued by some that even if peasants might be able to afford to adapt to the new varieties, they could not afford to accept the risk such varieties entailed and thus the rural income divide would widen.

In some respects, the results of the Green Revolution were correctly anticipated by critics of the policy. As Keith Griffin summarizes:

> The main beneficiaries in the rural areas have been producers who control optimal production environments, i.e., farms on good soils in well-irrigated regions, and in some countries optimal production environments are frequently controlled by the larger and better-off farmers.
>
> (Griffin 1989: 147)

Michael Lipton and Richard Longhurst, in their analysis of the effects of the Green Revolution, have isolated four phases of response to the issue of high yield varieties:

> First came the "green revolution" euphoria of 1967–70. In the second phase, there were growing fears that the MVs (modern varieties) enriched large farmers at the expense of small farmers and landowners at the expense of labourers. The later 1970s saw a third phase; several reassessments suggested that in MV-affected areas the poor gained absolutely, but lost relatively. Small farmers adopted after large ones – but did adopt and raised yields. Farmworkers

found that the effects of MVs in boosting the demand for their labour seldom brought much higher wage rates – but employment rose. Above all, poor consumers gained, as extra cereals supplied by MVs restrained food prices. The big exception to this rather happier verdict on the MVs was that producers in the non-MV areas, including many poor farmers, gained nothing from the new technology.

(Lipton and Longhurst 1989: 19)

The fourth phase began in the 1980s and seemed to promise a replay of the misplaced euphoria exhibited in the late 1960s during the first phase. This time the emphasis is on the promise of nitrogen fixation, coupled with breakthroughs in biotechnology, and the renewed faith that in breaking up the public sector and imposing the rule of the market (see Chapter 7), the dilemmas of the rural sector will be overcome at last. Skepticism, based on the limited impact of the Green Revolution, appears warranted. Nonetheless, the positive accomplishments of this technological burst also are beyond dispute: food yields did rise in many areas of the developing world. Still, the Green Revolution has not achieved the success that once appeared inevitable; in many poor regions, physical and social infrastructure is insufficient to support major yield increases. In these regions, farm advisers are lacking, roads can be non-existent, and the subsidies often needed to stimulate a shift in production technologies are unavailable (Goldman and Smith 1995).

Further, there is growing evidence of a slowdown in productivity in the Green Revolution areas of Asia. Many farmers shifted to rice intensification strategies – planting two or three crops per year instead of the customary one – and this practice has degraded the ecological system of the rice paddies. Many agricultural specialists have warned that Asia's great success with the Green Revolution is coming to an end. Investment in irrigation slowed in the 1990s as more investment went into land rehabilitation. Monocropping has led to a buildup in pests and a growing expenditure on pesticides. As fertilizer use and pesticide expenditures climb to maintain yield the gains of the Green Revolution are declining. In some instances farmers have increased their use of fertilizer at a 10 percent per year rate. India's public sector expenditures for fertilizer absorbed 80 percent of the subsidies devoted to agriculture in the early 1990s (Morris and Byerlee 1998: 470). Prabhu Pingali's research points to a number of growing weaknesses in the Green Revolution strategy. Among the problems he highlights are soil compaction, changes in soil composition, soil toxicity, increases in soil salinity due to flooding techniques employed in rice cultivation. Phosforous and potassium depletion in the soils has been a negative externality of intensive use of nitrogen fertilizers. Loss of these soil nutrients has given rise to an unbalanced soil composition. Perennial flooding, meanwhile, has leached out micronutrients such as zinc. Pests are showing increasing resistance to pesticides, and herbicides are under scrutiny due to indications of weed resistance. Across Asia Pingali found many instances of yield declines in the 1980s, compared to the 1970s. Where yields were maintained or increased the growing use of inputs (declining productivity) was often noted (Pingali 1998).

The developmental problems of cash crop farmers

Caught between the two extremes of the agrarian dualistic structure are the cash crop cultivators, typically with mid-sized farming operations. These cultivators produce almost entirely for the market with the aid of four to twelve agricultural workers hired on a permanent basis. Such farmers are important to any successful development strategy, both because they control a significant portion of the land (23 percent in Latin America, for example) and because they provide an even higher percentage of the food domestically produced and marketed. In short, such farmers normally constitute a vital source of food for the urbanized work force. Since food purchases constitute a very high portion of the expenditures of the industrial work force, quite often 50 percent or higher, the search for policies which attempt to harmonize the developmental needs of the cash crop farmers with those of the industrial work force is of utmost importance. Some of the factors that make cash-crop farming distinct from peasant agriculture are highlighted in Table 11.5.

Cash crop farmers face several alternatives in their decision to plant and market their output. In production, they can cultivate either **staples** of the population's basic diet, such as rice, beans, corn, wheat, lentils, oats, and manioc, or they can produce **speciality crops**, such as fruits and vegetables or export crops, including tropical products, such as coffee and tea or bananas, or non-traditional exports, such as fresh-cut flowers or wine destined for consumption at home by the more wealthy and in developed countries.

Staple production

Staple crops are often referred to as **wage goods**, because they form the bulk of the diet for working people in the industrial, government, and service sectors of the economy. In many developing nations, the government forms a purchasing board to set the price of such wage good crops. Often, the purchasing board's decisions reflect urban bias in that the "buy price" is set at an extremely low level. The one-sided logic of this strategy is to favor the industrial work force with cheap wage goods. Such a strategy allows employers to keep wages low, and profits higher,

Table 11.5 Peasant production conditions versus cash-crop farming

Concept	Peasant production	Cash-crop farming
Production objective	Survival of the family	Profit maximization
Labor force	Family members	Hired wage labor
Productivity of labor	Maximize output, without regard to labor quantity	Productivity > wage rate
Marketing	Home use plus cash crop (low level of specialization)	Production for market
Risk	Extreme risk-aversion	Risk accepted, based on estimated profitability
Technology	Extremely labor intensive, uneven adoption of new methods	capital intensive, dynamically adaptive

without affecting the urban standard of living, but this comes at the expense of both the cash crop farmers and their employees.

For the cash crop farmers, the low buy price paid by government, acting in its role as a **monopsonist**, creates a potent disincentive which can lead cash-crop farmers to switch production toward speciality and export crops. Then, to compensate for a shortfall in the domestic production of staples, the government may adopt a policy of importation of cereals and legumes to make up for the shortage of domestic production brought on by its own policies. Large-scale agribusiness corporations in the advanced industrial nations often can produce these crops at a lower average price than domestic cultivators, due to the use of more advanced levels of mechanization, chemically assisted production, and a variety of subsidies. When food imports form an important part of the consumption of basic foodstuffs in a developing nation, domestic cash crop farmers will tend to be driven from the market. A vicious circle may then ensue. Urban bias leads to a shift away from basic foodstuff cultivation, which leads to cheap food imports, which leads to a further reduction in the production and marketing of basic foodstuffs (Byerlee 1992). This can lead, in the future, to a crisis in the balance of payments if total imports exceed exports for too long.

Speciality crop production

When cash crop farmers shift production toward fruits and vegetables and meat and dairy products, they both avoid the urban bias implicit in government control of the staple food markets and are, at the same time, responding to the highly unequal distribution of income in most developing nations. Luxury meat and cheese products and wines, for example, may be readily available and relatively cheap by international standards, but at the same time, there may be shortages in the domestic production of food staples that must be met by imports. Rectification of this situation may entail difficult choices and policies, such as luxury taxes on certain food products, or income taxes which could be used to support targeted entitlement programs to transfer income to the poor, instead of utilizing a too-low "buy price" program to attempt to subsidize low-income consumers. Income transfers would increase the demand for food staples via an injection of purchasing power into the hands of the poor, and the quantity supplied of such staple products would be expected to increase as the market price received by producers would rise in the absence of a government-imposed "buy price."

Export crops

In addition to the problems created when cash crop producers shift from food staple production to fruits, vegetables, and food luxury items for high-income domestic consumers, cash crop producers can also switch to export crops. Once again, such a situation can be critical when policies which have been imposed to favor the urbanized population lead to a strong counter-reaction in the countryside. Emphasis on export crops can lead to a diminution of land planted to food staples, thereby necessitating expanded food imports. In such a situation, a nation may be forced to deal with a series of exchanges and structures (in the nations from which they now draw imported food staples) which it cannot control, and may not be able to influence, in order to provide basic foodstuffs. First, there is the difficulty of obtaining foreign exchange. Second, imported food products can be affected by export tariffs and quotas (from the supplying – exporting – nations) which are beyond the control of the importing nation. Third, the vagaries of planting and domestic consumption in the exporting nations can have a devastating impact on the food-importing nations. However, the difficulties inherent in food exports are hardly new; virtually all less-developed nations, because of their colonial history, are highly involved in the export of tropical food products, as we saw in Table 11.3. The issue, then, is normally not one of pure food self-sufficiency, but whether such nations should travel further down the path wherein much of their land, and a much higher portion of their best land, is devoted to exports.

Production problems in cash crops

Medium-sized cash crop producers face a variety of barriers to production that tend to increase their costs of production, three of which are briefly considered here.

Appropriate technology

Cash crop farmers combine the use of wage laborers with a certain degree of mechanization. However, most mechanized farm implements have been engineered for use in the advanced industrial nations, where relatively high wages prevail. Thus many available forms of agricultural capital tend to labor-saving in their design, to economize on wages. In the less-developed countries, however, labor tends to be relatively abundant compared to capital, so labor is relatively cheaper. This means that the optimal combination of labor and capital in production in most less-developed countries would utilize more labor relative to capital when compared to developed-country production techniques. Appropriate technologies in agriculture, that is, appropriate to the labor and capital mix of less-developed nations, can be of fundamental importance in finding new combinations of capital and labor which would both provide relatively more employment and capture the advantages of the relatively cheap labor so abundant in such economies. Furthermore, such technologies need to be "appropriate" in the sense that the mechanical devices in use should be relatively simple to operate, easy to repair, and durable. Sometimes, finding the appropriate technology is a simple matter of selecting off-the-shelf products. For example, in facing the issue of irrigation, there are several ways in which cultivators can proceed. To take a simple and perhaps overdrawn case, imagine that the options are between choosing a high technology or an intermediate technology. Under the high-tech scenario, laser-guided irrigation machines, integrated to computers, could be employed. Or, with intermediate technology, pipes and tubes, which can be locally produced and easily repaired without a reliance on foreign technicians and imported parts, can be employed with a much better "fit" in the developing society. Here we can view already existing alternative technologies in use, and one would suspect that few examples of the high-tech method would be utilized in the less-developed world.

In viewing the choice to plow a field, however, we do not actually see the appropriate technology. Instead, the choice is often between a modern tractor, and a team of oxen pulling a wooden plow. What less-developed countries require might be a particular type of tractor which is more versatile in the often uneven terrains of small, marginal farm land, and one less prone to needing repair than the machine which best fits the production needs in a more advanced nation. But it is the latter tractor which is likely to be available, not the former. Thus engineering of the alternative tractor is waiting to be done; it typically is not available on the market as a choice for the small- to medium-sized farmer. Creating such an alternative technology, however, entails a commitment to agricultural research, to mechanical research, and most particularly to basic education in the less-developed economies.

Yet, due to urban bias and many other factors discussed earlier, the commitment to agricultural research and development (R&D) is extremely small: In 1975 for every $100 of agricultural GDP production developing nations spent only 48 cents on agricultural R&D. Industrial nations spent $1.55 for every $100 of output in 1975, and $2.68 in 1995. Meanwhile, in 1995 developing nations spent only 62 cents per $100 of agricultural output (UNDP 2001: 110). Furthermore, it demands a commitment to the long term. Alternative technologies are too rarely developed precisely because of their distant pay-off, because of their smaller potential market, and because most less-developed nations have not yet created the required cadre of scientists and engineers who can adapt technologies to the needs of their countries. Those few scientists and engineers who are available in less-developed nations often have received their education abroad, and this education rarely prepares them for the task of confronting the particular production problems of poor nations. Compounding the problem is the **brain drain**; many promising students, once they have received their education abroad, decide to remain in the advanced industrial nation where they perceive they have greater opportunity (Adler 1987). Still, studies of the impact of 85 public research institutes in 81 developing countries found that the average rate of return on a dollar invested in agricultural research, over time, was 80 cents – nearly *twice* the rate of return achieved in agriculture in the industrial nations (UN, Department of Economic and Social Affairs 2000: 183).

Labor supply

Cash crop farmers are further constrained by the available labor supply in the rural areas. Landless peasants and smallholders will form the basis of their labor force. But due to the effects of urban bias, which severely limits educational spending in the countryside, the rural labor force will be likely to have limited educational skills, thus reducing their potential productivity. Irregularities in labor supply will also present a structural barrier to cash crop farmers who must compete for the labor-time of peasants who need to tend to their own small plots, particularly at peak times such as harvests. Landless peasants will often hire out to construction projects or in a variety of other activities such as unloading cargo, hawking products in nearby villages, selling artisan wares and so on, thereby further restricting the cash crop farmer's access to hired labor. Furthermore, low wage levels and the irregularity of employment of occasional workers, combined with the general lack of adequate public health care, again particularly acute in the rural areas, often translates into a work force which is burdened with malnutrition and chronic gastrointestinal disorders. As a consequence, the output per worker per day can be quite low, thereby creating major impediments to the efficiency of cash crop production.

Credit markets

The financial sector tends to reflect urban bias, in that bankers infrequently establish banks in the small- and medium-sized villages and towns near where cash crop farmers operate. Bankers are rarely trained in agricultural production or its special problems, and they are not necessarily receptive to the petitions of farmers for credit, particularly small- and medium-sized landholders. The formal credit market tends to be urban-based and sophisticated in terms of extending business loans, financing real-estate transactions, facilitating foreign investments, and investing in the local stock and bond markets. But rural lending tends to be outside the expertise, or interest, of urban center banks with loanable funds.

Credit, then, is too often of limited availability in rural areas. As a stop-gap measure, **informal credit markets** tend to develop; money lenders surface in the rural areas, who know their clients and their production capabilities and risks quite well. Two new barriers may arise, however, in dealing with this **kerb-side banking**, as it is sometimes called.

First, as local monopolists, the money lenders, who are often merchants or owners of larger farming operations, may be able to impose exorbitant interest charges which drain off a significant portion of the net proceeds of the farm income of small borrowers. Second, informal money lenders normally have a very limited supply of liquid funds to lend. Consequently, the level of borrowing from such sources will likely be highly constrained. Recognizing this, many governments have specifically channeled credit through **agrarian development banks**, the purpose of which is to target the borrowing needs of smaller cash crop farmers who lack access to formal channels of credit. Such a policy can be highly successful in meeting the special credit needs of farmers, but, as is true of so many other programs, it needs to be targeted carefully to meet the special needs of small- and medium-sized farm operators.

Large landholdings and agrarian backwardness

Throughout the less-developed world, large tracts of land owned by domestic landowners are rarely utilized to produce agricultural output in a purely capitalistic manner. What typically is found are two widespread forms of land usage, renting and sharecropping. Large owners may divide their lands into a multiplicity of small plots and either rent them out to small peasants for a fee or have sharecroppers who divide their output with the landowner. If the rental/sharecropping arrangement results in a lack of adequate mechanization, and/or increased erosion, and/or under-utilization of fertilizers because the renter, or tenant, is forced to take a very short-term view, then both the renter or tenant and the landlord are likely to be utilizing the land in a sub-optimal manner, both privately and socially.

The early classical economists, particularly Adam Smith and David Ricardo (see Chapter 4), criticized the "unproductive" landlord class and strongly believed that sharecropping and land rental farming was inefficient. Later, Alfred Marshall took much the same position, arguing that sharecroppers would have little incentive to make improvements to the land. Current research, however, is much more cautious in approaching the question of efficiency. Several studies and models have indicated that it is possible to have a relatively efficient land tenure arrangement involving tenants and landlords, or at least to have a production arrangement which does not fulfill the dire anticipations of Smith, Ricardo and Marshall (Stiglitz 1992).

Keith Griffin (1974), on the other hand, has emphasized the issue of land and *income distribution*, rather than that of optimal production, in his research on agriculture. He has drawn the conclusion that it is not land tenure arrangements per se which lead to agricultural retardation, but rather that the crucial issue is how the benefits of greater output are shared between renters or tenants and landlords.

> In our view, the problem in India and in other agrarian economies is not that some types of tenure systems are inflexible and inhibit innovation but that as long as the ownership of land is unequally distributed, and access to investment opportunities restricted, the benefits of whatever innovation does occur will be captured largely by the more prosperous landlords.
>
> (Griffin 1974: 91)

In Griffin's view, what *precedes* sharecropping – unequal power relations in the countryside – rather that the question of sharecropping per se is what is fundamental. He describes a situation in which, if production increases due to improvements made by sharecroppers, most or all the net increase in output ends up being captured by the landlord. Why? Because while the total yield may go up, the share received by the sharecroppers can be adjusted downward, to the benefit of the land owner. This can result when the supply of potential sharecroppers steadily increases every year, as more and more peasants are forced off their land, or have to engage in sharecropping as part of their survival strategy. Thus, the bargaining power of each individual tenant farmer declines as their total supply rises, allowing landlords to renegotiate distributive shares in their favor. Alternatively, the net amount of the harvest received by the tenant may remain relatively constant in spite of increased output, if the growth in production is achieved via mechanization and/or fertilizers and herbicides, with the landlord acting as the "middleman" in providing these inputs. Land owners also can gain a larger income share by requiring their tenants to rent tractors and to buy other agricultural inputs from them exclusively. It is via such processes that Griffin maintains that the benefits of technical change will be captured, in large degree, by the landlords and not the tenants, so that it is the distributive question which must logically precede the optimal production issue.

The issues surrounding the question of land ownership, however, continue to attract attention, and some researchers have found reason to continue to align themselves with the tradition of Smith, Ricardo, and Marshall, although not necessarily for the same reasons which those authors cited. For example, a recent econometric study of four districts in India, conducted by Radwan Ali Shaban (1987), compared sharecropping production results with the level of output achieved on land owned by small farmers. The results quite clearly show that where property and distribution rights are clearly defined, that is, on privately owned land, both the intensity of production and the level of output exceed the corresponding levels from less-secure production and distribution schemes, such as sharecropping:

- Both inputs and outputs were greater on the land owned by cultivators than on sharecropped land.

- After controlling for variables such as irrigation, plot value, and soil quality, it was found that output was 16 percent higher on the owned land.
- Family male labor use was 21 percent higher and female labor use was 47 percent higher on owned land.
- Draft animal usage was 17 percent higher on owned land.

Summarizing the results of this study, Stephen Smith concluded: "The theory and evidence considered in this study suggest that sharecropping is less technically efficient than owner-farming or fix-rent farming in many, but not all, instances" (Smith, S. 1994: 35). The dispute over the efficiency of different land tenure forms has not been resolved fully, but the dominant view may be once again shifting toward the classical economists' perception that the precise nature of the land tenure system and the property and distribution rights accompanying these are of fundamental importance in considering the efficient use of land.

The structuralist view

In Latin America, particularly through the 1960s, structuralist economists (see Chapter 6) argued that backward land tenure systems were at the heart of the lack of development in agriculture. Alain de Janvry nicely captures the essence of the structuralist argument.

> Structuralists claim that agricultural prices have not been particularly unfavorable in the last 40 years and that stagnation results from producer behavior under archaic land tenure systems. Survival of precapitalist relations of production imply rigidities in supply response; ... absentee management and autocratic, hierarchical labor relations impede the spread of innovations. The high degree of monopoly of productive resources and of institutional services (credit, information, etc.) permits the landlords to derive enormous economic rents and social advantages even while using the land highly extensively. As a result, behavior of the landed elite is oriented more toward maintenance of the economic and social status quo than toward profit maximization and capital accumulation.
>
> (de Janvry 1981: 146)

de Janvry strongly disputes this structuralist depiction of agrarian structures in Latin America, not as an institutional–historical description, but as an adequate analysis of recent trends. His research suggests that the social structures which were conducive in the past to the landed elite's misuse of land are quickly breaking down. The semi-feudal use of land is being replaced by capitalist land usage, as the last vestiges of a bygone era are swept away by the intrusions of the logic of the purely market-based economy. The old hacendado mentality, wherein land was a symbol of social stature, is being replaced by a new ethos wherein land is simply another capital asset, and the rate of return on land must be maximized through optimal production techniques.

If this is a correct depiction of current land usage, the dilemmas of development may, to some degree, be compounded rather than relieved. An unfettered capitalist strategy in agriculture will likely lead to the substitution of capital for labor, to further concentration in land ownership, and to the expulsion of large numbers of peasants from their small plots and from their status as intermittent farm laborers. A new dynamic then ensues: labor expelled from rural areas gravitates toward the urban areas, circling less-developed world cities in ever-expanding belts of misery and human degradation. Restructuring in the rural areas, then, may lead to increased yields in agriculture and an increase in the marketable surplus of crops either on the domestic or international market, as a result of the increasing displacement of small cultivators from the agrarian regions. Thus far, the employment absorptive capacity in most urban areas has been deficient in relation to the need to incorporate the population flow migrating from the rural areas. International migration has surged, too, as this process of creating landless workers has accelerated. And this new migration of labor from less-developed countries, some of it illegal, has created new forms of social stress and dissent particularly in Western Europe and the United States.

Transnational agribusiness

Since the Second World War, and particularly since the mid-1960s, a new link has been formed with some corporations in the advanced industrial nations and the agrarian sectors in the less-developed world. Modern agriculture is increasingly dependent upon research and development of herbicides, fungicides, insecticides, and synthetic fertilizers, most of which are produced by the huge petroleum transnationals through their enormous petrochemicals divisions. The bulk of the original research on these new chemical combinations was conducted during, or shortly after, the Second World War. At first, diffusion of the new products occurred principally within the advanced industrial nations. By the mid-1960s, however, market saturation led to the desire by the agro-transnationals to extend their sales into the less-developed world. This coincided with increasing concerns with a "population bomb" in the less-developed world and the need for agricultural output to increase faster than the rate of growth of population. Widespread usage of, and often dependence upon, new fertilizers, pesticides, and hybrid seeds provided by the new transnational agribusiness interests has sometimes been encouraged and financed by governments in the poor nations. Another source of such technological diffusion has been the spread of contract farming, whereby large and intermediate-sized farmers agree to plant, cultivate, and harvest according to the terms set by a contractor, often a large food-processing corporation based in the advanced industrial nations (see Box 11.4).

Agribusiness corporations also have made new incursions into the less-developed world in order to control cattle ranchers who are suppliers for the hamburger chains, such as McDonald's, and other fast food restaurants in the more developed nations. Thus vertical integration in the increasingly concentrated restaurant business has had a profound impact on certain less-developed nations, sometimes taking good agricultural land out of the available domestic supply in order to export beef, which requires a land-intensive form of production. In the process, such farming operations can contribute to deforestation, land degradation, and environmental pollution, ranging from soil erosion to global warming.

Finally, largely due to the increasingly sophisticated network of transportation, including automated docks, ship containerization, roll-on-roll-off truck trailers and

---

Box 11.4 Agriculture and the environment: property rights and resource depletion

Many environmental problems are traceable to issues of property rights and a lack of property rights enforcement. Throughout the developing world, vast tracts of land are held as **common property resources** and as state property. If policy regarding land use is ill-defined, either at the community level and/or at the level of the national government, environmental problems due to the overuse of resources are likely to arise, creating vicious circles of desertification, famine, and increasing poverty. This is the problem known as the **tragedy of the commons**.

In Africa, pastoral arrangements often allow for overgrazing, unbalanced forestry practices, and forest depletion due to the scavenging for fuel. In India, the rural poor derive as much as 20 percent of their income from foraging and from grazing their animals on commons areas. In Latin America, vast tracts of tropical forests are national property, but the use of this land is subject to little systematic management, and the predicted over- and misuse with which the tragedy of the commons literature abounds is the consequence. In Nepal, for example, population growth led to the expansion of peasant agriculture into forest regions, resulting in the loss of 20 to 50 percent of all forests within a decade.

Neoliberal economists have often argued that overgrazing, desertification, and deforestation on common and national lands can be resolved through the establishment of private property rights. Without well-defined private property rights, it is believed that individuals will have little incentive to conserve resources. Sometimes a compelling case can be made for the market-based solution which they advocate. In other instances, however, redefining communal practices, strengthening pastoral associations, or creating governmental oversight agencies can be a solution which strengthens long-standing institutional arrangements.

There are alternatives to simply privatizing all land, forests, and the seas to prevent overuse and the tragedy of the commons outcome. Nepal, for example, has reversed its policy of open access to woodlands by strengthening village and community control over these resources. Current research suggests that a resolution of these issues arises only when property rights are well-defined and enforced. Adequate management of such resources can proceed using either a private property-based distribution **or** a combination of communal and national ownership, but with a critical eye on the socially optimal use of such resources. What this implies if such resources are not privately held are either limits on use of commons resources and/or fees for use.

Source: Tomich *et al.* 1995: 33

---

cargo jets, exotic crops are increasingly being grown for the high-income recipients of the advanced industrial nations. Thus an array of both tropical products and traditional luxury fruits and vegetables are now generally available year-round to those who can pay. Ernest Feder described this new phenomenon as "strawberry imperialism," partly because a northern seasonal "exotic" such as strawberries could be air-freighted into Stockholm in the dead of winter from a distance of perhaps 4,000 miles via airfreight.

Unlike the older plantation economy arrangements, the new agribusiness conglomerates tend to make minimal commitments to high fixed cost assets such as land, docks, and railroads in the countries in which the production is derived. Rather, they emphasize contract farming, relying on existing infrastructure, rather than financing their own projects. Thus labor problems and the risks of weather, as well as long-term problems such as soil erosion or contamination of groundwater and streams, along with soil exhaustion, become the problems of the medium and large farmers who contract with the agribusiness TNCs, who can then simply contract out their purchases elsewhere. In the case of the new emphasis on cattle ranching for hamburger chains, many environmentalists have voiced concern over the tendency to push back rainforests in order to open up grazing land. The fear is that delicate environmental structures, where rainfall patterns are interrupted and where the holding capacity of the ground cover is now insufficient due to the elimination of much of the natural plant life, will be further adversely affected. Soil erosion can be an extremely serious **negative externality** in the cattle-ranching areas, as forests are cleared and grasslands lose their capacity to hold water. This can set up a vicious circle, whereby governments dispose of large tracts of rainforest for a modest payment, ranchers convert the land to cattle-grazing, erosion makes the land unsuitable within a few years, and the ranchers then pressure the government for access to new tracts of forest and savannah lands.

In the case of so-called exotic crops, though hard currency is earned via exports, a less-developed nation will have to share such new forms of revenue with the agribusiness transnational. Net foreign exchange earnings may well be quite modest, particularly when balanced against the opportunity costs of land shifted out of domestic food consumption and the possible adoption of cultivation practices which may not be sustainable, and/or which incur large external costs in the form of erosion which fouls stream beds, water supplies and fish-spawning areas, or environmentally important wetlands.

One example of a possible outcome under the new arrangements being formed by agribusiness TNCs in the less-developed world is that of Senegal's alliance with the giant Castle & Cooke operation.

> In 1972 Bud Antel Inc., a large California-based food conglomerate (taken over in 1978 by Castle & Cooke), formed a joint enterprise with the Senegalese government. The subsidiary, Bud Senegal is an affiliate with the House of Bud in Brussels. Bud Senegal grew vegetables, using a virtually labor-free drip irrigation system, with plastic tubes continuously supplying water to each plant individually, to tap the vast reserves of water just below the Senegal's dry soil. Three times a week from early December until May, a DC-10 cargo jet takes off from Senegal loaded with green beans, melons, tomatoes, aubergines, strawberries, and paprika. The destinations are Amsterdam, Paris, and Stockholm. The vegetables are not marketed locally, but in any event few Senegalese have enough money to buy them.
>
> Local people gained few jobs from the project, and in laying out the 450 hectare plantation Bud uprooted the indigenous baobab trees which were an important village resource, having previously provided local families with rope, planting materials, fuel, and wind erosion protection.
>
> (Dixon 1990:42)

Government in agricultural development

Although some economists have recently turned to free markets in the hope of accelerating the development process (see Chapter 7), major agricultural specialists have long maintained that a successful development strategy in agriculture must at a minimum have some state intervention to foment needed changes. In the forefront of this discussion is the research work of Bruce Johnston and John Mellor who, according to Peter Trimmer, advocate a "market policy" approach which would combine the advantages to be found through active government policies toward agricultural development with the benefits to be derived from properly channelled market forces.

> [The strategy] calls for government policy interventions into market outcomes but uses markets and the private marketing sector as the vehicle for those policy interventions. This "market policy" approach recognizes widespread "market failures" in agriculture as well as extensive "government failures" in implementation of economic tasks. The strategic dilemma is how to cope with segmented rural capital and labor markets, poorly functioning land markets, the welfare consequences of sharp instability of prices in commodity markets the pervasive lack of information about current and future events in most rural economies, and sheer absence of many important markets.
>
> (Trimmer 1989: 358)

One of John Mellor's major concerns has been the general lack of output response when increasing demands have been placed on less-developed world agricultural producers (this is the problem of low elasticity of supply). Mellor argues that in most instances higher prices and profits will not call forth much of an increase in the quantity supplied, as the neoliberals believe, because cultivators have tended to reach the limits of existing technologies and traditional inputs. Thus to increase agricultural output, a major shift toward new and appropriate technologies is needed, as well as massive investments in infrastructural elements that will relieve some of the bottlenecks on the supply-side of the agricultural sector. Mellor believes that a strategy which brings agricultural needs into the foreground will also have an impact on the demand for labor by increasing wages. This will, in turn, create more disposable income which will, for the most part, be spent on food.

While Mellor does not believe that a strategy of development which pushes agriculture into the foreground will solve the unemployment or underemployment dilemmas in agriculture, it will contribute to a significant reduction in the ranks of the unemployed. Mellor would, in fact, provide more governmental support to agriculture than to industry, and he emphasizes that the success stories in food production are to be found precisely in those nations where the state was actively involved in the diffusion of food-growing technologies, particularly through a technically competent extension service.

> Agriculture, with its small-scale orientation, is more in need of public-sector support than industry. The sharp turn-around in Asian agriculture – resulting in a 30 percent increase in growth rates in basic food-staple production from the 1960s to the 1970s – impressively demonstrates the results of turning the public sector's attention to the requisites of technological change in agriculture.
>
> (Mellor 1998a: 144)

While Mellor's emphasis on the need for technological diffusion and massive infrastructural investments in agriculture is certainly well-reasoned and supported by the successes of the East Asian economies and other examples, the problems of agriculture are not purely technological. The countryside needs to be understood as an arena where gross injustices have often been perpetrated, and the powerful have behaved with impunity, often for centuries. In this environment, it is important for those engaged in economic development to understand the grievances of small cultivators. This will not be easy for "outsiders" to comprehend, because small cultivators usually have nurtured a profound distrust of anyone who, in an official capacity, arrives in the countryside with the intention of "doing good" or "fostering development." Based on a study of agrarian issues in ten poor nations, David Lea and D.P. Chaudhri concluded that:

> To us it seems that the role of modern inputs, infrastructure and other enabling institutions is important but grossly exaggerated. More important than these inputs is local participation, local organization and skillful use of historical experience by the policy-makers. The role of the human element, individual and collective, can hardly be overstated in this respect.
>
> Rural development successes ... on a national scale are likely to be glaring exceptions and would be the result of a balanced growth strategy pursued by an enlightened and sensitive national leadership who can inspire confidence and a sense of participatory economic justice among the rural peasantry and landless poor. Such conditions cannot be created in a hurry. The strength of the past and continuity seems rather formidable. Change can be induced successfully if, and only if, the policy-makers and planners understand the working of the rural socioeconomic system and are prepared to hasten slowly.
>
> (Lea and Chaudhri 1983: 337–338)

Land reform

Land reform has been used to describe a very wide variety of changes in land ownership. For example, **colonization** programs, where land is given to small farmers who are willing to conquer wastelands, jungles and other unsettled areas of marginal productive value, often fall under this heading. Likewise, programs that are designed to partition extremely large neofeudal landholdings into smaller parcels, while leaving virtually untouched all other large landholders, have been considered as land reforms. And land reform has sometimes meant the break-up of village agrarian systems, where land is farmed in common without individual land title; such policies often also entail the sale of previously unclaimed forests and grazing lands which had been utilized on an as-needed basis by subsistence cultivators, much like commons lands had been used in Europe centuries before.

Nonetheless, the most common usage of the term land reform refers to the conversion of most, or all, large estates and privately held tracts of land to smallholder shares. Such a shift can, but need not, entail the direct entitlement of land ownership to smallholders. Rather, land title may reside in the hands of a village system; periodic redistribution can be made as the number of families grows or declines, and to suit other demographic changes at the village level. Normally, land reform sets strict limits on the maximum size of smallholdings. While some specialists argue that land reform is a dead issue, others believe that **negotiated land reform** may give new life to this issue. Under negotiated land reform there is an attempt to create a responsive market for large landholdings and to give both grants and loans to small-holder/peasants to buy land at fair market value. This approach, which demands the participation of either federal or state governments, avoids the politically explosive issue of condemnation and confiscation of large estates. Some countries are seriously engaged in negotiated land form, such as Brazil, Colombia, and South Africa (Deininger 1999).

In evaluating land reform schemes, it is important to keep in mind the fact that such programs typically seek to achieve a combination of political, social, and economic goals simultaneously. At the political level, land reform is often seen as a means to forestall or eliminate potential threats of a thorough-going social revolution by the landless. At the societal level, peasants may feel that the goal is social justice; they disregard the "big picture" issues such as "Is this socialism?" At the economic level, care needs to be exercised in assessing the outcome of a land reform program. Smallholders will, with the rarest exception, appropriate a larger share of agricultural output for themselves as they gain land and improve their own diets. This can mean, and often does mean, that the surplus of agricultural production above that which is consumed in the countryside can actually *decline* initially following land reform. For the mass of people living in the urban areas, and for the central government, land reform can create great difficulties if food scarcity becomes an issue. Such a situation can lead to a reliance on food imports and create a broad range of new political and social problems. Particularly if "urban bias" is present, critics will be quick to argue that land reform is a failure, though staying the course usually results in the marketable surplus rising.

Another issue of fundamental importance needs emphasis. The switching of ownership titles in the countryside, without an accompanying agricultural development *strategy*, will lead to failure and is not real land reform. Smallholders need not only title to their land; they also need the services, information, and training from agricultural extension services that can help to make them more productive. They need to be involved in research and development projects, and they need help in locating appropriate forms of mechanization, in learning about irrigation and water control projects, in gaining access to effective infrastructure, such as roads and schools, they need fertilizers and help in obtaining reasonable access to credit for future development.

In closing this chapter on agriculture, we will briefly examine two large land reform programs: Mexico's *ejido* system, which is generally regarded to have failed, and South Korea's model of agricultural development, known as the *Saemaul Undong*. But bear in mind that land reform has been achieved in a great number of other nations, such as Taiwan, China, Ethiopia, Bolivia, Eastern India, Chile, and Iran. Currently land reform efforts are underway in Zimbabwe, Malawi, South Africa, Guatemala, El Salvador, Brazil, and Colombia.

Land reform in Mexico

As a result of the Mexican revolution (1910–1917), which included widespread peasant revolts, particularly in land areas where plantation-style estates abounded, land reform was a *fait accompli* of the armed struggle. After the revolution, successive governments sought to complete the land reform, essentially breaking up tillable holdings in excess of 200 hectares. By 1976, 43 percent of land had been turned over to *ejidos*, which are village councils responsible for distributing land to their members. *Ejidos* were prohibited from renting, selling, or mortgaging the land. Unfortunately, the 28,000 *ejidos*, which provided land to 43 percent of all the farm families in Mexico, held only 16 percent of the irrigated land. The large landholders, a mere 2.5 percent of all landholders, were able to produce 40 percent of the food on 20 percent of the land. They were able to do so, because, despite land redistribution, they had managed to hold onto and control the best land. They were able to finance irrigation projects themselves or, in the more likely instance, to benefit from government-created irrigation projects specifically aimed at large farms. And the large landholders had a near monopoly on credit. For example, between 1956 and 1969, the private commercial farmers received 85 percent of all agricultural credits granted by financial intermediaries (de Janvry 1981: 215).

At first it appeared that the *ejido* system was a social, political, and economic success. From 1938 to 1951, agricultural output leapt ahead at an annual rate of 4.3 percent. From 1951 to 1970, agricultural output growth exceeded 6 percent per annum. Then, however, Mexican agricultural growth virtually stopped. From 1970 to 1976, agricultural output per capita fell by more than 15 percent (Cypher 1990: 90; de Janvry 1981: 217). Grain imports soared; between 1970 and 1979, they totalled 689,000 tons, and in the 1980–1989 period, they rose to 26 million tons (Russell 1994: 194).

The great failure of small-scale Mexican agriculture following land reform was due to several factors. In the 1970s, when greater emphasis should have been placed on agriculture because of the tightening of the "scissors" between land yields and population demands, the Mexican state became increasingly involved in industrial development, neglecting agriculture. Second, with the onset of the oil boom (1976–1982), the Mexican government took the position that it would be more efficient to export oil, which commanded a high price at the time, and import food. When the oil boom collapsed, however, and the debt crisis ensued, Mexico adopted neoliberal policies which reduced the size of governmental investments, particularly in the agrarian sector, and virtually eliminated the subsidized credits which had been allocated to the smallholders, or *ejidatarios*. Subsidies which had been granted on fertilizers were virtually eliminated, and electricity prices were increased by 60 percent under the "get prices right" or "real prices" doctrine of neoliberalism. In order to trim its budget, the government lowered the buying price of corn and other staples, further squeezing the *ejidatarios*. Not surprisingly, agricultural growth fell well below the rate of growth in population. In 1992, Mexico instituted sweeping changes in agriculture, essentially allowing *ejidatarios* to sell and rent their land and to use it as collateral for credit, while allowing corporations, both domestic and foreign, to buy such properties. In essence, by the 1990s, the Mexican effort at land reform had ended. Critics charge that these new trends will lead to a renewal of land concentration, expelling as many as 10 million rural residents from the countryside into Mexico's huge urban areas, or into international migration and ending the *ejido* system.

South Korea's Saemaul Undong

Prior to Japanese colonial rule in the early twentieth century, the rural landholding nobility in Korea, the *yangban*, had held both the land and the peasants in a vice-like grip for over 500 years. By the late nineteenth century, much of the Korean countryside had been swept with unsuccessful peasant revolts and risings. Japanese rule brought some limitations on the *yangban*, as some Japanese adopted Korean landholdings. For the peasants, however, conditions and land concentration, as described in the following citation, generally became worse under colonialism.

> In 1914, only 1.8 per cent of the households owned 51 per cent of the cultivated land. Rents ranged from 50 to 60 per cent of the crop with tenants, who bore the costs of production, left with 20 per cent or less of the final production. As in many Asian countries in the colonial period, the change from sharecropping to fixed rents in rural Korea meant in bad years there was no relief from starvation. Contracts were verbal and could easily be manipulated or terminated by landlords and protestors faced possible imprisonment by the colonial state.
>
> (Douglas 1983: 192–193)

In 1953, in the aftermath of the Korean war which had left ten million Koreans homeless in the devastated cities, a thorough-going land reform was instituted. Compensation paid to the *yangban* was minimal, 150 percent of the value of the annual harvest, with full payment spread over several years, an amount that was insufficient to compensate for the capitalized value of the land. Land was then distributed to the peasants, with an upper limit of three hectares imposed. Once instituted, the land ownership pattern in South Korea has remained stable.

In the early years, South Korean land reform had the appearance of a "title switching" program; peasants were forced to sell their surplus staples to the government, which redistributed them to the cities, with the price paid being so low that costs of production could not be covered. At first, Korean farmers were forced to compete with food-aid imports which came into Korea virtually free from the United States. Such difficult conditions in the countryside led to a massive outmigration of farmers. Such a demographic shift, however, was largely accomplished without an expanding underclass as the South Korean industrialization program, and its emphasis on maintaining labor-intensive production via export substitution (see Chapter 10), helped to absorb the inflow of former agricultural workers. Still, the relative neglect of agriculture, and the migration it fostered, was telling; in 1969, 29 percent of the dwellings in Seoul were classified as slum/squatter dwellings, where many former peasants resided.

> The neglect of agriculture created a poverty syndrome which had several dimensions. Low rural incomes meant ineffective demand for agricultural inputs.... Evidence for this period shows widening disparities between rural and urban incomes ... there is evidence to suggest that rural welfare, although not at the level of desperation of the 1950s, was not advancing. Real rural incomes stayed nearly the same for the decade (1960–70), while urban incomes doubled.
>
> (Douglas 1983: 190–191)

Fortunately, governmental planners recognized the critical conditions in the agricultural sector in the course of the 1960s, and reforms were introduced. For example, interest rates above 20 percent per year on crop loans were declared illegal, and there was a general expansion of irrigation facilities. In 1972, with the third five-year plan, the government turned to an integrated strategy of agricultural development, the *Saemaul Undong*, which has successfully moved the land reform from one of title switching to a genuine program of rural development. The strategies employed in South Korea contrast sharply with the growing neglect of small-scale producers in Mexico. The third five-year plan dealt with the slow growth in agricultural output – only a 2.3 percent increase per year in 1967–1971 – via four integrated strategies:

- the general diffusion of high yield varieties of seeds, the domestic production of fertilizers, and greater application of pesticides;
- the mechanization of agriculture;
- state management of grain storage facilities; and
- a program of housing construction, rural electrification and feeder road construction.

During this time period, the government allocated an extraordinary 28 percent of its budget to agricultural development. As a consequence, the differential between rural and urban living standards was greatly diminished. By the late 1970s, South Korea's program of agrarian development had been consolidated. In real terms, agricultural output increased over 500 percent between 1970 and 1991. Today, Korea has a relatively large population of 44 million in 1992, and a relatively modest population growth rate of 1.8 percent, projected to be less than 1 percent by the year 2000. With but limited land for cultivation – Mexico, for example, has nearly ten times the amount of land per capita – Korea has continued to import grains. But, with its tremendous strength in manufacturing exports, Korea can afford to sustain heavy grain imports as it creates true dynamic comparative advantage in production with greater value-added, while paying high wages.

While South Korea's experience with land reform and agricultural development has, of necessity, taken place within certain physical limitations, and while it has not eliminated the need to import cereals, it does demonstrate that a productive relationship between the state and the rural population can be achieved, within the context of a strong program of land reform. In Korea's case, the successes achieved in agriculture have always depended upon state intervention and a successful program of state-directed industrialization. Neoliberalism has played virtually no role in South Korea's success, nor has the program succeeded due to an "agriculture first" or an agriculture-led policy. Instead there has evolved a balanced policy of *both* agrarian and industrial development.

> To the extent that export-led industrial growth has made rural development possible, the use of such terms as "self reliant" to describe Korea's rural development is extremely misleading. The emphasis on private ownership has, in general, meant that increases in production have been generated by state intervention into the market rather than through an increase in a local corporate capacity to develop. It also suggests that the future of Korea's agricultural-cum-rural development will depend upon the ability to keep the export engine of growth in high gear.

> (Douglas 1983: 208)

Questions for review

1 In discussing appropriate technology for less-developed nations, we noted that given the relative labor abundance and relatively lower wages in the less-developed nations compared to the more developed economies, and the relatively higher price of capital, in many situations the optimal combination of labor and capital that should be used in the less-developed nations would be more labor-using and less capital-using compared to a higher-wage developed country. In a graph with the quantity of capital, K, measured along one axis and the quantity of labor, L, measured along the other, draw one convex-to-the-origin production isoquant, representing, say, 1,000 units of output for every combination of L and K on the curve. Now draw in an isocost line for a developed country which is tangent to the isoquant at some point. (You will remember that the slope of the isocost line is determined by the relative prices of K and L.) Note the quantity of K and L used on the axes. Now, assuming that the price of a unit of K in the less-developed country is the same as in the more developed, but the wage rate is lower, show that the optimal combination of K and L to produce 1,000 units of output in the less-developed nation would use more labor and less capital than in the more developed economy. Prove, too, that the less-developed country would be the lower cost producer of the 1,000 units. What difference does it make to the way you draw the isoquant if, now, we assume that not all combinations of labor and capital are technologically feasible to produce 1,000 units of output? What will the isoquant look like if there are only two different combinations of K and L available? What choice of technique (i.e., which combination of K and L) will the developed country and the less-developed country producer select?

2 Advocates of the Green Revolution have argued that the technologies employed are "scale neutral." That is, seeds and fertilizers are easily divisible, and no appreciable change in unit costs are involved in altering the quantities used. Therefore, they hypothesized, the Green Revolution should benefit both poor and wealthy farmers alike, without an appreciable relative advantage to one or the other in use. Contrast this technical view of the impact of the Green Revolution with a more "institutional" view. Assuming that the unit cost of inputs are nearly "scale neutral," why did the many institutionalists predict that the Green Revolution would increase intraregional and interregional income disparities rather than diminish them? What other considerations are there besides costs of the new inputs in deciding whether to use a new seed, a new fertilizer, or any new technology in agriculture? Can the response of poorer and richer farmers differ? Why?

3 Available research suggests that when peasant farmers are impacted by deforestation and desertification, women are particularly affected. Why is this so? How are women affected adversely?

4 Some peasants are quite "risk-averse," for reasons discussed in this chapter. Imagine a group of poor pastoralists struggling with the effects of a famine and drought. Why might it be "rational" for them to actively, if unintentionally, contribute to the acceleration of environmental degradation, and to their own famine, via overuse of grazing land, if they are concerned with guarding against the exhaustion of their animal herds? Is this situation an example of a market

failure? What could be done to prevent overgrazing of land? Are these people poor because they overgraze the land with the animals, or are they overgrazing the land because they are poor?

5   Explain, using supply and demand curves, how a low "buy price" (i.e., a price below market equilibrium) by government for a staple product, such as rice in India, may lead profit-oriented staple crop producers to switch to other crops. On the same graph, show the effect of targeted income subsidies to low income consumers on the quantity and price of rice traded in the market, assuming the "buy price" program is abandoned. Discuss the pros and cons of subsidized prices for staple commodities versus targeting income subsidies as strategies to help the poor to purchase staple food products.

6   How is true land reform different from a redistribution of landholdings? What political purposes might each have? What are the economic reasons for pursuing land reform? For a redistribution of landholdings that falls short of full land reform?

7   How important are improvements in the productivity of the agricultural sector relative to efforts to increase productivity in industry? Can a country become developed without an industrial and agricultural "revolution" in the economic sense of the term?

8   Are food imports necessarily an indication of weakness in the agricultural sector of an economy? Under what conditions might food imports, rather than domestic production, be desirable and economically rational? Under what conditions would rising food imports indicate a weakness in the overall economic strategy? Do countries have to produce everything they consume? Looking back at Table 11.1, for which countries would you guess that falling food production per person is an indication of problems and for which might such a result not be a problem?

Notes

1   Note, however, that declining per capita food production is not the same as declining per capita food consumption. For some newly industrialized nations, agricultural and food production should, with successful structural transformation, fall in relative terms compared to industrial and service production. The poorer a country, however, and the lower its level of human development, the less likely it is that the structural transformation has taken place. Thus the declining per capita food production for many African nations, is of great concern.

2   Note that this term is intended to signify extreme dependence on a very limited range of primary product exports, be they agriculture or raw material exports. It is not strictly intended to mean that an economy is literally dependent on only one export for its foreign exchange earnings.

3   It perhaps goes without saying that, though this phenomenon was only "discovered" at that time, this does not mean that the effects of commodity price swings had not been in operation for some time. This instability of prices, and the macroeconomic consequences, had been a focus of much of the critical concern of heterodox economists, as discussed in Chapter 6, for some time, and of policy-makers in the less-developed world who had to periodically confront such crises.

4   How can a country prevent a temporary and exogenous export price increase from having such adverse effects? One way is to sterilize the increased inflow of export revenues, to prevent an increase in the currency's exchange rate value vis-à-vis other currencies. This can be done if the central bank of the country sells more of its own currency, thus buying up

foreign exchange. This will increase the supply of its own currency, to balance the increased demand for that currency by non-residents resulting from the higher prices of the export. Effective sterilization also requires that government, with the increased revenues it earns and increased foreign exchange reserves, exercise restraint in spending these "savings."

5 Technically, the expected losses from the gamble failing exceed the expected gains from the gamble succeeding, where in this case, the gamble being considered is a change in peasant production (such as a new technology, or a new seed, or a new fallowing technique) where the probabilities of success and failure are still subject to some degree of uncertainty.

References

Barraclough, Solon (ed.). 1973. *Agrarian Structure in Latin America.* Lexington, MA: Lexington Books.

Barry, Tom (ed.). 1992. *Mexico: A Country Guide.* Albuquerque, NM: Inter-Hemispheric Resource Center.

Bliss, C.J. and N.H. Stern. 1982. *Palanpur: The Economy of an Indian Village.* Oxford: Clarendon Press.

Byerlee, Derek. 1992. "The Political Economy of Third World Food Imports: The Case of Wheat," pp. 305–326 in Charles Wilber and Kenneth Jameson (eds), *The Political Economy of Development and Underdevelopment*, 5th edn New York: Random House.

Cypher, James M. 1990. *State and Capital in Mexico.* London and Boulder, CO: Westview.

de Janvry, Alain. 1981. *The Agrarian Question in Latin America.* Baltimore, MD: Johns Hopkins Press.

Deininger, Klaus. 1999. "Making Negotiated Land Reform Work: Initial Experience from Colombia, Brazil and South Africa," *World Development* 27: 651–672.

Dixon, Chris. 1990. *Rural Development in the Third World.* London: Routledge.

Doolette, John and James Smyle. 1990. "Soil and Moisture Conservation Technologies," in John Doolette and James Smyle (eds), *Watershed Development in Asia.* Washington, DC: World Bank Technical Paper 127.

Douglas, Mike. 1983. "The Korean Saemaul Undong," pp. 186–214 in David Lea and D.P. Chaudhri (eds), *Rural Development and the State.* London: Methuen.

Eicher, Carl and John Staatz. 1998. "Agricultural Ideas in Historical Perspective," pp. 8–38 in Carl Eicher and John Staatz (eds), *International Agricultural Development*, 3rd edn Baltimore, MD: Johns Hopkins Press.

Fogel, Robert. 1994. "Economic Growth, Population Growth and Physiology," *American Economic Review* 84: 369–395.

Goldman, Abe and Joyotee Smith. 1995. "Agricultural Transformations in India and Northern Nigeria: Exploring the Nature of Green Revolutions," *World Development* 23 (March): 243–263.

Griffin, Keith. 1974. *The Political Economy of Agrarian Change.* Cambridge, MA: Harvard University Press.

—— 1989. *Alternative Strategies for Economic Development.* New York: St Martin's Press.

Hill, Polly. 1986. *Development Economics on Trial.* Cambridge: Cambridge University Press.

Lea, David and D.P. Chaudhri (eds). 1983. *Rural Development and the State.* London: Methuen.

Lipton, Michael. 1977. *Why Poor People Stay Poor.* Cambridge: Cambridge University Press.

—— and Richard Longhurst. 1989. *New Seeds and Poor People.* Baltimore, MD: Johns Hopkins Press.

Mellor, John. 1998a. "Agriculture on the Road to Industrialization," pp. 136–154 in Carl Eicher and John Staatz (eds), *International Agricultural Development*, 3rd edn Baltimore, MD: Johns Hopkins Press.

—— 1998b. "Foreign Aid and Agriculture-Led Development," pp. 55–66 in Carl Eicher and

John Staatz (eds), *International Agricultural Development*, 3rd edn Baltimore, MD: Johns Hopkins Press.

McCalla, Alex. 1998. "Agriculture and Food Needs to 2025," pp. 39–54 in Carl Eicher and John Staatz (eds), *International Agricultural Development*, 3rd edn Baltimore, MD: Johns Hopkins Press.

Morris, Michael and Derek Byerlee. 1998. "Maintaining Productivity in Post-Green Revolution Asian Agriculture," pp. 458–473 in Carl Eicher and John Staatz (eds), *International Agricultural Development*, 3rd edn Baltimore, MD: Johns Hopkins Press.

Pingali, Prabhu. 1998. "Confronting the Ecological Consequences of the Rice Green Revolution in Tropical Asia," pp. 474–493 in Carl Eicher and John Staatz (eds), *International Agricultural Development*, 3rd edn Baltimore, MD: Johns Hopkins Press.

Rostow, Walt W. 1960. *The Stages of Economic Growth.* Cambridge: Cambridge University Press.

Russell, Phillip. 1994. *Mexico Under Salinas.* Austin, TX: Mexico Resource Center.

Schejtman, Alexander. 1992. "The Peasant Economy: Internal Logic, Articulation and Persistence," pp. 276–304 in Charles Wilber and Kenneth Jameson (eds), *The Political Economy of Development and Underdevelopment*, 5th edn New York: Random House.

Schultz, Theodore. 1964. *Transforming Traditional Agriculture.* New Haven, CT: Yale University Press.

Schiff, Maurice and Alberto Valdés. 1998. "The Plundering of Agricultural Policy in Developing Countries," pp. 226–233 in Carl Eicher and John Staatz (eds), *International Agricultural Development*, 3rd edn Baltimore, MD: Johns Hopkins Press.

Shaban, Radwan Ali. 1987. "Testing Between Alternative Models of Sharecropping," *Journal of Political Economy* 95: 893–920.

Smith, R.E. 1972. *The United States and Revolutionary Nationalism.* Chicago, IL: University of Chicago Press.

Smith, Stephen. 1994. *Case Studies in Economic Development.* New York: Longman.

Stiglitz, Joseph. 1992. "The New Development Economics," pp. 261–275 in Charles Wilber and Kenneth Jameson (eds), *The Political Economy of Development and Underdevelopment*, 5th edn New York: Random House.

Tomich, Thomas, Peter Kilby, and Bruce Johnston. 1995. *Transforming Agrarian Economies.* Ithaca, NY: Cornell University Press.

Trimmer, Peter. 1989. "The Agricultural Transformation," pp. 358–361 in Gerald Meier (ed.), *Leading Issues in Development Economics.* Oxford: Oxford University Press.

—— 1998. "The Role of Agriculture in Indonesia's Development," pp. 539–549 in Carl Eicher and John Staatz (eds), *International Agricultural Development*, 3rd edn Baltimore, MD: Johns Hopkins Press.

UNCTAD. 1987. *Handbook of International Trade and Development Statistics.* Geneva: UNCTAD.

UN, Department of Economic and Social Affairs. 2000. *World Economic and Social Survey 2000.* New York: United Nations

UNDP (UN Development Program). 1993. *Human Development Report 1993.* Oxford: Oxford University Press.

—— 1994. *Human Development Report 1994.* Oxford: Oxford University Press.

—— 1995. *Human Development Report 1995.* Oxford: Oxford University Press.

—— 2001. *Human Development Report 2001.* Oxford: Oxford University Press.

World Bank. 1992. *World Development Report 1992.* Oxford: Oxford University Press.

—— 1994. *World Development Report 1994.* Oxford: Oxford University Press.

—— 1995. *World Development Report 1995.* Oxford: Oxford University Press.

—— 2000/2001. *World Development Report 2001.* Oxford: Oxford University Press.

—— 2001. *World Development Report 2001.* Oxford: Oxford University Press.

—— 2002. *World Development Report 2002.* Oxford: Oxford University Press.

12 Population, education and human capital

After studying this chapter, you should understand:

- the connection between population growth rates and the level and growth rate of income per capita;
- the importance and causes of the demographic transition and the effect on birth and death rates;
- the determinants of the fertility rate, particularly income per person and the level of education of women;
- the importance of education and human capital accumulation to economic growth and human development; and
- the role for government action to overcome market failure in the creation of human capital.

Introduction

The most malleable factor of production available to any economy is its population. Our consideration of endogenous growth theories in Chapter 8 and of the recent success of structural transformation of the so-called "high performance East Asian economies" (HPAEs) in Chapters 9 and 10 has highlighted the importance of an educated labor force to economic growth. Education is the means by which a nation is able to appropriate from and share in the gains arising from technological advances at the world level. A sufficiently educated labor force would seem to be absolutely necessary for sustained growth and for achieving full human development; even a nation that succeeds in avoiding all the other pitfalls of developing societies considered in the next part of the book but which neglects education will not succeed in developing as quickly or to such a high level as would be possible with more and better human capital.

The accumulation of a productive stock of human capital is thus one of the fundamental keys to the development process.[1] There is the question, however, as to how the growth rate of population and the growth of the labor force affect the level and pace of economic growth and development, and the pace of human capital accumulation itself. So, prior to considering in more detail the importance of the human capital input to development, it is necessary to briefly examine the nature of what is often called the "population problem."

The population problem

The so-called population problem is based upon an assumption that rapid population growth can cause the total population to exceed a nation's productive capacity so that real income per person falls or rises unnecessarily slowly. Deep down, what is called the population problem is simply a reassertion of the Malthusian spectre of population outstripping output growth already considered in Chapter 4. Reproducing equation 2.1,

$$\% \ \Delta \text{GNP per person} = \% \ \Delta \text{GNP} - \% \ \Delta \text{population} \tag{12.1}$$

The change in real income per person over time depends both on the growth rate of aggregate real income (measured by GNP or GDP) less the rate of population growth. Obviously the faster that GNP grows, population growth held constant, the more rapid will income per capita rise. The faster that population grows, the slower will be the expansion in income per person, for any given rate of aggregate GNP growth. This, however, does not mean that faster population growth *causes* slower growth in income per capita or that slower population growth *leads* to a faster increase in income per person. In fact, we shall argue that the relation between income and population is normally in the opposite direction, from income to population growth, and not vice versa.[2]

Within the groupings of countries and for most individual nations in Table 12.1, the population growth rate has tended to fall over time, though more slowly in some regions and countries than in others. In general, falling population growth rates seem closely associated with rising income levels, with a lag. That is, higher income per person leads to slower population growth, which, by equation 12.1, opens the door for more rapid increases in income per person in the future. This can be observed by noting that, in general, reading down the table from the low-income, to the middle-income and finally to the high-income groupings, population growth rates get progressively smaller.

Rather than an increase in income per person resulting in ever more rapid increases in population, as Malthus had predicted, the actual relation would seem to be the other way around. Income per person and population growth rates are inversely related, not directly related, for reasons we shall consider below. The best way to reduce population growth rates, then, is for a country to experience economic growth and higher incomes per person. Population growth is a fundamental consequence of the level of income.

The natural and the actual rate of population growth

What accounts for differences in population growth rates among countries and regions? In a purely accounting sense, the ***natural* rate of population growth** can be defined as

$$p_n = (\text{crude birth rate} - \text{crude death rate})/10 \tag{12.2}$$

where p_n is interpreted as an annual percentage change, the crude birth rate is the number of live births per 1,000 population and the crude death rate is the number of

Table 12.1 Actual population growth rates, by region and selected countries

	Population growth rate, annual percent			Share of world population[a]	
	1960–1970	*1970–1980*	*1980–2000*	*1980*	*2000*
Low-income economies	2.3	2.1	2.1	36.3	40.6
China	2.3	1.8	1.3		
India	2.3	2.2	2.0		
Pakistan	2.8	2.6	2.6		
Somalia	2.8	2.9	1.5		
Zimbabwe	2.6	3.0			
Middle-income economies	2.5	1.9	1.4	45.8	44.9
Argentina	1.4	1.6	1.4		
Côte d'Ivoire	3.8	4.0	3.3		
Jamaica	1.4	1.3	1.1		
Senegal	2.3	2.9	2.7		
South Korea	2.6	1.8	1.1		
High-income economies	1.1	0.8	0.7	17.8	14.9
Ireland	0.4	1.4	0.5		
Japan	1.0	1.1	0.4		
United Kingdom	0.6	0.1			
United States	1.3	1.1			
Less-developed regions					
East Asia and Pacific	1.9	1.5	1.4	31.5	30.6
Latin America and the Caribbean	2.4	2.0	1.8	8.1	8.5
Middle East and North Africa	2.9	3.0	2.6	3.9	4.9
South Asia	2.3	2.1	2.0	20.4	22.4
Sub-Saharan Africa	2.7	2.9	2.7	8.6	10.9

Sources: World Bank 1983: 184–185, Table 19; 1994: 210–211, Table 25, 2002a: 48–51, Table 2.1.

Note

a Total world population in 1980 was estimated as 4,429.3 million and 6,057.3 million in 2000.

deaths per 1,000 population.[3] Thus, for Côte d'Ivoire in 1993, with a crude birth rate of 49 and a crude death rate of 15, the natural rate of population growth was $pn = (49 - 15)/10 = 3.4$ percent. Crude birth and crude death rates are shown in Table 12.2 for the same countries and regions as in the previous table. The listings of the countries within each grouping is from the country with the lowest income to the highest. This is done to help us see if there are any patterns we can detect connecting crude birth rates (CBRs) and crude death rates (CDRs) to income levels.

The natural rate of population growth, p_n, calculated in Table 12.2, often is quite different from the *actual* population growth rates shown in Table 12.1. For example, in 1970, the p_n for Côte d'Ivoire is 3.1 percent, while the actual annual population growth rate over both the 1960s and the 1970s was well above this figure. The natural rate of population growth thus understates the actual rate of population growth for Côte d'Ivoire. Considering Somalia in 2000, just the opposite is true; the natural rate of population growth overstates the actual trend of population. For Japan, the natural rate of population growth predicts the actual population growth rate quite closely.

What accounts for the difference between the natural rate of population growth

Table 12.2 CBRs, CDRs, and the natural rate of population growth[a]

	CBR^b			CDR^b			$p_n,\%$		
	1970	1993	2000	1970	1993	2000	1970	1993	2000
Low-income economies	39	28	29	14	10	11	2.5	1.8	1.8
India	41	29	25	18	10	9	2.3	1.9	1.6
Pakistan	48	40	34	19	9	8	2.9	3.1	2.6
China	33	19	15	8	8	7	2.5	1.1	0.8
Zimbabwe	53	38	30	16	12	18	3.7	2.6	1.2
Somalia	50	48^c	51	24	17^c	17	2.6	3.1^c	3.4
Middle-income economies	35	23	18	11	8	8	2.4	1.5	1.0
Côte d'Ivoire	51	49	37	20	15	17	3.1	3.4	2.0
Senegal	47	43	37	22	16	13	2.5	2.7	2.4
Jamaica	34	21	21	8	6	6	2.6	1.5	1.5
Argentina	23	20	19	9	8	8	1.4	1.2	1.1
South Korea	30	16	13	9	6	6	2.1	1.0	0.7
High-income economies	18	13	12	10	9	9	0.8	0.4	0.3
Ireland	22	15	14	11	9	8	1.1	0.6	0.6
United Kingdom	16	13	11	12	11	11	0.4	0.2	0.0
United States	18	16	15	10	9	9	0.8	0.7	0.6
Japan	19	10	9	7	8	8	1.2	0.2	0.1
Less-developed regions									
Sub-Saharan Africa	47	44	39	20	15	17	2.7	2.9	2.2
East Asia and Pacific	35	21	17	9	8	7	2.6	1.3	1.0
South Asia	42	31	27	18	10	9	2.4	2.1	1.8
Middle East and North Africa	45	33	26	16	7	6	2.9	2.6	2.0
Latin America and the Caribbean	36	26	22	10	7	6	2.6	1.9	1.6

Sources: World Bank 1994: 212–213, Table 26; 1995: 212–213, 2002a: 48–51, Table 2.1.

Notes
a Countries are ranked in terms of their 1993 GNP per capita, from lower to higher incomes.
b Per 1,000 population.
c 1992.

and the actual? The actual rate of population growth shown in Table 12.1 depends not only on the natural rate, p_n, but also on migration flows between nations. We can define the actual rate of population growth, p_a, as

$$p_a = p_n + m \tag{12.3}$$

where m is net migration: m = (immigrants/100 population) − (emigrants/100 population) and p_a also is interpreted as a percentage. For countries with little immigration or emigration, or in which these flows are relatively balanced, the actual rate of population growth will be very similar to the natural rate. For countries with a high level of emigration relative to immigration, that is, with more people leaving the country than entering, the natural rate of population growth, p_n, will overstate the actual rate of population growth, p_a, as in Somalia. In countries, like Côte d'Ivoire, where net migration is positive, the actual population growth exceeds the natural rate, as population inflows exceed population outflows.

What is it that explains differences in CBRs and CDRs among countries, and hence population growth rates, and their trends over time? To understand this, it is helpful to consider the issue within a somewhat longer time frame. A look at the so-called demographic transition will illustrate the factors affecting population growth rates via the impact over time of various forces at work on the level of CBRs and CDRs.

The demographic transition

If we were to go back a century and examine natural population growth rates, we would find a quite different picture from that shown in Table 12.2. Crude birth and crude death rates were both higher, so that most countries had natural rates of population growth in the neighborhood of about 1 percent per year.[4] High death rates tended to nearly cancel out relatively high birth rates, so there was no "population problem." Births and deaths were in a sort of perverse balance, so that there was no population explosion. Natural population growth rates at 2, 3, and 4 percent are primarily twentieth- and twenty-first century phenomena.[5] What changed to make such rates of population growth possible?

What changed was the spread and speeding-up in some countries of the structural transformation toward industrialization and capitalist expansion (examined in Chapters 9 and 10) and higher levels of income and development, which contributed both to falling birth rates in the nations experiencing accelerated development and to a worldwide trend toward lower death rates in nearly every nation, rich and poor. For the nations on the road to industrialization, especially Western Europe, the United States, Canada, and Japan, crude birth rates *and* crude death rates fell relatively rapidly, so that their natural population growth rates remained close to 1 percent.

In the now-developed nations, rapid economic growth associated with fundamental structural change resulted in improvements in living standards, incomes and education which led people to choose to have fewer children, thus significantly reducing birth rates. Lower death rates, as improved economic conditions contributed to better health and longevity, fell along with the lower CBRs.[6] When modern medicine set out to tackle major public health hazards, like malaria, measles, smallpox, cholera, typhoid, diphtheria, poor sanitation, and so on, death rates fell even more rapidly.

The developed nations were in the process of completing what is called the **demographic transition**, whereby crude birth and crude death rates *both* decrease to levels below 20 per 1,000 of population. As a result of this transformation, population growth rates are at, or even below, 1 percent per annum.

In the less-developed nations, however, where the structural transformation toward more productive industrialization and capitalist development was either absent, very primitive or dualistic, crude birth rates remained high. On the other hand, crude death rates had decreased, often approaching the levels attained in the developed nations.[7]

The fall in death rates in the less-developed world was not wholly the result of economic, social and health improvements taking place within these nations. Instead, the sharp drop in worldwide crude death rates, especially after 1945, was the consequence of the public good characteristics of and positive externalities associated with the great strides in public health and sanitation measures, immunization for childhood diseases, pest control and similar measures that had originated in the developed world, the benefits of which were transferred to the less-developed world as well. The result was a growing gap in the less-developed nations between their birth rates, which fell only slowly as incomes rose slowly, and their rapidly declining death rates. This asymmetry led to an inevitable ratcheting upward in the rate of population growth in the less-developed nations as the gap between slowly falling but still relatively high CBRs and rapidly falling and low CDRs widened.

In effect, most of the less-developed countries have passed through but *one-half* of the demographic transition. Death rates have fallen significantly and are more in line with levels associated with higher incomes per person in more developed economies. In nearly every country of the world, CDRs have passed through the 20 per 1,000 population threshold. Birth rates, however, have remained relatively high in the less-developed economies, reflecting their relatively low income levels, though they are tending to fall as incomes increase over time. It is a cruel twist of fate, perhaps, that visits on the less-developed nations some of the best of the developed world – low CDRs – and the worst of the less-developed world – relatively high CBRs – simultaneously.

Figure 12.1 is a representation of the changes over time in crude birth and death rates and their effect on population growth. In Phase I, prior to the industrial revolution and the spread of capitalist methods of production within the now-developed world, both birth and death rates were high for all countries, so popu-

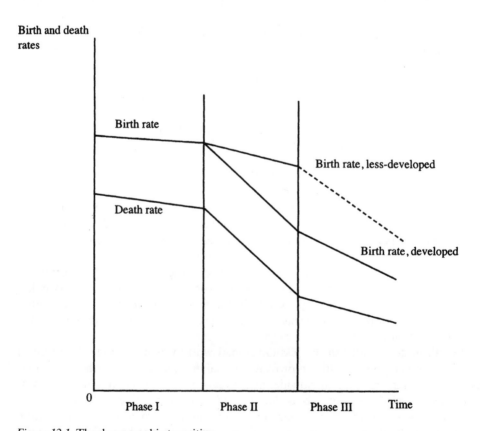

Figure 12.1 The demographic transition.

lation growth was relatively slow everywhere. The gap between the CBR line and the CDR line shows this rate of population growth.

In Phase II, death rates began to decline in the more-developed nations due to both localized effects of higher incomes but also as a consequence of worldwide health measures which brought mortality rates down for all countries, regardless of income level. In Phase II, the developed nations also experienced declining birth rates due to rising income levels at the same time that their death rates were decreasing, so population growth did not accelerate. The gap between the CBR line and the CDR line remained relatively stable.

In the less-developed nations, on the other hand, in Phase II crude birth rates remain high, falling only very moderately with slowly rising incomes. As a result, population growth rates actually begin to increase as the widening gap between the birth and death rates lines shows as the worldwide benefits of health measures reduce CDRs in the poor nations as well. It is only in Phase III, which has not yet been attained for most less-developed nations, that their birth rates also decline below 20 per 1,000 population and they also complete the demographic transition. For those less-developed nations which fail to make the necessary structural transformations and which have lagging per capita income levels, population growth will remain high as these economies remain mired in Phase II of the demographic transition with relatively high CBRs and relatively low CDRs.

Determinants of the crude birth rate

Whereas the crude death rate tends to vary within a relatively narrow band due to the spread of world public health measures, the crude birth rate exhibits a much greater degree of dispersion among nations as can easily be seen by reading down the CBR columns for any year in Table 12.2. This is because the crude birth rate is the consequence of more family-specific and national determinants than is the crude death rate. In particular, the primary determinants of crude birth rates have been found to be (a) family income and (b) the education level of women.[8]

There are, of course, cultural and religious factors which impinge on birth rates in particular nations and regions, but even when these are factored in, the evolution of family income and women's education are the most important determinants of birth rates over time. Reading down the CBR column in Table 12.2 for 2000 confirms the general tendency for the CBR to decline with higher income (in that table the countries are ranked from the lowest income to the highest as you read down the column). The connection between higher income and lower CBRs seems quite clear-cut.

Population growth rates thus depend on the evolution of CBRs and CDRs in any particular country. A key determinant of the CBRs is the average level of income in a country, as just discussed. Another significant factor affecting CBRs is the level of education of women and not simply because women become more aware of birth control. The issue is rather more complicated and economic at root, as is discussed more fully below. Both higher average income levels and higher education levels for women affect CBRs via fertility rates.

The total number of children that the average woman is expected to have is called the **fertility rate** (see Table 12.3). The fertility rate tends to be lower in regions with higher incomes and higher in regions with lower incomes. In other

Table 12.3 Fertility rates, income and women's education

	Total fertility rate[a]			Education ratio[b]		
	1970	1990	2000	1970	1990	1998
All regions						
Low-income economies	5.9	4.4	3.6	59	n.a.	79
Middle-income economies	5.1	2.6	2.2	n.a.	84	90
High-income economies	2.4	1.8	1.7	94	96	92
Less-developed regions						
Sub-Saharan Africa	6.6	6.1	5.2	58	79	80
East Asia and Pacific	5.7	2.4	2.1	n.a.	84	89
South Asia	6.0	4.1	3.3	51	n.a.	78
Middle East and North Africa	6.8	4.8	3.4	53	79	84
Latin America and the Caribbean	5.3	3.4	2.8	95	n.a.	99

Source: World Bank 2002b.

Notes
a Total fertility is the number of children that would be born alive to the "average" woman if she were to live to the end of her child-bearing years and have children according to the age-specific fertility rates as she ages.
b The number of females per 100 males in primary and secondary school.

words, there is an inverse relation between fertility rates and income and hence between the crude birth rate and income levels since the crude birth rate ultimately depends on fertility. Within all regions over the period 1970 to 2000, the fertility rate decreased. Those regions that have shown the fastest growth in income per capita and that have reached higher levels of income per capita, as in Latin America and the Caribbean and in East Asia, have demonstrated the most rapid decline in fertility and birth rates in the less-developed world (see Birdsall 1988).[9]

Table 12.3 also shows the number of females per 100 males attending primary and secondary school. Higher ratios in 1970, indicating a reduction of the education gender gap, are associated with lower fertility rates in 1990 and 2000, underscoring the importance of women's education as a means of reducing fertility and population growth rates.[10]

It will be noted that the Middle East and North Africa still has a relatively high fertility and population growth rate compared to the other less-developed regions, despite a narrowing of the education gender gap and a relatively high income level per capita compared to South Asia. This is likely due to distinct cultural factors, perhaps partly reflecting the role of women in Islamic societies, that have prevented as rapid a reduction in fertility and population growth than the impact of more female education and rising income would incline us to predict. Still, though the average fertility rate is higher than in other lower-income regions, this does not negate the importance of women's education or rising income to lowering fertility. From 1970–2000, the tendency for decreasing fertility with higher income and more education is clearly observed within the Middle East and North Africa region, confirming the positive impact of these two variables in reducing fertility rates.[11]

Family planning, the availability of and knowledge about contraception methods, social, moral, and legal views on and access to abortion services and a whole range of other factors can result in fertility and population growth rates that are higher or lower than might be expected given the income per capita levels or level of female education in any particular country. Such interventions can help to speed the process of reducing CBRs and help countries pass through the demographic transition threshold more quickly, but these measures are unlikely to be substitutes for the tendency of fertility rates and crude birth rates to be pushed downward by economic growth and the expansion of educational opportunities for women.

As family income and women's education rises, then, there is an unmistakable *tendency* for birth rates to fall, as was confirmed in Table 12.2.[12] This means that average *family* incomes will rise over time as per capita income in a country rises, assuming no strongly adverse changes in the income distribution, since family size will fall over time.[13]

The importance of the different "roles" of children in less-developed and developed economies

Though Table 12.3 suggests that fertility and hence birth rates tend to be inversely related to the level of per capita income and the education of women, the explanation for such a link needs to be clarified. At root, the reason is primarily economic.

We can formalize the relation between fertility rates and their determinants as

$$F = f(y, e, S) \qquad (12.4)$$

where F is the total fertility rate, y is per capita income, e is the number of females per 100 males in primary school, and S measures the social, cultural, and political factors specific to each country that also may affect fertility. It is expected that the first derivatives, f_y, $f_e < 0$, that is, fertility is negatively related to income and education levels, while the relationship between S and fertility (f_S) is indeterminate. The reason for expecting such an inverse relation between fertility and income is predicated on the different roles that children perform for their parents in low- versus high-income economies.

In economies at lower levels of per capita income, children play multiple roles for their parents. Even at young ages, children can provide an additional source of labor on family farms thus contributing to total family income. Within the household, older girls can care for younger siblings and help with the cooking, cleaning, fetching of wood and water, and other simple but essential tasks that contribute to the family's overall well-being.

Just as importantly, children often are a form of insurance for poor parents in their old age, ensuring that they will be provided for. This effect is strongest in countries lacking broadly based social security and old-age pension systems. It is for this reason that the so-called extended family, in which grandparents, parents, children, and perhaps aunts and uncles and cousins live in the same house or in very close proximity to one another is so much more common in the less-developed world than in more developed economies. Without an old age social security system in place, poor elder parents often are forced to live with their children and grandchildren as a means of survival, and the naturalness of such arrangements is deeply inculcated in all members of the family as a reciprocal relationship. It should be remembered, nonetheless, that such arrangements are borne out of necessity as much as they may seem to be desired social arrangements.

Another link between higher fertility rates and low incomes is found in infant and child mortality rates shown in Table 12.4. Families in many poor economies are aware that the probability of losing a child either at birth or at a young age is high, but they do not know precisely how many, if any, of their children will fail to reach maturity. According to the table, in Sub-Saharan Africa, the probability of losing any one child before that child reaches age five is still nearly 1 in 5 in 2000, and this probability is higher the poorer the family. Thus, to the extent that children are at least partly a form of old age insurance and given that the risk of losing a child is highest in Sub-Saharan Africa among all the less-developed regions, we would expect fertility rates to be higher there than other regions due to the greater risk of loss. And that is precisely what Table 12.3 confirms.

These multiple roles of children thus lead parents in poorer nations to "choose" to have more children for income and social security reasons. Children are an economic resource in the LDCs for poor families.

What is the "role" of children in richer economies? How does it differ? At higher levels of per capita income, fertility declines as the *cost* of having children rises in terms both of care required and educational expenses, but more importantly in terms of the opportunity cost of the parents, especially the mother. At higher levels of income, the time spent caring for, feeding, washing, taking children to and from school, dancing and sports practice, and so on is worth more than at lower levels of per capita income in terms of forgone income, particularly for working mothers. Simple economic analysis would suggest that the number of children "demanded" would decrease as income rises since the cost, or price, of children is greater at higher income levels.

Women, who remain the primary care-givers to children, bear the burden of this cost (see Focus 12.1 for another view of the role of women within the household). As their education level rises and their income-earning power increases and their relative contribution to family income grows, women choose to have fewer children since the opportunity cost of each child increases with growing income. Additional

Table 12.4 Infant and child mortality rates

	Infant mortality rate[a]			Under-five mortality rate[b]		
	1970	1990	2000	1970	1990	2000
All regions						
Low-income economies	134	88	76	209	127	115
Middle-income economies	79	39	31	125	49	39
High-income economies	21	8	6	26	9	7
Less-developed regions						
Sub-Saharan Africa	138	103	91	222	159	162
East Asia and Pacific	79	43	35	126	55	45
South Asia	138	87	73	209	121	96
Middle East and North Africa	134	56	43	200	72	54
Latin America and the Caribbean	84	41	29	124	49	37

Source: World Bank 2002b.

Notes
a The number of children who die before age one, per 1,000 live births.
b The probability of a newborn baby dying before reaching age five, per 1,000 live births.

FOCUS 12.1   WOMEN'S EDUCATION AND INCOME AND HEALTH

It is not only fertility rates that decline with higher levels of education for women. Health indicators, and hence family welfare, also improve.

In Africa, studies have shown that a 10 percent increase in female literacy rates reduced child death rates by 10 percent; by comparison, changes in men's literacy rates had no effect on child mortality rates. In Thailand, it was found that women with some primary education were 30 percent more likely to know how to treat diarrhoea in their children – using homemade salt and sugar solutions or other oral rehydration methods – than were mothers with no education, thus reducing infant deaths.

In studies in Indonesia, Kenya, Morocco, and Peru, the strong positive correlation of years of women's education and reduction in child mortality rates was confirmed again and again. In all instances, women's education was more important than men's education in reducing the death rate of children.

Further, income earned by women is spent differently within the household. In Jamaica, a household study found that women spend more of their income on goods for their children than do men (and less on alcohol). "In Guatemala, it takes fifteen times more spending to achieve a given improvement in child nutrition when income is earned by the father than when it is earned by the mother."

What do these results say about the role of men's and women's incomes and education levels within the household? What explains these differential effects? Why is the marginal contribution of men's income and education to household welfare less than women's?

Source: World Bank 1993a: 41–43

children mean more foregone income. At higher income levels, the lost income is greater than at lower income levels, so the number of children a family chooses to have is inversely related to family income. As family income rises, there are fewer children "chosen." At lower income levels, families "choose" to have more children since the cost of each is less in terms of any foregone income.

In richer countries, parents do not have children as either investments for their futures, as a substitute for social security, or as potential workers. As one of our more perceptive students once put it, in richer economies children might be better seen as a source of "entertainment" for their parents. They are doted on, dressed in designer clothes, groomed from infancy for pre-schools and beyond, and generally treated as objects of consumption rather than as investments as is the case in poorer economies.

As objects of consumption, children are expensive and are more expensive the higher the income of the family having them. Thus families choose to have fewer children as their income rises and as women get more educated and enter the work force, increasing their individual opportunity cost of having children. The prevalence of the "nuclear" family – mother and father and one or two children – is thus the norm in economies with higher average income as the economic need for the extended family tends to dissipate.

There is another reason why families in both poor and richer nations may have children: to carry on the family name. Since family names typically are carried to the next generation by male children, this results in a bias in favor of boy over girl babies. Nobel Prize-winning economist Amartya Sen has written passionately about how this bias has led to abortions of female children, what he calls "natality inequality." In a famous study of Asia, Sen writes of the "one hundred million" missing women (Sen 1990). At least partly the abnormally low number of women to men in India and Pakistan – roughly 93 to 100 rather than the more typical 98 – and other countries in Asia and Africa is due to the "role" of male children in transmitting the family name to the next generation which result in girls not receiving the same level of medical care or nutrition as boys, deficiencies that often are carried through life and contribute to higher mortality rates than would be expected.

Human capital accumulation: augmenting initial endowments

Beginning in the 1960s, economists began to seriously study labor not just as a homogeneous factor of production, L, but as a differentiated and moldable input to production, that is, as **human capital**. This suggested that nations could invest in people via education, work training, on-the-job training, nutrition, health care, sanitation, and so on to increase the *quality* of the employed labor force, just as investment could take place in not only increasing the quantity but also in improving the quality of physical capital via technological change. The dissatisfaction with the inability of neoclassical growth theories to fully explain the sources of economic growth by the accumulation of more physical capital and by the growth in the labor force led economists to consider more fully the other factors, especially education, training, and technology, which might account for more rapid growth in some economies than in others.

Our consideration of endogenous growth theories in Chapter 8 and the recent successes of the HPAEs confirmed the importance of a well-trained population and labor force within the development process. It is certainly not the only factor in successful development. Human capital accumulation is not sufficient to guarantee success (think of the former Soviet Union), but it certainly would seem to be necessary (for a critical view see Easterly 2001). In this section, we examine in greater detail the contribution that human capital accumulation, especially schooling, can have on the prospects for economic growth and human development.

The contribution of education to development

In the World Bank's study (1993b: 52–53, Table 1.9) of the HPAEs, they found that enrollments in primary education in 1960 predicted the following shares of growth over the period 1960–1985.

	% of total predicted growth
Hong Kong	86
Indonesia	79
Japan	58
South Korea	67
Malaysia	73
Taiwan	69
Singapore	75
Thailand	87

These are astounding and instructive results. The level of primary education was far and away the most important contributor to the predicted growth rates of the

HPAEs and Japan. Further, the accumulated and improving human capital stock of Hong Kong, Japan, Taiwan, and, to a lesser degree, South Korea contributed to the ability of these economies to be able to adopt, adapt, and indigenize the ever-expanding pool of "best practice" technological knowledge. As a consequence, in most of these economies, because of the qualities and relatively high level of training of the population and labor force, the levels of productivity and of "technical efficiency change" were able to grow quickly (see Table 8.4). In other words, most of the HPAEs were able to move closer over time to the ever-shifting-outward production possibilities frontier of "international best technological practice" by becoming more technologically efficient as they have had rates of **total factor productivity (TFP)** change that exceeded the rate of exogenous, best practice technological change.[14]

According to the World Bank's estimates, East Asia's rate of TFP was *double* that of any other less-developed region. Over the period 1960–1987, 28 percent of East Asia's output growth was due to increases in TFP. For South Asia, which includes India and Pakistan, TFP over the same period was responsible for 14 percent of total growth. In Africa and Latin America, there was *zero* TFP growth over the same period – that is, *all* their growth in output was due to increases in physical capital and labor usage. None of the average economic growth was the consequence of the more efficient utilization of inputs and improvements in efficiency due to human capital accumulation or to organizational and institutional changes needed for accelerated development (World Bank 1991: 45, Table 2.3). In other words, East Asia increased its output by producing more *intensively* and more efficiently, while Africa and Latin America produced more output, and at a slower overall pace, solely by producing *extensively*, that is, by adding more of the same quality inputs to the production process but not by using those inputs in a more efficient manner or by augmenting the quality of the overall human capital stock.

Table 12.5 provides some insight into the level and pace of human capital accumulation for various countries. Years of schooling is used as a proxy measure for the human capital stock.

The data in the table are quite suggestive. Countries were more likely to be middle- or high-income in 1993 if their 1970 level of primary education coverage was close to universal, that is 100 percent. Among the less-developed regions, East Asia and the Pacific had the second highest stock of human capital in 1970 if this is measured solely by primary school enrollments. Further, the mean value of schooling, shown in the last column of Table 12.5, is higher at higher levels of income and at higher levels of human development, as measured by the HDI (see UNDP 1994: 138–139, Table 5). For example, while Indonesia is ranked among the low-income economies, it is ranked as having "medium human development." South Korea, an upper-middle-income nation by the World Bank's income rankings, was ranked thirty-second among all nations on the HDI index and is among the countries with "high human development." The level of schooling is one important reason for these results.

Note that the "average years of school" measure is the mean value for adults aged twenty-five or more. To the extent that more years of school on average is a measure of greater human capital accumulation and potential, this trend augurs well, by itself, for the less-developed nations approaching universal

Table 12.5 Education and human capital accumulation

	Primary[a]		Secondary[b]		Tertiary[c]		Primary student teacher ratio		Average years of school[d]
	1970	1998	1970	1998	1970	1998	1970	1998	
Low-income economies	66	96	18	42	3	7[e]	43	42	
Bangladesh	54	122	n.a.	47	2	5	46	59	2.0
India	78	100	24	49	5	7[e]	41	72	2.4
Kenya	62	92	9	31	1	1	34	28	2.3
Indonesia	80	113[e]	16	56[e]	3	11[e]	29	22[e]	4.1
Middle-income economies	94	112	28	67	3	13	30	22	
Senegal	39	70	9	20	1	4	45	49	0.9
Jamaica	119	98	46	90	5	9	47	31	5.3
Mexico	106	114	23	71	5	18	46	27	4.9
South Korea	103	94[e]	42	102	7	68[e]	57	31[e]	9.3
High-income economies	100	103	77	106	27	59	26	17	
United Kingdom	104	102	73	156	14	58	23	19	11.7
Canada	101	97	65	105	53	58	23	18	12.2
United States	88	102	84	97	47	77	27	15	12.4
Japan	100	102	87	102	18	44	26	21	10.8
Less-developed regions									
Sub-Saharan Africa	51	78	6	26	1	4	43	40[e]	
East Asia and Pacific	90	107	24	62	1	8	30	23	
South Asia	71	101	23	48	4	6[e]	42	66	
Middle East and North Africa	70	97	24	60	4	22	34	24	
Latin America and the Caribbean	107	130	28	75	6	20	33	28	

Source: World Bank 2002b.

Notes

a Total enrollment in primary school as a percentage of primary school-age children (often 6–11 years). If this is greater than 100, it indicates that some children younger and/or older than the standard age are enrolled in primary school.

b Calculated the same as in the previous note, but as a percentage of secondary school-age children (often 12–17 years).

c Determined by dividing the number of students enrolled in all post-secondary education (college, university, technical, etc.) by the population aged 20–24.

d 1992, for population aged 25 and above.

e 1996.

primary school coverage. Of course, quantity is not enough; the quality of the education received is fundamental too, though this is inherently more difficult to measure.

The "Primary Student Teacher Ratio" in Table 12.5, which measures the number of students per teacher in primary schools, can be interpreted as one indicator of the quality of education. The ratio is positively related both to the mean years of schooling and to the level of income of the country. It suggests that those countries most focused on enriching and enlarging their stock of human capital will be those which strive to increase both the average number of years of schooling via *human capital broadening* and the quality of schooling via *human capital deepening*, as measured here by smaller class size.

Look at Bangladesh's record. From 1970, human capital broadening definitely took place at the primary school level as by 1998 universal education had become the norm. However, the primary student–teacher ratio shows that it is likely that the quality of education suffered as there was an average of 59 children per teacher in 1998 compared to 46 in 1970. The situation was even worse in India. And if one thinks of the other inputs to education – books, pencils, paper, desks – is it likely that either Pakistan's or India's teachers had sufficient numbers of these for the larger number of students they were trying to teach?

On the other hand, South Korea reduced the number of students per teacher over the period, suggesting that there was an improvement in the quality of education in each classroom on average.

So while universal primary education should be an important goal for countries wishing to increase the level of development, it is also important that sufficient financial and other resources be allocated to primary education so that the quality of such education is not compromised in the interests simply of increasing the coverage ratio. Though this is not noted in Table 12.5, but was discussed above, it is also of importance to maintain balance in the pursuit of universal primary school coverage, keeping in mind the need to address and reduce the gender education gap and the rural–urban education gap in designing human capital broadening and deepening programs.

Human capital accumulation and market failure

The evidence on the importance of education as a specific form of human capital to accelerating economic growth rates seems incontrovertible (but again see the view of Easterly 2001).[15] Nations with a larger stock of human capital are more likely to grow faster than those with less human capital, and they are able to reach higher levels of income per person. The endogenous growth models reviewed in Chapter 8 are unambiguous on this and much of the vast literature on human capital is dedicated to exploring the "value" of education to individuals and to society (see the classic articles by Mincer (1958) and Schultz (1960)). One of the important reasons why growth rates do not necessarily fall with increased human capital accumulation, that is, one possible reason for the absence of diminishing social returns to human capital investment, is that human capital accumulation creates substantial positive externalities.

When an individual receives schooling, that person is, of course, likely to earn more income over his or her lifetime as a consequence of the higher level of skills and knowledge which make that person more productive. There are unambiguous individual or **private benefits** to receiving an education and that is typically the personal motivation for undertaking increased years of schooling.

Furthermore, there are also **social benefits** that accrue to an economy as a whole as the result of individual decisions to go to school. Such social benefits can include: new knowledge which may be created by more educated individuals that adds to the well-being of others through new products, new medicines, safer production processes, and so on; more efficient workers who thus reduce the costs of production and prices paid to all consumers; a more educated work force which may be more inclined toward democratic processes; and more educated workers who are able to combine better with other workers, so that the level of productivity of all workers rises, increasing the incomes of all involved.

However, since the total benefits of education exceed the private benefits of education due to the existence of these social benefits and other positive externalities that might be listed, the choices of individuals as to the level of education to receive will result in less education on average than is socially desirable. This is a classic example of market failure, requiring some sort of government intervention to bring private and social benefits in line with one another for the social good.

Figure 12.2 illustrates the divergence between the privately chosen optimum level of education and that which would be socially optimum. The curve labelled $MPC = MSC = S$ assumes that the marginal private costs of education (MPC) to individuals are equal to the marginal social costs (MSC) of education, and that these can be viewed as the supply curve (S) of education, measured in terms of years of schooling on the horizontal axis.

The cost of schooling and the benefits are measured on the vertical axis. The market demand curve for education of a society's individuals is shown by the curve MPB, which measures the marginal private benefits of additional years of schooling accruing to private individuals as increased income and other benefits. If individuals choose education based on their own decisions, the quantity of education which is

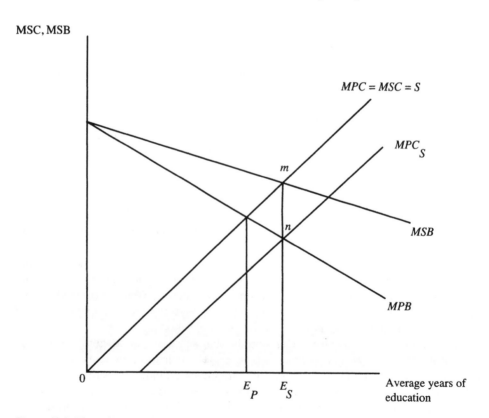

Figure 12.2 The private optimum and the social optimum level of education.

optimal for them to choose is the quantity E_P, where the supply curve, S, crosses the individual market demand curve, *MPB*.

As noted above, though, some of the benefits of schooling are received indirectly by others as higher incomes, via improved product quality, increased social cohesiveness, a higher level of technological development, and so on beyond what is received directly by the individuals who actually have undertaken the schooling. Thus the **marginal social benefit** (*MSB*) of education curve, which is *society's* demand curve for education, lies outside and to the right of the *MPB* curve, the *private* demand curve for education. The gap between the *MPB* and the *MSB* curve measures the value of the positive externality to society of any level of schooling. This gap widens as more years of education are accumulated, reflecting the presumption that learning-by-doing, association effects and other gains from increased education levels generate even more beneficial effects to society are greater than at lower levels of education.

The socially optimum level of education is E_S, where the supply curve of education crosses the marginal social benefits curve, that is, where society's supply curve intersects society's demand curve for education, *MSB*. For the socially optimum average level of education, E_S, to be reached, however, some sort of state intervention will be required to subsidize private decision-makers, since they will not, based on their own private maximizing calculations, accumulate education beyond the level E_P. A subsidy to private individuals equal to amount *mn* would induce private individuals to choose to undertake E_S years of education by lowering individual costs to the new subsidized marginal private cost curve, *MPCs*. Then, individuals would rationally choose the socially optimum level of education, as is desired, since the subsidized marginal private cost curve of education would cross the *MPB* curve, the private demand curve for education, at the socially desired average years of education, E_S.[16]

Figure 12.2 provides the theoretical underpinning for not requiring individuals to absorb the full cost of their education. There is an efficiency reason for society subsidizing the cost of education and, by simple extension, subsidizing a larger proportion of the costs the lower the income of the individuals being schooled. Even those who do not have children gain from the positive externalities of the children who do receive education. There is thus a rationale for taxing and then subsidizing education and other forms of human capital accumulation. The assumption of perfect markets and perfect information, often made in the more developed economies, is inappropriate in the less-developed countries. Poor households lack access to financial resources or the ability to borrow to capitalize future expected earnings from education, so the market failure problem is even greater than that caused by the divergence between private and social benefits the larger the number of poor in society. In fact, social returns to education are estimated to be nearly 20 percent to primary education. Given the imperfect markets and imperfect information facing the population in the less-developed economies, there is a strong case on efficiency and equity grounds for first providing free, universal primary schooling and, over time, extending this coverage to secondary education as well. In the World Bank study on the HPAEs it was noted that:

> the allocation of public expenditure between basic and higher education is
> the major public policy factor that accounts for East Asia's extraordinary

performance with regard to the quantity of basic education provided. The share of public expenditure on education allocated to basic (i.e., primary and secondary) education has been consistently higher in East Asia than elsewhere.

(World Bank 1993b: 197–203)

Thus it makes good economic sense, as well as contributing to improvements in equity via shared growth and in contributing to broader based human development, to allocate schooling expenditures first on primary education with a goal of universal coverage of males and females, and with secondary education close behind in terms of spending priority (see Focus 12.2). Post-secondary schooling, which is important for creating the indigenous capacity to adopt and adapt world-level best practice technological knowledge and for improving total factor productivity, should not consume too large a level of government resources at early stages of development. In fact, for low-income economies, there are alternative avenues for financing tertiary education besides large subsidies from the state. These can range from requiring university students, who are likely to be from higher-income families anyway, to pay the major portion of the full costs of their education via tuition and fees,[17] "targeting" state subsidies (via, say, scholarships) only toward those with both ability and financial need, to subsidizing, perhaps at a substantially lower cost, higher quality education for domestic students by sending them to study abroad.

FOCUS 12.2   PRIMARY EDUCATION IN BOLIVIA AND INDONESIA

In the early 1980s Bolivia and Indonesia were, superficially, at about the same level of development in terms of income per capita – in the low- to middle-$600 range. Illiteracy ran at about 20 percent of the population, and girls were especially disadvantaged. Both nations were predominantly agricultural. And both countries were spending an identical percentage of GDP on education: 2.3 percent. What each did with this share differentiates the two countries.

Indonesia spent 90 percent of its education budget on primary education. By 1987, 91 percent of rural children were enrolled in primary school, compared to the national average of 92 percent. And the gender gap between boys and girls in primary education had virtually disappeared. Free education was extended through to the ninth grade.

By contrast, Bolivia spent only about 41 percent of its education budget on primary education, so only 60 percent of primary school-age children attended school on average. In the rural areas, only 45 percent of schools even offered education to the fifth grade, with the remainder providing only three years of primary education. With such low attention to primary education, the gender gap was larger than in Indonesia consequently, and drop-out rates and grade repeatings by girls were significantly higher than for boys. Worse, the textbook ratio was only one per 10 students, indicating weakness in the quality of education and problems in human capital deepening.

Indonesia's income per capita grew at a 4.2 percent annual rate, 1980–1993, while Bolivia's growth rate of per capita income was −0.7 percent per year. While not all of the variance in growth rates can be attributed to differences in the attention paid to creating essential human capital resources via funding universal primary schooling, what we know about the importance of primary education to future economic suggests that Indonesia's policies were paying off.

Source: World Bank 1993a: 201, Box 5.1

Population growth and human capital accumulation

In the first part of this chapter, we saw that the rate of population growth for the less-developed nations has tended to rise because of the incomplete nature of the demographic transition in many nations. Death rates have declined rapidly, but birth rates, due to slower changes in fertility rates, have fallen much more sluggishly. Though family planning programs have had some success in some nations, the primary determinants of declining fertility and lower birth rates have been rising family income and an expansion of women's education.

Population growth should thus be considered a *dependent* variable rather than an independent, exogenous factor subject to easy manipulation. It is not so much that rapid population growth causes low incomes as it is that low incomes and low education levels are more likely to engender high population growth rates through higher fertility rates.

This perspective, however, does not deny that rapid population growth can create problems for less-developed economies and typically these are greater in those which can least afford them. One of the consequences of a rapid natural rate of population growth over an extended period of time will be a reduction in the average age-profile of the population.[18]

The *dependency ratio* is a convenient, if imperfect, demographic measure that provides some idea of the impact of population growth and demographic changes on society. It indicates for each potentially employed worker, the number of non-employed workers that must be supported by that worker's production. In Somalia with a high and rising population growth rate, the dependency ratio rose (Table 12.6). This means there was a rising proportion of young people in the population so that those who were working had to produce enough not only for themselves but for a growing proportion of the population that was young and non-productive. On the other hand, in South Korea with a slowing rate of population growth between 1970 and 2000, the dependency ratio fell dramatically, so that rising output per employed person could go to increasing per capita output and not solely to be spread over a larger number of non-workers.

Table 12.6 also shows the commitment of governments to education as measured by the educational expenditures as a percentage of gross national production (or gross national income). The World Bank study on the HPAEs (World Bank 1993b: 194–196) found that in South Korea, Thailand, and Singapore the absolute number of school age children actually fell, while in Sub-Saharan Africa the numbers of those of school age rose as a consequence of a more rapid pace of population growth. Thus, the increase in spending on education as a share of GNP for South Korea shown in the table was applied to a smaller number of students, and this permitted a focus on improvements in the quality of education and in the quality of the human capital being created. The large decrease in the average student–teacher ratio in South Korea (Table 12.5) is another quality indicator of the gains that can be attained from lower population growth rates on the capacity of a nation to accumulate human capital and hence to be able to both grow faster and to reach a higher level of income per person.

Other countries, such as Zimbabwe, also spent more of their government budgets on education (the last column of Table 12.6), but these were expenditures necessitated, at least partly, to keep pace with the growth of the school-age population so

Table 12.6 Dependency ratios, population age profile, and public expenditure on education

	% of population of working age (15–64 years)		Dependency ratio[a]		Public expenditure on education (% of GNP)	
	1970	2000	1970	2000	1970	2000
Low-income economies	54.8	58.7	0.84	0.71	2.36	2.83
India	55.9	61.5	0.79	0.63	2.47	3.35
Pakistan	54.6	54.5	0.98	0.82	1.01	2.39
China	56.0	68.3	0.79	0.48	1.20	2.03
Zimbabwe	48.6	51.6	1.08	0.76	3.26	7.47
Somalia	51.5	49.6	0.94	1.01	1.05	n.a.
Middle-income economies	56.3	66.0	0.79	0.52	2.48	3.76
Côte d'Ivoire	51.9	54.8	0.93	0.85	4.70	4.54
Senegal	52.6	53.2	0.90	0.91	3.76	3.44
Jamaica	47.5	61.3	1.11	0.61	2.58	6.84
Argentina	63.7	62.6	0.57	0.60	1.35	3.20
South Korea	54.6	72.1	0.83	0.39	2.62	3.38
High-income economies	63.5	66.9	0.58	0.49	4.17	4.81
Ireland	57.7	67.1	0.74	0.49	4.01	5.49
United Kingdom	62.8	65.3	0.59	0.53	n.a.	4.69
United States	61.8	66.0	0.62	0.51	4.49	4.70
Japan	68.9	68.1	0.45	0.47	2.87	4.63
Less-developed regions						
Sub-Saharan Africa	52.3	52.6	0.91	0.89	3.43	4.73
East Asia and Pacific	55.3	66.8	0.81	0.50	1.63	2.47
South Asia	55.3	60.3	0.82	0.66	2.27	3.09
Middle East and North Africa	51.3	58.6	0.96	0.69	3.97	4.75
Latin America and the Caribbean	53.4	63.1	0.88	0.59	2.67	4.21

Source: World Bank 2002b.

Note
a Calculated as (population < age 15 + population > 64 years of age) ÷ (population aged 15–64).

as to maintain the extent of coverage of primary and secondary schooling, making any increase in enrollment ratios (Zimbabwe now has universal primary coverage, but less than 50 percent secondary coverage) more expensive than would have been the case with slower population growth. Faster population growth and having a large share of the population young skews the need for spending in the direction of education and other social services aimed at younger persons, for example health care, just to keep pace with population growth, leaving less for other development purposes. These trends, however, are being mitigated as population growth slows with declines in fertility rates, as discussed above.

Final observations

This chapter builds upon the theory of the structural transformation which has been our focus since Chapter 7. Economic and human development seem to be inextricably linked to the structural transformation of poorer nations from their agriculture-based productive patterns to industrial and service-based economies. However, this structural transformation is not just one of changing what is produced, but of fundamentally altering how production takes place. Endogenous growth theories have alerted us to the importance of augmenting the stock of human capital, especially through education formation, since higher levels of human capital are strongly associated with higher income per capita, with higher rates of economic growth, with progress on the human development indicators, and with greater equity via shared growth.

In this chapter we have examined some of the details of human capital accumulation, drawing attention to universal primary and secondary coverage and reducing both the education gender and urban–rural gaps if less-developed nations are to build the base for future growth and development. At low levels of income and development, university education expenditures should not consume too much of the state's education budget; 25 percent might be the maximum warranted amount, leaving the remainder for primary and secondary funding. This chapter also reinforces the positive role for the state in not only overcoming market failure given the positive externalities arising from increasing the average level of education, but also highlights the guiding function a developmentalist state can perform in shaping the formation of an economy's human capital stock.

In this vein, university education should not just be left to the whims of either academics or to the current demands of students. Rather, part of the guiding function of the state is to direct government funding for tertiary education and to shape incentives so that a critical mass of scientists, engineers, and technicians are trained so that over time the human capital stock is augmented so as to be able to take advantage of the rapidly changing technological innovations occurring at the world level of applied knowledge as will be discussed more fully in Chapter 13. With the proper incentive structure via scholarships, employment, and so on government can contribute to the formation of a dynamic labor force capable of adding to the economy's level of development over the long term.

Questions for review

1 Using a recent edition of the World Bank's *World Development Report* or using the World Bank website (www.worldbank.org), calculate the natural rate of population growth for two additional countries not shown in this chapter. Then compare these values with their actual rate of population growth and calculate the value of net migration for each country.

2 Crude death rates in Table 12.2 tend to have a smaller range than crude birth rates. However, Sub-Saharan African countries like Zimbabwe and Côte d'Ivoire, have somewhat higher crude death rates than other nations. What might account for these higher death rates?

3 Note 8 to this chapter, and the accompanying discussion in the text, submits that the link between per capita income and crude death rates is much weaker than the relation between per capita income and crude birth rates. A simple econometric exercise would be to test this statement in two separate regressions.

Regress using Excel or some other program a cross-section sample taken from the data in a recent edition of the World Bank's *World Development*

Report or the UN's *Human Development Report* or from data at either of their web sites (www.worldbank.org and www.undp.org) with crude death rates as the dependent variable and income per capita as the independent variable and, separately, regress crude birth rates on income per capita. a) What are the expected signs of the coefficients on income in each regression? b) Do the actual coefficients on income have the expected signs in your regressions? c) Are the coefficients on the income variable statistically significant? d) What is the interpretation of the value of the coefficient on income in each of the regressions? e) How "good" is income as an explainer of crude birth and crude death rates, at least according to the adjusted R^2 values you obtained? Alternatively, if you do not have access to a simple regression program, draw two scatter diagrams for the data and fit, by hand, the best straight line to the data.

4   Choose two less-developed nations from two separate regions of the world and, using data on fertility rates, per capita income level, infant and child mortality rates, and female education levels from a recent edition of the World Bank's *World Development Report* or the UN's *Human Development Report* (or from data at their websites) explain the evolution of each country's fertility rate. Does each follow the expected path of lower fertility with higher income per capita, higher growth of income per capita, lower infant and child mortality rates, and more education for women? Are the changes in fertility over time greater or smaller than you would have guessed from the evolution of income and education alone for the two countries you have selected? What non-economic factors might be at work in affecting fertility, causing it to fall more rapidly or more slowly, in the two countries you have chosen?

5   If you have studied consumer indifference curves, try the following analysis of a family's decision about choosing the "optimum" number of children which can help you to understand better why income and fertility are inversely related from a neoclassical economic perspective. Measure the "number of children" on the horizontal axis and "income" on the vertical axis. Draw in a few normally shaped, convex-to-the-origin indifference curve. The shapes of the curve indicates that income (a proxy for "all other goods") and children are substitutes for a family in providing satisfaction or utility. Draw in a "current income" budget line and find the "optimum" number of children, given that income level, by the tangency of that budget line and the highest attainable indifference curve. Now, let income increase, but at the same time let the "price" of children also increase (in terms of the opportunity cost of lost income for time spent in caring for children by women with greater opportunities for employment). Thus the new budget line will both shift out and be steeper than the original line, indicating an increase in the relative "price" of children compared to all other goods as income rises. Show that it is quite possible to find a new optimum number of children such that fewer children are desired as the cost of children increases, as it is likely to do in urban areas as the structural transformation toward industrialization proceeds and as women are better educated and have expanded opportunities beyond the home.

6   Differentiate between human capital broadening and human capital deepening. Is one more important than the other?

7   Choose one less-developed country and one developed country and draw curves for each of their CBRs and their CDRs for the past twenty years, or more if you

can find the data. In which phase of the demographic transition is each country? Explain.

8 What has been the annual rate of total factor productivity in Zambia if: GDP has been growing at 0.9 percent per year: its labor force has been increasing at the rate of 3.3 percent per year; its capital stock has been rising by 2.5 percent per year; and the share of output produced by labor is 65 percent and by capital is 35 percent? (See note 14 for help.)

9 "There is no population problem in less-developed countries. There is a development problem." Discuss and evaluate.

10 One of the side-benefits of expanding education can be a reduction in equity or, at least, no strong increase in inequality. Extending primary and secondary education to all residents of a country contributes to individual productivity and individual incomes and may be important in creating a regime for shared growth. Compare enrollment rates and income inequality for five less-developed nations (use the ratio of income of the top 20 percent of income earners to the bottom 20 percent of income earners, or the Gini coefficient, as the measure of inequality). Do countries with lower enrollment coverage for primary and secondary education have more or less inequality than economies with higher enrollment ratios? Are there any systematic differences among the countries you have selected? Why, or why not? What other factors might be at work which contribute to or detract from the possibility for shared growth?

Internet exercises

1 Choose a country that interests you and list a) the CBR, b) the CDR, and c) then calculate the natural rate of population growth for 2000 using the following site http://devdata.worldbank.org/hnpstats/files/Tab2_1.xls.

2 Using the natural population growth rate calculated above, calculate in years the doubling time of the total population.

3 Given the above information, has your country passed through the "demographic transition." Explain on what evidence you argue that your country has, or has not, completed this transition. Has you country passed through any part of the transition?

4 Now, for your country:

a find the fertility rate for 1970–1975 and 1995–2000. [The fertility data is available at http://hdr.undp.org/reports/global/2002/en/indicator/indicator.cfm?File =index_indicators.html; you will need to go down that page to Number 5 and then click on the last two items in that section].

b Does the fertility rate for your country follow the pattern of change for the fertility rate discussed in the text? Briefly explain how it does or does not follow the pattern (and, what is the pattern, i.e., what factors account for a change in fertility?).

c What is the relationship between a country's fertility rate and its CBR, i.e., which affects which?

d What is the Maternal Mortality Ratio, 1985–1999 [you can find this at http://hdr. undp.org/reports/global/2002/en/indicator/indicator.cfm?File=index_indicators. html]. What does the MMR mean? What is the ratio for the US? Japan?

5   For your country, a) find the ratio of pupils to teachers in primary and second-
     ary school for two years, if that is available. b) Has there been "human capital
     deepening" over that period? Explain what that means. [Go to http://portal.
     unesco.org/uis/ev.php?URL_ID=5187&URL_DO=DO_TOPIC&URL_SECT
     ION=201 and then click on pupil–teacher ratio near the middle of the page.]

Notes

1 Easterly (2001: ch. 4, especially, but throughout) takes a decidedly contrarian perspective
   on the role of education. A close reading of his essays suggest, however, that education is
   important, but in the right context, which is what this book has suggested throughout.
   There is no single panacea that guarantees successful development.
2 We say the "normal" relation is from income to population growth, but there actually are
   instances of more rapid population growth leading to a quicker increase in output and
   income, as in the United States in the early to mid-1800s, or in Australia later in that
   century. In both cases, high population growth rates resulting from large inflows of
   migrants contributed to, rather than subtracted from, the expansion of production. New
   migrants helped to fill a void in labor supply and contributed to an increase in total output
   beyond population growth.
3 We divide by 10 in equation 12.2, because both the CBR and the CDR are stated per 1,000
   population. When we divide by 10, these are converted to rates per 100 of population, thus
   permitting us to interpret the difference as a percentage. Crude birth and death rates
   depend upon the age distribution of the population, death rates for different age groups
   (including infant mortality rates), the fertility rate of women, and other demographic
   characteristics of the population. The adjective "crude" is used as "average" would be.
4 Rapid population growth is a very recent historical phenomenon. It has been estimated
   that in AD 1, world population was about 300 million. It took 1,500 years for population
   to double from that level, an annual rate of population growth of less than 0.05 percent.
   From 1750 to the early twentieth century, world population grew at a rate of about 0.5
   percent, increasing the doubling time of world population to less than 150 years. From
   1950–1987, world population doubled from 2.5 billion to 5 billion, as the doubling time
   further decreased as world population grew at a rate approaching 2 percent per annum
   (Birdsall 1988: 479).
5 The average rate of population growth in the less-developed nations was 0.6 percent from
   1850–1900, rising to 1.3 percent by the 1920s, 2.0 percent in the early 1950s and to 2.6
   percent in the early 1970s (Reynolds 1986: 50). It is quite easy to determine, in an approximate fashion, how fast population doubles at these rates of growth by using the Rule of
   70, which is

      doubling time (in years) = 70 ÷ annual percentage rate of change of population.

      Thus, if population is growing at 2 percent per annum, population will double in
   approximately thirty-five years; at 3 percent per annum, the doubling time is reduced to
   twenty-three and a third years.
6 Maddison (1982: 189, Table B6) reports the following CBRs for a few of the now-
   developed countries, illustrating their trend rate.

	1820	1900
France	31.7	21.3
Germany	39.9	35.6
Japan	–	32.4
United Kingdom	30.3	28.7
United States	55.2	32.3

7 This can happen when, as is the case of a population that has been growing rapidly, a
   large proportion of the population is relatively young compared to that which is elderly.

A nation's CDR is a weighted average of the death rates of different age groups, so with a younger population the average death rate can be quite low, even for a poor economy given the large number of young relative to old persons.

8 In 1992, the CBR varied between 54 per 1,000 of population in Uganda and 10, in various countries, while the CDR varied only between 25 per 1,000 of population in Guinea-Bissau and 5 in a number of high-income economies. Of course the CDR has some association to per capita income levels, with countries with lower per capita incomes tending to have higher per capita CDRs. However, the link between income and death rates is significantly weaker than the link between income and birth rates. Infant mortality rates are strongly inversely correlated with women's education, just as birth rates are (World Bank 1991: 49).

9 Turn back to Table 1.2. Do the countries with the highest level of GNP per capita have the lowest levels of fertility? Do those with the fastest rate of growth of income per capita since 1990 show the greatest decrease in fertility rates?

10 Birdsall (1988: 514) notes that the inverse relation between women's education and fertility rates is found only for more than four years of schooling. For 0–4 years of education, women's education, and fertility tend to be positively related.

11 When CDRs are high, high rates of fertility and high CBRs are quite functional for maintaining the survival of entire populations. In such circumstances, cultural, religious, social, ideological, and family values have tended to advocate high birth rates and women's role as caretaker for the family. The already-developed nations had a longer time period, in some cases a century and more, during which the demographic transition was taking place at a more measured pace, so their religious and cultural value systems, particularly concerning the reproductive role of women, were able to evolve more in line with the falling rate of mortality. The less-developed nations, particularly those newly independent since 1945, have had much less time for their social value systems to catch up with changing economic and structural conditions.

12 The same trend for fertility rates to decline is observed when, instead of using average income as an indicator, the level of human development is used. Countries with a low HDI value in 1992 had an average fertility rate of 5.1; those with medium HDI values had an average fertility rate of 3.0; and in those nations with a high HDI value, average fertility was 2.8 (UNDP 1994: 174–175, Table 23).

13 All family incomes could theoretically rise even with a worsening income distribution if those with higher incomes have a faster rate of growth in their incomes than those with lower incomes. We simply want to focus here on the direct link between family income and lower birth rates, abstracting from income distribution changes, although such changes would be important to know and to analyze as to their impact on fertility and birth rates.

14 Total factor productivity can be estimated by subtracting from the total growth of a nation's output the share of growth due to: a) increases in the quantity of physical capital and b) increases in the labor force, each weighted by their input share to total production. Any positive remainder can be interpreted as the increase in total factor productivity. In other words, TFP measures the synergistic effect of combining an economy's physical capital and its human capital, which results in productivity increases beyond the contribution of increases in the physical quantities of the individual inputs. For example, if the annual output growth of a country over some period was 2.5 percent; physical capital grew by 3 percent per year and K made up 30 percent of the inputs; and the labor force, which accounted for 70 percent of the input to aggregate production, grew by 2 percent per year; then, 2.5 percent $- (3$ percent $\times 0.3) - (2$ percent $\times 0.7) = 0.2$ percent, which would be the annual estimated rate of TFP.

Countries able to combine both new capital, which typically embodies new technological knowledge, and a growing and improving human capital stock, which is better able to make use of and unlock the technological knowledge incorporated in new capital, will be better equipped to move toward and keep pace with the world production possibilities "best practice" frontier and will tend to have the highest rates of TFP. The World Bank (1991: 42) opined that "the main additional element (in explaining the growth of TFP) is the quality of labor," that is, human capital accumulation.

15 In Chapter 13 we shall consider the importance of scientists and engineers to continuing the process of development to higher levels of income and human realization, and especially to the process of technological change. It is thus not just universal primary education that is important over the long term though primary education provides the base upon which further progress can be made.

16 The subsidy amount of mn is found by determining the vertical difference between the MSB and the MPB curves at the socially optimum level of education, E_S.

17 Students from high-income families are more likely to attend university than are students from low-income families, both because the out-of-pocket costs for low-income families are a higher proportion of their income, and because the opportunity cost of attending university or other post-secondary education compared to total income is larger. Thus when post-secondary, particularly university, education is funded via low tuition fees to all students regardless of need, it is higher-income students, who could afford to pay a larger proportion of the actual costs, who disproportionately benefit from such subsidies. That is why targeted subsidies, rather than blanket subsidies extended to all regardless of need, tend to be both more efficient for the goals designed and tend to contribute to greater equity in society.

18 Rapid population growth caused by immigration often is the consequence of positive economic forces that pull migrants from low-wage, low-opportunity countries toward higher-wage, higher-opportunity economies. In these cases, as in the large migratory flows from Europe to North America, Argentina, and Australia in the 1800s, migrants are older, often bringing needed skills and education formed elsewhere. They add to the labor force and human capital pool of the receiving nation and contribute immediately to increasing aggregate output. This is different from the situation discussed here where the growth of population is due to natural forces and not to migration flows.

References

Birdsall, Nancy. 1988. "Economic Approaches to Population Growth," in Hollis B. Chenery and T.N. Srinivasan (eds), *Handbook of Development Economics*. Amsterdam: North Holland Publishers.

Easterly, William. 2001. *The Elusive Quest for Growth: Economists' Adventures and Misadventures in the Tropics*. Cambridge, MA: MIT Press.

Maddison, Angus. 1982. *Phases of Capitalist Development*. Oxford: Oxford University Press.

Mincer, Jacob. 1958. "Investment in Human Capital and Personal Income Distribution," *Journal of Political Economy* 66: 281–302.

Schultz, T.W. 1960. "Capital Formation by Education," *Journal of Political Economy* 68: 511–583.

Sen, Amartya. 1990. "More Than 100 Million Women are Missing," *New York Review of Books* 37 (December 20): 61–66.

UNDP (United Nations Development Program). 1994. *Human Development Report 1994*. NY: Oxford University Press.

World Bank. 1983. *World Development Report 1983*. New York: Oxford University Press.

—— 1991. *World Development Report 1991*. New York: Oxford University Press.

—— 1993a. *World Development Report 1993*. New York: Oxford University Press.

—— 1993b. *The East Asian Miracle*. New York: Oxford University Press.

—— 1994. *World Development Report 1994*. New York: Oxford University Press.

—— 1995. *World Development Report 1995*. New York: Oxford University Press

—— 2002a. *World Development Report 2002*. Oxford: Oxford University Press.

—— 2002b. *World Development Indicators 2002*. Oxford: Oxford University Press.

13 Technology and development

After studying this chapter, you should understand:

- what "technology" is;
- the distinction between an "independent technology learning capacity" (ITLC) and an "independent technology creating capacity" (ITCC);
- the connection between specific forms of human capital accumulation, technological progress and the level of development;
- the role of facilitating and obstructing institutions in the spread of technology;
- the imbedded nature of technology in a particular society's institutions and organizational structure;
- the importance of appropriate state action in helping to provide the complementary inputs for capturing the benefits of "best practice" technological change;
- the need for a strategy of "technological autonomy" based upon domestic sources of financial capital, entrepreneurship and science to create a dynamic "national technology."

Introduction

The significance of technological change to economic growth and development has been verified again and again in empirical studies. The endogenous growth theories considered in Chapter 8 and in the World Bank study (1993) of the East Asian economies confirmed these results. Even the research based on neoclassical growth models has found that the basic factors of production, capital, and labor, cannot explain all of economic growth. It is often the "residual," that is, the unidentified variables which contribute to increased productivity, including technology, organization, and institutional structures, which carry the weight of "explaining" economic growth over time and the differences among countries. In this chapter, we consider in more detail what is meant by technology, what preconditions are required if a country is to make effective use of technology as the structural transformation process proceeds forward, and what countries need to do to take better advantage of the ever-expanding world pool of technological opportunities.

What is technology?

Technology is knowledge applied to the production process. It permits an outward shift of a nation's production possibilities frontier (PPF) and creates the *potential* for greater output and income from the same resources. Technological progress reduces costs, increases productive efficiency, conserves on society's (and the world's) resources, and establishes the capacity for a higher standard of living for greater numbers of persons. It is primarily through technological advances that humankind has been able to progress to the extent that it has since the Industrial Revolution. Without technological progress, the spectre of hunger and deprivation that Malthus expected actually would have come to pass, as the law of diminishing returns worked its inexorable logic on fixed resources with unchanging productivity. However, by shifting the production possibilities curve outward and the aggregate production function upward, the static effect of diminishing returns has been overcome by technological progress that improves the productivity of all the factors of production. Thus the upward trend line of income per capita shown in Figure 3.1 following the Industrial Revolution was the consequence of the ever more intensive application of technology to production.

Nonetheless, technology is a difficult concept to define. This is because it is not any particular object, but rather is a *way of doing things and a way of thinking.* Technology involves not only the entire accumulated complex of scientific and machine-tool knowledge and the tools themselves which exist at the world level, but it also incorporates the *country-specific* human understanding, skills, education, and training essential for making use of such knowledge and tools. As Evenson and Westphal (1995: 2213) describe technology, it is

> tacit, not feasibly embodied and neither codifiable nor readily transferable. Thus, though two producers in the same circumstances may use identical material inputs in conjunction with equal information, they may nonetheless employ what are really two distinct techniques owing to differences in understanding of the tacit elements [of that technology].

Technology is *specific* to each country. The same physical manifestations of technology, such as a computer or a lathe, can have quite *different* effects on production and productivity since these must be combined with specific labor forces with specific skills, operating within a larger institutional and organization framework.

The more rapid technology is able to be adapted and put to work in an economy, the more rapid will be the pace of economic growth, but this requires that workers and entrepreneurs in a country have hands-on experience using such ideas in the act of producing. Slower technological progress means, *ceteris paribus,* slower economic growth and reduced possibilities for augmenting or creating the social mechanisms that promote greater equity and the higher level of human development that technological progress makes feasible.

What has not been well understood in thinking about technology is how some of society's social and economic institutions – including the existing class structure, land tenure relations, institutions for finance and banking, ideology, religion and superstition, the commitment of society to education and free inquiry, the openness of the state to change and to shared development, and the nature of the ties between industry and the scientific and educational infrastructure – are paramount forces in *determining* to what extent technology is able to perform its dynamic and transformative functions.[1] Many of the above are *Ayresian-type ceremonial institutions* (see Chapter 6). They tend to engender tradition-bound modes of behavior that operate on other than scientific principles. It is inconceivable, however, to have any socio-economic system where there are not some such ceremonial institutions, structures which are past-binding and status quo-oriented.

Nonetheless, in nations where the ceremonial structure is relatively weak, facilitating and complementary to change, or can be made so by appropriate state policies, technological knowledge has a better chance of being combined in the production process to contribute to greater productivity and to higher levels of output. On the other hand, in societies where the ceremonial institutional structure is retrograde, especially powerful and non-facilitating of change, and where the state does not act to *debilitate* these structures and ways of thinking, technology is less apt to be created or applied to production.

The importance of technology, and particularly the stock of human resources, have been widely identified as contributors to economic growth beginning with the empirical work of Edward Denison (1967: 299, 315), being responsible for over 40 percent of growth in the US and the UK over the period studied. Simon Kuznets' work (1966) also identified the significance of technological change, broadly interpreted, to productivity and economic growth. Solow (1988: 314) noted that perhaps over 90 percent of the increases in output can be accounted for by the combined forces of technology and education.

The magnitude of this effect should not be too surprising. In Chapter 8, we looked at how endogenous growth models have identified the importance of both technology and of human capital as fundamental *complementary inputs* affecting the rate of economic growth and the level of per capita income. The endogenous growth theories also showed how the ability to apply technological knowledge varies dramatically among economies, so that the convergence of income among economies does not take place in the simple fashion suggested by the neoclassical growth model. This way of looking at technology as something requiring social investment in specific human and organization inputs if it is to be utilized to its full effect, recognizes that there can be *technology gaps* among economies and that each economy develops its own relatively unique technological base. Technology is specific knowledge, not general knowledge which can be applied everywhere in the same way. Each country must make a substantial investment in its social and human resource capital base if it is to gain the capacity to do technology.

Prior to these recent theoretical contributions, many economists and economic models had envisaged technology as if it were an exogenous public good available to every economy, as in the Solow-type, neoclassical formulation, rather than understanding *technology as a process, as knowledge-in-practice*.[2] Technology is not something that just happens to economies, like some *dues ex machina*. It is a process that countries need to consciously and actively promote and nurture if the potential benefits of technological knowledge are to be effectively achieved. To an important extent, the current level of technology-in-use in any specific economy is *path dependent*, that is, it depends crucially on past decisions that affect current outcomes, though this lock-in on path dependency is never absolutely binding. Countries can do something about *adverse* path dependency in their use of technology by investing in the complementary inputs, particularly education and research and development (R&D), that contribute over time to each country's specific capability to effectively make use of technological knowledge. It is precisely these areas of social investment that can spell the difference between successful and less-successful development over time; they are the necessary preconditions for future progress.

A technological strategy of development

In a significant sense, then, it can be said that economic development is indistinguishable from the ongoing application of technological knowledge to production.[3] Without continuing technological change, economic growth slows and eventually development falters. In their comprehensive overview of technology, Evenson and Westphal (1995: 2216) quite unequivocally state that "[n]o LDC has to date achieved rapid economic growth without continued technological investment."

Technological change is the result of scientific discovery, experiment and innovation, all of which must be financed either by the private sector or the state. The successful introduction of technology into the domestic production process in any country, what can be called *domestic innovation*, requires a domestic scientific establishment capable, first, of understanding, processing, adopting, and adapting foreign-produced technological knowledge, including machines and tools, to local conditions and, later, of conducting its own research, designing its own experiments, and recognizing the potential and, sometimes, dangers of its own discoveries when applied to the domestic economy.

Ronald Dore (1984: 65–68) refers to these two distinct proficiencies as, respectively, an **ITLC** and an ITCC: an "independent technology *learning* capacity" and an "independent technology *creating* capacity." An ITLC might also be called, interchangeably, *technological autonomy*. Creating an ITLC and achieving technological autonomy is the first step toward greater self-sufficiency, a higher level of domestic efficiency and the creation of an internal dynamic for any economy. It is an ITLC that undergirded the Japanese, Korean, and Taiwanese development successes. The easy import substitution and easy export substitution phases of industrialization in those countries provided the creative space for domestic entrepreneurs and workers to be able to attain a higher level of skills that permitted them to become technologically competent. It is this learning capacity which permitted the East Asian economies to grow faster, on average, than other less-developed countries which apparently shared roughly the same initial endowments, such as the level of investment. Looking back at Table 8.4, with the exception of Singapore (which is a service-intensive economy), the East Asian economies did better at keeping pace or catching-up with international "best practice" technology than did nations in Africa or Latin America.

The ability to *create* technology and to add to the world pool of knowledge and practice, that is, for a country to have an ITCC, comes later with the further maturation and *deepening* of the ITLC process which preceded it. An ITCC is most likely to appear if sufficient resources are devoted to R&D and as countries complete secondary ISI and secondary export substitution and move into the knowledge-intensive phase of structural transformation (see Figure 10.1). An ITLC is *essential* to sustaining high rates of economic growth and to make progress on the path to fuller development. An ITCC may be necessary to continue this process over the longer term, after the gains from the ITLC strategy become more difficult to sustain and after a country has learned to be as efficient as world-level best practice techniques.[4] It is an ITCC that first Great Britain and then the US created and which contributed to their phenomenal progress over long periods, while each was the leading force for the creation of new technological standards and knowledge for the world.

Recent empirical studies of endogenous growth have found that a nation's research and development (R&D) expenditures are significant in explaining sustained growth rates over time. Other research has suggested that within the overall goal of increasing the stock of human capital, scientists and engineers (S&E) are an important sub-category of human capital which should be emphasized to better appropriate the benefits of technology. There is now little doubt that both R&D and S&E contribute to the creation of specific national technologies and to the learning required to be able to utilize technological knowledge effectively. Table 13.1 provides data on the number of scientists and indirect evidence on the R&D measure.

The story the table tells seems quite unambiguous. Countries at higher levels of development, here measured by the human development index (HDI), not only tend to have larger numbers of scientists and technicians in general, but they also have a significantly greater number of scientists and technicians directly involved in R&D activities with close links to the production process than do countries with lower HDI values.

Table 13.1 Scientists and engineers

	Scientists and technicians (per 1,000 pop.) 1986–1991	R&D scientists and technicians (per 1,000 pop.) 1990–2000
High Human Development (HDI > 0.75)	50.7	3.0
South Korea	45.9	2.2
Argentina	28.4	0.7
Chile	–	0.4
Singapore	22.9	2.2
Medium Human Development (0.50 < HDI < 0.75)	15.4	0.6
Mexico	–	0.2
Turkey	26.3	0.3
Sri Lanka	–	0.2
India	3.5	0.2
Low Human Development (HDI < 0.50)	1.7	–
Pakistan	4.0	0.1
Nigeria	1.0	0.02
Guinea	–	–
All Developing Countries	8.8	–
Industrial Countries (OECD)	84.9	3.4
Japan	110	4.9
US	55	4.1

Sources: UNDP 1994: 138–139, Table 5; 2002: Table 11.

South Korea's attention to R&D scientists is especially noteworthy among the less-developed countries, though all the less-developed countries have a stock of scientists that still falls well short of what has been achieved, on average, in the already developed countries. The relatively large number of scientists and technicians in Japan, even relative to the industrial country average, is suggestive of one of the reasons why Japan was so successful at catching up with the older developed nations.

While the rate of economic growth and technological change *are* path dependent in the sense of being the consequence of *past decisions* on the economic strategy, on expenditures for human capital purposes, on the exchange rate and inflation rate, and so on, modifications of the path are always possible when a country decides to make a change. What can be inferred from the South Korean and Japanese experiences is that, though the current rate of economic and human development may be path dependent, the future path has multiple branches at any moment in time.

The decisions the state private sector makes on expenditures for education, health, the military, on tariffs, on tax laws, on patents and other intellectual property rights, on the treatment of multinational corporations, and on a whole range of other factors today will determine along which path the economy and society will traverse in future. Private firms, individuals, and the state make decisions within the confines of the parameters for economic decision-making determined by the state and within the cultural and historical confines of each specific society. They *choose* the paths now via spending and other decision which affect future growth and development prospect's and the future path dependency of the economy.

While Table 13.1 does not prove causality, the endogenous growth models and research work by other scholars (see Grossman and Helpman 1994) do find that there is a *serendipitous effect*, what we would call a positive externality, associated with a larger number of scientists engaged in R&D activities who are then able to interact with others also possessing a high level of skill and knowledge. R&D scientists and technicians are one specific category of human capital which seems to be unambiguously associated with a positive pay-off for growth, all else the same.[5]

Table 13.2 provides more direct evidence on the relation between the level of technological capability and other key indicators. The 75 less-developed countries with Level 1 technological capacity have, at most, some industrial research capacity in the public sector, but not in the private sector where production takes place. In agriculture, the capacity for doing technology ranges from nil to relatively advanced.[6] There are only 20 less-developed countries with Level 2 technological capacity (all the East Asian economies were at this level), which means they have at least a basic technological capacity in key sectors of their economies.

It is clear from the first and second lines of Table 13.2, and even clearer from data that is even more finely disaggregated (see Evenson and Westphal 1995), that the level of technological capability was positively correlated with the pace of economic expansion over the period 1965–1990. For Level 2 less-developed countries, the rate of growth of aggregate GDP was higher than for the Organization of Economic Cooperation and Development (OECD) industrialized economies and was at least double the pace of growth for Level 1 countries.

The level of R&D as a share of GDP, of science expenditures as a percentage of GDP and of the availability of S&E compared to GDP clearly show the importance of these indicators for Level 2 countries compared to Level 1 economies. However,

Table 13.2 Technological capability and development capacity

	Level 1 LDCs	Level 2 LDCs	OECD DCs
Real GDP growth (1965–1990)			
Per capita	0.5–1.5	2.4–7.1	2.5
Total	2.5–2.8	4.7–8.1	3.5
R&D/GDP (1990)			
Public	0.2–0.3	0.4–0.6	0.7
Private	0.0–0.02	0.05–1.0	2.3
Science/GDP (1990)			
Public	0.02–0.03	0.04–0.10	0.40
Private	0.0	0.0	0.05
S&E/GDP	0.2–0.4	0.6–1.3	1.0
IPR (index)	0–1	2–4	5

Source: Adapted from Evenson and Westphal 1995: 2242–2243, Table 37.1.

Note
Level 1 less-developed countries have "traditional technology" to some "islands of modernization"; *Level 2* developing countries have technology ranging from "mastery of conventional technology" to newly-industrialized countries. *R&D/GDP* is the percentage of gross domestic product spent on research and development. *Science/GDP* is the percentage of gross domestic product spent on science. *S&E/GDP* is the availability of scientists and engineers relative to gross domestic product. *IPR* is an index measuring the strength of intellectual property rights; it ranges from 0 (no IPRs) to 5 (complete IPRs).

the share of GDP devoted to R&D in the private sector, even in the Level 2 countries, lags far behind what is spent in the OECD developed economies, suggesting that there remains a gap in technological effort and capability between even the highest tier less-developed countries, such as South Korea, and the developed economies. There is still space for improvement in these countries, as well.

The last line of Table 13.2 gives some notion of the institutional, including legal, support provided to R&D endeavors in terms of legal protection for intellectual property rights (IPRs), such as patents and copyrights. Most Level 1 countries have no patent protection for domestic IPRs and provide virtually no protection for foreign IPRs. In Level 2 countries, there are laws providing intermediate protection for foreign IPRs, but IPRs in the domestic economy remain weakly defined, except for the four East Asian economies. Protection of domestic intellectual property rights is particularly important as economies become more adept at adapting foreign knowledge to the domestic sphere.

Lacking such protection, private firms and private inventors may be hesitant to spend money to develop or introduce new ideas for fear of theft of their ideas. But more importantly, a well-developed legal apparatus which affords IPRs proper and needed protection is a signal that an economy recognizes the significance of technology and the application of new knowledge in the process of production. Laws concerning IPRs are complementary to efforts to build a technological capacity in other areas, and they reflect the attention to organization and institution-building characteristics of economies forging new paths toward a higher level of development. Thus the legal structure of economies must keep pace with efforts to augment other endowments for development, such as human capital resources.

Total factor productivity and national technology

Economists often assess the impact of various inputs to production on economic growth using a *growth accounting* methodology. Basically, this is an attempt to measure how much of any increase in output can be accounted for by additional units of physical capital (K) and additional labor (L) added to production (see Chapter 12, note for a representative calculation). Any economic growth left unaccounted for by increases in the quantity of the physical inputs is called *total factor productivity*, or TFP.[7]

TFP basically captures the impact of all the factors that contribute to the greater productivity of the inputs, K and L (or any broader definition of inputs used). Included in the TFP measure are: technological change and technological catch-up; improvements in the efficiency and learning capacity of the labor force due to human capital accumulation; the positive productivity effects of the structural transformation from agriculture to industry and other strategy switches; changes in state policy that contribute to greater efficiency, such as lower inflation rates or an improved tax structure; organizational and institutional alterations, such as better management practices and improved financial control mechanisms in the banking system, and so on. In a general sense, all of the variables which affect total factor productivity are related to an economy's acquisition of an ITLC and a national technological capacity to do technology and to be more effective users of resources.

Table 13.3 provides data on TFP estimates made by the World Bank. Part I shows annual rates of GDP growth, annual changes in the physical capital and labor inputs, and the resulting estimates of total factor productivity change over the period 1960–1987. Among the less-developed regions, East Asia's TFP growth rates were the highest, as one might expect from the larger number of scientists and the

Table 13.3 TFP estimates, 1960–1987 (percentages)

	GDP	Capital	Labor	TFP
Part I: Annual percentage changes				
Africa	3.3	6.3	2.2	0.0
East Asia	6.8	10.2	2.6	1.9
Latin America	3.6	6.3	2.6	0.0
South Asia	4.4	7.7	2.1	0.6
68 less-developed countries	4.2	7.2	2.3	0.6
Germany	3.9	4.8	−0.2	1.7
UK	2.4	3.1	−0.2	1.2
US	3.0	3.4	1.8	0.5
Part II: Total percentage of output growth due to changes in K, L *and TFP*				
Africa		73	28	0
East Asia		57	16	28
Latin America		67	30	0
South Asia		67	20	14
68 less-developed countries		65	23	14
Germany		23	−10	87
UK		27	−5	78
US		23	27	50

Source: World Bank 1991: 43, Table 2.2, 45, Table 2.3.

attention to R&D shown in Table 13.1. It will also be noticed that East Asia's rate of capital accumulation was more rapid than in any other region, and additions to the labor force were as high or higher than any other area.

All of these factors combined to give East Asia the highest rate of GDP growth among the regions and relative to the industrial economies listed. Faster physical capital accumulation, particularly to the extent that it embodied new knowledge, increased the pace of growth (see Focus 13.1 on the Salter Effect). A higher growth rate of labor, the quality of which was increasing over time, also contributed to the region's faster rate of growth. And all of the institutional, organizational, and policy decisions made by the state and the private sector contributed, on balance, to positive improvements in the efficiency with which the K and L inputs to production were utilized, hence the relatively large increase in TFP. In turn, TFP growth is strongly positively associated with rates of economic growth.

In Africa and Latin America, by comparison, *all* the growth in output was the result of simply adding more physical capital and labor to production. The lack of

---

FOCUS 13.1   THE SALTER EFFECT: THE IMPORTANCE OF PHYSICAL CAPITAL INVESTMENT

Acquiring an ITLC is not solely achieved via better education and augmentation of the human capital stock, though these are necessary. Knowing how to do technology requires experience gained primarily by actually producing. Best practice technological skills can only be acquired by using the most advanced manifestations of technology and of the ideas associated with them in production. This is the essence of learning-by-doing.

A significant proportion of new technological knowledge is *embedded* in the design of new physical capital equipment, such as computer-controlled arc welding devices or computer networks. Thus, the speed with which new capital replaces old capital will, to some extent, affect the pace at which best practice technological learning is integrated into local practice by becoming appropriated knowledge possessed by local human capital and entrepreneurs. This is another reason why export substitution strategies can contribute to more rapid economic growth. The faster the tempo of economic growth due to an expansion of manufactured exports and domestic production to accommodate such exports, the more new investment that will be required. Hence, to the extent that a more rapid pace of investment leads to the more rapid introduction of new physical capital embodying the latest technological knowledge, exporting contributes to the domestic learning process.

On the other hand, slow-growing economies, such as those who have not graduated from easy import substitution to begin to export manufactured goods to the international market, do not introduce as rapidly new capital with the latest embodied knowledge. Hence the speed at which technological knowledge is learned will be slower since any learning-by-doing effects in production will lag best practice technological knowledge.

The "**Salter Effect**" is the term applied to the speed at which new technological knowledge, embodied in new physical capital, is likely to be appropriated with economic growth. The faster the rate of economic expansion, the more rapid can be the rate of technological acquisition and hence future growth. The slower the pace of growth and investment, the slower the pace of technological learning and future growth. Thus exporting manufactured goods via an export substitution strategy, assuming the requisite human capital inputs have been created, can create a virtuous circle of technology learning, leading to altered path dependence.

Source: Salter 1969

complementary productivity-enhancing change, as registered by a zero TFP, is disconcerting. It points to the need for countries in Latin America and Africa to undertake the policies required to improve their human capital resources and to stimulate a higher level R&D if they are to move their economies and societies along a path of structural transformation which can more fully provide the opportunity for a higher level of human development. Both regions would clearly appear to need more coherent policies that can contribute to national technological learning that can permit the use of the world pool of knowledge more effectively.[8]

Part II of Table 13.3 reinforces this interpretation. None of Latin America's or Africa's growth rates was due to improvements in the efficiency with which the inputs were combined. In East Asia, 29 percent of the growth in output was the result of TFP growth. In South Asia, TFP contributed 14 percent to total output expansion. However, even for East Asia, though TFP *growth rates* are similar to those in the industrialized countries listed in Part I, the contribution of TFP to the region's growth was half or less than the contribution of TFP in the industrialized countries to total growth.

These data suggest that all of the less-developed regions continue to experience a technology gap relative to the more developed countries. There remains room for all less-developed countries to improve upon their national technological capacity. That this gap remains should not be too surprising. About 90 percent of all the world's technological R&D is done by the already developed nations, where most of the ITCC capability (the know-why) currently exists. Until that balance shifts, there will remain opportunities for increased R&D and human capital augmentation in the less-developed countries to build and consolidate their technology learning capacities, and thus the possibility of even more rapid growth is at least within the realm of possibility. It is this catch-up gap which Gerschenkron (1962) believed would permit late-developers to advance rapidly. This, however, is only true if those economies make the required investments in their initial endowments – basically, the training of labor and the proper incentives for individuals to be able to succeed – which results in more technologically sophisticated *augmented endowments*, which become the future's new initial endowments (Easterly 2001). Building a technological capacity, and the necessary human capital investment this requires, is about altering the nature of path dependency.

Technology-centered development versus capital-centered development

To capture the full benefits of the world pool of knowledge requires the utilization of best practice production techniques. If technology is viewed not as an exogenous given or as a public good freely available to all but as an *endogenous process* to some extent dependent on indigenous factors specific to each economy, then education and the improvement of human skills in general and the creation of a core R&D cadre must become an essential basis of any development strategy aimed at structural transformation. Ideally, efforts along this path should begin in the earliest stages of industrialization, beginning with easy ISI, so as to continually add to the stock of human resources and to the skills of entrepreneurs who can learn in the process of producing. This is why we do not take the strong view that easy ISI failed or that other countries should not do import substitution in future. Properly designed, as discussed in Chapter 9, import substitution industrialization is a vital training ground for creating technological competency, with its potential long-run positive external effects.

> Far more important [than physical capital to economic growth] in retrospect are the economic and social characteristics that reside in the capacities and skills of an economy's population, determine the efficiency of the institutions that direct the use of accumulated physical capital, and guide the current production into proper channels of consumption and capital investment.
>
> (Kuznets 1968: 272)

Technology exists as an intangible and accumulating body of knowledge *at the world level* capable of being utilized by any given country only *to the degree* it has developed a technologically sophisticated community, that is, an ITLC, which can use and adapt the existing pool of knowledge to employ the implements of production to further its own economic progress. It is thus not possible for countries to effectively borrow the *manifestations of technology*, such as physical capital, tools and implements which are so often the focus of the technology transfer literature, and expect to become developed if the human skills, culture, and institutions required to make effective use of this fragment of technology are absent or but poorly formed within the borrowing country. As one study put it, people, not tools, "are the real agents of technology transfer and diffusion" (Radhakrishna 1980: 170).

A technologically sophisticated community is composed not only of knowledge workers, like scientists, engineers, and researchers, but also of skilled workers on the shop floor who can utilize new ideas in the ways they are meant to be utilized, perhaps even improving upon them for use in their specific, local application. Just as importantly, there must exist or be created an *indigenous entrepreneurial nucleus* of determined agents capable of appreciating the potential of new ways of producing who are able and willing to make use of technology through constant innovation in the domestic production process.

The activities of the entrepreneurial nucleus will be concentrated predominantly in the private sector, but in some economies the state may be obliged to act as a collective entrepreneur to complement or substitute for missing private entrepreneurs. It is here especially that the state's macroeconomic policies, discussed in Chapter 15, can be either inhibitory or contributory to rapid development through their effects on human capital formation, on R&D and on the decisions made by the private sector to invest in creating the capacity to innovate. The state may also be involved in the actual production process in some countries via *parastatals*, which are publicly-owned enterprises, in key industries where "backward linkages" or positive externalities to the private sector are expected to be substantial. Parastatals in the steel industry in Brazil and Mexico are examples of state firms that generated positive externalities, as were South Korea's, Taiwan's, and Chile's publicly-owned banking systems (see Focus 13.2).

Technological diffusion via TNCs

Until quite recently, it was a common dogma that *technological diffusion* from the more developed nations to the less-developed economies could help poorer

FOCUS 13.2   TRANSACTIONS COSTS, THE STATE, AND TECHNOLOGICAL ACQUISITION

Gerschenkron's (1962) historical study and those of East Asian scholars, like Amsden (1989) and Wade (1990) on South Korea and Taiwan, found that developmentalist states were able to effectively contribute to the pace of technological acquisition and, hence, the level and rate of economic growth over time. Utilizing the concept of **transactions costs**, New Institutionalist Economics (NIE) analysis, building on the work of Nobel economist Douglass North, have argued that centralized state intervention was, in those instances, a lower cost means for achieving an ITLC than a market-based approach would have been.

It appears that when both effective and actual political power is concentrated within a developmentalist state bent on achieving economic growth, rapid progress is possible. If however, as in Pakistan in the 1960s, the political power does not reside in the state, no matter how strong or centralized it may seem, but rather actually belongs to powerful private classes in agriculture and trade with no interest in fundamental change, the state's ability to contribute to technological acquisition will be compromised. In Pakistan, the higher transactions costs of coordinating decisions and of searching for compromises, kept technological acquisition from being an attainable goal.

While research in the transactions cost vein applied to development is quite new, it does highlight the importance of specific institutional structures, of power groups and classes, and of a number of supra-market considerations which can and do impinge upon economic development via their impact on technological acquisition.

Source: Harriss *et al.* 1995: especially chs. 1, 2, 4, and 5

countries skip over stages of domestic technological development. In this way, they would be permitted to enter directly into the intensive stage of technology utilization without needing to "reinvent the wheel." It was believed that such diffusion could materially contribute to a more rapid narrowing of the income gap between the center and periphery. Many countries have attempted to follow this diffusion path by hosting within their economies transnational corporations (TNCs), the major source for cutting-edge knowledge, and yet they still have failed to become more developed and their rates of economic growth and development have lagged other economies which have not followed this strategy.

The failure of countries to become more developed by depending upon technological diffusion from the TNCs is not the result of any generalized conspiratorial plot by TNCs to keep the less-developed countries backward, as some commentators have argued. The problem is that many less-developed economies to which TNCs have brought, sold, or licensed technology have yet to create the requisite initial domestic technological culture and the domestic capacity for technological autonomy that would permit them to *capture* the benefits of tool and machine diffusion through learning and spread effects at the point of production. If technological borrowing were truly possible, the domestic environment of an economy and the idea of national technologies would be significantly less important, if not wholly irrelevant, for understanding the process of development. In that case the issue of how to develop would dissolve to one of increasing physical capital accumulation and technology transfers via foreign direct investment and other mechanisms, characteristic of the developmentalist foreign aid approach and the neoclassical economic growth models.

Albert Hirschman long ago warned of the inherent dangers of pursuing technological borrowing as the path to technological autonomy, particularly when technological knowledge is mediated by transnational corporate direct investment, as so
much of it has been in some countries. This has been a major issue in Latin
America, where the large-scale promotion of TNC investment was fundamental to
the (premature) introduction of the secondary ISI strategy (Chapter 10). Hirschman
cautioned that attempting to acquire technology through direct foreign investment
may do more to "harm the quality of local factors of production" than to act as a
spur to the expansion of the missing local inputs, such as innovating entrepreneurs
and skilled workers which such investment might be hoped to encourage
(Hirschman 1971: 227–229).

Rather than serving as a *complement* to local technological development and as a
boost to locally-controlled and locally-directed production and to the establishment
of a dynamic national technology, foreign inputs can become *substitutes* for the local
factors of production and for the building of a domestic technological capacity. This
is especially likely to occur in those countries where the necessary components of a
technological autonomy strategy have not been implemented, and particularly
where general education levels and technical education levels are low. The overwhelming influence and knowledge of the TNCs in such conditions is likely to
further stunt the development of the institutions and individuals capable of, and
necessary for, learning from the tool and machine implements of technology
developed and used by TNCs.

This factor substitution or **factor displacement and factor atrophy effect** is not
caused by the TNCs so much as it is permitted and even desired by some elements
of the local ruling elites in many less-developed countries who often are uninterested in seeing technological autonomy achieved in their countries.

> The dominant classes know that technological development cannot be intro-
> duced merely as an isolated input to production; but is part of a global process,
> which once started is very difficult to stop, and which endangers the stability of
> the social structure on which their privileges are based.
>
> (Herrera 1973: 35)

As Herrera (1973: 33) argued, then, it is not actually an absence of policies
toward science and technology and human capital creation in those areas which
characterizes most countries and which shows up in the small number of R&D scientists in Table 13.1 in many of the less-developed economies. Rather, it is the existence of an "implicit science policy" that is *hostile* to broader, uncontrolled
applications of science and technology that is the source of the imbalance. It is this
antagonistic attitude toward science and technology which inclines at least a
segment of the dominant classes in many less-developed countries toward technological dependency, precisely because more rapid economic and social change might
threaten the existing class structure. The position and privileges of the elite often
thrive on maintaining the prevailing configuration of inequality (for example,
powerful agricultural interests who view the structural transformation as a threat to
their wealth base).

External interests such as the TNCs, certainly have a stake in preserving control
over their own technological knowledge, which is expensive to produce. It is not

correct, however, to argue that technological dependency can be blamed exclusively or even primarily upon the TNCs or any other outside force. *Technological dependency and the absence of genuine efforts aimed at creating technological autonomy is something that the policies of a country create and perpetuate.* It is in the interests of a narrow, albeit powerful, elite and against the interests of the majority who lack access to power and to the state where overall development policy is made and where the spending priorities of the state are executed.

What is hopeful for change is that technological dependency is not in the interests of all members of the dominant elite. Many emerging industrialists in the infant ISI sector may be favorably predisposed toward a policy of technological autonomy and an ITLC. They increasingly require such technological knowledge if they aspire to be competitive on the world market as trade barriers are reduced. Where the influence of this modernizing fragment of the elite has been strong and growing, as it has been in Brazil and some other less-developed nations where the state had not already embarked independently on a path to technological autonomy, the changeover in state policies toward technology-creating institutions has been remarkable (Adler 1987).

Vigorous state promotion of technological progress, from education, to science policy and research, to support for R&D, to favorable treatment in the production process of local science and technology efforts *is essential* to the success of the pursuit of technological autonomy. Technological progress has substantial public goods characteristics, accompanied by significant positive externalities over the longer term, and the recurring problem of market and institutional failure obliges the state to take action to avoid clearly sub-optimal outcomes (Adler 1988). Until the state decides or is forced to decide to embark on the path of human capital creation and a better macroeconomic policy environment conducive to improving the national technological *learning* capacity, the pace of economic growth and development will be kept below its potential, regardless of the stage of structural transformation of the country and regardless of the orientation of economic policy, inward or outward.

Industrial innovation

Grossman and Helpman (1994: 24) have referred to "industrial innovation as the engine of growth" for the creation of a national technological capacity. Research and development is a purposive activity. It is one in which private firms will engage if they are: (a) encouraged to do so, for example by tax policies that treat R&D expenditures as tax credits or extend some other favorable treatment for such investments; (b) if they are compelled to so invest to be more competitive, for example, as a result of the opening of the economy to foreign competition over time with reduced infant tariff barriers, or when technological competency is necessary to increase a firm's exports as a condition of receiving loans or other rewards in contests for scarce state or private resources (as discussed in Chapter 10); or (c) if expected firm monopoly profits are predicted to cover such research and development costs *ex ante*.

To illustrate how the development of technology can be understood as part of an industrial innovation process, and one that requires continual investment and nurturing, rather than as a thing that can be appropriated easily or costlessly from other countries or firms, consider Grossman and Helpman's (1991) concept of a "quality ladder" faced by a firm. Each input to production has its own potentiality for improved productivity, or its own quality ladder, which is virtually unlimited. What firms do by engaging in R&D is to search for ways to move up the quality ladder for one or more of its inputs. When such investments, which are by their very nature uncertain, yield results, the discovering firm thus gains at least short-term economic (monopoly) profits over its rivals who have not discovered how to move up the technological track to higher productivity, lower cost production methods of production with that input, or at least not in the same way. And this is where the importance of the size of the stock of human capital, particularly of R&D human capital workers, becomes most important. Profit-maximizing firms, or cost-minimizing enterprises with target levels of output, will have an incentive to search for such input quality improvements by investing in new R&D, assuming that expected monopoly profits can be earned. As new industries emerge, firms will form research and development centers (assuming a modicum of competition *and* the availability of a critical mass of R&D scientists and technicians capable of adapting available knowledge to the domestic production process and the ability to appropriate any gains as at least short term above normal profits.

> [A]n increase in the magnitude of the typical quality improvement attracts additional resources into R&D. Then the growth rate [of the economy] accelerates, not only because the quality steps are larger, but also because advances come more rapidly.
>
> (Grossman and Helpman 1994: 34)

These are the positive externalities to R&D which begin to accrue beyond some critical threshold of R&D expenditure and given appropriate previous human capital accumulation. More innovations become possible and more technological innovation, including greater technical efficiency change and higher rates of TFP, will be the result of passing this threshold. But that critical threshold must be in place before such gains can begin to be appropriated.

Interestingly and importantly for our argument, the structural transformation process followed by different economies as presented in Chapters 9 to 11, has important consequences for the pace of technological progress. Some products and some sectors of production are likely to be better candidates for higher levels of technological change than are others. For example, the production of computers or other electronics products would seem to offer greater opportunities for new product innovation and improvements in factor productivity along a quality ladder than, say, the production of wheat or footwear. Then, assuming the requisite stock of human capital has been or is being accumulated, a country that has moved in the direction of more complex products and more capital- and knowledge-intensive production techniques would be expected both to do more R&D and to have a higher return to such investments compared to a country specializing in primary products or simpler manufactured goods predominately destined for a (small) protected domestic economy. For primary products or the most basic easy ISI products, cutting-edge technology may not be required or be important, especially if tariffs have remained high to protect ISI industries. And even if they have not, there may be a limit to the productivity of the inputs in these old lines of production.

Industrial policies to promote national technology

This view lends support to those state industrial strategies which target the promotion of knowledge- and technology-intensive industries as loci of dynamic comparative advantage, since the returns to R&D and hence to economic growth would be expected to be high and cumulative over the future in precisely those sectors. Such promotion may include not only infant industry protection measures but also special subsidies or contests for loans or other critical resources designed solely for firms in these sectors. As discussed in Chapters 7 and 10, such targeting of specific industries needs to be *performance based* if it is to have the desired effects. Firms should receive special treatment that reduces their costs and increases profits only on the condition that they meet certain objective standards which help the economy to reach its development objectives. Such targeting has been most successful when the *quid pro quo* performance standard has been based on the firm's ability to increase its exports over time.

Why is exporting an effective performance standard? Because it is a criterion that is implicitly based on the level of a firm's technological capacities. Firms which are able to export to the international market must be able to produce a product that at minimum meets international quality and price standards, and even factoring in state subsidies, this must mean that the firm is producing with, or very near, international "best practice" technology. In simple terms, such production must be efficiently produced and be of similar quality to close substitutes if the output is to be sold in the export market.

This is especially true as manufacturing production moves beyond simple non-durable consumer goods, such as textiles, and up the product ladder to more complex products, such as electronics. It is a bonus, perhaps, that exporting can contribute to domestic economic growth, but a fundamental motivation for encouraging firms to export and for rewarding such behavior is the contribution to the essential technological transformation that the ability to export imparts to the economy. As noted in Chapter 10, openness to the international economy, which can be measured by either the share of total exports to GDP or by the share of manufactured exports to total exports, tends to be positively correlated with economic growth. No doubt the effect of additional exports on total income directly contributes something to this positive relation through the income multiplier acting on increased demand. But as important as the direct export–income link is the domestic technological learning capacity that the ability to export enforces on producers and which is then, via positive spillovers, transmitted to other sectors of the economy, helping to extend the efficiency gains (Edwards 1992; also see Easterly 2001).

It is thus the effect on national technology acquisition which makes manufactured goods exporting such an important coordinating tool for most countries that want to speed economic growth and human development. Given that manufactured goods exporting requires a national technological capacity to be created and that such a technological learning capability requires the rapid accumulation of human capital, including R&D personnel, a strategy switch toward some kind of export substitution policy by the state will, if it is to be successful, compel state policy to carefully evaluate its spending priorities. Greater attention must be paid to those areas which relate to human capital accumulation, to the monitoring of macroeconomic policies, to improvement in the operation of state decision-making and the civil service, to evaluation of the legal framework, including intellectual property rights, to the appropriateness of policies to foster private sector initiative and so on.

In other words, an import substitution-cum-export substitution strategy along the general lines followed by the East Asian economies (Chapter 10) tends to oblige decision-makers to continually upgrade the national technological capacity if success is to be sustained. Of course, government policies may be poorly conceived and the human capital endowments and incentives may be insufficient for success, so the outcome of setting out on such a path is not certain. However, for a government to choose export substitution following an import substitution phase would seem to imply a recognition of the need for firms in the country to have the capacity to export. Since that will require managerial, financial and technological competence, the future path dependent direction of the economy dictated by such a decision is likely to enforce upon the state a greater degree of commitment to comply with its decisions to provide the complementary inputs and policies to make such a strategy switch viable.

Macropolicies and technological change

Part of what affects the level of TFP in any nation are the policies of the state as they affect the economy. Policies which create an environment in which private firms are enabled and encouraged to produce and invest in technological acquisition and to be efficient are likely to have a greater positive impact on output growth than policies that are less facilitating. In particular, macroeconomic policies can either encourage or discourage private entrepreneurs to innovate and change. For example, policies such as easy export substitution that tend to encourage the hiring of relatively cheap labor, increased expenditures aimed at expanding access to education among all groups and classes, and better health care, all tend to result in the sharing of the benefits of industrialization among more members of society, thus increasing the internal market and domestic sales and growth potential. Other policies that help to keep inflation rates and the balance of payments in check also would be expected to contribute to growth, national technological change, and development.

Table 13.4 presents some evidence on how macroeconomic policy relative to exchange rates, also discussed fully in Chapter 15, affects growth and technological progress. The table shows that when exchange rates are over-valued ("high distortion"), then this tends to reduce the returns to education to society as seen in the lower level of GDP growth and, especially, in lower TFP rates, regardless of the level of education. "Bad policy" thus reduces the efficiency of the economy's inputs, while "good policy" ("low distortion") raises efficiency all around. The table again highlights not only the importance of the level of education, but also that increases in the level of education, particularly in an environment of "good policy," adds significantly to national technological capacity, as measured by TFP. This accents an important issue; though human capital investment is necessary, it is not sufficient for higher rates of economic growth. Likewise, good macroeconomic economic policies are, by themselves, insufficient to guarantee progress.

Table 13.4 State policy, growth, and TFP

	Average annual GDP growth	Average annual TFP growth
Low distortion/high education level	5.5	1.40
Low distortion/low education level	3.8	0.25
High distortion/high education level	3.8	0.00
High distortion/low education level	3.1	−0.40
Low distortion/high change in education	5.3	1.30
Low distortion/low change in education	4.0	0.40
High distortion/high change in education	3.5	−0.16
High distortion/low change in education	3.4	−0.19

Source: World Bank 1991: 47, Table 2.4.

Note
High distortion refers to an exchange rate over-valued by more than 30 percent; *low distortion* refers to an exchange rate over-valued by less than 30 percent. *High education* means an average of more than 3.5 years; *low education* is 3.5 years average education or less. TFP measures the increased efficiency with which the labor and capital inputs to production are able to be utilized. TFP is an aggregate measure of the overall efficiency of an economy's policy environment.

Policy implications

Less-developed countries face the demands not only of initiating the structural transformation from agriculture to industry examined earlier if economic and human development are to be spurred. They also must confront the challenge of creating a "national technological capacity" and an "ITLC" as requisites for sustained progress. Much of the difference in incomes per capita among nations can be explained by the existence of technology gaps due to distinct capacities of different economies to do technology. Closing these gaps often compels a country to completely shift its development strategy, to implement new policies at the macroeconomic level, to re-order spending priorities of the central government and so on, all with the purpose of moving the country to a different path over the future.

What happens in an economy today, this month and this year is path dependent, being the result of past decisions and particular historical circumstances that affect macroeconomic policies, spending on education, research and development expenditures, the level of tariffs, the efficiency of domestic entrepreneurs and workers, and so on. This list of contributing factors easily could be extended, but the point is that past actions condition outcomes today. To change the rate of economic growth and the level of development in the future, it is necessary that countries make choices *now* that will shift the economy's path dependency to a higher efficiency, higher income track. This requires that greater attention be afforded those factors which can improve upon the acquisition and adaptation of the world pool of knowledge to domestic production processes. Emphasis on technical education and science and mathematics should increase as the level of development increases. Better state microeconomic industrial policies and macroeconomic policies can contribute in a complementary fashion to raising both private sector and public sector efficiency by rewarding technological competency, rather than connections or power.

In the effort to close the technology gap, decision-makers need to keep firmly in mind that this can only be done by creating a *national* technology and a *national* technological learning capacity. This requires that there be substantial *local control over* the production and learning processes. There must be an emphasis on forging genuine **indigenous** technological autonomy in which its domestic scientists, domestic entrepreneurs, and domestic skilled workers become the carriers and agents of technological knowledge. This knowledge can then be passed on to the next generation of domestic students and workers who become the future R&D scientists and technicians, the future entrepreneurs, and the future skilled workers.

This does not mean that each country must be independent of the rest of the world. Just the opposite is true. It means that each country must, however, develop the *productive independence* that comes with a domestic technological learning capacity that can permit the country to use the world pool of knowledge for local development needs. True technological independence, in the sense of not making use of knowledge created in the developed countries, would be a foolish and unattainable goal for a less-developed economy hoping to make genuine progress. But an independent technological learning capacity requires domestic inputs and domestic effort to attain such a degree of competence as to be able to make use of knowledge created elsewhere and apply it to local conditions.

American economist Alice Amsden (1989: 9, 21, 76) noted that South Korea "has entertained almost no direct foreign investment outside the labor-intensive sectors" and that "industrialization has occurred almost exclusively on the basis of nationally owned rather than foreign-owned enterprise." Direct foreign investment was viewed as another policy instrument to be selectively utilized in an effort to meet the growth and technological objectives of the developmentalist regimes in all the East Asian economies, and in Japan as well before them. Foreign investment was used to gain access to technological knowledge which foreign TNCs had created. TNCs also were a fulcrum around which domestic production linkages could be forged. But it was national capitalists and domestic finance which provided the base for the successful East Asian experience with both growth and shared development. This situation contrasts sharply with the experience of the major Latin American economies which have had *more than twice* the level of foreign direct investment as a share of total output, and substantially less success since initiating secondary ISI (see Focus 13.3).

FOCUS 13.3 INDIGENOUS LEARNING AND KOREA'S STEEL INDUSTRY

South Korea has been quite adept at learning foreign technology. With the initiation of a steel industry, foreign engineers were brought in to construct the earliest mills. Korean engineers served as observers. During the second and third stage of steel mill construction, Korean engineers assumed greater responsibilities relative to foreign consultants. By the time that the fourth generation of steel mills was built, Korean engineers worked without foreign engineers or consultants. Interestingly, there was an increase in the efficiency of operation of each successive vintage of steel mill constructed.

This is a further example of the learning-by-doing effects and the positive externalities that arise, but it also is an illustration of the importance of consciously building an indigenous cadre of scientists, engineers, and technicians who become increasing capable over time of performing closer to international best practice.

Sources: Enos and Park 1988; UNCTAD 1996

These differences, and Hirschman's observations above, suggest that foreign investment is not a perfectly substitutable factor input for domestic inputs in the development process. National development must be built upon national capital and national expertise (Evenson and Westphal 1995: 2237). In the next chapter, the possible benefits and costs of foreign direct investment are considered more carefully. But on one criterion, that of the acquisition of a national technological capacity, countries must be very careful and selective in their approach to transnational corporations. Too much foreign investment can prevent the creation of the technological autonomy that every country needs to sustain growth over the future. The TNCs provide no shortcuts to such autonomy unless a country has created the entrepreneurial core, the skilled workers and the scientists and engineers who can assimilate the knowledge potentially available from the TNCs. But it is also necessary that the proper state policies vis-à-vis the TNCs be in place, as discussed in the next chapter, if such learning is to be facilitated.

Questions for review

1   If technology is not a computer, or computer software, or a new machine, what is it? Are people part of technology? If so, in what sense? In what sense are technological knowledge and a nation's human capital inputs complementary to one another?
2   Some earlier development economists, like Alexander Gerschenkron, thought "late developers" would have an advantage compared to early developers in increasing their levels of per capita income, since they would be able to use the most advanced technology without having to re-invent such knowledge themselves. Under what conditions would such an optimistic perspective on "international technological diffusion" have validity for a late-developing economy? Under what circumstances would it be likely to be the case that international technological diffusion would *not* be of major benefit to an economy? Are there preconditions for successful transfers of technology? Explain. What role does government policy play in creating these preconditions and in augmenting an economy's initial endowments that might make technological acquisition and its use more productive for an economy?
3   Why would elites in some less-developed countries be opposed to national technological competence? In what lines of production and in what sectors might one expect to find such proponents of technological dependency? In what sectors might one expect to find supporters of a greater degree of technological autonomy?
4   Distinguish between an ITLC and an ITCC. What is required for an economy to have an ITCC? At what stage of technological acquisition are the East Asian economies? Most economies in Africa?
5   How can TNCs cause "factor atrophy" or "factor displacement"? Would this be more or less likely to occur if the country has already created an ITLC?
6   Explain how "openness" to the international economy, especially a growing capacity for local firms to export manufactured goods, might contribute to helping an economy create a national technological capacity.
7   In Luanda's economy, total gross domestic product has increased at an average annual rate of 4.7 percent over the last decade. The annual growth of the labor

force has averaged 2.2 percent and the increase in the physical stock of capital has increased an average of 2.5 percent per year. Labor's contribution to total output has averaged 30 percent over the period. Given these figures, what has been the annual rate of TFP in the Luandan economy?

8 If there were not "national technologies" specific to each country, but rather an international pool of technology available freely and equally to all countries, would you expect to find per capita income differences among nations persisting over time? Why or why not?

9 Why are domestic entrepreneurs, domestic capitalists, and domestic scientists and engineers so important to the development process? Why is it difficult, if not impossible, for foreign inputs to substitute for these domestic inputs without short-circuiting the development process?

Notes

1 In the neoclassical growth model (Chapter 4), technology is conceived as a public good available to all economies freely and with the same impact on productivity. In effect, the neoclassical model makes the not very likely assumption that all economies, rich and poor, have *exactly the same aggregate production function*. They do not differ in the technology they have available to them since it is a public good. Nor do they differ in their capacity to use technological knowledge. In other words, technology is defined as a "thing" that any society can appropriate without any preconditions. Economies differ as do income per capita, then, only in their level of saving and investment and in their population growth rates, not in the availability of technology or the specific ability of any country to make use of that technology to its fullest.

In the endogenous growth models (Chapter 8), technology is not viewed as a public good or a "thing" appropriable by any economy without preconditions. Technology (the $A(K)$ in equation 8.3) differs among economies, even though all potentially can tap into the same world pool of knowledge. The level and pace of technology differs in diverse economies, because of dissimilarities in human capital accumulation and the stock of human capital, because of economic policies of the state (for example, on inflation or on income distribution), because of different levels of management and financial skills of enterprises, and because of a whole gamut of other variables that constitute the "path" a country has been following to any point in time. In this view, there are *national technologies*, and the level and effectiveness of technology in each economy is dependent upon the resources each has devoted to technological appropriation.

2 This is not entirely true, as Fagerberg (1994: 1150 ff.) notes. Denison's (1967) early work had measured a "technological gap" that at least suggested the importance of country-specific efforts. The theoretical work on endogenous technical progress by Kenneth Arrow, H. Uzawa, Edmund Phelps, Solow, and others predates the current empirical work on the same sorts of issues. The major early articles on these themes are conveniently collected in Stiglitz and Uzawa (1969), a reading of which suggests that economists rediscover truths from time to time.

3 The pace of technological change is also related to the structural transformation discussed in Chapters 9 to 11. As a country begins to shift labor from agriculture and other rural production to urban, industrial pursuits, this typically results in higher productivity because of the higher level of physical capital and knowledge in use in industry. Thus the *structural transformation* from agriculture to industry beginning with easy import substitution is important precisely because it sets the stage for the *technological transformation* that can contribute to the transition to higher levels of development. However, the speed at which this technological transformation will be able to progress depends upon the attention paid to the proper human capital accumulation, to state policies on research and development, to the macroeconomic environment, to the skills of managers and entrepreneurs and to a range of institutional factors that can either support or retard the technological transformation.

4 ITLC involves both "know-*how*" and increasing progress on the path of "know-*why*," or "deep technological learning," to use Lall's distinction (Lall 1984: 116–117) for what are here called an ITLC and an ITCC. A schematic representation of the relations might look like the following:

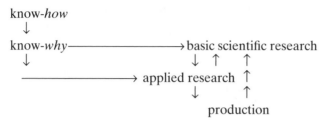

5 This does not change the conclusion of Chapters 8 and 12 on the importance for countries to pursue a more *generalized* human capital accumulation process in which universal primary and secondary education are extremely important. It does suggest, however, that resources do need to be directed to tertiary education as well, including funding specifically targeted at the training of essential R&D scientists and technicians, as the level of per capita income and the level of human development rises. Further, this argument underscores the importance, in the modern global economic environment, of primary and secondary education with a substantial *technical focus*, with both mathematics and science training given particular emphasis if today's students are to have the skills and adaptability which tomorrow's economy will demand.

6 Both Level 1 and Level 2 are further sub-divided into three sub-categories, making for six levels of technological capacity in the less-developed countries. This sub-division is due to the interesting work of Weiss (1990).

7 We actually first encountered the concept of TFP in Chapter 8. It is the name now given to the Solow residual in earlier growth accounting exercises. Calling the unknown factors influencing economic growth TFP certainly sounds more positive than referring to them as a residual, but that does not change the fact that TFP is measuring all the non-identified determinants of economic growth other than changes in the quantity of the inputs.

8 These are not the only changes that countries in these lagging regions need to undertake. We shall see in the following chapters, there are other policy failures that can derail progress. However, building a technological capacity via human capital accumulation and judicious R&D expenditures are necessary for progress over time. Overcoming other policy lapses will be ineffective in accelerating economic growth and contributing to human development without having put in place the necessary augmented human capital, R&D, and scientific endowments.

References

Adler, Emanuel. 1987. *The Power of Ideology: The Quest for Technological Autonomy in Argentina and Brazil*. Berkeley, CA: University of California Press.

—— 1988. "State Institutions, Ideology and Autonomous Technological Development," *Latin American Research Review* 23, 2: 59–60.

Amsden, Alice. 1989. *Asia's Next Giant: South Korea and Late Industrialization*. NY: Oxford University Press.

Denison, Edward. 1967. *Why Growth Rates Differ. Postwar Experience in Nine Western Countries*. Washington, DC: The Brookings Institution.

Dore, Ronald. 1984. "Technological Self-reliance: Sturdy Ideal or Self-serving Rhetoric," pp. 65–80 in Martin Fransman and Kenneth King (eds). 1984. *Technological Capability in the Third World*. Hampshire: Macmillan.

Easterly, William. 2001. *The Elusive Quest for Growth: Economists' Adventures and Misadventures in the Tropics*. Cambridge, MA: MIT Press.

Edwards, Sebastian. 1992. "Trade Orientation, Distortions and Growth in Developing Countries," *Journal of Development Economics* 39: 31–57.

Enos, John L. and Woo-Hee Park. 1988. *The Adoption and Diffusion of Technology: The Case of Korea*. London: Croom Helm.

Evenson, Robert E. and Larry E. Westphal. 1995. "Technological Change and Technology Strategy," ch. 37 in Jere Behrman and T.N. Srinivasan (eds), *Handbook of Development Economics*, volume IIIA. Amsterdam: Elsevier Science.

Fagerberg, Jan. 1994. "Technology and International differences in Growth Rates," *Journal of Economic Literature* 32, 2 (September): 1147–1175.

Gerschenkron, Alexander. 1962. *Economic Backwardness in Historical Perspective*. Cambridge, MA: Harvard University Press.

Grossman, Gene M. and Elhanan Helpman. 1991. *Innovation and Growth in the Global Economy*. Cambridge, MA: MIT Press.

—— 1994. "Endogenous Innovation in the Theory of Growth," *Journal of Economic Perspectives* 8 (Winter): 23–44.

Harriss, John, Janet Hunter, and Colin M. Lewis (eds). 1995. *The New Institutional Economics and Third World Development*. London: Routledge.

Herrera, Amilcar. 1973. "Social Determinants of Science Policy in Latin America: Explicit Science Policy and Implicit Science Policy," pp. 19–37 in Charles Cooper (ed.), *Science, Technology and Development*. London: Frank Cass.

Hirschman, Albert O. 1971. "How to Divest in Latin America and Why," pp. 225–252 in A.O. Hirschman, *A Bias for Hope*. New Haven: Yale University Press.

Kuznets, Simon. 1966. *Modern Economic Growth: Rate, Structure, and Spread*. New Haven: Yale University Press.

—— 1968. "Trends in Capital Formation," in UNESCO, *Readings in the Economics of Education*. Paris: UNESCO.

Lall, Sanjaya (ed.). 1984. Special issue on "Exports of Technology by Newly-Industrializing Countries," *World Development* 12 (May–June).

Radhakrishna, K. (ed.). 1980. *Science, Technology and Global Problems: Views from the Developing World*. Oxford: Pergamon Press.

Salter, W.E.G. 1969. *Productivity and Technical Change*. Cambridge: Cambridge University Press.

Solow, Robert. 1988. "Growth Theory and After," *American Economic Review* 78 (June): 307–317.

Stiglitz, Joseph E. and Hirofumi Uzawa. 1969. *Readings in the Modern Theory of Economic Growth*. Cambridge, MA: MIT Press.

UNCTAD (United Nations Conference on Trade and Development). 1996. *Fostering Technological Dynamism: Technology Capacity-Building and Competitiveness*. Geneva: UNCTAD.

UNDP (United Nations Development Program). 1994. *Human Development Report 1994*. Oxford: Oxford University Press.

—— 2002. *Human Development Report 2002*. Oxford: Oxford University Press.

Wade, Robert. 1990. *Governing the Market*. Princeton: Princeton University Press.

Weiss, C. 1990. "Scientific and Technological Constraints to Economic Growth and Equity," in Robert E. Evenson and Gustav Ranis (eds), *Science and Technology: Lesson for Development*. Boulder, CO: Westview.

World Bank. 1991. *World Development Report 1991*. Oxford: Oxford University Press.

—— 1993. *The East Asian Miracle*. Oxford: Oxford University Press.

Part 4

Problems and issues

14 Transnational corporations and economic development

After studying this chapter, you should understand:

- the variations in the types of transnational corporations (TNCs): resource dependent TNCs, commodity-trade controlling TNCs, "stand-alone" branch plants of TNCs operating under ISI programs, and integrated global production TNCs operating within core-subcontracting interfirm webs and commodity chains;
- the quantitative impact of TNCs on capital formation in poor nations;
- the qualitative impact of TNCs on capital formation, technology transfers and the organization of production;
- the costs of hosting TNCs in terms of transfer pricing, net long-term resource transfers, and diversion effects of TNCs;
- how "thin" globalization and weak backward linkages often result from hosting TNC activities;
- the reasons why hosting TNCs involves poor nations in monitoring environmentally risky and complex production processes;
- the potential for successful bargaining with TNCs, and the reasons why most host nations fail to reap the potential benefits of TNC investment;
- the role of export processing zones (EPZs), and their limited potential for contributing to successful strategies of development;
- the impact of EPZs on women workers; and
- why and how the impact of TNC activity has varied in Asia and Latin America.

Introduction

Transnational corporations, which are companies operating in two or more nations, are far from being a new or recent element of the structure of economic relationships which define the less-developed world. In the early colonial period (Chapter 3), TNCs such as the Dutch East Indies Company and the British East India Company played a major role in the economic life of Java, India, Holland, and England. Even prior to the Industrial Revolution, these early trading corporations were determined to reap profits from their near monopolistic control of certain trade routes and commodities. However, most of these early TNCs were involved in trade, not in the direct production of goods. With the onset of the second industrial revolution (1870–1910), giant vertically integrated corporations emerged in many branches of primary production, such as mining, and tropical commodities, such as bananas and rubber, and oil. Many of these vertically integrated companies established production and processing sites in the colonial areas, or in independent but poorer nations, such as in Latin America. These resource-specific transnationals often established a strong political presence, both within their nation of origin and within the host nation or territory.[1]

As noted in our earlier discussion of agriculture (Chapter 11), many nations in the less-developed world, particularly some of the poorest, remain virtual agricultural mono-exporters, depending for the bulk of their foreign exchange earnings on one or just a few export crops. Other nations are mono-exporters by virtue of their dependence on the marketing of one or just a few minerals or oil. In the international market for these commodities, huge buying TNCs, such as the grain transnational Cargill, or the oil transnationals such as Shell (with $69 billion in foreign assets and $54 billion in foreign sales in 1999, and 57,000 foreign employees) or ExxonMobil (with $99 billion in foreign assets and $116 billion in foreign sales, and 68,000 foreign employees) can exert strong pressure on the producing nations, particularly when they are among a handful of firms that dominate the buying, transportation and distribution of these products.

John Cavanagh and Frederick Clairmonte analyzed the state of the global commodities markets in the early 1980s.

> [I]n the last two decades the domination of primary commodity markets has passed from single commodity traders (e.g., the former United Fruit Company) to firms paramount in several global commodity markets. The trade in three commodities, by no means exceptional, illustrates the dimension of marketing leverage: the trade in bananas, where three conglomerates dominate 70–75 percent of global markets; the cocoa trade, of which six corporations account for over 70 percent; and the trade in tea and tobacco, where 85–90 percent is under the direct control of six transnational leaf buyers.
>
> The market power of the multi-commodity traders stems from their self-reinforcing modes of conduct that contribute to enhance their bargaining stance vis-à-vis developing countries. Most multi-commodity traders are private and largely non-accountable, not only in developing but also in developed market economy countries. Many are integrated backward into plantations and forward into processing, and hence are in an even stronger bargaining position vis-à-vis national marketing institutions with which they deal.
>
> (Cavanagh and Clairmonte 1982: 16)

Table 14.1 details the pervasiveness of the near monopoly and oligopoly structures in the global trade in primary commodities, much of which is controlled by transnationals.

Import substitution industrialization and the TNCs

After the Second World War, a third round of transnational activity began. In their search for viable development policies, many less-developed nations adopted, as we know, easy import substitution industrialization (ISI) strategies as the means to ini-

Table 14.1 Transnational control of global commodity trade, 1980

Commodity	Total exports (billions $)	Percentage marketed by top 15 TNCs[a]
Food		
Wheat	16.6	85–90
Sugar	14.4	60
Coffee	12.6	85–90
Corn	11.8	85–90
Rice	5.0	70
Cocoa	3.0	85
Tea	1.9	80
Bananas	1.2	70–75
Pineapples	0.4	90
Agricultural raw materials		
Forest products	54.5	90
Cotton	7.9	85–90
Natural rubber	4.4	70–75
Tobacco	3.9	85–90
Hides and skins	2.7	25
Jute	0.2	85–90
Ores, minerals and metals		
Crude petroleum	306.0	75
Copper	10.7	80–85
Iron ore	6.9	90–95
Tin	3.6	75–80
Phosphates	1.6	50–60
Bauxite	1.0	80–85

Source: Cavanagh and Clairmonte 1982: 17.

Note
a In most cases, 3–6 traders dominate the bulk of these markets.

tiate the structural transformation (Chapter 9). The ISI approach effectively locked out of the domestic market the products of many manufacturing companies of the advanced industrial nations, which, because ISI relied upon protective tariffs to encourage domestic manufacturing, found it more difficult to export to less-developed countries as a result. In response, many large manufacturing TNCs, particularly those domiciled in the United States, reacted, where they could, by "jumping the tariff walls" and setting up "stand-alone" branch plants in less-developed nations with reasonably large domestic markets.

It is conventional to associate easy ISI with nationalist policies adopted by governments in less-developed economies. And, indeed, during the peak ISI era, from roughly 1946 to the late 1970s, many nations sought to wrest control from TNCs. Nationalizations, in which foreign TNCs were taken over and converted to domestic ownership, were widespread from 1960 to 1980, with 587 recorded in various countries. These nationalizations were, however, largely concentrated in the areas of ore, minerals and metals, and in food and raw materials production, that is, they were largely directed at foreign investments which had for the most part been established during the colonial era in resource-specific or resource-dependent production. Furthermore, 76 percent of these nationalizations took place between 1966 and 1976, a decade when North–South tensions reached a zenith. Not only were the bulk of the nationalizations concentrated in time, they were also concentrated in place. A study of seventy-nine nations during the 1960–1985 period reveals a total of over 300 political regimes or governments, but a mere twenty-eight accounted for nearly two-thirds of all the expropriations of foreign transnationals (Kennedy 1992: 68–69).

Thus, during the time when ISI policies were being implemented, some less-developed nations did engage in "hostile" acts of expropriation. However, at the same time, the presence of other TNCs, particularly US TNCs in the manufacturing sector of the less-developed nations, was growing rapidly. As recent research has demonstrated, the growth of branch plant TNCs in manufacturing and the spread of easy ISI policies coincided for good reason. The largest US manufacturing corporations were not, in fact, in opposition to ISI, and the major less-developed nations were not hostile to *manufacturing* TNCs, even as they adopted and strengthened their ISI policies, at least partly to help create a domestic industrialist class.

During and particularly after the Second World War, the leaders of the largest corporations, and many policy-makers, were deeply focused on the difficulties of constructing a postwar international economic environment which would not degenerate into the fractious global struggle as had erupted prior to the Great Depression. Hanging over them was the realization that industrial capacity had leaped forward in the United States during the war. Policy-makers believed that a reinvigorated global system would be a necessity, and they accepted that the larger less-developed countries, as they adopted programs aimed at rapid industrialization, could help utilize the industrial capacity built up in the United States. As a result of such concerns, the United States, under President Truman, had promulgated the Point Four program (see Chapter 3) "not simply as an aid program but an effort to specify planning goals for Third World development. The numerous economic missions sponsored under the policy cost the U.S. little, but they had a substantial impact on the direction of less-developed world economic policy" (Maxfield and Nolt 1990: 58). During the Truman and Eisenhower administrations,

> U.S. technical aid missions were sent to most underdeveloped countries to help draft and implement ISI development plans. These plans specified the tariff, tax, and other incentives that would channel private investment into the targeted industries. They also became the basis for allocating U.S. and multilateral aid, and often local development resources, as well. This effort was an autonomous U.S. initiative; it was not simply a concession to less-developed world nationalists.
>
> (Ibid.: 49–50)

By 1960, US TNCs owned 49 percent of all of the direct foreign investment (DFI) spread around the globe (see Table 14.2). Some of the new-found strength of the United States arose as a result of its willingness to champion domestic ISI industrialization strategies, while simultaneously obtaining a preferred niche in many less-developed nations for US-based TNCs. Thus, even as the old-style mineral, food, and raw material TNCs confronted nationalization in the aftermath of often difficult transitions from colonialism to independence, US manufacturing TNCs were blazing a trail into new economic territory. Even though many of the new industrial plants were small, and therefore lacked economies-of-scale, they were profitable, because they were able to push prices upward in protected markets. Competing foreign-made goods often could be obtained only through imports, which often faced tariffs

Table 14.2 Share of the stock of world DFI (percentage of world total)

Country	1914	1960	1978	1992	2000
France	12.2	6.1	3.8	8.3	8.3
Germany	10.5	1.2	7.3	9.2	7.4
Japan	0.1	0.7	6.8	13.0	4.7
United Kingdom	45.5	16.2	12.9	11.4	15.0
United States	18.5	49.2	41.4	25.3	20.8

Source: UNCTAD 1994: 131; 2001: 307.

well above 100 percent, so there was plenty of room for increasing prices. While these new TNCs were often the subject of bitter controversy, they were rarely targets for nationalization. They tended to bring a new and more flexible corporate culture, adaptable to some degree to the development aspirations of the developing nations. In contrast, many of the older food, mineral, and raw material producers exuded an intransigent attitude which had often served them well in an earlier era, but which failed them in the 1960s and early 1970s.

The globally integrated production system

Beginning in the late 1960s, and accelerating throughout the 1990s, a fourth form of transnational economic activity could be noted. Global factories began to emerge, sparked by revolutions in communications, transportation, and information-processing technologies. Here the motivation for investment was not the domestic market, nor were the economic activities of these new TNCs resource- or location-specific. Rather, new manufacturing activities spread in less-developed economies based upon their cheap labor, the near absence of environmental restrictions relating to production activities, the absence of effective unions and labor laws, or other factors which essentially served to lower the costs of production. In the late 1960s and early 1970s, tariff barriers moved steadily downward, particularly in the developed nations. This helped facilitate the growth of truly global factories and shifted much of the emphasis in policy-making circles toward export-led industrialization and away from an over-emphasis on ISI. As the so-called East Asian "tigers" developed during this period, and as new possibilities for foreign investors and for expanding export activities opened up, ISI strategies came under attack (as we saw in Chapter 10). The institutions and technological processes needed to support the global factory system had not existed in the 1940s and the early 1950s, nor could they be quickly created. Thus the ISI era has been eclipsed by the era of **globally integrated production** as the nature of TNCs has evolved with advances in technology, from cellular communications to far-flung computer and data entry services. Without doubt, the age of the computer has accelerated the pace of change and the possibilities at the same time. Peter Evans describes the new era:

> The "new Internationalization" which has taken shape between 1973 and the present represents a different paradigm [from ISI]. Its production strategies are defined by global markets rather than local ones. Global production networks are typically constructed around a series of "strategic alliances" among TNCs but occasionally include Third World entrepreneurial groups. Manufactured

exports from the Third World back to rich country markets are central to the new paradigm, while flows from the advanced countries to the Third World increasingly take the form of services and intangibles. The new internationalization pervades all regions of the Third World but East Asia, not Latin America, is the archetypal site.

(Evans 1998: 197)

Why did the global factory system arise? Theorists have debated this point thoroughly. Some have emphasized "indivisibilities" of management and technologies, patents, and trademarks which can best be exploited by siting production and/or distribution facilities in more than one nation. Richard Caves has suggested that the motivation to "go global" often arises from the fact that firms own or control specific production processes, designs, styles, and other types of know-how. These "intangibles" are difficult to price, to divide-up, and are difficult to sell or license to other firms. Usually there is no orderly market, worldwide, for such in-house assets. Consequently, if these assets are not fully utilized within the domestic market, and/or if they can be adapted to higher production levels without incurring prohibitively rising unit costs, these firms can often increase their profits by operating additional production facilities abroad. Such firms might prefer to sell to foreigners these intangible assets to earn profits, but normally they cannot. Thus, their deeper utilization via foreign investment is one option; the alternative may be to completely forgo economic rents arising from the exploitation of the intangible assets they have created (Caves 1991).

Other theorists have emphasized the changing global conditions external to the individual firm, which have encouraged global production. For example, the average cost of ocean freight plus port fees dropped by more than 50 percent between the late 1940s and 1990. The price of an international call from New York to London fell ten-fold between 1970 and 1990. Airline fees per passenger mile decreased even faster and further than did ocean freight costs from the late 1940s to 1990. And satellite utilization charges had declined to one-tenth their 1970 cost by 1990 (World Bank 1995: 51). Neither the firm-specific theory of Richard Caves nor the perspective which emphasizes what might be called the global infrastructure approach are mutually exclusive. Both contribute to our understanding of recent trends in expanding TNC production.

A third group of theorists emphasize mega-changes in production systems, such as the "factory-of-the-future," where modern machinery can perform complex tasks previously necessitating skilled and experienced shop-floor technicians and workers. Deskilling of the labor force due to new production machinery and techniques has allowed many firms to retain a core group of technicians and managers in the industrial countries, while out-sourcing other production to less-skilled workers in the less-developed nations. For example, Nike, a US-based TNC with annual sales of $4 billion in 1993, directly employed 9,000 highly skilled workers involved in product design, data processing, sales, administration, product development, production design, marketing, and distribution. Nike also employed 75,000 workers via independent subcontracting arrangements in China, South Korea, Taiwan, Indonesia, Malaysia and Thailand, where labor-intensive production and assembly processes actually produce the final Nike product (UNCTAD 1994: 193) (see Box 14.1).

Box 14.1 Subcontracting in Indonesia

Subcontracting has become an important strategy increasingly adopted by transnational corporations in the 1980s and 1990s. As labor costs have risen in South Korea, Taiwan, and Singapore, many East Asian subcontractors have become small transnationals themselves, shifting their production and assembly operations away from nations such as South Korea, to new low-wage havens, such as Indonesia.

Depending on market demand, Nike Corporation contracts with four to six Indonesia-based South Korean subcontractors who employ roughly 5,000 Indonesian workers. According to the Nike Corporation, the advantage of locating in Indonesia is that a pair of shoes selling for $80 in the United States will involve direct labor costs in Indonesia of only $2.60. Thus there is greater opportunity for more profit.

Although the subcontractors who sell their output to Nike are pressured to pay a minimum wage of $52.50 per month, they often do not. For example, one twenty-two-year-old worker and his nineteen-year-old wife, both employees of a Nike subcontractor, earned a total of $82 per month. They rented one room for $23 per month. This housing, actually a six-foot-by-six-foot space, is described as follows:

A single bare bulb dangles from the ceiling, its dim glare revealing a plain bed, a single gas burner, and a small plastic cabinet. Their room, one of a dozen in a long cement building, is provided with one container of water daily. If they want more water, each jug costs about 5 cents.

Attempts by the workers to raise their pay above the current average of $2.62 per day have met with harsh treatment from the government. Independent unions and the right to strike are not recognized by the government.

Source: Gargan 1996

As a result of a complex process involving either the search to maximize the return on intangible assets, or the opportunity to take advantage of a global infrastructure, or to reap the advantages of labor deskilling and the potential gains by offshore outsourcing of production, by 1998, the transnationals of the advanced industrial nations were employing nineteen million workers (a 58 percent increase since 1992!) in the less-developed world, most of whom were working in global factories. However, this figure does not include subcontracting activities, such as those conducted by Nike described in Box 14.1. Including subcontracting, the World Bank estimated that the direct employment effect of TNCs could be 100 percent higher, suggesting total employment by TNCs of 38 million in 1998 (World Bank 1995: 62). Thus, following the estimates of the World Bank, the increased production activities of TNCs in the developing economies between 1985 and 1998 could have accounted for twenty four million new jobs created, including subcontracting.

Today, transnationals are to be found in most less-developed nations, their presence being felt under the four broad categories of transnational activity:

1   trading companies controlling the marketing process;
2   resource-intensive vertically integrated transnationals;
3   branch manufacturing plants; and
4   global factory production sites.

In any given nation, it is likely that more than one of the above forms of transnational activity will be present.

Direct foreign investment

Direct foreign investment (DFI) entails the ownership of productive assets by a corporation in another nation. Such ownership should be distinguished from the purchase of foreign stock or the lending of funds to foreign companies and governments. These latter forms of investment are known as portfolio investments. In 2000 the advanced industrial nations operated some **60,000** transnational corporations with approximately **820,000** foreign affiliates spread throughout the world (UNCTAD 2001: 9). These same industrial nations owned $6 trillion of foreign capital in 2000; of this total stock of DFI, $2 trillion was held in branches of production located in the developing regions: $1.1 trillion in East and South Asia, $607 billion in Latin America, $95 billion in Africa, and $60 billion in Western Asia. While one-third of the total stock of DFI of the developed nations was invested in the less-developed world, in recent years the *flow*, that is, the annual change in the stock, of DFI has increasingly been directed to the less-developed world. Between 1986 and 1993, the flow of DFI to the developing regions jumped from $16 billion to $80 billion, accounting for a record 41 percent of total DFI over that period (UNCTAD 1994: 1–19). But in the 1995–2000 period, due to the explosion in cross-border mergers and acquisitions in the industrial nations, the developing nations received only one-third of the *DFI flows*. Still, the total amount of such flows in the period came to an unprecedented $1.1 trillion.

In any given year, a relative handful of the developing nations receive the vast bulk of the DFI. In the period 1982–1992, for example, the top ten nations in a given year received over 70 percent of all the direct capital flows to the less-developed world. While there is some variation in the top ten nations over the ten-year period, eighteen nations have accounted for over 80 percent of such investment. With few exceptions, these eighteen nations were not the poorest; in Africa, where per capita income is extremely low, only Egypt, Nigeria, and Tunisia were among the top eighteen recipients of DFI. In 2000 the top ten recipient nations – four in Asia – received 76.7 percent of all DFI going to developing nations (UNCTAD 2001: 52). International capital flows tended to flow to countries where economic growth already was taking place, with only a handful of nations receiving such flows.[2]

Of the 60,000 TNCs with parent companies based in the developed nations, the top 100 firms accounted in any given year for roughly two-thirds of new DFI. In terms of asset size, the most important foreign productive activity of the top 100 firms is in the electronics sector, followed by mining and petroleum, motor vehicles, and chemicals and pharmaceuticals (UNCTAD 1994: 10). While US-based TNCs continue to dominate global production patterns, their relative significance has changed rapidly in recent years. Table 14.2 shows that while in 1960 US TNCs accounted for 49 percent of the total stock of DFI, by 1992, this share had shrunk to just 25 percent, falling again by 2000 to only 21 percent. Most of the relative gain was made by Japan, whose share increased from merely 0.7 percent in 1960 to 13 percent in 1992 – but then a decade of stagnation pushed Japan by 2000 to a relative level not seen since the 1970s. Germany too languished in the 1990s. The increasing national diversity of DFI tends to strengthen the relative bargaining position of host nations vis-à-vis the TNCs, since they are likely to have to deal with more than one potential group of national investors for a given project and that is, as we shall see, critical to the host country if it is to reap the potential benefits of TNC investment.

While trade between countries has historically received a great deal of attention in development economics (see Chapter 15), it is important to keep in mind the fact that the sales of foreign affiliates of the TNCs now *exceed* the total value of all exports of goods and services for the entire world (UNCTAD 1994: 20). In 2000, TNCs had sales from their foreign affiliates of $15.6 trillion, while the total value of world exports of goods and services stood at $7 trillion. About one-third of all TNC sales were intra-firm trades, a fact of some importance in our discussion of transfer pricing later in this chapter (UNCTAD 1994: xxi). Thus, in the view of many specialists, the role of the TNC has now eclipsed that of foreign trade as a factor determining the overall evolution of the global economic system. When UN researchers combined the domestic production of TNCs with their international production and sales, they arrived at the estimate that one-third of all global output is now under the direct governance of the TNCs (UNCTAD 1994: 135). Never, they state, has the influence of the TNCs been greater.

Who in the less-developed countries gains from DFI?

In neoclassical economic thinking, as characterized by the Solow, savings-centered theory, developing nations are viewed as deficient in physical capital investment. Consequently, it would appear that inflows of DFI could only have a positive effect on the growth rate of a poorer nation. On average, however, new DFI amounted to less than 3 percent of total investment throughout the less-developed world in the period 1980–1992. There are important exceptions, of course; Hong Kong received more than 10 percent of its investment from foreign sources during this period, Singapore over 20 percent, and Malaysia over 6 percent. From 1993–1999 reliance on DFI as a source of capital formation increased: In Asia it averaged 8.5 percent, in Africa 7.5 percent, and in Latin America 14.1 percent (UNCTAD 2001: 19, 24, 29). If the level achieved in the 1990s is sustainable it would suggest that DFI can make an important contribution to the overall investment level in many developing nations. Still, since this investment flow is concentrated among a few nations, most developing nations will receive only modest economic stimulus from DFI.

Furthermore, even when a nation is receiving large amounts of DFI, such flows do not always result in new capital formation. Existing plant and equipment are quite often the target of TNC investment for purchase, reducing the ownership and control of domestic capitalists. This effect has been referred to as denationalization, that is, the transfer of ownership of local capital to foreign capital owners (Gereffi and Evans 1981). While Mexico is considered one of the top receivers of DFI, 71 percent of such investment was devoted to the purchase of already existing Mexican companies in 2001 (Gazcón 2002: 15). Even if a so-called "greenfield" facility, that is, a new plant, is built by a TNC, this need not necessarily increase the total level of investment of a less-developed nation. Rather, the TNC may have raised the financial capital to make the required physical investment from within the poor nation itself, either from the banking sector or the equity markets, thereby diverting funds that would otherwise have been available to national entrepreneurs. In such cases, foreign DFI does not act as a *complement* to local investment, promising to increase the rate of expansion, but rather as a *substitute* for local capital ownership, local control, and perhaps for local learning.

If, with few exceptions, new DFI constitutes only a modest portion of total physical capital formation in any given year in less-developed economies, and if a part of the funding may derive from internal sources and thus not constitute a *net* addition to total capital formation, why has the role of the TNCs been so central to much of the recent development literature? The answer, clearly, must turn on considerations of the *qualitative* effects of DFI, rather than on considerations of quantitative relationships.

Collateral effects of TNCs: the modernization perspective

It has been suggested that TNCs, at least those associated with the ISI era and those that form part of the globally integrated system of production, can generate potential resource transfer effects through their activities in the forms of new capital, new product and process technologies, management/labor-training and other organizational innovations. Proponents of this modernization perspective believe it is largely a fruitless exercise to attempt to "unbundle" the multiple interactive stimuli that accompany DFI. But the modernization perspective rarely focuses on the important linkages between DFI flows, and flows from stock and bond purchases (portfolio investment), bank and corporate lending (private loans), bilateral aid institutions (such as the United States Agency for International Development) and multilateral institutions (such as the World Bank or the regional development banks) which make official loans and grants. It is important to be aware of such linkages, however, since nations that maintain a so-called good investment climate toward DFI, that is, a pro-business environment, will often reap substantial indirect resource transfers via such inflows of capital. In this section, we explore some of the research findings of those who analyze DFI from the modernization perspective, a view which focuses on the potential growth-stimulating role which TNCs may play through capital formation, technology transfers, and superior organizational production structures.

To begin, Table 14.3 summarizes the distribution of capital and other financial

Table 14.3 Net long-term resource flows into developing regions[a] (billions of dollars)

Type of flow	1991	1993	1995	1997	1999	2001[b]
DFI	**35.7**	**66.6**	**106.8**	**172.5**	**184.4**	**168.2**
Portfolio investment[c]	21.5	96.9	68.5	82.6	63.5	24.0
Bank loans	5.0	4.1	30.9	45.6	−23.3	−32.3
Official loans	62.6	53.4	54.1	40.7	47.4	36.5
Total	*124.2*	*220.9*	*260.2*	*341.4*	*271.8*	*196.5*
DFI/Total (%)	**28.7**	**30.1**	**41.0**	**50.5**	**67.8**	**85.6**

Source: World Bank 2002: www.worldbank.org/prospects/gdf2002/.

Notes
a Excludes IMF financing due to its short-term nature.
b World Bank estimate.
c Includes net purchases of securities by foreigners in domestic stock markets and bond financing as well as "other" debt flows.

flows in the 1991–2001 period. In observing this data it should be stressed that DFI amounted to only 26 percent of the net long-term flows to developing nations in the 1986–1990 period. Note that, in the last row of the table, DFI's share of total flows jumped upward all through the 1990s reaching a truly remarkable level of 86 percent of total flows in 2001. Heretofore developing nations relied heavily on (a) "official loans" from the World Bank and the regional development banks (such as the Asian Development Bank), (b) grants, and (c) bank lending. But in the 1990s these sources of funding atrophied ("official" forms of lending are analyzed in Chapter 17). Portfolio investment soared until the Asia Crisis of 1997, while DFI increased more than four-fold 1991–1999. Nearly 70 percent of DFI went to either East Asia (32 percent) or Latin America (35 percent – largely due to massive privatizations), with the Middle East attracting only 3 percent and Sub-Sahara Africa receiving only 6 percent. Table 14.3 demonstrates the rising importance of TNCs as well as the upward spiral of investment projects driven by their new enthusiasm for globally integrated production systems. Yet, the poorest nations rarely received any DFI – in 2000 the 49 least developed nations obtained a mere 0.3 percent of total DFI (UNCTAD 2001: 1).

Capital formation

While the absolute amount of capital formation provided by TNCs, in relation to total investment in a developing nation, is likely to be small, probably below 10 percent and usually less than half this amount, the qualitative significance of such investment can be much higher than one might assume using an aggregate approach. Such investment is often directed to a narrow range of industries that are important for economic growth, precisely because they are concentrated in manufacturing and services where new investment is associated with significant increases in productivity and production. Aggregate data can distort or even hide the role played by TNCs, a point well illustrated through the following summary of research on TNCs in India.

> In India, a study of 28 manufacturing industries in 1977–1978 found that in nine industries, including motor vehicles, electrical machinery, metal products, plastics, chemicals and pharmaceuticals, the foreign ownership share was greater than 20 per cent. A second study of TNCs in India found that foreign-owned firms accounted for more than 30 per cent of sales in manufacturing in 1975–76 and 1980–81. Foreign direct investment as a share of gross domestic investment has been very small in India, at 0.1 per cent in the period 1976–80 and only slightly higher – 0.2 per cent – in the late 1980s.
>
> (UN 1992: 119)

Furthermore, aggregate DFI data fail to reveal non-equity arrangements within the host nation which can have a substantial impact on productivity and output. Among such deals, which are often numerous, one finds franchising agreements, licensing, long-term subcontracting, and non-equity joint ventures with local capital. Any of these production linkages with TNCs may form a conduit for the diffusion of product and or process technologies and management/labor-skills, as well as providing opportunities for learning about more advanced organizational structures in marketing, advertising, finance, or research and development. It is often the case that indigenous business owners lack, as a group characteristic, an export culture, whereas manufacturing TNCs are likely to be quite proficient and dynamic in foreign marketing, almost by definition. To the degree that such skills are "spun-off" to the host nation through joint ventures and/or the turnover of management personnel working for TNCs or other transmission mechanisms, TNCs can be an important mechanism for augmenting and enhancing the proficiency of domestic managers, professionals, and perhaps skilled workers.

Since the scarcity of foreign exchange is likely to form a crucial bottleneck for many less-developed nations, curbing their development potential, the ability to expand into foreign markets can be of paramount importance to the nation. The domestic market is too small in many developing nations due both to the highly unequal distribution of income and the size of the population. Thus, foreign sales can be important in "widening" the market and in allowing firms to realize greater economies of scale in production. Such effects, when they do occur, can further assist the development process by lowering production costs, possibly further expanding the market as lower-income consumers could be brought into the market if lower costs translate into lower prices. Thus to the extent that TNCs transmit export skills to domestic producers, this is another potential benefit to the host country of such investment.

Table 14.4, below, reflects the new emphasis on global production, as well as the success of some Asian nations in building their own complex production facilities. Notice the dramatic drop in primary commodities exports from over one-half of the non-fuel exports in 1980 to a mere 19 percent in 1998. Meanwhile, world exports also shifted away from primary commodities, but not as dramatically as did developing nations. Still, the generalization that many developing nations find much of their economy dependent upon commodities exports should not be abandoned. We also see that relative to the overall level of world trade in 1998 (19 vs. 14.8 percent) developing nations as a whole are much more reliant on commodity exports than were developed nations in 1998. Low end labor-intensive production processes (assembly operations occurring commonly in Export Processing Zones) and resource-based manufacturing processes account for slightly more of total developing nations' exports in 1998 than in 1980. Note the dramatic rise in exports for low,

Table 14.4 Developing nations' exports – skill level, capital intensity (percentage share)

	Share of exports from developing nations		Share of world exports	
	1980	*1998*	*1980*	*1998*
Developing nations' exports[a]	–	–	*15.4*	*24.3*
Primary commodities	50.8	19.0	25.7	14.8
Resource-based labor-intensive manufactures	21.8	23.2	14.7	15.0
Low skill technology manufactures	5.8	7.3	10.1	7.6
Medium skill technology manufactures	8.2	16.8	26.4	29.6
High skill technology manufactures	11.6	31.0	20.2	30.2

Source: UNCTAD 2002: 55, 68.

Note
a Included are 225 production categories including raw materials, excluding fuels.

medium, and high skill production processes. Medium skill exports more than doubled their share of total developing nations' exports in only eighteen years, while a surprising 31 percent of all developing nations' exports are now accounted for through complex production systems that produce semiconductors, telecommunications and electronic equipment, and so on. And, it is in these areas, typically not associated with developing nations, where the transnational-corporation-driven production process is making its greatest gains in terms of the share of world exports.

Potential costs of TNCs to a host country

While there is evidence of situations where TNCs have enhanced productivity and economic growth in developing nations, the role of the TNCs has created a storm of controversy precisely because other research highlights the possible costs of TNCs to the host nations. In this section, we briefly consider how TNCs and DFI might deepen underdevelopment or facilitate a process of biased economic growth wherein the bulk of the economic benefits are retained by the TNCs.

Transfer pricing

TNCs buy many of their inputs from and sell much of their output to other branches or affiliates of the same TNC, though these often are located in different countries. The extent of such transactions varies from firm to firm and from industry to industry. Nonetheless, virtually all the research conducted on such TNC intra-firm transactions indicates that they are significant. Furthermore, since such transactions are not of an "arms-length" character between two independent economic agents who have agreed on the terms at which to buy and sell, the TNCs are in a position to set favorable intra-firm transfer prices when it is to their advantage to do so.

A transfer price is simply an accounting price that all firms use for intra-firm transactions of inputs and semi-finished final goods, particularly as these are shipped between different branches of the same firms or different divisions for either reprocessing or sale. In the normal course of business, transfer prices are necessary to allow firms to keep track of costs within divisions or branches of the firm and to measure the profitability and productivity of different divisions or branches. However, there exists the possibility, particularly in the intra-firm movement of inputs and semi-processed goods between countries, for TNCs to use transfer prices as a mechanism for avoiding taxes in one country or another and for avoiding any profit repatriation or other restrictions placed by any country within the company's global operations. Or, a firm might simply want to disguise the extent of its profits as a matter of public relations or in order to avoid adverse repercussions, which could range from labor tensions to nationalization. Then it is likely the company will have two sets of books; one for "real" transfer prices so the TNC can monitor the effectiveness of production globally, and another to "cook the books" so as to increase and move global profits of the TNC to the most advantageous location. In the modern age of computer operations, the movement of such financial capital is only a keystroke away.

Not all TNCs are engaged in devious transfer pricing schemes, of course. But in one important study of the pharmaceutical industry in Colombia, Constantine Vaistos found that 82 percent of the companies' actual profits were hidden in transfer pricing schemes. Another study of such practices in Kenya by the International Labour Office found that the actual outflow of profits and dividends was understated by perhaps 100 percent due to the over-pricing of inputs (these studies were from the 1970s, as cited by Crow and Thorpe (1988: 275–276)). In the latter case, it is easy to see how such over-pricing makes TNC profitability in Kenya seem lower than it really is; the TNC, however, increases its global profitability. Usually, such strategies are utilized to extract profits from a country where removing profits now or later might be difficult or subject to restrictions. With such transfer over-pricing, however, it is easy to see how profits and income actually created in Kenya are withdrawn in the form of higher costs. Since most less-developed nations have extremely weak tax-collecting agencies, porous tax laws and lax enforcement practices anyway, any loss of tax revenues from the TNCs due to such transfer pricing arrangements can be extremely serious. (For a detailed treatment of the issue see Plasschaert (1994).) Further, such practices tend to reduce the pool of potential domestic investment funds.

Income transfers via TNCs

While TNCs can contribute to net resource inflows to a developing nation, they also can contribute to net resource outflows in other ways beside transfer pricing. First, parent corporations in the developed countries commonly make loans to their subsidiaries in less-developed economies. In time, such loans will be repaid as interest and amortization, constituting a potential drain on the balance of payments and foreign exchange earnings of the less-developed economy.

Unless the subsidiary is earning foreign exchange via exports or saving foreign exchange by contributing to import substitution in the host country, the outflows of interest and principal can exceed the original inflow of financial capital, thus creating a net outflow over time. Likewise, declared profits often are repatriated to the parent corporation, though profits from the subsidiary may remain within the host nation either to be lent out or reinvested in the operations of the subsidiary.

TNCs often find that their relative strength is in the mastery and control of intangibles, such as organization and information technologies and product technologies. As unique owners of such technologies, they are in a position, should they choose to do so, to sell or lease such technologies and other intangibles via joint ventures, franchises and other interactions where there is no market for the product sold or leased, it being unique. It is presumed, therefore, that the price charged in such transactions does not represent only the cost to the TNCs of creating such unique information, but that the TNC also derives some degree of monopoly rent from such transactions. This, too, contributes to an outflow of income earned in the less-developed nation flowing to the TNC, presumably headquartered in a developed economy.

Diversion effects

Some evidence suggests that when TNCs enter an economy, indigenous research and development is curbed and redirected toward adaptive inquiry which merely follows the lead of the TNCs, rather than participating in the creation of knowledge. When such effects are present, there is a presumption that the indigenous technological base is narrowed and weakened. Thus the total effect of a strong presence of TNCs in an economy may be to either make no net addition to the R&D process or to divert that process away from appropriate domestic technologies, with an adverse impact on future growth possibilities (UN 1992: 148).

It has long been the claim of the structuralist economists that the TNCs employ capital-intensive production systems which are inappropriate in poorer nations where labor is both abundant and relatively cheap, and where the real rate of unemployment and underemployment may be alarmingly high, even if disguised by informal sector activities. Thus with more capital-intensive production techniques in use, TNCs contribute to urban unemployment and underemployment. Another diversion effect of the TNC may be an internal brain drain, whereby some of the top managers and best university graduates seek employment in the TNCs, leaving the indigenous industrial and agricultural firms with a relatively narrow cadre of managerial talent, and perhaps not always the best-trained.

Increasing industrial concentration

The presence of TNCs is generally associated with increasing industrial concentration. Thus, according to standard static microeconomic analysis, resources are more likely to be used sub-optimally as monopoly power is enhanced and the degree of control of oligopolies is expanded. As economic concentration increases, the distribution of income is further tilted toward those at the top. Thus, enhanced TNC activity can be associated with a greater polarization of incomes and a tendency to divorce economic growth from enhancement of economic well-being for the vast majority of the population (Newfarmer and Frischtak 1994). In a test of the hypothesis that DFI tends to worsen the distribution of income, Pan-Long Tsai reviewed the available research and concluded that virtually every study conducted on the subject had reached the conclusion that higher levels of DFI *were* associated with a worsening of the income distribution.

> The most striking result ... is the unambiguous positive partial correlation between (the stock of direct foreign investment) and the Gini coefficient.... Our results thus confirm previous findings and support the assertion of the dependency proponents. That is, continuing inflows of foreign capital into the LDCs is very likely to be harmful to the income distributions of the host economies.
>
> (Tsai 1995: 475)

Weak linkages, thin globalization

Much recent data, some of it recorded in Table 14.4 above, suggests that developing nations are making great strides in terms of rapidly attaining efficient production systems that allow for a major surge in exports from developing nations. This perception, however, needs to be understood in a broader context that includes the new systems of global production financed by TNCs. For national development the most telling indicator of successful incorporation of skill and technology transfers relates to the magnitude of the national linkages between the TNCs and the host economy. Since Mexico has regularly been one of the top ten nations in terms of DFI inflows in recent years it is instructive to note that current research does not suggest that Mexico's *national* industrial base has either grown, or diversified or deepened its capital and knowledge/skill levels to any serious extent (Cypher 2001). Rather than articulating a new dynamized industrial sector to the national economy, Mexico exhibits the characteristics of a "disarticulated" economy with a dynamic export sector, overwhelmingly dominated by TNCs and largely unlinked to the broader domestic economy. Kathy Kopinak refers to the huge maquiladora sector (employing well over a million workers in assembly operations) as an example of **thin globalization** (Kopinak 2003). By this it is meant that – while foreign capital has increasingly moved across borders and into Mexico – the degree of connectiveness between the export sector and the national economy is very low. This is an important generalization because it allows us to move beyond the stale "yes or no" debate as to whether "globalization" has been achieved. The modifier "thin" permits a critical understanding of the shallow level of spin off and assimilation of technology transfers that dominates the processes entailed in the integrated global production system. Thus TNCs and their joint-venture or strategic alliance partners may well achieve "thick" integration of their proprietary processes across national borders, while only loosely linking to subcontractors and domestic suppliers. The end result of the weak linkages scenario is to retain most of the value-added in manufacturing within the structure of the TNCs. (Value-added refers to the difference between the cost of all inputs into the manufacturing process, and the value of total output. High value-added activities normally are those wherein high skills and complex technologies are utilized in production.)

As we have seen in our discussion of Hirschman's concept of "backward linkages" (Chapter 5), major investments can create complex, interactive, virtuous circles of forces that will push an economy to a higher level of development. Recent research has centered on Hischman's concept in great detail. The 2001 *World Investment Report* encapsulated the meaning of Hirschman's concept in the following quote:

> [Backward linkages] are defined as transactions that go beyond arm's length, one-off relations and involve long-term relations between firms. In fact, a very large proportion of intra-industry transactions in every country involves linkages in this sense, marked by sustained exchanges of information, technology, skills and other assets. Linkages are of particular significance to developing host economies, because they provide a means of diffusing valuable knowledge throughout the economy – through direct flows to the linked firms as well as spillovers to and from the latter. The benefits provided through linkages with a foreign affiliates tend to be of greater competitive significance than those among domestic firms because of the stronger knowledge and skills base of many foreign affiliates.

(UNCTAD 2001: 127)

In the instances where these researchers find integral connections to the local production base two possibilities arise:

1   Core suppliers to the large transnationals are increasingly foreign-owned. These firms often exhibit the characteristics of cutting-edge suppliers sought by the

TNCs – mastery of quality control, capability of flexible "just in time" delivery, ability to independently design components and supplies at the level of original equipment standards, and – perhaps most important – the capacity to *jointly* address production problems with the contracting TNCs. Clearly, in this instance neither learning nor technology transfers occur with heightened DFI, and the domestic economy remains disarticulated from the accumulation process driven by the TNCs.

2   Deep linkages and dynamic technology and learning transfers occur normally when host nations intervene and set up their own "linkages promotion programs." As we have discussed in Chapter 7, the State can play a crucial role in tying together the forces of the TNCs and the national needs for rapid development. Not surprisingly, most successful linkage promotion programs have occurred in East Asia. Rather than passively receiving DFI, nations in East Asia have struggled to upgrade existing linkages, create new domestic sourcing possibilities and force TNCs to reorient their production toward linkages to higher value added activities. Six key processes have been encouraged by the state:

a   **Create** public/private sector forums to open a dialogue between the TNCs and unions, regional planners, national development agencies, business associations, supplier industry associations, and financial sector firms.

b   **Disseminate** to all parties information regarding successful examples of linkages.

c   **Limit and target** specific sectors or industries, bypassing areas where internationally integrated production systems are already dominant.

d   **Choose** to host foreign affiliates on the basis of their commitment to interact with and their potential to spin off crucial learning/technology to local suppliers.

e   **Select** suppliers based on their capability of meeting production standards, quality requirements, workforce skill requirements, and the commitment of local entrepreneurs to restructuring their operations to meet continually evolving standards set by by the contracting TNC.

f   **Monitor** and evaluate local suppliers, rewarding those that successfully conform to the above goals.

Nations with **Developmental States**, such as many East Asian nations, have been able to build strong backward linkages. Elsewhere, the lack of such States – particularly in Latin America – has led to a *passive* approach to hosting TNCs and the results have been that these nations are now enmeshed in a process of "thin" globalization wherein the national economy is largely disarticulated and a new "global" dualism has emerged – ultramodern TNCs operating in a nearly autonomous transnationalized sphere and a domestic economy mired in low productivity, poverty, social decomposition, capital flight, and massive unemployment exhibited by a burgeoning "informal" sector of "self-employed" day laborers who are, in reality the "disguised unemployed."

Table 14.5, below, documents the trends to be noted in the new integrated global production system. Many nations have dramatically increased their manufacturing exports, but most are not increasing their share of manufacturing value-added. Rather, as their exports rise so too do their imports of machinery equipment,

Table 14.5 Exports of manufactured products from developing nations (percentage)

	Share of world exports		Share of world manufacturing added	
	1980	*1997*	*1980*	*1997*
Developed nations	82.3	70.9	64.5	73.3
Developing nations	10.5	26.5	16.6	23.8
Latin America	1.5	3.5	7.1	6.7
(Mexico)	(0.2)	(2.2)	(1.9)	(1.2)
Newly industrialized Asian[a]	5.1	8.9	1.7	4.5
(Korea)	(1.4)	(2.9)	(0.7)	(2.3)
ASEAN-4[b]	0.6	3.6	1.2	2.6
China	1.1[c]	3.8	3.3	5.8

Source: UNCTAD 2002: 81.

Notes
a Honk Kong, Korea, Singapore, Taiwan.
b Indonesia, Malaysia, Philippines, Thailand.
c 1984.

technology, and intermediate supplies. In these nations it is common to note a process of deindustrialization as the export sector grows while the local manufacturing base shrinks and ownership shifts even more to the TNCs. The result of these processes is that value-added at the local level actually declines – meaning that there are few or no indirect or multiplier effects to be captured or enjoyed as DFI rises. But, this is not the whole story: in Asia the ability to insert a national strategy into the process demonstrates that there is no inevitable fate for host nations. As active participants they can increasingly experience the positive effects of DFI. Thus note the dramatically different patterns exhibited by the top Latin American exporters and the eight Asian nations that have actively pursued national linkage strategies. Note the standout position of Mexico, commonly hailed as *the* success story of free trade: "between 1980 and 1997 Mexico's share in world manufacturing exports rose tenfold, while its share in world manufacturing value-added fell by more than one-third, and its share in world income by about thirteen percent" (UNCTAD 2002: 80). In Asia only Hong Kong has been loosing ground in terms of value-added, and this may be due to its leanings toward the neoclassical free trade model and away from the developmental state approach.

Export promotion and the fallacy of composition

Critics of the TNCs have maintained that while the TNCs may well be in a position to expand exports, if a strategy of promoting DFI is employed at one time in a large number of nations, it must fail for all or many of these nations. The argument is straightforward. If the less-developed world, as a group, suddenly floods global markets with new manufacturing exports, prices will fall, and it is presumed that what is lost as prices fall will not be made up through the increasing volume of sales. In other words, the terms of trade for less-developed world manufactures would deteriorate, leaving the developing countries, as a group, worse-off. There is evidence that this has been occurring. International Monetary Fund data show that the terms of trade for less-developed country manufactured goods exports fell by -0.88 percent per year between 1967 and 1987 (IMF 1988). This is a disturbing trend. Not only do most low-income countries suffer from declining terms of trade for their primary products, but it appears that the tendency for the terms of trade to decline extends to the manufactured goods of the less-developed countries according to recent research by the United Nations:

> The empirical evidence strongly suggest that global competition for labor-intensive manufacturing activities has risen over the past few years. This coincides with the shift in the mid-1980s of several highly populated, low income economies towards more export-oriented strategies. The countries with the lowest proportion of technology-intensive manufactures and the greatest proportion of low-skill labor-intensive products in their manufactured exports have faced declining terms of trade in manufactures.
>
> (UNCTAD 2002: 119–120)

Long-term costs of TNCs: the potential for environmental degradation

The overall impact of TNCs on the environment is difficult to determine because research in this area is relatively recent and incomplete. Drawing inferences from the logic of transnational production is also somewhat problematic. On the one hand, it is very often true that TNCs have leverage with host governments which may allow them to engage in environmentally unsound activities which would be prohibited at home. From a cost-minimizing standpoint, they often have a strong incentive to function as environmental predators if permitted to do so. On the other hand, however, the TNCs are visible targets, and they have become deeply involved in presenting themselves as "environmentally conscious" producers in the advanced nations. As such they can be harmed by evidence of environmental insensitivity, both in their "home" market and in the less developed nations.

Furthermore, TNCs, particularly TNCs which operate stand-alone production facilities which often date from the early days of ISI policies, operate a full range of technologically diverse industries which tend to create most of the industrial pollutants found worldwide. For example, TNCs play a major role in the production of substances which account for approximately 80 percent of anthropomorphic greenhouse-gas generation (UN 1992: 226).

- TNCs are the primary producers and consumers of chlorofluorocarbons, the principal cause of stratospheric ozone depletion;
- TNCs account for at least 15 percent of greenhouse gas emissions;
- the twenty largest TNCs producing pesticides accounted for 94 percent of agrochemical sales in 1990 (UNCTAD 1994: 226);[3]
- TNCs have extensive involvement in the most highly polluting industrial activities, such as the production of industrial chemicals, synthetic resins and plastic products, non-ferrous metal products, iron and steel, petroleum production and refining, and paper manufacturing. The portion of DFI involved in pollution-intensive industries ranges between 20 and 50 percent (UN 1992: 231);
- several studies conducted in Asian nations indicate that TNCs maintain lower

environmental standards in developing countries than these same companies uphold in developed nations, but that these lower standards are nevertheless higher than those of locally owned firms (UN 1992: 233–234).

Host nations generally have strong laws and regulations governing environmentally damaging forms of production, but do not always have the versatile scientific capacity to actually monitor and enforce the laws which already exist. Depth of scientific know-how, particularly at the level of monitoring officials needed to supervise the TNCs, and local firms which are, in fact, much more numerous, is in short supply. Governing the environmental behavior of producers, including TNCs, is one of the most immediate and pressing problems facing developing nations today. Fortunately, consciousness of environmental degradation is spreading rapidly throughout the developing world (see Box 14.2).

Export processing zones and the problems of small nations

Critics of TNCs have highlighted the role of export processing zones (EPZs) for particular attention (Kopinak 2004), for they tend to illustrate the most undesirable

---

Box 14.2 TNCs in the logging business

Tropical forests are of two types. First, there are tropical rainforests which currently cover more than 1.5 billion hectares. Two-thirds of the rainforests are in Latin America, principally Brazil. Second, there are tropical dry forests, principally in Africa. They also occupy approximately 1.5 billion hectares of land.

In both types of forest, extensive ecological change is taking place. Current estimates suggest that 20 million hectares per year are being deforested, for a variety of reasons. Approximately 60 percent of the annual deforestation is due to conversion to agricultural uses. Access to this land often occurs as a result of logging operations. Land frequently is claimed by giant agribusiness TNCs or companies which contract with these TNCs. Another 20 percent of annual deforestation is due to the logging industry directly. The logging industry encroaches, directly or indirectly, on the forests at a rate of roughly 4 million hectares per year.

About 15 percent of the world's commercial lumber comes from the rainforests. The tropical dry forests are the main source of industrial wood products. Thus, the activities of the logging industry are particularly important to understanding the destruction of large regions of Africa.

The available research indicates that US TNCs had withdrawn from nearly all direct timber-cutting operations in the tropical forests by the early 1980s. In contrast, European TNCs remain extensively involved in much of the logging that is conducted throughout the developing world. This is particularly the case in Africa, where European corporations control 90 percent of the timber-cutting in Gabon, 77 percent of these operations in the Congo, nearly 100 percent of such activities in Liberia, and 88 percent of logging in Cameroon. The Japanese are extensively involved in logging operations throughout South-East Asia.

Aside from depletion of the forests, logging quite often leads to climatic changes which give rise to desertification or reduced rainfall. Silting of streams reduces or eliminates stream aquatic life, and could reduce fishing in oceans or lakes.

Sources: UN 1992: 228; World Bank 1992: 57–58

consequences which may arise when a less-developed nation uncritically turns to DFI hoping for the potential benefits (see Box 14.3). EPZs are special geographic areas, usually at or near ports or borders, where the normal "rules of the game" regarding foreign investors are relaxed by host governments. As a general rule, products entering and leaving EPZs are exempt from all import and export taxes, corporate and other taxes and licence fees are waived for firms operating in the zones, labor unions are excluded, and even existing labor laws are not enforced, including, sometimes, minimum wage laws (see Box 14.4). EPZs often attract foreign companies by offering a "tax holiday," suspending all corporate taxes for a multi-year period.

Furthermore, physical structures often are erected and leased at modest, typically below-market, rates in industrial parks in the EPZs. Good infrastructure, such as roads, is often offered at no cost or at highly subsidized rates. Such benefits can include below-market prices for electricity, gas, water, and waste disposal not

---

Box 14.3 Women workers in export processing zones

Between 70 and 80 percent of the workers in EPZs are women. They tend to be young, inexperienced, poorly educated and poorly trained, and single. Their employment condition is insecure, with extremely high turnover rates, sometimes 200 percent per year. Unions are usually non-existent, and those that exist are dominated by the employers in the zones.

The plants tend to be modern, clean, well-ventilated, and well-lit. Nevertheless, researchers have noted a wide range of employment-related problems, suggesting widespread hazardous working conditions. Some of the difficulties include exposure to radiation and toxic substances, chemicals used without adequate training or warnings, and inadequate safety equipment. Other research mentions common occurrences of eyesight deterioration, ulcers and other nervous disorders, puncture wounds, chemical burns, and electric shocks. The pace of work is demanding; workers sometimes repeat the same operations every five seconds, 7,200 times per day. Pay rates tend to be quite low by global standards, from approximately 45 cents (US) per hour to a few dollars per hour. But wages can also be much lower, with the National Labor Committee finding wages in the late 1990s at 9–20 cents per hour in Bangladesh, 25 cents per hour in Pakistan and ten cents per hour in Indonesia. With benefits, which can include one or two meals, transportation to and from work, and some medical care, the employee cost to the firm may, however, be closer to double the wage.

Employers have often mentioned factors such as "a pliant nature," "non-union," "nimble-fingered" and "docile" in stating their preference for women workers. One study of electronics TNCs operating in Mexico's EPZ found that women workers constituted above 70 percent of the labor force, with the average age ranging between eighteen and twenty-four years. Average education received was six years, the average experience level was three years, and direct wages were 85 cents per hour.

In comparison to employment outside the EPZs, the work day tends to be 25 percent longer, with wages as much as 50 percent less than the industrial wage paid in similar operations. Within the EPZs, women tend to do the direct assembly work, while men operate and maintain complex equipment. Some EPZs now operate high-tech plants where men are increasingly being employed in direct production in preference to women workers.

Sources: Barry 1992: 144; Shaiken 1990: 91; Sklair 1989: 172; UNCTAD 1994: 203

Box 14.4 Unions under integrated production systems

Unions can be effective agents for reducing economic discrimination against women workers and for enhancing the health and safety conditions of all workers in the workplace. One study of Mexican workers showed that, in the non-union sector, women with identical skill and experience levels were paid 18 percent less than male workers. But in the unionized sector, there was no difference in pay between men and women workers. Labor unions have demonstrated that they can play an active and forceful role in enforcing health regulations and work standards.

Unions, however, play a smaller role in developing nations because 40 to 80 percent of production takes place outside the formal economy. In both agriculture and the informal sector, labor contracts are non-existent. Within the formal economy, unions often have become well established in nations with TNCs within their industrial sectors. Research indicates that the stand-alone subsidiaries of manufacturing TNCs typical of the ISI era generally paid manufacturing workers substantially more than did local employers.

However, the recent rise of the globally integrated system of production raises deep questions regarding the relationship between TNCs and unions. Integral to the new system is widespread subcontracting, often in export processing zones. Subcontractors are small, formally independent firms, operating in a dense web of intra-firm production relations organized by large transnationals, particularly in electronics and textile production and assembly. Employing perhaps twelve million low-wage workers, subcontractors are not the visible nationalist targets which TNCs constitute. As small manufacturers, they rarely operate within a sector where laborers' interests are independently represented by a union, however. There is evidence suggesting that subcontractors, the instruments of the giant TNCs, tend to sidestep unions, ignore workplace health and safety standards, often pay sub-minimum wages, and often fail to follow labor standards.

A few large garment-making TNCs have voluntarily imposed corporate codes of conduct to try to ensure fair labor standards practices are adhered to by their subcontractors operating at the lower end of global commodity chains of production. Even consumer groups are getting involved, refusing to purchase products of major retailers whose suppliers refuse to conform to reasonable labor standards for their workers.

Sources: UNCTAD 1994: 193–194, 198–199, 201, 325–327; World Bank 1995: 76, 81

available to firms outside the zones. Sometimes labor training and housing for workers is provided and/or subsidized.

The incentive for nations to establish EPZs is that they gain often badly needed foreign exchange, though this typically is limited to labor's value added, that is, wage income, in production. Most of the employment is in labor-intensive manufacturing and assembly processes, thereby creating new jobs which can be very important to host nations. Unfortunately, EPZs generally fail to create either forward or backward linkages to local production; in fact, in most countries, firms located within EPZs are prohibited from having any but minimal sales to the internal market, so forward linkages are typically impossible. But neither do the firms locating in the EPZs form many backward linkages to potential supplying firms in the local economy. In one of the largest EPZ countries, Mexico, indigenous products other than labor constitute less than 5 percent of the value added of the production in the EPZs. Often the national contribution over and above direct labor consists of little more than janitorial services.

There were nearly 551 EPZs in developing nations 1998, employing nearly twenty-seven million workers. Some of these workers were in developed nations in North America and Europe or in transition economies in Eastern Europe – but the vast majority were in developing nations (ILO 1998a). Nearly one-third of the total number of workers employed by TNCs in the less-developed world were employed in TNC operations in an EPZ. In 1998, seventy-four nations had one or more EPZs, or were planning on adding such zones. While TNCs have played a crucial role in the establishment of the EPZs, in some of the older EPZs in Asia national businesses now play a vital role. Thus, not all of the workers in the zones are employees of the TNCs, their sub-contractors, or their subsidiaries. The EPZs continue to grow, sometimes very rapidly. For example, by 1995, over 600,000 workers were employed in such zones in Mexico, but by early 2001 there were one million three hundred thousand such workers. Malaysia had ninety-nine thousand EPZ workers in 1990, and two hundred thousand in 1997. Sri Lanka's EPZ employment soared from seventy-one thousand in 1990 to two hundred and eighty thousand in 1998. Outpacing all nations, China added one million one hundred thousand EPZ workers just between 1990 and 1992! In 1990 the number of EPZ workers was estimated at roughly four million (UNCTAD 1994: 190). Another sample covering only "large" programs with data drawn from the 1992–1994 period, detailing employment in only thirty-one nations found employment totals of five and one-half million (ILO 1998b: 27–29). We can see just how rapidly the EPZs are proliferating by noting that in the late 1990s the estimate of total employment had risen above twenty million – more than five times the level estimated in 1990 (ILO 1998c: 1). EPZs are scattered around the world, with the largest cluster in Asia, and a second much smaller cluster in Mexico, Central America and the Caribbean: in 1997 Mexico had 107 EPZs, Central America, and the Caribbean 92, South America 41, the Middle East 39, Asia 225, and Africa 47.

EPZs in small nations as a special case

EPZs have often been envisioned as the "starter" for the export engine of growth of an indigenous manufacturing sector. For this to occur, however, the TNCs operating in the EPZs must be embedded in a production structure which forges ever-more profound linkages to the national economy of the host nation. Only in South Korea and Taiwan has such a "virtuous circle" been created with export-oriented TNCs. Furthermore, in these nations, the EPZs became important sites for national capitalists to produce and export from, not simply for TNCs. What is most notable is the emphasis in South Korea and Taiwan on increasing the degree of local sourcing of inputs as a condition for firms remaining in the EPZs and reaping the benefits of the exclusions from taxes and tariffs. However, this reward structure should no longer surprise. South Korea's and Taiwan's industrial policies have been noted (see Chapter 10) for their monitoring of the effects of their policies and for the successful use of performance-based subsidy structures that reward results, in particular greater efficiency, while penalizing rent-seeking, unproductive behavior. Furthermore, as wages have increased in East Asia, these nations have proved adept at creating new forms of specialization to supplant the locational advantage of cheap labor which allowed them to attract DFI in those areas where DFI was desired.

When nations fail to force production linkages to the broader economy onto firms in the EPZs, as has most often been the case, then the EPZ becomes little more than an "export platform," and TNC investment will remain an enclave, disarticulated from other sectors of the local economy. What the local economy provides in such cases is limited to cheap labor power and an attractive investment climate, both of which contribute to a higher level of profit for the TNC, but without substantially improving the probability that a locally directed growth process will be initiated in the poor nation. This situation is particularly acute in small nations.

The vertically integrated manufacturing TNCs that small economies are able to attract maintain established, risk-reducing worldwide sourcing and distribution networks. These networks involve the transfer and sale of inputs, semi-processed goods and final products among far-flung subsidiaries of the parent corporation. Existing networks are quite difficult to penetrate, particularly for new or potential firms in a less-developed economy with limited experience in dealing with the immense corporate structures characteristic of the TNCs. Even when there is sufficient know-how, the TNC is not always ready to admit linkages with its subsidiaries, particularly when doing so increases the exposure of the TNC to local instability or, more likely, because in small economies the difficulty of attaining scale economies may raise the cost of locally produced inputs above those which the TNC can provide via its existing external supply network. Furthermore, the deficiency of a production culture among domestic entrepreneurs accustomed to a protected ISI climate will often be apparent by a low level of quality control and/or an inability to maintain production and delivery schedules, though these transitional inefficiencies can be overcome. Further, the indigenous infrastructural system may make it all but impossible to offer reliable deliveries, as roads, rail and waterway carriers can be extremely ineffective. In any case, the TNC often will resist local purchases under purely market-driven conditions, since to do so would be to reduce the profitability of a portion of their own productive apparatus. Such linkages were once forged through domestic content requirements or domestic hiring quotas in those areas for which the country feels it can provide inputs and from which the greatest possibility for positive external learning effects exist.

Creation of the World Trade Organization in 1994 has made it difficult for nations to utilize domestic content restrictions – but the WTO's strictures do not prevent nations from creating conditions wherein the local content rises. Nations need to encourage foreign affiliates of TNCs to (1) provide managerial and labor training to local supplier firms, (2) build an environment wherein foreign affiliates will be rewarded for sharing production information, (3) assist local suppliers by furnishing financial support – perhaps through advanced payment for production and/or prompt payment on delivery, (4) transferring technology and know-how to supplier firms. While this may sound utopian, case studies involving Malaysia, Thailand, China, and Singapore in the late 1990s demonstrate that a committed active state can engineer vital changes that lead to deep linkage effects in spite of the new barriers to local content legislation erected by the WTO (UNCTAD 2001: 149–214). Thus, in the 1990s local sourcing of electronics inputs were only 28 percent in Mexico, but were 62 percent in Malaysia and 40 percent in Thailand – the difference accounted for by the existence of policies to stimulate linkages in Malaysia and

Thailand (UNCTAD 2001: 135). The gap between those nations who have built linkage programs and the bottom-end EPZ nations is growing, with most nations able only to supply 5–10 percent from local content. Only nations with a broad development strategy are able to build linkage programs. More generally:

> Many TNCs have supplier development programmes in host developing countries.... The intensity of knowledge and information exchange in buyer–supplier relationships tends to increase with the level of economic development of host countries, particularly in complex activities, and where technological and managerial gaps with suppliers are not too wide.
>
> (UNCTAD 2001: xxii)

Vertically integrated TNCs and development prospects

The multiplier effects of backward linkages from TNC investments can be expected to be quite small unless a country is extremely diligent in helping local businesses to forge links with the TNCs. The International Labor Organization's research suggests that, generally, for every five EPZ jobs only one new (additional) job is created in the domestic economy – an extremely low job multiplier (ILO 1998b: 8). To the extent that export-platform promotion is a major component of a nation's overall development strategy, even wages paid will have a reduced multiplier effect when a significant part of consumption goods, including agricultural goods, are imported. To visualize this process, Figure 14.1 presents a stylized circuit of capital for a typical manufacturing TNC attracted to an EPZ in a small nation.

The production process is initiated outside the country in which the export subsidiary is located. Money capital (M) is used to purchase produced means of production and raw materials (MP) and labour (L), for the first stage of production (P_1). From this comes a partially transformed output or new means of production (C') with a value as yet unsold or "unrealized" greater than the initial outlay, M. With the completion of the first stage of production, C' is shipped by the TNC to its

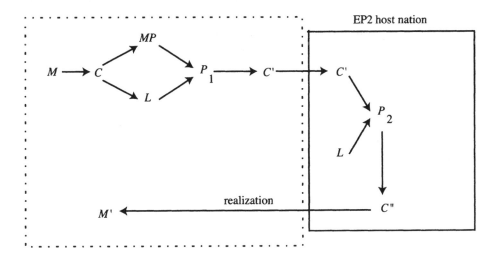

Figure 14.1 An EPZ circuit of capital.

export subsidiary in the small, export-platform economy. There the semi-processed product is combined in the local production process (P_2) with unskilled, cheap labour.[4] Now, the subsidiary of the TNC produces final or partially assembled commodities, C'', which are then re-exported. Their value is realized, and the profit from production is accumulated not in the country where the EPZ is located, but elsewhere within the international structure of the TNC. Production ($P = P_1 + P_2$) and realization take place only on an international scale, in which many individual subsidiaries of a TNC in widely scattered locations ultimately may participate. $C'' > C' > C$ and $M' > M$, where the difference $M' - M = S$, is the level of gross profit.

Structurally articulated *internally* with its own subsidiaries and already linked to established sourcing and distribution networks, the TNC's subsidiary (or affiliate) in a small nation is sectorally and structurally disarticulated from the local economic structure. The local economy is but a production point, and then for only a fragment, P_2, of the complete production process within the TNC. The manufacturing export-platform economy provides no more than a convenient physical location, albeit one that is frequently quite profitable. It is the non-specific locational bias of the purely export-oriented TNC, as opposed to the locationally specific food, raw material, mineral, and ISI manufacturing corporations of the past, which results in small host governments having reduced leverage when attempting to pressure the TNCs in EPZs to create or permit backward and forward linkages when they do not emerge spontaneously.

EPZs can create the appearance of industrialization and development in a country, without the substance. The location of the P_2 phase of production in a poor nation will almost always contribute to a higher GDP, though the *net* contribution of such production will be less than the gross effect to the degree that local production is adversely affected, especially in agriculture or other sectors which lose labor to urban areas near the EPZs where people migrate in hopes of finding employment. Moreover, the contribution of the TNC to the country's GNP will be less than its contribution to GDP by the level of repatriated profits, interest, and dividends. Even after taking such effects fully into account, the net contribution of the TNC will be overstated in a static analysis. Given that the P_2 process is not location-specific, it usually can be transferred rather easily by the "footloose" export-only manufacturing TNCs. And, to the degree that the new host nation provides a greater array of incentives to locate in its EPZs, the relocation costs to the TNC are correspondingly reduced. Furthermore, EPZs are unlikely to contribute to the breakdown of stultifying social structures which continue to thwart movement away from the low-productivity trap of the "plantation economies" still characteristic of many small nations. Enclave EPZs do not spontaneously contribute to the expansion of the "industrial arts" in a dynamic process of creative destruction that breaks down restraining internal barriers to progress. This is partly so because the TNCs seek to maintain the low-wage sector that, with reasonable levels of productivity, contributes strongly to their global profits.

Bargaining with the TNCs

There are, however, nations which have made substantial economic and social progress while selectively and constructively interacting with TNCs. In *bargaining* with TNCs, particularly TNCs of the "stand-alone" type which desire to enter a nation in order to sell in that nation's home market, the host nation can exert some leverage. This is particularly the case for a host nation which has achieved embedded autonomy, as demonstrated by their successful pursuit of not only ISI but export substitution strategies (see Chapters 7, 9, and 10). At the same time, some host nations have increasingly been able to exercise some bargaining strength due to the fact that there has been a rapid dispersion of the power formerly exercised by US TNCs. A quick glance back to Table 14.2 will demonstrate that, while US TNCs controlled approximately half of the stock of DFI in 1960, their share of this capital fell dramatically to one-quarter of the total in 1992. As a consequence of this shift, some host nations have been able to improve the terms of engagement with TNCs because, more and more, when foreign firms seek to become involved in these nations it is likely that TNCs from other nations will also be interested. This competition among TNCs to locate in any country can work in the favor of the host country.

In 1992, the United Nation's Transnational Corporations and Management Division published a benchmark work subtitled "Transnational Corporations as Engines of Growth" (UN 1992). This study drew together literally hundreds of research documents in order to address the crucial question of the links between DFI and economic development. Notice that the conclusions to this study, summarized below, do not address a number of thorny issues, such as the impact of TNCs on the environment (see Box 14.5), or the intermediate-term effects of DFI on the balance-of-payments discussed above under the heading "Income Transfers via TNCs," or transfer pricing issues. Some of their key conclusions are worth careful scrutiny, for there are major lessons to be learned. The following quotation and the subsequent summary deal only with the quantity and quality of physical capital formation:

> The evidence indicates that FDI (foreign direct investment) inflows make a positive contribution to the quantity of new physical capital in developing countries, and that this quantitative contribution appears more significant in industries that are crucial to growth and development, such as manufacturing. Local purchasing by TNCs has, in many host developing nations, provided a stimulant to local investment. Evidence of the qualitative contribution of TNCs to host country investment is less clear cut. ... TNC management practices provide a model for efficient organization of production that can be learned by host country producers.
>
> The evidence on TNCs and host countries suggests that the benefits from the presence of TNCs may depend as much on host country conditions as upon the assets brought by foreign firms. ... When TNCs produce largely in export processing zones, their ability to stimulate domestic production is reduced.
>
> The general conclusion is that TNCs have had a positive influence on domestic capital formation in host developing countries ... the evidence for such a conclusion is drawn from a small number of developing countries, most of which are large and have had some success in stimulating growth.
>
> (UN 1992: 124–125)

Box 14.5 Environmental problems in Mexico's EPZs

With more than one million employees (in 2002) working in over 3,000 foreign-owned plants along the nearly 2,000 mile US–Mexican border, the environmental effects of Mexico's EPZs have received considerable attention.

Mexico has a body of laws and an environmental ministry, SEDESOL, which attempt to regulate the environmental effect of production in the EPZs. At best, SEDESOL is able to inspect one-third of the assembly plants in a given year, and enforcement is lax. Some of the effects noted by researchers are as follows.

- The city of Tijuana, just below San Diego, California, has experienced a 119 percent population increase as workers have flocked to the more than 550 EPZ firms. Industrial waste from the plants and household waste from the population are beyond the sewage treatment capacities of the city. As a result, 12 million gallons of untreated waste flow daily into the Tijuana River and then into the Pacific Ocean.
- In Nogales, Mexico, seventy-five assembly plants, along with the supporting population, daily discharge 18 million gallons of untreated waste. The Nogales Wash contains mercury, lead, and a variety of industrial solvents utilized by furniture assembly companies. Carcinogenic chemicals found in underground aquifers have forced water-well closings ten miles north of the border.
- In Matamoros, one plant was found to be releasing xylene, an industrial solvent, at levels 6,000 times above that thought to be safe in drinking water. Another plant registered concentrations 53,000 times above the safe level. Releases of toxic hydrofluoric acid at one plant led to a ban on future worker settlements within one and half miles of the plant. Yet workers who already lived within this perimeter were permitted to remain there.

Passage of the North American Free Trade Agreement (NAFTA) in 1993 created new hope for an environmental clean-up of Mexico's EPZ plants. However, fraud and deception continue to overcome the attempt to control the disposal of toxic substances, with only 20 percent of the 12,500 tons of toxic solid wastes inspected for proper disposal.

Sources: Russell 1994: 254–260; Scheeres 1996

These summary conclusions are derived from several substantive findings.

- Manufacturing matters; attracting manufacturing TNCs can raise the total stock of capital available for production.
- Local sourcing of inputs matters; attracting foreign manufacturing capital is neither a necessary nor a sufficient condition for economic growth. The creation of backward linkages to the local production process is central to the benefits to be gained from TNCs. TNC capital must be compelled to link with local production sources.
- Host country conditions matter and are fundamental; host nations must be active participants in defining and revising the conditions under which foreign capital is permitted to operate in the domestic economy; market-driven passivity is inadequate if the potential gains from foreign capital investment are to have a chance of being realized.

- EPZs matter, but in a negative way; they have not been a viable basis for physical or human capital accumulation nor for sustained growth.
- Host country size matters; relatively large nations have, as a rule, been most successful in controlling the interactive process of foreign investment and in being able to reap more of the potential benefits of DFI; there are exceptions, however. The Latin American countries have been less successful in this regard, partly because of a more *laissez-faire* approach to DFI, rather than a more activist and cooperative approach.
- History matters; successful, or relatively successful, nations in dealing with TNCs have had a history of fostering development through ISI.

DFI in Asia and Latin America

As we have noted in earlier chapters, a great deal of comparative research has been conducted on the East Asian "miracle" economies and the largest Latin American nations. Another contrast to be noted is the manner in which the Asian nations have addressed the issue of the role of foreign capital. To begin to survey some of this research, it is useful to note the relative insignificance of TNCs at the top of the production pyramid in both South Korea and Taiwan in the 1980s. In contrast to the large Latin American nations, private nationally owned firms clearly dominate the most important sectors of production, with state-owned firms holding a rather distant second-place position (see Table 14.6). In Latin America, by contrast, the TNCs have a very strong position among the leading corporations, while nationally owned firms hold a relatively small share of production compared to South Korea and Taiwan.

In a recent attempt to account for the relatively strong performance of two of the Asian miracles, South Korea and Taiwan, in relation to the two largest Latin American nations, Brazil and Mexico, Barbara Stallings scrutinized the differing approaches to, and experiences with, foreign capital. She reached the conclusion

Table 14.6 Relative share of TNCs among the largest firms (percentage of total in each category, 1987)

Country	State-owned	National	TNCs
South Korea			
Top 10	10	90	–
Top 25	n.d.	n.d.	n.d.
Taiwan			
Top 10	40	60	–
Top 25	32	56	12
Brazil			
Top 10	60	10	30
Top 25	40	20	32
Mexico			
Top 10	40	20	40
Top 25	28	44	28

Source: Gereffi 1990: 92–95.

Note
n.d. = no data.

that "the issue at stake is whether the State's choice of development strategy determines the role of foreign capital or whether foreign capital determines development strategy" (Stallings 1990: 80). Stallings found that:

- in South Korea and Taiwan the overall importance of foreign capital had declined over time; DFI had continued, but at a moderate rate;
- in Latin America, the importance of foreign capital increased from the 1960s, with the implementation of secondary ISI, until the 1980s, when the debt crisis virtually halted such inflows;
- the East Asian nations have had a relatively lower reliance on DFI for capital and technology;
- the East Asia nations have favored borrowing from foreign governments, with relatively easy repayment requirements, to having DFI;
- the East Asian nations have been able to maneuvre between Japan and the United States, thereby improving their bargaining position in determining the conditions under which DFI has taken place;
- the East Asian nations had "strong" and cohesive states which were willing to operate strategically and plan strategically in pursuit of national development;
- the East Asian nations continued to weigh the relative merits of DFI against bank loans and other forms of credit, maintaining a balance between these in their favor;
- the Latin American nations tended to adopt one strategy regarding DFI, and foreign capital, to the exclusion of dynamic combinations regarding, first, openness to DFI versus protection and closure of certain key industries, and second, DFI versus bank loans.

Some of the creative and versatile strategies adopted by South Korea and Taiwan in their search to gain maximum advantage from DFI and foreign capital in general are summarized by Stallings:

[F]oreign capital took two main forms. One was direct investment, often in export processing zones that provided tax incentives and exemptions on import duties as long as output was exported. The other was marketing, typically through subcontracting arrangements with international retail chains.

Both the South Korean and Taiwanese governments were strong, centralized institutions, which used a combination of incentives and regulations to deal with foreign capital. The South Koreans had a more top-down approach and privileged loans over DFI since loans gave them greater control. The Foreign Capital Inducement Law of 1960 and its subsequent amendments set out procedures and guarantees for attracting foreign loans. Direct investors were also offered tax incentives, but they were never really encouraged during this period. In addition, the South Koreans were especially sensitive to the issue of dependency on the United States, and the normalization of relations with Japan in 1965 provided an opportunity to play off South Korea's two most important allies.... Taiwan was more willing to let foreigners acquire equity participation in the economy. Much of this was initially carried out through EPZs.... Nevertheless, the government maintained substantial control by ownership of upstream industries, including banking, and by targeting chosen sectors for investment. In both countries, the governments used their power to protect the interests of local firms as well as to regulate foreign participation.

(Stallings 1990: 77)

Analyzing the time period from the mid-1950s to the late 1980s, Stallings noted that the reliance on foreign capital increased in the Latin American nations, while domestic savings rose in South Korea and Taiwan, thereby lessening the need for foreign capital flows (see Box 14.6). In the 1950s and 1960s, the Latin American nations relied heavily on DFI, but they paid a price in terms of the loss of economic and political power by the central government and of a reduction in the importance of national capital. Meanwhile, the East Asian nations were able to access loans and aid funds which went directly to a clearly developmentalist state, as we saw in Chapter 10, thereby permitting the state to channel resources first toward an easy ISI strategy and later to provide the incentives for a strategy switch toward export substitution. Reviewing the differing growth experiences of the Latin American nations and the East Asian economies, Stallings arrives at an incisive conclusion regarding the role of foreign capital in economic development.

[The] differing trends over time, toward a lesser need for foreign capital in East Asia and a greater ability to control it, add up to an objective set of reasons for East Asian specialists to be more positive than their Latin American counterparts about the role of foreign capital. The key to understanding the different experiences centers on the issue of host country autonomy, an issue that also links the two debates being considered. Regardless of its form – direct investment, private bank loans, or public sector credits – the purpose of foreign capital is to further the interests of those who provide it. Development of the host country is a fortuitous side effect at best, which will only come about if the host government maintains enough autonomy and control to guarantee that the benefits are shared between providers and recipients of foreign capital.

(Stallings 1990: 82)

The integrated production system

Since the early 1980s, but with increasing emphasis, TNCs have turned to new forms of production, sometimes called flexible manufacturing, or "Japanese management techniques." While no two firms operate in an identical manner, many theorists of industrial organization believe that a blending of "just-in-time" inventory controls, total quality management techniques (JIT/TQM) and small-batch flexible production based on computer-aided designs and computer-aided manufacturing techniques (CAD/CAM), and, generally, "lean" production techniques capture the recent tendencies in worldwide, best-practice production technology. In a recent study examining the growth of new production forms in the less-developed world, John Humphrey defined "lean" production as having the following attributes:

Lean production involves three related transformations – the reorganization of production along JIT/TQM lines, the transformation of design, and the development of new relations with suppliers. It focuses not only on the factory, but also factors outside of the plant such as the design function and other firms.

Box 14.6 Management of DFI: the case of Taiwan

Taiwan's experience with foreign capital, particularly with DFI, is instructive. Taiwan constitutes an important case study of the potential benefit from having well-designed foreign investment guidelines concerning the terms of entry, interaction, and exit of foreign capital in the host nation.

Like Japan and South Korea, Taiwan has imposed important conditions on foreign capital, but these conditions have been somewhat less restrictive than in other countries of the region. When Taiwan has considered the entry of foreign capital, the state attempts to ascertain the degree to which such capital will contribute to new exports, particularly to the penetration of new markets. Other important considerations are the degree to which the foreign capital will create forward and backward linkages or input–output links and the likelihood of significant transfers of needed technologies. Taiwan is concerned with how a given investment project will enhance its chances of attracting future DFI which will fit into its development strategy.

Local content requirements

As has been the case in many other nations which have sought to manage DFI, Taiwan has emphasized **local content legislation** which has forced TNCs, even those operating in EPZs, to make significant and growing use of locally produced inputs. Research from the 1980s indicated that local content in the EPZs was slowly raised to approximately 20 percent. In Mexico, in contrast, local content has been trivial in the EPZs, less than 4 percent. (Since the creation of the World Trade Organization in 1994 it has become very difficult to impose foreign content legislation – but many nations in Asia have found creative ways to circumvent the WTO, requirements.)

Creating new comparative advantage

Taiwan has repeatedly revised its DFI conditions as the nation's economy has evolved. Thus in the 1970s it began to *discourage* labor-intensive DFI, while simultaneously working to provide a mass of well-trained engineers, scientists and managers which could spearhead a drive into high-technology, capital-intensive industrial activities of the secondary ISI/secondary export substitution stage of industrialization.

Export requirements

Nations with sizeable, if not huge, populations may find that the key to development rests with the expansion of domestic demand. Intermediate and small nations will generally find that exports must play a vital role, but not necessarily the central role, in a viable development strategy. As Robert Wade points out, Taiwan has made constructive use of export requirements when considering the admission of foreign capital, while simultaneously inhibiting access to the domestic market, which has been largely reserved for national firms.

Taiwan has sometimes been portrayed as a free trader, but is nonetheless willing to use both assured access to the domestic market and protection against imports to attract the kind of DFI which will enhance its growth strategy.

> Import protection is important too, and here the subtlety of the approval mechanism is valuable. Firms which are highly sought after may be told that since Taiwan is a free-trading country it cannot offer sizeable tariffs or import bans; but that the

government will ensure that the firm nevertheless gets an ample domestic market. What is being said, in effect, is that hidden protection via the approval mechanism will be given, while the outward appearance of little protection is maintained.

(Wade 1990: 152)

In summary, Taiwan has, thus far, demonstrated how trade-related investment measures (known as TRIMS) and a dynamic adaptation to new forms of comparative advantage can be combined in a successful development strategy. This does not mean, of course, that the Taiwanese experience can or should be duplicated exactly in other nations. But it does point to the possibilities of constructive interaction with foreign capital, indicating that a cohesive cadre of state managers can, as Robert Wade points out, *govern* the market, rather than adapting to a strategy of merely following and being buffeted about by market signals, as they are transmitted through the impulse of foreign capital.

Sources: Grunwald and Flamm 1985: 230; Wade 1990

These interrelated changes are held to create a new production system, based on principles which contrast with [early twentieth-century assembly-line] mass production. . . .

The core of reorganization within the firm along the lines of JIT/TQM can be captured in the term "minimum factory". . . . The aim of manufacturing production is to produce goods which satisfy the customer at the minimum possible cost. The ideal factory should have every stage of production oriented toward this overall aim, and all activities in the plant should contribute to transforming inputs into finished products which attend customers' needs. Any other activities are, in principle, a waste of resources. Such waste includes holding stocks, moving products around unnecessarily, producing items which are defective and reworking products. The ideal factory responds rapidly to customer demands, producing rapidly a range of products which satisfies customers' needs with the minimum possible inputs of energy, materials, capital and labor.

(Humphrey 1995: 150, 152)

JIT/TQM techniques are now being adopted widely, particularly in the newly industrializing countries (NICs), but also in countries such as Zimbabwe and the Dominican Republic. Unfortunately, it presently appears that successful adaptation to the new techniques seems to be the exception. Most countries, including some of the first-tier NICs, such as Brazil and Mexico, are not able to compete effectively on the basis of the emerging production systems. Clearly, cases of relatively successful adaptation are to be found, such as the new car plants in Mexico, but the likelihood of most nations being passed over by such technology is quite high. For, unlike the early ISI stage, the demands for JIT/TQM global factory production systems extend much deeper into the economic fabric of a less-developed nation. Early ISI branch plants were to a large degree "stand-alone" operations, importing some of their inputs, and relying on the parent company for design and production techniques, but largely operating independently from the parent on day-to-day production decisions.

Under the emerging system of "globally integrated production," there is a greater reliance on a web, or network, of sophisticated suppliers which must be close at hand or "just-in-time." This means that DFI intended to meet the standards of JIT/TQM production must be embedded in a network of sophisticated supplier firms offering a full range of inputs, as well as upstream services such as delivery, marketing, and transportation. As the list of items that must be provided outside of the factory grows, the likelihood that a given less-developed nation has the deep, complex, and quickly adjustable production support system to meet the expectation of the TNCs declines. Thus, it is feared that these new production systems will be adapted by a small number of NICs which are already relatively developed, leaving the rest of the less-developed world at risk of being further marginalized from "deep integration" and advanced production techniques. Thus JIT/TQM techniques may tend to reinforce the tendency toward "cumulative causation" and "backwash effects" discussed in Chapter 6. This, too, is the tentative conclusion of the United Nations which examined TNCs as "engines" of growth. Clearly, it is too soon to draw definitive conclusions regarding the new production systems. But just as clearly, the developing nations now face new and quite formidable challenges if they seek to attract and manage DFI and foreign capital in an ever more technological age. Evidence from the auto sector in Brazil and Argentina suggest that as integrated production systems expand, the role of local suppliers contracts and foreign-owned supplier firms arrive to service the high value added supply needs of the TNCs: "[D]omestic firms in developing countries supplying to affiliates that are part of integrated production systems typically belong to a lower tier and provide relatively simple inputs – cardboard boxes, plastic and foam rubber packaging materials, metal stamping, diemaking and simple assembly" (UNCTAD 2001: 137).

Conclusion

While FDI has expanded tremendously in the course of the 1990s it is impossible to demonstrate one unique pattern between host developing nations and TNCs. Outcomes vary primarily in accordance with the strategies and tactics adopted by host nations. A passive strategy yields meager results, while nations that actively engage TNCs have demonstrated that dynamic policies to capture gains from DFI are possible. It would be impossible to offer a superior summary of the lessons that have been learned regarding DFI and development than that of the *World Investment Report*:

> there is no ideal universal strategy on DFI. Any strategy has to suit the particular conditions of a country at a particular time, and evolve as it needs change and its competitive position in the world alters.... Making effective strategy requires above all a development vision, coherence and coordination. It also requires the ability to decide on trade-offs between different objectives of development. In a typical structure of policy-making, this requires the strategy-making body to be placed near the head of government, so that a strategic view of national needs and priorities can be formed and enforced.
>
> (UNCTAD 1999: 326)

Questions for review

1   Over the long period 1945–1995, global trade has generally grown much faster than the annual average rate of growth of global GDP. Proponents of an "export-led growth" strategy have argued that, with this growth of global trade, concerns over the "fallacy of composition" argument regarding trade as an engine of growth are exaggerated – that is, export growth has plenty of room for maneuver. Analyze this dispute, with particular reference to the possible duplications of the cases of Korea and Taiwan. What percentage of world exports currently is produced by less-developed countries?

2   Construct a chart listing the potential effects of inward direct foreign investment on developing nations. In one column, list the possible positive benefits of DFI; in a second column list the possible negative effects DFI can bring to a host nation. Some of these effects may be political, others economic, social, or environmental. Briefly explain each potential benefit and each potential cost.

3   You have been hired (at £1,000/day) to advise on the establishment of an export processing zone in a Middle Eastern nation. Your task is to write a brief (500-word) outline entitled "Pitfalls to Avoid and Benefits to Capture in an EPZ."

4   A large TNC, heavily involved in subcontracting its production to various low-income nations, has become the target of an adverse publicity campaign which has centered on the low labor standards of its subcontractors. Your task is to compose a "Code of Conduct" which the TNC will impose on its subcontractors in the future. What rules would you include?

Notes

1 For example, more than any other factor, the political economy of oil has determined the modern economic history of the Middle East. At the epicenter of a vast and complex historical transformation, one finds the overwhelming influence of the huge oil-producing transnationals. John Blair's classic, *The Control of Oil*, continues to be the best introduction to the role of the oil industry in the Middle East, and to the nature of the largest single group of TNCs, the oil and chemical corporations (Blair 1978).

2 This shows, too, why international convergence of income, as discussed in Chapter 8, is perhaps not evident. Poorer countries are different from more developed nations, even among the less-developed nations themselves, there are differences. They do not have the same production functions, so the fact that they have less physical capital does not mean that the return to capital is higher, as the law of diminishing returns would suggest. Physical capital in the poorest countries is less effective, because the complementary inputs, like human capital, technology, government policies, and so on, that make such capital more productive are missing or but poorly formed.

3 Drawn to India by the market potential for fertilizers created by the Green Revolution, one pesticide manufacturer, Union Carbide, began production of chemicals and pesticides in Bhopal in 1970. In December 1984, Bhopal became an international symbol of environmental catastrophe when a pesticide product, methyl isocyanate (MIC), was released into the air in massive amounts. Safety conditions at the plant were totally inadequate, and 200,000 people in the city of 800,000 suffered from gas inhalation. Thousands died, and over 25,000 were treated by medical professionals. No one knows the long-term effects on the survivors, many of whom can no longer work (Gupta 1988: 55).

4 Wages in the EPZs tend to be one-tenth or less than average hourly wages in the advanced industrial nations for roughly similar work. Although productivity measured as output per hour is usually lower in the EPZs – often half that of the advanced nations and sometimes above 80 percent – the profitability of such production can be quite high.

References

Barry, Tom (ed.). 1992. *Mexico: A Country Guide*. Albuquerque, NM: The Inter-Hemispheric Education Resource Center.

Blair, John. 1978. *The Control of Oil*. New York: Vintage Books.

Cavanagh, John and Frederick Clairmonte. 1982. *The Transnational Economy*. Washington, DC: The Institute for Policy Studies.

Caves, Richard. 1991. "The Multinational Enterprise as an Economic Organization," pp. 146–160 in Jeffrey Frieden and Anthony Lake (eds), *International Political Economy*, 2nd edn New York: St. Martins.

Crow, Ben and Mary Thorpe *et al.* 1988. *Survival and Change in the Third World*. Oxford: Oxford University Press.

Cypher, James. 2001. "Developing Disarticulation within the Mexican Economy," *Latin American Perspectives* 28 (May): 11–37.

Evans, Peter. 1998. "Transnational Corporations and Third World States: From the Old Internationalization to the New," pp. 195–224 in Ricard Kozul-Wright and Robert Rowthorn (eds), *Transnational Corporations and the Global Economy*. London: Macmillan.

Gargan, Edward. 1996. "An Indonesian Asset is Also a Liability," *New York Times* (March 16): 17–18.

Gazcón, Felipe. 2002. "Para fusiones y adquisición de empresas, 71% de la IED," *El Financiero* (8 de mayo): 15.

Gereffi, Gary. 1990. "Big Business and the State," pp. 90–109 in Gary Gereffi and Donald Wyman (eds), *Manufacturing Miracles*. Princeton, NJ: Princetown University Press.

Gereffi, Gary and Peter Evans. 1981. "Transnational Corporations, Dependent Development, and State Policy in the Semiperiphery: A Comparison of Brazil and Mexico," *Latin American Research Review* 16: 31–64.

Grunwald, Joseph and Kenneth Flamm. 1985. *The Global Factory*. Washington, DC: The Brookings Institution.

Gupta, Avijit. 1988. *Ecology and Development in the Third World*. London: Routledge.

Humphrey, John. 1995. "Industrial Reorganization in Developing Countries," *World Development* 23 (January): 149–162.

ILO (International Labor Organization). 1998a. *Labour and Social Issues Relating to Export Processing Zones*. Geneva: International Labor Organization.

—— (Bureau of Multinational Enterprise Activities). 1998b. "Export Processing Zones: Addressing the Social and Labour Issues." 1–31. http://www.transnationale.org/pays/epz.htm

—— 1998c. "Export Processing Zones Growing Steadily," *Press Release of ILO* (September 28) 1–5. www.ilo.org/public/english/bureau/Inf/pr/1998/34.htm.

IMF (International Monetary Fund). 1988. *IFS Supplement on Trade Statistics*, no. 15.

Kennedy, Charles. 1992. "Relations between Transnational Corporations and Governments of Host Countries," *Transnational Corporations* 1 (February).

Kopinak, Kathryn. 2003. "Maquiladora Industrialization of the Baja California Peninsula: The Coexistence of Thick and Thin Globalization," *International Journal of Urban and Regional Studies* 27 (June): 319–336.

—— (ed.). 2004. *Social Costs of Industrial Growth in Mexico*. San Diego, CA: Center for US–Mexico Studies, University of California, San Diego.

Maxfield, Sylvia and James Nolt. 1990. "Protectionism and the Internationalization of Capital," *International Studies Quarterly* 34: 49–81.

Newfarmer, Richard and Claudio Frischtak (eds). 1994. *Transnational Corporations, Market Structure and Performance*. London: Routledge.

Plasschaert, S. (ed.). 1994. *Transnational Corporations: Transfer Pricing and Taxation*. London: Routledge.

Russell, Philip. 1994. *Mexico Under Salinas*. Austin, TX: Mexico Resource Center.

Scheeres, Julia. 1996. "Waste Repatriation to the US," *El Financiero International* January 8–14: 5.

Shaiken, Harley. 1990. *Mexico in the Global Economy*. San Diego, CA: Center for US–Mexico Studies, University of California, San Diego.

Sklair, Leslie. 1989. *Assembling for Development*. Boston, MA: Unwin Hyman.

Stallings, Barbara. 1990. "The Role of Foreign Capital in Economic Development," pp. 55–89 in Gary Gereffi and Donald Wyman (eds), *Manufacturing Miracles*. Princeton, NJ: Princeton University Press.

Tsai, Pan-Long. 1995. "Foreign Direct Investment and Income Inequality," *World Development* 23 (March): 469–484.

UN (United Nations Transnational Corporations and Management Division). 1992. *World Investment Report 1992*. Geneva: United Nations.

UNCTAD (United Nations Conference on Trade and Development). 1994. *World Investment Report 1994*. Geneva: United Nations.

—— 1999. *World Investment Report 1999*. Geneva: United Nations.

—— 2001. *World Investment Report 2001*. Geneva: United Nations.

—— 2002. *Trade and Development Report, 2002*. Geneva: United Nations.

Wade, Robert. 1990. *Governing the Market*. Princeton, NJ: Princeton University Press.

World Bank. 1992. *World Development Report 1992*. Oxford: Oxford University Press.

—— 1995. *World Development Report 1995*. Oxford: Oxford University Press.

—— 2002. www.worldbank.org/prospects/gdf2002/.

15 Macroeconomic equilibrium

The external balance

After studying this chapter, you should understand:
- how fixed, floating, and managed float exchange rate regimes function and the impact of changing economic conditions on exchange rates;
- how exchange rates are affected by inflation;
- the importance of the balance of payments and the components of the current and capital accounts of the balance of payments;
- the importance of official foreign exchange reserves;
- the interrelation between exchange rates and the balance of payments;
- the impact of over-valued and under-valued exchange rates on the balance of payments and on economic progress;
- the connections between internal macroeconomic disequilibriums (inflation and the fiscal deficit) and external macroeconomic disequilibriums (exchange rates and the balance of payments);
- the concept of the "twin deficits" and the connection to the balance of payments;
- the difference between "good" and "bad" current account deficits; and
- the importance of monitoring the balance of payments accounts so as to anticipate potential crises.

Introduction

In an increasingly global economy, where barriers to trade and financial flows among nations have tended to be reduced since the early 1970s, policy-makers must be ever vigilant in ensuring that their country's balance of payments and exchange rate evolve in ways that create the possibility of expanded and sustained economic growth and development. In modern economies linked by virtually instantaneous and twenty-four-hour flows among the world's financial markets in London, Paris, Frankfurt, Tokyo, Hong Kong, Seoul, Sydney, Mexico City, Buenos Aires, Toronto and New York, disequilibrium situations that are not corrected fairly quickly can lead to severe crises over the longer term.

It is no exaggeration to suggest that in the current context of economic policy-making, it is the external equilibrium conditions imposed by the balance of payments which are the ultimate binding constraint facing every economy. If these constraints are not prudently respected, a balance of payments disequilibrium can thwart virtually all other positive steps policy-makers and society have taken on the road to becoming more developed. This is why an understanding of the workings of the balance of payments accounts is essential for coming to grips with the challenges facing many economies today.

This chapter considers the relation between a country's exchange rate, its balance of payments position and the links between the macroeconomic *internal* balances, especially the rate of inflation, and the *external* balances. To understand how balance of payments difficulties may arise, it is necessary to consider exchange rate determination under different possible exchange rate regimes – floating, fixed, and managed float – and then the connection between a nation's exchange rates and its balance of payments position.

Exchange rates

A country's **nominal exchange rate** is the number of units of a foreign currency that can be obtained for each unit of the domestic currency or, alternatively, the number of units of the domestic currency required to buy one unit of some foreign currency.[1] Table 15.1 shows the nominal exchange rates for a number of different currencies, stated in terms of US dollars.

The table tells us, for example, that one Pakistan rupee exchanged for $0.01671, or almost two US cents on 4 February 2002. Alternatively, one US dollar exchanged for a bit more than 63 Pakistan rupees.

Each country has a multiple number of bilateral exchange rates, one for each country with which it trades, has financial transactions, or in which its citizens travel or from which visitors arrive. The table lists only a few bilateral exchange rates between various countries with the United States.

Table 15.1 Nominal foreign exchange rates, selected countries[a]

	Units of foreign currency received for US$1	Units of US$ received for 1 unit of foreign currency
Argentina	2.025 (peso)	0.49505
Bangladesh	59.478 (taka)	0.01824
Cambodia	4,026 (riel)	0.0002754
China	8.2866 (renminbi yuan)	0.12097
Ethiopia	8.8109 (birr)	0.12466
Ghana	7,797.9 (cedi)	0.0001429
India	48.41 (rupee)	0.02072
Kenya	79.05 (shilling)	0.01278
Malaysia	3.805 (ringgit)	0.26350
Mexico	9.153 (peso)	0.10931
Pakistan	63.023 (rupee)	0.01671
South Korea	1,318 (won)	0.0007649

Note

a Exchange rate values quoted at interbank rates for February 4, 2002 from http://www.oanda.com/convert/classic. Local currency names in parentheses.

Types of exchange rate regimes

Exchange rate values are determined in different ways for different countries. Exchange rates can be regulated solely by the free market (floating exchange rate) or solely by a government decision to set a value relative to other currencies (fixed or pegged exchange rate) or by some intermediate means of some mix of government regulation and the forces of supply and demand in the market. The way in which exchange rate values are determined for a particular country is referred to as its *exchange rate regime.*

Floating exchange rates

If a country operates with a freely **floating exchange rate** regime, the nominal value of the exchange rate relative to other currencies will depend solely upon the demand for and the supply of the domestic currency on the foreign exchange markets. This can be illustrated in Figure 15.1, which shows the market demand curve, $D_\$$, and the market supply curve, $S_\$$, for US dollars in Sri Lanka. The vertical axis tells us the cost (the exchange rate) in terms of the number of Sri Lankan rupees that must be given up to buy one US dollar by those in Sri Lanka who wish to exchange their rupees for dollars. It cost 93.665 Sri Lankan rupees to buy one US dollar on the foreign exchange market (ignoring service costs of exchange currencies) on February 4, 2002. The horizontal axis of the graph shows the quantity of dollars being demanded and/or supplied in the Sri Lankan exchange rate market.

Who in Sri Lanka might wish to exchange their rupees for US dollars? That is, who is supplying rupees and demanding dollars?

1   Importers of goods into Sri Lanka who need to exchange their rupees for dollars to be able to purchase goods from suppliers;

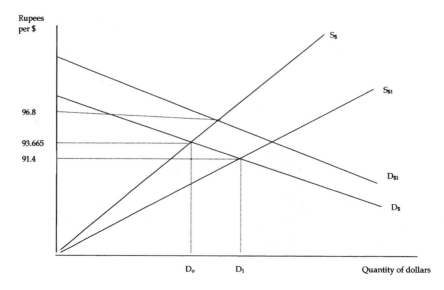

Figure 15.1 Exchange rate determination, floating rates.

2   Sri Lankans wishing to invest in the US stock or bond markets, to make
     deposits in US banks or to otherwise invest in the US (or any location where
     dollars might be used);
3   Sri Lankans traveling abroad who will need dollars;
4   Anyone else currently holding Sri Lankan rupees who wishes, for whatever
     reason, to hold dollars rather than rupees.[2]

As for most demand curves, it is reasonable to presume that as the number of
rupees that must be given up to buy one dollar decreases (i.e., as the price of dollars
falls in terms of rupees that must be given up), the quantity demanded of dollars will
rise, since this means that travel in the US for those holding rupees now will be
cheaper, goods imported from the US will cost less in terms of rupees given up, and
so on. Thus the demand curve for dollars is drawn sloping downward to the right as
for $D_\$$.

What determines the supply of dollars entering the Sri Lankan foreign exchange
market? It is more or less the obverse of the factors influencing the demand for
dollars.

1   The desire of importers holding dollars in, say the United States, who wish to
     exchange them for rupees to pay for goods of Sri Lankan producers;
2   US citizens, or anyone with US dollars, who travel to Sri Lanka and who
     exchange dollars for rupees at the airport, their hotel, local banks, or currency
     exchanges;
3   Investors in the United States, or anyone holding dollars, wishing to make a
     deposit in a Sri Lankan bank or to otherwise invest in the economy who needs
     rupees to do so and thus who supply their dollars to the Sri Lankan foreign
     exchange market.

As for other normally shaped supply curves, it seems reasonable to presume that
as the number of rupees that can be obtained for each dollar increases, the quantity
supplied of dollars will be larger. Thus the supply curve $S_\$$ is drawn with an upward
slope.

The equilibrium exchange rate between the United States dollar and the rupee is
determined by the intersection of the two curves, $D_\$$ and $S_\$$, at a value of 93.664
rupees per dollar. To buy (demand) one dollar costs holders of rupees 93.665 rupees
in exchange. Alternatively, selling (supplying) one dollar by holders of dollars
results in the receipt of 93.665 rupees.[3]

This is the exchange rate toward which the foreign exchange market will tend at
any point in time if there are no barriers to such adjustments (as, we shall see, there
are when exchange rates are not freely floating), and given the demand curve $D_\$$
and the supply curve $S_\$$. The equilibrium price of one dollar $= 93.665$ Sri Lanka
rupees will prevail as long as demand and supply remain constant. What happens,
however, if one or the other or both of the curves shift?

An increase in the supply of dollars, shown by the rightward shift of the supply
curve to $S_{\$1}$, results when those holding dollars wish to trade them for more rupees
at all possible prices or exchange rates. This may happen because those living in the
US wish to purchase more Sri Lankan goods as their incomes rise or because investment opportunities have improved for some reason in Sri Lanka. Or, a tourism push

by the Sri Lankan government may succeed in attracting more visitors from the US who need to exchange dollars for rupees to pay for their hotels, meals, and other expenditures. Whatever the reason, the shift to the right of the supply curve of dollars means that there are more dollars entering the Sri Lankan foreign exchange market than before at all possible exchange rates.

The shift of the supply of dollars (which is simultaneously an increase in the demand for Sri Lankan rupees since the dollars are being exchanged for rupees) will, with freely floating exchange rates, result in a new equilibrium value of the nominal exchange rate. With the increased supply of dollars, and assuming the demand for dollars ($D_\$$) remains unchanged, the nominal exchange rate value of the dollar will *depreciate* as the number of rupees that can be obtained in exchange for US\$1 declines from 93.665 to 91.4 rupees.[4]

At the same time that the dollar's value depreciated, the value of the Sri Lankan rupee has *appreciated*. Each rupee now is worth more than before the shift in the supply of dollars. This is because it now takes fewer rupees to purchase each dollar. When the rupee appreciates in value relative to the dollar, purchasing anything priced in dollars will now cost less in terms of the number of rupees that must be given up, even when the dollar price of what might be purchased remains unchanged. Thus, when rupees appreciate in value relative to the dollar, it encourages Sri Lankans to import US goods and services, to travel to the US and to increase their investments in the United States.

On the other hand, if the demand for dollars in the Sri Lankan foreign exchange market were to rise (what factors might cause such an increase in demand?) from $D_\$$ to $D_{\$1}$ and $S_\$$ remained the same, the nominal value of the dollar would now *appreciate* from its value of 93.665 rupees per dollar to 96.8 rupees per dollar as more rupees could be obtained in exchange for each dollar in the foreign exchange market. Of course, the other side of this appreciation in the value of the dollar is the depreciation in the value of the Sri Lankan rupee, as it takes more rupees to buy each dollar.

This depreciation in the relative value of the rupee will have the effect of: (a) discouraging imports from the United States to Sri Lanka, since everything priced in dollars now requires more rupees in exchange; (b) encouraging Sri Lankan exports to those holding dollars, since it is easier to obtain rupees than before; (c) decreasing travel from Sri Lanka to the United States and encouraging travel in the reverse direction; and (d) discouraging Sri Lankans from converting rupees to dollars for investments outside the country, while encouraging those with dollar holdings to bring dollars to Sri Lanka where now more rupees can be obtained in exchange for each dollar.

Fixed exchange rates

At the other end of the spectrum from a fully floating exchange rate regime is a **fixed or pegged exchange rate** regime. Until the early 1970s, most countries operated with fixed exchange rates set in cooperation with the International Monetary Fund (IMF) as part of the Bretton Woods institutional arrangements for international trade and finances established at the end of the Second World War (see Chapter 17). Following a series of crises, first in the United States and then the oil crisis of 1973, many countries, and most importantly the United States, elected to adopt floating or some intermediate exchange rate regime, leaving the fixed exchange rate era behind. However, many less-developed nations continue to operate with fixed, or quasi-fixed, exchange rate systems. Typically, the exchange rate is linked to the currency of the largest trade partner(s), often the former colonial power.

When nominal exchange rates are fixed, however, the adjustment to a new equilibrium exchange rate value shown in Figure 15.1 (when either or both the demand and supply of dollars change) *cannot* take place, since the exchange rate value is fixed at some nominal level. Let us assume that the nominal value of the exchange rate of the Sri Lankan rupee is fixed by the Sri Lankan government at 93.665 rupees per dollar, as shown in Figure 15.2, an exchange rate value which happens to coincide with the current equilibrium value.

What happens when the demand or supply (or both) of dollars changes, or the current nominal exchange rate does not, by chance, coincide with the intersection of the supply and demand for dollars shown in Figure 15.2?

For example, if the demand for dollars increases to $D_{\$1}$ for reasons discussed above and the supply curve of dollars is $S_\$$, there will be an unmet demand for dollars in the Sri Lankan foreign exchange market. This is because the quantity of dollars brought to market by those wishing to trade dollars for rupees, Q_S, is less than the quantity of dollars demanded, Q_D, by those who wish to exchange their rupees for dollars at the prevailing fixed exchange rate of 93.665 rupees per dollar. Not enough dollars will be made available by those exchanging dollars for rupees to meet the demand for dollars in the Sri Lankan foreign currency market at the fixed exchange rate value. A shortage of dollars in the market (equal to $Q_S - Q_D$) and a simultaneous surplus of rupees at the current fixed nominal exchange rate is the result.

What happens to the excess supply of rupees? Where does it go? Alternatively, how is the problem of the shortage of dollars handled?

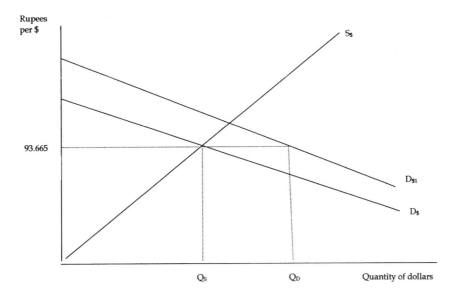

Figure 15.2 Exchange rate determination, fixed rates.

The shortfall of dollars can be met and the surplus of rupees absorbed, and hence the fixed nominal exchange rate of 93.665 rupees per dollar maintained if the Sri Lankan government *sells* US dollars from its **official foreign exchange reserves** in an amount equal to the shortage. Those official foreign exchange reserves, accumulated in the past by exporting more than importing or as a result of other net dollar flows into Sri Lanka, are a part of the Sri Lankan government's savings of official foreign exchange reserves. When, as in Figure 15.2, the quantity demanded of dollars exceeds the quantity supplied of dollars at the fixed nominal exchange rate, the Sri Lankan government can buy the excess supply of rupees, and it does so by selling off some of its dollar reserves.

If insufficient dollars are held as official foreign exchange reserves by the Sri Lankan government to trade for the excess supply of rupees that Sri Lankans wish to exchange for dollars or if the Sri Lankan government for some reason refuses to supply the quantity needed to cover the shortage, the supply of dollars available on the foreign exchange market will have to be *rationed* to those wishing to exchange rupees for the limited supply of dollars available.

For example, requiring *import licenses* as a prerequisite for exchanging rupees for dollars is one way to allocate the limited supply of dollars relative to the larger quantity demanded at the fixed exchange rate value. Limits on the number of rupees that can be exchanged for dollars is another way to restrict the quantity demanded to some value closer to the quantity supplied of dollars. These are all examples of **administrative means** that can be devised to ration the limited quantity of dollars among those demanding them in exchange for rupees.

Other administrative mechanisms for allocating the limited supply of dollars in the foreign exchange market based on a priority listing might include giving precedence in exchanging rupees for dollars to those importing essential goods from the United States with importers of non-essential goods from the United States having secondary priority for buying dollars. Then any dollars still available could be allocated to Sri Lankans traveling on business to the United States and then to regular tourists to the United States. Speculators interested in transferring some of their financial assets to the United States might be last in the queue for exchanging rupees for dollars. The government could utilize such a priority ranking to determine how to allocate the limited dollars available in the Sri Lankan foreign exchange market at the fixed exchange rate and thus avoid having to dip so deeply into its dollar reserve holdings.

There is a risk in using such administrative efforts to control the exchange of currencies. Some who hold Sri Lankan rupees and wishing to exchange them for dollars but who find themselves unable to do so under the administrative rules because of the limited quantity supplied relative to the demand will look for alternative avenues for obtaining dollars in the local market. Illegal and quasi-legal foreign exchange markets, so-called "black or parallel markets," will begin to emerge. The greater the discrepancy between the fixed exchange rate value and its equilibrium value, the greater will be the quantity of transactions taking place as the market will be further from its equilibrium value with more unmet demand (see Focus 15.1).

If no administrative means to limit the demand for dollars to the smaller quantity supplied are utilized and the government wishes to prevent the emergence of parallel foreign exchange markets, the ability of the Sri Lankan government to maintain the fixed exchange rate of 93.665 rupees per dollar will be determined by the quan-

FOCUS 15.1 PARALLEL MARKET EXCHANGE RATES VERSUS OFFICIAL EXCHANGE RATES

One way to gauge the misalignment of official exchange rates is by comparing them with the **parallel market** exchange rate. The parallel market includes an estimate of black market exchange rate values and exchange rates prevailing at non-official, but legal, foreign exchanges. In the following table, the parallel market exchange rate premium is the per cent difference between the parallel market rate and the official exchange rate.

	1981–1986	1990–1991
Sub-Saharan Africa		
Mozambique	2,110.8	62.6
Tanzania	248.8	74.5
Zambia	46.3	149.7
The Gambia	13.8	21.3
Nigeria	232.7	25.1
Zimbabwe	81.3	23.5
Kenya	15.1	7.3
Others		
Argentina	32.8	42.4
Bolivia	136.2	1.5
Indonesia	4.2	2.6
Mexico	13.0	6.8
The Philippines	12.3	7.1
Thailand	−2.2	2.0
Venezuela	110.3	5.2

A positive value indicates by how much the parallel market exchange rate exceeded the official exchange rate and is an approximate measure of the extent of over-valuation of the official exchange rate. Over the period 1981–1986, for example, Nigeria's official exchange rate was over-valued by more than 200 percent. In general, economies in Sub-Saharan Africa had somewhat higher levels of exchange rate over-valuation than have had countries in other less-developed regions. Note Thailand's *under-valued* exchange rate in the first period and the mild over-valuation in the later period.

With the exception of the Gambia and Argentina, there was a tendency to reduce the degree of over-valuation of official exchange rates between the two periods. This has meant *depreciations and devaluations* of official rates bringing them closer to their equilibrium values.

Over-valued exchange rates make exporting more difficult and encourage importing. While maintaining over-valued exchange rates is not a priori bad policy, extreme over-valuation can lead to stagnant, over-protected domestic production and a weak export sector. That is the worst of all possible worlds.

In examining Sub-Saharan Africa, the World Bank found that for those countries that had depreciations of their real exchange rate of 40 percent or more, growth rates of per capita income averaged 2.9 percent. For countries with smaller depreciations, per capita growth rates averaged −0.4 percent. And for those countries where real exchange rates become more over-valued, per capita growth rates averaged −2.7 percent.

Large exchange rate over-valuation thus tends to impact negatively on the competitiveness of an economy and can dramatically slow economic growth. Exchange rate over-valuation is not, however, the only factor which can impede growth and adversely affect competitiveness, though it is important. *continued*

In a detailed study of Mexico, UNCTAD found that from 1990 to 1994, the real exchange rate became severely over-valued by more than 50 percent. Not surprisingly, Mexico's international competitiveness in manufacturing decreased, with the index of competitiveness rising from 136.5 in 1990 to 197.4 in 1993. (The index measures the unit labor cost of production in constant US dollars. An increase in the index indicates a decrease in competitiveness.) At the same time as the exchange rate was becoming over-valued, real wage increases outstripped increases in labor productivity by nearly four times (+70 percent v. +18 percent).

Over-valuation of the exchange rate thus was not the only factor affecting Mexico's decreased international competitiveness. Internal structures and slow productivity growth relative to income growth also contributed. The latter effects may reflect the inadequacy of Mexico's past human capital accumulation efforts and weak technological acquisition skills. Further, the failure of Mexico to pursue export substitution policies in the climb up the structural transformation ladder and the premature initiation of capital-intensive, higher wage secondary import substitution have contributed to the inability of Mexico to sustain economic growth and development.

Sources: UNCTAD 1995: 85; World Bank 1994: 228, 242

tity of official foreign exchange reserves and the willingness of the government to continue to support the fixed exchange rate value despite losing such reserves. As foreign exchange reserves are reduced below some acceptable level, the Sri Lankan government will be forced to **devalue** the rupee (i.e., to increase the number of rupees required to buy each dollar) to a new value closer to the equilibrium value where $D_{\$1}$ intersects with $S_\$$, thus eliminating or reducing the dollar shortage problem.[5] For example, if the rupee is devalued to its new equilibrium value of 96.8 rupees per dollar, then the dollar shortage disappears as the quantity supplied of dollars (which is also the quantity demanded of rupees) exactly matches the quantity of dollars demanded (and which is also the quantity supplied of rupees). The major risk to a country of maintaining a fixed exchange rate is that changes in the supply and the demand for foreign currency may result in a run-down of official foreign exchange reserves.[6]

A managed float exchange rate regime

Somewhere between freely floating exchange rates and fixed exchange rates lies the **managed float**. With a managed float exchange rate regime, a government allows changes in the supply of and demand for its currency to have an effect on the spot market exchange rate, but it may intervene to prevent full and complete adjustment of the exchange rate toward its equilibrium value.

For example, in Figure 15.2, if Sri Lanka had a managed float exchange rate regime, then the shift in the demand for dollars to $D_{\$1}$ might result in a change in the exchange rate from the initial value of 93.665 rupees per dollar to an intermediate value of, say, 94.5 rupees per dollar rather than a full adjustment to the new equilibrium value. The rupee still has *depreciated* in value – it now takes more rupees than before to buy one dollar – just not by as much as the full adjustment to the equilibrium value. This decreases the shortage of dollars in the foreign exchange market compared to what would prevail with a fixed exchange rate and thus reduces the pressures on official foreign exchange reserves and other measures required to maintain a fully-fixed exchange rate regime.

There remains, however, a shortage of dollars supplied to the Sri Lankan foreign exchange market relative to the demand that will need to be filled through the depletion of official foreign exchange rate reserves. A managed float reduces but does not eliminate the need for the Sri Lankan government to supply dollars from its foreign exchange reserves (or impose other rationing measures, as discussed above) to sustain the exchange rate at a value other than its new equilibrium value. With a managed float, a country exercises some degree of control over its exchange rate value, not letting it just be buffeted about by market forces. This may be done to foster greater stability in the value of the exchange rate over time so as to permit those involved in international trade and investment to project with less uncertainty the future value of the currency. But as with any non-floating exchange rate regime, a managed float may put pressure on official foreign exchange reserves if changes in the supply and demand for foreign exchange markets change in ways that create unmet demands for foreign currencies.

Other exchange rate regime types

Other possible exchange rate regimes are a **crawling peg** and a *band* exchange rate system. With a crawling peg, which is a more transparent type of managed float, the government fixes – pegs – the currency's value vis-à-vis foreign currencies. The pegged value is regularly adjusted downward, typically because the country's inflation rate exceeds the inflation rate of its major trading partners. As we shall see in the next section, the crawling peg may help to keep the *real* value of a country's currency from becoming over-valued if the "crawl" downward of the pegged value is of the proper amount.

A band exchange system is a kind of modified float/modified peg. The value of the currency is allowed to fluctuate freely according to market forces of supply and demand, but only *within* an agreed upon range of upper and lower values vis-à-vis other currencies. The government commits to maintain the value of the currency within that band, so there may be times when it will be necessary either to sell off foreign exchange reserves or to accumulate such reserves to preserve the currency's value within the predetermined range.

Few governments have freely floating exchange rates at all times. Most floating exchange rate regimes are potentially some form of a managed float depending on the circumstances. In today's electronically integrated world economy, where twenty-four hour trading in currencies is not only possible but a reality, few countries are willing to let temporary disturbances in the foreign exchange markets completely dictate day-to-day spot exchange rates because of the potentially adverse affects these can have on trade and financial flows and domestic income and production. Thus virtually all countries, developed and less-developed alike, utilize a managed float system, directly or indirectly, to avoid wide and unproductive swings in the value of their exchange rates.

FOCUS 15.2   EXCHANGE RATE REGIMES

Different countries have different exchange rate regimes: floating, managed float, pegged, fixed and so on. For an explanation of the different types of exchange rate regimes in use and to discover which exchange rate regime is used by any particular country go to http://www.mof.go.jp/english/if/if043k.htm.

Real versus nominal exchange rates

The nominal exchange rate is the current or spot value of a currency. Let us consider why the nominal and **real exchange rate** (RER) values might differ by looking at the foreign exchange market for Mexican pesos traded for US dollars. What is the impact on the exchange rate if there is a difference in the rate of inflation between the United States and Mexico?

The real exchange rate will diverge from the nominal exchange rate if such a difference in inflation exists unless there is a freely floating exchange rate regime in effect. For example, suppose that during the course of 2003, prices in Mexico rose by 20 percent while prices in the United States remained constant. If Mexico had a *fixed* nominal exchange rate regime so that 12 pesos traded for US$1 throughout the year, at the end of December 2003 the RER of the peso would be 10 pesos per dollar [(12 pesos/US$1) × (100/120)]. In other words, the real value of the peso would have *appreciated*. It was cheaper, in real terms, to buy US dollars with pesos at the end of the year than it was at the beginning of the year. With the fixed exchange rate and rising prices in Mexico, prices of US goods and services became relatively cheaper and were easier to buy than before the inflation. This is one example of how a currency can become *over-valued*.

With price inflation in Mexico 20 percent higher than in the United States over the year, for the nominal exchange rate to have maintained the same real value, the end-of-year exchange rate would have had to change to 14.4 pesos for US$1 [determined as: 12 pesos/US$1 = ? × (100/120)]. The intuition behind this calculation is as follows. Since prices in Mexico rose by 20 percent while prices in the United States remained unchanged, the nominal exchange rate would have to fall by 20 percent in terms of its ability to purchase dollars. If the real exchange rate value between the dollar and the peso is to be maintained, Mexicans should need to give up 20 percent more pesos to buy one dollar after the inflation as before. What is 20 percent of 12 pesos? It is 2.4 more pesos, or a total of 14.4 pesos, that should be required to buy each dollar if the real value of the exchange rate is to be maintained.

Equivalently, holders of dollars should receive 20 percent more pesos per dollar so that the same number of dollars can buy the same quantity of Mexican goods after the inflationary episode when prices are 20 percent higher if the real exchange rate value is to be maintained. To pay for the higher priced Mexican goods after 20 percent inflation, more pesos per dollar must be received in exchange to maintain the same purchasing power for the US dollar after the inflation as before. Again, the required nominal bilateral exchange rate needed to maintain a constant RER would be 14.4 pesos for US$1.[7]

If exchange rates are freely floating, the market and the forces of supply and demand will tend to maintain the real exchange rate value of currencies so that any inflationary differentials between countries will be compensated for by movements of the nominal bilateral exchange rate in the proper direction.[8]

On the other hand, if a country has a *fixed* exchange rate and its domestic rate of inflation exceeds that of its trading partners, its real exchange rate relative to those of its trading partners will appreciate. This means that the currency is becoming over-valued, stimulating spending outside the country and deterring spending from abroad in the nation with the higher rate of inflation. Contrariwise, if a country has a fixed exchange rate and an inflation rate that is *lower than* its trading partners, the real exchange rates will depreciate and the domestic currency will be worth less (it will be under-valued relative to its equilibrium value). This will discourage spending in the higher inflation nations and encourage the high inflation nations to spend in the country with lower inflation (as their exchange rate will have appreciated).

With a managed float system of exchange rates, if a country has inflation that exceeds the rate of inflation for the countries with which it has financial and trade relations, then it will be necessary to allow, or force, a depreciation, or announce a devaluation, of the nominal value of the exchange rate by the amount of the inflation differential to prevent an over-valuation of the exchange rate. For those countries with *lower* inflation rates than their trade and financial partners, however, a decision as to whether to allow their currency to remain under-valued with a managed float will depend upon the nature of the trade and financial flows with their partners and, of course, the actions of the bilateral trade and financial partners to their now over-valued exchange rates.

If a high-inflation country is a major importer of goods from a country with lower inflation, an under-valued exchange rate in the low-inflation nation will encourage even further the purchase of its exports. A country with an under-valued exchange rate often has little incentive to make any adjustments if it is a major exporter. However, if low inflation nation imports essential goods from a higher-inflation country, maintaining an under-valued exchange might be counter-productive to economic growth and/or economic welfare by making such imports artificially expensive relative to the equilibrium value. In such a circumstance, forcing an appreciation of the exchange rate might very well be the appropriate policy decision. For managed exchange rate regimes, the nominal value a country defends will depend on the importance of exports and imports to the economic structure of that particular economy relative to its trade and financial partners.

Countries with fixed exchange rates that have inflation rates that differ substantially from those of their trade and financial partners will be aware quite quickly that their bilateral exchange rates are either over- or under-valued. The greater the divergence in inflation among countries, the larger the likely disequilibrium in the external balance that is likely to emerge if exchange rates remain fixed. Countries that choose to have a fixed exchange rate system will be compelled to keep their own rate of inflation equal to, or even below, that of their most important trade and financial partners. If they do not do so, the country can experience a continual drain on its official foreign exchange reserves as its currency becomes over-valued. Alternatively, frequent devaluations or mini-devaluations would be required, thus in effect, creating a managed float regime.

Some economists actually support fixed exchange rates for some countries precisely for the internal fiscal and monetary discipline it engenders, specifically the need to maintain in close check inflationary pressures. In reality, countries with fixed exchange rates do have other options besides exhausting their official foreign exchange reserves when inflation gets out of hand: rationing of foreign exchange; borrowing on the international market; and periodic devaluations, so the discipline of fixed rates is not absolute. For nations unable or unwilling to manage their economic affairs properly, there always seem to exist, for a time anyway, means to avoid the required adjustments that can facilitate growth and development by more sustainable and less *ad hoc* methods.

The balance of payments

For most countries, a severe disequilibrium in the balance of payments is often the ultimate binding constraint on the economy. Good policy-makers learn to monitor their country's balance of payments accounts for signs of impending difficulties, and they take steps to modify their economic, social, fiscal and monetary policies to correct problems before they erupt into full-blown crises. In effect, good policy-makers use the evolution of their balance of payments accounts as a *signaling device* for judging the effectiveness of their other interventions into the economy. The ability to adjust to disequilibrium situations in an agile fashion seems to have been one of the hallmarks of the success of the East Asian economies in a wide range of situations, and adjusting to balance of payments problems before they reach a crisis stage is another of those instances.

What is the balance of payments? Very simply, the balance of payments accounts measure the inflows and outflows of foreign currencies across the national borders of a country in transactions with the rest of the world over some period of time, usually a year. Simplifying somewhat, the balance of payments measures what a country earns and "borrows" from the *rest of the world* (ROW) and what it spends in and "lends" to the ROW. A nation's spending in the ROW will be exactly equal to what it earns from the ROW plus any net borrowing (= borrowing − lending) from the ROW. Nations thus ultimately can only import goods or their citizens can travel or invest in other countries to the extent that other countries purchase their exports or travel to or invest in their country. In the final analysis, spending in the ROW by any country is, over time, limited to the income earned from the ROW.

The balance of payments (B of P) of any country is composed of four parts: the *current account balance*, the **capital account balance**, the *financial account balance* and *net errors and omissions*. Because of double-entry accounting, the following is true always:

B of P = current account balance + capital account balance + financial account
balance + net errors and omissions[9] = 0   (15.1)

What, then, can it possibly mean to say that a country has a balance of payments *problem* if there is always a zero balance no matter what policies a country may follow? Before answering that question, we shall quickly review the elements entering into the different parts of the balance of payments accounts.

The current account balance

The *current account* of the balance of payments measures the outflow of expenditures and the inflow of receipts ("income") of a country vis-à-vis the rest of the world for current transactions and market exchanges such as the purchase of cars or insurance or contracting services. Table 15.2 shows the major components of the current account.

For most countries, the largest item in the balance of payments is the *balance of trade*. The balance of trade measures the net trade of all goods and services of a country with the ROW; these are entries A to D in Table 15.2. If there is a *surplus in the balance of trade*, that means that the monetary value of all exports sold to the

Table 15.2 The current account of the balance of payments

Item	Transactions creating an inflow	Transactions creating an outflow
I. Trade		
A. Merchandise exports	✗	
B. Merchandise imports		✗
A − B = *Balance on merchandise trade*		
C. Service exports	✗	
D. Service imports		✗
C − D = *Balance on service trade*		
A − B + C − D = *Overall balance of trade*		
II. Income		
E. Receipts from ROW of interest, profit and dividends and employee compensation	✗	
F. Payments to ROW of interest, profit and dividends and employee compensation		✗
III. Current transfers		
G. From ROW	✗	
H. To ROW		
A − B + C − D + E − F + G − H = *Balance on the current account*		✗

ROW exceeded the monetary value of all purchases of imports from the ROW (trade surplus = $\$X - \$M > 0$). When a country spends more on imports than it is able to export, the country will have a trade deficit ($= \$X - \$M < 0$).

It usually is of some interest to disaggregate the balance of trade, so many countries also determine their balance on *merchandise trade* and their balance on *service trade*. The balance on merchandise trade (items A and B in Table 15.2) includes the export and import values of all real, tangible goods, such as motor cars, oranges, rice, computers, computer programs, mattresses, golf clubs, or whatever. The balance on service trade includes exports and imports of services (items C and D) that create flows of money between countries, such as banking, insurance, advertising, film, television, video rentals, technology and product licensing, contracting and building services, and shipping plus all flows of money due to tourism.[10]

Section II of the *current account* in Table 15.2 (items E and F) is concerned with the payments of, and income earned from, flows of interest, profits, and dividends and employee compensation that are the result of previous loans and investments made in, or by, other countries. For example, borrowing by the Brazilian government from US banks in the 1970s created an outflow of currency on Brazil's current account as interest payments were paid to the United States. At the same time, the United States had an identical transaction created on its current account, albeit as a positive inflow of currency (and comparable to the income earned from exporting a good or a service).

In a similar way, countries which are hosts to foreign transnational producers or which have foreign investors involved in their domestic stock or bond markets are likely to experience an outflow of money (an "expenditure") on item F of the current account as payments to the foreign owners of those assets. These are income flows to pay for the *current value* of the services of past loans and investments. We shall see in Chapter 16 and in Focus 15.3 below that such movements of income payments can be quite important for some countries, especially those which incur fairly large external debts that then must be serviced.

Items G and H of the current account measure any other *current transfers* that may take place between nations. These are *unilateral* financial flows between nations measuring one-way flows of money. There is no corresponding equal and opposite flow of a good or service in the other direction, as is the case for all other items of the current account balance. For example, when Great Britain provides a

FOCUS 15.3   CURRENT ACCOUNT BALANCES

While aggregation can hide what is happening to individual countries, it is still useful to consider the evolution of current account balances, in billions of US dollars, by region.

	1987	1988	1989	1990	1992	1993	1994	1995	1998	2001
Africa	−4.4	−9.7	−7.5	−3.0	−9.1	−9.1	−12.6	−17.3	−20.0	−2.1
	−14.2	**−15.2**	**−15.0**	**−17.3**	**−15.2**	**−13.8**	**−13.9**	**−14.6**	**−18.7**	**−22.5**
Latin America	−11.1	−11.5	−5.9	−2.0	−35.1	−44.9	−47.9	−31.2	−90.7	−54.4
	−31.9	**−35.4**	**−38.7**	**−38.4**	**−34.3**	**−38.4**	**−39.4**	**−45.2**	**−47.8**	**−60.8**
Four East Asian economies	32.8	30.7	27.0	17.0	12.8	18.0	11.2	12.1	67.4	60.1
	−0.6	**1.5**	**3.1**	**4.1**	**4.6**	**2.6**	**3.3**	**6.0**		

Note
Figures in bold are "net factor service payments."

Africa and Latin America have incurred persistent current account deficits, while the four East Asian countries (Hong Kong, Singapore, Taiwan, and South Korea) have run current account surpluses. One important contributing factor to current account deficits in Latin America and Africa has been interest payments on external debt (discussed more fully in Chapter 16). The figures in bold type are the *net income payments* for each region, which includes the net sum of payments and receipts of *interest*, *profits*, and *dividends* (and small amounts for labor services). The largest component of factor service payments is interest on *external debt*.

Even though Latin America had a positive *trade* surplus of $26.6 billion in 1990, this net income earned from the ROW was smaller than the net factor service payments to the ROW, resulting in an overall current account deficit. Thus, past current account deficits that resulted in borrowing from abroad, can contribute to future current account deficits, requiring further borrowing or other financing. On the other hand, the East Asian economies have had positive net inflows (except for 1987) of factor service payments, even though they too, especially South Korea, have incurred external debt obligations in the past.

The differences in the evolution of the current account balances and net income payments, between Africa and Latin America, on one side, and the East Asian economies on the other, highlight once again the importance of past decisions on structural transformation, the industrialization strategy, human capital accumulation, technology acquisition and a good policy environment for successful development. One does not have to go back too far in time to find the East Asian economies with persistent large current account deficits. Apparently, they ran "good" deficits (discussed below) that allowed a transition to a higher level of development, and now, the East Asian economies are able to run current account surpluses, with the positive dividends which derive from such net earnings from the ROW.

Sources: IMF 1995: 159–160; 2002: 195–198

no-strings package of aid worth £50 million to Kenya to build an electrical generating facility for the capital city of Nairobi, this would appear as a positive inflow on Kenya's current transfers account and a negative entry on the UK's current transfers account.

Another example of a current transfer would be the remittances that Turkish immigrant workers in Germany or Mexican immigrants in the United States send to their families back home in their native countries. Such remittances create an outflow for the German and US current transfer balance while creating an inflow of money ("income") from the ROW for Turkey and Mexico in their current transfer balance. We have encountered these flows before, since they affect the value of gross national product of nations, as distinct from gross domestic product.

Deficits and surpluses in the current account balance

There is a *deficit in the current account balance* when $A - B + C - D + E - F + G - H < 0$. In a very rough but reasonable sense, a country with a current account deficit has spent more on what it has purchased from the ROW than it has earned from the ROW on goods and services of all types. Current expenditures in the ROW thus exceed current income from the ROW.

How can a country spend more in the ROW than it earns from the ROW? Just as for a family or business, current expenditures of a country in the ROW can only exceed current income from the ROW if the difference (a) is borrowed, (b) is financed out of past savings, and/or (c) is financed by selling off some assets or wealth and using the proceeds for current expenditures above income. In other words, a country that runs a current account deficit can only do so by going into debt or reducing its existing international assets to be able to spend more than its current income. There are no other alternatives. We shall examine what this means below.

In a similar fashion, a current account surplus means a country has earned more from the ROW than it has spent in the ROW. A *surplus on the current account* occurs when the sum of $A - B + C - D + E - F + G - H > 0$. Such a country will find that it has accumulated savings (= income from the ROW not spent in the ROW), some of which may be lent to other countries needing to finance current account deficits. Countries running a current account surplus will be accumulating international assets vis-à-vis the rest of the world (see Focus 15.3). They will have income earned from the ROW that is not spent on goods and services in the ROW.

The capital account and financial account balances

From equation 15.1 above, we know that if a country is running a current account deficit of some given size, the sum of the capital account balance and the financial account balance will be positive and of the same value (ignoring, for the moment, "net errors and omissions"). If a country is running a current account deficit equal to, say, −$15 billion, then there must be a capital account balance + financial account balance equal to +$15 billion to maintain the balance of payments identity in equation 15.1. Since a current account deficit can only be financed by borrowing from the ROW or by reducing savings or selling off accumulated international assets, the capital account and the financial account balances identify the mix of net borrowing and international asset reduction a country had done to finance its current account deficit.

In a like manner, a country running a current account surplus will have the sum of the capital account balance + financial account balance of the same value but with a negative value (ignoring, again, "net errors and omissions"). A net deficit on these two accounts actually means that the country will be a net accumulator of assets vis-à-vis the ROW. Countries with a capital account deficit may be lenders to countries with current account deficits or they can be accumulating, in the form of foreign exchange reserves at the nation's central bank, the excess of income over expenditures earned from the ROW on their current account transactions.

Table 15.3 shows a summary of the items included in the capital and financial balances.

While the overall capital account balance is important, it is in the financial account that some of the most important long-term flows of assets across national borders are recorded and that show more clearly the implications of a country's balance of payments position.

Items J and K measure the inflows and outflows of currency resulting from international loans. When one nation receives a loan from another nation or when an individual, business or government acquires a loan from a foreign bank or other financial intermediary or even another individual located in a foreign country, a positive inflow of foreign currency is recorded on the financial account of the borrowing economy. For the lending country, there is an outflow on the financial account equal to the amount of that lending. For example, when Mexican citizens buy US Treasury bonds in the US bond market, Mexico is making a loan to the United States that creates a foreign currency inflow to the United States and an equivalent outflow from Mexico.

Table 15.3 The capital account and the financial account

Item	Transactions creating an inflow of money	Transactions creating an outflow of money
IV. *Capital account*		
I. Net Capital transfers[a]	✗	**or** ✗
I = Balance on the capital account		
V. *Financial account*		
J. Loans from ROW	✗	
K. Loans to ROW		✗
L. Investments from ROW[b]	✗	
M. Investments in ROW[b]		✗
N. Sale of official foreign exchange reserves[c]	✗	
O. Purchase of official foreign exchange reserves[c]		✗
J − K + L − M + N − O = *Balance on the financial account*		

Notes
a This includes debt forgiveness and other types of capital movements not captured by the Financial Account balance.
b Investments include both foreign direct investment (FDI) and portfolio investment.
c These are purchases and sales by the central bank of foreign currencies, gold and IMF special drawing rights (SDRs), a kind of international currency created by the IMF and allocated to nations for use in settling transactions between countries.

Similarly, items L and M measure investment transactions that create inflows or outflows of foreign currency as the result of financial portfolio investment or FDI in productive facilities. An inflow of investment actually can be considered to be a specific type of loan as it contributes to total investment in the country, increases income and thus, potentially, permits an expansion of current consumption and investment. Note that when a country has a positive inflow on items J or L in the financial account, this will contribute to an outflow of currency in the "Income" portion of the current account *in the future* as these loans and investments are repaid and as the profits and dividends they generate are repatriated to the lending country.

Items N and P are equally important to understand. Item N measures the sale of official foreign exchange reserves by the government from its existing holdings of foreign currencies or gold and SDRs. Such sales actually create an *inflow* of international currency into an economy as foreign reserves are traded for domestic currency on the foreign exchange market. This means the country is returning some of its previously accumulated international currency assets held by the central government to the economy to be used for some other purpose, be it to pay for imports or to finance some other expenditure.

What exactly are official foreign exchange reserves? Very simply, they are holdings by the central bank of currencies of other countries plus gold and SDRs. They represent the accumulation of international assets from the past when the country earned more than it spent vis-à-vis the ROW, thus representing a form of saving for a nation vis-à-vis the ROW.[11] Countries always desire to hold some quantity of foreign exchange reserves, often the equivalent of at least three to four months of imports, for emergency situations such as unexpected downturns in export earnings or unforeseen but temporary, increases in import spending.[12] When a country runs a current account deficit due to spending exceeding income, these official reserves can be sold to the public to provide the additional foreign exchange required to finance spending in the ROW in excess of what is earned from the ROW when other inflows of financial assets (e.g., loans and FDI) are not sufficient to pay for a current account deficit.

Item O in Table 15.3 has the opposite interpretation to item N. It represents an *increase* in the official foreign exchange reserve holdings of a country obtained by exchanging domestic currency for foreign currency in the foreign exchange market.

Countries via their central bank and the normal legal channels where foreign exchange deals are transacted are continually both selling from their foreign exchange reserves and adding to them. What is most important is the change in the *net* position on official foreign exchange holdings over time – that is, the difference between the value of N and O. When $N - O > 0$ – meaning sales of foreign exchange from official reserves exceed purchases of foreign exchange added to official reserves – the country will suffer a net *decrease* in its official foreign exchange assets. Perhaps this seems counterintuitive, but a net positive value means that foreign exchange has entered the economy, just as all positive values in the balance of payments indicate an inflow of foreign currency into the economy. It is just that in this case the inflow into the economy comes from the government itself, which had been holding these reserves from circulation. Since this foreign exchange is coming from the government's official foreign exchange reserves, this must mean that those reserves will be smaller than they were. A decrease in official foreign exchange reserves is equivalent to dissaving by the country and occurs when $N - O > 0$.

When $N - O < 0$, a country experiences a net *increase* in its official foreign exchange reserves. A net negative value for the change in official foreign exchange reserves means that foreign exchange is leaving the economy. In this case does not leave the country completely, as typically is the case, but is added to the *government's* official foreign exchange reserves. An increase in official foreign exchange reserves represents a form of national saving taken out of circulation of the local economy.

The twin deficits and the balance of payments

The origin of a current account deficit or a current account surplus in the balance of payments can be easily seen in the concept of the **twin deficits**. Equation 15.2 is a simple national income identity, where Y is total national output ($=$income), C is consumption of final goods and services, I is gross domestic investment, G is government spending, T are taxes, X is total exports, and M is total imports, all calculated in monetary terms.

$$Y = C + I + G + (X - M) \tag{15.2}$$

With some simple rearrangement of terms,[13] we can rewrite equation 15.2 as

$$(S - I) + (T - G) = X - M \tag{15.3}$$

Assume, first for simplicity, that $(T - G) = 0$, that is, government has a balanced budget so there is no fiscal deficit or fiscal surplus. Then, if the first expression on the left-hand side, $S - I$, is <0, that is, if gross investment spending exceeds domestic saving, then $X - M < 0$ by definition and by necessity. Why by necessity? Because when $S - I < 0$, the country is investing more in new capital than it has released resources for such investment purposes from total national production. In other words, domestic consumption is "too high" when $S - I < 0$ such that not enough domestic output is available for the desired level of investment. The only way that actual investment can exceed domestic saving is if imported goods make up for the shortfall of domestic production, that is, only when $X - M < 0$.

A nation can spend more than it has income or consume and invest more than it has produced *only* if there is a trade deficit that makes up the discrepancy. Hence, the idea of the "twin deficits." When "not enough" domestic saving is being done to provide the resources for the actual level of investment taking place, and that happens when domestic spending exceeds domestic income, then this *internal* deficit must be matched by an equal and balancing *external* deficit in international trade that provides the additional goods to be consumed but which are not produced in the domestic economy. Obviously, if the term $(T - G) < 0$, too, the size of the external deficit will have to be correspondingly larger to meet the excess internal demand for goods. We know that for this to happen borrowing or a reduction in the nation's official foreign exchange reserves must occur to finance the excess of spending above total national production.

What is a balance of payments problem?

What does it mean for a country to have a balance of payments problem? If the sum of the Current + Capital + Financial + Net errors and omissions parts of the balance of payments always sum to zero, how can a country have a problem?

Any country running a current account deficit will be obliged to either borrow *foreign* exchange or reduce its own official foreign exchange reserves to finance any spending above income due to a current account deficit. Whether borrowing takes the form of loans from foreign governments, banks, other corporations, individuals, or some other institution, the loan is for foreign currency and must be repaid in foreign currency. If the borrowing takes the form of portfolio or direct foreign investment, there is still a foreign exchange obligation in the future to pay for the outflow of foreign currency such investments imply as these investments reap profits that are returned to the original, foreign investor.

If a country cannot borrow foreign exchange from the usual sources in the international market or its foreign exchange reserves become dangerously depleted, then it will be unable to run a current account deficit. While it is not correct to claim that *every* current account deficit is a problem, persistent and large current account deficits may be signals of future problems and of underlying weaknesses in the economy that lead to such deficits. Since current account deficits require external financing or a decrease in official foreign exchange reserves, they can lead to a build-up of debt or a decrease in domestic saving that may become a drag on future domestic growth possibilities if such borrowing is not properly managed or not used prudently, as Chapter 16 explores.

On the other hand, countries that run current account surpluses are unlikely to have future balance of payments problems though not every current account surplus is necessarily a good thing.[14] So, even though the accounts in the balance of payments always sum to zero, what the specific values are in each account and why they are those specific values remain important to examine to be able to grasp when there may be potential problems and when there are not. More will be said on this below in considering "good" and "bad" current account deficits.

Exchange rates and the balance of payments

There is a close relation between a nation's exchange rate, its exchange rate regime (fixed, floating or managed float) and the balance of payments accounts. After all, the flows of money that end up in a country's foreign exchange markets are transactions that are captured somewhere in a country's balance of payments accounts.

Balance of payments adjustment with floating rates

If a country's exchange rates are fully floating – that is, if their value is determined by the market forces of supply and demand – it is technically impossible to have a balance of payments problem. Why is this?

Imagine that Pakistan, at the current spot nominal exchange rate, is running a current account deficit. This may be due to the fact that Pakistanis wish to spend more on imports than is earned from Pakistani exports or any reason that results in current expenditures in the ROW exceeding current income from the ROW.

The quantity supplied of rupees to the foreign exchange market by those wishing to buy imports will then exceed the quantity demanded of rupees by those as payment for Pakistan's exports, as shown in Figure 15.3.

At the current exchange rate of $0.04 per rupee, there is a surplus of rupees (equal to *mn*) on the foreign exchange market as a consequence of the current account deficit. If exchange rates are freely floating, however, this surplus will be but a very temporary phenomenon. At the current exchange rate "too many" rupees are being offered for exchange relative to the quantity desired. This means that the current nominal exchange rate of rupees is too high. The result will be a deprecia- tion of the rupee to its equilibrium value of $0.03 to 1 rupee. This is the typical result of an adjustment to the equilibrium price whenever there is a surplus of a good in a competitive market.

As the exchange rate of rupees falls and the cost of purchasing a unit of foreign currency rises for Pakistanis, two important effects will result. The willingness of holders of rupees to buy imports falls since it is now more difficult to buy dollars than before. It takes more rupees to buy each dollar. Imports of goods become more expensive in terms of the rupees that must be given up. As a result, the quantity sup- plied of rupees declines. On the other hand, the desire of foreigners to buy Pakistani exports increases as their prices in terms of foreign currency fall since it is easier to buy rupees with dollars and thus the quantity demanded of rupees rises.

Pakistan's exports will increase and its imports will decrease, and this will con- tinue until the current account is brought into balance with the value of exports equal to the value of imports or, more generally, until the outflows of expenditures are balanced by an equivalent income flow, evaluated at the floating rate which will automatically adjust to remove any temporary imbalances.

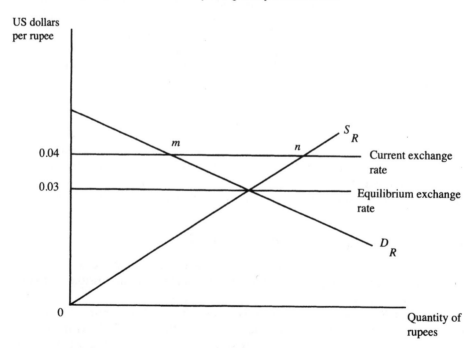

Figure 15.3 Floating exchange rates and the balance of payments.

Likewise, differences in the inflows and the outflows on the capital and financial accounts will result in similar equilibrating tendencies, so that the freely floating exchange rate will tend toward balance in all the parts of the balance of payments accounts. As a consequence of these exchange rate movements, there will be no systematic tendency for a country's foreign exchange reserves to either increase or decrease over time. There may, of course, be temporary changes in these balances, but these will be smoothed out over time so that once a country has reached its desired level of foreign exchange reserves, a floating exchange rate regime will tend to maintain those foreign exchange reserves relatively intact over time.

Balance of payments adjustment with fixed exchange rates

If Pakistan operates with fixed exchange rates, then the imbalance between the supply of and demand for rupees in Figure 15.3 created by an exchange rate value that is "too high" and is reflected in a current account deficit is more problematic. At the nominal exchange rate of $0.04 per rupee, the rupee is *over-valued* relative to its equilibrium value. If the exchange rate and the supply and demand curves remain the same, there will be a persistent current account imbalance created as spending outside Pakistan is encouraged and spending inside Pakistan by foreigners is discouraged by the over-valued exchange rate. If the current account is now in deficit, the deficit will be worsened; if the current account is in surplus, the surplus will shrink over time and may turn into a deficit.

Let's assume that the current account is already in a deficit situation. Maintaining the exchange rate at the fixed value of Figure 15.3 likely will require a financial account surplus. Borrowing or inflows of direct foreign investment from the ROW will be required to compensate for the excess spending relative to income on the current account. In future periods, such borrowing and investment will exacerbate any current account deficit, as income payments for interest, dividends, and profits (item F in Table 15.2) are required to service the current borrowing inflows. Alternatively, or most likely in conjunction with such financial inflows, the government will need to use some of its foreign exchange reserve holdings to finance the excess supply of rupees brought to market in search of dollars as a result of the current account deficit exacerbated by the over-valued exchange rate.

Currency over-valuation and the balance of payments

From this brief description of the impact of an over-valued fixed exchange rate on the balance of payments accounts, one can see why policy-makers need to be very vigilant in monitoring the balance of payments. At least two alternative general scenarios can be imagined as resulting from an over-valued exchange rate with quite distinct effects.

A beneficial current account deficit

A current account deficit due to currency over-valuation can allow a country to import at a lower cost for critical goods and services that may be required for accelerating economic development: capital goods, new technologies, foreign technicians who train local experts, training abroad for scientists, engineers and health professionals, and so on. An over-valued exchange rate can help a country purchase vital inputs relatively cheaply, since over-valuation reduces the price of imports artificially.

In particular, during the easy import substitution industrialization (ISI) stage over-valuation can be a means to cheapen the costs of production and has the same effect as a subsidy by reducing direct costs of production. When accompanied by other measures discussed in Chapter 9, over-valuation can contribute to the overcoming of transitional inefficiencies which make infant industry protection necessary in the first instance. By lowering the costs of production and contributing to technology acquisition, over-valuation can contribute to the desired goal of having new domestic enterprises reach levels of international competitiveness more quickly.

If such a strategy is to be successful over time and not thwart progress, the exchange rate will need to be adjusted downward toward or even below its equilibrium value at some time in the future, just as infant industry tariffs need to be removed. The enhanced ability to produce created during the transition period of over-valued exchange rates must be translated into a capacity for the nation to export an expanding array of goods to foreign markets and to produce import substitutes at prices competitive with foreign imports. In the best of all circumstances, this productive transformation will push the current account into surplus. At a minimum, a successful transitional over-valuation strategy will result in a stable or shrinking current account deficit.

For less-developed nations, such an evolution of the current account and of the exchange rate from over-valuation to equilibrium can provide for a more rapid pace of economic growth and the possibility for greater equality and development. With proper management of a short-term external imbalance caused by a slightly over-valued exchange rate and the current account deficit it encourages, there can be strongly positive effects on aggregate economic growth and employment.

Policy-makers walk a thin line in following this policy, however. Timely mini-devaluations, carefully managed to guard against speculative attacks on the currency, can help to create the conditions for the success of this strategy. Much like the programed reduction in infant industry tariffs, over-valuation as an indirect subsidy to industries which buy imported inputs should be programed for phase-out as well. For such a strategy to work, however, the other pre-conditions for economic development discussed in the previous chapters must be in place, from the human capital base, to technology capacity, to policy-making effectiveness.

A debilitating current account deficit

A current account deficit resulting from an over-valued exchange rate may result in eventual crisis. If protected industries do not become more efficient, the financial account borrowing required by the current account deficit will have been wasted. When funds borrowed from the ROW are not directed to productive investments that have the potential to *increase* future export income or to *reduce* future import expenditures, then such borrowing will, if sufficiently large, eventually lead to a crisis. Sooner or later, increased payments of interest, dividends, and profits to service past borrowing will push the current account deficit to limits that are difficult or perhaps impossible to finance with new loans from abroad. When that happens, more and more of the country's foreign exchange reserves will need to be used in an effort to maintain the over-valued fixed exchange rate. There is, of course, a limit to any government's official foreign exchange holdings, and when those are exhausted or when the government finally appreciates the unsustainability of the over-valued exchange rate, action will need to be taken to bring the exchange rate and the balance of payments accounts into line (see Focus 15.4).

One such step will be a devaluation to bring the exchange rate closer to its equilibrium value. A forced, sharp devaluation will almost always result in a slow-down and often a reversal of economic growth. Devaluation is required to stimulate export sales and to simultaneously discourage import purchases. However, if a country has failed to invest in export industries, any growth in export income from devaluation will be less than it could have been if future export capacity had been strengthened by the proper use of the borrowed funds. Often, to be able to achieve a current account balance or even a surplus sufficient to generate the foreign

---

FOCUS 15.4   TRADE IN ENVIRONMENTAL SERVICES: TOXIC WASTE

Burdened with large current account deficits, some countries have begun to "export" environmental waste disposal services to the already-developed countries as a means of earning income. In effect, in return for a foreign exchange inflow, countries agree to accept toxic waste materials from more developed countries which have encountered difficulties in disposing of such substances at home. "Hazardous waste is defined as waste which, if deposited in landfills, air or water in untreated form will be detrimental to human health or the environment."

Where does such hazardous waste end up? Latin American countries, with their large current account deficits (see Focus 15.3), have recently been a key destination. And African nations have accepted substantial inflows of toxic materials in recent decades.

- Guinea-Bissau received 15 million tonnes of waste from the UK, Switzerland, and the US over a period of five years.
- The Congo received more than 1 million tonnes of solvents and chemical wastes from the US and Europe in one year alone.
- Nigeria had nearly 4,000 tonnes of mixed chemicals and other waste from Europe dumped, illegally, in the country.
- Equatorial Guinea received 2 million tonnes of chemical wastes from Europe for a landfill on Annoban Island.

Less-developed countries typically have fewer restrictions on the dumping of hazardous materials, at least partly because they have had less experience with them given their lower level of development. And, given the foreign exchange that can be earned, the temptation to accept trade in unsafe materials is large. For example, Guinea-Bissau was offered by two British companies an amount per year equal to one-half the country's total GNP for burying hazardous chemicals on its soil!

The capacity of less-developed countries to monitor and control the effects of such toxic waste disposal is low, if it exists at all. In recognition of this, the Organisation of African Unity (OAU) called for a ban on hazardous waste imports in 1988, but it apparently has been ignored by many member states on the continent. Given their need for foreign exchange earnings and the lack of overall development, many less-developed nations with current account deficits may be tempted to provide relatively low-cost dump sites for developed world wastes. With better economic policies in the future, this Faustian choice would cease to be so attractive.

Source: Elliott 1994: 35–37

exchange earnings required to service past borrowing, imports will need to be repressed severely. How can that be accomplished?

Import repression is achieved via austerity measures designed to provoke a domestic recession that reduces the propensity to import by reducing total national income. Besides a currency devaluation, other austerity measures that may be introduced, sometimes in consultation and at the urging of the multinational lending institutions like the IMF and the World Bank (see Chapter 17) are:

1   a reduction in the rate of inflation via greater control over both the fiscal deficit and the money supply that create and perpetuate inflation ("stabilization policies");
2   an increase in domestic interest rates and a reduction in trade barriers with the ROW ("adjustment policies");
3   limits on wage increases to less than the inflation rate;
4   lay-offs of government employees; and
5   privatization of state enterprises, to name a few.

"Good" external imbalances

The previous discussion demonstrates something of great importance: at times, the correct external *im*balance can result in substantial positive growth dividends in the future in terms of contributing to improving a country's internal balances. A "good" external imbalance can contribute to a nation's progress where it counts, that is, in stimulating and increasing domestic employment, income, and human development.

In the last section, we saw that a current account deficit and an over-valued exchange rate – external imbalances – can contribute to more rapid economic growth and development – an improvement in the internal balances – if the borrowing from the ROW to finance current account deficits is used productively to expand export production or increase import substitution production. However, this can be a transitional strategy only. Over time, the fixed or managed float exchange rate value will have to be adjusted downward toward and perhaps below its equilibrium value. As the net gains from an over-valued exchange rate strategy reach exhaustion, devaluation becomes necessary to preserve the gains of the disequilibrium development strategy.

This is an example of what MIT economist Alice Amsden (1989) has called "getting prices right by getting some prices wrong," that is, promoting more rapid growth and development via fomenting selective disequilibria, a strategy that harkens back to Albert Hirschman's "unbalancing" recommendation for initiating development (Chapter 5). However, the appropriate institutional structure and the other pre-conditions for successful structural transformation must be in place for this strategy of a *managed external disequilibrium* to have a chance to work. Further, it is necessary to effectively monitor the external disequilibrium and know when the time has come to alter policies that can shift the external accounts, as the East Asian economies apparently have been successful in doing, even after the 1997 financial crisis (Wade 1990; World Bank 1993). The transition from easy ISI to easy export substitution followed by South Korea and Taiwan and by other East Asian producers, considered in Chapter 10, was part of this strategy to "unbalance" and expand exports so as to gain the growth advantages of a good external imbalance.

A second type of "good" external imbalance often supplants the prior "good" imbalance. Policy-makers may opt for an under-valued exchange rate, as shown in Figure 15.4, after having had for some time an over-valued exchange rate, and they are especially likely to do so, or at a minimum to substantially reduced over-valuation of the exchange rate, when export substitution becomes an integral part of the overall development strategy.

Given the supply, $S_\$$, and the demand, $D_\$$, for the United States dollar in the South Korean foreign exchange market, the fixed (or managed float) value of 780 won to the dollar is "too low" – that is, it is taking more wons to buy one dollar than it should at the equilibrium exchange rate value. The dollar is over-valued relative to the won, so that more won are received for each dollar. The under-valuation of the won relative to the dollar will discourage, by making more expensive, the purchase of imports from the United States, and it will encourage, by making relatively cheaper, the sale of Korean exports to the United States market. Of course, the stimulation of exports and the discouragement of imports will tend, all else equal, to increase economic growth and employment in South Korea, and that may be one strategy to follow for a country wishing to push its new exports into the international market.[15]

If under-valuation persists and is the norm with the most important of South Korea's trading and financial partners, a current account surplus will, sooner or later, likely result, meaning that Korea will be earning more from the ROW than Korea spends in the ROW on goods and services, unilateral transfers and on profits, dividends, and interest. The other side of the current account surplus would be a capital and financial account *deficit*, indicating that South Korea would be accumulating net assets vis-à-vis the ROW through the extension of loans, through portfolio and direct foreign investment or via the build-up of its foreign exchange reserves. This accumulation can be seen in Figure 15.4 as the excess supply, k_1k_2, of dollars,

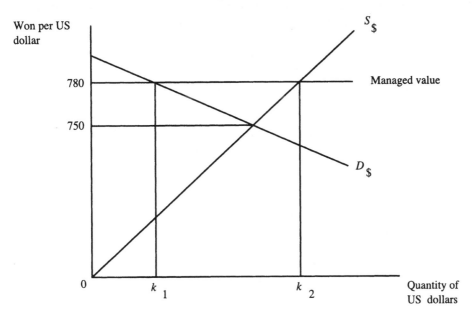

Figure 15.4 An under-valued exchange rate.

which measures the additional quantity of US dollars supplied to purchase Korean exports, for travel, and for investment in South Korea relative to the smaller quantity demanded (k_1) of dollars.

Interestingly, a good disequilibrium brought on by a conscious under-valuation of a country's exchange rate does *not* impose upon policy-makers the same binding economic need to eventually remove the source of the disequilibrium. A current account surplus disequilibrium is actually sustainable through time. There is thus an **asymmetry** at work in the impact of exchange rate misalignment on the balance of payments. Eventually, an over-valued exchange rate, beyond mild over-valuation, *must* result in a devaluation, since it is impossible for less-developed countries to sustain a current deficit indefinitely through external borrowing or the running down of official foreign exchange reserves. An under-valued exchange rate and a current account surplus may, however, be economically sustainable through time (though they may not be *politically* sustainable, as Japan's problems over trade with the United States illustrate).

Monitoring the balance of payments

Countries must carefully monitor what is happening to their balance of payments accounts. There is no a priori means of determining if a current account deficit per se is "good" or "bad." It depends upon how the excess of spending financed by the capital and financial account surplus is being used. If international borrowing is dedicated to improving productivity via technology development, research and development, funding new physical capital purchases for export producers, financing more human capital training, or other such expenditures that contribute to increased efficiency in the economy, then such a deficit can be a "good" deficit in terms of its contribution to economic growth. A "good" current account deficit also will not result in the depletion, or at least will not contribute to any significant deterioration, of the central bank's foreign exchange reserves. A fail-safe early warning sign for any government that it has a balance of payments problem is any sustained deterioration in its official foreign exchange reserves.

Recurring and chronic current account deficits accompanied by decreasing official foreign exchange reserves most often reflect underlying problems in a nation's overall development strategy and the failure to promote the needed structural transformations. It is true that there may be temporary *external* shocks to an economy that can create a balance of payments crisis. However, over a longer time frame of two to three years, the causes of continuing crises are most likely to be found in *internal* failures of economic policy, in the design of such policies and in their implementation.

Countries have the option of following different paths and of making decisions about their future. The evolution of a country's balance of payments accounts over time can be an important indicator as to whether those internal economic decisions, within the given external environment, are on the correct course or not. Those countries that successfully climb the structural transformation ladder discussed in Chapters 9 to 13 are more likely to avoid creating unsustainable current account imbalances.

Questions for review

1 Table 15.1 shows bilateral exchange rates for various countries in terms of US dollars. Each country actually has bilateral exchange rates between its currency and the currencies of all of its trade and financial partners. Choose three countries from the table, then calculate all possible bilateral exchange rates among these three countries from the bilateral rates provided in the table.

2 Looking back at Figure 15.1, what factors – economic and political – might cause a *decrease* in the demand for rupees and a downward shift of $D_\$$, assuming $S_\$$ constant? Assuming floating exchange rates, what effect does the decrease in the demand for rupees have on the exchange rate for rupees? (Does it appreciate? Depreciate?) What effects would you expect such a change in the exchange rate to have on Sri Lanka's exports? Its imports? Its total national output and total national income? Now consider, what factors – again economic and political – might cause the supply of rupees, $S_\$$, to decrease assuming $D_\$$ remains unchanged? What would happen to the exchange rate value of the Sri Lankan rupee in that case? To Sri Lankan exports? Imports? Travel in Sri Lanka? Foreign investment in Sri Lanka?

3 For years, many less-developed countries have suffered from "capital flight," as richer individuals, banks, and large companies have converted their domestic assets into foreign currencies and eventually foreign assets, such as bank accounts or shares on foreign stock markets or land, usually to escape high inflation, expected devaluations and unstable domestic economic conditions. What effect does the *return* of capital flight money to less-developed countries have on their exchange rates? Does the return of financial capital affect the demand or supply curve? Show, using a graph. What economic incentives might countries provide to encourage the return of flight capital?

4 Assume that the current nominal exchange rate between the British pound and Belizean dollar is £1:$B2, and that this is the "correct" real equilibrium value. During the year, inflation in Britain is 10 percent, while in Belize it is 20 percent. What new nominal exchange rate will maintain the real exchange rate value of the two currencies constant? (Hint: What will the new rate of exchange be for £1?)

5 What will cause a currency to depreciate in value? To appreciate in value? To be devalued? To be revalued? Which terms should be used in referring to falling exchange rate values when there are fully floating rates, depreciation, or devaluation? When there is a change in the exchange rate of a currency whose value is determined by a managed float? When there is an increase in the value of a fixed exchange rate currency: appreciation or revaluation?

6 According to the theory of the "twin deficits," what happens when a country saves more than it invests, assuming the central government budget is balanced? What would this suggest about the capital account of the balance of payments for that country? What sort of exchange rate regime might such a country be using: fixed, managed, or floating?

7 What are the risks of having an over-valued exchange rate? Are there any situations under which an over-valued exchange rate might be beneficial to economic growth?

8 Use the following information to determine (a) the balance of trade and the

current account balance, (b) the capital account balance, (c) the change in official foreign exchange reserves and (d) the statistical discrepancy of the balance of payments for this country [ROW = rest of the world]

> Service exports, $3.6 billion; total foreign exchange reserves, end of the year, $33.4 billion; merchandise imports, $17.3 billion; net unilateral transfers, $3.2 billion; profits, interest, and dividend earnings from the ROW, $4.2 billion; service imports, $2.4 billion; total foreign exchange reserves, beginning of the year, $34.6 billion; foreign loans extended to ROW, $1.8 billion; merchandise exports, $13.6 billion; profits, interest and dividends paid to the ROW, $5.8 billion; foreign loans received from ROW, $2.8 billion.

9 Morocco is currently running a current account deficit equal to −$12 billion per year. (a) Explain the likely reasons for such a deficit. (b) Explain what such a deficit implies about Morocco's capital account balance and/or foreign exchange reserves. (c) Discuss some possible steps Morocco might undertake to reduce the size of the current account deficit in the future, explaining the specific impact you would expect each measure to have in correcting the current account deficit balance.

10 Carefully explain what it means to say that a country has a "balance of payments problem." What parts of a country's balance of payments accounts might alert one to the possibility of a balance of payments crisis? Explain.

Notes

1 We will only be concerned here with the **spot exchange rate**, that is, with the current rate of exchange for currencies in the market on a daily, or current, basis. There also are future values determined for many exchange rates, such that one can buy or sell many foreign currencies to be traded at some fixed time in the future. These exchange rates also are reported in the major financial papers, such as *The Wall Street Journal* or *The Financial Times*, on a daily basis, as well as in the business sections of all major newspapers. If you have access to the Internet, exchange rates can be found at http://www.oanda.com/convert/classic.

2 Sri Lankans and others holding rupees and who exchange them for dollars in the Sri Lankan foreign exchange are simultaneously supplying rupees and demanding dollars. We could just have easily drawn Figure 15.1 showing the supply and demand for rupees rather than for dollars.

3 We are ignoring here, for simplicity, the transactions costs involved in foreign currency exchanges. As anyone who has traveled abroad knows, the "buy" and "sell" prices of currencies are never the same, the difference being a measure of the transactions costs of such exchanges. Here we assume such costs are zero.

4 Thus, someone trading 100 dollars after the increase in the supply of dollars on the foreign exchange market in Sri Lanka would receive 9,150 rupees compared to 9,366.5 before the shift in supply. The same quantity of dollars is worth less than previously in terms of the number of rupees that can be bought. In other words, the value of the dollar has fallen or depreciated.

5 Fixed exchange rates are thus not necessarily constant at some given value forever. A country that has fixed exchange rates may find it necessary to change the fixed value of its currency vis-à-vis other currencies from time to time, when severe imbalances between the quantity supplied and the quantity demanded of currencies persist. Fixed exchange rates do not, however, respond automatically, as do floating rates, to changes in the

supply of, and the demand for, foreign exchange. Fixed rates are determined by government fiat and only are maintained by government intervention of one sort or another.

6 Of course it is also conceivable that changes in the supply and demand curves are such that official foreign exchange reserves increase due to the excess supply of dollars in the Sri Lankan market relative to the demand for dollars. This means that the equilibrium value of the currency would result in appreciation relative to the fixed exchange rate value. While this is possible, most often LDCs encounter the problem of maintaining over-valued exchange rates as was discussed in the case of Sri Lanka.

7 Consider the following example. Assume that a US importer was buying handkerchiefs from a Mexican company and that the price of each handkerchief was 12 pesos in January 2003. The US importer would need to exchange US$1 for each handkerchief imported to obtain the 12 pesos needed to pay the Mexican exporter. After the inflationary episode, and assuming that the price of handkerchiefs increased at the 20 percent rate of inflation in Mexico, the Mexican exporter's price per unit would have risen to 14.4 pesos per handkerchief simply due to the inflation (12 pesos × 1.2). To maintain the real value of the exchange rate, the United States importer would now need to receive 14.4 pesos for each dollar exchanged. At this rate, US$1 continues to be able to buy one handkerchief just as before the inflation. If the exchange rate had remained at 12 pesos to US$1, each handkerchief would have required the United States importer to pay $1.20 to obtain the 14.4 pesos needed to pay for each handkerchief, which would be a depreciation in the value of the dollar and an appreciation in the value of the peso.

8 Why does this adjustment take place automatically with floating exchange rates? Assume that the nominal exchange rate of the Mexican peso has not yet reached the 14.4 pesos to US$1 equilibrium value but that the exchange rate is determined solely by market forces. Let's suppose that the current market rate is 13 pesos to US$1. This will mean that, given Mexico's inflation of 20 percent, the nominal exchange is still *over-valued* compared to its equilibrium value. This will make imports from the United States, travel to the United States, and Mexican investment in the United States cheaper than they were before the inflation. This will tend to increase the demand curve for dollars by Mexicans, and assuming all else is unchanged, this outward shift will continue until the real rate of 12 pesos to US$1 is restored at the nominal exchange rate of 14.4 pesos to US$1. In fact, the supply curve of dollars will also be decreasing at the same time, as holders of dollars are less willing to trade them for pesos due to the higher real price of Mexican goods with inflation (remember, for holders of dollars, until the real value of the exchange rate is restored, the dollar has *depreciated* in value), so the adjustment to any inflation differential between the two countries will be even more rapid.

This adjustment with floating exchange rates to conserve the real value of the exchange rate works to maintain *purchasing power parity* among countries, so that the same traded goods in each country in terms of a common currency would sell at roughly the same price when prices are converted to a common currency. If the purchasing power parity condition is violated, the prices of traded goods in one country will differ from those in another measured in terms of a common currency. Conversely, when such differences in traded good prices are observed, this may be evidence of the absence of fully adjusting, fully floating exchange rates.

9 The "net error and omissions" is of whatever value necessary to make equation 15.2 equal to zero. It is a measure not only of those legal transactions that get missed in some way in the normal collection of statistics and due to errors of bookkeeping, but also of a whole range of foreign currency transactions between one country and the rest of the world, many of them illegal, that no official statistics will ever be able to catch: illegal drugs and narcotics, gun-running, money-laundering operations, and capital flight. In fact, variations over time in the size of the these net errors and omission are one means by which governments track the illegal drug trade and illegal movements of financial funds to and from a country.

10 When a French resident travels to Spain on holiday, this is the equivalent of Spain "exporting" a service to France, thus creating an inflow of income for Spain on its current account. The French traveler injects spending into Spain for lodging, food, drinks, entertainment, and other expenditures; the same expenditure creates an outflow of money, or an import of tourism, in the French balance of payments accounts of an exactly equivalent amount.

11 By explicitly separating out the net movements of financial capital between nations from net changes in official reserves, it is sometimes easier to get an early warning of potential problems arising in the balance of payments accounts. If the change in official reserves is strongly and persistently *positive*, indicating a decrease in foreign exchange reserves or a reduction in gold and SDR reserves, this can be a sign of the likely need for a devaluation in the exchange rate, for a reduction in the internal rate of inflation or an entire change in economic strategy. We would argue, though, that policy-makers should constantly be monitoring *all* the major components of the balance of payments for signals of possible problems: a persistent current account deficit may be a sign of weaknesses in the relationship between exporting and importing. A capital account surplus, even with no net changes in official reserves, or even if these are accumulating, may result in an excessive amount of foreign debt and other obligations over time that can slow growth and development and result in an outflow of official reserve assets at a later date.

12 We also saw in the section on exchange rates that foreign exchange reserves may be needed to maintain the current nominal value of an exchange rate above its equilibrium value. In such circumstances, the volume of foreign exchange required will be even larger than for countries which have fully floating rates.

13 $(Y-C-T)-I-(G-T)=X-M$; remembering that by definition saving, S, is any income not consumed, then $Y-C-T=S$, so substituting: $(S-I)-(G-T)=X-M$. Rearranging the second term on the left-hand side so there is a positive sign between the two parenthetical expressions gives us expression 15.3 in the text.

14 A severe recession can depress a country's import spending such that $X>M$ to such a degree that a current account surplus materializes. Obviously, this is not a "good" current account surplus.

15 By simple national income accounting,

$$Q = Y = C + I + G + (X - M),$$

where Q is the value of national output, Y is income, C is total consumption, I is gross investment, G is government spending, X is export value and M is import value. Clearly, increasing X and decreasing M, as an under-valued exchange rate tends to do, will increase Q and Y, all else equal. Two of the important "all else are equal" assumptions are (1) that any imports discouraged are not essential to the domestic production process (e.g., technology, new capital) or that compensating policies (e.g., subsidies) neutralize such effects and (2) that the economy is not at full production, or else increases in X will simply subtract from domestic C or I.

References

Amsden, Alice. 1989. *Asia's Next Giant: South Korea and Late Industrialization*. New York: Oxford University Press.

Elliott, Jennifer A. 1994. *An Introduction to Sustainable Development*. London: Routledge.

IMF. 1995. *World Economic Outlook* (May). Washington, DC: IMF.

—— 2002. *World Economic Outlook* (April). Washington, DC: IMF.

UNCTAD (United Nations Conference on Trade and Development). 1995. *Trade and Development Report, 1995*. Geneva: UNCTAD.

Wade, Robert. 1990. *Governing the Market: Economic Theory and the Role of Government in East Asian Industrialization*. Princeton, NJ: Princeton University Press.

World Bank. 1993. *The East Asian Miracle*. Oxford: Oxford University Press.

—— 1994. *Adjustment in Africa*. Oxford: Oxford University Press.

16 The debt problem and development

After studying this chapter, you should understand:
- the origins of the external debt crisis for many less-developed nations;
- petro-dollar recycling, OPEC's absorption problem and the nature of the resource transfer from oil importers to oil exporters leading up to the 1980s debt crisis;
- when it is prudent for a country to borrow funds externally to finance a current account deficit or an investment project;
- how to measure the burden of the external debt and external debt-servicing costs;
- the continuing adverse impact of the excessive external debt build-up, or "debt overhang," of the 1970s on current and future growth possibilities for many LDCs; and
- some possible solutions to the debt problem.

Introduction

Throughout this text, we have examined fundamental action areas for countries wishing to accelerate their pace of economic growth and human development. We considered the critical need for greater attention to education and human capital accumulation. Universal primary education and progress toward universal secondary education are important benchmarks for future advances in growth and development. Tertiary education, we saw, must be geared to turning out a larger number of research scientists and technicians so that the needed focus on technology is implanted.

The creation of an efficient and honest civil service must also be one specific goal of a country's education and training policies. These efforts require that the central government take an active role in setting priorities, in mapping future projects carefully, in monitoring results, and in devoting sufficient public resources to all levels of education and professional training so that the goals which have been set have a reasonable chance of being achieved.

The importance of maintaining moderate or low rates of inflation, of carefully limiting central government budget deficits within sustainable boundaries, of avoiding severely over-valued exchange rates, of not running a persistently large current account deficit in the balance of payments, and so on also were identified as fundamental policy areas requiring particular attention by any nation interested in improving the pace of economic progress and human development. Of course, all of these suggestions are premised on the assumption that the key government decisionmakers of a country truly are interested in achieving a higher level of economic welfare that promotes greater equity and human progress. It is also presumed that leaders in the central government with such a vision will create the necessary mechanisms and find the human talent to carry out their mission, even against the wishes of elites with a vested interest in maintaining the status quo. The *desire* to develop must be firmly a part of the vision of the central government and other leaders or there can be little hope for sustained progress.[1]

However, even if a country with visionary leaders begins to set a new path for the future and seemingly follows all the rules and avoids the pitfalls of inflation, overvalued exchange rates, budget deficits and so on, there still may be a barrier that makes progress extremely difficult to achieve for some economies: excessive external debt accumulation inherited from the past.

This has been the dilemma confronting many Latin American and Sub-Saharan African countries since the early 1980s when the most recent international debt crisis erupted (the 1997 Asian financial crisis was more locally contained and less pervasive). The stock of external debt accumulated is not subject to the sorts of internal policy modifications that allow countries to correct for inflation, for balance of payments problems, for central government budget deficits, or even to choose to move along an entirely new development path. Yet existing external debt can undo even the best-laid plans for the future of the most visionary country. External debt accumulated by earlier, often non-democratic and military regimes can haunt the efforts of later democratic governments seriously interested in promoting economic growth and equity in their nations. External debt can constitute a serious internal barrier to further necessary structural transformation, but one that is not particularly amenable to domestic manipulation.

Origins of the external debt dilemma

For many less-developed nations lacking adequate domestic oil reserves, the decision in October 1973 of the Organization of Petroleum Exporting Countries (OPEC) to substantially raise the price charged for a barrel of oil marked the beginning of the external debt crisis. The price per barrel of Saudi Arabian light crude oil, a benchmark for other prices, rose from $2.59 on January 1, 1973 to $5.18 on November 1, 1973 and then to $11.65 on January 1, 1974. From 1973 to 1980, the export price of oil rose by about 500 percent after another spike in price in 1979–1980 (Vernon 1987: 290; Wee 1976: 133).

OPEC had been in existence since 1960, but it had never previously been able to effectively act as a cartel to set and maintain monopoly prices until 1973. Given that the bulk of the world's internationally marketed petroleum originates in OPEC nations, as long as the OPEC cartel's higher prices remained in effect every economy that required imported oil to generate electricity to run its factories and other industries – not to mention to fuel its motor cars, trucks, and trains – found that its import expenditures were now substantially greater.

For most less-developed nations, the OPEC price hike resulted in a larger trade deficit as import expenditures grew beyond export revenues. For most countries this also meant a larger current account deficit in the balance of payments. From the previous chapter on external macroeconomic equilibrium, you will remember that a current account deficit must be financed by a corresponding surplus on the sum of the capital and financial accounts. Thus the higher oil import bill due to the higher price of petroleum forced oil-importing nations to face, in the short term, the need for increased external borrowing, including foreign investment, and the running down of accumulated official foreign exchange reserves to cover the current account imbalance.[2]

It needs to be said that there did exist another option to running larger trade and current account deficits and undertaking further external borrowing. Oil-importing economies could have reduced their oil and other import expenditures sufficiently to maintain their trade and current account balances as they were prior to the oil price hike. This decision, however, would have meant slower rates of economic growth as there would have been fewer imported inputs used in production, and the effect would have been stronger the deeper the import cut-back. Such *adjustment policies* were pursued voluntarily by only a very few economies in the 1970s. Perhaps not surprisingly, those economies that best adjusted to the oil crisis were East Asian economies like South Korea that did not encounter a debilitating debt crisis, despite a high level of debt accumulation.

With higher oil prices, oil-importing nations thus found themselves in a difficult situation. They were forced to choose between slower economic growth or accumulating external debt to pay for more expensive oil. Far too many countries ended up making decisions that continue to have negative effects on their current development prospects. External debt accumulation, when not handled correctly, is another example of the effects of adverse path dependence that can extend far into the future.

Petro-dollar recycling

Fortuitously but unfortunately in the final analysis, the initial OPEC price increase brought its own solution for meeting the increased need for borrowing by petroleum-importing nations. Rapidly rising oil revenues created a so-called *absorption problem* for most of the OPEC nations. One of the motivations for raising prices in the first instance was to allow oil exporting nations to share in the wealth of their own natural resources – rather than selling it cheaply to other countries to spur economic development elsewhere – and to use the increased revenues for improving infrastructure, education, technology, and in a myriad of other uses. However, the increase in revenues flowed in so quickly after the price increases there simply were not enough immediate outlets in the OPEC economies for spending the additional oil income fast enough.

Many OPEC nations, such as Saudi Arabia, Iraq, and Kuwait, deposited their excess export earnings in international banks in New York, London, Tokyo, and Frankfurt in so-called Euro-dollar or Euro-currency markets where they could earn interest until appropriate private or public uses for the funds could be initiated. This helped to solve the OPEC nations' need to make productive and profitable use of their large and growing oil export revenues. However, the large inflow of OPEC deposits represented a challenge to the private international banking system which needed to find sufficient additional borrowers for this large volume of loanable funds if they were to be able to pay the interest on these new deposits (see Focus 16.1).

What the private banking system did to resolve this contradiction was to create a new class of borrower, the so-called **sovereign borrower**. This new class of borrower was none other than the petroleum-importing countries themselves who became the recipients of aggressive efforts to provide them with loans to finance their growing current account deficits as the price of oil increased.[3] In effect, a portion of the earnings of the OPEC oil-exporters deposited in private international banks was loaned back – recycled – to the petroleum-importing countries from which the increased revenues had been derived in the first place!

Petro-dollar recycling refers to this circulation and re-circulation of petroleum revenues from the oil-importing nations to the OPEC economies to the private international banks and then back again to the oil-importing nations in the form of loans, only to make the round again and again (Devlin (1989) is an excellent source for the full story of the private international banking system's marketing of loans to sovereign borrowers). The private international banks loaned to the petroleum-importing nations the funds that permitted them to continue to import petroleum and other imports at roughly the same levels as prior to the OPEC price increase.

FOCUS 16.1   OPEC'S ABSORPTION PROBLEM

The increase in oil prices in 1973 resulted in a huge resource transfer from oil-importing to oil-exporting economies. One measure of the size of this transfer can be seen in the evolution of the current account balances of importers and exporters of petroleum (figures are in billions of US dollars).

	1973	1974	1975–1978	1979	1980	1981
Middle East oil exporters	6.5	55.9	33.8	61.9	99.6	56.3
Developing countries	−9.1	−21.0	−39.5	−51.7	−68.0	−105.1

For the Middle East oil exporters, current account surpluses grew dramatically following each oil price increase, first in 1974 and again in 1979–1980. These current account surpluses occurred even though the Middle East oil exporters increased their own expenditures on imports from $3.5 billion in 1972 to more than $52 billion in 1982. These numbers give some idea of the large flows of financial capital and goods that the oil price increases set in motion from importers of oil to exporters of oil.

The other side of the current account surpluses of the Middle East oil exporters was a financial resource transfer from the oil importing developing countries, as measured by the evolution of the current account deficits of the oil importers shown above, from small to large negative balances.

The OPEC oil exporters could not absorb in productive uses all the new income at the rate at which it was being earned. There was a need to look for alternative investment alternatives. In 1974, 51 percent of $56.2 billion invested internationally by OPEC nations found its way to private international banks, particularly in Europe (other uses of these funds was in direct foreign investment, bonds, real estate in Europe, and so on). When oil prices were increased again in 1979, bank deposits absorbed 65.2 percent of the $62.1 billion invested internationally by the OPEC economies. In 1980, $100.2 billion was placed internationally, 44.2 percent of which went to private international banks.

Sources: World Bank 1985: 33, 89; Zanoyan 1995

Later, additional money was lent to oil importers to be used not just for import purchases but also to repay the interest and principal coming due on past debt obligations. And so began the cycle of debt accumulation.

Dimensions of the debt crisis

Table 16.1 shows the growth of external debt accumulation after 1970 for a few of the severely and moderately indebted nations. External debt accumulation was especially rapid for some countries, particularly those in Latin America and especially for Mexico, Brazil, and Argentina. But external debt also rose quite rapidly in the 1970s and into the early 1980s for South Korea as well.[4] The table also shows whether a country has a severe external debt problem (an S after the country), was moderately in debt (M), or was less indebted (L) as of 1999.

As the table shows, the first major episode of external debt accumulation occurred during the 1970s and into the 1980s. Since 1985, debt has continued to rise for many countries, especially in Argentina, Brazil, India, Mexico and South Korea (see Focus 16.2 for data on aggregate external debt accumulation over an earlier period). In some heavily indebted Sub-Saharan African countries, and for very special reasons, total external debt has shown a tendency to fall. Korea's debt rose more than three times between 1993 and the 1997 Asian financial crisis, but the South Korean economy has been able to avoid the crises of debt that other countries have experienced (Amsden 2001: 254–255).

In the 1970s, it was the private international banks which provided an increasing proportion of new loans to cover foreign currency shortfalls, especially to the largest

Table 16.1 Total external debt, 1970–2000 (millions of US$)

	1970[a]	1980	1985	1993	2000
Argentina (S)	1,878	27,157	44,444	74,473	146,172
Brazil (S)	3,236	71,012	106,730	132,749	237,953
Chile (M)	2,060	12,081	20,221	20,637	36,978
Congo (S)	135	1,526	1,760[a]	5,071	4,887
Côte d'Ivoire (S)	256	7,445	8,446	19,146	12,138
Ghana (M)	489	1,407	1,170[a]	4,590	6,657
India (L)	7,940	20,582	35,460	91,781	100,367
Kenya (M)	313	3,394	4,219	6,994	6,295
Malaysia (M)	390	6,611	13,384[a]	23,335	41,797
Mexico (L)	3,206	57,379	97,429	118,028	150,288
Pakistan (S)	3,059	9,936	12,965	26,050	32,091
South Korea (L)	1,797	29,480	47,996	47,203	134,417
Sudan (S)	319	5,163	5,086[a]	16,193	15,741
Tanzania (S)	248	2,476	3,60	9,522	7,445
Zimbabwe (M)	233	786	2,143	4,168	4,002

Sources: World Bank 1983: 178–179, Table 16; 1987: 232–233, Table 16; 1995b: 200–201, Table 20; 2002: 264–266, Table 4.16.

Notes
Letters in parenthesis after countries indicated degree of external debt in 1999: S = severely indebted; M = moderately indebted; and L = less indebted. The classification depends on the present value of debt compared to exports and income (see Table 16.2).
a Includes only *public* external debt. Other years include both public and private external debt.

FOCUS 16.2　THE EVOLUTION OF EXTERNAL DEBT ACCUMULATION

In 1970, the external debt of the less-developed countries totalled $68.4 billion. By 1980, external debt had multiplied by nearly ten times, reaching a total of $635.8 billion. Debt rose less rapidly in the 1980s, but the total nearly doubled by 1990, reaching $1,298.7 billion. By 2000, estimated external debt for the low- and middle-income nations totalled $2,492.0 billion, nearly forty times larger than in 1970.

Debt burden ratios, calculated as total external debt divided by total export income have shown a tendency to fall over the 1990s for all regions except Africa and quite significantly in South Asia. Yet for all regions, the debt to export ratio was higher in 1999 than in 1980 prior to the outbreak of the debt crisis. The ratios measure debt as a percentage of the total income earned to repay debt, that is, external debt foreign exchange obligations as a share of total foreign exchange received due to exports, the primary source of a country's foreign exchange earnings.

	1980	*1990*	*1999*
East Asia	81.8	114.3	99.9
Latin America	201.8	279.7	230.9
South Asia	160.5	380.8	216.0
Sub-Saharan Africa	91.7	219.3	224.2

What are the costs of such debt expansion? Zambia, for example, was forced to spend *thirty times more* to make its debt payments in 1994 than it spent on education! For other regions above, the debt to GNP ratio declined, as total economic growth outpaced debt accumulation, but individual countries still experienced crises related to this debt overhang, from Nicaragua to Mexico.

Sources: World Bank 1997: 247, Table 17; 2001: 250–253, Table 4.15;
2002: 266, Table 4.16

debtors in Latin America, so that they could pay for more expensive imports. Nearly two-thirds of all new capital in Latin America over the period 1977–1981, and an even larger percentage of total borrowed capital, was provided by the private banking system (Ffrench-Davis and Griffith-Jones 1995: 240).

These loans were extended at market and variable rates of interest as the risk of inflation was transferred to the sovereign borrowers, who found that their repayment obligations varied with the level of world inflation.[5] On the other hand, most Sub-Saharan African countries, being quite poor and higher-risk borrowers, tended to receive the bulk of their external debt in the form of **concessional** loans. These were loans made available at below-market interest rates and with extended periods for repayment, often thirty years or more. Concessional loans were provided by bilateral lending institutions such as the African Development Bank (AfDB) or multi-lateral institutions, like the World Bank and the International Monetary Fund (IMF) (see Chapter 17 for more details on the lending activities of these institutions).

When to borrow externally

When does it make sense for a country to borrow externally, that is, when is it suitable to incur debt denominated in foreign currencies? External borrowing will be necessary to finance any part of a current account deficit not covered by direct foreign investment inflows, aid inflows, or a reduction in a country's official foreign exchange reserves.[6] In fact, a country cannot incur a current account deficit without having the ability either to borrow foreign currency or without having accumulated sufficient official foreign exchange reserves to cover any spending in the current account of the balance of payments greater than export and other income items.

One acceptable reason to borrow externally can be to finance what is expected to be a *short-term* current account deficit. This may occur as a the result of some temporary imbalance in which expenditures for imports exceed export earnings, perhaps due to an unexpected drop in export prices or any other unforeseen, but transitory situation, in which import expenditures exceed export earnings. External borrowing in such circumstances can help a country avoid unnecessary disruptions to production, employment, and smooth consumption over the short term. Once export revenues recover or import expenditures return to normal levels, then the need for external borrowing will have ended. Under such circumstances, external borrowing can help to smooth import purchases over time and stabilize economic conditions, thus contributing to greater social welfare.[7]

For example, if the OPEC petroleum price increases in 1973 had been expected to be temporary so that the larger current account deficits which resulted would be closed in the near future, then external borrowing to get past that short-term disruption, even to pay for the import of consumer durable and non-durable goods, might reasonably have been justified.[8] In fact, this is precisely one of the original reasons that the IMF was created: to assist in the financing of temporary and transitory balance of payments disequilibria. However, after a few months had passed and the price of petroleum remained at its higher level and then was increased again by OPEC in 1974, the justification for external borrowing simply to pay for roughly the same physical quantity of imports no longer applied. Clearly the price increase had become something beyond a temporary disturbance that was going to go away quickly.

When the need for external borrowing to finance a current account is expected to be a *recurring long-term* likelihood given current or expected levels and prices of imports and exports and the magnitude of other capital and financial account inflows and outflows, then the decision to borrow externally needs to be appraised very carefully. Long-term external debt accumulation *must* contribute either to foreign exchange savings or to foreign exchange earnings in the future. In other words, if the need to borrow externally is not a short-term exigency to smooth transitory cyclical movements in the current account of the balance of payments, then such borrowed funds must be dedicated to expanding *import substitution* industries which, in the future, can reduce the nation's import expenditures or such borrowing needs to be dedicated to the expansion of *export production* which increases future foreign exchange earnings.[9]

If external borrowing is to take place, it should be undertaken for productive investments that will expand the output of *tradable goods and services*. Obviously export goods are tradables, but so too are all import substitution commodities. If the output of import substitute industries were not being produced domestically, they would be imported, that is, traded. Thus producing goods and services to replace imports is a way to save on foreign exchange needs. Borrowing to finance infrastructure that can contribute to either greater export earnings or import substitution production by lowering costs also could be acceptable. Investments in roads, communications systems, electricity, water, and perhaps even the legal system might qualify as foreign exchange earning or foreign exchange saving investments that can justify external debt accumulation.

The key issue in deciding on the wisdom of external borrowing over the long term is determining whether such borrowing is dedicated to investments that are expected to generate foreign exchange earnings or foreign exchange savings in the future that will be sufficient to pay-down the external debt undertaken. The issue is not whether external debt accumulation contributes to the overall economic growth of an economy; that is an insufficient criterion. The question is whether such external borrowing contributes sufficiently to the growth of the tradables sectors. If it does, external debt may be advisable; if not, external debt accumulation is not recommended since the so-called "transformation problem" of generating sufficient foreign exchange to repay the debt will not be met (World Bank 1985: 48).

External borrowing to finance the expansion of production in non-tradable output – for example construction of new homes, shopping malls, and hospitals – are certainly important to the well-being of the population. However, investing in these kinds of goods and services does not contribute to the ability to repay external debt since the output created does not generate foreign exchange earnings. These are goods and services sold and traded in the internal market only and they only generate funds in the domestic currency. Therefore, external borrowing to finance such investments cannot be justified. Neither can many other types of expenditures, such as national defense. External borrowing other than for short-term disruptions to the balance of payments should only in the most extreme of circumstances be undertaken to cover expenditures for current consumption, since, by definition, no foreign exchange earnings or savings are generated.

Both replacing imports and expanding exports can help to close a trade gap and contribute to a smaller current account deficit by increasing the domestic production of tradable goods. There may be, nonetheless, some preference for using external debt to finance export expansion projects over import substitution purposes, since there is a natural limit to the foreign exchange savings that can be expected over time from the latter. Not all imports can be replaced by domestic production, so the potential savings of foreign exchange from import substitution ultimately is limited. The expected earnings from export expansion, however, can continue to grow over a longer time period and at a higher rate, though there is no guarantee here either. Market conditions can change, new exporters can enter the same market thus reducing each country's effective demand and so on. But there is definitely a limit to foreign exchange savings derived from import substitution while foreign exchange earnings via the export of tradables are not subject to an absolute upper limit.

Whether external borrowing is dedicated to tradables that expand export earnings or which create import savings, the expected increase in foreign exchange holdings should be sufficient to cover repayment of the principal (*amortization*) and interest on the external debt incurred over the life of the loan. For this relation to hold, the annual rate of increase in foreign exchange earnings from "growing" exports plus the rate of foreign exchange savings from reducing imports must be greater than the average rate of interest charged on a country's external loans.

As Focus 16.3 suggests, external borrowing should be done extremely cautiously, and any guesses about future export prices and future import prices should err on the side of understating them in attempting to determine the wisdom of accepting

FOCUS 16.3 THE MEXICAN DILEMMA

When OPEC raised the price of petroleum in 1973, Mexico was an oil importer despite having significant domestic oil reserves controlled by the public corporation, PEMEX. One group within government argued that higher petroleum prices created an opportunity for Mexico to begin to export oil that could help to finance increased economic and social development over the future. It was suggested that the increased external borrowing required to modernize the petroleum industry and to increase its productive capacity for export purposes could be paid for out of the expected increased revenues from oil exports over the future.

Others in Mexico feared, however, that if the price of petroleum were to decrease significantly in the future, then lower export revenues would be available for economic and social development purposes. If the price decrease were at all sharp, external debt repayment might even require that Mexico export an ever-larger quantity of petroleum (since oil export income equals the price of oil multiplied by the quantity of oil exported) in order to be able to earn the needed revenues to meet the increased external debt obligations. This group within and outside of government argued against any expansion of oil production that needed to be financed by external debt accumulation paid out of expected future petroleum exports. The fear was that since petroleum is a non-renewable commodity, that is, non-producible, Mexico would be unable to regulate the pace at which its oil was used up if the country's oil reserves had been pledged as the means to repay external debt obligations. Falling oil prices would trigger a more rapid rate of oil depletion, as a larger physical quantity of oil would need to be exported at a lower price of oil to earn the necessary foreign exchange to service the debt.

The pro-debt forces prevailed, and external debt accumulation to finance the expansion of petroleum exports took place at a rapid pace. Public spending financed by external debt jumped from 30 percent of GDP in 1978 to nearly 50 percent in 1982. The government's fiscal deficit more than doubled from 8 percent of GDP in 1980 to 18 percent in 1982. Total Mexican exports came to be dominated by oil exports that grew rapidly over time, but when the price of oil collapsed in the 1980s, the need to further expand the physical quantity of petroleum exports to service debt obligations increased, as more cautionary voices had foreseen. In 1981, oil exports accounted for 69 percent of all exports. By 2001, however, only 8 percent of total exports were oil, as manufacturing exports grew dramatically.

Mexico's oil "patrimony" was in danger of being depleted just to repay past debt in the early 1980s, leaving little to be used to fuel the social and economic development that had motivated the expansion of oil production in the first instance. It was only due to a change in economic strategy that fueled the growth of manufactured exports, including the introduction of the North American Free Trade Agreement, that the oil gamble did not result in crisis.

Sources: World Bank 1985: 63; World Bank Country Data: http://www.worldbank.org/cgi-bin/sendoff.cgi?page=%2fdata%2Fcountrydata%2Fict%2Fmex_ict.pdf

higher levels of debt. This caution is counseled because, as we shall see below, countries that find themselves with "too much" external debt relative to their ability to repay can find their future growth and development prospects to be seriously comprised. Thus, in considering whether to borrow to expand exports, the estimation of future expected export earnings should be based on a presumption that the future prices of exports will be *lower*, perhaps significantly lower, than they are in the present. Likewise, in estimating expected future import expenditures, it should be assumed that future import prices will be higher than current import prices. Such *discounting* will tend to make the standard for borrowing externally to finance export expansion or import substitution more rigorous, such that the incentive to borrow is reduced. This disincentive will be greater the larger the discounting factor.

What, then, are the lessons of the Mexican dilemma discussed in Focus 16.3? If export expansion is to be financed by external debt expansion, it is perhaps advisable that these exports be *renewable* commodities, that is, goods or services that are capable of being produced and not simply exhausted, like petroleum. Second, and as argued above, higher prices today for an export are no guarantee of higher prices in the future. In fact, just the opposite is as likely to be true. Borrowing large amounts over an extended period of time increases the likelihood of over-borrowing that, in the future, can adversely affect economic growth and human development if export prices decline, making repayment of debt more onerous in terms of the quantity of output which must be exported.

There is one further consideration. Even when countries do borrow for the right reasons, such borrowing may be less than effective, as Focus 16.4 points out.

External borrowing, adjustment policies, and savings

The foregoing caveats concerning external loans refer to decisions to borrow to finance persistent current account deficits. Such disequilibria may arise from external events, such as the petroleum price increase. But they also may be a reflection of underlying, and often quite severe, problems and failures of internal economic policy. Policy errors that result in high levels of inflation and over-valued exchange rates can create situations in which the current account of the balance of payments is in deficit, requiring a compensating inflow of external financial resources on the

---

FOCUS 16.4   INEFFECTIVE USE OF EXTERNAL DEBT

Even when borrowing for the right reasons – export expansion or import substitution – investments funded by external debt still can be inefficiently utilized. In a study of the Philippines, Argentina, and Morocco, the World Bank found that incremental capital–output ratios in all three countries rose substantially during the period in which external borrowing was taking place.

For example, Argentina's ICOR increased from 4.4 in 1963–1972 to 11 over the period 1973–1981, indicating that to generate an additional unit of output the amount of physical investment required rose from 4.4 to 11 units. Thus, physical capital investment was *less effective* in producing output due to an increase in capital-intensive production. Even worse, virtually none of the $35 billion Argentina borrowed between 1976 and 1982 resulted in a *net* addition to investment.

The same tendencies were noted in the Philippines, where the ICOR doubled, and in Morocco, where the ICOR rose from 2.6 in 1965–1972 to 6.7 in 1979–1982 as external debt was being incurred. What these trends indicate is the difficulties in producing output, some due to microeconomic and others to macroeconomic inefficiencies, in these economies. What is certain is that such inefficiencies make it more difficult to repay external debt. By comparison, South Korea's ICOR remained at about 3 as external debt grew, indicating greater efficiency in the overall production process in generating output from new investment. The structural transformations pursued by South Korea examined in previous chapters, combined with good state policy, helped avoid severe and lingering debt problems.

Source: World Bank 1985: 52, 68

capital account, some of which may be in the form of external debt owed to private banks or to bilateral or multilateral lending institutions.

At a more fundamental level, a persistent imbalance in the current account may reflect the failure of an economy to successfully negotiate the series of "strategy switches" in economic policy that contribute to the necessary structural transformations on the path toward greater industrialization and diversification of production discussed in Chapters 9 to 11. It is in those instances, where external financing is used to attempt to *maintain* the status quo and to avoid the costs of better economic policy-making, that external debt is economically inadvisable, though it may be the preferred political choice. The Latin American debtor countries followed this path of least resistance, using external debt to finance current consumption or military expenditures or to repay old debt. This had the effect of perpetuating economic structures and policies that badly needed to be changed. In particular, external debt accumulation permitted the continuation and deepening of import substitution industrialization and the omission of the export substitution stage of industrialization. The failure to develop the capacity to export manufactured goods to the world market was reflected in the inefficiencies in production, as measured by both low aggregate growth rates and non-existent rates of total factor productivity, as we saw in Chapter 10, which have stifled progress in Latin America since the 1960s.[10]

The twin deficit and productive borrowing

On the other hand, if external borrowing to finance a current account deficit is properly used to expand the production of tradables, then such borrowing can be an important contributor to the adjustment policies in any attempt to transform the economic structure in a direction that is sustainable in the future. In such cases, external borrowing is not only justifiable, but such debt, being self-liquidating, can be integral to an effort to support the required structural transformation of the economy which results in greater efficiency and a more technological focus by financing needed investments, both public and private.

Even if a country does not have a current account imbalance requiring inflows of capital, external borrowing could still be warranted if used productively. Recalling the concept of the twin deficit from Chapter 15, it will be remembered from equation 15.3, and assuming that there is no central government deficit, that the following relation must hold if there is no external debt accumulation:

$$S - I = X - M = 0 \qquad (16.1)$$

This states that if savings equals investment then there will be no trade gap and no need for external financing. In a country without access to external sources of financing including direct foreign investment, the overall level of investment will be constrained by domestic savings. On the reasonable and usual assumption that $S = s(Y/L)L$, s is likely to be smaller the lower is per capita income, so that low-income countries are likely to generate low levels of total savings.[11] Low levels of saving mean that the bulk of an economy's production goes to consumption, leaving little left over for investment. Low levels of investment, including financing for investment in human capital like education and health care and technology, result in low levels of income per person in future. Thus, a vicious cycle of poverty is reinforced, with poor countries remaining poor because they begin poor lacking sufficient capital of all types for expanding productive investments over the future.

However, if domestic savings, S_D (our S in statement 16.1), can be supplemented by foreign savings, S_F, via external borrowing, then total investment can be pushed above what would be achieved from domestic resources alone. When this occurs via borrowing on the capital account of the balance of payments, statement 16.1 becomes:

$$S - I = X - M < 0 \qquad (16.2)$$

Statement 16.2 shows that for domestic investment to be greater than domestic saving, the equivalent value of additional investment goods must come from an excess of imports over exports. In other words, foreign borrowing can help a country to finance this twin deficit by boosting the level of domestic investment and financing the import of investment goods and other inputs to production. This creates the possibility of a *virtuous* cycle of foreign borrowing, domestic investment and increases in domestic production. Of course, our admonition that such borrowing be channeled toward tradables, be they export production or import substitution goods, still applies. If this condition holds, external borrowing can contribute to higher economic growth rates and to structural transformation in the production process along the lines suggested in Chapter 10, permitting poorer nations to supplement domestic resources in short supply with foreign resources.[12]

The debt burden

Given that external debt can only ultimately be repaid using foreign exchange earned from exporting, it is often convenient to use the ratio of total debt divided by total exports (D/X) as a measure of the *debt burden*. Another measure of the severity of external debt is the *debt service ratio,* calculated as the share of export income used for repaying principal and interest on the debt. Table 16.2 shows the total debt to export ratio and the debt service ratios for the same countries listed in the previous table.

Let us first consider Mexico's debt service ratios to see what these mean. In 1980, the equivalent of half of all Mexico's export revenues were required to pay current amortization and interest on the external debt. The debt service ratio had decreased by 1990 to about a fifth of export income only to rise again in 1999 to a fourth of export earnings. The contrast between the years in terms of the cost to the Mexican economy of external debt servicing is striking, however. In 1980, prior to the international debt crisis which began in mid-1982 (discussed in the next section), Mexico still was able to borrow externally from the private banks that provided the bulk of the new loans to the largest debtors. So even though the equivalent of half of Mexico's export income apparently was absorbed by debt service, much of the actual debt service was paid by simply "rolling over" old debt by incurring new debt. This meant that debt servicing in 1980 did not have a particularly adverse effect on Mexico's ability to import other goods and services, since very little of actual export income needed to be used to pay amortization and interest payments on past debt.

The last column of Table 16.2 shows the total debt to export ratio for Mexico in 1999 as 108, substantially less than the 175.6 ratio that prevailed as recently as 1993

Table 16.2 Debt service ratios and total debt to export ratios

	1970	1980	1990	1999	D/Xª
Argentina	18.2	37.3	37.0	75.9	456
Brazil	31.9	63.1	22.2	110.9	399
Chile	27.2	43.1	25.9	25.4	175
Congo	9.2	10.6	35.3	1.4	265
Côte d'Ivoire	6.8	38.7	35.4	26.2	220
Ghana	9.1	13.1	36.9	19.9	190
India	20.9	9.3	32.7	15.0	104
Kenya	17.1	21.0	35.4	26.7	193
Malaysia	3.1	6.3	12.6	4.8	48
Mexico	28.2	48.1	20.7	25.1	108
Pakistan	23.6	17.9	23.0	30.5	252
South Korea	13.1	19.7	10.8	24.6	71
Sudan	5.0	25.5	7.5	6.5	1,717
Tanzania	7.2	25.9	32.9	15.6	370
Zimbabwe	4.4	3.8	23.1	25.3	159

Sources: World Bank 1983: 178–179, Table 16; 1987: 236–237, Table 18; 1995b: 178–179, Table 9, 206–207, Table 23; 2001: 258–260, Table 4.17.

Note
a Net present value of total external debt as a percentage of total exports, 1999. Debt service ratio = ($amortization + $interest)/$exports.

when total external debt was 1.75 times total exports. This ratio has shown a tendency to fall as Mexico has given special attention to debt reduction measures and as Mexico's exports have risen faster than debt accumulation. By contrast, Brazil's and Argentina's debt burdens are quite high and higher than in the early 1990s, at least partly a reflection of the low level of exports compared to GDP sold in international markets. This, however, reflects more fundamental underlying failures of these two large Latin American debtors to make the necessary structural transformation, including the formation of human capital and technology acquisition capabilities discussed in previous chapters, that have handicapped two promising economies in their ability to make progress.

By contrast, consider what has happened to the debt service ratio in South Korea. Between 1980 and 1990 South Korea's debt service ratio fell dramatically, amounting to but slightly more than 10 percent of export income though it rose sharply by 1999 as total accumulated external debt increased rapidly at least partly due to the Asian financial crisis of the late 1990s (Table 16.1). The reduction in debt servicing into the early 1990s was due primarily to South Korea's rapid expansion of exports (at the rate of 12.3 percent annually, 1980–1993) that made repayment easier over time. It is likely that South Korea's debt to export ratio of more than 70 percent will fall over time, as the adverse short-term impact of the financial crisis of the late 1990s passes. In 1993, the ratio had been only 46.2 percent, the second-lowest debt burden among all countries at that time. Still, being able to repay, theoretically at any rate, all external debt out of one year's export revenues suggests that South Korea (and Malaysia) have managed to avoid the excessive build-up of external debt that has had such an adverse effect on the progress of other debtor nations, especially in Latin America, but also in Africa. Sudan's debt to export ratio is a matter of grave concern, even though the debt-service ratio is low due to extraordinary efforts of the international community to delay current repayments. The potential income from exports to pay for such a level of debt is just not there.

The debt crisis

The onset of the international debt crisis is usually dated as beginning when Mexico announced its decision to suspend payment on its scheduled external debt payment in August 1982. Other countries soon followed suit. What set off this moratorium on debt obligations that for a time threatened the stability of the international financial markets?

By mid-1982, the private international banks had begun to dramatically reduce their petro-dollar recycling to sovereign borrowers as a consequence of a slow-down in the rate of growth of the international economy. Stringent monetarist policies to reduce inflation introduced by the United States and British central banks under pressure from Presidents Carter and Reagan in the United States and from the Conservative government in Great Britain had resulted in sharp recessions that spread quickly through the global economy.[13] As income in the developed countries declined so too did their import purchases, including imports from the less-developed oil-importing nations.[14]

With the decline in export revenues being earned by the oil-importing nations, the private international banks decided that sovereign borrowers were no longer the good risks they had been judged to be since 1973. The commercial banks thus quickly tried to reduce their lending exposure to the debtor economies, as the perceived riskiness of further lending increased. Since many borrowing nations had been using new loans to pay their debt-service obligations as they came due and had been putting relatively little borrowed money to productive uses in tradables that would have saved or earned foreign exchange in future, when the so-called loan window of the private banks closed, debtor nations faced a potential crisis given the current account deficits being run by so many of them.[15]

Without access to new loans to finance current account deficits and with finite official foreign exchange, debtor countries were soon confronted with difficult decisions. With the global recession rapidly reducing their export earnings, it was becoming impossible to both service past debt *and* continue to import at the same level, especially after access to external funds was ended. Any reduction in imports to save on foreign exchange that would then be used to make loan payments would mean a lower current living standard, particularly if critical inputs to industry were affected, since all foreign exchange to pay for debt servicing would now need to come from export earnings (or official reserves). Mexico's announcement of a moratorium on its debt service immediately reduced the size of its current account deficit that required financing by an amount equal to the sum of the deferred debt servicing. This meant that without having to dedicate any export earnings to debt repayment more goods and services could be imported than if Mexico's debt service obligations had been met on time. Soon, other indebted nations followed suit, declaring a debt-servicing holiday so as to conserve any foreign exchange earned from exporting for import purchases.

The debt servicing moratorium had the effect of mobilizing the private international banks and their governments to attempt to find the means to get Mexico and other nations to continue with their debt service repayments before any loans were declared "bad" or non-performing, a financial status which threatened many large international private banks with bankruptcy due to excessive lending. A fundamental defining feature of the 1980s debt crisis, as already noted, was the exceptionally high level of private bank debt held by the largest borrowing nations.[16] While it was individually rational for each private bank to cease lending as the riskiness of new loans increased, it was **socially irrational** for them *all* to suspend lending simultaneously. In fact, it was this *lack* of coordination of international financial flows – combined with a healthy dose of greed on the part of the banks – that led the private banks to *over*-lend before the outbreak of the crisis and then to *under*-lend when the United States and United Kingdom-administered global recession resulted in the sharp decrease in world trade after 1980.

In at least partial recognition of this divergence between private and social benefits and the seriousness of the market failure problem in international lending, an important part of the effort to minimize the damage to the private banking system was a concerted effort by the IMF and the United States Treasury to force the large private banks to re-initiate so-called *involuntary lending* to the major debtor countries. In effect, as a condition of being repaid, the banks would provide new loans precisely for that purpose. This allowed debtor nations to more easily adjust to the changed policy environment that lower levels of bank lending implied.

In making such loans and in providing other concessions to the debtor nations such as lower interest rates and longer repayment schedules, albeit without much enthusiasm, the larger private banks avoided the worst effects that a full-scale default would have implied. They provided "bridge loans" that made continued repayment to the large private lenders possible and avoided technical defaults by the debtor economies. Many smaller banks were, however, left out of the international reorganization deals and quite a few collapsed when their debts went unpaid as a result of their being closed out of the re-financing process. The difficulty faced by many of the indebted nations in not being able to repay on their borrowing obligations, given prevailing interest rates, world trade patterns, the short maturity period of their loans, the lack of domestic productive efficiency and so on, did for a time, however, threaten to spill over into a full-blown banking crisis, especially for some large US banks like Chase Manhattan and Citibank, and there was no shortage of doomsday scenarios as to the impact of such financial collapse on the world economy (Pastor 1987).

Efforts to overcome the debt crisis[17]

International efforts to overcome the debt crisis focused on measures that might enable potentially defaulting countries to continue to be able to service their debt obligations without unduly affecting long-term economic growth. These measures have included the involuntary lending discussed above. There have also been numerous negotiations to lengthen the maturities of commercial loans, to reduce interest rates charged and to capitalize overdue payments by adding them to the principal value of the loans. Some write-downs, or cancellations, of loans have occurred, but these have not been particularly significant to the overall total of external debt from commercial banks. Turning loans into long-term bonds, even perpetual bonds never requiring repayment of principal, is a proposal still worthy of more widespread application, especially for the most deeply indebted economies (World Bank 1985: 29).

Multilateral (e.g., World Bank loans) and bilateral (e.g., government-to-government) debt has been somewhat easier to reschedule or even cancel. Various rounds of talks by the Paris Club, where negotiations among governments take place on external debt, have had some success in reducing non-commercial debt of the 25–30 poorest of the most indebted nations (having GDP of less than $500 or debt-to-export ratios exceeding 350 percent), most of which are in Africa. Under the 1994 Naples terms of the Paris Club discussion, up to 67 percent of non-commercial public external debt is potentially eligible for long-term rescheduling and even, in some instances, cancellation (UNCTAD 1995: 36–39). The goal is to reduce the debt service ratios of the poorest debtors to below 20 percent. However, debt reduction or extensive stretching-out of maturities is not enough. It is also necessary to correct whatever it is that resulted in excessive debt accumulation in the past, and for most countries it begins with a failure to have properly initiated and carried through the required structural transformations discussed in Chapters 9 to 11.

There have also been a variety of innovative **debt swaps** in which an indebted country trades something to a holder of its debt in return for debt reduction. For example, a debt-for-equity swap involved the holder of Mexican debt with a value of, say, $1 million trading that debt to the Mexican government for a share of ownership in a newly privatized, formerly state-owned, company. The holder of the Mexican debt might receive the equity value in the company equivalent to $1.2 million, though that equity would now be denominated in pesos, not in dollars. It is clear that there are potential gains to both parties to the transaction. The holder of Mexican debt with a face value of $1 million is able to "buy" $1.2 million worth of equity in a Mexican company at a discount. The Mexican government is able to retire $1 million worth of debt denominated in dollars with a peso expenditure, thus reducing its debt servicing requirements and the outflow of foreign exchange on that debt.

Other kinds of "swaps" also have been completed. Debt-for-nature swaps have been used to encourage countries to set aside rainforests or other land areas as protected reserves. In these swaps the holder of the debt might be an organization like the World Wide Fund for Nature (WWF) or some other non-governmental organization with an interest in preserving the natural environment. How would such a group come to be a holder of, say, Brazilian debt that could be swapped for rainforest preservation? They might very well have purchased Brazilian debt on the **secondary debt market**. The secondary debt market is a "discount" market for sovereign debt instruments. Banks or other primary providers of loans to sovereign borrowers can reduce their exposure to default by selling debt to others willing to accept the risk in the secondary market. Chase Manhattan, for example, may have Brazilian debt with a face value of $20 million it would like to remove from its portfolio of loans because of concern over the likelihood of repayment or to reduce its exposure in the external debt market. In the secondary market in 1989, for example, the discount on such Brazilian debt was in the neighborhood of 70 percent, so the WWF could have purchased $20 million worth of Brazilian debt instruments for about $6 million. Then, the WWF could "swap" this debt with the Brazilian government for an agreement that sets aside the equivalent of, say, $10 million worth of Brazilian rainforest from future economic development by transferring ownership to a trust, to a government agency, or even to the WWF. In this way, the WWF is able to protect $10 million worth of Amazonian rainforest from overuse at a cost to its members of $6 million. The Brazilian government reduces its external indebtedness at a 50 percent discount (by giving up the equivalent of $10 million of Brazilian forest to retire $20 million of external debt), though the actual cost may be significantly less than this, since there is no outflow of foreign exchange associated with this swap (see Focus 16.5).

There was even some hope, for a time, that approaches such as the Brady Plan, proposed in 1989, might actually lead to a voluntary reduction of the external debt burden of the most deeply indebted nations as commercial banks and other institutions were encouraged to write-down their debt holdings. That has not happened to any great extent, however, and many countries continue to be saddled with large debt burdens that make further adjustment policies that might contribute to the necessary structural transformations required for further development even more difficult to achieve. Mexico, for example, after apparently taking all the right steps, at least in the eyes of many economists at the IMF and the World Bank, toward liberalization of the economy, the stabilizing of the inflation rate, and a shift in economic policies toward exporting, found itself in late 1994 in a severe currency, and then economic, crisis. While many would say that this was the consequence of a political crisis, a view which we would not necessarily contradict, the underlying forces pushing the Mexican economy toward political and economic crisis can at least partly be found in the continued debt overhang in the economy that makes long-term growth and debt repayment a tricky balance at best.

Debt overhang and future economic growth

For many countries in both Latin America and Sub-Saharan Africa, poor economic policy decision-making in the past led to further bad decisions in the 1970s to accumulate large external debts to finance unsustainable current account deficits. All too

---

FOCUS 16.5 THE FIRST DEBT-FOR-NATURE SWAP

The first debt-for-nature swap took place in 1987 and involved Bolivia and a non-governmental organization called Conservation International. Conservation International purchased $650,000 of Bolivia's external debt on the secondary market for $100,000, a discount of 85 percent. This was swapped for the equivalent of $250,000 of Bolivia's currency to be used in setting up and operating the Beri Biosphere Reserve to protect forest land from logging and other destructive practices. Bolivia reduced its external debt obligation by $650,000 in hard currency terms, but without using foreign exchange to do so. Instead, via the swap, this debt was retired using domestic currency.

Other countries also have done such swaps. Brazil had $100 million of debt-for-nature swaps in 1991. Mexico and Costa Rica also have been parties to such transactions. These swaps are no panacea for either developing country debt reduction or for protecting the environment, as the totals are small relative to the total debt of any country. On the other hand, such swaps are innovative means to try to combine efforts to increase the level of development and to protect threatened natural resources simultaneously.

Source: Elliott 1994: 55–56

often, such external debt was not used to promote the adjustment of the economy to a more productive economic structure but was used to maintain the status quo and inequitable structures and policies, often carried out by non-democratic governments that over-spent during their tenure in power. In some of the highly indebted countries, particularly in Latin America, new governments emerged in the mid- to late-1980s with reformist and more democratic agendas. These are governments, often at the urging and with the assistance of the IMF and the World Bank, interested in altering the economic structures of their economies, in making them more efficient, more technological, and more independent by fostering structural transformation. However, the **debt overhang** of accumulated external debt and its repayment facing many countries has hampered this effort at transformation, making economic growth substantially more difficult and costly for the population and more protracted than it need be.

The debt overhang, that is, the need to continue to service debt accumulated in the past for some indefinite time into the future, can adversely affect investment decisions of potential investors. They may fear higher taxes or periodic domestic economic recessions will be necessary to find the funds required to repay these external obligations. This thus may discourage productive investment from taking place (on debt overhang, see Chowdhury (1994); Cohen (1995)). Table 16.3 provides some indirect evidence of the impact of past debt accumulation on investment and the possible effect on future growth prospects.

Particularly for heavily indebted Latin American countries like Argentina and Brazil and for African economies, the decrease in gross investment in 1985 from the values reached in 1980 is indicative of the costs to future production arising from the debt crisis. Brazil, for example, continued with investment rates below the level that had been reached in 1970; the same is true for Argentina, which continues to suffer very low rates of capital formation. South Korea and Malaysia have managed to keep their investment rates high and even rising (though the effect of the Asian financial crisis was still being felt in 2000), fueling higher economic growth. As seen in Table 16.2, the burden of debt in those countries is not so severe, and they have

Table 16.3 Gross capital formation (as percentage of GDP)

	1965	1970	1980	1985	1990	1993	2000
Argentina	19	24	25	18	14	19	16
Brazil	25	21	23	19	20	21	21
Chile	15	19	21	17	25	27	23
Congo	22	24	36	30	16	29	24
Côte d'Ivoire	22	22	27	13	7	8	12
Ghana	18	14	6	10	14	22	24
India	18	17	21	24	25	21	24
Kenya	14	24	25	22	20	18	13
Malaysia	20	20	27	25	32	38	26
Mexico	22	23	27	21	23	21	23
Pakistan	21	16	18	18	19	21	16
South Korea	15	25	32	30	38	36	29
Sudan	10	13	15	9	7	–	14
Tanzania	15	23	22	–	17	23	13

Sources: World Bank 1982; 118–119, Table 5; World Development Indicators 2002.

been able to avoid recurring economic crises or recover relatively quickly when they have struck.

What is apparent from the data for some of the African countries is the instability of investment rates in many countries. In some years, investment rates have been respectable, but they seem not to be sustainable. The recovery in investment rates in the Congo is probably due at least partly to the fact that, as for Mexico, the Congo is an oil exporter. For the severely indebted economies, particularly those which remain primary product exporters, like Argentina and Côte d'Ivoire, debt overhang continues to make any desire by government and the private sector to initiate the desirable structural transformation toward a more sustainable, productive and efficient economy more difficult to attain as valuable foreign exchange is drained to pay external debt obligations.

In one comprehensive study the effect of debt overhang on economic growth was estimated to become negative when the debt to export ratio reached 160–170 percent of exports and 35–40 percent of GDP (Pattillo *et al.* 2002). From Table 16.2, that would include most of the countries listed there, with the exception of India, Malaysia, and South Korea. For the others, the total of debt would be expected to put downward pressure on economic growth as is reflected in the lower investment rates in Table 16.3.

The social effects of servicing debt can be devastating. A 1996 Oxfam report found that "For less than is currently being spent on debt, it would be possible by the year 2000 to make social investments which would save the lives of around 21 million African children, and provide 90 million girls with access to primary education." The amount spent by governments in Sub-Saharan Africa to service debt amounts to *four times* what is spent on health care and *exceeds* the total amount spent on primary education and primary health care combined. It is the poorest debtors, particularly those in Africa, such as Mozambique and Zambia, which find that their debt payments, even when external debt is not fully serviced, greatly exceed spending on social infrastructure.[18]

Some way must be found to relieve the pressure of debt overhang, perhaps through new forms of lending that convert old debt into perpetual bonds never requiring repayment of the principal. This will at least open the possibility that such economies, if they follow desirable structural transformation policies in future will not be bound by poor policy decisions from the past. This step is all the more urgent, because many of these loans were undertaken by non-democratic governments from which few in the population benefitted.

Questions for review

1   Table 16.1 shows the total debt accumulated by a number of debtor nations. However, in comparing total debt among nations, such a gross comparison may be a bit deceptive. Countries with larger populations will be more likely to be able to repay a given sum of debt than a country with a smaller population. Calculate in the following table per capita external debt using population figures from a recent edition of the *World Development Report* or some similar source. Then rank the countries by debt per person, using 1 for the country with the highest debt per person and 15 for the country with the lowest debt per capita. How do the rankings for total debt differ from the rankings for debt per capita?

	2000	*Ranking*
Argentina		
Brazil		
Chile		
Congo		
Côte d'Ivoire		
Ghana		
India		
Kenya		
Malaysia		
Mexico		
Pakistan		
South Korea		
Sudan		
Tanzania		
Zimbabwe		

2   We learned in the section on "When to borrow externally" that, in estimating the expected gains from incurring external debt, it is best to err on the side of caution given the inherent uncertainly about future prices coupled with the certainty of debt repayment. In evaluating expected future (net) foreign exchange earnings from export expansion, it was suggested that the future prices of exports should be assumed to be lower than current prices and the future prices of imports to be higher than current prices. This procedure tends to make any export expansion project to be financed by external borrowing less desirable than if the calculation were made at current prices.

Now consider what future prices should be used if the purpose of external borrowing is to finance a potential import substitution project rather than an export expansion project. Should the future import prices used be higher or lower than current prices? Should the future export prices of the current array of exports be estimated as higher or lower than current prices? Explain what difference such a calculation will have on the desirability of accumulating additional external debt.

3   Country X has a current external debt of $22,000 million, on which an average rate of interest of 6.2 percent is charged. Country X's exports are currently equal to $31,000 million and are growing at a rate of 5.5 percent per year. Calculate Country X's current debt/export ratio and, assuming no new external debt accumulation, the debt/export ratio in one, three and five years' time.

4   What effect does a deterioration in a country's terms of trade have on its ability to service its external debt obligations? What effect does a devaluation or depreciation of a country's currency have on its ability to service its external debt obligations denominated in foreign currencies? If you can, use some simple numerical calculations to show these effects. (For example, when the value of the Mexican peso fell from roughly 3 pesos: $1 to 6 pesos: $1 in early 1995, did this depreciation make repayment of Mexico's debt easier or more difficult? Were more or fewer exports, in physical terms, required for a fixed amount of debt service?)

5   Explain what a debt service ratio of 47 percent means? If a country exports $5.3 billion and imports $5.3 billion of goods and services, where does the foreign

exchange come from to repay external debt service? Can a country have its exports and imports equal (that is, no trade deficit or surplus) and still service its external debt? How (Hint: think back to the balance of payments accounts)?

6 What sorts of changes in economic policy would you recommend to the most indebted countries? What are they doing wrong or did they do wrong in the past? What adjustment policies would you recommend? What pre-conditions might be required for such adjustment policies to be effective? If you have information about a particular country that could make your discussion more specific, please include that. (Hint: think of the discussions in Chapters 8 to 15, plus any political, social or other pre-conditions you might think necessary.)

7 Explain petro-dollar recycling.

8 Under what conditions might it make sense for a country to increase its external debt, i.e., what are **acceptable** reasons for incurring external debt? Explain.

Notes

1 This is a political pre-condition that we have, admittedly, not specifically addressed, not because we think it unimportant, but because it would take us too far a field from our current inquiry. Unfortunately, it would appear that in many circumstances, governing elites are not truly concerned with improving the economic and social conditions for a broad range of the population, but rather would seem to be more interested in consolidating specific gains for a narrow segment of a ruling elite. Under such conditions, the economic know-how about development will be less important than will be political changes which can strengthen democracy and participation in the decision-making process of the country.

In some instances, such political change will need to be quite revolutionary, certainly in the sense of displacing former centers of political and economic power, if not also literally in the sense of overthrowing corrupt and non-democratic regimes. Such fundamental political changes preceded the rapid progress observed in South Korea and Taiwan after the 1950s. In other countries with entrenched ruling classes wielding economic and political power, the nullification of powerful interests may be as important for the future as are low inflation rates and human capital accumulation.

2 **External debt** is borrowing denominated in a foreign, typically a **hard** or stable international, currency. US dollars were the key currency for external debt. Anywhere from 65 percent to more than 75 percent of external public debt was denominated in dollars over the period from 1974 to 1983 (World Bank 1985: 22). External debt is incurred when governments or businesses borrow from foreign governments, from foreign private banks, from foreign businesses, from individuals in other countries, or from a multilateral lending agency, such as the World Bank or the IMF. External debt can be repaid only by earning foreign exchange, that is, by exporting goods and services.

By contrast, **internal debt** arising, for example, from the central government's need to borrow to cover a budget deficit, is most often denominated in the country's own currency. While the possibility, and the danger, of simply printing money to repay an internal debt exists, thus making repayment assured, such a possibility is not available for servicing external debt payments. External debt repayment requires that foreign exchange be earned; printing money to repay external debt is not an option.

3 Sovereign borrowers were thought to be better risks than other borrowers. The thinking by the private banking community was that, as independent and sovereign countries, the oil-importing borrowers would always be able to repay, on the assumption that countries "do not go bankrupt." Of course sovereign borrowers were different from other borrowers in another significant sense, too. They did not provide any collateral to the private banks when they borrowed.

As we shall see, the banks made a logical error. While it may be true that sovereign nations do not go bankrupt in the usual sense of the term, they certainly can decide to not make payments on their external loans on time (a **moratorium**) or at all (a **default**). The international banking system's thinking also demonstrates its lack of "memory." Very similar banking crises had erupted in the 1890s and in the 1930s with almost the same cast of bad debtors, particularly the larger Latin American countries (see Stallings 1988). It might be worthwhile to remember Keynes' dictum in this regard: if you owe the bank $100,000, you have a problem. If you owe the bank $100 million, the bank has a problem. The truth of this the private banking system discovered when debtor nations stopped paying on their obligations.

4 Just prior to the outbreak of the debt crisis, in 1982, South Korea was the third-largest debtor nation, at least in terms of total external debt, after Brazil and Mexico.

5 In 1974, 18.4 percent of all public external debt was in floating interest rate loans; by 1982, 51.2 percent of public external debt had been contracted at variable rates of interest (World Bank 1985: 21, Table 2.4).

6 We are here concerned with the *practical* arguments for incurring external debt, as opposed to the *theoretical* rationales often found in the economics literature, particularly those concerned with the free flow of capital between nations. (We are also concerned with the issue of capital inflows resulting from borrowing, as distinct from capital inflows that result from foreign aid or from multinational direct foreign investments there are discussed in Chapters 14 and 17.)

For example, it is often argued that when financial and physical capital flow to less-developed nations from more developed nations, these contribute to an increase in the level of world efficiency, as capital moves from regions with lower rates of return, that is, more developed economies with relatively large stocks of capital, to regions with higher rates of return, that is, the less-developed nations with smaller stocks of capital. In this way, as we saw in earlier chapters, external sources of savings can add to internal savings, thus permitting lower-income countries to grow more rapidly. These efficiency and mobilization-of-savings arguments are often put forward as compelling reasons for countries to rapidly open the capital and financial account of their balance of payments, that is, to allow the free flow of financial capital with the international economy without government interference with such flows. However, as Stiglitz (1993) has argued, the flow of financial capital is not at all like the flow of goods, and any market imperfections can result in too much or too little movement of capital. In fact, Stiglitz makes the case that when financial markets are imperfect, government oversight of capital flows can actually increase economic efficiency. Recognizing, then, the complexities of external capital flows, we are considering the rationale for such borrowing, assuming an imperfect world with imperfect information.

7 Alternatively, it might well be argued that one of the reasons countries hold foreign exchange reserves is to have the ability to undertake precisely such import consumption smoothing.

Borrowing for consumption smoothing is a situation when a short-term need to borrow due to the excess of imports over exports that results in a current account deficit is roughly matched on the other side of the business cycle by an excess of exports over imports and a surplus on the current account that permits repayment of previously accumulated external debt obligations.

8 And there were many, including many economists, who did believe that the OPEC price increases would be transitory. This is because, as a cartel which artificially set a monopoly price for its product by getting each member to agree to limit the quantity sold on the international market, economists believed there would be a tendency for OPEC members, especially smaller producers, to cheat on the output-restricting agreement. It was thought that some members would attempt to sell slightly more than their individual quota at the higher price, an action that would increase their export revenues even further but with a negligible effect in the overall market. If the incentive to cheat is strong enough, however, all members would be expected to do so eventually, and then the effort to hold the price high by restricting output would collapse. It was this sort of reasoning which led many to prophesy that the OPEC price increase could only be temporary. This way of abstract thinking, while unimpeachable in its logic, did not, however, count on the political resolve of the OPEC members to stick to the agreement. And for well over a

decade and a half, this political purpose of OPEC, particularly for the Middle Eastern producers, outweighed any economic advantage members might have felt pulling them apart.

9 There is another significant factor to be considered in evaluating the desirability of incurring external debt: the rate of interest charged on such debt. As we shall see below, one of the measures of the burden of external debt is the ratio of total external debt to exports (D/X). If the average interest rate charged on the total debt, D, exceeds the rate of growth of export earnings, X, then D/X will increase over time, assuming a constant total debt. Contrariwise, if the interest rate is lower than the rate of export income expansion, then D/X will fall over time, reducing the burden of the external debt.

10 The political economy of the problem of external debt accumulation is even more complex than considered here. At least a part of the reason for the twin deficit discussed in the next section and for a persistent current account imbalance in many less-developed nations, and certainly many Latin American economies, is related to income inequality. A narrow but wealthy stratum of the population has a high propensity to import. The demand of this elite for imported consumer goods and, indirectly, for imported inputs of domestic capital-intensive industries, adds to the import bill and reduces the share of any export earnings that might be dedicated to other uses.

One possibility for dealing with recurrent current account deficits might, then, involve a tax on high-income families, which will reduce import demand and the external borrowing requirement. Such tax revenues could provide a source of funds for financing the structural transformation and the expansion of export substitution production, further reducing external borrowing requirements.

11 S is total savings, Y is total national income (say, GNP), L is total population, Y/L is per capita income, and s, which is the proportion of income saved, has a value of $0 < s < 1$.

12 The full twin deficit equation, $(S - I) + (T - G) = X - M$, demonstrates another possible cause of the need to borrow externally. If the central government runs a budget deficit such that $T - G < 0$, then, assuming $S - I = 0$ or $S - I < 0$, an external borrowing requirement is also created by the fiscal deficit. This reinforces the need for prudent government finance and oversight of internal macroeconomic policy. Internal debt can lead to external debt accumulation. On the other hand, government may find it wise to borrow externally when loanable funds are short at home, but only if such borrowing meets the same requirements of expanding tradables in the future. However, such state spending may be directed to a broader range of investments which can have such an effect: education, research and development, international marketing research, and so on.

13 Basically, by reducing growth in the money supply, interest rates were pushed upward dramatically, thus discouraging borrowing and investment. This induced a slow-down in economic activity which resulted in a slower pace of inflation as aggregate demand fell.

14 This is because, as we saw in Chapter 15, imports (M) are a function of the level of income (Y): $M = f(Y) = mY$, where $0 < m < 1$.

15 In 1981, all of the countries listed in Tables 16.1 and 16.2 had substantially larger current account deficits than had prevailed in 1970 prior to the OPEC price increase. For example, Mexico's current account deficit had risen from $1,068 million in 1970 to $12,933 million in 1981; Chile's from $91 million to $4,814 million; Kenya's from $49 million to $736 million (World Bank 1983: 74–75, Table 14). Part of the increased current account deficit was due to higher oil costs; part, however, was the consequence of the larger external debt service obligation itself that created an outflow of foreign exchange in the current account. External debt incurred to finance a current account deficit itself also added to future current account deficit financing needs due to the outflow of interest and principal repayment required for debt servicing. In many countries, particularly in Latin America, with weak or non-existent restrictions on movements of financial assets, capital flight seriously exacerbated the need for external borrowing beyond that reflected in the current account imbalance alone.

16 This was particularly true for the Latin American debtor nations and in East Asia. For most African economies and South Asian borrowers, the bulk of their external debt had been provided by multilateral agencies such as the World Bank or the IMF or by other governments at concessional rates of interest and with easier repayment schedules.

In 1980, 74.4 percent of South Asia's external debt was concessional; 27.0 percent of Sub-Saharan Africa's was concessional, but only 4.4 percent of external debt in Latin America was concessional (World Bank 1995b: 206–207, Table 23). The world recession adversely affected the African and South Asian countries' ability to repay as well. However, the effect of any default on multinational lending agencies or on other governments that had extended concessional loans was quite different from a default impacting on *private* banking institutions' balance sheets and accounting rules. The debt crisis was a real crisis situation since it threatened the financial stability of major private banks and their economies (see Felix (1987) for a historical perspective on earlier debt crises affecting Latin America).

17 For a readable and informative overview of views on external debt reduction, see "Symposia" (1990).

18 For example, between 1990 and 1993, Mozambique was only able to meet about 10 percent of its scheduled debt repayments, equal to about $70 million per year. Yet this amount alone would have been sufficient to pay for ten times the number of textbooks required for all the country's primary schools.

References

Amsden, Alice H. 2001. *The Rise of "The Rest": Challenges to the West from Late-Industrializing Economies*. Oxford: Oxford University Press.

Chowdhury, Khorshed. 1994. "A Structural Analysis of External Debt and Economic Growth: Some Evidence from Selected Countries in Asia and the Pacific," *Applied Economics* 26 (December): 1121–1131.

Cohen, Daniel. 1995. "Large External Debt and (Slow) Domestic Growth: A Theoretical Analysis," *Journal of Economic Dynamics and Control* 19 (July): 1141–1163.

Devlin, Robert. 1989. *Debt and Crisis in Latin America: The Supply Side of the Story*. Princeton, NJ: Princeton University Press.

Elliott, Jennifer A. 1994. *An Introduction to Sustainable Development*. London: Routledge.

Felix, David. 1987. "Alternative Outcomes of the Latin American Debt Crisis: Lessons from the Past," *Latin American Research Review* 22 (2): 3–46.

Ffrench-Davis, Ricardo and Stephany Griffith-Jones (eds). 1995. *Coping with Capital Surges: The Return of Finance to Latin America*. Boulder, CO and London: Lynne Rienner Publishers.

Pastor, Robert A. (ed.) 1987. *Latin America's Debt Crisis: Adjusting to the Past or Planning for the Future*. Boulder, CO and London: Lynne Rienner Publishers.

Pattillo, Catherine, Hélène Poirson, and Luca Ricci. 2002. "External Debt and Growth," *Finance and Development* 39 (June): 35–38. http://www.imf.org/external/pubs/ft/fandd/2002/06/padillo.htm.

Stallings, Barbara. 1988. *Banker to the Third World: U.S. Portfolio Investment in Latin America, 1900–1986*. Berkeley, CA: University of California Press.

Stiglitz, Joseph. 1993. "The Role of the State in Financial Markets," *Proceedings of the World Bank Annual Conference on Development Economics*, vol. 2. Washington, DC: World Bank.

"Symposia: New Institutions for Developing Country Debt." 1990. *The Journal of Economic Perspectives* 4 (Winter): 3–56.

UNCTAD (United Nations Conference on Trade and Development). 1995. *Trade and Development Report 1995*. Paris: UNCTAD.

Vernon, Raymond (ed.). 1987. *The Oil Crisis*. New York: W.W. Norton & Co.

Wee, Herman Van der. 1976. *Prosperity and Upheaval: The World Economy, 1945–1980*. Berkeley, CA: University of California Press.

World Bank. 1982. *World Development Report 1982*. Oxford: Oxford University Press.

—— 1983. *World Development Report 1983*. Oxford: Oxford University Press.

—— 1985. *World Development Report 1985*. Oxford: Oxford University Press.

—— 1987. *World Development Report 1987*. Oxford: Oxford University Press.

—— 1995a. *Annual Report 1995*. Washington, DC: World Bank.

—— 1995b. *World Development Report 1995*. Oxford: Oxford University Press.

—— 1997. *World Development Report 1997*. Oxford: Oxford University Press.

—— 2001. *World Development Indicators 2001*. Washington, DC: World Bank.

—— 2002. *World Development Indicators 2002*. Washington, DC: World Bank.

Zanoyan, Vaban. 1995. "After the Oil Boom," *Foreign Affairs* 74 (November/December): 2–7.

17 International institutional linkages

The International Monetary Fund, the World Bank, and foreign aid

After studying this chapter you should understand:

- the functions and evolution of the International Monetary Fund and the World Bank and their lending programs;
- what an IMF stand-by loan is and its purpose;
- the theory supporting, and the purpose of, IMF austerity and adjustment programs;
- the effectiveness of IMF austerity and adjustment programs;
- the difference between World Bank project loans and structural adjustment loans (SALs);
- the focus and limitations of foreign aid; and
- the nature of donor bias in aid giving.

Introduction

As we have seen in the previous chapters, developing nations have to make a wide range of choices regarding their development strategies. For sustainable development, we have seen that, in the final analysis, countries must draw primarily upon their own resources and capabilities. However, since virtually all less-developed nations are members of the IMF and the World Bank (IBRD, the International Bank for Reconstruction and Development), and since almost all of the poorest and some of the not-so-poor nations draw significant supplements to their savings and production capabilities from foreign aid, it is necessary for every student of economic development to acquire a basic understanding of the role of these institutions in the development process.[1]

When sovereign nations turn to the multilateral institutions such as the IMF and the World Bank, or when they accept foreign aid, they then are able to extend their production capabilities by supplementing domestic savings and investment with foreign resources. But while such access creates an opportunity, it also presents a challenge to the developing nations, since the international institutions never lend or grant funds without also attempting to influence the course of events and the economic dynamics of the less-developed nations. When international institutional linkages improve on the overall developmental potential of the recipient nation, there is little reason for concern. Unfortunately, in the opinion of virtually all observers of aid, including the lending institutions themselves, this fortuitous outcome has too rarely been achieved. Consequently, the role and effects of international institutional linkages have long been a subject of much debate and sometimes confusion.

It is often difficult to penetrate to the core of this debate, because the recipient nation may find it convenient to exaggerate the impact of the international institutions on their development trajectory in order to avert criticism of its own policies. Meanwhile, the lending and donor agencies have operated with varying degrees of secrecy, making it extremely difficult for development economists to evaluate objectively the impact of these international institutional linkages. Of all the various international institutions involved in development issues, the IMF is by far the most opaque in its operations. We will turn to this entity first, then to the World Bank, and finally to bilateral foreign aid. Little specific attention will be paid to the regional development banks, the main ones being the InterAmerican Development Bank (IDB), the Asian Development Bank (ADB), and the African Development Bank (AfDB). These regional banks are important, and they function much as does the World Bank, but with a mandate limiting their activity to a geographic region.

The IMF

Both the IMF (or "the Fund") and the World Bank were conceived at the Bretton Woods conference held at the Mount Washington Hotel in Bretton Woods, New Hampshire in 1944. This conference brought together representatives of forty-four nations in an attempt to think through and plan out a new international financial and trade system. The new system needed to be both stable enough to maintain confidence and able to avoid the international economic chaos of the 1920s and 1930s, and yet be flexible enough to accommodate changing circumstances. It is somewhat ironic that John Maynard Keynes dominated the conference, because in most respects the two main prodigies of the conference, the IMF and the World Bank, have never demonstrated a strong affinity for Keynesian-type approaches to economic issues. Most of the proceedings of the Bretton Woods conference were devoted to the creation of the IMF, with the World Bank idea left semi-defined and much in the background.[2]

The IMF officially came into existence in late 1945, whereupon thirty-nine countries pledged quotas totaling $7.4 billion. According to the Articles of Agreement of the Fund, voting power was directly related to a nation's quota, expressed as a percentage of the total subscribed quotas, with each country's individual quota being determined jointly by its level of economic income and population size. (The World Bank also shares this structural characteristic.) Powerful and economically advanced nations, particularly the United States and Britain, pledged the largest amounts to the Fund, and consequently received a proportionately larger vote, usually enough to veto any actions that might be proposed by the Fund which the United States and Britain strongly opposed. The majority of the nations joining the Fund were poor and developing, and they lacked the level of economic development and the hard currency reserves or gold necessary to create a strong position in the IMF's voting structure.

Fund membership has grown steadily, reaching 184 members in July 2002 (see Figure 17.1). The IMF's capital stock grew to $270 billion as Horst Köhler, the IMF's recently appointed managing director, swept away an entrenched management team that long-time director Michel Camdessus (1987–2000) had built.

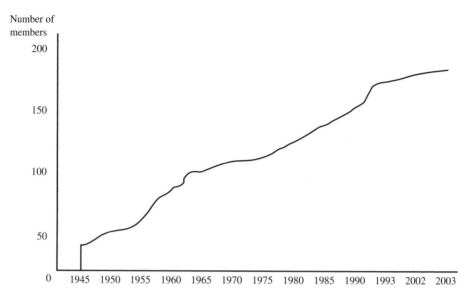

Figure 17.1 Growth in membership of the IMF.

Spearheading the new team was Ann Krueger who became the First Deputy Managing Director of the Fund in September 2001.

In 2003, the United States continued to be the Fund's largest participant, holding 17.1 percent of the voting power. Yet, US influence in the Fund has steadily diminished, as other nations vie for world economic dominance. In 1982, for example, the United States held 19.6 percent of the voting power. As the United States' influence within the Fund has declined over the years, so Japan's share has steadily advanced. Nonetheless, the United States' role is extremely important, since major changes in Fund policy can only occur when there is 85 percent of the voting power in favor of such changes. Thus, though relative US dominance in the Fund has been reduced, the United States retains ultimate veto power over any major decision it might wish to block.

History of the IMF

From 1946 to 1955 the Fund lent virtually nothing to its members, restricting its actions largely to technical assistance to European member nations which were in the process of achieving full convertibility of their currencies (see Figure 17.2). During this period, the Fund was attempting to reach agreement in interpreting its charter and mandate, much of which was not fully defined until 1952. Of note at this juncture was the creation of the Stand-by Arrangement, which articulates the policies and procedures to be utilized when a nation seeks access to the Fund's resources in excess of 25 percent of its quota (or first credit tranche). Borrowing below the 25 percent limit is freely allowed without approval or condition, since this amount represents the hard currency reserves and gold each country pays in to the IMF.

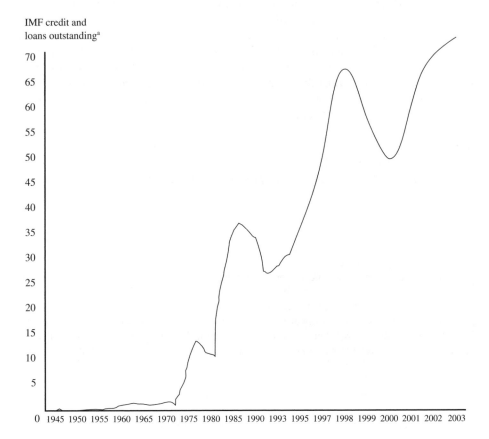

IMF credit and
loans outstanding[a]

Figure 17.2 IMF lending.

Note
a In billions of dollars.

A nation goes to the IMF to borrow to cover a current account deficit or because of exchange rate problems requiring foreign exchange reserves. Typically, resort to IMF financing reflects an inability on the part of a country to access more normal channels of international financing. In other words, going to the IMF is tacit recognition of currently unsustainable economic policies, due either to internal policy failures or to external changes in the international economy that adversely affect an economy. In theory, the Fund's loans are short term and were conceived as "bridges" for resolving short-term balance of payments and exchange rate difficulties.

Stand-by arrangements

A "stand-by arrangement" is a two-part process, whereby a member nation can draw from its quota over a period of twelve to eighteen months.[3] The first part of the stand-by arrangement consists of a process whereby a *letter of intent* is signed by both the borrowing nation and the representatives of the Fund. In order to prepare for such an agreement, a nation desiring Fund resources must first accept the visit of an IMF delegation, which makes its own assessment of the conditions of the borrowing nation and the macroeconomic difficulties which have led to the need for a request for international assistance. At this stage of negotiation, both the potential borrower and the Fund will engage in extensive bargaining, with each side seeking to guide and control the borrowing process. The Fund will demand "conditions" for its willingness to make a loan thus the term, **conditionality** for such requirements while the borrowing nation will attempt to ensure that conditionality is as mild as possible (see Box 17.1). How draconian the stand-by loan conditions are depends on many factors, of which the negotiating skill of the borrowing nation is of particular importance.[4]

Once a letter of intent has been signed, "drawing" of the quota can begin. In this second stage, the Fund reviews the progress the borrowing nation has made on meeting

---

Box 17.1 What is conditionality?

For a country to make use of IMF financial resources, it first must meet, or at least agree to, certain macroeconomic policy conditions. These **conditionality** requirements range from rather general commitments to cooperate with the IMF in setting policies to formulating a specific, quantified plan for financial and fiscal policies.

Conditionality seeks to ensure that members using IMF resources will adopt the policy measures the IMF believes are needed to improve the balance of payments positions and to resolve their exchange rate difficulties. It is also important that the country be able to repay the IMF in a timely manner.

For "high-conditionality" arrangements, that is for upper credit tranche* stand-by and extended arrangements, four conditions are generally included:

- a letter of intent, which outlines the government's policy intentions during the program period;
- policy changes, known as "prior actions," that must be taken before approval of the arrangement;
- performance criteria, which are quantitative targets for certain policies, such as limits on the budget deficit or on the money supply, that must be met on a quarterly or semi-annual basis for drawings to be made and which serve as a monitoring device; and
- periodic reviews during the life of the lending arrangement, another device through which the Executive Board of the IMF assesses the consistency of policies with the objectives of the adjustment program.

Befitting the unsettled nature of Fund policies in recent years, the IMF has decided that its policies on conditionality have often *contributed* to further economic turmoil. The Fund in 2002 openly discussed the "growing intrusiveness of conditionality" stressing that recipient countries should "own" any restructuring program. The new conditionality guidelines mandate that the Fund will work in "more of a cooperative venture" with borrowing nations, reduce the number of conditions and work more closely with the World Bank on structural changes imposed as conditions for loans.

*A "tranche" is a credit "slice" equal to 25 percent of a nation's quota, with upper tranches being defined as borrowing above 25 percent of the quota.

Sources: IMF 1995d: 234; IMF 2002: 390

the agreement's conditions every six months, with subsequent drawings dependent upon meeting the conditions imposed. Failure to meet the conditions may, and sometimes does, result in suspension of a stand-by arrangement. A "drawing" from the Fund consists of a transaction whereby the Fund sells "hard" currency, like the United States dollar or the euro, to the borrowing country in exchange for its own currency, which is deposited at the Fund in the country's account. To repay the loan, the borrowing country must "buy back" its own currency by using hard currencies to repurchase what it deposited, thus replenishing the Fund's supply of hard currencies.[5] Under a stand-by arrangement, the more a nation borrows, the greater the scope of the conditionality and the greater the restrictiveness.

In the early years of the Fund, borrowing was never extensive. In the period 1947–1967, half of the borrowing actually was done by the advanced nations. It was not until the late 1960s, and particularly the early 1970s as a result of the first oil shock, that the Fund became oriented toward lending to the developing nations. To be sure, the Fund continues to wrestle with issues of currency stability and financial balance on a global scale – its original mission – but increasingly the Fund has become an institution specializing in the problems of the developing nations. In mid-1995, the IMF had active stand-by arrangements (or similar loans, to be discussed below) with sixty-two nations (see Figure 17.2). During the period 1979–1993, the Fund financed 353 separate programs, suggesting that relatively few less-developed nations were exempt from the Fund's direct influence in recent years (Killick 1995: 60). The Fund appeared invigorated by its vastly expanded role, envisioning much larger programs for the twenty-first century. These anticipations, however, were steadily undermined by a wave of crises in the late 1990s. The Asian Crisis (1997) and the Russian Crisis (1998) pushed lending to new heights – by 2002 lending amounted to nearly twice the peak level achieved in 1985–1986 (Figure 17.2). The Fund turned defensive as critiques of its policies and program abounded – from the far right of the political spectrum through the middle ranks and on to the left. The Fund's new role, providing mega bail-outs with surprising frequency, raised the visibility of an institution that had long been comfortable with a very low public profile. In November 1998, for example, the Fund pledged a $41.5 billion loan to Brazil for release in 1998 and 1999. Then, in August 2002, the Fund approved another loan to Brazil in the amount of $30 billion. An unprecedented 1995 mega-loan to Mexico (discussed below) had unleashed a firestorm of criticism and commentary. The August 2002 loan to Brazil caused little notice and even less dissent (outside Brazil). In this new environment the Fund grappled with the stresses of a new era burdened with the sudden and unanticipated economic breakdowns that befell some of the largest and most important developing nations. The confidence of the early 1990s had been replaced by a guarded wariness as the Fund sought to revise many strategies and programs.

Other lending facilities of the IMF

In 1963, the Fund created a new lending source, the Compensatory Financing Facility, which would supplement resources borrowed under stand-by arrangements. This new Facility signaled both a change in the direction of the Fund's concerns toward the developing nations and the fact that the Fund would continue to reinterpret and amend its original mandate under its Articles of Agreement. The new

Facility became one of eight to be created in the period 1963–1993, with three new lending facilities created during the turbulent years 1974–1975, designed to increase the amounts that could be lent to borrowing nations above the original quota amount.

The **Compensatory Financing Facility** allows member nations to borrow for the specific purpose of coping with external shocks to export earnings and/or food imports. In effect, the Fund acknowledged that a broad range of developing nations, which remained primary commodity exporters to the international market, often faced sudden and uncontrollable movements in export earnings due to the intrinsic instability of global markets for primary commodities and their terms of trade, particularly agricultural goods.[6] Such concerns also were echoed by the creation of the **Buffer Stock Facility** in 1969, which was designed to help stabilize the prices of raw materials from the cyclical volatility so characteristic of many primary products.

Further, as a result of the spike in oil prices in the early 1970s, many poor nations which were totally bereft of petroleum resources were particularly impacted, with fuel import costs soaring, as we saw in Chapter 16. The Fund reacted quickly by creating two other lending sources to facilitate borrowing due to petroleum price changes: the **Oil Facility** and the **Extended Fund Facility**. The Extended Fund Facility allowed countries that had used all of their regular quota drawing rights to continue to receive supplementary funding from the Fund.

These five new Facilities were all addressed to the particular problems of the less-developed nations and, taken together, demonstrated the new orientation of the Fund as an entity which was primarily involved with the problems of the poorer countries. Through the 1980s and into the 1990s, the Fund continued on this trajectory. It has created three new **Structural Adjustment Facilities**, which lend over a multi-year period in order to change the productive and institutional structures of the poor nations. (Structural adjustment lending actually was originated by, and continues at, the World Bank, as is discussed later in the chapter.) In early 1995, the Fund once again demonstrated its ability to innovate and evolve when it signed an unprecedented $17.8 billion stand-by arrangement with Mexico, following the massive devaluation of the peso at the end of 1994. This huge loan was 50 percent larger than all other current stand-by loans combined, and ten times greater than Mexico's quota! The Fund justified this loan as necessary to stabilize the fragile emerging financial markets of the less-developed nations, not only in Latin America, but in Asia as well, which reacted quickly and adversely to the Mexican peso crisis. In doing so, the IMF widened its scope of authority and influence, once again.

Yet, the deepening difficulties the Fund faced from 1997 onward forced further adaptations – thus in 1997 a **Supplemental Reserve Facility** was created to deal with 'financial contagion' problems. Loans of this nature – beginning with a $13.1 billion loan to Korea in 1997 and a $5.3 billion loan to Russia in 1998, are included in Stand-By Arrangements. *Anticipatory lending*, a new and novel concept, was created through the **Contingent Credit Lines program** in 1999. Breaking new ground, the IMF is now willing, in principle, to provide loans to nations without *any* balance of payments or foreign reserves problems if either the nation or the Fund felt they could *anticipate* a forthcoming crisis. This is an important threshold step for the Fund, which will allow member nations to borrow up to 500 percent of their quota to deal with a 'contagion' threat. Also in 1999 the **Enhanced Structural**

Adjustment Facility was rechristened as the **Poverty Reduction and Growth Facility** (PRGF). Access to this fund is restricted to "low income" members with loans lasting up to 10 years. In 2003 thirty-eight nations, many African, had PRGF approved credits that totaled $6 billion (IMF 2003a: 14; IMF 2001: 12–13).

While stand-by arrangements continue to be the primary focus of Fund lending, it is important to recognize that increasingly the IMF has become concerned with lending for periods well beyond the 12- to 18-month focus of the typical stand-by arrangement. Indeed, in the 1991–1995 period, stand-by arrangements accounted for only 45 percent of Fund loans, while longer-term loans of up to approximately five years accounted for the remainder of all approved loans, demonstrating the importance of the expanded lending facilities. Table 17.1 records the IMF's lending activities in recent years.

Fund surveillance

While the Fund is most active with a nation when it seeks, accepts and draws a loan, the Fund exercises its influence in other ways, notably through what is termed *country surveillance*. Each year, every member country must undergo an annual surveillance consultation which, according to a 1977 amendment to the Articles of Agreement of the Fund, is to include "a comprehensive analysis of the general economic situation and economic policy strategy of the member" (IMF 1995c: 154). Surveillance is a process which can allow the Fund to exert leverage over economic policy-making, even when a nation is not seeking a loan from the Fund. Of course, a country may largely sidestep the recommendations of the Fund at this stage, but this may lead to more difficult negotiations, and more stringent limits, on any loans which are sought from the Fund at a later date.

Objectives of the IMF

When the Fund lends to a less-developed nation, what does it hope to achieve? In the view of the IMF, borrowing nations are largely responsible for their own economic duress. Consequently, the Fund loans and intervenes so as to impose conditions which it believes will lead to greater economic stability. Thus, except for the periods of the oil spikes of the early and late 1970s, the Fund's basic position is and

Table 17.1 New IMF loans, calendar year (billions of SDRs)[a]

	1985	1990	1995	2000	2002
Total new loans	4.0	4.8	18.3	7.7	26.6
Stand-by (+ other General Resources Account)	4.0	4.27	17.0	7.18	25.24
Structure adjustment facilities (+ PRGF funds)	0.0	0.53	1.3	0.52	1.36

Source: International Monetary Fund "Past Disbursements and Payments."

Note
http://www.imf.org/external/np/tre/tad/extrep1.cfm.
a One SDR = $1.37 USD in March 2003; $1.28 in August 2001; $1.32 in January 1997.

has been that it is fundamentally *endogenous*, rather than *exogenous*, factors which explain the need for Fund intervention.

From the perspective of the IMF, nations are forced to make appeals to the Fund because they have mismanaged their resources. In particular, the Fund concentrates on a nation's exchange rate and its balance of payments position. Nations which seek out the Fund's assistance have virtually exhausted their official hard currency reserves to finance a trade or other current account deficit. But why do nations run a trade or current account deficit? Largely ignoring exogenous factors such as the terms of trade, the Fund argues that troubled nations have deliberately over-valued their currency, in effect, pricing themselves out of the market for exports, while drawing in too many products from the international economy via imports. Nations which are in financial trouble with unsustainable external macroeconomic imbalances, then, are essentially living beyond their means. Excess aggregate demand is the underlying macroeconomic cause leading nations to seek loans from the Fund in this way of looking at the situation.

To begin to solve the problem of such an imbalance, in the Fund's perspective, a **stabilization program** must be introduced that typically results in **compression** of the economy. Excess demand and spending by consumers and government must be wrung out of the system, and therefore a short-term economic downturn must be imposed. Once the so-called fundamentals of the economy, that is, the key economic variables, are stabilized and brought into equilibrium, the Fund believes that the economy will bounce back, but with a stronger foundation for economic expansion, especially if stabilization is followed by a fundamental adjustment process in the way the economy functions so that disequilibrium situations are less likely in future. In the Fund's view, adjusting the "fundamentals" requires several steps:

1   a devaluation of the currency to its sustainable, equilibrium value to stimulate exports and discourage imports;
2   control of the rate of growth of the money supply in order to stem inflationary pressures which lead to over-valuation of the currency and excess aggregate demand in the economy;
3   a reduction of government spending, especially to control the *fiscal deficit*, to restore the balance between the public and private sector's roles in the economy and to reduce inflationary pressures;
4   a reduction in real wages (that is, of inflation-adjusted wage payments) in order to make exports more attractive on the world market and to mitigate internal aggregate demand at the same time. By reducing real wages, the profit share of industry is expected to rise, as will the profit rate. A higher profit rate will attract more direct foreign investment, which will provide a net addition to the capital stock, thereby strengthening the export capability of the economy and reducing the external borrowing requirements.

While the relative emphasis on the above four components varies somewhat from nation to nation, they constitute the essence of what is generally known as an IMF **austerity package**. It is worthwhile to briefly review each of these components of an austerity program.

Devaluation

Unquestionably, the Fund's view that exchange rate over-valuation is a significant underlying factor contributing to current account deficits and economic crisis often has a solid basis, as was argued in Chapter 15. Poor nations far too often do have a tendency to over-value their currencies. Why? Necessary imports of machinery and equipment and intermediate products can be acquired relatively cheaply via over-valuation, and this may speed the development process, particularly during the import substitution phase of industrialization (see Chapter 9). Unfortunately, however, superfluous luxury consumer good imports and foreign travel also are made cheaper for domestic elites with over-valuation. A politically weak government may appeal to the middle class, proffering travel and imported luxuries at low prices in exchange for their political support. Thus there are tempting political and economic reasons for currency over-valuation, particularly in countries lacking a strong democratic tradition.

In the Fund's view, devaluation of the currency will accomplish two desired objectives: imports will decline, while exports will increase, closing the trade gap and reducing the current account deficit. While this is true in theory, as we saw in Chapter 15, in real time exports may not respond strongly to a devaluation due to a low price elasticity of demand, particularly if such exports are primary products.[7] Thus, the bulk of the austerity package's effect from devaluation tends to fall heaviest on import compression via higher import prices. The foreign trade account may well come into balance with time, but often only by under-cutting the productive base of the economy due to the increased cost of importing needed capital and intermediate goods for industry. In the longer term, the effect of a devaluation may well be to reduce the capacity to export to the extent that imported inputs enter into the production of export industries, thus creating precisely the opposite result from that sought by the Fund.

We are not arguing, let it be clear, against devaluation per se, or in favor of maintaining import substitution industrialization beyond the time period when ISI can usefully be sustained, as the discussions in Chapters 9 and 10 made abundantly manifest. Nor are we arguing in favor of over-valued exchange rates, as Chapter 15 hopefully made clear. We are suggesting that, at times, a devaluation, particularly a sharp and large devaluation, actually may interfere with a nation's trajectory of structural transformation, rather than supporting it. By asymmetrically and adversely affecting import substitution industries more rapidly and more severely than contributing to export expansion, a devaluation, if not carefully considered, and perhaps bolstered with compensatory programs, such as public investment, may actually inhibit the desired adjustment process that the IMF would wish to encourage, aimed at altering the productive structure of the less-developed country. Thus, current research shows, in repeated cases, that one of the consequences of acceptance of a Fund program is a *decline* in investment. Another affect, to be expected when investment declines, is that GDP growth turns *significantly negative* during the period when nations are under Fund programs (Bird 2001: 1851–1852). Adam Przeworski and James Vreeland found in a recent study covering a wide number of cases or "observations" that GDP growth was *lowered* by an average amount of 1.5 percent per year while nations were participating in IMF programs (Przeworski and Vreeland 2000). As Graham Bird notes, "On the positive side IMF programs do seem to be associated with a statistically significant and enduring depreciation in the real exchange rate. Perhaps connected with this, they also appear to be associated with some significant strengthening in the balance of payments" (Bird 2001: 1852).

Inflation

According to the IMF, domestic inflation is a major cause of currency over-valuation. The Fund anticipates that a country with an over-valued currency is simultaneously one wherein the domestic rate of inflation has been so high, relative to the world average, as to create over-valuation, particularly if exchange rates are not freely floating. Inflation is viewed by the IMF as a monetary problem, one of "too much money chasing too few goods." This excess demand arises from many sources, but two are considered primary: first, the governments of less-developed nations attempt to expand spending too rapidly relative to the effective tax base, providing social services and engaging in poorly thought-out spending programs. The resulting "fiscal deficit" is believed to crowd out the private sector, by pushing up interest rates as government borrows to finance expenditures above revenues, thus absorbing the limited amount of investment funds. Second, workers, particularly unionized workers and government employees, who also may be unionized, push up wages beyond justified productivity increases in an economy that already suffers from excess demand conditions.

So, behind the balance-of-payments crisis, the IMF finds over-valuation of the currency; behind over-valuation lies excessive inflationary pressures; and behind high inflation is profligate government spending on development and social projects, without proper regard for the limited resources of the developing nation. Given this interpretation, the Fund imposes limits on the growth of the domestic money supply, requires a tightening of bank credit, and imposes a ceiling on wage increases, typically well below the rate of inflation. This is part of the IMF's overall view of the need for reining in excessive state involvement in the economic activity of less-developed economies.

Government spending

Less-developed nations often run central government budgets that are in deficit, contributing to the inflation process. The Fund views the government's deficit as prima facie evidence of excess demand and therefore imposes strong cuts on government spending as a condition of receiving loans. Governments in the developing world often provide subsidies on basic goods such as food staples, milk and meat products, fuels, and pharmaceutical products. The Fund generally will impose a "get prices right doctrine" and call for the elimination of such subsidies, letting market-determined prices prevail. As a consequence, austerity programs often impose an inordinate burden on those in society who can least afford the effects of income and spending compression. (Ironically, by deregulating the prices of basic goods, inflation often surges.) Other targets for government cut-backs can vary widely from nation to nation, but governments often reduce their educational budgets and/or physical infrastructural outlays, which will, unfortunately, reduce the supply capacity of the developing nation in the future. Nonetheless, in searching for ways to reduce state spending and the government deficit, these are often where cuts are made, rather than in military spending, because of political pressures from domestic elites and the military itself.

The Fund requires cuts in central government spending as a condition for its loans, given its competitive equilibrium approach, which leads it to argue that resources released, that is, not spent, by the public sector will be more productively employed by the private sector.[8] This assumption, however, is often unwarranted when the private sector is structurally weak and competition, in the economic sense, is absent. As a result, the institutions of society, from banks to private businesses operating in the private sector are not well developed and do not respond well or quickly to investment resources freed-up by the public sector. Business interests may react to the general downturn in the economy brought on by reduced government expenditure, in fact, by reducing production and investment. Or, as is sometimes the case, these business interests may have drained much of their liquid funds from their own nation in anticipation of the devaluation which the Fund will surely impose. *Capital flight* often may be more appealing to business interests than higher levels of investment or the expansion of domestic productive capacity and the social capacity to do technology.

Again, we do not wish to invite misunderstanding. There is no denying the culpability of many governments in running unsustainable fiscal deficits, in poor project design, and in unnecessary and wasteful spending. But IMF demands to simply cut state spending, without some fundamental analysis of the structural and institutional transformations desired for that particular society, can inhibit further progress. No doubt many blanket subsidy programs for staple foods or for utilities are wasteful, providing benefits not only to the poor, but also to non-poor who could afford to pay more. Targeted subsidy programs by government would retain the spirit of such spending measures by helping those who needed them most, thus reducing the cost of such programs without eliminating them. Cutting back indiscriminately on central government, educational, health, and certain infrastructural expenditures would not seem to be advised, certainly not on the basis of the new growth theory evidence examined in Chapters 8 and 12. What we are suggesting is that the IMF's condition requiring a cut in government spending so as to reduce the fiscal deficit and hence inflationary pressures has been too often a terribly blunt instrument, cutting into areas of social investment with substantial positive external effects. More attention also could be placed on better and more effective tax collection measures. Reducing the fiscal deficit is a two-sided objective, and it can be achieved by reducing government expenditures and/or raising tax revenues.

Wage repression

Wage cuts have their counterpart in a reduction in total consumption and that tends to reduce total national income. Thus it becomes problematic to argue that an increase in the profit rate alone, created by wage cuts, will be sufficient to stimulate additional production, since reduced demand is likely to follow lower wages. If additional production can be easily exported, however, wage repression may result in a net increase in output, but it may not if the export sector is weak.[9] It is also difficult to determine how foreign investors may respond to lower wage costs, as there are many other factors that enter into a decision to commit to an investment abroad besides the cost of labor. The Fund posits that a nation that is in the process of stabilizing its economy and which is serious about adjusting its economic structure will attract foreign capital. But if the domestic economy is in a shambles, and export markets show weak growth, foreign capital may choose to stay on the sidelines. James Vreeland conducted a massive study involving 110 countries that underwent IMF programs from 1961–1993. He concluded that IMF programs have a *negative* affect on manufacturing labor and therefore shift the distribution of income from labor to capital. On average, controlling for many factors, Vreeland shows that labor's share of income in the manufacturing sector under IMF programs falls from 39.8 percent to only 36.4 percent – and this is found within the context of a *falling* GDP (Vreeland 2002: 121–130). One of Vreeland's most interesting findings, long argued by opponents of IMF austerity programs with little evidence, is that the degree of income redistribution toward capital is so great that industrialists are actually better off under the IMF programs than they would have been had economic growth been satisfactory. Table 17.2, below, summarizes Vreeland's startling findings in three cases.

Compression effects versus expansionary effects of IMF programs

Having now traced out some of the possible effects of an IMF austerity package, it is important to add a significant qualification regarding the compression effects of the Fund's program. While the Fund's approach, in and of itself, would seem to point to an induced economic downturn for the borrowing nation, the Fund also injects hard currencies into the economy when it lends, and this should act as a stimulus to economic expansion, moderating the various dampening effects of the components of the austerity program. Furthermore, and this is a very important point, nations which consummate a loan arrangement with the Fund are able, by virtue of now being under the guidance of the Fund, to essentially alter their country risk status in the eyes of international lenders and often gain access to new credits from abroad. This is a second possible stimulus working to counteract the adverse affects of a domestic austerity program. A third stimulus will almost surely come from the World Bank (discussed below) which will lend because the Fund has lent, as usually will the relevant regional development bank for that country, such as the African Development Bank for African countries and the InterAmerican Development Bank in Latin America. In addition to this three-

Table 17.2 The impact of IMF austerity programs: capital's share and labor's share

Country	Years	Δ GDP (%)	Δ Capital's Income[a] (%)	Δ Labor's Share[a] (%)
Congo	1985/1986	−2.99	+9.5	−8.5
Uruguay	1989/1990	−1.03	+2.0	−2.7
Ecuador	1982/1983	−5.7	+36	−18.0

Source: James Vreeland 2002.

Note
a Manufacturing sector income.

fold injection of hard currencies from the Fund, from the international financial markets, and from the World Bank and/or the regional development bank, if the borrowing nation is quite poor, it is likely to receive some financial grants from bilateral foreign aid entities, such as the United States' Agency for International Development (AID). However, in a significant study Graham Bird's evidence demonstrates that IMF programs *generally do not* serve as a catalyst to attract either private or bilateral or other forms of multilateral financial flows (Bird 2001: 1856–1862).

If equity investments (DFI) are arriving, and a variety of new loans and grants are extended, the stimulus effects may well outweigh the compression effects of the austerity program. However, new DFI may introduce other problems for a less-developed nation (Chapter 14), grants may come at the price of other concessions to a powerful and wealthy neighbor, and new loans will surely cause a poor nation to exchange short-term liquidity for longer-term financial obligations which create an outflow on the current account. Only if the nation actually becomes a better producer, that is, only if the inflows of financing contribute to structural transformation and a fundamental adjustment of the economy along the lines set out in Chapters 9 to 13, will the loans, grants, and investments make any long-term developmental sense, as was argued in the previous chapter concerning external debt. These positive effects *can* materialize, but these new-found sources of liquidity may merely be utilized by the borrowing nation as a short-term expedient, while the structural problems of the nation remain unaddressed, again as occurred during the debt crisis. Consequently, even if, under the best of circumstances, GDP growth is quickly resumed in the aftermath of the imposition of an IMF austerity package, it is also necessary to analyze the post-compression debt levels, and to take account of the manner in which DFI and new foreign aid grants impact the productive capacity of an economy.

In any given year, the IMF does not loan immense sums of money, certainly in comparison to the problems the Fund hopes to address. As we have seen in Table 17.1 in 2000 the Fund made loans in the amount of 7.7 billion SDR's (approximately $10 billion US$), but received repayments in that year of 15.8 billion SDR's. Thus, the net effect of the Fund's lending in that year was to *contract* global liquidity by about $10.5 billion US$. In 2002, by contrast, the Fund was a net contributor to global liquidity (IMF 2003b). What the Fund really has to offer to a nation in difficult straits is its *imprimatur*, the Fund's stamp of approval to the international financial community, from which other loans, grants, and DFI will flow, in varying proportions, to the beleaguered nation, or so it is argued. And, the Fund strongly believes, good technical economic advice, particularly concerning macroeconomic policy, will be another major benefit arising from an IMF program.

Do IMF programs work?

The answer to this question depends on how we interpret it. If we take it to mean that, once the less-developed nation reaches an agreement with the IMF, follows IMF conditionality to the letter, and undergoes a "successful" stabilization and adjustment of the economy whereby inflation is thereafter controlled, the currency is thereafter realistically valued in terms of hard currencies, the trade account remains in balance, investment remains high, and the economy grows and prospers, the answer (in most instances) is assuredly "no."

The IMF has been very interested in posing and answering this question. In their most recent attempt at self-evaluation, the Fund's research economists studied forty-five stand-by and Extended Fund Facility arrangements which the Fund approved between mid-1988 and mid-1991 in thirty-six countries. According to the Fund, the results were as follows.

- Improvement was most notable on a pre-loan, post-loan comparison basis for exports. With the imposition of a Fund agreement, exports improved strongly, but over time export strength weakened.
- Only approximately half of the countries benefitted from additional capital inflows.
- Regarding inflation, "a few countries achieved dramatic reductions from very high initial rates, but many continued to experience moderately high inflation; a few even recorded upward trends."
- Regarding growth, "few if any countries shift[ed] to a distinctly more rapid pace of growth backed by higher savings ratios."
- Regarding investment, "few countries saw any increase in overall investment ratios, although private investment rates rose as public investment rates fell" (IMF 1995b: 234).

Clearly, the results of the Fund's study, which largely parallels numerous studies done previously both by the Fund and independent researchers, portray the IMF's impact in a less than flattering light. Hostile critics of the Fund would have a difficult time mounting a more severe critique than the Fund has made of the consequences of its own policies. But the Fund seems unburdened by these findings. Undismayed and undeterred by this latest report indicating that the IMF's model has failed to come to grips with the persistent problems of the less-developed nations, the Fund's Executive Directors drew two inferences from this study: first, that the Fund should warn nations which undergo adjustment that they cannot expect improvement on both the external balance of payments account and in short-term improvement in growth and investment; second, that the Fund should lend for a longer period of time, that is, the Fund should continue to shift its programs away from stand-by arrangements, lasting twelve to eighteen months, toward intermediate adjustment program loans with a duration of three to five years.

Of the many studies conducted on the effectiveness of the Fund by independent researchers, a 1992 study headed by Tony Killick broadly confirms the IMF's in-house study cited above, while adding new dimensions worth noting. Killick and his associates analyzed the effects of 266 Fund programs in the 1980s, 220 of which were stand-by arrangements. Forty-eight percent of the stand-bys were never completed, indicating that the recipient nation was unwilling or unable to comply with the conditionality demands of the Fund.[10] Thirty-three percent of the discontinued programs broke down almost immediately. And, in the 1988–1990 period, the non-completion rate on stand-by loans reached 88 percent. Why? According to Killick, easier credit conditions allowed the less-developed nations to go elsewhere for loans, and thereby to avoid IMF oversight and conditionality. Another important finding is the prevalence of recidivism: "no less than nineteen countries had six or more programs approved by the Fund, encompassing 131 programs or 44 percent of the total for the period" (Killick *et al.* 1992: 590).

On a somewhat more positive note, Killick and his research associates *did* find in a study of IMF arrangements in the 1979–1985 period that Fund adjustment programs led to improvements in the balance of payments, without any long-term "strangulation" of imports. But the study of the 266 Fund programs, referred to above, found that, over time, net capital inflows did not improve as "Fund credits were often used to repay other creditors." Killick argues that, although countries under a Fund program may, and probably will, attract new financing from the World Bank, the regional development banks, and foreign aid donors, "there appears to be no general catalytic effect on private flows" (Killick 1995: 179). Meanwhile, 40 percent of the completed programs were associated with *increased* rates of inflation. And, most important for considerations of economic development, "the brunt (of adjustment) falls on the fixed investment ratio, which declines substantially and significantly over the whole period. Overall, the programs appear unable to exert any appreciable squeeze on private and public consumption" (Killick *et al.* 1992: 593–595).

In summing-up the complex state of the evaluative literature on the IMF a number of conclusions appear to be accepted by both critics and supporters of the Fund.[11]

- Short-term improvements in the balance of payments are significant, even for countries which abandon the IMF programs (Killick 1995: 68).
- IMF compression and austerity are most often associated with compression of wage income, compression of social services and compression of investment, but without any compression of overall consumption, which implies that upward income redistribution occurs.
- One of the strongest effects of IMF programs, as Manuel Pastor's research on Latin America clearly demonstrated, is a decline in the wage share of GDP (Pastor 1987). Pastor's results are particularly applicable to workers in the state sector and wage workers in the formal sector, who feel the brunt of wage compression in a standard IMF program. Peasant producers, on the other hand, *may* find that the emphasis on devaluation and export promotion increases their earnings.
- While in the short term some countries do find that the rate of growth of GDP rises modestly, in relation to the situation immediately preceding the crisis which precipitated the IMF program, over a somewhat longer period of time the basic capacity to sustain growth often appears to be *undermined* by reductions in public- and private-sector investment. This, apparently, helps to explain why many nations which have either completed or abandoned IMF programs subsequently enter into new programs with the IMF.

Some critics and observers of the Fund, citing studies such as the two summarized here, argue that the IMF is an inept institution which should either cease to do business or radically recast its approach. Others maintain that the IMF does, in fact, serve its purpose and meet its objectives. To these observers, the Fund's objectives are not really tied to the improvement of the performance of the less-developed nations, but to the long-term improvement of conditions which allow major participants in the international economy, such as the transnational corporations, relatively free access to the widest possible range of production and sales sites in the global economy (Pauly 1994: 204–215; Crow *et al.* 1988: 310–330). In this view, the IMF is a "mechanism of integration," bringing the less-developed nations into a new international division of labor and ensuring the repayment of international bank loans which soared in the 1970s. If this, indeed, is the criterion by which the Fund should be evaluated, high marks are surely to be awarded. Certainly the Fund has been consistent in its hostility to import substitution industrialization, at least since the early 1970s. And it has unquestionably advocated a more open trading regime around the world.

Prior to the Asian Crisis of 1997 the Fund was a supremely confident, even swaggering, institution. But, in the early years of the twenty-first century the IMF found itself the target of some very influential sources – among them Joseph Stiglitz, whose book *Globalization and Its Discontents* opened with a blistering two chapter critique of the IMF informed by Stiglitz's years as chief economist of the World Bank (Stiglitz 2002: 3–52). Also breaking ranks, the United Nations' *Human Development Report 2002* focused on the "democratic deficit" of the Fund (and the World Bank along with the World Trade Organization), noting that only seven of the 184 nations in the IMF controlled 48 percent of the voting power of the institution. While the Fund urged "transparency" and "good government" and "participation" on the member nations during IMF austerity programs, the United Nations noted in some detail the lack of these crucial elements *within* the organizational structure of the IMF (United Nations 2002: 112–117). Stung and seemingly confused by these critiques, high level Fund officials who rose to prominence in the 1980s and 1990s were less than convincing in their statements that critics really did not understand the complexities and intricacies of high-level economic theory, and that time had (or would) prove IMF policies correct (Boorman 2002: 241, 245–248). While widely disparaged, the Fund continues to exert *tremendous* influence – at the close of 2002 the IMF held vital influence over the lives of hundreds of millions of citizens of fifty-three developing nations through the IMF's programs. A global superpower in itself, the Fund's pivotal role in development issues is beyond dispute.

The World Bank

Like its twin Bretton Woods institution, the IMF, the World Bank was created in late 1945 and commenced lending on a very modest scale in 1947. The International Bank for Reconstruction and Development (as the Bank was originally, and still officially is, known) loaned an average of slightly more than half a billion dollars per year from 1947 to 1967, a relatively meager sum when spread over the many nations that sought to receive Bank support. Until the 1970s, one distinguishing characteristic of the Bank was that it loaned "long," that is, for a multi-year period, while the Fund loaned "short," for periods of twelve to eighteen months.[12]

Another distinction between the Fund and the Bank in the early years was that the Bank offered *project* loans and technical expertise to promote large-scale capital-intensive mega-investment projects in less-developed nations. Highest on the list for loans was water projects such as dams, irrigation systems, flood control, and hydro-power installations for promoting agricultural development and electricity generation for industry. Until 1968, when Robert McNamara became World Bank president, the most notable change at the World Bank was the creation of the International Development Association (IDA) as a new component of the World Bank Group. The IDA was assigned to be the entity to make long-term loans to nations which otherwise could never receive funding in adequate amounts from the Bank, due to their general financial weakness. IDA loans are concessional, meaning that a significant portion (more than 25 percent) of the interest cost of the loan is waived and other easier terms, such as grace periods for the repayment of interest, can be built into the loan. Under its charter, the Bank may lend only to governments. With the exception of the IDA loans, it expects to, and does, make a respectable profit. It is not, therefore, in the strict sense of the word, an aid institution. Still, the Bank is not just another financial institution, because it does lend to nations for the long term on unproven projects, often with substantial externalities, and for which private sources are usually reluctant to make loans. Even after the IDA came into existence, the World Bank attracted little attention. Lending from the IDA amounted only to a modest average of one quarter of a billion US dollars per year up to 1967 (see Box 17.2).

US influence at the Bank

Since its inception, the Bank has had only US citizens for its presidents. (In a mirror image of this tradition, and reflecting international power relations which prevailed when these institutions were created, only Europeans have headed the IMF.) As in the IMF, the United States has been the dominant shareholder in the World Bank. Yet, its sway over the Bank has diminished somewhat over the years, as its share of the Bank's capital subscriptions, and consequently its share of the voting power within the IBRD, has fallen from 35 percent in 1947 to 21 percent in 1981, and then 16.5 percent in 2002. Once again, it has been Japan which has gained the largest relative share of influence in the Bank in recent years, though it held only 7.9 percent of the voting share in 2002. Much of the money lent by the Bank to less developed nations also has served to stimulate production in the United States economy and in the other advanced nations. On average, roughly 60 percent of all loans and credits consist of orders for equipment and supplies furnished by the economies of the advanced nations.

The McNamara era and the basic human needs approach

As an institution, the Bank rapidly changed under the leadership of Robert McNamara (1968–1981). With McNamara the Bank moved to center stage in the development dialog. It built up a vast cadre of highly trained economists, reaching 6,100 full-time staff in 1994, with 1,375 consultants or temporary staff. McNamara changed the Bank in practically every way imaginable. Its funding vastly expanded, its orientation changed radically, and its "mission" was completely and dramatically redefined. Heretofore, the Bank had modest goals. But McNamara accepted a new approach to development, known as the **Basic Human Needs** approach, first advocated by the International Labor Organization in the late 1960s. Now, the central focus of the Bank would be to put an end to world hunger, poverty, and misery. Thus, the Bank leaped from its modest objectives of placing a few selected loans in the developing nations to attacking the most intractable and broadest of

---

Box 17.2 The World Bank Group

The International Bank for Reconstruction and Development: Until the 1980s, the IBRD, known popularly as simply the World Bank or "the Bank," lent for specific development projects, usually with a seven-year cycle from planning to completion. In its early years, the IBRD definitely reflected an "engineering" orientation. From 1947 to 2002, the Bank made cumulative loans of $371 billion to ninety-four nations. Loans normally have a five-year initial grace period, after which they are to be repaid over a period of fifteen to twenty years, at the market rate of interest. The Bank does not reschedule or cancel its loans. Borrowing governments have an outstanding record of paying off these loans, since failure to repay the Bank would virtually destroy the credit rating of a developing nation. The IBRD has always achieved a substantial rate of profit on these loans.

The International Development Association (IDA): Established in 1960 to forestall the creation of a similar agency at the UN, the IDA lends to nations which cannot qualify for IBRD loans under the usual lending rules. Only the poorest nations are eligible for IDA loans. In 2002 the IDA had 79 nations (2.5 billion people) as potential candidates for its "credits." Over 41 percent of the $135 billion in IDA loans issued from 1961 to 2002 went to India, China, Bangladesh, and Pakistan. Formally the IDA does not issue loans, but rather "credits." These "credits" have a nominal interest rate of 0.75 percent, a grace period of ten years, and repayment over the following forty years. In 2002 IDA lending reached a record level of $8.1 billion (47 percent for Africa).

The International Finance Corporation (IFC): Created in 1956, the IFC supports private-sector development, functioning as a co-investor and assisting the private sector to obtain debt and equity financing in the international financial markets. In 2002, for example, the IFC created 204 new projects in seventy-five nations – up from fifty-one nations in 1992. With an emphasis on small- and medium-sized businesses, the IFC has become more significant since the 1970s as a result of changes in policy orientation at the World Bank. Nonetheless, the IFC is much smaller than the IBRD and the IDA; its total outstanding loans amount to $21.6 billion. The World Bank has continued to prioritize the IFC with growth in annual lending more than doubling from 1992 to 2002.

The Multilateral Investment Guarantee Agency (MIGA): Since 1988, the MIGA has functioned to guarantee direct foreign investments against non-commercial risks, such as nationalization, and has given policy advice, particularly to potential foreign investors. The MIGA organizes international conferences to promote investment opportunities in developing nations and also trains nationals in poor nations on methods of investment promotion. In 2002 the MIGA guaranteed $1.4 billion which supported investments of over $4 billion for that year – up from $313 million in guarantees in 1992.

---

developmental objectives. McNamara and his close associates became advocates of the basic human needs approach which sought to channel development funding to programs in less-developed nations that would directly benefit the poor, particularly the poorest 40 percent of the population. This meant a vast new role for the IDA, and a new emphasis on housing projects, water sanitation, the Green Revolution, schooling, and related matters (see Box 17.3).

Between 1967 and 1993, the IBRD lent $224 billion on over 3,000 separate loans, while the IDA lent an additional $76 billion. Just as important, however, was the fact that *co-financing* allowed the Bank to vastly increase its importance, because other entities, particularly international banks, lent funds for Bank-approved loans. Co-financing can expand the reach of the Bank by 80 percent or more; in 1992, for example, the Bank loaned $16.4 billion, but also generated $13.3 billion in co-financing. Thus, in terms of its importance in generating long-term capital flows into the less-developed nations, the Bank can be nearly twice as significant as its annual lending numbers would suggest.

Box 17.3 The World Bank and the environment

Beginning in the late 1970s, prominent environmental groups began to carefully examine the lending policies of the World Bank. Their mounting critique helped push the Bank into issuing an official statement in 1984 mandating that the Bank would no longer finance projects which "cause severe or irreversible environmental degradation."

In 1987. with criticism of the Bank's environmental commitment mounting, Bank President Barber Conable announced that he would create an Environmental Department and increase the Bank's research on environmental degradation, desertification, and environmentally threatening forestry practices. By 1989, Conable had introduced the Bank's first environmental review process to screen some loans and projects for their potential environmental impact. From 1989 to 1993, 300 projects were evaluated for their environmental impact. Critics charged that the majority of loans and projects, however, were not subject to adequate environmental review. But by 1992 the Bank was employing 279 full-time analysts to work on environmental issues.

In 1993, the Bank indicated that its commitment to environmental concerns was deepening. A new Vice-President for Environmentally Sustainable Development was created with the objective of helping "Bank operational staff better understand the linkages between poverty and the environment and to view social, environmental, cultural, and agricultural concerns as more interrelated." Between 1992 and early 1995, the Bank devoted nearly 10 percent of its funding to projects with environmental objectives.

The Bank is also the implementing agency for the Global Environmental Facility (GEF), created in 1991 and restructured in 1994. The GEF is a financial mechanism under the combined trusteeship of the World Bank, the United Nations Environmental Program, and the United Nations Development Program. By mid-1995, the GEF had funded projects with a combined worth of $558 million, while committing to lend $2 billion from 1994 to 1997. These project loans address a range of broad environmental issues, such as climatic change, depletion of the ozone layer, and land degradation.

Does all this constitute a "Greening" of the Bank? Critics are not sure, but they do acknowledge that the Bank has made serious steps toward addressing environmental issues which it long ignored or down-played. Some critics are less sure:

> The environmental movement has won some project-by-project skirmishes but it has been strategically and ideologically outflanked. Through a combination of reassuring rhetoric and some genuine improvements, the Bank has distanced itself from outright hostilities with the opposite camp.
>
> Sources: George and Sabelli 1994: 183; World Bank 1984: 4; 1995a: 26, 28

Table 17.3 records total Bank lending and co-financing for recent years. Note that these figures are in current, rather than inflation adjusted, dollars. Adjusting for inflation, and after soaring in 1999, Bank lending actually fell somewhat from 1990 to 2002.

The rise of structural adjustment lending: 1979–2002

By the late 1970s, McNamara's vision had gone beyond that of meeting basic human needs. He now believed that successful economic development would require that the Bank itself provide much of the guidance and implementation of a development program to less-developed nations. In this view, these countries would have to share, if not relinquish, decision-making powers over a vast array of economic policy matters which heretofore had been considered strictly the sovereign province of independent nations. With these new loans, which McNamara never completely defined prior to stepping down in 1981, the World Bank once again recast its "mission"; now, it would guide the economic trajectory of entire nations in their quest for development. The new-style comprehensive loans were termed **structural adjustment loans** and **sectoral adjustment loans**. These loans have continued through 2002 to be a prime focus of the World Bank's activities.

The global economic crisis of the late 1970s had altered McNamara's perspective. In his view, as he expressed it in his annual presidential address to the World Bank in 1980, the debt crisis, the rise in oil prices, and the slow growth in aggregate demand in the advanced nations were all working to undermine the development prospects of the less-developed nations. Consequently, the basic human needs approach was not enough; it was not possible to rely on the less-developed nations to define their paths to development, while the Bank attempted to care, through its lending, for those who had been left out of the process of economic growth. Rather, now it was necessary to help build, adjust, and remould the economic foundations of the developing nations. A wide range of issues which, previously, the World Bank had left to the determination of the borrowing nation would now be upper-most in the Bank's analysis when it considered which countries were eligible for loans and credits.

From the late 1970s, when the first structural adjustment loans, called SALs, were made, through to 1986, the role of SALs within overall Bank lending grew to the point where approximately one out of every three dollars in lending was for the

Table 17.3 World Bank lending and co-financing (billions of US dollars, fiscal years)

	1990	*1993*	*1995*	*2000*	*2002*
Gross disbursements					
IBRD	13.9	12.9	10.4	10.9	11.5
IDA	3.9	4.9	5.7	4.4	8.1
Total	**17.5**	**17.8**	**18.4**	**15.3**	**19.6**
Co-financing	n.a.	11.6	8.2	7.0	4.7

Source: World Bank, *World Bank Annual Report* (Washington, DC: World Bank, various years). www.worldbank.org./annualreport/.

purpose of structural adjustment. In 2002 *total adjustment loans* accounted for *64 percent* of all lending, with 48 percent of loans going either to restructuring the Public Sector or the Financial Sector! In essence, a SAL is granted not to build anything in particular, but to change national economic policies in some desired direction. Consequently, the borrowing nation has some discretion on where and how it will spend the SAL funds, unlike project loan funds from the Bank which are very much under the control of the Bank for a specific undertaking. Depending on circumstances and the nation involved, SALs attempted to address a broad range of macroeconomic problems. Once a SAL has been arranged, funds are disbursed over time in a conditional manner, much as for the IMF, being dependent on the success of the economy in making fundamental changes in pre-selected policy areas. Between 1980 and 1986, the average SAL had conditions in ten of the nineteen policy areas which the Bank wished countries to address. The most frequent conditions were to "improve export incentives" (76 percent of all SALs incorporated this as a condition), to "reform the government's budget or taxes" (70 percent), to "improve financial performance of public enterprises" (73 percent), "to revise agricultural prices" (73 percent), and to "strengthen capacity to formulate and implement public investment programs" (86 percent) (Mosley *et al.* 1991: vol. 1, 44).

Adjusting the state sector

It is clear from this brief summary of the most common conditions for SAL loans that the role of the state was at the epicenter of the Bank's analysis regarding what most needed to be "adjusted" in the poor nations. This orientation reflected the so-called "new political economy" perspective of Anne Krueger, who was for a period in the 1980s the Chief Economist of the World Bank, as well as reflecting the views of many other influential economists within the Bank. As will be recalled from our earlier discussion in Chapter 7, the focus of neoliberal economists has been upon what they believe has been the excessive role of the state in the economy which, they argued, constituted a serious impediment to economic development. Thus, it comes as less than a surprise to find that the central thrust of the SALs was largely concentrated on paring-back the role of the state intervention, particularly through the sell-off, or privatization, of state-owned firms via programs often financed and directed by the Bank.

The ultimate aim of the Bank was to achieve a new form of macroeconomic management which would successfully integrate the borrowing nation into the global system of trade, finance, and investment. Any nation which sought to hold on to the vestiges of import substitution industrialization did not receive much assistance from the Bank; dismantling ISI and instituting export production became a virtual *sine qua non* for obtaining Bank assistance. In striving for a complete reorientation of the economies of many nations, the World Bank ventured into territory which had long been the sole domain of borrowing governments, such as the size of the public administration apparatus, the organization of the civil service, and the general structure of the public sector, labor regulations, and public investments. In every instance, the Bank sought to remold the society and economy to create an environment it believed would be more encouraging to the private business sector, including international corporations.

By 1987, the Bank was ready to formalize its shift to structural adjustment lending via what it termed its "integration policy," which sought to coordinate all Bank programs within a nation in order to obtain consistency under the umbrella concept of structural adjustment. In effect, then, even though loans formally defined as SALs remained at the level of roughly one-third of annual outlays, in nations where "integration" was adopted, all loans, including project loans, were intended to be coordinated within the framework of the SAL concept. Furthermore, under **cross-conditionality**, nations could only receive SALs if they had stand-by arrangements with the IMF. And, they could only receive stand-by support from the IMF *if* they accepted SALs from the Bank. (Meanwhile the IMF itself began to enter into SAL lending with the creation of the Structural Adjustment Facility in 1986 and the Enhanced Structural Adjustment Facility in 1987.)

Did SALs speed the development process?

One survey of the effectiveness of World Bank SALs was conducted on 241 such loans conferred upon thirty-three African nations between 1980 and 1989. The results were that average per capita income fell on average 1.1 percent per year in these nations, while per capita food production declined overall. The purchasing power of the minimum wage fell by an average of 25 percent. Government expenditures for education declined by 36 percent, and the total number of elementary school students decreased by 14 percent. Not surprisingly, the numbers of the poor increased steadily (George and Sabelli 1994: 141). These are not particularly encouraging outcomes, though one might argue that the special problems of the poor African nations makes this an unfair measure of success or failure of SALs, as other adverse forces also were at work. On the other hand, the Bank never suggested that some countries, in Africa or anywhere, might find a deterioration of economic progress to be the outcome of accepting SALs.

An independent research team composed of Paul Mosley, Jane Harrigan, and John Toye attempted to evaluate the effects of SALs via a detailed study of nine nations from countries in Africa, Asia, and Latin America. They buttressed this sample with a broader comparison of twenty countries that had received SALs between 1980 and 1987 with twenty similar nations which had no SAL loans over the period. Their findings were largely similar to the study conducted on Africa, cited above. Their four main conclusions were:

1   SALs had a positive impact on exports and on the balance of payments;
2   overall investment declined under the SALs;
3   SALs failed to increase the economic growth rate and the flow of international capital, but they did not decrease either growth or international capital flows over the period prior to the SALs;
4   living standards for the poor, however, declined under SALs (see Box 17.4).

Box 17.4 Women and "invisible adjustment"

Women have proven to be more vulnerable than men to the loss of household income following the implementation of structural adjustment loans (SALs). To compensate, women have adopted new survival strategies, increasing their workload and engaging in prolonged periods of greater self-sacrifice. This process has been termed "invisible adjustment," since such strategies are normally not included in the evaluation of the effects of SALs.

The process of "invisible adjustment" is complex. One aspect concerns the need for adaptive strategies in the face of sizeable reductions in public spending, which normally are required as a condition for receiving an SAL. When public health spending is reduced, for example, women must attempt to adapt by increasing the time they spend as informal medical aides, nurturing and nursing sick children and other family members who, prior to the SAL, might have been treated at rural health clinics or urban hospitals.

With food subsidies eliminated or reduced, women often must spend more time shopping and preparing food, and the food they have available after an SAL may have a significantly reduced protein content. Even relatively poor women in many less-developed countries sometimes employ "servants," usually young girls, to help with the labor-intensive tasks of food preparation and washing-up. But when household income falls, this "luxury" is quickly eliminated, and women and girls in the family perform these tasks.

This helps set up a vicious circle, since a restricted diet for children often means increased vulnerability to illness and longer periods of recovery. Furthermore, a reduced diet means that family workers will have much less energy to devote to remunerative labor, thereby risking dismissal due to lower productivity or increased absenteeism.

SALs often include restrictive monetary policies designed to create higher unemployment and thus reduce real wages. In the formal sector, women are more vulnerable to such unemployment effects, and they often are forced into the informal sector where compensation is lower and the effort to survive is typically greater. In an attempt to compensate, women often increase their hours of work. For those women working outside of the home, their increased absence often necessitates that older children care for younger siblings. Under such circumstances, it is usually older girls who lose the advantage of an education in order to provide child-care at home. One study of a major urban area of Ecuador found that during a period of structural adjustment, the share of women working in the informal sector jumped from 3 percent in 1988 to 21 percent in 1992.

SALs appear to impose a three-fold burden on women: time devoted to market activities (in either the formal or informal sectors) increases; household labor increases; and nurturing labor (helping with sick children and relatives) increases.

Sources: Henshall Momsen 1991: 97–99; World Bank 1995b: 106–108

Their overall evaluation of SALs was little short of devastating:

> By contrast with the Bank's generally acknowledged success in project lending (e.g., an average *ex post* rate of return of 17 percent across all projects between 1960 and 1980), it is not even clear whether the net return, in terms of growth of gross national product, on the $25 billion which the Bank has so far invested in policy-based ending is positive or negative.
>
> (Mosley *et al.* 1991: vol. 1, 302)

Critiques of World Bank and IMF SALs

Criticism of the SAL strategy has fallen into two distinct categories. First, some observers, including many from the developing nations, have felt that the World Bank and the Fund have abused their vast powers by overstepping their proper boundaries and usurping a considerable share of national sovereignty at a time when the developing nations were particularly vulnerable to pressure, due to the decline in primary commodity prices and the ravages of the debt crisis. Second, other observers have argued that the Bank and the Fund have operated from false premises and assumptions derived from the neoliberal school, which maintains that by "freeing-up" resources from the public sector and orienting the economy toward the export sector, the economy will expand at a much higher rate. With the Bank seemingly impervious to the early critical work on SALs, and with the focus on SALs increasing through 2002, the Bank – under considerable pressure from citizens' groups and non-governmental organizations – consented to a joint World Bank–Civil Society review of SALs with their participation. The report of the Structural Adjustment Participatory Review group – which examined the impacts of SALs on Bangladesh, Ecuador, Ghana, Hungary, Mexico, the Philippines, and Zimbabwe was sufficiently devastating that the Bank – reached the following key conclusions regarding structural adjustment lending:

- Trade liberalization has been pushed through indiscriminately, allowing import growth to surpass that of exports-destroying domestic firms;
- Lack of meaningful participation of national stakeholders in the design and implementation of trade policies have rendered these measures technically inefficient;
- Financial assets have become more concentrated;
- [Financial] reforms have promoted short-term speculation and investment in non-productive activities;
- Employment levels have worsened and real wages have deteriorated and income distribution is less equitable today;
- Women have suffered the most as a result of labor-market reforms;
- Employment has become more precarious;
- The elimination of universally provided subsidies for essential goods has negatively affected the poorest (SAPRIN 2002).

Regarding the first of these propositions, while it is true that the World Bank and IMF SAL programs have effectively sought to usurp a portion of national sovereignty, it would be a mistake to view the borrowing nations as passively accepting the various conditions of the SALs. Rather, as the research of Mosley, Harrigan and Toye has shown, the borrowing nations have used the new SAL format as a basis for carrying on sophisticated bargaining with the World Bank and the IMF. Most recipient nations have not fully complied with the intent of the SALs, and they have sought to bend the conditionality of the SALs to their best advantage (whether this advantage accrues to a narrow elite or to the nation as a whole is debatable and, ultimately, the real issue). Desiring influence, the World Bank, at least, has reluctantly accepted the fact that the issue of governance of a nation will not be willingly handed over to a group of World Bank economists. Failing to find the leverage which they sought, the World Bank has been forced to settle for *some* influence, rather than maximum influence.

At the same time, non-compliance by countries has left advocates of SALs as effective instruments of change, a convenient escape route when SALs have failed to demonstrably improve the overall macroeconomic environment in borrowing nations; they have argued that, *had* the borrowing countries followed World Bank and IMF advice to the letter, matters would have turned out differently.

Sustainable development, comprehensive development framework, and a knowledge bank?

In 1991, when the World Bank selected its eighth president, Lewis Preston, the evidence regarding the weaknesses of the SAL approach had mounted, and there was a growing chorus of voices decrying the Bank's apparent abandonment of the world's poor. Some of those voices came from within the World Bank itself, where many of the top research economists simply did not share the ideological fervor of the neoliberal economists who had proposed and advanced the SAL agenda so rigidly, and often with little regard for the particular history of individual nations. Troubled by signs of weakness in many aspects of the Bank's past accomplishments, Preston called for a full evaluation of the Bank's lending practices to be headed by then Bank Vice President, Willi Wapenhans. In 1992 the "Wapenhans report," entitled "Effective Implementation: Key to Development Impact," was presented. Its results exerted a strong, perhaps unprecedented, influence on the Bank, at least up until 1995. The main conclusion of the Wapenhans Report was that, compared to the early 1980s, the Bank's loan portfolio had suffered a rapid decline in performance. Wapenhans found that in the early 1980s, the Bank had classified only 11 percent of its loans as "troubled," but by 1991, 37.5 percent fitted that category. In only 22 percent of the cases had borrowers fulfilled all of the agreements of a loan. Preston reacted rather quickly by bringing the concept of "sustainability" to the foreground, much as McNamara had emphasized the basic human needs approach throughout most of his tenure.

Sustainability shares with the basic human needs approach an emphasis on the poor, but in addition the Bank was to seek to insure that its loans were consistent with environmental concerns (for details, see Chapter 2 on "sustainable development"). A third pillar of the Bank's sustainability concept is population control. Preston reoriented the Bank towards sustainability, so defined. The dual track approach of the Bank's thrust (SALs + sustainability) became a complex mix of SALs + *sustainability + comprehensive development framework + social capital + good government + a knowledge bank* under James Wolfensohn who took over the Bank's presidency in 1995. While the above terms will not be detailed here, suffice it to say that one critic charged that under Wolfensohn the Bank has suffered from "a burgeoning agenda ... and a concomitant overload of objectives and conditionalities" (Kapur 2002: 69). While others find evidence of "loss of control over its agenda" an "operational loss of focus" and the embrace of "mission creep and accelerating goal proliferation" as the Bank has continued to deepen its commitment to SALs while simultaneously attempting to focus on sustainability, transparency, accountability, participation based on country "ownership" of programs, and "institution building" most under the heading of the **comprehensive development framework** (Pincus and Winter 2002: 20).

Much of this approach – critics label it a diversion – is well tied to the sustainability concept in the Bank's annual *World Development Report 2003* devoted to "Sustainable Development in a Dynamic World" (World Bank 2003). Here readers can follow the Bank's text as vague issues such as "interpersonal networks, share values and trust" are entertained (World Bank 2003: 19). Many critics have argued that the Bank, beset by the same barrage of criticism as the IMF, has sought to partially commit to a plethora of goals to deflect the criticisms (largely well documented) leveled against the Bank from the early 1990s onward. One informal group of trained observers has called for a return of the Bank to its earliest role as a *Development Bank* (see Focus 9.3), dropping the structural and sectoral loans, stepping back from the comprehensive development framework because the Bank lacks the operational framework and resources to pursue the plethora of goals it has now set forth (Pincus and Winter 2002). It would probably be an overstatement to argue that the Bank is currently in a "crisis," but the institution is challenged as never before by its constituents, its observers/critics and its funders.

Foreign aid

The term **foreign aid** is often loosely and incorrectly applied to programs that are not concessionary, such as loans from the IBRD or the IMF, or to bilateral programs that are essentially military or strategic in nature. All foreign aid is concessionary; it comes either in the form of concessionary loans or outright grants. The major source of foreign aid is bilateral assistance from the advanced nations to a selected number of poorer nations. Virtually all foreign aid is intended for the purpose of economic development; relatively little in a given year will be for the purpose of "emergency assistance," such as food, clothing, and emergency medical care for victims of disasters, war, and famine. Food aid is normally less than 10 percent of all aid. Multilateral organizations such as the United Nations certainly play a role in the decisions made and funds expended for foreign aid, but their programs are smaller than the sum of the bilateral programs of developed countries.

Among the many misconceptions regarding foreign aid, one in particular tends to stand out above all: contrary to popular conception, the really poor and destitute nations do not receive much of the foreign aid in any given year. This fact is brought to light in a summary of some of the known research regarding the recipients of foreign aid presented in the United Nations Development Program's (UNDP) *Human Development Report 1993*. In discussing the unique role played by the NGOs in transferring aid to the poor nations, the UNDP stated some of the more disturbing characteristics of foreign aid programs: "If government and official aid programmes usually fail to reach the poorest 20% of income groups, most NGO interventions probably miss the poorest 5–10%.... On the whole it is easier for NGOs to reach the not-so-poor than the very poorest" (UNDP 1993: 96). Why is this so? Because aid programs tend to be designed for those that already have some assets, such as small farmers, rather than, say, landless farm laborers or informal service workers. Even a self-help housing program designed for the poorest of the poor may put aid officials in an awkward position, since these destitute families often will be "squatters" on land owned by others. Providing assistance to such families would place the aid-giving group in direct opposition to the guardians of the property laws in the aid-receiving nation, and they thus shy away from such projects and controversy.

In 2000 total "official" foreign aid, or Official Development Assistance (ODA), from the advanced nations and OPEC (some of which was transferred to the World Bank's IDA and to other multinationals such as the UN) came to roughly $55 billion (UNDP 2002: 202, Table 15). In addition an estimated $8 billion was raised by NGOs. As these funds are distributed foreign aid allows for about 5 cents (US) per day of external support in the poorest nations of the world.

Targeted directly to the best projects in a few of the poorest nations, ODA can make a difference, helping to set a society on a new path. But this can only happen when programs actually reach the poor, when programs are well designed and crafted to meet the very specific needs of a recipient country, *and* when overall ODA outflows rise to the growing challenge of global poverty. None of this appears now to be happening. ODA, adjusted for inflation, reached its peak in 1992, and by 1997 aid flows had fallen 23.7 percent in relation to 1992 (Hjertholm and White 2000: 85–86). In 2000 – estimating the effects of inflation – official aid was well below the 1992 level, and on a rough par with that of 1997. Commentators explain this serious drop in aid as a result of the end of the Cold War which had actually given the poorer nations some leverage with the superpowers of the era, and *"aid fatigue"* arising from unexplained causes but thought to be based in the intractable nature of many of the most pressing problems in poor nations.

In 1998 the World Bank published a highly influential study *Assessing Aid* which essentially argued that aid did not help poor nations in many instances, and that in the future donor's should direct their aid funds to nations that had "good" government and "good" policies – which essentially seemed to mean market-friendly neoliberal governments and policies (World Bank 1998). Aid fatigue was encouraged by the study's findings that only 29 cents of every US dollar intended for aid expenditures actually went to such ends (World Bank: 1998: 19, 21). Aid, then was *fungible*, suggesting that the remaining 71 cents of each dollar intended for aid was wasted or misspent or misappropriated. This conclusion, however was not demonstrated in the study. In many cases, perhaps, recipient nations used the additional funds to support high priority projects that yielded a satisfactory social return. Serious study of this issue remains to be conducted.

In the US strident criticism has come from the right of the political spectrum, particularly through the Metzler Commission formed by the US Congress in 1998 to analyze the role of international financial institutions – particularly the World Bank and the IMF (Sanford 2002: 747–751). The Commission was hostile to the international financial institutions seeking either major reductions or the elimination of both the IMF and the World Bank. The Commission was also hostile to aid, buttressed in its views by the very critical analysis presented in *Assessing Aid*. As a result, the US government, adopting much of the Metzler Commission's views, has called for the conversion of 50 percent of the IDA's funding from loans to grants. This, of course, would eventually end the IDA as it currently relies for much of its ongoing financing from the repayment of loans (20 to 40 years after the loans have been issued).

Aid, which had been a rather undiscussed matter in development economics, became a major area of dispute after 1997. The *Journal of Development Studies* devoted an entire issue to the controversies stirred by *Assessing Aid*, finding weaknesses in the key econometric studies that the report was based on. Researchers urged that aid not be restricted to nations that had embraced neoliberal policies, but rather that aid should be used to build good policies instead of restricting aid to nations that had already adjusted their institutions and policies to the neoliberal model (Hermes and Lesink 2000: 1–15).

But, as suddenly as aid was disparaged in many powerful quarters it was aggressively re-embraced by the World Bank and even the US government after the UN sponsored the *Millennium Summit* in 2000. The UN, pushed into a background position on aid issues, has steadily regained prestige and momentum after it began publishing the Human Development Index (see Chapter 1) in the early 1990s. Under Kofi Annan's leadership as Secretary General of the UN, the industrialized nations signed-on to the *Millennium Development Goals* in September 2000. To meet the goals – which include (1) the eradication of extreme poverty and hunger, (2) the achievement of universal primary education, and (3) reduction of child mortality rates by two-thirds, *all by 2015* – ODA would have to roughly triple to $175 billion a year (in current dollars). Given the context set by *Assessing Aid* and the Metzler Commission, the abrupt *volte face* regarding aid policy issues was extreme. Observers attributed the success of the Millennial Conference to the underlying weakness in the global economy first exhibited with the Asian Crisis of 1997 and to the polarizing effects of globalization. The Millennial Conference was subsequently supported by the 2002 Monterrey (Mexico) Conference sponsored by the UNDP – where the US Administration announced that it would raise ODA spending by 50 percent in the next three years! On the way to the Monterrey Conference, the World Bank issued a staunch defense of its role as an institution involved in aid assistance, thereby distancing itself from the paradigm suggested in *Assessing Aid*.

This dizzying chain of events seems to suggest three things: first, the UN has gained a new voice, new legitimacy, and new urgency in leading with the Millennium Goals project. Second, the World Bank is now officially supporting the program, claiming that the "goals have been commonly accepted as a framework for realizing development progress" (World Bank 2003: 1). Third, the US's position in favor of converting IDA to grants as an indirect way to end development aid has undermined its own legitimacy, creating a new political space for Europe and Japan in the debate over aid (Sanford 2002: 754–757). *Aid fatigue is no more.*

Table 17.4 presents a range of data regarding ODA flows of some of the major donor nations comparing outlays in 1970 with those of 1991 and 2000 as a share of gross national product (GNP). Note that while the United States is the second largest donor nation in absolute size, it is by far the *smallest* contributor among the wealthy nations when viewed from the standpoint of the share of ODA to GNP. The UN has set a target of 0.7 percent of GNP as a goal to be achieved by the donor nations for their aid contributions; all donor nations fall well below that UN benchmark, as Table 17.4 demonstrates. Indeed, by 2000 the "aid commitment" level had fallen to only 0.22 percent of GNP – 33 percent below the level of 1991, the lowest registered since 1973 (IMF 1996: 1, 7).

When aid is directed to the poorest nations and to the poor in the less-developed nations, serious difficulties often arise with the process of delivery. This is most painfully obvious in the case of emergency assistance. Press reports of food piled up at docks in the midst of a famine are common. Road and rail transport is too often in insufficient supply; the food may have come from thousands of kilometers, while

Table 17.4 ODA flows of selected advanced nations

	2000 outlays (billions of US dollars)	Percentage GNP			Per Capita	
		1970	*1991*	*2000*	*1991*	*2000*
Japan	13,508	0.23	0.32	0.28	77	102
US	9,955	0.31	0.17	0.10	44	35
Germany	5,030	0.33	0.41	0.27	92	71
UK	4,501	0.42	0.32	0.32	99	79
France	4,105	0.46	0.54	0.32	115	80
Total or average ODA	**53,737**	–	**0.33**	**0.22**	**75**	**67**

Source: UNDP 1993: 203; 2002: 202.

the distance between the starving and the food supply on arrival may be only a few kilometers, but it might as well be ten thousand. Maybe it is a case of roads being destroyed, of bridges gone, or of the government or a tribal leader pilfering the food for individual profit. Whatever the reason, failure to deliver the aid is the outcome.

In other instances the same problem of an inhibiting institutional structure arises, but in a more subtle form. Agricultural aid is a good example of this situation, where new technologies, such as the Green Revolution discussed in Chapter 11, cannot be diffused because the recipient nation lacks the necessary technically trained cadre of farm advisers who can communicate with the peasantry and overcome their doubts. Indeed, studies of agricultural aid in India have shown strongly positive results, only because of a relatively large number of technically literate individuals who were able to fill the gap between the technology and knowledge and those who would *use* the technology. India's success has rarely been duplicated elsewhere, particularly in Africa. Consequently, it is necessary to recognize, once again, that a vicious circle of poverty is hard to overcome merely by providing one or only a few of the necessary ingredients for development. Aid programs that are not well integrated into the wider complex of social institutions within the less-developed nation may succeed in spite of the odds against them, but the probability of success is typically low. This lack of an *absorptive capacity* for aid is perhaps obvious enough to students of economic development, but it is too often overlooked in the broad, politically charged, debates surrounding aid giving.

Donor bias

Most aid is disbursed via bilateral programs, the largest being US AID, with outlays of approximately $10 billion in 2000. Most bilateral aid reflects the biases of the donor nation. Donor bias arises from the following considerations.

Commercial interests

Most foreign aid is **tied**, meaning that a proportion of the aid funds must be spent in the donor nation. This often results in more capital-intensive projects than necessary. Sometimes the pressure to accept tied aid is more subtle, amounting to *strategic non-lending* for nations which have previously received aid, but failed to buy their inputs primarily from the donor nation. In other instances, commercial inter-ests shift the focus from product sales to the maintenance of prices and production; this is particularly the case with food aid, which pushes surplus agricultural com-modities off the domestic and global market into non-market aid channels, thus helping to keep market prices higher than they might otherwise be. Unfortunately, food aid can undermine production by local producers of competing commodities in the aid-receiving nation by undercutting local demand. No one can compete against food products which are either given away or sold below their cost of production. This process can force many local producers from the market, perhaps contributing to a dependence on imported food staples from the developed countries.

Spheres of influence

Most of the large donor nations distribute their aid with a high emphasis on main-taining positive relationships with former colonial regions and/or regions where they have historically maintained a degree of political and economic hegemony. Another consideration may be national strategic leverage in a region. Such considerations largely explain why Egypt was the number one US aid recipient in 1991; the United States has based much of its Middle East strategy on maintaining Egypt as a friendly Arab nation, leading it to contribute most of the $4.6 billion in ODA funds received by this nation.

Procedural imperatives

In many instances, aid programs are allocated for one or only a few years. Yet in order to foster development, a multi-year aid commitment would be necessary. It may be procedurally necessary to limit aid programs due to budgetary considera-tions, or due to changes in political rule in the donor nation, leaving the recipient nation without the follow-through to make a project viable.

Ideological imperatives

When ideology drives the aid process, as it often does, the neediest nations and the best projects may be overlooked, or under-funded. Since the late 1970s, aid agencies have, for the most part, emphasized the desirability of private-sector development, a reflection of the dominance of neoliberal thinking. Nations which have resisted this orientation have often found that aid funds are difficult to obtain.

Aid and the multilaterals

While most aid is bilateral, the largest donor nations generally work closely with the IMF and the World Bank. Nations that are deemed to be unwilling to cooperate with the Fund and the World Bank are often considered to be unworthy of bilateral aid. Thus, in the 1980s when the Bank and then the Fund placed such emphasis on structural adjustment and neoliberal economic doctrine, the aid agencies and gov-ernments generally followed the lead of the multilaterals. This new tendency toward a three-way interlocking of the IMF, the World Bank, and bilateral aid is explained by IMF Deputy Director Mark Allen:

ODA is increasingly channeled to countries with IMF- and Bank-supported adjustment programs. The donor community finds that the existence of such programs
gives an assurance that aid will be invested more productively. If we compare
1990–93 with the previous three years, nominal ODA to countries with IMF-supported programs increased by 35 percent, while that for countries without such
programs rose by only 6 percent. Thus, continued financing from the IMF and the
Bank is a catalyst for considerably large ODA flows to these countries.

(IMF 1995a: 339)

Since neoliberal economic advice often resulted in a reduction of programs and
expenditure which were most likely to reach the neediest, aid often became a supplement to structural adjustment, attempting to fill in some of the gaps in the social
fabric created by the SALs. The UN Economic Commission for Latin America and
the Caribbean conducted a study of income distribution changes in the course of the
1980s; all but one of the eight nations studied experienced strong shifts toward
greater income inequality. Only two countries stood out as exceptions; Uruguay's
income distribution was essentially unchanged, while Colombia's improved
(ECLAC 1994: 1). Absent from the study was Mexico, the nation with the second
largest population in Latin America. It too experienced a dramatic shift toward even
greater income inequality. Mexico, it will be remembered, was the World Bank's
largest single experiment with SAL programs.

With Mexico's recovery after the peso crisis of 1995 that nation was upheld as a
shining example of the new era of the 1990s: "Trade, not Aid!" Yet, predictably, the
World Bank/IMF/US "Washington Consensus" view on Mexico crumbled along
with the Mexican economy in late 2000. The Mexican case had been taken as proof
of the benefits of unrestrained opening to trade and investment. But this shallow
perspective was not really based in the realities of the Mexican economy which had
long exhibited deep pathological traits before the export-led boom evaporated in
late 2000 (Cypher 2001: 11–37).

Conclusion

By 2003 the situation regarding aid and the multilaterals had changed fundamentally
– the World Bank was touting aid as the chief force behind the 20-year increase in
life expectancy in poor nations since 1960, while cutting their illiteracy rate by 50
percent (Kahn: 2002 W1, 7). The "Washington Consensus" was widely disparaged,
the critical thrust of *Assessing Aid* was no longer a touchstone for a radical policy
shift and the Millennium Development Goals suggested the possibility that the UN's
"Sustainable Human Development approach" could move into a position of dominance in development policy. Much more threatening to the neoliberal "Washington
Consensus" approach was the possible rise of what Charles Gore termed the
"Southern Consensus." Gore envisioned a possible new development paradigm
based on the understanding of the process of development as experienced in East
Asia and upon the critical analytical work of the UN's research centers such as
CEPAL (ECLAC) and UNCTAD. This *neostructural* consensus would call for the
strategic integration of developing nations with the world economy based on a carefully *sequenced* opening of the trade sector. Strategic integration would call for
limited capital account liberalization and safeguards against "hot money" flight from

developing nations leading to massive currency devaluations. Under this approach inbound FDI would be constrained to activities that actually contribute to building the productive base of the developing nation. Dynamic comparative advantage would form the basis of integration while trade policy would emphasize improvements in supply capacity, education and training of the labor force and independent technological capabilities. Policy-making would be *embedded* while capable policy-makers would formulate dynamic policy incentive based in performance criteria for national firms (Gore 2000: 789–804). Which way will development economics go now? Toward an entrenched neoliberalism, a "growth with equity" approach based in Sustainable Human Development fulfilling the Millennium Development Goals or toward a new "Southern Consensus"? Perhaps the near future will hold a bit of each approach – and the debates over development economics will continue.

Questions for review

1   You have been selected as the chief negotiator to represent your country, which is facing an economic crisis and must seek assistance from the IMF. You must draw-up a draft version of a letter of intent and a secret document which will represent the bargaining position of your nation as negotiations open with the IMF. First, describe the economic conditions which have created a crisis for your nation. Second, explain the "policy actions" which will be undertaken by government to improve the functioning of the economy during the program period. Third, what "prior actions" is your government willing to undertake in order to obtain an IMF stand-by loan? How does your position differ from that which the IMF will probably present? How will you attempt to bargain with the IMF in order that your nation is adequately represented?

2   "The Fund and the World Bank tend to assume that endogenous, policy-related errors lie at the base of a nation's difficulties. In fact, exogenous difficulties are usually more of a factor. Consequently, adjustment programs fail to address the causes of an economic crisis. Such problems are invariably brought-on by structural problems." Discuss this statement. Do you agree? Why, or why not?

3   Based on your reading of this chapter, identify five major public misconceptions regarding foreign aid.

4   How might a typical IMF stand-by program, or a typical World Bank structural adjustment loan, contradict some or all of the basic objectives of "sustainability"? Imagine that this SAL is applied to a nation which has little industrial or manufacturing capability. How might a structural adjustment loan lead to new burdens being placed upon the environment of the nation?

5   "Governments often achieve objectives they have long-held, but have been unable to achieve, while operating under an IMF or a World Bank adjustment program." Why might this be so?

Notes

1   Foreign aid is defined as the receipt of concessional lending and grant funds, as well as technical assistance. "Concessional lending" involves loans that are received at a discount of 25 percent or more below the normal market rate of interest. Normally, a concessional loan will also have a longer-than-average repayment period, with a "grace" period of several years when no payment of interest or principal is required. A "grant" is aid

received which never requires repayment. "Technical assistance" constitutes advice and guidance, as well as training, offered by a donor and received by a developing nation.

Most foreign aid is bilateral, that is, direct donor-to-recipient assistance. But, some foreign aid comes via the World Bank and the regional multilateral development banks, such as the InterAmerican Development Bank. A third source of foreign aid funds comes from the non-governmental organizations (NGOs), such as Oxfam and others. The NGOs are of growing importance in the distribution of aid; in 1990, they channeled $7.2 billion into the less-developing nations, of which $2.2 billion came from donor governments, and the rest came from funds directly raised by the NGOs.

2 A third pillar of the Bretton Woods conference, the World Trade Organization (WTO), designed to mediate trade disputes and to eliminate trade wars and reduce tariffs among nations, was not ultimately approved. Instead, a looser organization, known as the General Agreement on Tariffs and Trade (GATT), became the means by which trade and tariff disputes were resolved and through which freer trade has been achieved since 1945. Only in 1995 was the WTO finally reborn as a vehicle for managing international trade disputes, following a period in which the world economy had passed through more than a decade of crisis from the debt débâcle of the 1980s to the global slow-down of the early 1990s.

3 When members borrow hard currencies under stand-by arrangements, they can have access to 100 percent of their quotas. In addition, such members may be able to access other so-called "Facilities" of the Fund, such that during a three-year period, they could, at a maximum, have access to an amount equivalent to 600 percent of their subscribed quota, through stand-by drawings and special facility loans.

4 It may not, however, be a simple task for a less-developed nation with limited resources and few trained professionals to successfully bargain with the Fund; the IMF has vast resources, which include a staff of 2,600 highly trained professionals, who endeavor to impose the Fund's preferred package of conditions, if possible.

5 "Hard" currencies are those that are readily convertible into other currencies and which are relatively stable in value over time. As a rule, the US dollar and the pound sterling meet these general conditions, but preference for the strongest, or hardest, currencies is subject to change, with the Japanese yen and the German mark being held in high regard in the early 1990s. "Soft" currencies are more volatile in value and are potentially more difficult to convert into hard currencies; in other words, with soft currencies, there is a risk of devaluation which is carried by the holder of such currencies.

6 The continued importance of primary product exports reflects the difficulty, or unwillingness, of less-developed nations to transform their productive and export structures more toward secondary and tertiary commodities. You will remember from Chapter 6 the term of trade problems that being a primary product exporter and a manufactured good importer can impose on less-developed nations.

7 This is part of the so-called J-curve phenomenon. With devaluation, export income may not grow by much for a time, due to the slower response of export sales to the lower unit price of exports, in real terms, that a devaluation implies. Thus total export income may not rise by much very quickly. On the other hand, total expenditure on imports can actually increase after a devaluation, depending on the price elasticities of demand. With higher import prices, if the quantity of imports purchased does not fall by more, in percentage terms, than the price has risen, the import bill will grow. Thus, it is quite possible that a devaluation, in the short-term at least, will result in a deterioration of both the trade deficit *and* the current account deficit.

8 The theoretical assumptions and the model employed by the Fund to analyze the difficulties of the borrowing nation are important to explore in any serious assessment of the Fund's activities. Basically, the Fund assumes away the problem of economic development by treating the potential poor borrowing nation *as if* it already had a fully articulated and developed market economy. There is no place for economic dualism in the Fund's analysis; all factors of production are assumed to be fully employed, and there is complete mobility of factors of production within the economy. Lewis' dualism and the reservations of Prebisch and Singer and other developmentalist economists (Chapters 5 and 6) have no role to play in the model employed by the Fund.

The Fund's approach largely derives from the large body of work of a little-known Fund economist, Jacques J. Polack, who, in 1943, developed an analysis known as the "Polack Model," which we have described above, albeit in a non-rigorous manner. Readers wishing to have access to Polack's highly influential work (spread over fifty years!) should consult the two-volume work by Polack (1994).

9 In a completely closed economy with no trade, wage repression that leads to an increase in the share of total income going to profits would unambiguously reduce the overall level of output and income, as long as the usual assumption holds that the marginal propensity to consume out of profits (MPC_P) is less than the marginal propensity to consume (MPC_W) out of wages.

10 Updating this research through 1993, Killick has determined that of 305 programs examined between 1979 and 1993, 53 percent were never completed (Killick 1995: 60–61).

11 Studies done of IMF programs often do not clearly indicate why a given sample of nations has been chosen, or why particular dates have been utilized. Many studies do not adjust for size of the nations involved, or other variables which would permit the results to achieve greater reliability. Furthermore, although the Fund prefers to present its programs as being guided by the principle of "uniformity of treatment," it has often bent the rules regarding conditionality in order to lend to governments which either the Fund or the major donor nations support as a result of their ideological stance or because of their strategic influence. The most recent example of the role which ideology, and even personal ties, can play in determining how the Fund will react to a nation in economic difficulties is that of the $17.8 billion Mexican loan in early 1995. The Fund's Managing Director, Michael Camdessus, acknowledged that he had become a personal friend of some of the top economic policy-makers in Mexico, particularly Mexico's influential Finance Minister, and that as a result his professional objectivity regarding Mexico's looming economic disaster had been compromised. Camdessus admitted that the inconsistencies revealed in the Mexican situation were not unique and that the Fund's unwillingness to impose adequate surveillance on Mexico in 1994 pointed to "a global problem with the culture of the Fund" (Gerth and Sciolini 1996: A6).

Given this "political element," quantitative tests of the "effectiveness" of the Fund's programs become more problematic. If uniformity of treatment is violated because of special relationships the IMF forges with some countries, it becomes very difficult to determine on the basis of comparative empirical studies of Fund programs what the general effect of a program may be.

12 This distinction, however, has increasingly been blurred, due to the fact that the Fund has drawn the conclusion that its stabilization programs have performed badly because of their short-term orientation. The Bank has, since the late 1970s, increasingly shared the theoretical perspective of the Fund and has sought to link short-term stabilization programs of the Fund to long-term lending programs at the Bank. When this linkage occurs, it is known as a cross-conditional program.

References

Bird, Graham. 2001. "IMF Programs: Do They Work?," *World Development* 29, 1: 1849–1865.

Boorman, Jack. 2002. "Interview with Jack Boorman," *IMF Survey* (August 5): 241, 245–248.

Cypher, James. 2001. "Developing Disarticulation Within the Mexican Economy," *Latin American Perspectives* 25, 6 (May): 11–37.

ECLAC. 1994. "Social Panorama of Latin America," *CEPAL News* (July): 1–3.

George, Susan and Fabrizio Sabelli. 1994. *Faith and Credit: The World Bank's Secular Empire.* London: Westview Press.

Gerth, Jeff and Elaine Sciolini. 1996. "IMF Head: He Speaks and Money Talks," *New York Times* (April 2): 1, A6.

Gore, Charles. 2000. "The Rise and Fall of the Washington Consensus as a Paradigm for Developing Countries," *World Development* 28, 5: 789–804.

Henshall Momsen, Janet. 1991. *Women and Development in the Third World.* London: Routledge.

Hermes, Niels and Robert Lensink. 2000. "Changing the Conditions for Development Aid: A New Paradigm?," *Journal of Development Studies* 37 (August): 1–16.

Hjertholm and Howard White. 2000. "Foreign Aid in Historical Perspective," pp. 80–102 in Finn Tarp and Peter Hjertholm (eds), *Foreign Aid and Development.* London: Routledge.

IMF. 1995a. "Coordinated Approach to Multilateral Debt," *IMF Survey* (October 23): 338–339.

—— 1995b. "Record IMF-Supported Adjustment Programmes Assessed," *IMF Survey* (July 31): 233–236.

—— 1995c. "Strengthening IMF Surveillance," *IMF Survey* (May 22): 153–156.

—— 1995d. *IMF Survey* (July 31).

—— 1995e. "IMF Provides Financing for Macroeconomic and Structural Adjustment," *IMF Survey* (September Supplement): 10–14.

—— 1996. "Official Financing Fell in 1994," *IMF Survey* (January 8): 1, 7–8.

—— 2001. "IMF Financial Facilities," *IMF Survey* (September Supplement): 12–13.

—— 2002. "New Conditionality Guidelines," *IMF Survey* (December 16): 390–391.

—— 2003a. "Standby, EFF, and PRGF Arrangements," *IMF Survey* (January 20): 14.

—— 2003b. "Past IMF Disbursements and Repayments," *IMF* (March): www.imf.org/external/tre/tad/extrepl.cfm.

Kaptur, Devesh. 2002. "The Changing Anatomy of Governance," pp. 54–75 in Jonathan Pincus and Jeffery Winters (eds), *Reinventing the World Bank.* Ithaca: Cornell University Press.

Kahn, Joseph. 2002. "World Bank in Report Defends the Use of Aid," *New York Times* (March 12): W1, W7.

Killick, Tony. 1995. *IMF Programmes in Developing Countries.* London: Routledge.

Killick, Tony, Moazzam Malik, and Marcus Manuel. 1992. "What Can We Know About the Effects of IMF Programmes?," *World Economy* 20 (September): 575–597.

Mosley, Paul, Jane Harrigan, and John Toye. 1991. *Aid and Power: The World Bank and Policy-Based Lending,* 2 vols. London: Routledge.

Pastor, Manuel. 1987. "The Effects of IMF Programmes in the Third World," *World Development* 15 (February): 249–262.

Pauly, Louis W. 1994. "Promoting a Global Economy: The Normative Role of the International Monetary Fund," pp. 204–215 in Richard Stubbs and Geoffrey Underhill (eds), *Political Economy and the Changing Global Order.* New York: St Martin's Press.

Pincus, Jonathan and Jeffery Winters. 2002. "Reinventing the World Bank," pp. 1–25 in Jonathan Pincus and Jeffery Winters (eds), *Reinventing the World Bank.* Ithaca: Cornell University Press.

Polack, Jacques J. 1994. *Economic Theory and Financial Policy.* Aldershot: Edward Elgar.

Preworski, Adam and James Vreeland. 2000. "The Effect of IMF Programs on Economic Growth," *Journal of Development Economics* 62, 385–421.

Sanford, Jonathan. 2002. "World Bank: IDA Loans or IDA Grants?," *World Development* 30, 5: 741–762.

SAPRIN (Structural Adjustment Participatory Review International Network). 2002. *The Policy Roots of Economic Crisis and Poverty.* (April) SAPRIN: www.saprin.org/globalrpt.htm.

Sheehy, Thomas. 1994. "The Index of Economic Freedom: A Tool for Real Reform of Foreign Aid," *The Heritage Foundation Backgrounder* No. 986 (May 6): 1–18.

Stiglitz, Joseph. 2002. *Globalization and Its Discontents.* New York: Norton.

UNDP (United Nations Development Programme). 1993. *Human Development Report 1993.* New York: Oxford University Press.

—— 2002. *Human Development Report 2002.* Oxford: Oxford University Press.

Vreeland, James. 2002. "The Effect of IMF Programs on Labor," *World Development* 30, 1: 121–139.

World Bank 1993. *World Development Report 1993.* New York: Oxford University Press.

—— 1984. (Office of Environmental and Health Affairs). *Environmental Policies and Procedures of the World Bank.* Washington, DC: World Bank.

—— 1995a. *The World Bank Annual Report 1995.* Washington, DC: The World Bank.

—— 1995b. *World Development Report 1995.* New York: Oxford University Press.

—— 1998. *Assessing Aid.* Washington, DC: World Bank.

—— 2003. *World Development Report, 2003.* Washington, DC: World Bank.

Index

The index is in word-by-word alphabetical order. Page references relating to information in tables or illustrations are given in *italic*. F or B following a page reference refers to a Focus or Box feature, respectively.